Emperor and Priest
The Imperial Office in Byzantium

This is a revised and translated edition of Gilbert Dagron's *Empereur et prêtre* (1996), an acknowledged masterwork by one of the great Byzantine scholars of our time.

The figure of the Byzantine emperor, a ruler who sometimes was also designated a priest, has long fascinated the western imagination. This book studies in detail the imperial union of 'two powers' against a wide background of relations between Church and state and religious and political spheres.

While in the medieval West the empire was broken down into its various temporal realms, leaving spiritual matters to the papacy, the Byzantine East preserved the structures of an empire whose ruler – the anointed successor of David – received directly from God his mission to lead his Christian subjects. In this sense, the emperor was a priest, albeit 'of another priesthood' or a quasi-bishop. Historians have continued the debate on this subject since the time of the Reformation, declaring 'caesaropapism' to be a malady of the East. Yet the ambiguities and nuances of this divided imperial role can still be perceived today. Presenting much unfamiliar material in complex, brilliant style, as much for western medievalists as for Byzantinists, it will attract all historians concerned with royal and ecclesiastical sources of power.

... a profound exploration of wide-ranging aspects of Byzantine thought and perception – a veritable pilgrim's guide to the Byzantine soul ... This is a very significant book for Byzantine specialists, one of the most stimulating to appear for some time, but it will also be of great use to those outside the field of Byzantine studies ... Indeed, no one interested in the varieties of earthly sovereignty should be unaware of it. (John W. Barker in *Speculum*)

GILBERT DAGRON is Professor Emeritus of Byzantine History and Civilisation at the Collège de France, Honorary President of the International Committee on Byzantine Studies and a member of the Institut de France.

D1595855

Past and Present Publications

General Editors: LYNDAL ROPER, *University of Oxford*, and CHRIS WICKHAM, *University of Birmingham*

Past and Present Publications comprise books similar in character to the articles in the journal *Past and Present*. Whether the volumes in the series are collections of essays – some previously published, others new studies – or monographs, they encompass a wide variety of scholarly and original works primarily concerned with social, economic and cultural changes, and their causes and consequences. They will appeal to both specialists and non-specialists and will endeavour to communicate the results of historical and allied research in the most readable and lively form.

For a list of titles in Past and Present Publications, see end of book.

Emperor and Priest

The Imperial Office in Byzantium

GILBERT DAGRON
Collège de France

Translated by
JEAN BIRRELL

CAMBRIDGE
UNIVERSITY PRESS

CAMBRIDGE UNIVERSITY PRESS
Cambridge, New York, Melbourne, Madrid, Cape Town, Singapore, São Paulo

Cambridge University Press
The Edinburgh Building, Cambridge CB2 8RU, UK

Published in the United States of America by Cambridge University Press, New York

www.cambridge.org
Information on this title: www.cambridge.org/9780521801232

Originally published in French as *Empereur et prêtre: Etude sur le "césaropapisme" byzantin* by Éditions Gallimard 1996 and © Éditions Gallimard. First published in English by Cambridge University Press 2003 as *Emperor and Priest: The Imperial Office in Byzantium* English translation © Cambridge University Press 2003

First published 2003
This digitally printed version 2007

A catalogue record for this publication is available from the British Library

ISBN 978-0-521-80123-2 hardback
ISBN 978-0-521-03697-9 paperback

Contents

Plates

Plans

Acknowledgements

This book continues and completes research carried out over many years at the Collège de France: it is therefore appropriate that I should mention here all those who, by their presence and their comments, have helped me to bring to fruition an initially tentative project. I am also indebted to Mme Ghislaine de Feydeau for her careful reading of the text and to M Constantin Zuckerman for revising the notes; to both my thanks.

I had talked to my old friend Pierre Nora about the king-priests and priest-kings who fascinated me, though I was far from confident that they would interest readers accustomed to keep their distance from Byzantium. He was brave enough to read the typescript and propose its publication in the *Bibliothèque des Histoires*.

It is a great honour for me to see this English version of my book, with a few corrections and additions, appear in a prestigious series published by Cambridge University Press. I would like to express my deep gratitude to Professor Judith Herrin of King's College London for suggesting and encouraging this project. A translation, it is sometimes said, is a betrayal; in this case it has produced a new book, which owes much to the skill, intelligence and patient labour of Jean Birrell, to whom I offer my warm thanks. In venturing, so to speak, onto their own ground, and addressing them in their own language, I would like to pay tribute to the brilliant school British Byzantinists have created and sustained at a high level, to evoke my personal contacts with many of them and to record my admiration for their learning, their culture and, of course, their humour.

Bibliographical abbreviations

AASS   Acta Sanctorum

ACO   Acta conciliorum oecumenicorum

Anal. Boll.   Analecta Bollandiana (Brussels)

BHG   F. Halkin, *Bibliotheca Hagiographica Graeca*, 3rd ed., I–III, Brussels, 1957, completed, *Novum Auctarium Bibliothecae Hagiographicae Graecae*, Brussels, 1984

Bonn   *Corpus Scriptorum Historiae Byzantinae*, Bonn, 1828–97

Byz.   Byzantion (Brussels)

ByzForsch.   Byzantinische Forschungen (Amsterdam)

ByzSlav.   Byzantinoslavica (Prague)

BZ   Byzantinische Zeitschrift (Munich, then Cologne)

CJ   Corpus Iuris Civilis, II: *Codex Iustinianus*, ed. P. Krüger, repr. Berlin, 1963

CTh.   Codex Theodosianus, ed. T. Mommsen and P. M. Meyer, repr. Berlin, 1954

CSCO   Corpus Scriptorum Christianorum Orientalium

CSEL   Corpus Scriptorum Ecclesiasticorum Latinorum

DACL   Dictionnaire d'Archéologie Chrétienne et de Liturgie, I–XV, Paris, 1907–53

Darrouzès, *Regestes*   J. Darrouzès, *Les Regestes des Actes du Patriarcat de Constantinople*, I: *Les Actes des Patriarches*, fasc. 4: *Les Regestes de 1208 à 1309*; 5: *Les Regestes de 1310 à 1376*; 6: *Les Regestes de 1377 à 1410*, Paris, 1971–9

De cerimoniis   Constantini Porphyrogeniti imperatoris De cerimoniis aulae byzantinae libri duo, ed. I. I. Reiske, Corpus Scriptorum Historiae Byzantinae, Bonn, 1829, vol. I. For chaps 10–106 of book I, the numbering is from the manuscript, with, in brackets, the misleading numbering of the Bonn edition, which conceals a gap of nine chapters.

Dig.   Corpus Iuris Civilis, I. *Iustiniani Digesta*, ed. T. Mommsen and P. Krüger, repr. Dublin-Zurich, 1966

Dölger, *Regesten*   F. Dölger, *Regesten der Kaiserurkunden des oströmischen Reiches von 565–1453*, I–III, Munich-Berlin, 1924–33, repr. (1 vol.) Hildesheim, 1976

DOP   Dumbarton Oaks Papers (Washington)

DS   Dictionnaire de Spiritualité, Ascétique et Mystique (Paris, 1937–)

DTC   Dictionnaire de Théologie Catholique, I–XV, Paris, 1930–62

EEBS   Epeteris Hetaireias Byzantinon Spoudon (Athens)

FHG   Fragmenta Historicorum Graecorum, ed. C. Müller, I–V, Paris, 1874–85

Goar, *Euchologion*   J. Goar, *Euchologion, sive Rituale Graecorum*, Venice, 1730, repr. Graz, 1960

GRBS   Greek, Roman and Byzantine Studies (Duke University)

Grumel, *Regestes*   V. Grumel, *Les Regestes des Actes du Patriarcat de Constantinople*, I: *Les Actes des Patriarches*, fasc. 1: *Les Regestes de 381 à 715*, 2nd ed., Paris, 1972

Grumel-Darrouzès, *Regestes*   V. Grumel, *Les Regestes des Actes du Patriarcat de Constantinople*, I: *Les Actes des Patriarches*, fasc. 2 & 3: *Les Regestes de 715 à 1206*, 2nd ed. revised and corrected by J. Darrouzès, Paris, 1989

Histoire du christianisme   Histoire du christianisme, ed. J.-M. Mayeur, C. L. Piéti, A. Vauchez and M. Venard, IV: *Evêques, moines et empereurs (610–1054)*, ed. G. Dagron, P. Riché and A. Vauchez, Paris, 1993; V: *Apogée de la papauté et expansion de la chrétienté (1054–1274)*, ed. A. Vauchez, Paris, 1993

Inst.   Corpus Iuris Civilis, I: *Iustiniani Institutiones*, ed. P. Krüger, repr. Dublin-Zurich 1966

JAC   Jahrbuch für Antike und Christentum (Munster)

Jaffé, *Regesta*   P. Jaffé, *Regesta Pontificorum Romanorum*, 2nd ed. revised and added to by G. Wattenbach *et al.*, I–II, Leipzig, 1885–8, repr. Graz, 1956

Janin, *Constantinople byzantine*   R. Janin, *Constantinople byzantine. Développement urbain et répertoire topographique*, 2nd ed., Paris, 1964

Janin, *Eglises et monastères   La Géographie ecclésiastique de l'Empire byzantin*, I: *Le siège de Constantinople et le patriarcat oecuménique*, III: *Les Eglises et les monastères*, by R. Janin, 2nd ed., Paris, 1969

JÖB   Jahrbuch der österreichischen Byzantinistik (Vienna)

JRS   Journal of Roman Studies (London)

Justinian, *Novellae   Corpus Iuris Civilis*, III: *Novellae*, ed. R. Schöll and G. Kroll, repr. Berlin, 1963

Koukoules, *Byzantinon bios*   P. Koukoules, *Byzantinon bios kai politismos*, I–IV, Athens, 1948–57

Mansi   *Sacrorum conciliorum nova et amplissima collectio*, ed. J. D. Mansi, I–XXXI, Florence/Venice, 1757–98

MGH   Monumenta Germaniae Historica inde ab a. C. 500 usque ad a. 1500 (Hanover)

OCP   Orientalia Christiana Periodica (Rome)

Oikonomides, *Listes*   N. Oikonomides, *Les Listes de préséance byzantines des IXe et Xe siècles*, Paris, 1857–66

PG   Patrologiae cursus completus, Series graeca, ed. J.-P. Migne, Paris, 1857–66

PL   Patrologiae cursus completus, Series latina, ed. J.-P. Migne, Paris, 1844–64

PLRE   The Prosopography of the Later Roman Empire, I: *A.D. 260–395*, by A. H. M. Jones, J. R. Martindale, J. Morris (Cambridge, 1971); II. *A.D. 395–527*, by J. R. Martindale (Cambridge, 1980); IIIA and B: *A.D. 527–641*, by J. R. Martindale (Cambridge, 1992).

PO   Patrologia Orientalis

Rhalles–Potles, *Syntagma*   G. Rhalles and M. Potles, *Syntagma ton theion kai hieron kanaon*, I–VI, Athens, 1852–9

RE   Pauly-Wissowa-(Kroll), *Real-Encyclopädie der Classischen Altertumswissenschaft*

REB   Revue des Etudes Byzantines (Paris)

REG   Revue des Etudes Grecques (Paris)

SC   Collection des Sources Chrétiennes

TM   Collège de France, Centre de recherche d'histoire et civilisation de Byzance, Travaux et mémoires (Paris)

VizVrem.   Vizantijskij Vremennik (Moscow)

Zepos, *Jus*   J. and P. Zepos, *Jus Graecoromanum*, I–VIII, Athens, 1931

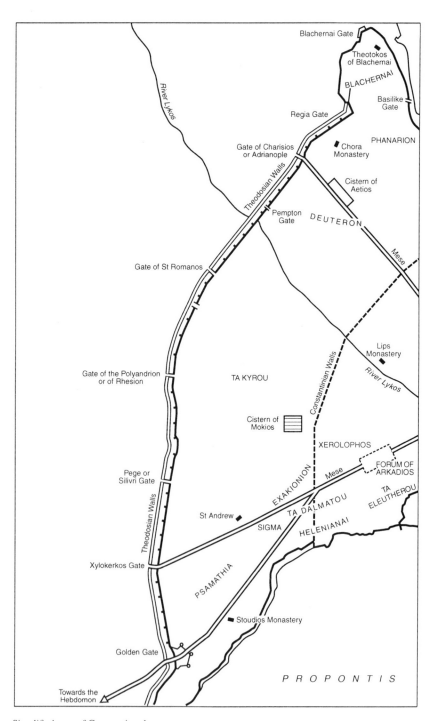

Simplified map of Constantinople

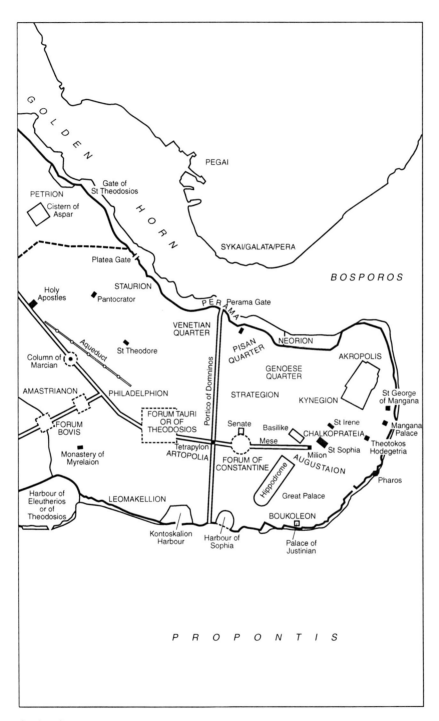

GOLDEN HORN

PEGAI

Gate of
St Theodosios

PETRION

Cistern of
Aspar

Platea Gate

SYKAI/GALATA/PERA

BOSPOROS

STAURION

Holy
Apostles

Pantocrator

PERAMA Perama Gate

VENETIAN
QUARTER

PISAN
QUARTER

NEORION

Aqueduct

St Theodore

GENOESE
QUARTER

AKROPOLIS

Column of
Marcian

Portico of Domninos

STRATEGION

KYNEGION

St George
of Mangana

AMASTRIANON

PHILADELPHION

FORUM TAURI
OR OF
THEODOSIOS

Senate

Basilike

St Irene

CHALKOPRATEIA

Mangana
Palace

FORUM
BOVIS

Mese

Milion

St Sophia

Theotokos
Hodegetria

Monastery of
Myrelaion

Tetrapylon
ARTOPOLIA

FORUM OF
CONSTANTINE

AUGUSTAION

Pharos

Harbour of
Eleutherios
or of
Theodosios

LEOMAKELLION

Hippodrome

Great Palace

BOUKOLEON

PROPONTIS

Kontoskalion
Harbour

Harbour of
Sophia

Palace of
Justinian

Continued

Introduction

No one today would still talk about Church and state as two institutions, or concepts, which common sense or history have conclusively taught us to distinguish. We are better equipped now than at the beginning of the twentieth century to appreciate the connections and interrelations that would be concealed by too rigid a division between the sacred and the profane, the spiritual and the temporal, clergy and laity. The political rituals and imagery of the most republican past now seem to us loaded with religious significance or nostalgia. Ethnology teaches that any actual power only becomes rightful power by being sacralised, most of all royal power, source of all other, whose every manifestation is a theophany. From sacredness to priesthood is only a small step. The Indo-European vocabulary and myths tell us that the king rules not only relations between humans but relations between humankind and the gods,[1] and that the king synthesises in his person the warrior, priestly and productive functions.[2] Marc Bloch's *The Royal Touch* and Kantorowicz's *The King's Two Bodies*, two seminal works I mention here by way of dedication, have accustomed us to the idea that the Christian sovereigns, too, had *charismata*, and that they cannot simply be ranked as laity.

The state is sacred and the Church is power. If their separation constitutes an undeniable advance and deserves to be preserved as a moral principle and, above all, a guarantee of freedom, this is not a natural phenomenon but a legacy of history, and therefore problematic. Many are the human societies where there is no sign of this separation, thanks not to some alleged psychology of peoples – though the notion lingers in the subconscious – but to circumstances. Antiquity had its priests, but there was no pagan Church on the margins or at the heart of the state; in the case of Judaism and Islam, two religions of the Book where the

---

[1] E. Benveniste, *Le Vocabulaire des institutions indo-européennes*, II (Paris, 1969), pp. 57–69.
[2] G. Dumézil, *Mythe et épopée*, II (Paris, 1971), p. 358; see also D. Dubuisson, 'Le roi indo-européen et la synthèse des trois fonctions', *Annales, Economies Sociétés Civilisations (ESC)*, 33 (1978), pp. 21–34; J. Le Goff, 'Les trois fonctions indo-européennes, l'historien et l'Europe féodale', *Annales, ESC*, 34 (1979), pp. 1187–1215.

message does not fundamentally differ from that of Christianity, the synchronism between religious revelation and political organisation is so total that the distinction between Church and state becomes almost meaningless. In utopian or supposedly ideal societies this same duality is always denied or abolished; all fundamentalism seeks to establish a Church state and all totalitarian ideology a state Church. In the case of Christianity, too, we have to allow for the influence of history. When he uttered the famous words: 'Render therefore unto Caesar the things which are Caesar's; and unto God the things that are God's' (Matthew, 22: 21), Christ was in the somewhat contradictory historical situation of a Jew obliged to live his monotheism in a polytheistic empire. Later, it was the geographical break up of Roman power that favoured the emergence of a 'theory of the two powers', one temporal and established in Constantinople, the other spiritual and remaining in Rome. But as soon as an eastern Church was organised round the emperor and his patriarch, or the empire was reborn in the West with the Carolingians and the Ottonians, the schema ran into difficulties and the theory of the two powers was confronted by another theory, or rather by another model: that of an earthly monarchy conceived in the image of divine monarchy, incarnated in a sovereign to whom God had directly delegated the government and the salvation of men, and whom he had legitimated by unction. The separation of powers was resisted not so much by fundamentalism as by a nostalgia for unity.

Was this emperor, or this king (we should remember that *basileus* may be translated by either word), in his own way, a priest? The question is usually posed only at the conclusion of a systematic analysis of the legitimate or illegitimate interventions of the temporal power in the Church, with the claim to priesthood representing the extreme and shocking degree of unbridled autocracy. It seemed to me, on the contrary, that it was better to begin with this problem and as far as possible confine myself to it. It indicates the most difficult, but also the most direct and most reliable, way of evaluating links between the political and the religious. Rather than drawing up an endless and groundless inventory of the emperor's rights in ecclesiastical matters, which postulates a distinction, let us take advantage of the exceptionally rich documentation provided by Byzantium to examine the many resonances of the concept of king-priest, postulating a unity.

The Church–state opposition and its derivatives, incautiously applied to the Christian middle ages, have led to no end of confusion, anachronism and error. To speculate about an equilibrium between the spiritual and the temporal is to adopt a shortsighted or self-deluding approach; it is to think in institutional rather than power terms, to presume an implicit constitution and a near consensus about principles, and to accept the existence of tensions and contraventions and a gulf between theory and practice, but not to see them as questioning a conventional separation of roles. One may understand in this way the domain of municipal magistrates or imperial functionaries, who had a power of representation or of delegation and were themselves only cogs in a wheel; but the language can no longer be the same when one approaches the top of the hierarchy, the emperor who governs or the hierarch who 'binds and looses'. The notion of institution is then replaced by that of power, a tactic of separation by a strategy of unity. Power, unlike institutions, carries its own justification; it does not make it possible to establish the traditional difference between the person and the function, but only to see in the same person what might be called, using the vocabulary of Christology, 'two natures' or, using the political vocabulary of the England of 1600, 'two bodies'.

The real question is whether the emperor was or was not, in his own way, a priest. It cannot be avoided, but, in the Christian context, a positive response is tainted with doctrinal error. For the most part, one finds only anecdotal or rhetorical allusions accompanied by a disclaimer. Constantine the Great called himself 'a bishop over the outside', but this was only a manner of speaking; it was rumoured that Herakleios, victorious over Persia, had become a priest,[3] but the story lacked all foundation; Leo III declared: 'I am emperor and priest', but he was a heretic; Leo VI held the rank of lector or deacon, but only according to Arab writers seeking to explain why his remarriage had been prohibited. The priesthood of kings seems to be an obvious truth to which any reflection on the foundations of a universal monarchy leads, but which cannot be expressed openly without being condemned, and which must be camouflaged by anodyne comparisons. Both the fact and the camouflage probably date back to Constantine the Great, that is, to the very beginnings of an empire which was suddenly identified with Christianity present and future, whose history was from then on measured by the yardstick of Christian time – a sort of countdown bringing the eschatological climax daily a little closer – and whose ruler became the manager of an economy of salvation. This emperor with a mission to convert and to fulfil the prophecies had then to be recognised as possessing the special priesthood, outside the strictly liturgical domain, which had been that of the mysterious Melchizedek of Genesis, or of Saul, David and Solomon, predecessors of the *basileis* at the head of a chosen people.

Everything turns on this, less in the coherence of the ideas than in the superimposing of models. Among the latter, for cultural reasons which mask deep-seated prejudices, historiography has always favoured those that derive from antiquity. As a result, with regard to the problem which is our concern here, it has too exclusively evoked the sacredness of the Hellenistic kings and attached exaggerated importance to the rather anodyne title of *pontifex maximus* borne by the pagan emperors, leading to the simplistic conclusion that the empire of Constantine and his successors had been only imperfectly Christianised.

---

[3] CSCO, Scriptores Syri III, 4, *Chronica minora*, ed. I. Guidi, I, p. 24.

In actual fact, the Old Testament was far more influential than antiquity. I hope to show this by suggesting that the transition to Christianity had as much impact in the political as in the religious sphere, in a way that was almost equally visible but rather more problematic. This influence was particularly marked and decisive in the East, because of the presence there of Jerusalem, and because it was in the East that the most highly structured and enterprising Jewish communities were found and that it was hardest to forget the Judaic roots of the other 'religions of the Book' – even if this forgetfulness was sometimes more deliberate than elsewhere, for example at the time of the 'orthodox' reaction against an iconoclasm accused of Judaising. In good sacred history, the emperors of Christian Byzantium inherited from the Old Testament kings a power not only sacred and divine, which was already the case with Hellenistic and Roman power, but priestly or quasi-priestly. It was this that gave substance to the very notion of a Christian empire, but also made it ambiguous; for Christianity no longer permitted a realistic reading of the history of the Jewish people, their kings and their relations with their jealous God, but only a metaphorical one. When the age of Law was succeeded by the age of Grace, the Old Testament lost all historical reality to become only the projection of a future to be decoded, a repertoire of situations and behaviour which could no longer serve as a basis for any legitimacy. These rather transparent views gave a precise but disembodied and slightly deceptive image of the *basileia*. Between the emperors of Constantinople, who saw themselves in the mirror of the Old Testament, and the Christian Church of which they formed part, there existed a gulf which is revealed by the ceremonial that took the sovereigns from their palace to St Sophia. The debate which resulted belonged to exegesis and not to ideology, and formed part of the more general contradiction in which Christianity was both the continuation and the abolition of Judaism. It endlessly revolved round the insoluble problem of the king-priest, but rarely tackled it head on. It was muted, but periodically revived by an extreme sensibility to certain words, images and gestures. The inevitable but inadmissible notion of royal priesthood clung on to a few texts or rituals, going deeper to ground as the refutations became stronger and the balance of power between the emperor and the ecclesiastical hierarchy evolved. It was both what could not be said and what it was impossible not to think. The denials were more numerous than the affirmations, and many historians have been taken in by this arithmetical imbalance.[4]

This, briefly summarised, is the central thesis which justifies the title of my book. But reliance on a specific documentation demands certain precautions and

[4] In particular L. Bréhier, the only historian to devote a brief study to this subject: 'Hiereus kai Basileus', in *Mémorial Louis Petit. Mélanges d'histoire et d'archéologie byzantines* (Bucharest, 1948), pp. 41–5.

respect for the reader imposes certain obligations. A knowledge of Byzantium cannot be assumed, even on the part of contemporary medievalists, for whom it is not a prime concern. I have therefore deliberately chosen a fairly wide-ranging approach and made each chapter to a degree independent, within a whole in which chronological order is important but not all-important.

I propose to approach the problem by three different routes. One, the most majestic but also the most encumbered, is that of the imperial succession. On this point, Byzantium had to battle with all its heritages, lacking a theory, conceiving an opposition between unction and blood and between the legitimacy of rupture and the legitimacy of continuity, and seeking above all to develop complex practices which would neutralise the dilemma. Priestly kingship was already an element in this ambiguity; it also existed, as has recently been shown, in the early medieval West,[5] though without producing the same results or raising the same issues. For any attempt to understand the meaning of the verb 'to succeed', the eastern *basileia* offers an incomparably richer panorama. But it is not enough on its own; it is also necessary to read the Old Testament and to observe what Islam took from it.

A second approach is through coronation, that is, the ritual in which one would expect to find, behind formulae, gestures and insignia, a definition of sacred kingship and of the sovereign's relations with God and with the Church. This is probably true of the West; in the East, however, the trail quickly runs dry, or rather leads off in another direction. It emerges that coronation was slow to be ritualised, and that the role of the clergy in it was kept to a minimum; it might assume many forms and remained almost the only event that really mattered, namely, the assumption of power, planned or sudden, peaceful or bloody. Coronation prolonged or mimed this, gave it the security of popular consensus and ecclesiastical blessing, but also preserved or restored to it its charge of violence, and recognised that direct link between the emperor and God which we have already noted and which was as good as priesthood.

It is a different ceremonial that takes us to the heart of the debate, one that was much more common; repeated at every major festival, it took the emperor from the heart of his palace to the gates of St Sophia, and from there into the interior of the sanctuary, which he entered in the company of the patriarch, just as Moses had entered the 'tabernacle of the congregation' with his brother Aaron. This procession, punctuated by halts and by the crossing of thresholds, demonstrates better than any constitution the limits and the true nature of imperial power, the proximity that united kings and priests and the distance that separated them, and the conditions and the mutations that were necessary before the Old Testament sovereign could acquire Christian legitimacy. Each stage of this highly

---

[5] A. W. Lewis, *Royal Succession in Capetian France: Studies on Familial Order and the State* (London, 1981).

organised scenario had attached to it, in the collective memory and imagination, a group of stories, legends and images which emphasised its meaning and served as a reminder that those participating in or watching the ceremony might at any moment step out of their preordained roles, break the rules and perform an act so dysfunctional as to create what was called a 'scandal'.

One cannot mix centuries with impunity and, to avoid the illusion of stability which Byzantine civilisation so easily creates in those who succumb to its fascination, it is at least necessary to focus on a number of points ranged over time, and show how permanence and change interact.

Some reference to Constantine was inevitable, if not without its dangers. A book would hardly have been long enough for a full discussion of the religious policy of the first Christian emperor, and this was not my aim. Instead, I have tried, on the basis of the rectifications rapidly made to his projects, speeches and the *Life* by Eusebios of Caesarea and of the development of legends which made him a saint without ever wholly eradicating an undertow of stubborn hostility, to bring out the ambiguities inherent in the very notion of a Christian empire. Every effort has been made to get rid of Constantine: by sterilising his ideas in a rhetoric of 'as if', by neutralising the man himself in sainthood and by finding in the legend of Pope Sylvester and the Roman baptism, the first step towards the *Constitutum Constantini*, a way of inverting the roles and of distancing an *imperium* and a *sacerdotium* which no one knew how to reconcile. Constantine was thus disposed of, but the great Constantinian themes remained, and it was from this source that the 'New Constantines' sprang, successors against whom the Church kept the doors of sainthood firmly shut.

It is not far from Constantine to Antichrist, as became clear in the age of iconoclasm (730–843), that crucial period in Byzantine history that revealed the depth of a schism which had long been open, and was never again wholly healed, between the imperial power and the Church. All the grievances accumulated against the Christian emperors erupted, and they were ranked among the persecutors or found to give off more than a whiff of sulphur. This was a spectacular process, carefully stage-managed and effectively dramatised. Reforming emperors were travestied as heretics; sovereigns imbued with their religious role were caught in the trap of exegesis. When the phrase 'Am I not emperor and priest?' was attributed to Leo III, a nerve was touched, the enigmatic figure of Melchizedek, who had haunted the imagination for centuries, was conjured up and a question was posed to which there could be no answer.

Iconoclasm marked a rupture. With it ended the great age of the emperor-priest; after it strategies of piety were developed which, by means of ceremonial, religious architecture and the distribution of holy relics and imperial insignia, defined what may be called a religion of the emperors. The dynastic policy of the first Macedonian emperors – Basil I (867–86), Leo VI (886–912) and

Constantine Porphyrogenitus (913–59) – may appear chaotic when studied through the events of their reigns, but makes perfect sense in the context of the world of sanctity, that invisible but nearby world where the only sure alliances were made. There was no more speculation about Melchizedek; that direct route towards the claim to priesthood, if not entirely closed, was definitively prohibited. Nor did the Christian sovereigns now attempt to define their place theoretically in an overall ecclesiology; this was done, and as restrictively as possible, by the hierarchs and this zone, too, had become a minefield. Their aim was now more modestly and more concretely to remodel the religious landscape, to impose a system on it and to trace in it a topography and itineraries that would restore to the emperors what they had lost in the unfortunate dispute of iconoclasm. The patriarchs, generally submissive and easily replaced if they were not, gave no real cause for concern; but the patriarchate as an institution had become a threat, and it was here that a sacred space had to be recaptured. The great works of the tenth century which, like the *Book of Ceremonies*, claimed to preserve from oblivion a venerable tradition, should rather be seen as books written for the occasion, which attempted, with some success, to establish a new equilibrium in this sphere.

The last three chapters will be devoted not to the emperors, since they were no longer the source of new ideas, but to the clergy, who, from iconoclasm on, organised, wrote, argued and sometimes sought to erect the patriarchate as counter-power. A much richer and more varied documentation provides a few 'constitutional' markers: in 806, a letter from Theodore of Stoudios to the emperor Nikephoros, which sketches the first portrait of an ideal and legitimately elected patriarch; in 879–80, the first canon of the 'Photian' council, which extended patriarchal jurisdiction over the whole of eastern Christianity; at the same period, the first three titles of the juridical collection of the *Eisagoge*, in which the temporal power and a spiritual power which aimed to eclipse it were placed in false symmetry; in the mid-eleventh century, the texts which described the 'schism' of the patriarch Michael Keroularios and his battles with the imperial power. A 'clerical' rather than 'royal' reading of the history of the Jewish people encouraged this theocratic dream; but it was above all Rome which, in spite of the disagreements and the ruptures between the patriarchate and the papacy, served as model. The legend of St Sylvester baptising Constantine as he left for Constantinople and his receipt of imperial privileges, known and accepted in the East, may have sown the seed of a 'royal priesthood' conceived as the opposite to a 'priestly kingship'. New Rome recalled that it had in principle the same rights as Old Rome, and the rare patriarchs who carried this notion to its logical conclusion set up as rivals, in the same capital, the 'two powers' whose geographical separation to the two poles of Christendom had been consecrated by the Sylvestrine legend.

I will look, lastly, at the canonists and liturgists, beginning with Balsamon. He was the first, at the end of the twelfth century, to pose the problem of the emperor's 'episcopal *charismata*', to consider not only the limits of his intervention in the Church but the nature of his power, and to marshal the arguments. The time was ripe for this lucidity, which has been seen primarily as subservience; the age of the Komnenoi saw the starkest contrast between an elite of Constantinopolitan clergy and an oligarchy of metropolitans. Writing as the thoughts came into his head, Balsamon noted some particularities which made it impossible to regard the emperor as simply a layman: he entered the sanctuary in order to present his gifts, and had the right to cense the faithful and instruct them. These hasty thoughts, endlessly repeated and expanded, culminated in a theory with unction as its keystone, an 'Old Testament' unction that was all the more effective in that it was symbolic and that the sovereign received it without priestly intermediary. It conferred on him 'priestly *charismata*'. After 1204, this hypothesis collapsed. Royal unction was soon no more than a 'sacramental', as in the West; a vague symbolism invaded the ceremonial, cut it off from its roots, and avoided recognising the Davidic references. The Byzantine emperor was no more than a layman on whom was conferred only a purely formal grade of half-cleric, as with the kings studied by Marc Bloch.

This book would perhaps not be wholly without value if it did no more than add an eastern dimension to the works of western medievalists devoted to the same subject. But it has another aim. I hope to show that it was in Byzantium that were forged, tried out and appraised most of the formulae that were later re-used in the medieval and modern West, where they had neither the same depth of meaning nor, above all, the same justification. I hope, in particular, to expose the mechanisms of a historiography which describes a Christian world divided from the beginning into two cultural zones, one western, where the temporal and spiritual 'powers' were differentiated, the other eastern, where they were combined. This will be the subject of my last chapter. It begins with an analysis of the notion of 'caesaropapism', which was meant to stigmatise a typically Byzantine perversion of the relations between state and Church, but which can easily be shown to have been a product of the most contradictory religious movements of modern Europe. Nor is the 'theory of the two powers', which is contrasted with imperial interventionism, perhaps as simple or as clear as is claimed. It is a product of a mixture of warring elements and superposes the Christian distinction between the spiritual and the temporal, the functional separation between the affairs of the Church and those of the state, and the political recognition of a clerical power independent of lay power. Here, too, western Europe seeks to distance itself from the East and projects on to the writings and age of Pope Gelasius I (492–6), elevated to theoretician, a political

Augustinianism which long served it as a doctrine in a context of historical rupture and the fragmentation of power.

In Byzantium, where the illusion of continuity prevailed, the same problems had a different resonance. They started with the birth of a Christian empire and made it impossible to conceive of a Christianity where the *imperium* and the *sacerdotium* were independent of each other; they remained linked to a timescale and an ecclesiology which had as its keystone the emperor, from David to the age of Grace, then from the First to the Second Coming. Alongside the Church, for which the patriarchs and the metropolitans alone were responsible, there was this sacred history, which was perceived through the succession of the emperor-priests.

Power, it is true, changed its nature with the Incarnation. But are we to believe that Christ definitively separated the temporal and the spiritual power which had previously been merged or, on the contrary, that He finally united for the last stage in human history the priesthood of Levi and the kingship of Judah?

In one of the early chapters of *The Brothers Karamazov*, that most Byzantine of novels, Dostoevsky expresses our problem in the form of a paradox. Ivan Karamazov, revolutionary intellectual and atheist, has written a treatise on the ecclesiastical courts, in which he rejects the principle of the separation of Church and state. He is questioned on this subject by companions who between them express a whole spectrum of opinions: Miusov, another layman, a landowner, westernising and sceptical; Father Paissy, representative of Orthodoxy; and the Elder, who speaks the language of the heart. Ivan justifies his position by explaining that the confusion between Church and state, however unacceptable, will always exist, because normal relations between the two are impossible and because 'its very basis is false'. But, instead of asking what should be the place of the Church in the state, one should rather ask how the Church will be identified with the state to establish the Kingdom of God on earth. When the Roman empire became Christian, it naturally incorporated the Church, but the latter, so as not to renege on its principles, cannot but seek in its turn to control the state.

Miusov observes that this is a utopian dream and hardly serious, 'something like socialism, I suppose'. The Elder hesitates for another reason; he fears that, in a world where the law and love are merged, the criminal will no longer deserve pity, as he no longer deserves it – or so the Elder believes – in 'Lutheran countries' and in Rome, where the Church has proclaimed itself state. But he foresees nevertheless a far-off day when the Church will reign:

> 'But, good Lord,' cried Miusov, as though suddenly losing his self-control completely, 'what are you talking about? The State is to be abolished on earth and the Church is to be raised to the position of the State! Why, it's no longer

Ultramontanism, it's arch-Ultramontanism! It's more than Pope Gregory the Seventh dreamed of!'

'You've got it all wrong, sir', Father Paissy said severely. 'It is not the Church that is to be transformed into the State. Please understand that. That is Rome and its dream, that is the third temptation of the devil. On the contrary, the State is transformed into the Church, it rises to it and becomes a Church all over the world, which is the complete opposite of Ultramontanism and Rome and your interpretation of it, and is only the great predetermined destiny of the Orthodox Church on earth. This star will shine in the East!'[6]

This is how the issue was being debated in the Russia of the 1870s, with some confusion of theocracy and caesaropapism. There may have been forebodings about the ideological drift of a state–Church, but this was seen, all in all, as closer to the spirit of Orthodoxy than the spiritual treason of a Church–state. The only point quickly accepted was that a distinction in principle between the two powers rested on a lie. But what was that lie?

[6] F. M. Dostoevsky, *The Brothers Karamazov* (London, 1958), pp. 73–4.

Part 1

The Principles

1. *Heredity, legitimacy and succession*

Yet later, when they began creating princes through hereditary succession and not by election, the heirs immediately began to degenerate from their ancestors ... a prince will also see through the reading of this history [that] ... when the empire lapsed into hereditary succession, it came again to ruin.

Niccolo Machiavelli, *Discourses on Livy*
(pp. 24, 49 of trans. by J. C. and P. Bondanella,
Oxford, 1997)

POWER AND DYNASTY

Foreigners who visited Constantinople or who observed Byzantium from afar were no doubt impressed by the pomp that surrounded the imperial office, but also surprised by its chronic instability. A Chinese traveller of the seventh/eighth century noted:

Their kings are not men who last. They choose the most capable and they put him on the throne; but if a misfortune or something out of the ordinary happens in the Empire, or if the wind or the rain arrive at the wrong season, then they at once depose the emperor and put another in his place.[1]

In the middle of the ninth century, the Khazars dispatched an envoy to Constantine/Cyril, who was arriving in their country to evangelise it, and this 'astute and clever' man asked the missionary, 'Why do you persist in the bad habit of always taking as your emperors different persons, coming from different

---

[1] *Xin T'ang shu* (ancient history of the Tang, compiled in the mid-tenth century on the basis of older accounts of embassies and merchants), ch. 198, ed. Zhonghua shuju (Beijing, 1975), pp. 5313–14, quoted in F. Hirth, *China and the Roman Orient* (Hong Kong, 1985), p. 52. There are echoes of this Chinese author, at roughly the same period, in an observation of Theophylaktos Simokattes, who notes that the kings of Taugast (China) knew neither popular uprisings nor sedition, 'because with them it is the family tie that dictates the choice of leader': *Historiae*, VII, 9, 2, ed. C. de Boor and P. Wirth (Stuttgart, 1972), p. 261.

families? We, for our part, do it according to family.' Cyril replied by quoting the example of David, who succeeded to Saul, though not of his family but chosen by God.[2] Many things are said or suggested in these two brief stories: a surprising turnover of emperors; the quasi-legitimacy of famine or bread riots (when an adverse wind prevented the annual fleet from reaching the capital, or when the Nile floods were insufficient, or when a drought caused prices to soar); the decisive influence of the inhabitants of the capital; a monarchy in principle elective but where being chosen by God, rather than by the people, merely legitimated success; an absolute power 'tempered by the legal right of revolution';[3] and the superimposing of Old Testament models on the Roman heritage.

Had they been better informed, our foreigners would have been forced to accept that imperial power was often transmitted from father to son, and been surprised only that this practice was not based on any officially recognised principle. In fact, already in their day and even more in subsequent periods, the history of Byzantium can be presented as a series of dynasties which tried to establish themselves but were quickly cut short, lasting sometimes for three or four generations, but rarely longer than a century. That of Herakleios barely exceeded this limit (610–711); that of the Isaurians, starting with the iconoclast emperor Leo III, lasted eighty-five years (717–802); that of Amorion failed to reach fifty. The Macedonian dynasty, the longest lasting and most famous, survived from the seizure of power by Basil I (867) until the death of Theodora, daughter of Constantine VIII (1056). But it was only with the Komnenoi, from the end of the eleventh century, that the empire really became identified with a family and with the legitimacy of blood rights. Previously, while 'dynastic feeling' was clearly quite widespread, it lacked any institutional or ideological support. When an emperor transmitted power to his son, he was careful to say to him: 'It is not I who have chosen you, it is God; and it is the people, the senate and the army who have elected you'; the fiction of divine or constitutional choice discreetly concealed hereditary transmission.[4] The people of Constantinople

[2] *Life of St Constantine-Cyril*, 9, in F. Dvornik, *Les Légendes de Constantin et de Méthode vues de Byzance* (Prague, 1933), pp. 343–80, especially p. 360.

[3] J. B. Bury, *The Constitution of the Later Roman Empire* (Cambridge, 1910), p. 9, repeating an expression of Theodore Mommsen.

[4] This was also the case when someone from outside the family was chosen as emperor. When Justin II was close to death, he crowned his adopted son, Tiberius, declaring: 'It is not I who gives you the crown, but God by my hand': Simokattes, *Historiae*, III, 11, 8, ed. de Boor and Wirth (n. 1), p. 132, repeated by Theophanes, *Chronographia*, ed. C. de Boor (Leipzig, 1885), p. 248 (trans. C. Mango and R. Scott, *The Chronicle of Theophanes Confessor* (Oxford, 1997), p. 368). Similarly, Michael III crowning Basil I: 'In appearance, it was the hand of he who then reigned [Michael] who gave the diadem, in reality, it was the right hand of the Most High which had given it to them [Basil and Eudokia Ingerina]': Leo VI, *Funeral Oration of Basil I*, ed. and trans. A. Vogt and I. Hausherr, 'Oraison funèbre de Basile Ier par son fils Léon VI le Sage', *Orientalia Christiana*, 26.1 (Rome, 1932), p. 56; see also Theophanes Continuatus, *Chronographia*, ed. I. Bekker (Bonn, 1838), p. 240.

often demonstrated a deep attachment to the reigning family, its crowned heirs or its frustrated descendants, even succumbing to the appeal of several 'false tsarevitches': such as Theodosios, son of Maurice, persistently rumoured to have escaped the massacre of his family in 602 and to be wandering from town to town;[5] or Beser who, at Edessa, passed himself off as Tiberios, son of Justinian II;[6] or Gebon who is said to have claimed, about 858, to be the son of Theophilos and Theodora;[7] or the blinded child whose rights were defended, about 1261, by peasants who took him for John Laskaris.[8] But these same people instigated or arbitrated in frequent usurpations, which sometimes failed and were deemed 'tyrannical', and sometimes succeeded, allowing another family to acquire legitimacy. This was the very 'Roman' mechanism which made it possible to combine, without really reconciling, the two notions of usurpation and dynasty.[9]

If, in order to respond to the perplexity of the Chinese traveller, the Khazar envoy or even the historian of today, we seek texts of a 'constitutional' nature, in which Byzantine authors or jurists set out to describe their political system and give a legal basis to the exercise of power, we will be disappointed. Such texts are extremely rare, and they never explicitly discuss rules of succession.

It is true that a thousand years of Byzantine history produced a few scattered texts of this type, evidence of a desire to impose some order on its contradictory heritage – Hellenistic, Roman, Jewish and Christian.[10] But they nearly all ran counter to the historical tide and have the air of vain protests or utopias more than of attempts to lay even the provisional foundations of a political order. In the first third of the sixth century, a treatise of political science (*Peri politikes epistemes*) proposed that one organic law should regulate the appointment of emperors, a second should define the role of the senate and the status of the senators, a third should standardise the enthronement of bishops, a fourth should control the allocation of offices and dignities, and a fifth should ensure the safety and stability of the law.[11] This bias towards legalism (*dikaiarcheia*)

---

[5] Simokattes, *Historiae*, VIII, 13, 4–6, ed. de Boor and Wirth (n. 1), p. 309; Kedrenos, *Historiarum Compendium*, ed. I. Bekker (Bonn, 1838), I, p. 709.

[6] Michael the Syrian, *Chronicle*, trans. J. B. Chabot (Brussels, 1899–1910), II, pp. 503–4; *Chronicon ad annum 1234 pertinens*, 165, trans. J. B. Chabot, CSCO, Scriptores Syri 56, pp. 242–3.

[7] Niketas Paphlagon, *Life of the Patriarch Ignatius*, PG 105, col. 505.

[8] Georgios Pachymeres, *Historiae*, III, 12–13, ed. and trans. A. Failler and V. Laurent, *Relations historiques* (Paris, 1984), I, pp. 258–67.

[9] P. Lemerle, *Annuaire du Collège de France, 1972–3* (Paris, 1973), pp. 494–5.

[10] The discussion that follows is taken, slightly amended, from G. Dagron, 'Lawful society and legitimate power', in A. E. Laiou and D. Simon (eds.), *Law and Society in Byzantium, Ninth–Twelfth Centuries* (Washington, 1994), pp. 27–51, especially pp. 29–35.

[11] *Menae patricii cum Thoma referendario De scientia politica dialogus*, ed. C. M. Mazzucchi (Milan, 1982); see also A. S. Fotiou, 'Dicaearchus and the mixed constitution in sixth century Byzantium', *Byz.*, 51 (1981), pp. 533–47. Long attributed to Peter the Patrician, this work was probably written between 507 and 535 by a patrician by the name of Menas.

was soon brushed aside by the 'innovations' of Justinian (527–65), which the author of the treatise had probably been trying to counteract or forestall: the transformation of the senate into a court aristocracy and the strengthening of imperial omnipotence. Between 879 and 886, a legal handbook previously promulgated by Basil I (the *Prochiron*) was reissued in a new version (the *Eisagoge*). This gave the patriarch Photios the opportunity to preface it with 'titles' on justice, the emperor and the patriarch, that is, to transform it into a sort of institutional schema with the emphasis on law, and in which the emperor was subject not only to a superior justice but to the Roman legal tradition (that is, to the laws of the codification) and was faced with a rival in the person of the patriarch.[12] This was another vain attempt to check a trend which gave quasi-sacerdotal privileges to the *basileus*, and which caused Leo VI (886–912) to say, some years later, to mark a break with the Roman past, that 'the solicitude of the emperor will in future extend to all things and that his "foresight" [*pronoia*, a word which can equally mean divine 'providence'] controls and governs everything'.[13] In the eleventh and twelfth centuries, when the imperial office lost some of its sacred aura as it fell into the hands of the great families, the problem of the proper balance between monarchy, aristocracy and democracy in a Christian political order was debated once again;[14] but these reflections went no further than criticism of the Komnenoi and in particular of Manuel I. In 1305/6, a letter from Manuel Moschopoulos evoked a sort of social contract based – sign of the times – on a double oath of loyalty, a 'political oath' (*horkos politikos*) binding the members of the national community to each other, and an 'imperial oath' (*horkos basilikos*) binding his officials and paid soldiers to the emperor[15] (an attempt to give a constitutional appearance to a feudal society).

These attempts were few and their lack of success is evident. They always came to grief over the same issue: the impossibility of confining power within a juridical equation. Despite a lexical analogy apparent in Greek, the notions of 'lawful society' (*ennomos politeia*) and 'legitimate power' (*ennomos arche*) were, in good Roman imperial tradition, two very different matters. A

[12] The *Eisagoge* regards the law as the only principle capable of harmonising the material and spiritual elements of which man is made, and also the temporal (the emperor) and spiritual (the patriarch) powers: see A. Schminck, *Studien zu mittelbyzantinischen Rechtsbüchern* (Frankfurt-am-Main, 1986), pp. 4–10. The first Titles of this legal compilation are analysed below, pp. 229–351.

[13] Novel 47; see also, on the same subject, Novels 46, 78 and 94: *Les Novelles de Léon VI le Sage*, ed. and trans. P. Noailles and A. Dain (Paris, 1944), pp. 182–7, 270–1, 308–11.

[14] P. Magdalino, 'Aspects of twelfth century Byzantine *Kaiserkritik*', *Speculum*, 58 (1983), pp. 326–45.

[15] Ed. L. Levi, 'Cinque lettere inedite di Emanuele Moscopulo (Cod. Marc. Cl. XI, 15)', *Studi italiani di filologia classica*, 10 (1902), pp. 64–8 (letter 5); I. Ševčenko, 'The imprisonment of Manuel Moschopulos in the year 1305 or 1306', *Speculum*, 27 (1952), pp. 133–57, with a translation and commentary of the same letter.

'lawful society' is a civilisation where social relations are regulated by rules and procedures, where contracts are made before witnesses and by notarial acts, where the citizen has access to courts and to judges to pursue a complaint if he is wronged, and where these judges base their decisions on a body of written texts or established customs inspired in one way or another by the old adage of distributive and egalitarian justice, *suum cuique tribuere*.[16] This notion is based on a reality. Byzantine civilisation, descended from Greece and Rome, had a legislative tradition, conserved a legal system and made use of the expertise of notaries to draw up the most important documents of social life (wills, marriage contracts and commercial agreements); there is no question but that it gave priority to civil law and had little interest in political organisation. For instance, 'to live according to the law' (*kata nomous politeuesthai*) was given at the end of the twelfth century as the ultimate and invariable definition of the *Romaioi* under Arab or Turkish rule.[17] The notion of 'legitimate power', which seems to be the counterpart of the notion of 'lawful society', has, in reality, very different implications. It involves not limiting absolute power by constitutional rules, but rather taming it, by disciplining, rationalising and moralising the violence in which it originated.

This is why the few pages devoted to political science turn easily into 'mirrors of princes' or verge on related genres (eulogies or collections of aphorisms), whose function was not to articulate theories but to formulate moral advice.[18] The *Sentences* (*Kephalaia parainetika*) assembled by the deacon Agapetos in the sixth century,[19] or those attributed to Basil I in the ninth century,[20] offer a

---

[16] *Dig.* I, 1, 10 (= *Inst.* I, 1; *Basilica* II, 1, 10): 'Iustitia est constans et perpetua voluntas ius suum cuique tribuendi.'

[17] Balsamon, *Canonical Answers to the Patriarch Mark of Alexandria*, 4, Rhalles–Potles, *Syntagma*, IV, p. 451.

[18] H.-G. Beck, *Res Publica Romana. Vom Staatsdenken der Byzantiner*, Bayer. Akad. d. Wiss., Philos.-hist. Klasse, Sitzungsb. 1970, 2 (Munich, 1970), p. 18. On the 'mirrors of princes', see in particular H. Hunger, *Die hochsprachliche profane Literatur der Byzantiner* (Munich, 1978), I, pp. 157–65; G. Prinzing, 'Beobachtungen zu "integrierten" Fürstenspiegeln der Byzantiner', *JÖB*, 38 (1988), pp. 1–31; and for the treatises of relevance here: I. Čičurov, 'Gesetz und Gerechtigkeit in den byzantinischen Fürstenspiegeln des 6.-9. Jahrhunderts', in *Cupido legum*, ed. L. Burgmann, M. T. Fögen and A. Schminck (Frankfurt-am-Main, 1985), pp. 33–45.

[19] PG 86, cols. 1164–85; see also K. Praechter, 'Der Roman Barlaam und Joasaph in seinem Verhältnis zu Agapets Königsspiegel', *BZ*, 2 (1893), pp. 444–60; P. Henry III, 'A mirror for Justinian: the *Ekthesis* of Agapetus Diaconus', *GRBS*, 8 (1967), pp. 281–308; W. Blum, *Byzantinische Fürstenspiegel* (Stuttgart, 1981), pp. 32–9. Agapetos wrote between 527 and 548.

[20] The sentences are supposedly addressed by Basil to his son Leo, and date from 879/86: PG 107, cols. XXI–LVI; see also Blum, *Byzantinische Fürstenspiegel* (n. 19), pp. 39–41; I. S. Čičurov, 'Tradicija i novatorstvo v politčeskoj mysli Vizantii konca IX v. (mesto *Poučitel'nyh glav* Vasilija I v istorii žanra)', *VizVrem.*, 47 (1986), pp. 95–100; A. Markopoulos, 'Autour des *Chapitres parénétiques* de Basile Iᵉʳ', in *EVPSYCHIA. Mélanges offerts à Hélène Ahrweiler* (Paris, 1998), II, pp. 469–78.

picture of 'legitimate power,' one of delegation and reproduction which owes much to Hellenistic Greece.[21] The emperor ought to be an image of God so as to embody in himself an image offered for the imitation of men; he ought to be governed by the laws of God so as to be able to govern his subjects legitimately;[22] he ought to impose on himself a respect for the law, knowing that no one can force this on him;[23] he ought to endeavour to see himself as the 'companion in earthly slavery' (syndoulos) of other men, made of the same dust, as he was supposed to be reminded by the pouch filled with earth that he held in his hand, the akakia.[24] These mirrors or maxims did not offer a political ideology, that is, an organised system, which had perhaps existed in the Hellenistic models on which they were more or less loosely based; in the Roman and Byzantine period, in any case, the genre was closer to the spiritual exercises made fashionable by the Stoics.[25] Nor did they amount to an independent and theoretical reflection on the nature of power; they aimed rather to provide whoever exercised power with an antidote which would protect him against the dangers to which he was inevitably exposed, to subject his thinking and his sensibility to a moral experience and to lead him, by means of memorable maxims and incantatory formulae, towards a meditation on himself. It may seem ironic that these 'mirrors' often served as alibis for absolutist regimes, that they are associated with the name of unscrupulous autocrats like Justinian and Basil, and that they enjoyed their greatest success in tsarist Russia and the courts of European monarchs[26] – but this was no accident. For the purpose of these works was to provide a cure for the inevitable diseases of absolute power not by a change of political system but by the personal 'conversion' of the prince.

The aim was to convert brute force (to theriodes, therion alogon, in the words of Agapetos and Basil)[27] into legitimate power, and the historical sources often allude to this conversion. If Theophanes described Leo V, in 814, as 'most

[21] See in particular the Treatise on Kingship of the neo-Pythagorean Ekphantos, ed. L. Delatte, Les Traités sur la royauté d'Ecphante, Diotogène et Sthénidas (Liège/Paris, 1942), and Eusebios of Caesarea. But the borrowings from these works, like those from Philo or more probably a pseudo-Philo, were made through the intermediary of some unknown florilegium; see also Praechter, 'Der Roman Barlaam und Joasaph' (n. 19); Henry, 'A mirror for Justinian' (n. 19); I. Ševčenko, 'A neglected Byzantine source of Muscovite political ideology', Harvard Slavic Studies, 2 (1954), pp. 141–79, repr. in I. Ševčenko, Byzantium and the Slavs in Letters and Culture (Cambridge, Mass./Naples, 1991), pp. 49–87, with bibliography, pp. 726–7.

[22] Agapetos, 1, PG 86, cols. 1164–5; Basil, PG 107, cols. XXIX–XXXII.

[23] Agapetos, 27, PG 86, cols. 1172–3; Basil, PG 107, col. XXXVII.

[24] Agapetos, 21, 71, PG 86, cols. 1172, 1185; Basil, PG 107, cols. XXVIII, XLIV–XLV.

[25] P. Hadot, Exercices spirituels et philosophie antique (Paris, 1981), especially pp. 13–74.

[26] For the diffusion of the Sentences of Agapetos in Russia, see Ševčenko, 'A neglected Byzantine source' (n. 19); I. Ševčenko, 'On some sources of Prince Svjatoslav's Izbornik of the year 1076', in Orbis Scriptus: Dmitrij Tschizewskij zum 70. Geburtstag, ed. D. Gerhardt, W. Weintraub and H.-J. Winkel (Munich, 1966), pp. 723–38, repr. in Ševčenko, Byzantium and the Slavs (n. 21), pp. 241–61.

[27] Agapetos, 40, PG 86, col. 1176; Basil, PG 107, col. XXVIII.

legitimately emperor of the Romans',[28] it was to indicate that this general, summoned to the empire by war and popular acclaim, had succeeded in making the changes that turned him into a legitimate sovereign – not rushing things, allowing the patriarch to act, ceasing to be an army leader, submitting, not to constitutional rules which did not exist, or even to procedures that were more than a little vague, but to a process that enabled him to quit one role, that of general approved by plebiscite, and assume another, that of emperor elected by God. If, on the other hand, Michael Attaleiates and his contemporaries doubted whether Isaac I Komnenos, in 1057, had successfully negotiated the transition from 'tyranny' to 'legitimate power', in spite of his probity and his courage, it was because he was unable to rid himself of the warlike fury that had given him power but not sacredness. Once emperor, he had himself depicted on the coinage with an unsheathed sword; he had confiscated, like a tribal chieftain, the property of his enemies; in short, he had not 'converted' himself into a legitimate sovereign.[29]

It was not power that was legitimate; but whoever appropriated power could be made legitimate by choosing to respect the law. This simple idea had been cast by the ancient tradition in the form of a paradox, its first term borrowed from Hellenistic literature – the emperor is not subject to the laws because he is himself 'living law'[30] – and its second applying a corrective – but a legitimate sovereign ought to choose to conform to the laws.[31] In short, legitimacy was achieved through a conversion to legality. This paradox seems at first sight a rather lame device to reconcile the irreconcilable and to pass fraudulently, by way of morality, from law to politics; but a number of jurists attempted to give it substance. When Balsamon, at the end of the twelfth century, developed the same principle of an emperor's superiority in relation to the civil laws

---

[28] *Chronographia*, ed. de Boor (n. 4), p. 502, line 24 (pp. 685–6 of Mango and Scott translation). Theophanes could hardly have guessed, when he wrote, that Leo V would revive iconoclasm.

[29] Michael Attaleiates, *Historia*, ed. I. Bekker (Bonn, 1853), pp. 59–62; Skylitzes Continuatus, ed. E. T. Tsolakes (Thessalonike, 1968), pp. 103–6; Zonaras, *Annales*, ed. M. Pinder (Bonn, 1897) III, pp. 665–8.

[30] For the emperor as 'living law', see in particular H. Hunger, *Prooimion, Elemente der byzantinischen Kaiseridee in den Arengen der Urkunden* (Vienna, 1964), pp. 117–22; Beck, *Res Publica Romana* (n. 18), pp. 31–3; D. Simon, 'Princeps legibus solutus. Die Stellung des byzantinischen Kaisers zum Gesetz', in *Gedächtnisschrift für Wolfgang Kunkel*, ed. D. Nörr and D. Simon (Frankfurt-am-Main, 1984), pp. 449–92.

[31] The idea is ancient and has been expressed in many different ways. Among the Hellenophone theoreticians and rhetors, the Pythagorean Diotogenes was already using the formula: 'The king is either animate law or legitimate power': Delatte, *Traités sur la royauté* (n. 21), pp. 37–8, 245–9; see also Dion of Prusa (= Chrysostomos), *Orationes*, III, 43, ed. G. de Budé (Leipzig, 1916), pp. 51–2; Libanios, *Orationes*, ed. R. Förster (Leipzig, 1908), LIX, 12–13. In the juridical sources: *Inst.* II, 17, 8 ('Licet legibus soluti sumus, at tamen legibus vivimus', a phrase attributed to the emperors Severus and Antoninus); *CJ* I, 14, 4 and VI, 23, 3; *Epitome legum*, I, 29, Zepos, *Jus*, IV, p. 290; Kekaumenos, *Strategikon*, ed. B. Wassiliewsky and V. Jernstedt (St. Petersburg, 1896), p. 93; Manuel Komnenos, Novel 63 (1159), Zepos, *Jus*, I, pp. 385–6; Andronikos II, Novel 38 (of 1296), Zepos, *Jus*, I, p. 560.

and the canons of the Church, which he did not exactly present as his own
but analysed with obvious approval, he justified this imperial privilege in two
ways: by 'economy' (*oikonomia*), that is, by the possibility always open to the
emperor to cease to apply a rule on grounds of a higher interest and to introduce
an exception that did not disprove the rule; and by the emperor's 'episcopal
privileges' (*archiepiskopika dikaia*), that is, by the quasi-sacerdotal nature of
his office.[32] Balsamon provided the empty paradox with a content that might
be interpreted as a theory of power. At almost the same period, Chomatianos
offered another theory in a passage where he distinguished, in rather vague
terms though his meaning is clear, between *to dikaiotikon* and *to exousiastikon*;
between on the one hand, a natural law that governs social relations, gives
priority to the legislative heritage and defines the ideal of the 'lawful society'
(*ennomos politeia*), and on the other, the freedom conferred by 'legitimate
power' (*ennomos arche*) to govern by decreeing norms that responded to the
needs of the moment.[33] This is a system of thought which opposed, in terms
that would not have been disowned by the sulphurous Carl Schmitt, norm and
decision, legal or institutional constraints and freedom to rule, lawful state and
a 'state of emergency'.[34]

In Byzantium, this duality received from Christianity a distinctive character
and a justification it would otherwise have lacked. The concept of *eunomia* is not
specifically Christian; those of an internalisation of norms and of a legitimacy
acquired by conversion would be more so, and that is why the 'mirrors of
princes' could so easily be Christianised on the surface. What is specific to
Christianity, on the other hand, is to put the problem of law in a historical
perspective, or rather to contrast the present age of Grace with a bygone age of
Law, as St Paul did when he wrote: 'Moreover the law entered, that the offence
might abound. But where sin abounded, grace did much more abound'. Adam's
disobedience provoked the law, which Moses received from God; but Christ's
coming freed men from both the rule of law and that of sin.[35] The paradox of
the Incarnation gave a temporal dimension to that of the 'living law' and made
it easier to conceive of two legislative orders intended to complement each
other, like the Old and the New Testaments: on the one hand the codifications

---

[32] Commentary on canon 16 of Carthage, Rhalles–Potles, *Syntagma*, III, pp. 349–51; Simon, 'Princeps legibus solutus' (n. 30), pp. 475–6. For *oikonomia*, see G. Dagron, 'La règle et l'exception. Analyse de la notion d'économie', in *Religiöse Devianz. Untersuchungen zu sozialen, rechtlichen und theologischen Reaktionen auf religiöse Abweichung im westlichen und östlichen Mittelalter*, ed. D. Simon (Frankfurt-am-Main, 1990), pp. 1–18; for the emperor's 'episcopal rights', see below, pp. 258–69.
[33] J. B. Pitra, *Analecta sacra et classica Spicilegio Solesmensi parata*, VI (Paris/Rome, 1891), pp. 458–9; Simon, 'Princeps legibus solutus' (n. 30), pp. 450–9 (with revised text and commentary).
[34] C. Schmitt, *Politische Theologie. Vier Kapitel zur Lehre von der Souveränität*, 2nd ed. (Berlin, 1934, repr. 1985).
[35] Romans, 5: 12–21.

(that of Justinian repeated in the *Basilika*), a juridical heritage safeguarded but dehistoricised; on the other the Novels, acts of government by a sovereign of the age of Grace and not the age of Law, word of an emperor who, in a 'a state of emergency', was required to respond to the needs of the moment, orient the law in the direction of the 'love of men' and do everything in his power, by imitating Christ, to keep humanity on the path of an 'economy of salvation'.

In this difficult reconciliation of power and law, theories and ideologies could serve only as masks. The legitimacy accorded by men or by God could be accorded only to individuals. Whether the emperor was subject to the law or made a 'living law endowed with speech' and a providential saviour, there was nothing to justify the delegation of sovereignty to one family on a lasting basis. The problem of succession, therefore, remained unresolved and was never tackled head on. It was the weak point, spotted by both the Chinese traveller and the Khazar envoy. When it was transmitted, a moment of danger and fascination, power – I mean imperial power, source of all other – seemed like an absolute and almost magical phenomenon, a sort of theophany; there were no institutional criteria to test its legitimacy, only historical and moral references, accumulated examples which eventually came to constitute a rule of the game, with innumerable variations, and tacitly to define transgressions in the absence of a procedure. Each new emperor had to observe these rules if he wanted to achieve legitimacy.

Among the models which did not found a right was that of a sovereignty transmitted from father to son; though in practice compatible with it, its formulation offended against an old 'republican' sensibility,[36] the dual conviction that power was received by delegation (from the people or from God) and that it was exercised in the context of a *res publica* or state. It was indubitably because the concept of state was in abeyance that the medieval West came officially to base a political order on family structure. The history of medieval France, for example, shows how a patrimony was gradually turned into a kingdom and how a family *honor* became a crown. Even if historians now qualify this traditional picture,[37] it remains the case that with feudalism the family became the basis of a state organisation. But where there was no feudal revolution, as in Byzantium, it was, conversely, the family which tried to find a place in a political system which did not allow for it and had difficulty accepting it. The empire existed independently of the emperors who came to power and who attempted to found a dynasty. It existed in the Roman form of a vast administrative and juridical construction which the sovereign dominated and whose cohesion he ensured without ever becoming entirely identified with it. It also existed within

[36] See, for example, the quotation from Machiavelli at the head of this chapter.
[37] Notably Lewis, *Royal Succession* (see introduction, n. 5).

the great temporal structure set out in the Old and New Testaments and their apocalyptic continuations, in which divine choice passed from the Jewish people to Rome, and in which the Incarnation of Christ providentially corresponded to the accession of Augustus, and His return on the Day of Judgement to the voluntary abdication of the last emperor of Constantinople. It also existed in the half Hellenistic, half Christian symbolic form of the *basileia*, of a kingdom of all the earth which was only the reflection of the celestial kingdom, ruled by a sovereign here below who was only the provisional delegate of the one on high. These and some other representations gave substance and meaning to the empire; they prevented it from being equated with one family and led to a distinction being drawn, as sharply as today, between the imperial office and its holder.

All the same, in a structure too lofty and too rigid to recognise blood rights, there was nothing to prevent the sovereigns of Constantinople, like their Roman precursors, from developing family strategies. It was regarded as natural for an emperor, once he had received or seized power, to try to transmit it to his children, at the risk of implicating them in his fall. An emperor who did not attempt to get his son crowned would not have lived up to expectations and would probably have lost all credibility. Only one emperor made a show of wishing to resist such pressure. Leo IV, an emperor of total legitimacy, son of Constantine V and grandson of Leo III, in 776 refused to make his sole heir, the future Constantine VI, co-emperor on the pretext that if he himself were to die prematurely, his son risked being assassinated, whereas if he remained simply a private person he stood a reasonable chance of leading a quiet life. But this was a manoeuvre designed to raise the stakes and to obtain from the representatives of the constituted bodies (circus factions, army, guilds and senate) a written commitment to accept as emperor no one but Leo himself, his son Constantine or their descendants.[38] The initial refusal made it possible to take a further step towards the establishment of a dynastic system; but it also emphasised that an emperor could in principle exclude his son from the succession and that, paradoxically, the greatest assurance of a hereditary transmission of power was an oath that linked each of the social bodies personally to the emperor and his family. The rather strange procedure of the 'oath', which was tending to spread,[39] makes it clear that dynastic logic was foreign to the empire and

---

[38] Theophanes, *Chronographia*, ed. de Boor (n. 4), pp. 449–50 (pp. 620–1 of Mango and Scott translation), and see below, pp. 76–8.

[39] See N. Svoronos, 'Le Serment de fidélité à l'empereur byzantin et sa signification constitutionnelle', *REB*, 9 (1951), pp. 106–42; A. Pertusi, 'Insegne del potere sovrano e delegato a Bisanzio e nei paesi di influenza bizantina', in *Settimane di studio del Centro italiano di studi sull'alto medioevo*, 23 (1975), *Simboli e simbologia nell'alto medioevo* (Spoleto, 1976), II, pp. 529–35, who discusses other oaths intended to assure the rights of under-age successors (Michael II, Theophilos and Leo VI); see also Theophanes Continuatus, *Chronographia*, ed. Bekker (n. 4), pp. 78–9; Ioannis Skylitzes, *Synopsis Historiarum*, ed. I. Thurn (Berlin, 1973), pp. 191–2.

was part of a strategy of power. It was negotiated between the emperor and his subjects, and not always without precautions. The brutality with which Michael II, in 820, demanded from the senators a written commitment to defend to the death his future wife and his descendants provoked this reaction on the part of one chronicler:

> In this way he believed he would retain power, not only as long as he himself lived, but also after his death, whereas everything depends of necessity not on them [the senators], but on the hand of God, 'by [whom] kings reign' [Proverbs, 8: 15], and tyrants enslave the earth.[40]

In 912, the dying Leo VI was more respectful of the forms when he made the senators swear 'to retain their goodwill towards his wife and his son'.[41]

A dynasty was never, in Byzantium, more than the unpredictable pursuit of an individual destiny, an extension to the family of a personal adventure. The Byzantine sources say this, in their way, by taking up the biblical idea that God demonstrated his approval or disapproval of a 'king' by bestowing or withholding from him the joy of seeing his children and his grandchildren accede to the throne. John of Nikiu, writing about Herakleios and his religious policy, reports the following prediction of Severos of Antioch: 'No son of a Roman emperor will occupy the throne of his father as long as the Chalcedonian sect rules the world.'[42] When the chroniclers tell how Leo V ascended to the throne in 813 and then revived iconoclasm, they assume that he reasoned as follows (which he may well have done within his entourage): 'Those of my predecessors who honoured images saw their reign cut short by a brutal death; those, in contrast, who suppressed the worship of images, like Leo III and Constantine V, enjoyed long reigns and transmitted the empire to their children and grandchildren; it is they, therefore, whom I should copy.'[43] The dynastic succession was here not a natural right of the descendants, linked to the definition of the empire, but a blessing granted by God to an emperor whose religious and political legitimacy was so strong that it assured him not only a long personal reign, but an extension of his *basileia* to descendants who received and sought to preserve it. What we call for convenience a 'dynasty' was no more than a prolongation of the legitimacy of an emperor 'to the third, fourth or fifth generation'.[44] This had been the aim of Leo V. This, in the *Book of Ceremonies* (where we will search in vain for even a glimmer of a dynastic theory, although the imperial

---

[40] Theophanes Continuatus, *Chronographia*, ed. Bekker (n. 4), pp. 78–9.

[41] Skylitzes, *Synopsis*, ed. Thurn (n. 39), pp. 191–2.

[42] *The Chronicle of John, Coptic Bishop of Nikiu*, 116, trans. R. H. Charles (London, 1916), p. 185 (concerning Martina and the succession to Herakleios).

[43] *Scriptor incertus de Leone Armenio*, ed. I. Bekker (Bonn, 1842), p. 349; Theophanes Continuatus, *Chronographia*, ed. Bekker (n. 4), pp. 26–7, where the advice is attributed to a pseudo-monk.

[44] For a parallel with the West, see Lewis, *Royal Succession* (see introduction, n. 5), pp. 50, 36 (St Valery or St Riquier appears to Hugh Capet to tell him that his heirs will retain the crown until the seventh generation).

family is ubiquitous), was the wish of the senators when they congratulated the emperor on the birth of a son 'born in the purple' and hoped that he would 'know the children of the children of the porphyrogenitus and see the porphyrogenitus himself, advanced in years, inherit power and the paternal kingship'.[45] This was the eulogy which the rhetoricians Themistios and Libanios wove into their speeches when they addressed Constantius II, heir to the throne to 'the third generation' (*ek trigonias*).[46] And it was the assumption of Psellos and his contemporaries when they praised, in the middle of the eleventh century, the five generations of emperors (the *pentagonia*) which made Zoe and Theodora, daughters of Constantine VIII and last descendants of the Macedonian dynasty, the potential heiresses of the 'imperial patrimony' (*basileios kleros*).[47]

FAMILY AND DYNASTY

Family and empire are concepts, if not irreconcilable, at least heterogeneous. It was not enough for a family to seize power for a dynasty to be founded. Byzantine history demonstrates this by offering an almost complete spectrum of cases, which correspond to different conceptions of the imperial office and of imperial legitimacy.

The first is that of marriage. This was used to integrate into a family which was regarded as legitimate individuals who were fighting their way up to the summit of power. The Tetrarchy relied almost exclusively on this solution. To try to prevent the break up of the empire and encourage harmony among the many and inevitably rival emperors, they resorted, in true Roman fashion, to marriages, that is, to women. Galerius became Diocletian's son-in-law; Maxentius, son of Maximian, became the son-in-law of Galerius. Constantine himself took as his second wife Fausta, daughter of Maximian and sister of Maxentius, and gave his half-sister Constantia in marriage to Licinius. Later, to bind more closely to the immediate family a branch suspected of dissidence, Constantine's daughters, Helena and Constantina, were married to his half-nephews, the former to Julian, then Gallus, sons of Julius Constantius, the latter to Hannibalianus, son of Flavius Dalmatius.

In the second, 'patrimonial', model power was reserved to the members of a family, at the risk of it being shared as with a patrimony. This is well illustrated by Constantine the Great, who ended the system which had promoted him and who seems to have envisaged a partition of the empire between his

[45] *De cerimoniis*, II, 21, p. 616.
[46] Themistios, *Orationes* I, 2b, ed. H. Schenkel and G. Downey (Leipzig, 1965), I, p. 4; Libanios, *Orationes*, ed. LIX, 13 (of 348), R. Förster (n. 31), p. 215; see also Julian the emperor, *Orationes* IV, 131c, ed. and trans. J. Bidez (Paris, 1932).
[47] Psellos, *Chronographia*, ed. and trans. E. Renauld (Paris, 1967), I, pp. 67, 99; Skylitzes, *Synopsis*, ed. Thurn (n. 39), p. 416; Zonaras, *Annales*, ed. Pinder (n. 29), III, p. 609.

descendants or relatives.[48] After 317, he gave the rank of caesar successively to his sons Crispus, Constantine, Constantius and Constans, and even to his half-nephew, Hannibalianus. It is not clear whether Constantine had a clearly formulated plan for the succession at the time of his death in 337,[49] but the situation he left behind led to a division of the empire, or at least to a division of territorial responsibilities within it. Britain, Gaul and Spain went to Constantine II, Italy, Africa and Pannonia to Constans, the east to Constantius II, and eastern Illyricum to Hannibalianus. If this plan had been carried out, Constantine would have recreated within his own family the Tetrarchy which he had destroyed by eliminating all his rivals and establishing what the sources freely call his 'monarchy'. Between 337 and 340, wars and assassinations simplified this partition, leaving only two brothers, Constans in Rome and Constantius in Constantinople; this 'fraternal' duality lasted for more than a century because it adapted the principle of partition to geographical reality, that is, the two *partes*, and to the need for a degree of political unity. From this period on, 'to have the empire as inheritance' was much more than a customary metaphor to signify that an emperor's son had a good chance, if not the right, to succeed his father.[50] This expression, in a highly legalistic society, revealed a conception of the empire more patrimonial than authentically hereditary or dynastic. It also lent itself to ambiguity, because it suggested an appropriation of the *res publica* and renunciation of any elective principle and, even more, because, in good Roman and Byzantine law, a patrimony was divided between all the children. The empire-patrimony was an empire whose indivisibility was challenged with every succession and which, after being reunified in the hands of the 'father', risked falling apart whenever there was more than one heir. The danger was real at a time when the empire had two capitals and many imperial residences. But even when the East alone remained and the fate of the emperor was definitively linked to that of Constantinople, the spectre of a partition of the 'imperial patrimony' re-appeared from time to time, as either a territorial partition of the empire or, much more difficult to avert, a division of imperial power.

Marriage alliances and patrimonial succession were often combined in a highly pragmatic fashion. This was the case for several decades with what is incorrectly called the 'Valentinian–Theodosian dynasty' (fourth to fifth centuries). The 'Valentinian dynasty' continued for a while in the West while soon disappearing in the East; but Theodosius I attached himself to it by taking as

---

[48] All the sources, beginning with Eusebios of Caesarea, emphasise the fact that Constantine made the empire a 'patrimony' to be transmitted to his children; see below, p. 145.

[49] E. Stein, *Histoire du Bas-Empire*, French ed. by J.-R. Palanque, I (Bruges, 1959), pp. 131, 485; and more recently, R. Klein, 'Die Kämpfe um die Nachfolge nach dem Tode Constantins des Grossen', *ByzForsch.*, 6 (1979), pp. 101–50.

[50] Thus it is said, in the *Life of St Irene Abbess of Chrysobalanton*, 3, ed. and trans. J. O. Rosenqvist (Uppsala, 1986), pp. 8–9, that Theodora had Michael III as 'heir to the empire'.

his second wife Galla, daughter of Valentinian I and sister of Valentinian II. Contemporary sources all emphasise the ties of kinship by marriage on which the *unanimitas imperii* was based, once again, even if the catastrophes which engulfed the West gave this phrase more the status of wishful thinking than a description of reality. Valentinian the Great appeared at the head of a 'genea-logy' which circulated in the East and included several crowned heads.[51] But the *basileia* was not devolved to a family, rather it was a family which had authority to appropriate all those who acceded to the *basileia*. Agnellus, in the first half of the ninth century, reports that the Augusta Aelia Galla Placidia, one of the most representative figures of the age, daughter of Theodosius I and Galla, half-sister of Honorius and Arcadius, had after a vow decorated the church of St John the Evangelist in Ravenna with mosaics representing, around herself and her children (Valentinian III and Honoria), the reigning cou-ple (Theodosius II and Eudokia), emperors connected by family ties (Gratian, Valentinian II, Theodosius I, Arcadius and Eudoxia), and also Constantine the Great and Constantius II.[52] This was a strange hotchpotch, in which succession and kinship were deliberately confused and which seemed to recognise in the first century of the Christian empire a sort of familial logic, in the absence of a dynastic structure. What had made it possible to impose a semblance of order on this chaotic process was its culmination. Theodosius II, third-generation Theodosian in direct line, model of the legitimate heir and model, for better or worse, of the young prince 'born in the purple', was proclaimed emperor almost from birth and married to the 'most beautiful young woman' in the empire.[53] It seemed reasonable to hope that from this series of marriages a dynasty would emerge.

But for a dynastic succession to be established, it had to escape the ill luck or biological misfortune which could suddenly, in any royal line, cause the reservoir of male heirs to dry up.[54] When Theodosius II died without leaving a son, Byzantium suffered from such a dearth for more than 150 years. The very principle of the hereditary transmission of power was lost behind more or less constitutional rules, which were actually only procedures for arranging a replacement. In 450, the succession was assured by a fictive and sterile marriage between the sister of Theodosius II, Pulcheria, and an obscure soldier, Marcian (450–7), who was soon replaced by another, Leo (457–74). Leo and his wife

[51] It is appended to the *Chronographikon Syntomon* of Nikephoros the Patriarch, ed. C. Boor *Nicephori . . . opuscula historica* (Leipzig, 1880), pp. 102–4.

[52] *Liber pontificalis Ecclesiae Ravennatis, MGH, Scriptores rerum Langobardicarum*, p. 307; com-pleted by the *De dedicatione ecclesiae Sancti Iohannis Evangelistae*, an anonymous work of the thirteenth or fourteenth century, ed. in L. A. Muratori, *Rerum Italicarum Scriptores*, I, 2 (Milan, 1725), pp. 570–1. See also A. Grabar, *L'Empereur dans l'art byzantin* (Paris, 1936), pp. 28–9 (which needs correction on several points).

[53] See below, pp. 41–8.   [54] Lewis, *Royal Succession* (see introduction, n. 5).

Verina had the son they had prayed for but he died almost immediately.[55] A grandson, child of their daughter Ariadne, lived just long enough to legitimate the accession of his father, the Isaurian Zeno (474–5, 476–91); but Zeno in his turn died childless, and Ariadne persuaded the senate to elect, and herself married, the aged Anastasios (491–518), a sixty-year-old *silentiarius*, who left three nephews, all quickly removed from the scene. This lack of dynastic perspective and this ageing of the empire – in some ways comparable to the gerontocracy of the last years of the Soviet empire – gave the role of arbiter to the senators and the soldiers for a while. Justin I was himself aged sixty-eight at the time of his accession (518) and could only, when close to death (527), adopt his nephew Justinian to make him his successor; similarly Justinian (527–65), who was unable to have children, transmitted power to a nephew, Justin II the *kouropalates*, at the end of a long reign which ended in a sinister doomsday atmosphere. Justin II (565–78), who was afflicted with madness a few years later, shared power with his wife the augusta Sophia, then adopted as his son and named caesar, that is designated successor, an officer from among his friends, Tiberios. He, in his turn, made caesar, then, as he lay dying on 13 August 582, named augustus Maurice, a forty-three-year-old general whom he had chosen as his son-in-law.

In his *Ecclesiastical History*, John of Ephesos dwells at length on this dearth of heirs in order to explain why the birth of a male child, on 4 August 583, the year after Maurice's accession and marriage, made such an impression on contemporaries.[56] The heir was fêted. The choice of his name provoked a war of slogans between the demes, the Blues opting for 'Justinian' on account of that emperor's longevity, the Greens, successfully, for 'Theodosios', to recall the only hope, soon dashed, nurtured by the eastern empire since Constantine of becoming established in one family.[57] An acclamation painted on a wall in Aphrodisias confirms that the child was hailed as a 'New Theodosios'. He had as of right all the honours that his birth 'in the purple' had earned the last of the Theodosians. The festivities accompanying his marriage, in February 602, lasted for a week. Maurice was soon the father of at least six sons and three

---

[55] G. Dagron, 'Le fils de Léon Ier (463). Témoignages concordants de l'hagiographie et de l'astrologie', *Anal. Boll.*, 100 (*Mélanges B. de Gaiffier and F. Halkin*) (1982), pp. 271–5.

[56] *Historiae ecclesiasticae pars tertia*, V, 14, trans. E. W. Brooks, CSCO 106, pp. 199–200. For a more detailed analysis, see G. Dagron, 'Nés dans la pourpre', *TM*, 12 (1994), pp. 105–42.

[57] An old scholium in the ms. *Vaticanus gr.* 977 (tenth century) shows that the choice of forename set the Greens against the Blues: 'I have found', wrote the scholiast, 'in a book of St Isaac, that Justinian lived a little more than ninety years. It says there: Constantina, wife of Maurice, gave birth to a son, whom Maurice named Theodosios, being his first born. The Blues shouted that he ought to be called Justinian, the Greens that he ought to be called Theodosios, because Theodosios had been orthodox and had lived for many years. The Blues riposted by saying: "May God give you in peace as many years as he gave to Justinian", that is ninety years and more, whereas Theodosios lived for only fifty years.' P. Maas, 'Metrische Akklamationen der Byzantiner', *BZ*, 21 (1912), p. 29, n. 1.

daughters;[58] his philoprogenitive powers were satirised in street songs,[59] but with a secret relief that the age of succession problems was over. John of Ephesos is careful to record that the birth of the 'New Theodosios' was regretted by ambitious men who had hoped, as in the past, to strike lucky thanks to an insecure reign, and that it was hailed in the Hippodrome by popular acclamation: 'It is good that God has given you [to us] and that you have liberated us from the servitude of many!'

A superfluity of heirs made the hereditary transmission of power possible; but for a patrimonial or hereditary succession to be transformed into a proper dynasty, it was also necessary for the selective principle of primogeniture to be added, tacitly or explicitly, to the general principle of community of blood. This alone made it possible to avoid confusion when there were numerous heirs and to ensure that the empire did not become the common property of the male members of the family,[60] but passed, with each generation, to whoever was the oldest or the 'most suitable'. It is not known how Maurice was proposing to arrange his succession before the massacre on 27 November 602 in which he and his sons were killed. He may have intended to crown only the oldest, or he may have planned a 'patrimonial' partition of the empire on the Constantinian model.[61] At all events, throughout the period that followed, under Herakleios and his descendants (610–711), the difficult process of transforming the reigning family into a dynastic lineage was as serious a problem within the empire as, outside it, were the problems of the Persian and Arab war, which reduced the empire by half, or the long religious debate about Christ's wills, which eventually split eastern Christendom.

The impression is given of a family that from the outset seized power, in 610, and then perpetuated itself under two names and their diminutives: the name of the exarch of Carthage, Herakleios, father of the new emperor, and the name of the holy founder of the Christian empire, Constantine, which added

---

[58] *Chronicon Paschale*, ed. B. G. Niebuhr (Bonn, 1832), p. 693, which gives the names of six male and three female children still living in 602.

[59] John of Antioch, *frag.* 218c, *FHG*, V, pp. 35–6; Theophanes, *Chronographia*, ed. de Boor (n. 4), p. 283 (p. 408 of Mango and Scott translation); G. Dagron, *Constantinople imaginaire. Etudes sur le recueil des 'Patria'* (Paris, 1984), pp. 179–80.

[60] For the Merovingians, the Carolingians and even the Capetians to begin with, this conception of patrimonial empire and the custom of partition, attributed too exclusively to the 'Frankish mentality', is analysed by Lewis, *Royal Succession* (see introduction, n. 5); J. Barbey, *Etre roi. Le roi et son gouvernement en France de Clovis à Louis XVI* (Paris, 1992), pp. 19–20.

[61] Theophylaktos Simokattes says that Maurice, when sick in the fifth year of his reign (596), drew up a will, rediscovered under Herakleios, which provided for a partition of the empire between his children, on the Constantinian model: to the eldest, Theodosios, Constantinople and the East, to the second, Tiberios, Rome and Italy, and 'to the others the rest': *Historiae*, VIII, 11, 9, ed. de Boor and Wirth (n. 1), pp. 305ff. J. B. Bury presumed that Illyricum and Africa would have gone to two younger sons, Peter and Paul: *A History of the Later Roman Empire from Arcadius to Irene* (395 AD to 800 AD), II (London, 1889), p. 94, n. 2.

legitimacy. The women who conveyed heredity assumed a particular importance. They, too, took family or dynastic names. The sources relate that, on
6 October 610, Herakleios received from the hands of the patriarch Sergios
both the imperial crown and the crown of marriage, taking as his wife Fabia,
who became the augusta Eudokia.[62] When she died, on 13 August 613, leaving a son and a daughter, the latter, Epiphaneia, then just a year old, was in
her turn crowned augusta and took the name Eudokia (4 October 613);[63] it
was almost as if the empire could not now manage without an empress or, as
Michael II was later to say, 'the senators' wives without a mistress'.[64] *Romanitas*
adopted a new image and shed some of its old finery. The *imperator Caesar
Augustus* became the *basileus*, a title long unofficial but officially attested for
the first time in a protocol of 21 March 629, when the fall of the Persian empire left it vacant. The imperial dignity was no longer seen as the topmost
rank of a hierarchy, but as a sort of divine grace, a symbolic unction which
attached the chosen few to a line of Davidic sovereigns and extended to their
family.[65]

It looked as if Herakleios was instituting a dynasty and making provision for
his succession. He baptised and crowned as co-emperor (on 25 December 612 or
22 January 613) his only son by his first wife, Herakleios the New Constantine,
then about eight months old;[66] later, he gave the surviving sons of his second
wife – his niece Martina, whom he had married and immediately proclaimed
augusta around 622[67] – the imperial dignities of caesar and *nobelissimos*, inherited from the old *cursus* and not normally leading to the exercise of power.[68]
But this fragile equilibrium was broken when, on 4 July 638, one of the sons
of his second marriage, Heraklonas, was in his turn made co-emperor.[69] It then
looked as if the two marriages had produced an empire with two heads, and
that Herakleios had stalled midway between two institutional systems, one old,
the other new. He had established not so much a dynasty as a family collective,

[62] Bury, *Later Roman Empire* (n. 61), p. 299.
[63] Theophanes, *Chronographia*, ed. de Boor (n. 4), p. 300.
[64] Theophanes Continuatus, *Chronographia*, ed. Bekker (n. 4), pp. 78–9.
[65] See in particular S. Spain Alexander, 'Heraclius, Byzantine imperial ideology, and the David
    plates', *Speculum*, 52 (1977), pp. 217–37.
[66] Nikephoros, *Breviarium*, 5, ed. and trans. C. Mango, *Nikephoros, Short History* (Washington,
    1990), pp. 42–3; Theophanes, *Chronographia*, ed. de Boor (n. 4), p. 300 (p. 430 of Mango and
    Scott translation). For a discussion of the dates, see ed. Mango, *Breviarium*, Introduction.
[67] According to Theophanes, end of 613 or beginning of 614, but in reality later, perhaps in 622,
    at all events before 624. This incestuous marriage caused a scandal and earned Herakleios
    ecclesiastical censure.
[68] Theophanes, *Chronographia*, ed. de Boor (n. 4), pp. 301, 335; Nikephoros, *Breviarium*, 19, 27,
    ed. and trans. Mango (n. 66), pp. 68, 76. That Martinos was named only *nobelissimos* and not
    caesar emerges from the acclamations in the *De cerimoniis* (II, 29, p. 630), which preserves the
    protocol of the ceremonies of 4 January 639.
[69] *De cerimoniis*, II, 27, pp. 627–8; Nikephoros, *Breviarium* (n. 66), 25, 27, ed. and trans. Mango,
    pp. 74, 76.

sanctioned by his will which laid down that his two crowned sons would be 'equal emperors' and that they should 'honour Martina as a mother and an empress', in other words, share power with her.[70]

This was to conceive of the empire as the common property of all the males in the family, the *basileia* as a latent virtue which coronation only activated in individuals united by blood, and power as something to be shared or competed for among relatives. It was not a fortuitous deviation; contemporaries saw it as a political system and it enjoyed genuine popular support.[71] Nor was it unique to Byzantium, since it was also found in the Frankish and Merovingian monarchies. It persisted in the Carolingian empire and only disappeared entirely from France with the Capetians.[72] But it was a source of instability and crises, since at each generation it was necessary to eliminate by force the younger sons who had become inconvenient brothers or uncles who fomented rebellion.[73] The iconography of the coinage is the best evidence of the difficulties associated with this familial collegiality. The issues of Herakleios broke with the previous Roman tradition, which had not permitted the junior emperor to be shown on regular issues. The family began to appear on the gold, that is, the most official coins (*nomisma*); Herakleios had himself represented with his son, Herakleios New Constantine, then with the latter and Heraklonas (the three emperors sharing the same title of augustus); Constans II first appeared alone, then sometimes with his eldest son Constantine, with his two other sons on the reverse, and sometimes

---

[70] Nikephoros, *Breviarium* (n. 66), 27–8, pp. 76–8.

[71] When his half-brother died (poisoned?), Heraklonas was urged by the people of Constantinople to crown the son of the dead man, Constans II, as co-emperor: Nikephoros, *Breviarium*, 30–2, ed. and trans. Mango (n. 66), pp. 80–5.

[72] Lewis, *Royal Succession* (see introduction, n. 5), pp. 154ff.; J. Dhondt, 'Election et hérédité sous les Carolingiens et les premiers Capétiens', *Revue belge de philologie et d'histoire*, 18 (1939), pp. 913–53.

[73] When Constans II became sole emperor after a family battle, he reverted to pluralism by crowning not only his eldest son Constantine IV, in 654, but also his two other sons, Herakleios and Tiberios, in 659: Abu'l Faraj Bar Hebraeus, *The Chronography*, trans. E. A. W. Budge (London, 1932), I, p. 99. Along with the coinage, the acts of the sixth ecumenical council (680–1) show, in a dating formula repeated many times, that it was Constans II himself who raised Herakleios and Tiberios to the rank of co-emperors (Mansi, XI, pp. 208–9, 217, 221, 229, 316, 321, 328, 332, 377, 388, 456, 517, 549, 584, 601, 612, 624). Perhaps, as suggested by A. Christophilopoulou ('Ekloge, anagoreusis kai stepsis tou byzantinou autokratoros', *Pragmateiai tes Akademiai Athenon*, XXII, 2 (Athens, 1956), pp. 123–30), Constantine IV was both crowned and 'proclaimed' emperor, whereas his brothers were only crowned. Constans II was also obliged to react to the claims of a brother, Theodosios, who was offended that he, too, was not called to the *basileia*, and whom he got rid of by making him enter orders and then executing him for high treason, to the horror of the populace: Theophanes, *Chronographia*, ed. de Boor (n. 4), pp. 347, 351 (pp. 485, 490 of Mango and Scott translation). Herakleios himself had to take action against a brother and a nephew, both called Theodore, who plotted against him: Nikephoros, *Breviarium* (n. 66), 20, 24, ed. and trans. Mango, pp. 68–9, 72–3. When Constantine IV became emperor 'together with his brothers' in 668, it all had to be done again: Theophanes, *Chronographia*, ed. de Boor (n. 4), p. 352 (pp. 491–2 of Mango and Scott translation).

alone with all three sons on the reverse.[74] The horizontal family prevented the portrayal of the vertical structure of a lineage, and the pre-eminence of the eldest son was marked only by his position on the obverse instead of the reverse, or by a place of honour within the family group. The problem of the succession was only really settled by the great-grandson of Herakleios, Constantine IV; though obliged, for the first half of his reign, to allow his brothers, Herakleios and Tiberios, privileges which made them competitors, and a place on the reverse of the *nomisma*, he at last succeeded, in 681, in stripping them of their titles, denying them their place on the coinage and having their noses cut off, in order to safeguard the rights of his son.[75] It was this slow motion *coup d'état* which marked the transition from the horizontal family, with its inevitable superfluity of collaterals, to the dynastic lineage with primogeniture. The collegiality of the *basileis* was then replaced by a hierarchy, with a more rigid distinction between the 'great emperor *autokrator*', sole holder of power, and the 'junior emperors' kept in reserve, and between the indivisible empire and a shared *basileia*.[76]

Such a long apprenticeship was necessary before the family could become a dynasty. This is clear in the case of the Isaurians. This was the period when the imperial office was becoming increasingly sacralised, and when it was claiming, as we will see, a quasi-priestly character and bolstering itself with Old Testament references; it was when the term 'porphyrogenitus' appeared and

[74] P. Grierson, *Catalogue of the Byzantine Coins in the Dumbarton Oaks Collection and in the Whittemore Collection*, II, 2 (Washington, 1968), pp. 402–3, 427–35, plates XXIV–XXV; C. Morrisson, *Catalogue des monnaies byzantines de la Bibliothèque nationale* (Paris, 1970), I, pp. 255–6, 328.

[75] Ibid., pp. 373–5; Abu'l Faraj Bar Hebraeus, *The Chronography*, trans. Budge (n. 73), I, pp. 101–2; Michael the Syrian, *Chronicle*, ed. Chabot (n. 6), II, pp. 454–6. Constantine IV was forced to accept this partition of the *basileia* which the soldiers of the theme of the Anatolikon wanted to turn into, effectively, a cumbersome collective, which they compared to the Trinity: 'We believe in the Trinity. Let us crown all three!': Theophanes, ed. de Boor (n. 4), pp. 352, 360 (pp. 491, 502 of Mango and Scott translation). Christophilopoulou ('Ekloge' (n. 73), pp. 72–3, 127–8) is probably right in thinking that the soldiers were asking not for the 'crowning' of Herakleios and Tiberios, who had already been crowned by their father, but for their 'proclamation'; both George the Monk (ed. C. de Boor and P. Wirth, *Georgii Monachi Chronikon* (Stuttgart, 1978), p. 728) and Zonaras (*Annales*, ed. Pinder (n. 29), III, p. 222) interpret Theophanes in this way. The opposition of the thematic army should perhaps be dated to 680: Grierson, *Catalogue of Byzantine Coins* (n. 74), II, 2, pp. 512–13, 525–32, plate XXXII.

[76] For the change in title, see E. Stein, 'Postconsulat et *autokratoria*', *Annuaire de l'Institut de Philologie et d'Histoire orientales et slaves*, 2 (*Mélanges Bidez II*) (1933–4), pp. 869–912, criticised justifiably and at length by F. Dölger in a review (*BZ*, 36 (1936), pp. 123–45) and an article ('Die Entwicklung der byzantinischen Kaisertitulatur und die Datierung von Kaiserdarstellungen in der byzantinischen Kleinkunst', in *Studies Presented to D. M. Robinson*, II (1953), pp. 985–1005, both repr. in F. Dölger, *Byzantinische Diplomatik, 20 Aufsätze zum Urkundenwesen der Byzantiner* (Ettal, 1956), pp. 102–51. See also Christophilopoulou, 'Ekloge' (n. 73), pp. 134–8; A. Christophilopoulou, 'Peri to problema tes anadeixeos tou byzantinou autokratoros', *Epistemonike Epiteris tes Philosophikes Scholes tou Panepistemiou Athenon*, 12 (1961–2), pp. 471–92.

was applied for the first time to Leo IV, in Neapolitan sources;[77] it was when the people and the army first expressed a strong attachment to the reigning family; and lastly, it was when the hereditary principle found its necessary complement in primogeniture. The monetary iconography shows that this was a conscious policy. The type adopted by the Isaurians was in marked contrast to that of Herakleios and his family. The successors of Leo III (Constantine V, Leo IV and Constantine VI) had the reigning emperor and his eldest son, associated as co-emperor, represented on the obverse, and on the reverse, the dead ancestors, father, grandfather and great-grandfather, with a legend indicating the direct family descent over two, three or four generations.[78] For the first time, there was a representation of the notion of dynasty in all its verticality. The unchallenged rights of the eldest son were emphasised by association at an early age, already customary but now systematic. Constantine V was crowned, on 31 March 720, when barely two years old; Leo IV, on 17 May 751, when just over a year old; the people of Constantinople were surprised that Constantine VI, at the age of five, had still not received the diadem from his father's hands. Attempts were made to find outlets for the ambitions of the other members of the family and distance them from power. Constantine V, who had six sons from two of his three marriages, and whose succession might have created the same problems as that of Herakleios, was careful to crown as co-emperor only his eldest son Leo IV, and to give the other five sons titles which were reserved to the imperial family but which excluded them, in principle, from real power.[79] These ranked promotions did not, however, entirely prevent disputes. We know that Leo IV, in the very year that he crowned his son, learned of a revolt by his half-brother the caesar Nikephoros, while Irene, a little later, cut short the attempted usurpations of the caesars and *nobelissimi*, brothers of her dead husband, by having them tonsured and made to enter orders, although they nevertheless persisted in their scheming until they were blinded and dragged from one exile to another.[80]

All these various types of succession could result from the grafting of the family on to the empire. They seem to form a progression from which a settled dynasty

[77] The first of these documents dates from 1 March 763: see B. Capasso, *Monumenta ad neapolitani ducatus historiam pertinentia*, I (Naples, 1881), p. 262, no. 1; P. Bertolini, 'Le serie episcopale napoletana nei sec. VIII e IX. Ricerche sulle fonti per la storia dell'Italia meridionale nell'alto medioevo', *Rivista di storia della chiesa in Italia*, 24 (1970), pp. 356–7 and n. 29.

[78] Grierson, *Catalogue of Byzantine Coins* (n. 74), III, I, pp. 293, 300, 325–6, 328–33, 337, 340–1, 344, plates VIII, XII, XIII; Morrisson, *Monnaies byzantines* (n. 74), II, pp. 450, 466, 483–4, 489–90. The example was later followed by the son of Michael of Amorion, Theophilos, who had his father represented on the reverse of the *nomisma*: ibid., pp. 514–16.

[79] Christophoros and Nikephoros became caesars on 2 April 769, and Niketas *nobelissimos* the same day; Anthimios became *nobelissimos* during the lifetime of his father (that is, before 775); Eudokimios, the youngest, received the same title in 780.

[80] Theophanes, *Chronographia*, ed. de Boor (n. 4), pp. 443–4, 450–1, 454, 468, 473–4, 496 (pp. 621, 627 of Mango and Scott translation).

emerged in the age of iconoclasm. But there is an element of arbitrariness in this presentation. In practice, all these models remained possible, concurrent, a product of circumstances and usually overlapping. This can be seen in 867, when Basil the Macedonian brought the 'Amorian dynasty' to an end by murdering Michael III, and himself founded what is conventionally called the longest 'dynasty' in Byzantine history, since it managed to survive, through women, until 1056. Basil did not slip furtively into an existing institution; he set out to renovate it and to found a new regime, with his children. That this was a family takeover of power is stated by the sources in various ways: 'When Basil seized Roman power with his sons', we read in the *Life of St Theophano*.[81] Constantine Porphyrogenitus explains his grandfather's haste in propelling his children to the head of the empire as soon as they were old enough by the desire to put an end to any dissidence or plotting; they were, he tells us, the increasingly numerous roots which attached the Macedonian family to the empire, or the branches sprouting from a graft. Three sons (Constantine, Leo and Alexander) were named emperor in order to identify the empire with a hereditary patrimony; the fourth (the future patriarch Stephen) was 'offered' by his father to the Church,[82] in preparation for the time when this institution would lose its independence as a counter power and when it, too, would fall under family influence. Basil's four daughters were sent to the Constantinople monastery of St Euphemia of Petrion, which he himself had founded or rebuilt and was now, at all events, a family possession. He was acting out of piety, perhaps, but no doubt also to avoid having sons-in-law who might, in the next generation, emerge as rivals to his sons, like Artabasdos, son-in-law of Leo III, in 742.[83]

The empire seemed to have been taken over, to have become officially patrimonial. When he was seeking to recover the trust of Basil I, Photios could think of nothing better than to forge a prophecy promising power to a mysterious progeny by the name of BEKLAS (the initials of Basil himself, his wife Eudokia, and his four sons, Constantine, Leo, Alexander and Stephen).[84] There were images to accompany this familial publicity: of Basil and his family on the first pages of the *Parisinus gr.* of 510;[85] mosaics in the Kainourgion, in the Great Palace, showing Basil enthroned with his wife, Eudokia, and 'their children',

[81] Chapter 8, ed. E. Kurtz, *Zwei griechische Texle über hl. Theophano, die Gemahlin Kaisers Leo VI* (St. Petersburg, 1898), p. 5.
[82] As Isaac was sacrificed to God by his father Abraham, wrote Constantine VII, repeating an image from Leo VI's funeral eulogy of Basil.
[83] Constantine Porphyrogenitus, *Vita Basilii*, 34–5, in Theophanes Continuatus, *Chronographia*, ed. Bekker (n. 4), p. 264; Skylitzes, ed. Thurn, *Synopsis* (n. 39), p. 134; Zonaras, *Annales*, ed. Pinder (n. 29), III, p. 419. For St Euphemia, see Janin, *Eglises et monastères*, pp. 127–8.
[84] Niketas Paphlagon, *Life of the Patriarch Ignatios*, PG 105, cols. 565–8.
[85] *Homilies* of Gregory of Nazianzus, copied and illuminated for Basil I (between 879 and 883?); see the catalogue of the Louvre exhibition, *Byzance. L'art byzantin dans les collections publiques françaises* (Paris, 1992), pp. 346–8, with brief bibliography. See also below, pp. 193–4 and plates 7–8.

like luminous stars, painted all round the room, also clothed in imperial robes and adorned with diadems. The sons hold rolls on which are written the 'divine precepts' and the daughters hold the Gospel to show that they, too, can read and are not entirely unversed in theology.[86] Even piety, religious ceremonial and processions were gradually modified to accommodate family cults.[87] Basil's sons were in different situations and had, in any case, little liking for each other, but contemporary chroniclers were not in error in presenting them as a group. Not only did Basil break with the dynastic tradition started by the Isaurians by elevating to the empire two or three of his sons and not only the eldest, but he broke with the custom adopted as long ago as the seventh century of distinguishing between the 'senior' and 'junior' emperors. The documents leave few doubts on this score.[88] At the anti-Photian council of 869–70, Basil, Constantine and Leo were merged in one and the same imperial entity.[89] At the council of 879–80, Leo and Alexander were described, like Basil, as augusti, 'great emperors', *synautokratores*. The text promulgating the *Prochiron* puts Basil, Constantine and Leo on the same plane. The coinage shows who held real authority and who was in favour, but the effigies were always accompanied by the same legend: *Augusti Romanorum/Basileis Romaion*.[90] This *isotimie* (equal honour) of the founder's children is not without echoes of the descendants of Herakleios and it provoked almost equally acute tensions; it ceased only with the death of the last son, Alexander, on 6 June 913, even though Leo VI had tried to enforce a dynastic logic, emphasised by his deliberate decision to name his son 'the Porphyrogenitus', which seems to have caused some surprise.[91]

---

[86] *Vita Basilii*, 89, in Theophanes Continuatus, *Chronographia*, ed. Bekker (n. 4), pp. 333–4. It is possible that the 'roll' which each son holds in his hand is the *akakia* which Constantine Porphyrogenitus interprets elsewhere as symbolically representing the 'tome of divine legislation', that is, the Christian precepts inscribed on a roll: *De cerimoniis*, II, 40, p. 638.

[87] See below, pp. 204–7.

[88] The sources are collected and analysed by Christophilopoulou, 'Ekloge' (n. 73), pp. 93–8; Christophilopoulou, 'Peri to problema' (n. 76), p. 488.

[89] After 6 January 870, date of Leo's coronation: Mansi, XVI, cols. 309, 344, 357, 389.

[90] Grierson, *Catalogue of Byzantine Coins* (n. 74), III, 2, pp. 474–6, 487–90, plate XXX; Morrisson, *Monnaies byzantines* (n. 74), II, pp. 538–9.

[91] Leo VI enjoyed effective power after the death of his father in 886, but never succeeded, throughout his reign, in ridding himself of his brother Alexander. In their titles, the documents treat them as equal; the *Kletorologion* of Philotheos (899) makes only minor differences between them in ceremonial: Oikonomides, *Listes*, pp. 83, 220–1, 222–4. Leo crowned his only son Constantine on 15 May 908 and had him represented together with himself on the gold and silver coinage, whereas he shared with Alexander only certain issues of the *follis*. But in the end, he was obliged to designate as his successor his brother, already *autocrator*, begging him to look after his son and to make him too, in due course, an emperor *autocrator*: Zonaras, *Annales*, ed. Pinder (n. 29), III, p. 455. A contemporary text which is highly polemical but surprisingly accurate has Leo VI asking representatives of the Church and the army 'not to proclaim at his death either Alexander or any other person, but only the Porphyrogenitus, as he himself had acquired the habit of calling him'; then trying to have Alexander murdered and chosing a guardian from outside the family for the young Constantine, but at the last moment he was

Once this hurdle had been overcome, it seemed that the Macedonian family would become a lineage and that the relative stability of the empire was based on the principle of the transmission of power to the eldest son (or oldest surviving son) and on the attachment of the people and most of the dignitaries to a dynastic legitimacy. But it soon becomes clear, on closer inspection, that the system of succession which was being established was far more complex. The reigns of the porphyrogeniti (Constantine VII (913–59), his son Romanos II (959–63) and the latter's children, Basil II and Constantine VIII) alternated or overlapped with those of prestigious military leaders who occupied centre stage, thanks to the minority of the princes of the blood and their own merits, and who were too sure of their rights to be regarded simply as usurpers (Romanos Lekapenos (920–44), Nikephoros Phokas (963–9) and John Tzimiskes (969–76)). The legitimate princes had to cede real power to the newcomers, and the newcomers acquired a veneer of legitimacy by allying themselves, or seeking to ally themselves, with the dynasty by marrying into it. They tried to push into the background or downgrade in the hierarchy the porphyrogeniti of whom they were, in principle, the protectors, but they were unable to impose their own descendants, that is, to found new dynasties. The legitimate emperors resisted and seized the earliest opportunity to rule alone, but the empire adapted to this chronic divorce between legitimacy and real power until Basil II (976–1025). On reaching adulthood Basil managed to assume both roles simultaneously, that of porphyrogenitus (which he was to the fourth degree) and that of conqueror. After the interlude of Constantine VIII (1025–8), last male of the Macedonian dynasty, his two daughters Zoe and Theodora emerged from a prolonged retreat to legitimate five successive emperors by marrying them or by adopting them as sons (Zoe, in her fifties, married Romanos Argyros, then Michael IV, adopted Michael V and finally married Constantine Monomachos; the dying Theodora adopted Michael VI). They also secured the succession when necessary by a brief personal reign (jointly in 1042, Theodora alone in 1055–6).

The age of the Macedonians, therefore, illustrates not so much the triumph of the dynastic ideal in Byzantium as its ambiguities and its limitations. It began with the brutal appropriation, share out within the family and superfluity of heirs that characterise the empire-patrimony and familial collegiality. The equilibrium which was achieved over the next five generations was based not on a purely dynastic system, but on a mixed system which managed to combine or juxtapose blood rights and marriage alliances, legitimacy of continuity and legitimacy of rupture.

obliged to face facts and accede to the remonstrances of the senate, not without prophesying: 'Things will be difficult for the next thirteen months!', that is, for Alexander's brief reign, in 912–13: B. Flusin, 'Un fragment inédit de la "Vie d'Euthyme le Patriarche"?', *TM*, 9 (1985), pp. 128–9.

LEGITIMACY OF RUPTURE AND LEGITIMACY
OF CONTINUITY

Expressions that compare the empire to a transmissible patrimony appear everywhere in the sources, with the ambiguities we have noted. References to
biological heredity as a principle of succession are, in contrast, much rarer. The
phrase 'child of royal blood' sometimes appears in a text to emphasise a hereditary succession, fitness to reign or, more vaguely, the 'nobility' of a lineage
equipped with a historical or legendary origin; but it did not explicitly create
a 'blood right', at least before the Komnenoi. It was simply a term of praise,
and this praise had its downside. The collections of *Sentences* and mirrors of
princes are full of formulae to the effect that no one should pride himself on his
birth, least of all the emperor, in whom this moral fault risked compromising
his political legitimacy, and to whom the moralists tirelessly repeated that he
was moulded from the same clay as other men and would return to the same
dust. A cloth pouch filled with earth, the *akakia*, was placed in his hand at the
same time as the insignia of power to remind him of this truth, in case he got
carried away and lost the sense of a fundamental equality.[92] It was through the
dignity with which he had been provisionally invested that the emperor was a
'divine icon'; through his body and his birth he was only an 'icon of mud'.[93]
Here, the Greek conjuration of hubris encountered Roman egalitarianism to
become the Christian virtue of humility. This enduring tradition is enough to
explain why, in good morals as in good politics, the theme of *eugeneia* (good
birth) was always discreet and more aristocratic than imperial.

Western dynasties provided themselves with invented genealogies which
traced their descent back to the Carolingians or to the heroes of Troy,[94] but
this was less common in the East. His panegyrists may have fabricated a royal
descent going back to the Arsacids and Artaxerxes for the parvenu Basil I, and
through them to Constantine the Great.[95] But when his son Leo VI rather half-
heartedly repeated this fabrication in his funeral oration for his father, delivered
in 886, he invoked the authority of an 'ancient' who was supposed to have said:
'It is better to be the originator of a race [*genos*] than to attach oneself to another

---

[92] The *akakia* or *anexikakia* was a sachet of purple silk in the form of a roll of parchment, containing
earth or dust. In certain solemn circumstances, the emperor held the cross or the sceptre in his
left hand and the *akakia* in his right; the *akakia* was defined by Symeon of Thessalonike as
'dust in a handkerchief, to signify the perishable nature of power and the humility which [the
emperor] should feel': *De sancto templo*, 148, PG 155, col. 356.

[93] Agapetos, 21, 71, PG 86, cols. 1172, 1185; Basil, PG 107, cols. XXVIII, XLIV–XLV.

[94] Lewis, *Royal Succession* (see introduction, n. 5), especially pp. 104–22.

[95] For the Arsacids: Niketas Paphlagon, *Life of the Patriarch Ignatios*, PG 105, cols. 565–8; Pseudo-
Symeon Magister, *Annales*, ed. I. Bekker (Bonn, 1838), pp. 689–90. For Constantine the Great:
Constantine Porphyrogenitus, *Vita Basilii*, 3, in Theophanes Continuatus, *Chronographia*, ed.
Bekker (n. 4), p. 215; Genesios, *History*, ed. A. Lesmüller-Werner and I. Thurn (Berlin, 1978),
pp. 76–7. And see below, p. 201 and n. 39.

origin', and chose, unworried by the contradiction, to present Basil I both as the descendant of a royal line and as a new man who conferred rights of succession on his own descendants.[96] This may have been scepticism regarding the true ancestry of the first of the Macedonians, or it may have been a skilful combination of two antithetical themes which had long been part of the rhetorical repertoire. Either is possible; but these two themes were probably not seen as truly contradictory. They operated at very different levels: descent from a royal *genos* was the anodyne praise of a panegyric, addressed to women as readily as to men; to found a family of emperors was a true proof of legitimacy. If there was a contradiction, it was inherent in the political system itself.

This twofold eulogy was matched by two models which might be conflicting or complementary: on one hand, the son of the emperor, 'born' (or simply raised) 'in the purple' (*porphyrogennetos*), who had known no other condition than the imperial and was destined to succeed his father; on the other, the ordinary man, the private person (*idiotes*), who might accede to power by choice or by force. The latter was not necessarily seen as inferior to the former, and court rhetoric might well, instead of lauding the precocious sacredness and legitimacy of the porphyrogenitus, take a different tack and oppose merit to the purple. In 361, Libanios took this line on behalf of Julian the Apostate and against Constantius II, son of Constantine, presented as a man of the palace surrounded by eunuchs.[97] The pro-Macedonian chroniclers later mined the same seam by describing Michael III, authentic porphyrogenitus, as a drunkard, mad on horses, and by contrasting this puppet lacking physical and moral substance with Basil I, the 'new man' who had tamed a wild horse, seized the empire and founded a dynasty.[98] Even in the eulogy of Leo VI, as we have seen, the legend of his father's 'royal' origin counted for less than the powerful image of the 'renovator'. Much later in Byzantine history, John III Vatatzes (1222–54), son-in-law and successor of Theodore Laskaris, was praised for being a 'private person, son of private persons', from a long line of commoners, and not one of those degenerate heirs corrupted by luxury and flattery.[99] According to circumstances, commonplaces were mobilised on either side, which is not to

---

[96] Leo VI, *Funeral Oration of Basil I* (n. 4), pp. 44–5. He went on to say that it was God who had chosen his father Basil to reign; then he lauded the nobility of the family of his mother, Eudokia Ingerina, descended from the Martinakioi, and also destined by God for the empire, before concluding with the familar formula: 'But what good is the empire of all the earth to him who in an instant will sleep close to the slave, prey to the whip!': ibid., pp. 50–3, 66–7.

[97] *Orationes* XIII (to Julian), 7, ed. Förster (n. 46), II, p. 65; see also Themistios, *Orationes* XIV (to Theodosius I), 182b, ed. Schenkel and Downey, I (n. 46), p. 262.

[98] P. Karlin-Hayter, 'L'enjeu d'une rumeur. Opinion et imaginaire à Byzance au IXᵉ s.', *JÖB*, 41 (1991), pp. 85–11, especially p. 97.

[99] A. Heisenberg, 'Kaiser Johannes Batatzes der Barmherzige', *BZ*, 14 (1905), pp. 196–7 (§§5–6); on the sanctity of John Vatatzes, see R. Macrides, 'Saints and sainthood in the early Palaiologan period', in *The Byzantine Saint*, ed. S. Hackel (London, 1981), pp. 69–71.

say that they were totally artificial. A legitimacy based exclusively on natural blood rights and hereditary succession, even camouflaged as prenatal unction, was no more satisfactory than the violent accession of someone without
family.

The chroniclers, consequently, reported a number of historical examples
which can all be analysed as an artificial or temporary rupture of the dynastic
link, intended to strengthen legitimacy as the sole qualification of an heir to the
throne. Let us look at a few examples.

This had been the purpose of the proposal put forward by Leo IV in 776,
and discussed above; the emperor threatened to make his son, Constantine VI,
porphyrogenitus son of a porphyrogenitus, a 'private person', and the protests
this provoked allowed him to transform dynastic legitimacy into a sort of social
contract.[100]

After his accession in 829, it was said that Theophilos decided to punish
those who had assassinated Leo V, in 820, in order to give the crown to his
father, Michael II. He let it be known that he had promised the latter on his
deathbed to reward them, which would, in fact, have been justified by dynastic
zeal; but when the murderers appeared, Theophilos had them put to death, 'not
for having stained their hands with murder, but for having laid hands on the
Lord's anointed'.[101] The dynastic link was not altogether rejected, but another
link, over and above that of blood, was established with the lineage of the
emperors to whom God had given the supernatural legitimacy of unction. In
presenting himself as the *diadochos tes basileias*, Theophilos was playing on a
word which could equally well mean 'successor' or 'heir'; he was pretending
to invoke the gratitude he owed to his natural father while actually thinking of
his duty to his father's predecessor, who was probably also his godfather, that
is, his 'spiritual' or 'adoptive' father.[102]

The *Life* of St Theophano, first wife of Leo VI (and herself of 'imperial
blood'), is clearer still. The author, a contemporary, elaborates on the actual
historical episode of Leo's disgrace, when he was stripped of his imperial title
and imprisoned by his father, Basil, in 883, as a result of a slander, then solemnly
rehabilitated as heir to the throne in 886. He uses this episode to make his heroine
utter a surprising tirade. Leo, who 'had received unction already in the womb',

---

[100] See above, pp. 22–3.
[101] Theophanes Continuatus, *Chronographia*, ed. Bekker (n. 4), Bonn, pp. 85–6; George the Monk
Continued, *Vitae imperatorum recentiorum*, ed. I. Bekker, p. 791; Skylitzes, *Synopsis*, ed. Thurn
(n. 39), pp. 49–50; Genesios, *History*, ed. Lesmüller-Werner and Thurn (n. 95), p. 36, according
to whom, Michael II, on his deathbed, begged his son to pay a fair price to the assassins he had
armed.
[102] Theophanes Continuatus, *Chronographia*, ed. Bekker (n. 4) pp. 23–4, who says that Leo V,
soon after his accession (10 July 813), 'adopted' the son of Michael II; see W. Treadgold, 'The
problem of the marriage of the Emperor Theophilus', *GRBS*, 16 (1975), p. 337.

had no idea what hardship and poverty were; in the purple, he had known only luxury and flattery; by the adversity he had suffered, God had wished to test him before making him the heir to his *basileia*.[103] Leo's imprisonment by his father and his spectacular rehabilitation on the occasion of the St Elijah procession are here clearly interpreted as a temporary rupture in the dynastic link, followed by a joint choice of the emperor and God.[104] In the *Life*, the episode of imprisonment, which might have been seen as a humiliation, is neither passed over discreetly nor played down but presented as an initiation rite; Leo himself made it an important date in the commemorative calendar, with thanksgivings to St Elijah and a special race for the inhabitants of Constantinople.[105] The legitimacy of the porphyrogenitus son had needed this supplementary legitimating process.

Both approaches are equally valid: the transmission of imperial power ought not to be left solely to the accident of a natural relationship, that of blood; but only the ties of this natural relationship made it possible to legitimate the violence or the arbitrariness which had preceded the seizure of power. The political ideal which Rome had bequeathed to Byzantium assumed a certain balance between rupture and continuity. It needed a rebellious relative, like Julian the Apostate, or a new man who had become part of his predecessor's family by marriage, like John Vatatzes, or an emperor's son with another justification to offer than blood rights. These contradictory requirements are explicable in terms of Roman history and the legacy of 'Roman ideas' (or at least of a moral reading of Roman history, like that of Machiavelli),[106] but they had a more general validity. Kingship was structurally twofold. Far from Byzantium in space and time, there also existed a 'magic' kingship which acquired power through the real or symbolic elimination of the predecessor, and a hereditary type of kingship, devolved to a family which could claim an illustrious ancestor, sacred or divine. In the case of hereditary kingship, lineage created a right. In the case of 'magic' kingship, succession supposed a challenge, an exploit and rupture. Even when it was the son who succeeded to his father, it was after a simulated murder or incest, and the ideal successor was not so much the son as the son-in-law, that is, the man of daring who gained entry to the lineage from outside

---

[103] *Life of St Theophano*, 14, ed. Kurtz (n. 81), p. 9. Leo VI was not exactly in prison, but deprived of his liberty within the palace of 'the pearl'. For the dates, see R. J. H. Jenkins. 'The chronological accuracy of the Logothete for the years AD 867–913', *DOP*, 19 (1965), pp. 102–3.

[104] All the more so given that, according to the hagiographer, Leo had been stripped of his royalty when he was imprisoned.

[105] *Kletorologion of Philotheos* (899), in Oikonomides, *Listes*, pp. 214–19 ('on the 20th of the month, we celebrate with a religious procession within the palace the memory of St Elijah, and with it the end of the internment of our pious emperor').

[106] See the quotation at the head of this chapter.

as a result of a contest or an obligatory test, such as the chariot race which, in the Greek myth of Oenomaos and Hippodamia, gave Pelops both the daughter and the kingdom of his father-in-law.[107]

In the Byzantine context, the result was a 'mixed' or 'alternate' system. When an emperor wanted to appoint his son to succeed him, he had him adopted by the empire, associated him in his power as he would have done with a stranger and was careful not to flaunt the dynastic link. When the reigning sovereign chose a stranger, he adopted him or integrated him into his family by marriage, as Augustus had done when he forced Tiberius to divorce in order to marry his daughter Julia. When a fortunate usurper ended a dynasty or when a new man was entrusted with the empire, he looked for or was obliged to make a marriage into the fallen imperial family or one of those which had preceded it. Marcian, summoned to the throne in 450, married Pulcheria, sister of his predecessor, Theodosius II; Zeno and then Anastasios married Ariadne, daughter of Leo I. Michael II of Amorion, who seized power by force in 820 and conveniently became a widower, made an early remarriage to the (porphyrogenitus) daughter of Constantine VI, brought out of a convent for the purpose. He declared to the senators, on this occasion, that 'it was impossible for an emperor to live without a wife', just as it was impossible for the senators' wives to live 'without a mistress and empress', and he made them sign a pledge to remain faithful, even after his death, to his wife and any children she might bear him.[108] The most remarkable example is that of Zoe and Theodora, the daughters of Constantine VIII referred to above; last descendants of the Macedonians and hence sole repositories of dynastic legitimacy, they transmitted the empire three times by marriage and twice by adoption, and the people of Constantinople called them 'our mamas' (*Mannai*).[109] Psellos tells how the inhabitants of the capital rose up when Zoe was banished by her 'adopted son', Michael V Kalaphates, in 1041, and how they demanded the return of 'the only free woman among women, the sovereign of the whole family, she who in full legitimacy had the prize of power, she whose father had been emperor, and whose father's father had been emperor, and even the father of her father's father'.[110]

It is, of course, the absence of male heirs that explains the role played by the heiresses of the dynasty; but the situation occurred so frequently that it is tempting to see it as a model, not unique but relatively stable, in which the dynastic continuity of the empire was naturally assured by women, while it

---

[107] See in particular L. de Heusch, 'Pour une dialectique de la sacralité du pouvoir', in *Le Pouvoir et le sacré*, Annales du Centre d'études des religions de l'Université libre de Bruxelles 1 (Brussels, 1962), pp. 15–47.

[108] Theophanes Continuatus, *Chronographia*, ed. Bekker (n. 4), pp. 78–9.

[109] Skylitzes, *Synopsis*, ed. Thurn (n. 39), p. 434.

[110] Psellos, *Chronographie*, ed. and trans. Renauld (n. 47), I, p. 102; P. Lemerle, *Cinq études sur le XIe siècle byzantin* (Paris, 1977), p. 253.

was men who seized power and exercised it on a temporary basis. Liutprand of Cremona was yet again ill informed when he wrote that, to evaluate nobility, 'the Greeks' took no interest in the mother, but only in the father.[111] The Byzantine sources say almost the opposite; not only do they record the aristocratic origins of the wives or mothers and their eventual membership of an imperial family, but they distinguish true female dynasties. An Arab is said to have predicted to the emperor Theophilos, in 837, that the family of the Martinakioi (with which he himself was connected) would retain the throne for a long period of time;[112] this was a female lineage, which was the starting point for the Macedonian dynasty and later made many alliances with it. Nor should we be particularly surprised at the importance of women in the business of succession. According to the physiological conceptions of the age, it was they who transmitted the blood;[113] in practice, it was on the occasion of marriages, and usually through the wives, that the larger part of the patrimony was transmitted. It is not difficult, therefore, to understand why political legitimation conformed to the rule and why a certain tendency to matriarchy can be detected.

The notion generally associated with any praise or criticism of the hereditary transmission of power was that of 'birth in the purple', which emphasised the legitimacy – or inadequacy – of a child born when his father was already emperor, and the hope – or fear – that this birth would extend the reign into a dynasty.[114] Such hopes were invested in Theodosius II in 402, and in the 'New Theodosios', son of Maurice, in 583. It is significant that the very term 'porphyrogenitus', which expresses the idea of 'birth in the purple', appeared at the same time as the first true dynasties, those of the Isaurians and the Amorians. It became more than just a surname or prestigious qualifier for those descendants of the Macedonian family, men and women (Constantine VII, Basil II, Zoe and Theodora), who had to remember that their birth made them the sole repositories of dynastic legitimacy, even if their youth or circumstances had obliged them to share power with 'parvenus'. It is easy to show, however, that, at least until the eleventh century, the particular sacredness recognised in the children of a crowned emperor and the principle of the hereditary transmission of imperial power by primogeniture did not necessarily coincide and had, in any case, neither the same origin nor the same implications.

The birth of a porphyrogenitus symbolised dynastic success, the grafting of a family on to the empire; most of all, however, it conferred a sacred character

---

[111] *Antapodosis*, V, 14, ed. P. Chiesa, *Liudprandi Cremonensis opera omnia*, Corpus Christianorum, Continuatio Mediaevalis 156 (Turnhout, 1998), p. 130.

[112] Theophanes Continuatus, *Chronographia*, ed. Bekker (n. 4), p. 121; Genesios, *History*, ed. Lesmüller-Werner and Thurn (n. 95), p. 49. For the Martinakioi, see C. Mango, 'Eudocia Ingerina, the Normans and the Macedonian dynasty', *Zbornik Radova*, 14–15 (1973), pp. 20–1.

[113] Pseudo-Kaisarios, *Dial.*, III, 150, PG 38, col. 1052: the Hippocratic theory Christianised.

[114] Here I summarise the argument of my article 'Nés dans la pourpre' (n. 56), pp. 105–42.

on the newborn child, divine unction in its mother's womb. It was, in fact, conception that counted, or ought to have counted, in the strict definition of the porphyrogenitus, birth being adopted for reference, as in horoscopes, only for convenience. In a letter to Robert Guiscard, written in the name of the emperor Michael Doukas, Psellos speaks of 'conception and birth after the emperor's accession'.[115] In order to explain to Leo VI that he was a porphyrogenitus without experience of unhappiness and poverty, Theophano told him: 'You were anointed in the womb'.[116] In the preamble to the *De administrando imperio*, Constantine VII used the same expression when he addressed his son, Romanos: 'God himself has chosen you and decided as early as the womb to give you his kingship by reason of your excellence'.[117] Andronikos II (1282–1328) declared in a Novel that 'God, supporting him from his mother's womb, had placed him on the elevated throne of power'.[118] The words are distinctly Old Testament in tone; just as the prophet Isaiah could say that the Lord had 'made mention of [his] name', that is, had chosen and adopted him, 'from the bowels of [his] mother',[119] so the porphyrogenitus could claim that God had formed him to be emperor and conferred on him the 'unction of kingship' from his conception by allowing him to be fathered by an already anointed emperor. Birth was a dynastic matter, conception a sacred matter, because the naming of the prophet or the anointing of the young prince signified that, from the beginning, divine adoption had replaced natural and family ties.[120]

These distinctions were of little consequence when the eldest son of the emperor was himself porphyrogenitus, since dynastic practice and the sacredness of birth in the purple then combined to assure the pre-eminence of one child. But what happened when a porphyrogenitus had to give precedence to an older brother, born before their common father's accession to power? Here, the distinction of birth in the purple did not reinforce but contradicted primogeniture, that necessary complement and steadying element in the dynastic system. The problem was not purely academic; it was faced in particular by Basil I, and it is noticeable that the term porphyrogenitus seems to have been applied to the

---

[115] *Ep.* 144 (1073), K. N. Sathas, *Mesaionike Bibliotheke*, V (Athens/Paris/Venice, 1876), p. 390. This was in connection with a proposed marriage between Konstantios Doukas, youngest brother of the emperor, and the daughter of Robert Guiscard, when Psellos had to explain the meaning of the word porphyrogenitus.

[116] *Life of St Theophano*, ed. Kurtz (n. 81), 14, p. 9.

[117] Preface, lines 35–6, ed. and trans. G. Moravcsik and R. J. H. Jenkins, *Constantine Porphyrogenitus, De administrando imperio* (Washington, 1967), I, pp. 46–7.

[118] Novel 38, Zepos, *Jus*, I, p. 559.

[119] Isaiah, 49: 1. The predestined, prophets or kings, were modelled by God 'in the womb': Ecclesiastes, 49: 7 and 50: 22; Jeremiah, 1: 5; Judges, 16: 17; Psalms XXII [XXI]: 10–11 and LXXI [LXX]: 6.

[120] For the general significance of unction, see H. Lesêtre, 'Onction', in *Dictionnaire de la Bible*, IV, 2 (1907), cols. 1805–11; E. Cothenet and J. Wolinski, 'Onction', *DS* XI (1982), cols. 788–819. And see below, pp. 49–50 and 267–76.

children of his second marriage (Leo, Alexander and Stephen) only after the death of their older brother (Constantine), who had been expected to succeed his father.[121] There were no instances in the late empire or Byzantine period when a porphyrogenitus was preferred; the principle was invoked, however, in at least two cases, as it had been, long before, in Achaemenid Persia,[122] to disqualify the incumbent and justify a rebellion. In 479, Marcian, son of Anthemios, based his claims to the empire on the fact that he had married a daughter of Leo I, Leontia, born *after* the accession of her father, whereas the emperor Zeno had married the elder daughter, Ariadne, born *before* Leo came the throne.[123] In a *Passion of St Artemios* set in the reign of Julian but very probably written in the age of iconoclasm, the persecuting emperor explains his rebellion against Constantius II by telling the future martyr

> You know that it is rather to our family that the empire should normally have come. For my father Constantius was born of the marriage of my grandfather Constantius [Chlorus] to Theodora, daughter of Maximian, whereas Constantius [Chlorus] had Constantine [I] by Helena, a woman of no consequence, a sort of prostitute, when he was not yet caesar and was simply a private person [*idiotes*].[124]

Other attempted usurpations may have invoked this pretext or this justification, in the absence of official recognition of primogeniture.[125] But there is at least one other case where, without apparent conflict, 'birth in the purple' was a factor. At his accession in 1059, various sources say that Constantine X Doukas

---

[121] See above, pp. 33–4.

[122] Herodotus (*The Histories*, VII, 2–3) tells of the 'fierce dispute which arose between the sons of Darius with regard to the royalty'; before acceding to the throne, Darius had children by a first marriage, the eldest of whom was Artabazanes, and also by a second marriage, after becoming king, the eldest of whom was Xerxes; the latter, advised by Demaratus, former king of Sparta, claimed 'that he was born to Darius when Darius was already king and in possession of the empire of the Persians, whereas Artabazanes had been born when Darius was only a private person'. The argument reappears in Plutarch: *Lives*, 'Artaxerxes', II, 4.

[123] Theodoros Anagnostes, *Epitome*, 419, ed. G. C. Hansen, *Kirchengeschichte* (Berlin, 1971), p. 116; Theophanes, *Chronographia*, ed. de Boor (n. 4), p. 126 (p. 195 of Mango and Scott translation). Other sources mention the revolt but without giving an explanation.

[124] *Passio S. Artemii* by the 'monk John' (*BHG* 170), 41, PG 96, col. 1289. The passage is repeated with only slight changes in the metaphrastic Passion (*BHG* 172), 25, PG 115, cols. 1188–9, but not in the old Passion (*BHG* 169yz) ed. J. Bidez, which follows the *Historia ecclesiastica* of Philostorgios. The tetrarch Constantius Chlorus was, in fact, married twice: by his first wife, Helena, in 272, he had the emperor Constantine the Great, and by his second marriage, to Theodora, daughter of Maximian, he had Constantius, father of Gallus and Julian.

[125] The custom of chosing the eldest son as successor was never made official and could always be ignored. For example, John II Komnenos explained at length, in a discourse-will, in 1143, why he chose Manuel rather than the elder of his two surviving sons to succeed him (Kinnamos, *Epitome*, ed. A. Meineke (Bonn, 1836), pp. 26–9); Manuel himself persuaded the synod to regulate his succession in favour of his elder son, as if this might pose a problem: I. Medvedev, 'He synodike apophase tes 24 Martiou 1171 hos nomos gia te diadoche sto throno tou Byzantiou', in *Byzantium in the 12th Century: Canon Law, State and Society*, ed. N. Oikonomides (Athens, 1991), especially p. 236.

wished to found a dynasty. He had three surviving sons by his wife Eudokia, in order of birth, Michael, Andronikos and Constantius. The Skylitzes Continuator, revealing a slight uncertainty regarding the order of precedence, noted that 'among them, only Constantius was porphyrogenitus, *but* that their father proclaimed them all emperors'.[126] Zonaras repeats this, adding that Constantius was invested with the imperial insignia soon after his birth and before his two older brothers.[127] Psellos, happily, is more explicit:[128]

> After his [Constantine X Doukas] accession to power, the sun had not yet completed a full year's revolution when a child was born to him, who was judged worthy of the empire. As for the other brothers, as their birth had preceded the accession of their father to power, the admirable Michael and his younger brother Andronikos were both simple 'private persons' [*idiotai*], but, not long after, he who was both the oldest and the handsomest of his sons, by which I mean the most divine Michael, received from his father the imperial diadem. The emperor put this young prince, whom he was soon to install on the throne, nobly to the test to see if he was fitted for the empire.

So chroniclers and historians, in this particular case, drew a distinction between the porphyrogenitus Constantius, who received, at birth and by right, the name of emperor, and the two *idiotai*, Michael and Andronikos, the first associated with the throne after Constantius, as if by choice and to test his ability to reign, the second not receiving the imperial title during his father's lifetime. It was the eldest of the sons, Michael, who, though second to be crowned, was generally regarded as the designated successor; but the youngest, the porphyrogenitus Constantius, comes between the eldest and the middle brother in official acts,[129] and on the coinage.[130] This contravention of the order of birth seems to have continued in the reign of Romanos Diogenes (1068–71), even though Andronikos was promoted to the rank of co-emperor;[131] it only disappeared in

---

[126] Skylitzes Continuatus, ed. Tsolakes (n. 29), p. 118, lines 5–8.

[127] Zonaras, *Epitome Historiarum*, XVIII, 9, 19–20, ed. M. Pinder and T. Büttner-Wobst (Bonn, 1897), III, p. 681.

[128] Psellos, *Chronographia*, ed. and trans. Renauld (n. 47), II, p. 148.

[129] This was the hierarchical order of naming in a solemn oath pronounced by Eudokia in 1067: N. Oikonomides, 'Le serment de l'impératrice Eudocie (1067). Un épisode de l'histoire dynastique de Byzance', *REB*, 21 (1963), pp. 101–28 (the text of the document is at p. 106).

[130] This is the hierarchy made clear on the *nomismata histamena* of the regency of Eudokia (May–December 1067), where the empress is shown with Michael on her right and Constantius on her left: Morrisson, *Monnaies byzantines* (n. 74), II, p. 648 and plate 89 (where Constantine = Constantius).

[131] The *nomisma histamenon* then represented on the obverse Christ crowning Romanos and Eudokia, and on the reverse Michael in the centre, Constantius on his right (in second place) and Andronikos on his left (ranked third): ibid., p. 649, plate 89 (with the same correction). The seals of Romanos and Eudokia had exactly the same disposition: V. Laurent, *Les Sceaux byzantins du Médailler du Vatican* (Vatican, 1962), p. 9, no. 12; G. Zacos and A. Veglery, *Byzantine Lead Seals* (Basel, 1972), I, 1, no. 93, with references to published seals of the same type.

favour of a purely dynastic hierarchy in that of Michael VII, the *idiotes*,[132] who avoided giving Constantius his true imperial title, but opportunely remembered his porphyrogenitus status when negotiating his marriage to the daughter of Robert Guiscard.[133]

Primogeniture prevailed, therefore, without serious difficulties, and the notion of birth in the purple had only minimal impact, institutionally speaking. But it resisted dynastic logic, opposing a practice without a theory (an unavowed *jus sanguinis*, the automatic succession of the eldest son) to a sort of theory without practice (an ineffective *jus unctionis*, a purely formal preference for the child born after his father's accession). We are driven to the conclusion that, in a political ideology which was reluctant to accept the hereditary nature of the imperial office, the notion of porphyrogenitus made it possible to evade the issue. The child conceived in the purple and at once acclaimed was, of course, the son of the emperor, but the blood ties which made him a potential heir to the empire were immediately replaced by those of divine 'election' by unction. The *basileia* had to strip itself of all the overly 'natural' features which would have made it simply a *dynasteia*. Although it was never wholly superposed on heredity, 'birth in the purple' supplied it with an indispensable alibi.

This was not all; divine adoption by 'unction in the womb' was combined, in the ceremonial laid down in the tenth century for the birth, baptism and tonsure of a porphyrogenitus, with a sort of popular adoption. Let us summarise the chapters in the *Book of Ceremonies* which describe this process.[134]

In chapter II, 21, it is stated that on the day of the birth, the senators came to the palace to congratulate the emperor and to wish that he might know the children of the children of the porphyrogenitus and see the porphyrogenitus himself, advanced in years, heir to the paternal power and kingship, so that the *basileia* and the *politeia* of the Romans would be well ruled and governed. On the 'third day of the birth', the four demes organised a first session of acclamations.[135] On the fifth day, their representatives and those of the *tagmata*, a total of 200 persons nominated by the *praepositus*, gathered at the Hippodrome to acclaim the child, calling him by 'whatever name' had already been chosen but which it was their privilege to utter for the first time, 'according to the ancient ceremonial

---

[132] The three sons of Constantine X appear again at the foot of the Chrysobull of 1074, which they signed jointly, but this time in 'natural' order: Michael now emperor *autocrator*, Andronikos, Constantius: *Michaelis Pselli Scripta minora*, ed. E. Kurtz and I. Drexl (Milan, 1936), p. 334 (where Constantine should read Constantius).

[133] One of the letters drawn up for this negotiation presents the porphyrogenitus as a 'model of royalty' and emphasises the fact, well illustrated by what preceded it, that his name came immediately after that of the principal emperor: Psellos, *Ep.*, 144 (of 1073), ed. Sathas, *Mesaionike Bibliotheke* (n. 115), V, p. 390.

[134] *De cerimoniis*, II, 21–3, pp. 615–22.

[135] Chapter I, 51 [42], pp. 216–17 may preserve a protocol of the acclamations laid down for this occasion.

and the old custom'. On the eighth day, a priest entered the narthex of the church (probably a chapel in the palace) to say a prayer over the child and to 'give him the name which had been spoken by the demes'. There followed a procession of the dignitaries and their wives to honour the child by greetings and acclamations similar to those which were addressed to the emperor.[136] Throughout the week following the birth, there were distributions of drinks or 'birth-cakes'[137] at the portico of the Hall of the Nineteen Couches for the officers of the *tagmata*, the *scholae* and the fleet, the leaders of the Greens and the Blues, representing the 'political', with the guilds. And at the crossroads of the Mese, from the Chalke to the Forum of the Bull, the same distributions were made to the poor, 'our brothers in Christ'.[138]

In chapter II, 22, we learn that for the baptism of a male child of the emperor, the officials, bureaucrats and senators assembled; they walked in procession to the 'great baptistery' of St Sophia, where those who had been named as godparents (*anadochoi*) 'received' the child (*dechontai hoi anadochoi*).[139]

According to chapter II, 23, the tonsure (*koureuma*) was a separate ceremony where the child's hair was offered to God. The emperor convened the senate and summoned the patriarch, the metropolitans and the archbishops. Together, they went into the sanctuary chosen by the emperor, where they were joined by the senators and by 'all those who, in their role as godparents, ought to receive the hair of the imperial child'. The *praepositus* brought a piece of cloth made of stitched squares. He himself held the first square, into which the cut hair would fall; the other squares were each held by one of the 'tonsure godparents'. At this point, the author interpolates a memory: for the tonsure of the porphyrogenitus Leo, son of Basil I, which took place in the chapel of St Theodore, the chosen sponsors included not only the *strategos* of the Anatolikon and the *strategos* of Cappadocia, but all the officers of these two themes down to the rank of *droungarios* and *comes*, some fifty persons in all. As a result, the piece of cloth and the chain of godfathers holding it stretched from the chancel barrier to the portico of the Chrysotriklinos.

---

[136] P. 619, lines 1–3. These acclamations were enough in themselves for it to be said that the newborn child was 'proclaimed emperor from the moment his mother gave birth' (Marc the Deacon, *Life of Porphyrios, Bishop of Gaza*, 44, ed. and trans. H. Grégoire and M. A. Kugener, *Vie de Porphyre, évêque de Gaza* (Paris, 1930), p. 37), even when the coronation proper was postponed.

[137] The word *lochozema* meant the beverage given to the new mother so she would have plenty of milk and to help her recover, which was also distributed as a sign of rejoicing; for parallels with modern customs, see P. Koukoules, *Byzantinon bios*, IV, p. 332.

[138] That is to say, at the places and crossings of the western arm of the Mese beginning at the palace: Forum of Constantine, Tetrapylon, Forum Tauri or of Theodosius, Philadelphion, Amastrianon and Forum of the Bull (before the Xerolophos or Forum Arcadius).

[139] The verb *dechomai/anadechomai* and the noun *anadochos* have, in this ritual as in that of confession, a very concrete meaning which emphasises the value of 'adoption' in the former and the account of the sinner's faults to his confessor in the latter.

The stages which are distinguished here (first benediction and birth greetings, choice and fixing of a name, baptism, tonsure) were laid down for all the children and marked in the *Euchologion* by a number of prayers and liturgical acts which survive little changed into modern times.[140] When the child was a porphyrogenitus, the feasts were simply more solemn and confirmed the common character of the different ceremonies, that of adoption rituals. The point was to have the imperial child adopted by as many as possible of the representatives of the social body on which his future and perhaps even his survival depended. The naming by 200 selected representatives, who enjoyed the privilege of calling the child by his name for the first time, created a link of this type. The choice of the name was only a pretence, but even so the *Book of Ceremonies* imposed a duty of protection with regard to the porphyrogenitus on the demes, that is, symbolically on the people of Constantinople, who were so important in the process of legitimating or toppling emperors, and on certain elements in the army;[141] for whoever named the child became a godfather, that is, an adoptive father. The sponsorship of baptism was an occasion for more subtle strategies, often intended to defuse family hatreds or latent political conflicts through the tie of a spiritual paternity. The offering of hair, then distinct from baptism, served a similar purpose, as, since pagan and Jewish antiquity,[142] to offer a man or a god hair cut from a child was to place that child under his protection. The porphyrogenitus was privileged, in this case, because the whole of the social body was associated in the various ceremonies that followed his birth; the people of Constantinople, the dignitaries and the army were attached to the child by a tie of adoption which it would be sacrilege to break in case of revolt or violence. Instead of recognising the right of the son to succeed his father by virtue of natural kinship, a multitude of ties of symbolic kinship were created, which made the porphyrogenitus not only the son of the emperor, but the adoptive son of the empire, just as unction in the womb made him the adoptive son of God; as a precaution and with foresight, certainly, but also in order to avoid any unseemly reference to blood rights.

This analysis of the rituals of infancy could be extended to the time of marriage. For a period in the eighth and ninth centuries, the choice of the wife of a porphyrogenitus, or more generally of a young 'prince heir', was the occasion for a curious 'beauty contest', which is described in a dozen or so independent sources. These accounts, though they turn readily into moral fables and borrow all sorts of symbolic elements from universal folklore, seem largely to be true. When the sources are compared, it becomes impossible to dismiss

---

[140] Goar, *Euchologion*, pp. 261–71.

[141] In the West as in the East, the child was often named after the godfather; for contemporary Greece, see Koukoules, *Byzantinon bios*, IV (n. 137), p. 58 and n. 4.

[142] See for example A. Michel, 'Tonsure', *DTC* XV, 1 (1946), cols. 1228–35; H. Leclercq, 'Tonsure', *DACL* XV, 2 (1953), cols. 2430–43.

them as pure fiction, and the reported episodes form a coherent series from 788 to 882,[143] that is, exactly the period when the notion of porphyrogenitus was developing and becoming sacralised. What happened, we are told, is this. When the *porphyrogenitus* or the son of the reigning emperor awakened to physical love and was old enough to take a wife (between the age of sixteen and twenty), imperial envoys and palace eunuchs embarked on a systematic search 'throughout the territory of Romania'. A number of young girls were selected on the criteria of beauty and bearing. On their arrival in Constantinople, and after a further selection process, these 'candidates', a dozen in all, lived for a while in close contact with the empress, who examined them carefully, and the young emperor saw them before making his choice. At the end of the contest, the happy victor was prepared for her role as empress and some of the more glamorous losers were provided with dowries and married to dignitaries or foreign princes. In practice, the search was limited to a few towns or provinces, the selection was confined to the great families and clan interests heavily influenced the choice. But what is significant is the importance attached to giving these princely marriages the appearance of a largely open 'contest'; it was probably intended to recreate the same combination of elements as when a parvenu emperor took a wife from within the imperial family, but in reverse. In this case, it was not the wife of high birth who brought to the *idiotes* the imperial blood he lacked, it was the 'son of the emperor' who required from a wife 'without birth' the indispensable complement constituted by election and excellence. The competition rewarded not the boldness of a man of ambition but the beauty of a candidate; dynastic legitimacy came from the emperor and it was hoped that the legitimacy of rupture would come from the future empress and would be evaluated in purely feminine terms, just as the courage of the *idiotes* was evaluated in purely masculine terms. In both cases, there was an attempt to resolve a contradiction which stemmed from the very nature of power by giving complementary roles to the emperor and the empress.

There was no legitimacy without this improbable equation, which succeeded in reconciling dynasty and usurpation, heredity and merit, kinship and adoption, blood and unction.

SUCCEEDING TO . . .

When Constantine/Cyril (or the hagiographer who put the words into his mouth) replied to the Khazar's criticism of the instability of the imperial office in Byzantium by invoking the Old Testament, it was much more than a way

[143] As noted by W. T. Treadgold, 'The bride-shows of the Byzantine emperors', *Byz.*, 49 (1979), pp. 395–413. Other historians believe them to be a fiction: L. Ryden, 'The bride-shows at the Byzantine court: history or fiction?', *Eranos*, 83 (1985), pp. 175–91. See also Dagron, 'Nés dans la pourpre' (n. 56), pp. 137–40.

of ending the debate with an authoritative argument. The missionary and all his contemporaries, believing that the Romans were the new chosen people, searched for and found in the history of the Jews ideas that made it possible to adapt the political structures of Rome to its new mission. The New Testament offered them only a prudent distinction between religion and the state, and between an emerging Christianity and a still pagan empire; it was to the Old Testament, therefore, that they turned, not, certainly, to take up the heritage of the 'deicide' people, but to receive the precepts which God had *apparently* given to the Jewish people while foreseeing that they would *actually* apply to the Christian empire.

Kingship, its origins and the nature of the office, sacerdotal or not, is one of the principal subjects of the Old Testament, and a Byzantine reader could take from it a number of key ideas. First, that kingship – that is, kingship over a chosen people, one engaged in a divine plan of 'economy' – could only be a gift of God. It was God who had indicated Saul to Samuel by saying to him: 'Tomorrow ... I will send thee a man out of the land of Benjamin, and thou shalt anoint him to be captain over my people Israel, that he may save my people out of the hand of the Philistines' (I Samuel [I Kings] IX: 16). This divine choice, which leads to the emergence of a charismatic leader, was, in fact, combined, a little later, with popular designation by acclamation (I Samuel [I Kings] XI: 15); the two levels of legitimacy coincided but were not confused. Another lesson learned by the Byzantines was that unction made the sovereign 'another man' (I Samuel [I Kings] X: 6), the adopted son of God, with the double consequence of a downgrading of dynastic heredity and the definition of a sacred kingship.[144] Divine election by unction made it possible to choose from outside the reigning family, a *mutatio regni*,[145] though it did not preclude dynastic succession. As Constantine/Cyril observed, David succeeded to Saul without being related to him, but God promised David that he would 'stablish the throne of his kingdom for ever', that his 'mercy' would not 'depart away from him, as I took it from Saul', that 'thine house and thy kingdom shall be established for ever' (II Samuel [II Kings] VII: 13–16), and 'his throne as the sun before me' (Psalm LXXXIX [LXXXVIII]: 5). Nevertheless, though one can speak of a Davidic dynasty and of a divine 'alliance' with the house of David, the hereditary transmission of royal power was not recognised as a principle; it was accepted only in the kingdom of Judah, not in Israel; it was not accompanied by recognition of primogeniture,[146] and each enthronement consisted in principle of a renewal of

---

[144] Useful summaries in H. Cazelles, 'Royauté sacrale et la Bible', I: 'Royauté sacrale et désacralisation de l'Etat dans l'Ancien Testament', in *Supplément au Dictionnaire de la Bible*, X (Paris, 1985), cols. 1056–77.

[145] Of the type that survived in the West with the recognition of the royal title to Pepin the Short in 751.

[146] Solomon was allegedly the tenth son of David.

the Davidic alliance and an adoption by God of the new sovereign. The right given by unction to exercise certain religious functions already distinguished Saul from Samuel and remained ever after a permanent source of conflict. Like kingship, the priesthood was recognised as twofold. The charismatic kingship of unction was distinguished from the hereditary kingship of the national leader, a priesthood reserved to the priests from a royal priesthood.[147]

One need only read the exegetes and historians of the biblical world to understand how the Byzantines were able without undue strain to find in the Old Testament text not only situations with certain analogies with the recent past or the present of the empire, but a guiding principle in the most complex debates of the day; not only a repertoire of rhetorical themes that made it possible to praise the legitimacy of a 'New David' and the fairness of a 'New Solomon', or denounce the blindness of a 'New Ahab' and the persecutions of a 'New Amalekite', but ready-made 'types', to which the present reality could be made to correspond. No new event was wholly true nor any new emperor wholly authentic until they had been recognised and labelled by reference to an Old Testament model.[148] In Byzantium, the Old Testament had a constitutional value; it had the same normative role in the political sphere as the New Testament in the moral sphere. The history of the Jews, carefully dehistoricised and dejudaised by this Christian reading, was made to prefigure what would or should be the conduct of the empire, and to explain in what conditions and by conforming to which biblical figure a ruler could win or lose his legitimacy, a son inherit his father's power or a king be able to call himself a priest.

Conceived in this way, which is common to the 'religions of the Book' but which can be applied to other societies, the term 'succession' has two meanings. One succeeds *to* a king or *to* an emperor, and the most ordinary and safest succession practice is then probably hereditary transmission; but one succeeds *in* a role and an office, and *in* a series to which one is summoned by God. The role had been written for David; the series was that inaugurated by the first Christian emperor, Constantine, who was both a dynast and David *redivivus*. Each successor who found a place in this series was, in the words of the ceremonial acclamations, a 'New David' and a 'New Constantine', as well as the heir or virtual founder of a dynasty. In Byzantium, one was emperor at these three levels.

[147] On kingship in the Old Testament, see in particular R. de Vaux, *Les Institutions de l'Ancien Testament*, I (Paris, 1958), pp. 141–3, 145–50, 155–8; A. Caquot, 'Remarques sur *la loi royale* du Deutéronome', *Semitica*, 9 (1959), pp. 21–34; T. Veijola, *Die ewige Dynastie. David und die Entstehung seiner Dynastie nach der deuteronomistischen Darstellung* (Helsinki, 1975); B. Halpern, *The Constitution of the Monarchy in Israel* (Ann Arbor, 1981); A. Lemaire, 'The united monarchy: Saul, David and Salomon', in *Ancient Israel: A Short History from Abraham to the Roman Destruction of the Temple*, ed. H. Shanks (Washington, 1988), pp. 85–108; S. Horn, 'The divided monarchs: the kingdoms of Judah and Israel', *Ancient Israel*, pp. 109–49.
[148] G. Dagron, 'Judaïser', *TM*, 11 (1991), pp. 378–80.

Islam, which felt the influence, either directly or by way of Byzantium, of Old Testament models provides an illuminating parallel. As specialists tell us, the Arab language has at least two words to indicate the sovereign:[149] *malik* (from the old Semitic root *mlk*), the holder of a dynastic kingship without any particular sacred quality,[150] and *khalifa*, the successor or representative who exercises 'in his turn' or 'by delegation' a sacred power, without this excluding or affirming a hereditary right. In the Koran, God establishes Adam and, above all, David as 'caliphs' on earth:

When your Lord said to the angels:
'I will create a *khalifa* on earth',
the angels said:
'Will you place there one who will make mischief
and shed blood
while we sing your praises
and proclaim your holiness?' (Chapter 2: 30)

The angels protested because they made the mistake of confusing *malik* and *khalifa*:

O David, we made you a *khalifa* on earth,
so judge men in truth and justice;
do not follow your lusts,
they will lead you away from the path of God. (Chapter 38: 26)

There exists, then, in the Koran, the distinction between two conceptions of monarchy which specialists had already noted in the Old Testament and which I have tried to show in Byzantium. Many stories, often invented, try to define, with regard to what the Muslim caliph should be, what distinguishes the *khalifa* from the *malik*.[151]

Tabari reports a dialogue between the caliph Umar and the first Muslim of Persia, Salmân. Umar asks Salmân: 'Am I a *malik* or a *khalifa*?' And Salmân replies: 'If you have taxed the lands of the Muslims one dirhem, or more or less, and if you have used this dirhem for purposes contrary to the law, then you are a *malik* and not a *khalifa*.' Umar wept.

---

[149] See, in particular, B. Lewis, *The Political Language of Islam* (Chicago, 1988), especially pp. 43ff., 53–6, 97–9; also D. S. Margoliouth, 'The sense of the title Khalifah', in *A Volume of Oriental Studies presented to E. G. Browne*, ed. T. W. Arnold and R. A. Nicholson (Cambridge, 1922), pp. 322–8; R. Paret, 'Signification coranique de *Halifa* et autres dérivés de la racine *halafa*', *Studia Islamica*, 31 (1970), pp. 211–17; R. Paret, '*Halifat Allah – Vicarius Dei*. Ein differenzierender Vergleich', in *Mélanges d'islamologie. Volume dédié à la mémoire d'Armand Abel par ses collègues, ses élèves et ses amis*, ed. P. Salmon (Leiden, 1974), pp. 224–32; D. Sourdel, A. K. S. Lambton and F. de Jong, 'Khalifa', in *Encyclopédie de l'Islam*, IV, pp. 970–85; A. Al-Azmeh, *Muslim Kingship, Power and the Sacred in Muslim, Christian and Pagan Polities* (London/New York, 1999), which seeks to show that Islam, despite its distinctive features, fits easily into the system of 'royal' ideologies of antiquity and the early middle ages.
[150] Thus the 'prince of princes' Bagratid, whose sovereignty over Armenia was recognised by the Arabs, was regarded as a *malik*.
[151] Quoted in Lewis, *The Political Language of Islam* (n. 149).

After the *rashidun* ('rightly guided') caliphs, as the Umayyad and Abbasid dynasties became established, a contamination occurred between the two sorts of monarchy, and this disillusioned prediction was attributed to Muhammad: 'the caliphate after me will last for thirty years, to be followed by monarchy' (that of the *malik*). The sources also attribute to Mu'awiya, who made the caliphate hereditary, this observation: 'I am the first king [*malik*]' of Islam.[152]

The stricter Muslims criticised the title *khalifat Allah*, God's caliph or lieutenant, which was assumed by certain caliphs of the Umayyad period (such as Abd al-Malik 685–705) and the Abbasid period (such as al-Mamun 813–33), and which presumed a monarchy by divine right, a sort of 'vicariate of God'. The following story began to circulate. A man spoke to Umar, addressing him as *khalifat Allah* (representative of God). 'No', replied Umar, 'God's representative is David.' The man then addressed him as *khalifatu Rasul Allah* (successor of the Envoy of God, that is, Muhammad). 'No', replied Umar, again, 'the successor of God's Prophet is Abu Bakr.' The man then gave him the precise title of *khalifatu khalifati Rasul Allah* (successor of the successor of the Envoy of God). 'That is correct', said Umar, 'but it is very long, and the title can only get longer; better call me *Amir al-Muminin* [Commander of the believers].'

This delightful story invites us at least to qualify excessively theoretical schemas for the theological basis of the caliphs' power. It brings out the ambiguity of the word *khalifa*, which, according to circumstances and never indiscriminately, had the meaning of successor and of representative; that is, it could sometimes mean 'succeed to' and sometimes 'succeed in'. It also suggests a sort of de-escalation by distinguishing successive but quite separate levels of authority: God, His representative, His Envoy, the successor of His Envoy, the successor of the successor of . . . Unless one referred directly to the community of believers of whom the caliph was leader, one was obliged to count, one by one, all the links in this chain of succession to find the precise place, title and legitimacy of each sovereign. The repetition, by meticulously measuring the temporal distance which distanced the power exercised in the present from its divine origin, prevented this power from hardening into theocracy pure and simple, but it also led, by the ruptures it suggested, to an interpretation of the succession to the caliphate as a series of reproductions rather than as a natural transmission over the course of time.

I will here make only the briefest of comparisons with Byzantium. Like the sovereign of Baghdad, the sovereign of Constantinople hesitated between a definition of *malik* and a definition of *khalifa*, between a succession performed in time, which caused dynasties to be born, and a perpetual chain of delegations,

---

[152] See R. G. Khoury, 'Calife ou roi: du fondement théologico-politique du pouvoir suprême dans l'Islam sous les califes orthodoxes et omeyyades', in *La Syrie, de Byzance à l'Islam, VIIe–VIIIe siècles*, ed. P. Canivet and J.-P. Rey-Coquais (Damascus, 1992), pp. 323–32.

which defined the David *redivivus* or, in the most common Greek phrase, 'the emperor of each period'.[153] The empire-patrimony could, at a pinch, be transmitted according to the tacit rules of natural succession; but the sacred *basileia*, which came from God and had been invented *for* the empire of the Christians *through* the intermediary of the chosen people before the 'time of grace', was not a power that could be transmitted. It was a role into which one entered always provisionally and by proxy. The Byzantine empire, rather like the Arab caliphate, was hereditary from the instinct for self-preservation, sacred and priestly, hence elective, by a projection of the 'Jewish antiquities'.

---

[153] This expression in the singular, *ho kata kairous basileus*, would surely have delighted Kantorowicz if he had known of it.

2. *Proclamations and coronations*

A MODEL CORONATION

This is how the *Book of Ceremonies* of Constantine Porphyrogenitus described an imperial coronation towards the middle of the tenth century, synthesising various protocols and, according to the rules of the genre, removing the proper names and dates in order to transform a historical document into a model.[1]

The civil and military dignitaries, in ceremonial dress and with the insignia, wait at the palace, ready to escort the sovereign. He emerges from the state chamber of the Augusteus, wearing the *skaramangion*, a narrow floor-length tunic, and the purple *sagion*, a short cloak. As he makes his way towards the gates of the palace, he is 'received' by the patricians, the consuls and the rest of the senate. He leaves by the military quarter of the *scholae* and, along his route, in their accustomed places, the representatives of the demes (Greens and Blues) make the sign of the cross for his benefit. On arriving at the Horologion and the south vestibule of St Sophia, the emperor changes his clothes, putting on more imperial robes in a space concealed behind a portière (the *metatorion*): a silk tunic called a *divetesion* and an embroidered mantle which was given the name, probably Khazar in origin, of *tzitzakion*.[2] Next comes the 'entry' with the patriarch, when they pass together through the imperial door of the narthex towards the central nave; this is described in detail in the first chapter of the *Book* and we will examine it in ch. 3. The sovereign prays before the 'Holy Doors', those in the chancel barrier separating off the sanctuary, but does not go through. After lighting candles, he and the patriarch mount the ambo, where, laid out on a portable altar, are the insignia of kingship: the *chlamys*, the fibula with which it was fastened on the right shoulder and the crown.[3] The

---

[1] *De cerimoniis*, I, 47 [38], pp. 191–6; ed. and trans. A. Vogt, *Constantin Porphyrogénète, Le Livre des cérémonies* (Paris, 1939), II, pp. 1–5.

[2] Rarely worn, it seems to have appeared only in the eighth century, after the marriage of Constantine V to Irene, a Khazar whose name was Čiček (Flower).

[3] The old diadem, a band of silk joined behind, had been replaced by the *stemma* of gold encircling the head, similar in shape but rigid, decorated with gems, pearls or emeralds, with at the front

patriarch says a prayer over the crown (the ceremonial does not give the words, as this was a liturgical matter),[4] takes it up and places it on the head of the sovereign. The people then shout: 'Holy, holy holy![5] Glory in the highest and peace on earth!', followed by 'Many be the years of such and such, great emperor *autokrator*[6] ....' Wearing the crown, the emperor descends the ambo, enters a second *metatorion* located at the easternmost end of the south aisle,[7] and sits on a portable throne (*sellion*); here, in successive batches, twelve in all, the dignitaries come to greet him in order of hierarchy, falling to the ground and kissing his two knees. The *praepositus* then says: 'At your service', and all shout 'For many and good years', before withdrawing. The ceremony continues with the kiss of peace, communion and the exit, according to the order laid down for the great religious festivals, described in the first chapter.

Next in the collection comes a protocol of acclamations which actually comes from a different ceremony, since the crowned emperor is not a 'senior emperor *autokrator*', but a 'junior' co-emperor. In the ambo, the patriarch 'prays over the *chlamys* before handing it to the senior emperor', and it is the latter who puts it on the co-emperor; 'next, the patriarch says the prayer over the crowns and, with his own hands, crowns first the senior emperor, then hands the other crown to the senior emperor, who crowns the newly consecrated emperor'. The factions shout 'Worthy' and the insignia or flags are dipped.[8] Alternately, the choirs and the people then salute the sovereigns:

Glory to God in the highest and peace on earth ... Goodwill to Christians, because God has had pity on his people ... this is the great day of the Lord, this is the day of the salvation of the Romans ... this day is the joy and the glory of the world, when the crown of the empire has been worthily placed on your head.

It is all rather disappointing. Where one had hoped for a fine historical evocation, there is only a museum piece. Where one might have expected to find, in this synthesis of protocols, if not a definition of the *basileia*, at least the description of a truly royal ritual with a route, participants, significant gestures and words, there is only this imprecise and characterless text which says almost nothing of importance and is valuable chiefly for the critique it inspires.

---

a large coloured stone, usually surmounted with a cross, and trimmed with ear-length pendants (*prependoulia*). The *stemma*, which I have called a 'crown', did not yet incorporate a cap.
[4] This short prayer is given below.
[5] For the meaning of this triple exclamation, see below, pp. 155–6.
[6] It describes, therefore, the coronation of a 'senior emperor' with *autokratoria*, not that of an associate 'junior emperor'.
[7] For this space, which served as an apartment for the emperor actually inside St Sophia, see below, pp. 92–7.
[8] As a mark of respect; but, as we will see, in the fifth-century ceremony, the flags were, in contrast, raised as a sign of rejoicing and renewal when the new emperor was proclaimed; see below, pp. 60–1.

First, it is not dated, and cannot be dated with confidence;[9] the determination of the compiler to eliminate anything that might locate the account in history has impoverished it in a way that only emphasises how much the actual ceremony of investiture, as described in other sources, depended on the personality of each new emperor and the circumstances of his accession to the throne.

Second, it carelessly juxtaposes the protocol of the coronation of a senior emperor and that of the acclamation of an associate emperor, incidentally emphasising the extent of the difference between the two legitimacies we have already described; that of the new man directly promoted as *autokrator* and crowned by the patriarch, and that of the heir or successor associated with the *basileia* and crowned by the 'senior emperor' himself.

Third, the other participants are reduced to symbols; the people, *laos* or *demos*, consist only of a handful of dignitaries or carefully selected representatives, lining the shortest route between the private space of the palace and the semi-public space of St Sophia. The town and its inhabitants, whose importance in choosing emperors is well documented, are deliberately sidelined.

Further, the principal role seems to be devolved to the church, terminus of the itinerary, and to the patriarch, who places the crown on the head of the new sovereign or blesses the crown which the emperor will place on the head of the associated crown prince. Admittedly, the compiler is recording only the religious aspect of the ceremony; but in so doing, he strips it of all specificity and simply describes the imperial procession, as laid down for any great festival, already described in detail and which he admits he is only summarising.[10] Neither the *mutatio vestis* in the propylaea of the narthex,[11] nor the salutations in the *metatorion* of the south aisle are in any way exceptional; only the coronation in the ambo introduces a specific element into the normal liturgy of the emperor's 'entry' (*eisodos*) into the church of Christ, which was, in fact, as we will see, the fundamental ceremony with the highest institutional and symbolic significance.

---

[9] G. Ostrogorsky and E. Stein ('Die Krönungsordnungen des Zeremonienbuches. Chronologische und verfassungsgeschichtliche Bemerkungen', *Byz.*, 7 (1932), pp. 185–233) believed that I, 47 [38]a might be the protocol of the coronation of Michael I (2 October 811), Leo V (11 July 813) or Michael II (25 December 820), and that I, 47 [38]b concerned an appointment as associate emperor that took place after 812, since it includes the expression 'emperor of the Romans', perhaps the coronation by Theophilos of one of his sons, Constantine (in 830) or Michael III (1 September 840). F. Dölger (*BZ*, 36 (1936), pp. 149–51) prefers, for I, 47 [38]a, the accession of Leo V, which the sources present as a sort of model of constitutionality, and rightly observes that, in the case of I, 47 [38]b, the formula 'emperor of the Romans' does not provide a *terminus post quem*, because it was in use well before the ninth century. He thinks the association may even have been that of Romanos II, crowned by his father, Constantine Porphyrogenitus, on 6 April 945.

[10] *De cerimoniis*, I, 1, pp. 5–35; ed. and trans. Vogt, *Constantin Porphyrogénète* (n. 1), I, pp. 3–28.

[11] For the importance of the *mutatio vestis* in imperial rituals, see A. Alföldi, 'Insignien und Tracht der römischen Kaiser', *Mitteilungen des deutschen archäologischen Instituts, Römische Abteilung*, 50 (1935), pp. 5–9.

But because the dates of imperial coronations were deliberately made to coincide with great religious festivals, the coronation was only an episode tacked
on, and sometimes tacked on by surprise, as when Michael III associated Basil
I on the throne. On 26 May 866, Whit Sunday, the chroniclers tell us,[12] Michael
came to St Sophia according to the normal ceremonial but the congregation
were surprised to see him enter the church and climb the first steps of the ambo
wearing the crown, whereas custom required the emperor to remove it before
passing through the Imperial Doors of the narthex. The explanation was not long
in coming; Michael took advantage of the religious festival to crown Basil. This
story shows not that Constantine Porphyrogenitus's chapter is inaccurate, but
that he chose to reproduce a minimal ceremony, or a blessing, the wearing of
the crown and a few acclamations making a promotion to the empire official
without constituting a true royal consecration.

Lastly, this chapter on the coronation occupies a surprising place within
the structure of the *Book of Ceremonies*, that is, at the head of a section
devoted to civil ceremonies (I, 47–72 [38–63]) – as opposed to religious
ceremonies (I, 1–46 [1–37]) – and the promotions of dignitaries. The emperor
and the augusta were thus placed at the top of a hierarchy which descended to the
level of office head and *protospatharios*, making the *basileus* a sort of top civil
servant. This pyramidal presentation is largely an illusion. In fact, there was a
break in the court hierarchy before or after the *kouropalates*. The caesar and
the *nobelissimos* were invested with imperial dignities which were intended –
like that of *kouropalates* – to satisfy the ambitions of members of the imperial
family and which retained – unlike that of *kouropalates* – an echo of the *basileia*
in the term indicating the promotion (*cheirotoneia*, that is, 'consecration', not
proagoge), in the epithets repeated in the acclamations (*eutychestatos* for the
caesar, *epiphanestatos* for the *nobelissimos*) and in the acts of homage (one
kissed the two knees of the emperor, one knee of the caesar and the hand of
the *nobelissimos*). Elsewhere Constantine Porphyrogenitus gives the protocol
of the elevation by Herakleios, on 4 July 638, of his son Heraklonas from the
dignity of caesar to the *basileia* and of his son David to the rank of caesar;[13] and
he probably took as his model a 'consecration' as caesar and *nobelissimos* from
the protocol of the ceremony of 2 April 769, during which three of the children
of Constantine V had been promoted to the rank of caesar (Christophoros and
Nikephoros) and *nobelissimos* (Niketas).[14] He knew from personal and historical experience that since the seventh century the *basileia* had become a sort of

---

[12] Leo the Grammarian, *Chronographia*, ed. I. Bekker (Bonn, 1842), pp. 245–6; George the Monk
Continued, ed. Bekker (see ch. 1, n. 101), pp. 831–2.

[13] *De cerimoniis*, II, 27, pp. 627–8.

[14] Ibid., I, 52–3 [43–4], pp. 217–29. The dating of these anonymous protocols, which goes back
to C. Diehl, has been accepted by all commentators, notably by Ostrogorsky and Stein, 'Die
Krönungsordnungen des Zeremonienbuches' (n. 9), pp. 224–31.

latent virtue, a symbolic unction extending to the progeny of the sovereign and distinct from the *autokratoria*, that is, effective power. It is surprising, therefore, that he here connives at a confusion and, in a book entirely devoted to the glorification of the *basileia*, presents the 'coronation' as the promotion of a higher dignitary, on whose head a crown is placed on the occasion of a feast in the religious calendar.

Even if we complete the *Book of Ceremonies* by the prayers of the *Euchologion*, we are still a long way from the great rituals which made the new king 'another man', those *ordines* which ethnologists rather naively interpret as a global representation of kingship,[15] and to which, in form at least, the chapter devoted to the 'coronation of the emperor' in the *Treatise on the offices* of the Pseudo-Kodinos (fourteenth century), comes closer.[16] The prayers of the patriarch in the ambo are brief and relatively banal in spite of their Old Testament tone:

> Before the *vestitores* invest the emperor with the *chlamys*: 'Lord our God, King of kings and Lord of lords, You who, through the intermediary of your prophet Samuel, chose your servant David and, by unction, made him king of your people Israel, hear also today our supplication, look down from your holy dwelling on high on we who are unworthy, deign to anoint with the oil of gladness your faithful servant,[17] a man it has pleased you to establish as emperor over the holy nation which you have made your own by the blood of your only Son. Endow him with power from on high, put on his head a crown of precious stones, bless him with a long life, place in his right hand the sceptre of salvation, establish him on the throne of righteousness, gird him with the weapons of your Holy Spirit, give strength to his arm, subject to him all the barbarous nations, instil into his heart fear of you and compassion towards his subjects, preserve him in an unspotted faith, make him a scrupulous defender of the teaching of the holy catholic Church: so that he may judge your people fairly and the poor with justice, defend the children of the poor and inherit thy heavenly kingdom. For yours is the power, the kingdom and the glory.'

> Before placing the crown, or causing it to be placed, on the head of the new emperor and proceeding to the liturgy of the presanctified, the patriarch says a second prayer: 'Before you, the only King of men, he to whom you have entrusted the earthly kingdom bows down the neck, with us. And we beseech you, Master of all, keep him under your protection, strengthen his kingdom,

---

[15] See, for example, J. L. Nelson, 'Inauguration rituals', in *Early Medieval Kingship*, ed. P. H. Sawyer and I. N. Wood (Leeds, 1977), pp. 50–71.

[16] Ed. and trans. J. Verpeaux, Pseudo-Kodinos, *Traité des offices* (Paris, 1966), pp. 252–73. This text is analysed below, pp. 279–80.

[17] This was a symbolic anointing accorded by God and not, at least before the late twelfth or early thirteenth century, an actual anointing performed by the patriarch. See below, pp. 273–5.

grant that he does your will in all things, make justice and an abundance of peace flourish during his lifetime; may the peace of his reign enable us to lead a sweet and tranquil existence in all piety and honesty. For you are the King of peace and the Saviour of our souls and bodies, and we glorify you.'[18]

PROTOCOLS OF THE FIFTH AND SIXTH CENTURIES

It was perhaps to compensate for this obvious banality that the tenth-century compiler added a few accounts of coronations chosen by a master of the offices (*magister officiorum*) of Justinian I, Peter the Patrician,[19] author of a lost work on the administration, the *Peri politikes katastaseos*, now known to us only through the borrowings in the *Book of Ceremonies*. In preserving the ceremonial, Peter the Patrician probably intended, as John the Lydian assumed, and as Constantine Porphyrogenitus himself professed to be his aim, 'to restore the honour of the Roman name' and to save the empire from the 'folly' of uncontrolled innovation;[20] but, with greater intelligence than his tenth-century imitator, Peter did not confine himself to a single model. He noted the differences between an ancient ceremonial, longer and starting from the military parade ground situated at the seventh milestone from Constantinople, the Hebdomon,[21] and a modern (end fifth/sixth century) ceremonial concentrated on the Hippodrome and St Sophia. Above all, he distinguished between situations: that of the new man chosen as emperor after the death of his predecessor and proclaimed either according to the ancient formula (Leo I succeeding Marcian on 7 February 457)[22] or the modern formula (Anastasios succeeding Zeno on 11 April 491);[23] that where the accession of the new sovereign took place amidst confusion and improvisation (Justin I appointed almost by chance on 10 July 518);[24]

---

[18] Goar, *Euchologion*, pp. 726–7. His version is based on the ms. *Barberini* 336 (Biblioteca Vaticana), which has the oldest text.

[19] Peter the Patrician, *magister officiorum* 539–65, was the author of other lost works: a history of the Roman empire which stopped with Constantius II, a history of the office of *magister officiorum* and stories or reports of diplomatic missions in Persia, used by Menander Protector: *PLRE* III, pp. 994–8 (Petrus 6); H. Hunger, *Die hochsprachliche profane Literatur der Byzantiner*, I (Munich, 1978), pp. 300–3; more recently, P. Antonopoulos, *Petros Patrikios* (Athens, 1990). E. Stein (*Histoire du Bas-Empire*, French ed. by J. R. Palanque, II (Bruges, 1949), pp. 723–9) dates the composition of Peter the Patrician's book on ceremonies to between 548 and 552.

[20] Ioannes Lydos, *De magistratibus*, II, 26, ed. and trans. A. C. Bandy, *On Powers or The magistracies of the Roman State* (Philadelphia, 1983), pp. 122–5; prefaces to books I and II of *De cerimoniis*, pp. 3–5, 516–17.

[21] Janin, *Constantinople byzantine*, pp. 446–9.

[22] *De cerimoniis*, I, 100 [91], Bonn, pp. 410–17. H. E. Del Medico ('Le couronnement d'un empereur byzantin vu par un juif de Constantinople', *ByzSlav.*, 16 (1955), pp. 43–75) found in a tenth-century collection in Hebrew, the *Yossipon*, the description of a coronation which he believed to be that of Leo; but P. E. Schramm (*Könige und Päpste*, III, pp. 360–8) has shown that it was an interpolation referring to the coronation of a Germanic emperor.

[23] *De cerimoniis*, I, 101 [92], pp. 417–25.   [24] Ibid., I, 102 [93], pp. 426–30.

the very different situation where 'an emperor is appointed by another emperor' (the very young Leo II crowned by his grandfather Leo I on 17 November 473);[25] and that, lastly, of the reigning emperor, which could not be passed over in silence even though the ceremonial was pared down to essentials (Justinian I, who had exercised real power for some time, but who was only proclaimed emperor by his uncle, Justin, on his deathbed, on 1 April 527).[26] Peter the Patrician justified this spectrum of reproduced or summarised protocols not by the scrupulousness of a historian but by the desire to 'permit each [future emperor] to choose, when the time comes – may God long delay that day![27] – the ceremonial which is most orderly and pleasing to him'.[28] It is made clear that the proclamation of an emperor did not lend itself to a uniform ceremonial; rather, it was a solemn event which could and should take different forms according to the political circumstances of the enthronement and the personality of each new ruler. We must first, therefore, examine these differences, which owe far more to the conditions in which power was assumed than to historical developments, and take note of the structural permanencies.

Chapter I, 100 [91] chooses, in order to describe the 'ancient' ceremonial in its most developed form, the investiture of an emperor who was in no way exceptional. When the all-powerful Aspar came looking for him in the hope of ruling through him, Leo I was commanding troops stationed in Selymbria as *comes et tribunus Mattiariorum*.[29] He was a soldier, chosen by the army. On 27 January 457, after Marcian's death and a sham vote in the senate, the officers and soldiers of the *scholae* and the army gathered at the Hebdomon with, notably, the archbishop of Constantinople, Anatolios (449–58) and the master of the offices, Martialis.[30] The *labara* and standards were laid on the ground to signify the despondency of the empire temporarily deprived of an emperor. In a beautiful monody, all those present then asked God to approve the choice of men:

> Hear us, O God, we beseech you; hear us, O God! Let Leo live. Hear us, O God! May Leo be emperor! God, you who love mankind, the republic asks for Leo as emperor. The army asks for Leo as emperor. The laws uphold Leo.[31] The Palace upholds Leo. This is the wish of the Palace. This is the request of the military. This is the wish of the senate. This is the wish of the people. The world awaits Leo. The army supports Leo. Let our fine common [choice] approach, Leo! Let our wise common [choice] reign, Leo! Hear, O God, we beseech you!

[25] Ibid., I, 103 [94], pp. 431–2.   [26] Ibid., I, 104 [95], pp. 432–3.

[27] Since Justinian was extremely old, though still living, the author denies wishing for or predicting his imminent death.

[28] *De cerimoniis*, I, 100 [91], Bonn, p. 417.   [29] For Leo I, see *PLRE* II, pp. 663–4 (Leo VI).

[30] Ibid., p. 729 (Flavius Areobindas Martialis).

[31] Corippus, *In laudem Iustini Angusti minoris*, I, v. 148, ed. and trans. Averil Cameron (London, 1976), p. 41: 'Te iura vocant, te sustinet aula'; the parallel is noted by S. MacCormack, *Art and Ceremony in Late Antiquity* (Berkeley, 1981), p. 249.

Suddenly, the *comes* Leo was led to the tribunal (*tribounalion*), a first commander (*campiductor*) placed his torque (*torques/maniakes, maniakion*) on Leo's head and a second placed his in Leo's right hand.[32] The *labara* were raised amidst a shout of joy:

Leo Augustus, you are victorious, you are pious, you are venerable. God has given you, may God protect you! In venerating Christ, you are always the victor. May Leo reign for many years! May God protect the Christian reign!

Then, under cover of a testudo formed by the *candidati* with their shields, and still on the tribunal, the new emperor donned the imperial cloak (*chlamys*), placed the diadem on his head and appeared to the people, who prostrated themselves; he seized a lance and a shield and was acclaimed in this warlike posture. An address written in advance on a *libellarion*[33] was read to his 'comrades in arms',[34] granting them, in particular, a donative of five *nomismata* and one pound of silver each, distributed immediately afterwards. The acclamations that punctuated the reading of this text praised imperial generosity: 'Through you come honours, through you come goods. May your happy reign provide us with golden centuries.'

The original protocol stops short at the end of this investiture by the army and in the presence of civil and ecclesiastical dignitaries, adding only that Leo 'entered the town' and that 'the rest of the ceremony', the *adventus*, 'took place according to the usual form'. But the compiler, probably Peter the Patrician himself, did not stop here and describes in detail an 'entry' which is either that of Leo himself or that of an emperor of the same period.[35]

On leaving the tribunal of the Campus Martius, the emperor proceeded on foot to the nearby church of the Hebdomon,[36] removed his crown and said a prayer. The patriarch and his clergy were no longer with him, as they had

---

[32] For this *Torqueskrönung*, see, among others, Alföldi, 'Insignien und Tracht' (n. 11), pp. 52–3, who refers in particular to the coronation of Julian in Gaul by a *draconarius*: Ammianus Marcellinus, XX, 4, 17–18; Julian, *Orationes*, V, 11, ed. and trans. Bidez (see ch. 1, n. 46), I, 1, p. 232; Libanios, *Orationes*, ed. Förster (see ch. 1, n. 31), XVIII, 99, II, p. 278; Socrates, *Historia ecclesiastica*, III, 1, PG 67, cols. 373–6.

[33] In the time of Leo VI and Constantine Porphyrogenitus, the emperors, even if they were not from the army, addressed the soldiers as their *systratiotai*.

[34] The *libellarion/libellarium* was the little book containing the text of the sovereign's address, read by one of the *libellesioi/libellenses*, unless by a senior functionary such as the *quaestor* or *magistros*: *De cerimoniis*, I, 101 [92] and 102 [93], pp. 418, l. 21, 423, ll. 18–19, 429, ll. 13–14.

[35] There is an obvious break between the two documents, noted by Bury, *Later Roman Empire*, I (see ch. 1, n. 3), p. 312; O. Treitinger, *Die Oströmische Kaiser- und Reichsidee nach ihrer Gestaltung im höfischen Zeremoniell* (repr. Darmstadt, 1956), p. 10, n. 9; M. McCormick, *Eternal Victory: Triumphal Rulership in Late Antiquity, Byzantium and the Early Medieval West* (Cambridge, 1986), pp. 210–11, n. 101.

[36] It must be St John of the Hebdomon, often referred to in connection with imperial processions (Janin, *Eglises et monastères*, pp. 413–15; G. Dagron, *Naissance d'une capitale. Constantinople et ses institutions de 330 à 451*, 2nd ed. (Paris, 1984), pp. 98–102), rather than SS. Carpus and Papylus, as has sometimes been supposed, on the grounds that it was situated on the route leading from the Golden Gate to the Helenianai.

returned to the Great Church to await the arrival of the procession. The second stage took the emperor, riding on a white horse and again wearing his crown and escorted by the dignitaries, to a sanctuary of St John the Baptist, which was probably by the Golden Gate, the monumental gate of Constantinople built into the Theodosian walls.[37] There followed further devotions, the crown again being removed and placed on the altar (at the same time as offerings, a sign of submission and homage) and then put back on. A third stage took the procession, still on horseback, to the quarter of the Helenianai, where the keeper of the Palace came to prostrate himself before the emperor,[38] and where the latter found a cross held by *vestitores*, which would accompany him for the rest of the route. Here, he dismounted and entered a *metatorion* to put on a purple *chlamys*, a white *divetesion* and consular sandals, the *kampagia*;[39] it was in these new robes that, mounted on a chariot, in the middle of a civil and military procession, he passed through the 'gate' of the ancient walls to reach the Forum of Constantine,[40] where he was received by the city prefect and the senate. The 'first' of the senate handed him the traditional 'golden wreath' (*modiolon chrysoun, aurum coronarium*), tax or homage.[41] He climbed back into the chariot alone, senators and dignitaries lining the route as far as the Augustaion, the Horologion and the atrium and narthex of St Sophia. There followed the customary ceremonial and liturgy of the 'entry' into the church (the second St Sophia, that of Theodosius II, inaugurated in 415, and not yet that of Justinian); the emperor removed his crown and gave it to the *praepositus*, passed through the barrier of the sanctuary with the patriarch and placed gold and valuable gifts on the altar. He then proceeded to the place prepared for him in

---

[37] The text, which seems here to have been interfered with, makes no reference to the passage through the Golden Gate.

[38] Was this the keeper of the Helenianai palace? It could equally have been the keeper of the Great Palace, whom the emperor appointed as he left and who had come to meet him on his return, when he had reached the quarter of the Helenianai, that is, was almost at the gate of the old ramparts of Constantine, for the last 'entry'. At the end of the chapter, it is specified that officers of the *scholae* remained in the palace so that it was not left undefended. The *metatorion* referred to here might be that of another sanctuary dedicated to the Precursor, that of 'the old gate': Janin, *Eglises et monastères*, pp. 420–1. For the Helenianai, see V. Tiftixoglu, 'Die Helenianai nebst einigen anderen Besitzungen im Vorfeld des frühen Konstantinopel', in *Studien zur Frühgeschichte Konstantinopels*, ed. H.-G. Beck (Munich, 1973), pp. 49–120.

[39] Alföldi, 'Insignien und Tracht', (n. 11), p. 65 and n. 7.

[40] *De cerimoniis*, I, 100 [91], p. 416, ll. 16–17. This is an addition probably dating from the time of Constantine VII (see n. 11).

[41] See T. Klauser, 'Aurum coronarium', in T. Klauser, *Gesammelte Arbeiten zur Liturgiegeschichte, Kirchengeschichte und christlichen Archäologie, JAC*, Ergänzungsband 3 (Münster, 1974), pp. 292–309. Useful update on the now ritualised offering of the *aurum coronarium/oblaticium* in McCormick, *Eternal Victory* (n. 35), pp. 211–12. In the ceremonial of the emperor's triumphal return, it was stipulated that the emperor would also receive from the senators a gold crown, but would offer in return the equivalent value in gold coins: the texts are edited by J. F. Haldon, *Constantine Porphyrogenitus. Three Treatises on Imperial Military Expeditions* (Vienna, 1990), C 694–8, 771–7, pp. 138, 142–4.

the south aisle, heard the Gospels and, if he wished, attended the office. Lastly, he received his crown again from the hands of the patriarch (a gesture signifying only that the emperor, leaving the church of Christ, resumed his sovereignty, and in no way comparable to a coronation), distributed gifts to the clergy and returned to the Palace.[42] Just before passing through the door, in the main road leading up to it, the emperor was welcomed by the officers of the *scholae*, who had remained in their places so as not to leave the palace undefended, and by the senators and the city prefect; they gave him a 'bond' (*pittakion*) of a thousand pounds of silver, soon returned as a 'counter-gift'.[43] The final stages took place inside the Consistorium, where the prefects, senators and dignitaries assembled, in the Chamber (*cubiculum/kouboukleion*) into which only the patricians followed the emperor, in the Great Triklinos, where a banquet was held, and, next day, at the Hippodrome, where the emperor decreed there would be races, if the Christian calendar permitted.[44]

It is clear that this ceremonial comprised two distinct and complementary parts: a proclamation outside the walls and a triumphal entry into the city. The proclamation itself mimes a military takeover like those which had swept Constantine to power, or Julian in Gaul; a general was 'chosen' by his troops, decided to risk a 'usurpation', received as a crown the military leader's torque, was arrayed in a length of purple fabric and then raised on a shield, and made it his first task to distribute silver to his 'companions in arms'. In the case of Leo I, the *comes et magister utriusque militiae* Aspar imposed his candidate, admittedly, but in Constantinople itself and in a more or less normal political context. If, therefore, the ritual was performed in the setting of a Campus Martius and given the appearance of improvisation, it was as a reminder that power was seized by force and that the coronation which followed was the beginning of a process that was irreversible even if its outcome remained uncertain. Of course, every effort was made in 457 to play down this sense of violence; it was the senate, it was said, which had chosen, and civil dignitaries were present – at least as bit players – at the Hebdomon, as were the patriarch and his clergy. By asking God in a spellbinding scene to approve the choice of men, the unanimity of the army, the senate, the palace, the law and the people was evoked; the torque soon became a crown and the newly elected emperor was raised on a dais, rather than on a shield. But it was still the act of the two *campiductores* placing their torques on Leo's head and in his hand that was regarded as marking the moment when God responded favourably to the prayer, when the ordinary

---

[42] This ceremony is described in *De cerimoniis*, I, 1, and analysed in ch. 3. The text of Peter the Patrician makes it clear that the ceremonial, transposed into the St Sophia of Justinian, remained substantially the same. The main difference was that the atrium of the Theodosian church became the south vestibule (or 'propylaea of the narthex').

[43] *De cerimoniis*, I, 100 [91], p. 415, line 22.

[44] That is, if the day did not fall on a Sunday, or on one of the 'feasts of the Lord' or during Lent.

man became instantaneously an emperor, and when, with the raising of the *labara* and standards, the empire itself was restored in his person.

The coronation proper was over, but the fortunate general become emperor still had to enter, by stages, the heart of the city and establish himself in his palace. This *adventus principis* was not a ceremony unique to an imperial investiture, but the triumphal or simply solemn entry of an emperor into an imperial city, defined as a defensive perimeter, a consecrated space and a civil community ruled by institutions.[45] That the sovereign's arrival in a city should give rise to a special ritual and distinctive iconography is itself worthy of attention and open to various explanations. Ernst Kantorowicz emphasised the eschatological and soon Christianised meaning of this epiphany; the saviour king appears to the people of his city surrounded by supernatural signs, preceded or followed by the genius of the empire, a Victory or an angel.[46] In this case, he had at his side a great processional cross, probably that reproducing the vision of Constantine the Great when he was preparing to fight Maxentius at Rome or when preparing to besiege the ancient Byzantium.[47] The jubilant crowd welcomed with flowers and garlands this *deus praesens*,[48] its liberator and its defender, who was visiting the city during the course of a campaign or returning to it for a while after a temporary absence, and who soon gave proof of his generosity and the prosperity of his reign by scattering gold as he passed (*sparsio*), sometimes also remitting taxes or dedicating trophies.[49] But agreement was not so easily reached between such disparate parties as the emperor in arms and the peace-loving city, always personified by a woman. It had to be reaffirmed at every opportunity as a reminder that the violence which had given power to the former had been pacified and guaranteed by the latter. It was this aspect that dominated in an imperial investiture and which led to the static and instantaneous ceremonial of proclamation outside the walls being complemented by the dynamic ceremonial of an entry by stages.

At Constantinople, the itinerary of the *adventus* might vary,[50] and the protocol of Leo I's proclamation contains some oddities, which may be due to the poor state of preservation of the text. But the overall schema is of a progress with

---

[45] For the *adventus* and the triumph, see MacCormack, *Art and Ceremony* (n. 31); McCormick, *Eternal Victory* (n. 35) (who draws extensively on the proclamation protocols of the *De cerimoniis*); Haldon, *Constantine Porphyrogenitus* (n. 41).

[46] See E. Kantorowicz, 'The "King's Advent" and the enigmatic panels in the doors of Santa Sabina', *The Art Bulletin*, 26 (1944), pp. 207–31, repr. in E. Kantorowicz, *Selected Studies* (New York, 1965), pp. 37–81.

[47] Dagron, *Constantinople imaginaire* (see ch. 1, n. 59), pp. 87–9. For this cross, see *De cerimoniis*, I, 1; II, 15 and 40, pp. 8–10, 591, 640.

[48] See R. Turcan, 'Les guirlandes dans l'Antiquité classique', *JAC*, 14 (1971), pp. 92–139 (pp. 121–4 for the triumphs).

[49] See the images and texts discussed by MacCormack, *Art and Ceremony* (n. 31), pp. 46–79.

[50] For a topographical study of these variations, see McCormick, *Eternal Victory* (n. 35), pp. 209–20.

a halt, a metamorphosis and a prayer at each of the walls which protected the town: those which had defined its urban perimeter since Theodosius II, crossed at the Golden Gate; those constructed by Constantine, which demarcated the sacred perimeter of its foundation, crossed at the 'Beautiful Gate'; and those defining the rebellious city which the founder had been required to conquer in order to 'romanise' it, crossed a little beyond the Forum.[51] The *Patria* of Constantinople include many legendary texts which emphasise the capture of Byzantium by Constantine and the violent scenes which had accompanied it, or which, in order to keep alive in the imperial capital the 'memory' of a lost liberty, imagined that the forum retained the circular shape of the emperor's tent when he had besieged the city.[52] The scenario of the *adventus*, as it was mimed at Constantinople, would have been that of the rape of the city by a conqueror who forced its triple historical defences, ransomed it and imposed his own law, except that, at each stage of his 'entry', the conqueror lost a little more of his warlike ferocity, becoming more generous than avid and more civil than military and, at the end of his journey, was careful to humble himself before the one true King, who reigned in Heaven. This metamorphosis, which gave the emperor not power, which he already possessed, but legitimacy, which he still lacked, was marked by a series of changes in his conduct and his dress: when he dismounted from his warhorse to climb into a carriage, vehicle of officials, or to walk on foot like a citizen, when he returned the tribute given him, when he removed certain items of his military apparel in favour of elements of senatorial and consular dress and when he removed the crown from his head, gave it to the *praepositus* (who held it, with covered hands, over the altar) and received it back from the patriarch.

From the time when, in the words of Peter the Patrician,[53] 'they took it into their heads' to perform the proclamations in the Hippodrome, the ceremonial was altered in ways that transformed its organisation and its symbolism. This was partly a matter of fashion, but even more of circumstances.

The investiture of Anastasios is the first instance described (I, 101 [92]).[54] The evening after Zeno's death (9 April 491), when the dead emperor's body was still in the palace, the dignitaries and senators assembled, at the portico in front of the Great Triklinos,[55] with the archbishop of Constantinople (Euphemios, 490–6), while the people took up 'their positions' in the Hippodrome (the tiers

---

[51] Dagron, *Naissance d'une capitale* (n. 36), p. 100; for the *antiquissima pulchra porta* of Buondelmonti, see C. Mango, *Le Développement urbain de Constantinople (IVe–VIIe siècles)*, 2nd ed. (Paris, 1990), pp. 24–5.

[52] *Patria*, II, 45, ed. T. Preger, *Scriptores originum Constantinopolitanarum* (Leipzig, 1901–7), p. 174; Dagron, *Constantinople imaginaire* (see ch. 1, n. 59), p. 85.

[53] *De cerimoniis*, I, 100 [91], p. 417, ll. 7–9.

[54] See the analysis of Christophilopoulou, 'Ekloge' (see ch. 1, n. 73), pp. 39–44.

[55] The portico of the Triklinos of the Nineteen Couches.

of the Blues and the Greens) and the soldiers in the area reserved for them in front of the imperial box (the *stama*); all proclaimed their hostility to the dead emperor. The three groups on whom the choice of a new emperor depended were not in conflict but in secession, each confined to its own institutional space. To break the deadlock, the dignitaries dispatched to the Hippodrome Zeno's widow, the empress Ariadne, wearing the *chlamys* and surrounded by all those designated by protocol to watch the races with the emperor and by some eunuchs of the Chamber and the patriarch Euphemios. The other civil and military dignitaries occupied their usual places on the tiers below the tribune. Behaving like a true emperor, Ariadne addressed the crowd, who acclaimed her through the intermediary of a *libellesios* positioned in front of the throne and behind the chancel barrier. Without waiting for the 'request' of the people and the soldiers,[56] she had ordered the dignitaries, senators and officials to meet before the Holy Gospels and in the presence of the holy patriarch, to choose a new emperor, impartially and in submission to God; the proclamation, which affected the 'salvation' of the world, would take place during Easter week, after Zeno's burial. In reply, the crowd approved the date of Easter, celebrated the 'victory' of Ariadne and declared that the 'kingship is hers', asking her, incidentally, to expel 'the thieving city prefect' (which she at once did) and predicting that all would be for the best under a 'Roman' (*Romaia*) empress, if 'no foreigner was added to the Roman race'.[57]

The augusta then returned to the imperial chamber of the Augusteus, but the dignitaries, senators and officials who were deliberating close by decided to leave the decision to her, and she chose the *silentiarius* Anastasios. This response, relayed by the patriarch, met with general approval, and Anastasios was immediately taken and placed in safe keeping in the Consistorium. The next day (10 April), was devoted to Zeno's funeral, and the ceremonial of investiture took place the day after. The civil and military dignitaries, summoned the day before, came to the palace in white *chlamys* and were received in the Consistorium, as was the patriarch. Anastasios went to the portico of the Great Triklinos, where he was required to swear the oath to govern conscientiously and justly, then to the imperial box of the Hippodrome, which was part of the palace. He first entered the *triklinos* of the box, a sort of private room, put on the *divetesion*, the *toubia* and the *kampagia*,[58] then appeared on the tribunal, facing the soldiers in the *stama*, whose flags and standards were lying on the ground, and the people in the tiers; all acclaimed him. Anastasios was raised on a shield

---

[56] *De cerimoniis*, I, 101 [92], p. 419, 1 ll. 7–8. Every imperial appointment was supposed to issue from an instant popular 'demand', as we see, for the proclamation of the emperor in *De cerimoniis*, I, 102 [93] and for the promotions of caesar and *nobelissimos*, ibid., 52–3 [43–4].

[57] *De cerimoniis*, I, 101 [92], p. 420, ll. 15–16, allusion to Zeno's Isaurian origins.

[58] Golden sandals and linen bands encircling the leg like stockings, which were part of consular, triumphal and then imperial costume.

and a *campiductor* placed his torque on his head. The flags and standards were immediately raised. The coronation over, the new emperor descended from the shield and returned to the *triklinos* of the imperial box, where the patriarch, after pronouncing the *Kyrie eleison*, robed him in the *chlamys* and placed a crown on his head. Anastasios then returned to the tribunal of the *kathisma*, hailed by the crowd who acclaimed him with the title of augustus. There were no unusual features in the rest of the procedure; the emperor made an address through his spokesman, the *libellesios*, awarded the soldiers the expected donative, processed to St Sophia for a short office and, returned to the palace, where he dismissed everyone except those who had been invited to the final banquet.

A number of peculiarities might have attracted the attention of Peter the Patrician. The first is the role devolved to Ariadne on the death of the hated emperor, her first husband, in order to assure continuity and the transmission of power in a dangerous situation of crisis and rupture. What the various parties had agreed on was not the name of Anastasios (which might have given rise to the traditional and symbolic popular 'demand'), but the free choice of the augusta; she had then assumed for some hours the posture and the language of an emperor *autokrator*, even *triumphator*, before resuming a more usual role, that of an heiress of the blood legitimating a 'new man' by a second marriage. Equally noteworthy is a new power structure, with two poles constituted by the Hippodrome, where the soldiers were present alongside the people, and the palace, where the civil and military dignitaries deliberated in close proximity to the imperial apartments and the *scholae*. Direct communication between them was possible; thanks to the *kathisma*, first Ariadne and then Anastasios had no need to leave the palace to address the representatives of the people or the army and receive the crown. In this condensed and more static, but perhaps more intense, ceremonial, the Campus Martius of the Hebdomon was reduced to the tiny perimeter of the imperial box and the space in front of it (the *stama*), and the *adventus* was no more than an appearance without risk of popular demonstrations; but the same elements were present.

Lastly, it is noticeable that the Christian element was stronger. It was becoming traditional to chose as far as possible the date of one of the great religious festivals for the coronation (Easter, in this case, which symbolised the salvation of the ecumenical empire); as at meetings of councils, the Gospels placed on display reminded the dignitaries of their moral responsibilities; the patriarch was involved throughout, seated among the dignitaries, deputed by them to communicate with the augusta, accompanying her to the Hippodrome, investing Anastasios with the *chlamys*, placing the crown on his head and then presiding over the brief ceremonies in St Sophia. This Christianisation of the ceremonial was significant, but the omnipresence of the patriarch did not mark an institutional recognition of the role of the Church, which simply guaranteed the orthodoxy of the new ruler, who was suspected of sympathy for the

Monophysite heresy. Euphemios was no more than a rather special dignitary. The true coronation was still that performed by the *campiductor* and not the handing to the emperor, by the patriarch, in the secrecy of a *triklinos* concealed from public view, of insignia which his new dignity authorised him to put on.

The accession of Justin I (I, 102 [93])[59] added only one new element to this scenario, a 'disturbance',[60] a timely reminder that a ceremonial of proclamation was only ever a historical process which those in power wished to ritualise, but which might escape their control. On the death of Anastasios, during the night of 9–10 July 518, there was neither an emperor to crown a successor nor an augusta to assure a transition. The rupture which had threatened in 491 was this time a reality and the situation became, even during the course of the ritual, 'almost uncontrollable'.[61] The *magistros* Celer and the *comes* of the Excubitors, Justin, were summoned to the palace, where each harangued his troops.[62] The people, meanwhile, gathered in the Hippodrome, cheered the senate and demanded 'for the army and the *oikoumene* an emperor chosen by God'. Seats were placed in the portico adjoining the Great Triklinos, and the dignitaries and the patriarch tried in vain to reach agreement on a name. In the face of this continuing dissension, the Excubitors, soldiers of one of the palace guards, caused to be acclaimed in the Hippodrome and raised on a shield a tribune by the name of John,[63] a friend of Justin (he later became bishop of Herakleia – apparently the only way he could survive after this abortive proclamation). For their part, in the Triklinos of the Nineteen Couches, the soldiers of another body of guards, the *scholae*, made the *magister praesentalis* Patrikios,[64] whom they hoped to crown (a variant of shield-raising) climb onto the couch in the middle, which was reserved for the emperor. Fighting broke out in the palace, during which Patrikios was only rescued with great difficulty from the hands of the Excubitors. The latter, now in control, then proposed candidates by repeatedly knocking on the ivory door leading from the Triklinos to the imperial apartments and demanding from the *cubicularii* the imperial insignia for the candidate in question, which were refused each time. The support of the senate finally tipped the balance in favour of Justin himself, who was surprised and forced to accept, though not before his lip was split by the soldiers of the scholae in a final outburst of rioting.

All the institutional elements were in place; the dysfunction was restricted to the palace, where divisions emerged between the indecisive dignitaries and

---

[59] *De cerimoniis*, pp. 426–30. For Justin, see *PLRE* II, pp. 648–51 (Iustinus 4); for his accession, see Stein, *Histoire du Bas-Empire*, pp. 219–20 of vol. II of French trans. by Palanque (see ch. 1, n. 49).

[60] *De cerimoniis*, p. 426, ll. 3–4.   [61] Ibid., ll. 5–6.

[62] There was rivalry between the *scholarii* and the Excubitors. For Celer, see *PLRE* II, pp. 275–7 (Celer 2).

[63] Ibid., p. 609 (Iohannes 65).

[64] Ibid., pp. 840–2 (Fl. Patricius 14); Reiske did not understand that this was a proper name.

senators, the rival soldiers and the *cubicularii* who held the insignia. The ceremonial then proceeded in conformity with the previous model; Justin ascended to the box of the Hippodrome with the dignitaries and the patriarch, who had only recently taken up office (John II), and was then raised on a shield and crowned with the torque of a *campiductor* at the foot of the *kathisma*. The only variant of significance is that he did not return to the *triklinos* of his box to put on the insignia which the *cubicularii* had decided to hand over; the soldiers made a testudo with their shields to conceal him from view while the patriarch 'put the crown on his head' (and probably also handed him the *chlamys*). This detail confirms that the patriarch did not crown the new emperor; rather, he presided over a discreet *mutatio vestis* which did not create the new emperor but transmitted to him the insignia kept in the imperial Chamber.

'It also seemed necessary to explain how an emperor is created by another emperor', wrote Peter the Patrician in lapidary fashion,[65] before briefly summarising the coronation of Leo the Younger by his grandfather Leo I, on 17 November 473 (I, 103 [94]), and that of Justinian by his uncle, Justin I, on 1 April 527 (I, 104 [95]). These acts were not dynastic, but the transmission *in extremis* of the empire by an emperor on the point of death to a relative, a grandson who would play only a bit part (Leo II)[66] and a nephew who already exercised real power (Justinian). The ceremonial was reduced to essentials. In the first case, the titular emperor appeared at the box of the Hippodrome with the patriarch on his left and the caesar on his right. The patriarch said a prayer which the crowd concluded with an 'Amen', and Leo crowned his grandson. After which came the acclamations, the gift by the city prefect and senate of the *modiolon chrysoun*, and the donatives to the soldiers. In the second case, it was in the Tribunal of the Nineteen Couches (that is, the courtyard of Delphax), during a *silentium* open only to the dignitaries and before a symbolic representation of the army, that the same scene was enacted, with the patriarch performing the same role.

From the ceremonial point of view, the transfer of the proclamation from the Hebdomon to the Hippodrome and the transformation of the *adventus* into a procession from the palace to St Sophia reveal a degree of contraction; but structural analogies persist. The principal divide, also found in the Byzantine period and corresponding to the two conceptions of kingship we have distinguished, lay between the 'new' emperors, for whom a process of seizing power was followed or mimed, and the 'heirs', who received the crown from the hands of their predecessor.

[65] *De cerimoniis*, I, 103 [94], p. 431, lines 3–4.
[66] Son of Ariadne and Zeno, Leo the Younger was born in 467, made caesar in October 473, and consul for the year 474. Having become sole emperor on the death of Leo I, on 18 January 474, he crowned his father Zeno on 9 February and died later that year at the age of seven: *PLRE* II, pp. 664–5 (Leo 7).

FROM CEREMONIAL TO HISTORY

There are obvious differences of period and style between the protocols of
Peter the Patrician and the conventional chapter in the *Book of Ceremonies*.
The ritual had, of course, evolved; still very much alive in the fifth century, it
was becoming schematised in the sixth – as Peter the Patrician observed with
regret, noting the importance then assumed by the Hippodrome – and fossilised
in the tenth. But the changes were slight and are not, in any case, what is of
most importance. The medieval text reveals a tendency to greater formalism,
but above all a difference of approach. His prejudices inclined Constantine
Porphyrogenitus, for personal reasons, to present imperial power as normally
hereditary and dynastic, standing apart from all turbulence. Whereas the high
functionary of the sixth century selected a whole spectrum of models as close
to concrete and dated situations as possible, the tenth-century compiler looked
only for the common denominator of all possible coronations. Finding nothing
more significant, he was content with the final episode, the visit to St Sophia,
necessary but insufficient.

In fact, it is Peter the Patrician who was right; to each emperor his own proclamation. Even after the sixth century, the models he presented continued to be
valid or at least available for the choice of those who acceded to the empire;
they could be used selectively and left room for improvisation and innovation.
The brief indications regarding proclamations and coronations found in the historical sources primarily confirm the great difference, which Peter the Patrician
emphasises and which the *Book of Ceremonies* cannot quite manage to conceal,
between he who received a power left vacant by the natural or violent death of
his predecessor and he – usually an heir of the blood – who was associated with
the *basileia* by his predecessor in his lifetime.

When the emperor was a new man who was chancing his arm or was swept
to power by a popular revolution, it was generally the long ceremonial that
was adopted, and adapted to an often confused situation, with a clear distinction and sometimes a longish delay between the 'proclamation' (*anagoreusis,
anakeryxis*) and the 'coronation' (*stepsis, stepsimon*).

This was the case for Phokas, who, the *Paschal Chronicle* tells us, 'was
crowned by Kyriakos, patriarch of Constantinople, in the holy church of St John,
at the Hebdomon', on Friday 23 November 602, soon after the precipitate flight
of Maurice and his family, and who entered the capital two days later, on Sunday
25 November, seated on a chariot, in the midst of a crowd in which there were no
longer any opponents, and followed a classic itinerary of Hebdomon, Golden
Gate, Troadesian Porticos,[67] Mese and Palace.[68] There had, of course, been

[67] That is, the western section of the Mese; see Mango, *Développement urbain de Constantinople*
(n. 51), pp. 28, 30, n. 44.
[68] *Chronicon Paschale*, ed. Niebuhr (see ch. 1, n. 58), p. 693.

an earlier proclamation by the soldiers, before the coronation by the patriarch, which was performed at the Hebdomon and not in St Sophia in order to speed up the usurper's legitimation and allow the 'entry' to be delayed until the Sunday, when division would have given way to consensus. This is one example among others where revolt, civil war and ceremony followed one after the other, almost without transition.

It was more difficult still to construct a normal ceremonial from the series of events marking the victory of the revolt led by Herakleios against Phokas. To manage this, the *Paschal Chronicle* missed almost everything out and sum-marised: 'At the ninth hour of this Monday [5 October 610], Herakleios was crowned emperor in the very holy Great Church by the patriarch of Constantino-ple, Sergios. And the Tuesday following there was a meeting at the Hippodrome, during which...'[69] Nikephoros the Patriarch attempted to distinguish two in-stitutional stages; after the scenes of rioting and the entry into the town of the victorious Herakleios followed, a 'proclamation' by the senate and the people, which he would have us believe took Herakleios by surprise, and a coronation by the patriarch.[70] Theophanes gives a longer, but more confused, account. Herakleios arrived at Abydos where he was joined by the enemies of Phokas, and proceeded to Herakleia, where he received a crown (sent by the metropoli-tan of Cyzicus, who had taken it from a church of the Virgin); having reached Constantinople by sea, he disembarked at the Sophia harbour and, when the violence had died down, had himself crowned by Sergios in the chapel of St Stephen in the Palace; 'and his fiancée Eudokia was crowned augusta the same day; and both received the same day from the patriarch Sergios the crowns of marriage: thus, on the same day, he was recognised *autokrator* and husband'.[71] Was Theophanes so carried away by his *bon mot* about the two crowns, that of marriage and that of the empire, that he confused St Sophia and the palace church of St Stephen, where imperial marriages were, indeed, held? It is unclear, but it was certainly in the chapel of St Stephen that Heraklonas was crowned in 638, before processing to St Sophia.[72] In any case, it is revealing that in this account the first elements of the ordinary ceremonial go back as far as the rebellion, and the solemnity of the coronation is merged with a private, family festival.

For the accession of the ephemeral Artemios/Anastasios II (4 June 713), the brief account of the deacon Agathias describes events as follows: the day after the blinding of his predecessor (3 June 713), Whit Sunday, the new emperor, a former palace secretary (*asekretis*), was 'invested' (*anakeryttetai*) by a vote and

---

[69] Ibid., p. 701; the chronicle gives the date as Monday 6 October, which is incorrect as the 6 October fell on a Tuesday; either the day or the date is incorrect.
[70] *Breviarium*, II, ed. and trans. Mango (see ch. 1, n. 66), pp. 36–9.
[71] Ed. de Boor (see ch. 1, n. 4), pp. 298–9 (p. 428 of Mango and Scott translation).
[72] *De cerimoniis*, II, 27, p. 628.

scrutiny (*psepho tini kai dokemasia*) by the senate, the whole of the clergy, the soldiers and the 'politic people', after having been 'proclaimed' (*anagoreutheis*) at St Sophia and crowned (*stephtheis*) inside the sanctuary by the patriarch John.[73] The events and the participants are clearly distinguished, but the stages are in reverse order. The upheaval was real, if we are to believe the other sources; in the turbulence of the rioting and under threat of the Bulgar invasion, the 'people' assembled in the Great Church to perform the proclamation.[74]

The classic case is that of the general proclaimed emperor by his troops outside Constantinople on the occasion either of a personal success or of a setback endangering the empire, who then set out for Constantinople and entered it as a victor to have himself crowned, gradually transforming a military takeover into a ceremonial of legitimation. After Phokas and Herakleios, it is illustrated by Leo III, *strategos* of the Anatolikon, who was proclaimed by his troops in April 716, and made a traditional entry into the capital, through the Golden Gate, on 25 March 717, after securing a purely formal 'election'.[75]

Another variant: on 11 July 813, after the defeat of the imperial army by the Bulgars of Krum at Versinicia, the *strategos* of the Anatolikon, Leo, was appointed by his peers to succeed Michael I, but was careful not to hurry things; he allowed the patriarch room for manoeuvre, signed a declaration of orthodoxy, had the army's choice confirmed at the Hebdomon and only then entered the city by the Charsian Gate; he spared the lives of his predecessor and his family, took possession of the palace and received the crown, next day, in the ambo of St Sophia. The providential saviour had succeeded in becoming 'most legitimately emperor'.[76]

A century and a half later, in 963, Nikephoros Phokas assumed power in similar circumstances, and we are fortunate in that the organiser of his accession, Basil the Parakoimomenos, was also the author of a revision of the *Book of Ceremonies*. He added to the protocols of Peter the Patrician (if it was not he who had inserted them into the collection) a detailed account of the proclamation and coronation of Nikephoros, which he considered, with good reason, exemplary. Since the death of Romanos II (15 March 963), the dynastic succession had been assured by the dead emperor's two sons, Basil and Constantine, both crowned but only five and three years old; the augusta Theophano acted as regent and the *parakoimomenos* Joseph Bringas exercised real power.

On 2 July, Nikephoros Phokas, then *magistros* and *domestikos* of the *scholae* of the East, was proclaimed emperor in his military camp of Cappadocia

[73] Mansi, XII, col. 192; see Christophilopoulou, 'Ekloge' (see ch. 1, n. 73), p. 76.
[74] Nikephoros, *Breviarium* (see ch. 1, n. 66), 48, ed. and trans. Mango, pp. 114–17. Theophanes, *Chronographia*, ed. de Boor (see ch. 1, n. 4), p. 383 (p. 533 of Mango and Scott translation).
[75] Nikephoros, *Breviarium* (see ch. 1, n. 66), 52, ed. and trans. Mango, pp. 120–1.
[76] Theophanes, *Chronographia*, ed. de Boor (see ch. 1, n. 4), p. 502 (pp. 685–6 of Mango and Scott translation).

(*en to kampo*, as might have been said of the Campus Martius of the Hebdomon).
The soldiers dragged him from his tent and raised him, in spite of himself, on
a shield. He was now emperor, but he still refused, out of calculated restraint,
to wear the crown and the imperial robes, except for the red shoes. He made
contact with Constantinople and protested his good intentions with regard to the
two young emperors, but could not prevent Joseph Bringas from organising a
resistance, reinforcing the town's defences, declaring the rebel 'anathema' and
attempting to seize his father, Bardas, who had taken refuge in St Sophia. From
10 to 13 August, fighting raged; Leo Phokas (brother of Nikephoros) entered
the city and Bardas Phokas (his father) took control of the palace. Nikephoros
himself, meanwhile, had arrived at Hiereia on the other side of the Bosphorus
on 14 August; he was joined there next day by the Chief Eunuch of the Chamber
(*parakoimomenos*), Basil, the *praepositus* of ceremonies, John, and some chosen dignitaries, whose role was clearly to organise the entry, coronation and
installation of the new sovereign. In fact, the revolt turned into a ceremony. On
16 August, the date he had chosen, Nikephoros crossed the Sea of Marmara at
dawn with the imperial dromon and landed not far from the Golden Gate, at the
quay of Pege,[77] where a crowd had gathered to welcome him. He proceeded
along the outside of the wall to reach the paved road (*plakote*) leading from
the Hebdomon, and made his first devotions at the monastery of the Virgin of
the Abramites, outside the walls.[78] Here he put on the imperial *skaramangion*
and rode on horseback to the Golden Gate, which he reached at the third hour,
where the demes acclaimed him and celebrated his victories over the Arabs.
He passed through the gate and, still mounted, followed the Mese as far as
the Forum of Constantine, where he prayed in the church of the Theotokos
of the Forum,[79] and put on the *divetesion*, the *kampagia* and the *campotuba*
before walking in procession to St Sophia behind the cross. At the Horologion
of St Sophia he was once again received by the two demes, with acclamations
very similar to those which had preceded the proclamation of Leo I at the
Hebdomon. In the Great Church, after changing his tunic and putting on the
tzitzakion, Nikephoros made a solemn entry with the patriarch as far as the chancel barrier; then, in the ambo, he was robed in the *chlamys* and crowned by the
hierarch.

Here is clear proof that the ceremonial remained fundamentally unchanged,
and that what divided Peter the Patrician and Constantine Porphyrogenitus
was primarily a difference of approach. The accession of Nikephoros Phokas,
some twenty years after the first edition of the *Book of Ceremonies*, certainly
culminated in a coronation in St Sophia similar to that described in Chapter I,
47 [38] of the *Book*, but it began with a military proclamation, an *adventus*

[77] Janin, *Constantinople byzantine*, pp. 234–5.   [78] Janin, *Eglises et monastères*, pp. 4–6.
[79] Ibid., pp. 236–7 (church built by Basil I).

and an 'entry' that were fairly similar, give or take a few details, to the long schema of the proclamation of Leo I in 457. In fact, the ceremonial was inspired by a model which was not that of a coronation but a triumph, more precisely that of Basil I returning victorious from Tephrike and Germanikeia in 878 (or 879), the protocol of which is preserved in the same manuscript as the *Book of Ceremonies*;[80] it has the same itinerary and the same stages. There is nothing surprising about this. When power was not transmitted by the hereditary route but fell to a 'new man', any imperial proclamation looked like a triumph; conversely, when an emperor was involved, any triumph merited an imperial proclamation or reiterated an earlier proclamation. Indeed, it is possible that the founder of the Macedonian dynasty took advantage of his triumph of 873, or that of 878–9, to have himself crowned a second time and to efface by a ceremonial 'in the old manner' (as the protocol puts it) the ceremonial of simple transmission by which, in 866, he had hurriedly received the crown of co-emperor from the hands of Michael III.[81]

In the case of a simple transmission of power by a reigning emperor to a co-emperor, the ceremonial naturally had as its centre the Palace and provided only for a possible appearance at the Hippodrome, then a very short journey to St Sophia. The examples given by Peter the Patrician precede the consolidation of the first Byzantine dynasties, but it was with Herakleios, that is, with the custom of associating with the empire children of very young age, that the ritual began to become fixed.

The *Paschal Chronicle*, an excellent witness, describes the coronation of Herakleios-Constantine (Constantine III), at the age of eight months, as follows:

This year [613], on 22 of the month of Audynaios, January according to the Romans, the child Herakleios New Constantine was crowned *basileus* by his father Herakleios at the Palace. And afterwards he went to the Hippodrome and there, wearing the crown, he was venerated by the senators as *basileus* and acclaimed by the factions; and then, with his father, he left to go to the Great Church, carried by Philaretos. And it was ordered, from this 22 January on, to write [on official acts], after 'in the name of . . .', 'of the reign of the very divine masters and very great benefactors, always augustas and *autokrators*,

---

[80] Haldon, *Constantine Porphyrogenitus* (n. 41), pp. 140–6, who opts for the date 878 rather than 879; for the two triumphs of Basil I (873 and 878/9), see McCormick, *Eternal Victory* (n. 35), pp. 154–7, 169.

[81] The *Vita Basilii* specifies that for each of the two triumphs Basil received 'the crown of victory from the hands of the patriarch, like the ancient emperors': 40 and 49, in Theophanes Continuatus, *Chronographia*, ed. Bekker (see ch. 1, n. 4), pp. 271, 284; the protocol of the triumph of 878/9 refers to a crown of gold offered by the prefect 'as in the past', that is, as in the time of Justinian, the protocol of whose triumph of 559 is given earlier in the same treatise. We should perhaps draw a parallel with the passage in Genesios on a new coronation (*History*, ed. Lesmüller-Werner and Thurn (see ch. 1, n. 95), p. 80); see below, pp. 80, 198; McCormick, *Eternal Victory* (n. 35), pp. 156–7.

the very pious Flavios Herakleios third year – and second year after his consulate – and Flavios Herakleios New Constantine, his son protected by God, first year'.[82]

We should note that the coronation did not take place in St Sophia, and that the formula which made the reign of Herakleios' eldest son begin with his very precocious association appears as a novelty. This was indeed the case, because Herakleios was the first to associate the name of his eldest son with his own in the official regnal formula, which had not been done by Maurice (even though he had suppressed the intermediary level of caesar, or rather reserved it, as we have seen, for younger sons who were not expected to reign).[83]

This was probably the case with Heraklonas, born later of Herakleios' second marriage, who was first appointed caesar, but whom his father then decided to promote *basileus* on a level with Herakleios-Constantine. The protocol of this elevation, preserved in the *Book of Ceremonies*,[84] merits close attention as the situation was exceptional and the ceremonial not yet stabilised:

Let it be known that, on 4 July of the eleventh indiction [638], the *autokrator* and great emperor [Herakleios], wishing to promote his son Herakleios [Heraklonas] from the dignity of caesar to the state of *basileia (eis to schema tes basileias)*, proceeded in the following manner. The patriarch and all the members of the senate were summoned.[85] And the patriarch entered the house of the emperor, who had beside him the lord Constantine [Herakleios-Constantine, co-emperor], blood brother [of Heraklonas].[86] The prayer took place at St Stephen of Daphne,[87] and they removed from the head of the caesar the *kamelaukion* (headgear) he was wearing to put on the imperial crown. And after another prayer had been said for the lord David, [Herakleios] raised the latter to the dignity of caesar by placing on his head that same *kamelaukion*. Then the very glorious patricians were summoned according to tradition and entered the Augusteus, and they received the senior emperor and his sons [Herakleios-Constantine and Heraklonas], the caesar [David] standing with them. When they had all withdrawn,[88] from the rank of consul to that of *illustris*, they took up places standing on the steps of the *area*,[89] the doors of the military quarter were opened,[90] and all the standards, the *scholae*

---

[82] *Chronicon Paschale*, ed. Niebuhr (see ch. 1, n. 58), pp. 703–4.
[83] See above, pp. 28–9.   [84] *De cerimoniis*, II, 27, pp. 627–8.
[85] The patriarch was Sergios, who died on 9 December of the same year.
[86] Actually his half-brother.
[87] According to Theophanes, it was where Herakleios himself had been crowned.
[88] That is, after the greetings, the dignitaries withdrew from the Augusteus into the court of the Tribunal (*area*), where they stood on the steps.
[89] This was the inner court formed by the Tribunal of the Nineteen Couches.
[90] The word *harma* sometimes has this meaning in the *Book of Ceremonies* (pp. 392 l. 15, 558 l. 2, 628 line 15, 676 l. 15); R. Guilland, *Etudes de topographie de Constantinople byzantine* (Berlin/Amsterdam, 1969), I, p. 3.

and the demes entered. At the same time, the patriarch left, and after all had acclaimed the emperor, he at once went to the Great Church with his children, and everything took place in the Great Church according to tradition.

The procession to St Sophia was only the conclusion of a ceremonial which took place wholly within the palace, where the role of the patriarch was to say a prayer during the coronation in St Stephen, and where the greetings of the dignitaries were followed by a sudden eruption into the court of the Tribunal of the standards, the soldiers of the *scholae* and the representatives of the demes, which evokes the scenes at the Hebdomon or Hippodrome described by Peter the Patrician.

A little later, in September 641, the accession of Constans II, son of Herakleios-Constantine, led to what Peter the Patrician called a 'disturbance'. Heraklonas was forced by popular pressure to elevate his nephew to the *basileia*, but he performed this duty with obvious reluctance. He went to the sanctuary (St Sophia) with the patriarch Pyrrhos, mounted the ambo and gave orders (to the patriarch) for Constans II to be crowned. 'But the crowd forced him to perform the task himself. He then took the crown of his father Herakleios to the church and did the job.'[91] The coronation by the patriarch, necessary when the imperial throne was vacant, was thus regarded as an anomaly, an insult or a rejection when the emperor *autokrator* was living and able to do it himself. A tradition was gradually established; the coronation took place in the ambo of the Great Church on the occasion of a solemn festival, Christmas, Epiphany, Easter or Pentecost.[92] It was the 'senior emperor' who crowned his descendant and designated successor. Although the Greek expression is sometimes ambivalent, we should understand that the role of the patriarch was as defined in the second protocol of Chapter I, 47 [38] of the *Book of Ceremonies*. He said the prayer over the crown and the *chlamys* but did not himself perform the coronation or the robing.

The unusual manner in which Leo IV, son and grandson of emperors, made his own son, Constantine VI, co-emperor in 776 emphasises the procedure and the significance of the coronation of an heir. The emperor, as we have seen,[93] postponed the day and told those who expressed concern about this that he

---

[91] Nikephoros, *Breviarium* (see ch. 1, n. 66), 31, ed. and trans. Mango, pp. 82–3.

[92] Grierson, *Catalogue of the Byzantine Coins in the Dumbarton Oaks Collection* (see ch. 1, n. 74), II, 2, p. 402; W. Treadgold, 'The chronological accuracy of the *Chronicle* of Symeon the Logothete for the years 813–845', *DOP*, 33 (1979), pp. 166–7 and n. 34. Constans II was probably crowned at Easter 654, Constantine V at Easter 720, Leo IV at Whitsuntide 751, Constantine VI at Easter 776, Staurakios son of Nikephoros I probably at Christmas 803, Theophylaktos son of Michael I at Christmas 811, Constantine son of Leo V at Christmas 813, Basil I at Whitsuntide 866, Constantine first son of Basil probably at Epiphany 868, Leo VI at Epiphany 870, Constantine VII at Whitsuntide 908, the children of Romanos Lekapenos at Whitsuntide 921 and Christmas 924, Romanos II at Easter 945, Basil II at Easter 960 and Constantine VII at Easter 962.

[93] See above, pp. 22, 38.

wanted to retain for his son the possibility of leading the life of a 'private person'. It was regarded as abnormal, it seems, for the association of a dynastic heir to be delayed until he was six years old, the age of Constantine VI when Theophanes was writing.[94] Well-orchestrated demonstrations were held at the Hippodrome from Palm Sunday to the Thursday of Easter week, at the end of which the emperor obtained from the representatives of the various social groups (army of the themes, central army, senate dignitaries, representatives of the people and of the crafts) an oath on the wood of the Cross, later confirmed in writing, of loyalty to the dynasty – more particularly to the direct descendants of Leo IV, as the main danger came from a usurpation by the emperor's brothers. This oath-swearing took place on Good Friday. Next day, Leo IV promoted his youngest brother, Eudokimos, to the dignity of *nobelissimos* in the Tribunal of the Nineteen Couches, then went to St Sophia with the caesars (his brothers Nikephoros and Christophoros) and the *nobelissimi* (his brothers Niketas, Anthimios and Eudokimos); after changing the altar cloth, as was customary on this liturgical date, he mounted the ambo with his son and the patriarch, had the oaths of loyalty placed on the altar by all those who had signed them, and declared: 'See, Brothers, that I accede to your request and give you my son for emperor. See that you receive him from the Church and from the hand of Christ.' All shouted: 'Confirm to us in response, Son of God, that we receive from your hand the Lord Constantine as emperor, to protect him and to die for him!'. This was a prayer by which those present conventionally requested a divine sign validating the choice of men, and which was comparable to that which preceded the raising of the standards in the proclamation of Leo I at the Hebdomon.[95] Next day, Easter Sunday (24 April),[96] the emperor went at dawn to the Hippodrome with the patriarch. A portable altar was erected and, in full view of all present, in the *kathisma*, the patriarch said the traditional prayer over the imperial symbols and the emperor crowned his son. There followed a procession to St Sophia, with the two caesars, the three *nobelissimi* and the empress Irene, wife of Leo IV and mother of Constantine VI.

The choice of the Hippodrome rather than St Sophia for the coronation was permitted by tradition and made possible a wider popular involvement, which Leo IV clearly desired. The role of the Church was not, as a result, diminished. The patriarch was present at the emperor's side throughout and gave his religious approval to a political act. Christ was guarantor of the oaths of loyalty pronounced on the wood of the Cross, confirmed in writing by the name and autograph cross of the signatories, and solemnly deposited on the altar of his church. Perjury would, in consequence, be a major religious sin, potentially

[94] Ed. de Boor, pp. 449–50; see above, p. 22.
[95] *De cerimoniis*, I, 100 [91], pp. 410–11.
[96] 14 should be corrected to 24 in Theophanes' text.

punished by excommunication or anathema. The scenario prepared by Leo IV was made subtly to coincide with the stages in the Easter liturgy. When the 'great emperor' said on Easter Saturday: 'I give you my son', and when he crowned him on Easter Day, the parallel with the son of God crucified and re-surrected was obvious to all; all the more so, perhaps, in that Judas was present in the shape of one of Leo IV's brothers, implicated a few months later in a plot.

CONCLUSIONS

At the end of this 'case review', it is easier to understand the perplexity of Constantine Porphyrogenitus when he wanted to provide a model of an imperial coronation and the rather lame synthesis found in the *Book of Ceremonies*. Rather than a gradually established ceremonial with room for a few variations, there existed a few elements of ritual which each emperor organised into a more or less theatrical ceremonial, which bore his imprint or was inspired by one of the earlier protocols, chosen as a historical or political reference point. These structural elements were the expectant wait of the people who asked for an emperor, punctuated by acclamations and entreaties, and the appearance of the crowned emperor on a shield or tribune or in the ambo of a church. The participants – people, army and senate dignitaries – could be kept apart, regrouped or fused into a single unit. The significant places – Hebdomon, Tribunal of the Nineteen Couches, Hippodrome, St Sophia or palace church – were always the same, but the ritual switched easily from one to another, and the coronation itself might take place in any one of them, with the patriarch involved as required. Peter the Patrician's conclusion was absolutely correct; it was a matter of circumstance and choice. The ceremonial served only to relay the event; it put the emphasis, in each case, on the process which led from real power to imperial legitimacy, so giving each proclamation its own character.

Justinian's master of the offices was equally correct when, among the proto-cols he chose, he distinguished those where 'an emperor is appointed by another emperor'. In his day, this method of transmitting power owed more to its Roman associations than to Byzantine dynastic practice. It is all the more interesting to note that the distinction had become clearer rather than more blurred, and that the investiture ceremonies of an emperor who had risen from the ranks and those of an emperor born in the purple now had little in common. The former, as we have seen, resembled an *adventus* and a triumph that culminated in the religious confirmation of a power already acquired, the latter an ordinary procession during which legitimate power multiplied almost spontaneously in the setting of St Sophia, the Hippodrome or simply the palace. This lack of specificity in a ceremony which was supposed in principle to change the na-ture of a man by investing him with the sacred function of 'king' is probably to be explained by the priority acknowledged to *de facto* power. The usurper on whose head his soldiers placed a torque and the child born of an emperor received by that fact alone, whatever the future held, the mark of the *basileia*. The ceremonial confirmed, but did not confer, this mark; it did no more than indicate one of the possible routes to legitimation – a long route for the emperor appointed on the battlefield, received and civilised by the city and submitted by the Church to God, a short route for the son of an emperor legitimated by his birth, regarded as 'God's anointed' if he was a porphyrogenitus, receiving at a very young age a crown which only prolonged the power in place for a new generation.

Association was an old practice, which acquired a new significance in Byzantium. In Rome, it had made it possible to avoid the power vacuum at the time of the ruler's death and the disturbances which always threaten autocratic regimes in such circumstances; it also had the advantage of favouring hereditary successions while escaping the censure of the 'republican reflex'. But the successor designated in this way was not promoted directly to the highest dignity and had to await the death of his predecessor before passing from the rank of caesar to that of augustus. For the western monarchs who occasionally or systematically resorted to association, its purpose might be to strengthen a heredity that gave only an insecure right by a precocious 'election', to protect the dynastic rights of the eldest son against the possible claims of his siblings, or simply to allow the son to be initiated into the administration of the kingdom and assist his father;[97] but it was only with the death of the king, however, that the new reign formally began. It was different in Byzantium. The purpose of association was very much the same; to favour heredity and to transmit, as it were from hand to hand, a power of which the various social groups (army, senate, people and Church), now only symbolic participants in the 'proclamations', were no longer the true guardians. But access to the *basileia* was no longer in stages, and the co-emperor, even if the title of 'junior emperor' indicated that he did not yet exercise real power, was *basileus* as of right.

The *autokratoria*, the accession to and assumption of effective power, was normally used to count the years of the reign and was recognised by some modifications to the more official titles, but seems not to have been the occasion of any investiture ritual in the case of emperors who had previously been crowned. At least, the *Book of Ceremonies* says nothing on this subject, except perhaps in a chapter known only from its title, on the 'accession of Romanos II' (II, 17). It reports only the reception and dinner which were held on the anniversary of the accession (*tes autokratorias*), as of the coronation (*tou stepsimou*, if it was different from the accession), birth (*tes genneseos*) and marriage

---

[97] For association and its meaning under the Capetians up to the thirteenth century, see Lewis, *Royal Succession* (see introduction, n. 5).

(*tou stephanomatos*) of the emperor, and gives the text of the greetings laid down for these situations: 'May God grant you the blessing of reigning for a hundred years in peace and of celebrating for a hundred years the present day of your accession'.[98] And the *Kletorologion* of Philotheos confirms this double anniversary in the case of Leo VI and his brother Alexander, both born in the purple and crowned in their infancy, hence *basileis* when their father, Basil, died on 29 August 886, but acclaimed also *autokratores* the day after, 30 August.[99] Admittedly, on the death of the senior emperor, the planned succession was not always automatic; there might be hesitation, consultation between dignitaries, family disputes, the reading of the will of the deceased emperor (as on the death of Herakleios),[100] popular unrest or the emergence of a usurper under cover of a regency. The sources sometimes speak of 'proclamation' (*anagoreusis*), especially when the succession initially planned for was disrupted or might be contested (when Heraklonas was declared emperor on the death of Herakleios-Constantine,[101] when Constantine VI put aside his mother to take personal power,[102] or when Michael III succeeded to Theophilos),[103] but this was not a special ceremony – a simple acclamation seems to have been enough. Only Basil I, to my knowledge, received from the hands of the patriarch, like a newly promoted emperor, the 'crown of autokrator' (*autokratorikon stemma*), but this was to efface the memory of his first coronation by Michael III and, in the words of the historian Genesios, who was conscious of this anomaly, so that 'he himself might establish another beginning to his *basileia*'.[104]

Historians have long debated which emperor was the first to be crowned by the patriarch.[105] The question is difficult to answer for a number of reasons. The rather later sources, beginning with Theophanes (early ninth century), are

[98] Note, however, that *De cerimoniis* (I, 71, 72, 74 [62, 63, 65]) gives the ceremonial for the eve and the day of a reception with 'ballet' which is more precisely, according to the acclamations, an anniversary of *autokratoria*; it also gives some indications regarding the promotions and distributions which were made on the occasion 'of the *autokratoria*, coronation, birth and marriage' of emperors (II, 33 and 53).

[99] Oikonomides, *Listes*, pp. 221 and notes 265, 225, 229.

[100] Nikephoros, *Breviarium* (see ch. 1, n. 66), 28, ed. and trans, Mango, pp. 76–9.

[101] Ibid., 30, pp. 80–1.

[102] Theophanes, *Chronographia*, ed. de Boor (see ch. 1, n. 4), p. 466 (pp. 640–1 of Mango and Scott translation).

[103] Genesios, *History*, ed. Lesmüller-Werner and Thurn (see ch. 1, n. 95), pp. 51–2; Skylitzes, *Synopsis*, ed. Thurn (see ch. 1, n. 39), p. 79.

[104] Genesios, *History*, ed. Lesmüller-Werner and Thurn (see ch. 1, n. 95), p. 80; see above, p. 74 and below, p. 198.

[105] W. Sickel thought that Marcian was the first emperor to be crowned by the patriarch: 'Das byzantinische Krönungsrecht bis zum 10. Jahrhundert', *BZ*, 7 (1898), p. 517; this view has been criticised by W. Ensslin ('Zur Frage nach der ersten Kaiserkrönung durch den Patriarchen und zur Bedeutung dieses Aktes im Wahlzeremoniell', *BZ*, 42 (1943–9), pp. 101–15, 369–72 (complete version, Würtzburg, 1947) and Christophilopoulou ('Ekloge' (see ch. 1, n. 73), pp. 65–6). O. Treitinger thinks that the emperor had no need of being crowned by the patriarch: *Kaiser- und Reichsidee* (n. 35), pp. 27–31.

guilty of anticipation and project on to the fifth century the customs of their own day; also, they often use the verb 'to crown' metaphorically in the sense of 'proclaim emperor', or with constructions which leave it unclear whose was the principal role in the coronation. When, for example, they say that the emperor crowned his own son 'by the patriarch', should we understand by this 'through his intermediary' or 'with his assistance'?[106] Above all, the process of enthronement, which in principle involved a choice by the senate, a proclamation by the army and/or the people, with 'raising' and 'acclamations', and a religious confirmation with coronation, can be summarised by a variety of formulae which preserve only a part of the whole. With regard to Marcian, in 450, Theodore Lector says that he was proclaimed at the Hebdomon by the army, Malalas that he was 'crowned' by the senate',[107] the *Paschal Chronicle* that he was appointed augustus there by the demes,[108] and Theophanes that Pulcheria summoned the patriarch and the senate in order to proclaim him emperor.[109] None of them was wholly wrong. With regard to Leo I, Theophanes summarised by stating that he had been crowned by the patriarch Anatolios.[110] On this occasion, he was misled or is misleading us.

The protocols we have examined make it possible for us to define the precise role of the patriarch and of the Church in the proclamation and coronation of an emperor. For Leo I, in 457, Anatolios was present among the dignitaries at the Hebdomon, but it was the emperor himself who, in the Tribunal, put on the *chlamys* and placed the crown on his own head under the testudo formed by the shields of the *candidati*; the head of the Church appeared only later, at St Sophia, where he received an emperor who had already been crowned. For the succession of Zeno, in 491, Euphemios accompanied Ariadne to the Hippodrome, transmitted the message from the dignitaries to the empress, passed on her reply and said a prayer before robing Anastasios in the *chlamys* and crowning him inside the imperial box of the Hippodrome. But this act did not, as we have seen, amount to an official coronation; it was only a blessing, in private, of the insignia of a kingship that had already been conferred. Justin I, in 518, received the crown from the hands of the patriarch John at the Hippodrome, but under a testudo of shields. In the cases where the *basileia* was transmitted by a reigning sovereign to a co-emperor, for Leo II in 473 and

---

[106] See, for example, Theophanes on the coronation of Theophylaktos by his father Michael I (*Chronographia*, ed. de Boor (see ch. 1, n. 4), p. 494, p. 678 of Mango and Scott translation), or Skylitzes on the coronation of Constantine VII by his father, Leo VI (*Synopsis*, ed. Thurn (see ch. 1, n. 39), p. 189).

[107] Theodoros Anagnostes, *Historia ecclesiastica*, ed. G. Ch. Hansen (Berlin, 1995), p. 100; Malalas, *Chronographia*, ed. L. Dindorf (Bonn, 1831), p. 367.

[108] *Chronicon Paschale*, ed. Niebuhr (see ch. 1, n. 58), p. 590.

[109] *Chronographia*, ed. de Boor (see ch. 1, n. 4), p. 103 (p. 159 of Mango and Scott translation).

[110] Ibid., p. 110 (p. 170 of Mango and Scott translation); Malalas wrote: 'After the reign of Marcian, the most divine Leo was crowned by the senate' (n. 107).

Justinian in 527, the patriarch was at the emperor's side, at the Hippodrome or Delphax, but confined himself to saying a prayer. It is clear, therefore, that in the second half of the fifth century and in the sixth, the patriarch was a dignitary who was better placed than the others to serve as intermediary between the senate or people and the imperial family, and who was called on to bring down the grace of God by his prayer and his blessing, but played no institutional role, except when he received from the new emperor, occasionally from the time of Anastasios and systematically after the iconoclast crisis, a written and signed profession of orthodox faith.[111]

The proclamation was made out in the open and the coronation, as we have said, might take place anywhere. The removal of the ceremony from the tribune of the Hebdomon or the box at the Hippodrome to the ambo of St Sophia, mentioned explicitly for Constans II in 641,[112] unarguably strengthened its religious character; but it gave the Church as an institution no right over a power which the emperor received directly and without intermediary from God. If the Church gained in importance in the process of legitimating the sovereign, it was because it could give a degree of credibility to the oath of loyalty sworn by the dignitaries and the representatives of the people by transforming a future perjury into sacrilege (as we see from the example of Leo IV), and because it could impose on the emperor a humility before God which alone limited his power. Also, in the religious part of the ceremonial, the removal of the crown was more important than the coronation. By removing then resuming the crown at each entry into a sacred place, the emperor was recognising that the delegated power which he had personally received from God ceased wherever God had his residence on earth, just as it would cease when Christ returned, on the Last Day, the Day of Judgement. The crown was only on loan. When the body of the sovereign was about to be sealed in its tomb, the master of ceremonies said to it: 'Remove the crown from your head', because God, the King of kings, was calling him to leave earth in order to join him in heaven; and the *praepositus* tied round his head a simple purple band, remembrance of a kingship which had also died.[113] Many accounts show that the ultimate destination of imperial crowns was usually a sanctuary.[114]

It is revealing that the majority of emperors, at least after iconoclasm, arranged for their own coronation or that of a co-emperor in St Sophia to coincide

[111] The patriarch, suspecting Anastasios of sympathy for the Monophysites, imposed this condition on his coronation; the same for Phokas in 602, Leo III in 716, Michael I in 811 and Leo V in 813: Theophanes *Chronographia*, ed. de Boor (see ch. 1, n. 95), pp. 136 (Anastasios), 289 (Phokas), 390 (Leo III), 493 (Michael I), 502 (Leo V) (pp. 205, 413, 540, 675, 685 of Mango and Scott translation); Genesios, *History*, ed. Lesmüller-Werner and Thurn (see ch. 1, n. 95), p. 20 (Michael II). The oath itself is preserved in Pseudo-Kodinos, *Traité des offices*, ed. and trans. Verpeaux (n. 16), pp. 252–4.

[112] Nikephoros, *Breviarium* (see ch. 1, n. 91), 31, ed. and trans. Mango, pp. 82–3.

[113] *De cerimoniis*, I, 69 [60], pp. 275–6.   [114] See below, pp. 104–5, 214–16.

with one of the great festivals of the 'Lord', or at least to take place on a Sunday, as if grafting it on to the liturgical calendar was necessary to give a religious character to a political event. This was to acknowledge that the ceremonial did not of itself confer a sacred character; that it did not create, but at most recognised, an emperor who had received his power either on the day of his conception in the purple or on the day when his political ambition had been made public, with the backing of popular approval or acceptance from on high.[115] In the West, at the end of the fourteenth century, there was a relative downgrading of royal consecration under the influence of theoreticians of the *jus sanguinis*, who asserted that the child was king by its birth and that anointing with the chrism added nothing.[116] In Byzantium, the trend was in the opposite direction; there was no sacred element, strictly speaking, until the time when Davidic unction, instead of being regarded as conferred automatically by God on the heir or on the new man, without either priest or ceremony, was actually administered by the Church. But this change did not come about before the end of the twelfth or beginning of the thirteenth century.[117]

That is why Constantine Porphyrogenitus, when he came to the chapter on coronation, was reduced to banalities.

[115] What certain texts call 'to receive the oracle of kingship': see below, p. 193.
[116] J. Barbey, *Etre roi. Le roi et son gouvernement en France de Clovis à Louis XVI* (Paris, 1992), pp. 37–42.
[117] See below, pp. 273–4.

3. Ceremonial and memory

FROM THE PALACE TO ST SOPHIA

It was not, therefore, by chance that Constantine Porphyrogenitus put first among all the court ceremonies the one which solemnly conducted the emperor to St Sophia and then back to his palace after the service (see plans 1, 3 and 4).[1] The ceremony described, with minor variations, was that of all the great feasts of the Christian calendar; it contained a basic schema, referred to throughout the compilation by a phrase such as 'and events then proceed as described above', but also the most solemn and most significant ritual, which, each time it was repeated, described the origins and nature of imperial power, confirmed its legitimacy and suggested certain of its limitations. The ceremony comprised several stages.

Lengthy and detailed preparations were first made within the palace. The day before, orders were given and the emperor was briefed. On the day itself, before dawn, the personnel of the Chamber assembled the robes and the insignia; the *vestitores* brought from the palace chapel consecrated to St Theodore,[2] the most venerated of the military saints, the 'rod of Moses', illustrious relic and symbol of command;[3] other *cubicularii* assembled the robes and the crowns, the *spatharii* brought the imperial arms, the shields and the lances. Before the solemn robing, the sovereign went to pray in the apse of the great octagonal hall, the Chrysotriklinos, where, above the human throne, Christ in majesty was portrayed on his divine throne. Like a toreador about to enter the arena, the emperor made his devotions in different sanctuaries: in the Theotokos,[4] in

---

[1] *De cerimoniis*, I, 1, pp. 5–35; trans. Vogt, *Constantin Porphyrogénète, Le Livre des cérémonies* (see ch. 2, n. 1), I, pp. 3–28. For the itinerary of the procession and the topography of the palace, see, while awaiting a new edition in preparation, A. Vogt, *ibid., Commentaire*, I, pp. 5–78, and the plan reproduced here, which makes no claims to exactness.

[2] Janin, *Eglises et monastères*, pp. 149–50 (no. 7).

[3] See, in particular, Pertusi, 'Insegne del potere sovrano e delegato' (see ch. 1, n. 39), pp. 515–21; the rod of Moses and the insignia derived from this illustrious model were kept in the church of St Theodore: *De cerimoniis*, II, 40, p. 640. See below, pp. 98, 216.

[4] Janin, *Eglises et monastères*, p. 208 (no. 86).

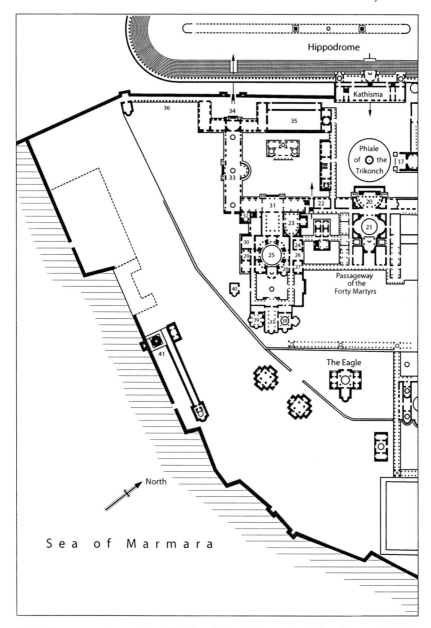

Plan 1. Reconstructed ground plan of the Great Palace of Constantinople (based on a version in A. Vogt, *Le livre des cérémonies*)

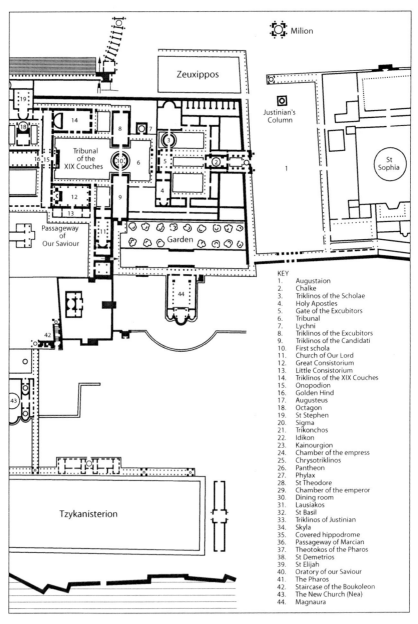

Milion

Zeuxippos

Justinian's
Column

St
Sophia

19

14

8   7

3

Tribunal
of the
XIX Couches   10   6   5   2

1

16 15

18

4

12   9

13

Passageway
of
Our Saviour   Garden

44

42

43

Tzykanisterion

KEY
1.   Augustaion
2.   Chalke
3.   Triklinos of the Scholae
4.   Holy Apostles
5.   Gate of the Excubitors
6.   Tribunal
7.   Lychni
8.   Triklinos of the Excubitors
9.   Triklinos of the Candidati
10.   First schola
11.   Church of Our Lord
12.   Great Consistorium
13.   Little Consistorium
14.   Triklinos of the XIX Couches
15.   Onopodion
16.   Golden Hind
17.   Augusteus
18.   Octagon
19.   St Stephen
20.   Sigma
21.   Trikonchos
22.   Idikon
23.   Kainourgion
24.   Chamber of the empress
25.   Chrysotriklinos
26.   Pantheon
27.   Phylax
28.   St Theodore
29.   Chamber of the emperor
30.   Dining room
31.   Lausiakos
32.   St Basil
33.   Triklinos of Justinian
34.   Skyla
35.   Covered hippodrome
36.   Passageway of Marcian
37.   Theotokos of the Pharos
38.   St Demetrios
39.   St Elijah
40.   Oratory of our Saviour
41.   The Pharos
42.   Staircase of the Boukoleon
43.   The New Church (Nea)
44.   Magnaura

Plan 1. *Continued*

Plan 2. Reconstruction of the Great Palace of Constantinople (based on a version in A. Vogt, *Le livre des cérémonies*)

Plan 2. *Continued*

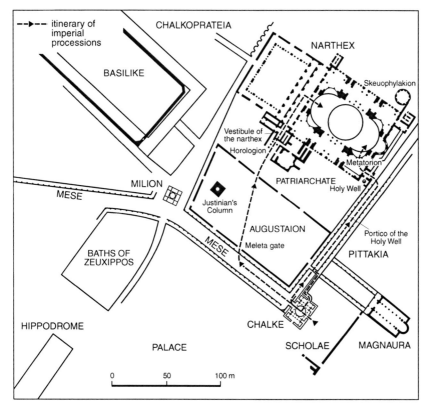

Plan 3. Itineraries from the Great Palace to St Sophia (based on C. Mango, *The Brazen House*)

the oratory of the Trinity which adjoined it,[5] and in the baptistery, where the three 'great and beautiful crosses' were kept, and to which candles were fixed. The procession then continued to the Augusteus, the hall of the old palace of Constantine, where the emperor was 'received' by the dignitaries of the Chrysotriklinos and the officers of the guard; he then went into the 'octagonal hall', where his robes lay ready and where the staff of the Chamber greeted him. Next, he entered the church of the protomartyr Stephen, situated just opposite, where he venerated the large, beautiful and precious cross of St Constantine the Great.[6] Then, in the apartment of Daphne, he waited for an ecclesiastical official, the *referendarios*, to come on behalf of the patriarch to bring him the instructions regarding the order of the religious ceremony. This formal wait,

[5] Ibid., p. 487 (no. 2).
[6] Ibid., p. 473–4 (no. 3). This was the principal church of the old palace. *De cerimoniis*, II, 40, p. 640, confirms that the cross of Constantine and the insignia connected with it were kept in St Stephen's.

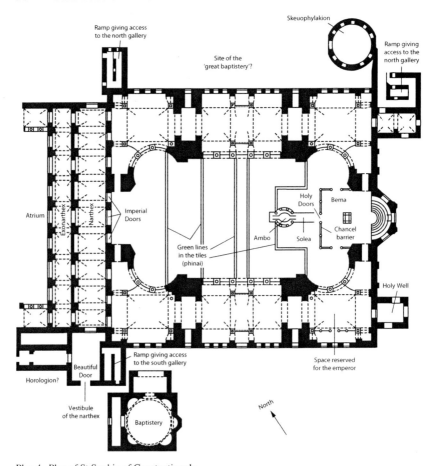

Plan 4. Plan of St Sophia of Constantinople

and the intervention of a sort of ambassador from the Great Church, who laid down its conditions, indicated that the ceremonial was regulating an encounter between two powers, each master of its own ground.

Only then did the *praepositi* place the crown on the emperor's head and the procession set off, not to leave the palace immediately, but to make a tour of the palace world and to complete the image of a warlike sovereign who was invested with the *chlamys* – the imperial cloak – by the *vestitores* in the Octagon, and with his weapons by officers in the Onopodion. The procession then moved to the Great Consistorium, where the rod of Moses and the cross of Constantine had, meanwhile, been placed, so that the emperor could take them up. Waiting for him here were the civil officials of the chancery and departments, *protosekretis*, notaries and *chartularii*. The procession continued towards the military quarter proper, the *scholae*, with a pause in the *triklinos* of the *candidati*, hall of the first of the palace guards, where the clergy of the church of Our Lord were assembled.[7] The emperor crossed the rotunda with its eight columns, which marked the first *schola* and, after venerating a silver cross placed in his path, passed into the hall of the Excubitors, another ceremonial body. Lined up here were the standard-bearers and ensign-bearers of the various troops, who would accompany him into the church with the most traditional emblems of Roman power: *vexilla* surmounted by the eagle or by the *tyche* ruling the world, Constantinian standards and *labara* adorned with the chrismon. Lastly, the procession crossed the *Lychni*, chamber of the lamps which held the 'image of Persia',[8] 'another silver cross' and a seven-branched candelabra.

The presence of the demes and the alternating 'receptions' entrusted to the Blue and Green factions show that, from the quarter of the *scholae*, the procession had embarked on the long process of leaving the palace and crossing, at least symbolically, the city. The people were only represented, but it was they who dictated the rhythm of events, as at the Hippodrome, that of a twofold alternation of Blues/Greens and 'peratics'/'politics'.[9] Beneath the dome of the Tribunal, on leaving the Lychni, it was the leader of the 'peratic Blues', identified with the *domestikos* of the *scholae*, who received the sovereign and handed him the booklet of the acclamations chanted by his deme. The chamber was decorated with carpets, silks and precious objects provided for the occasion by the cloth merchants and goldsmiths; here were assembled foreign visitors (for example, Liutprand of Cremona during his stays in Constantinople), members of the guilds, the eparch and his staff and the logothete of the praetorium, all those who symbolised production, trade and regulation. The sovereign next stopped at the *triklinos* of the *scholae*, under the propylaea of the church of the Holy Apostles,[10] where the democrat of the 'peratic Greens', in other words the *domestikos* of the Excubitors, conducted with his deme a second reception in

---

[7] Another palace church, where the imperial standards were kept: Janin, *Eglises et monastères*, pp. 511–12 (no. 12).

[8] That is, the original or a replica of the *mandylion*, the towel upon which Christ had impressed his features, brought from Edessa to Constantinople in 945.

[9] For the four 'factions', demes or 'colours', their organisation and their activities, see, in particular, for the early period Alan Cameron, *Circus Factions: Blues and Greens at Rome and Byzantium* (Oxford, 1976). In the period which interests us, the seditious activities of the demes had ceased, but not the horse races, and the representatives of the colours were integrated into the official ceremonial. See also G. Dagron, 'L'Organisation et le déroulement des courses d'après le Livre des cérémonies', *TM*, 13 (2000), pp. 1–200, where the whole system is described.

[10] Janin, *Eglises et monastères*, p. 50 (no. 4).

perfect symmetry with the first. The 'peratic Blues' and their leader performed the third, in the presence of the medical corps and the gymnasts, under the dome of the Chalke, only a few steps from the famous 'Bronze Gate', but still inside the palace.[11] And, to emphasise a transition, the sovereign, having 'left' to the sound of organs, was received by the demarch of the Blues at the head of the faction of the Whites (that is, the 'politic Blues') outside the railing situated in front of the Gate. This was the fourth 'reception'. The fifth was entrusted to the demarch of the Greens with the faction of the Reds ('politic Greens') and took place at the gate opening onto the Augustaion;[12] the sixth and last reception fell once again to the demarch of the Blues and the deme of the Whites, who welcomed the emperor when he reached the Horologion of St Sophia,[13] a sundial or a mechanical clock corresponding to an entrance, its precise location unknown, on the north side of the Augustaion, within the perimeter of the Great Church.

From the Horologion, the sovereign entered the south vestibule of the narthex (the 'propylaea of the narthex') by the Beautiful Door.[14] Here, the *praepositi* removed his crown behind a curtain suspended from the roof, a space called a *metatorion*.[15] The emperor, without his crown, then crossed over the threshold of the narthex, where the patriarch was waiting for him with his clergy.[16] He venerated the Gospels held by the archdeacon, greeted and kissed the patriarch and walked with him as far as the Imperial Doors, which gave access to the central

---

[11] For the Chalke, its topography and its history, see C. Mango, *The Brazen House: A Study of the Vestibule of the Imperial Palace of Constantinople* (Copenhagen, 1959), pp. 73–107.

[12] Janin, *Constantinople byzantine*, pp. 59–62; Mango, *Brazen House* (n. 11), pp. 42–7. This square, more or less enclosed and annexed to the palace, had to be crossed to reach St Sophia. It was the site of the equestrian statue of Justinian on top of a column. The ancient Tetrastoon may also have stood in this square, between the palace and the church. The patriarchate and its dependencies were situated on the north side of the Augustaion.

[13] Janin, *Constantinople byzantine*, pp. 102–3. For a description by Harun Ibn Yahya of the mechanism which caused a different figurine to appear every hour, see A. A. Vasiliev, *Byzance et les Arabes* II, 2 (Brussels, 1950), p. 392.

[14] For the doors of St Sophia, see in particular C. Strube, *Die westliche Eingangsseite der Kirchen von Konstantinopel in justinianischer Zeit* (Wiesbaden, 1973), pp. 46–52, 68. While it is true that the 'Beautiful Door', in the singular, is used in the *De cerimoniis* for the bronze gate of the south vestibule opening onto the narthex, the expression the 'Beautiful Doors' (*horaiai pylai*) is found in numerous texts to mean what the *De cerimoniis* calls the 'Imperial Door' leading from the narthex to the central nave.

[15] St Sophia had two *metatoria*, that in the vestibule, a simple hanging to shield the area from onlookers, and the suite of rooms reserved for the emperor in the south aisle and the corresponding gallery: see J. B. Papadopoulos, 'Le Mutatorion des églises byzantines', in *Mémorial Louis Petit. Mélanges d'histoire et d'archéologie byzantines* (Bucharest, 1948), pp. 366–72; Strube, *Die westliche Eingangsseite* (n. 14), pp. 72–81, who draws a parallel between St Sophia and the other Constantinopolitan churches to which the emperor processed.

[16] Goar, *Euchologion*, pp. 733–4, gives two prayers spoken by the patriarch each time he encountered the emperor.

nave;[17] here, candle in hand, prostrating themselves three times, they together gave thanks to God. There followed the 'entry' (*eisodos*), the beginning of the liturgy strictly speaking. The standard-bearers and the officials and dignitaries of the senate went first and formed a line the length of the nave and *solea*. The cross of Constantine was placed on the right side of the sanctuary. The patriarch and the emperor passed in their turn through the monumental doors. After this second crossing, the earthly sovereign and the leader of the Church walked in step the length of the central nave, from the Imperial Doors to the Holy Doors, those let into the chancel barrier and giving access to the sanctuary. When the emperor arrived via the *solea* at the round plaque of marble of porphyry called the *omphalion*,[18] the patriarch went first. He 'went alone inside the railings' (of the chancel barrier) and stood in the holy doorway on the left (a side door in the chancel barrier).[19] The emperor prostrated himself three times, entered in his turn, prostrated himself before the patriarch and went with him to the altar. He kissed the altar cloth (that is, the representation of Christ embroidered on the cloth), which was held up to him by the patriarch so that he did not touch it; he venerated the liturgical vessels and the relics which were presented to him on the table (chalices, patens, corporals, holy swaddling-clothes of Christ) and then placed his gifts on it, heavy bags of gold coins or precious objects (altar cloths, chalices, crowns...). A short procession then took the emperor and the patriarch into the circular space behind the altar, where they venerated a great cross of gold which the pilgrim Antony of Novgorod believed he saw miraculously raised on the feast day of Constantine and Helena, in 1200.[20] The emperor censed the cross with the censor which was handed him by the patriarch, then 'entered' directly into another *metatorion*, much larger than the simple curtained off area in the vestibule, as it consisted of a suite of rooms created at the easternmost end of the south aisle to permit the emperors to pray while following services, receive people and change their robes.

The liturgy of the 'entry' was followed by the office strictly speaking, during which the emperor moved three times. For the offertory, he left his *metatorion* by the 'right side of the church', that is, by the south aisle, went behind the ambo

---

[17] Elsewhere than the *De cerimoniis*, they are sometimes called, as noted above, *horaiai pylae*, or *pylae megalai*, *mesoi pylones: Typikon of the Great Church*, ed. and trans. J. Mateos, *Le Typikon de la Grande Eglise*, Orientalia Christiana Analecta 165–166 (Rome 1962–3), I, p. 144, II, pp. 62, 88.

[18] Treitinger, *Kaiser- und Reichsidee* (see ch. 2, n. 35), p. 60.

[19] For the arrangement of these features, see S. G. Xydis, 'The chancel barrier, solea, and ambo of Hagia Sophia', *The Art Bulletin*, 29 (1947), pp. 1–24; K. Kreidl-Papadopoulos, 'Bemerkungen zum justinianischen Templon der Sophienkirche in Konstantinopel', *JÖB*, 17 (1968), pp. 279–89; G. P. Majeska, 'Notes on the archaeology of St Sophia at Constantinople: the green marble bands on the floor', *DOP*, 32 (1978), pp. 299–308.

[20] Trans. B. de Khitrowo, *Itinéraires russes en Orient* (Geneva, 1889), pp. 94–5.

and accompanied the oblations, proceeding, via the *solea*, to the Holy Doors, but 'keeping outside' them with his procession of standards; he then returned to the *metatorion* by proceeding along the *bema* on the right, but outside the chancel barrier. In other words, he did not pass through the sanctuary, in which there were now only clergy. For the 'kiss of peace', the patriarch stood on the right side of the *bema*, near the *metatorion*, but remained inside the chancel barrier, whereas the emperor climbed the steps of the *bema*, but without entering the sanctuary; they were then at the same level but separated by the chancel barrier when they kissed. It was from the same position that the sovereign then kissed the 'hierarchs present', then once again the patriarch; he descended the steps in the direction of the nave to kiss the dignitaries of the senate before returning, by the same route, to the *metatorion*. For communion, the same positions were adopted: the emperor left the *metatorion* in the same way, by the south aisle, reached the right of the *bema*, communicated outside the chancel and, after kissing the patriarch, returned to the *metatorion*, where he proceeded to dine with his entourage.

When the meal was over and the emperor was ready to leave the church, the patriarch was brought into the *metatorion*, kissed the sovereign, proceeded with him to the 'small door giving onto the Holy Well',[21] and stood alongside him in the doorway for the distribution of money to members of the clergy and to some poor people. Behind a curtain suspended in the Holy Well, the patriarch returned to the emperor the crown which the latter had removed before entering the narthex, and gave him consecrated bread and perfumed oil that came from the lamps and was consequently sanctifying; he received in return heavy purses full of gold (*apokombia*). After they had kissed one last time, the emperor left the Holy Well. The return journey was less formal than that of the arrival, taking him through the east portico of the Augustaion and the 'iron gate' giving onto the 'narrow passage' of the Chalke. The 'receptions' by the demes were also more modest. The first took place outside the Holy Well, with the demarch of the Blues and the deme of the Whites, the second under the dome preceding the 'iron gate', with the demarch of the Greens and the deme of the Reds, the third at the gate leading from the Chalke to the *scholae*, with the democrat of the Blues and the peratic deme of the Whites (= the Blues), the fourth at the propylaea of the Holy Apostles, that is, at the *scholae*, with the democrat of the Greens and the peratic deme of the Reds (= the Greens), and the fifth at the Tribunal with the democrat of the Blues and the peratic deme of the Whites (= the Blues). The emperor then proceeded through various rooms in the palace, removed his crown and his *chlamys* in the place where they would be stored and went to pray in the apse of the great hall, the Chrysotriklinos, where, above his own throne, he could see the 'theandric' image of Christ in majesty.

---

[21] For the Holy Well, see Mango, *Brazen House* (n. 11), pp. 60–72.

This was the ceremonial for Easter, Pentecost, the Transfiguration, the Nativity and Epiphany, dates often chosen, let us remember, for coronations. The chapters concerning the regulation of other feasts are not fundamentally different. The emperor might enter other places of worship, reach St Sophia by the Holy Well or leave by the galleries; the overall balance remained the same.[22] The most interesting variant is perhaps that recorded for the Sunday of Orthodoxy, celebrating the end of iconoclasm and the restoration of images: 'On that day, the emperor does not enter the sanctuary'; he left the patriarch at the Holy Doors and went straight to the *metatorion*; he did not leave the *metatorion* for the offertory, but only for communion. This break with tradition, on the occasion when the Church was commemorating its victory over a heresy that was reputedly imperial, could be interpreted as a penance imposed on the emperor and a public affirmation of the privilege of the clergy; but Constantine Porphyrogenitus knew of it only from old documents, and is quite specific that it had disappeared from the ceremonial of his day and that the emperor once more entered the sanctuary and kissed the altar cloth.[23]

SPACES, COMMUNICATIONS AND TRANSITIONS

Constantinople had three great institutions: the imperial power, the people and the Church. Each occupied its own space, and relations between them – simple or complex – were expressed in topography and ceremonial by communications – easy or difficult – and by stages, halts and transitions. The Great Palace was closely connected to the two main sources of legitimacy: the Great Hippodrome, where the emperor was confronted with the *populus romanus* in a ritual of horse races that renewed his *tyche*, and the Great Church, where he encountered the patriarch and Christ in another ritual of confirmation. It is convenient to note here, so as not to have to return to the subject, that the analogies do not stop there. The emperor, whether he was going to St Sophia or to the Hippodrome, made lengthy preparations and 'waited' in his palace, either for the patriarch to inform him of the order of the religious ceremony or for the organisers of the games to communicate the *kombina*, that is, the detailed programme of the races with precise information about the horses, their places in the teams and their starting positions. The emperor reached his box at the Hippodrome without leaving his palace, by a spiral staircase, the *mystikos kochlias*, which conveyed him there 'secretly', but this architectural device turned the box into an enclave of the palace in public space and ensured only visual communication between

---

[22] See, for example, *De cerimoniis*, I, 1, pp. 26–33, for the Nativity of the Theotokos; I, 31 [22], pp. 124–8, for the Exaltation of the Cross; I, 32 [23], pp. 128–36, for Christmas; I, 36 [27], pp. 147–54, for the Purification of the Virgin, etc.
[23] *De cerimoniis*, I, 37 [28], pp. 159–60.

emperor and people. The long journey which took the sovereign to St Sophia may seem very different, but the church could be reached in three different ways (see plan 4):[24] by the most solemn itinerary, punctuated with frequent halts, which crossed a small portion of 'urban' space; by the less official route laid down for the procession's return, which connected the apse of St Sophia and its annex of the Holy Well to the side gate of the Chalke (the 'iron gate'); and by a direct and 'secret' route which left from the Chalke or the Magnaura, followed a raised gallery of the portico of the Augustaion, the *diabatika*, a sort of *cryptoporticus*, and led to the box built into the easternmost end of the south gallery of St Sophia or, thanks to another *mystikos kochlias*, to the Holy Well. This last itinerary formed a sort of long umbilical cord linking the palace to the church and was suited to sudden arrivals and rapid departures. The links were more complex, therefore, in the case of St Sophia than in that of the Hippodrome, and a public, a semi-public or a strictly private access could be chosen. The slow unfolding of the ceremonial aimed to give the impression of a certain distance between the palace and the church, whereas the 'secret' passage suggested the possibility of a rapid intrusion, avoiding all obstacles or thresholds. But the problem was still that of connecting the palace to an imperial enclave in popular or ecclesial space; the south-eastern *metatorion* of St Sophia formed, like the *kathisma* at the Hippodrome, a sort of mini-palace on two floors, integrated into the structure of God's temple, but where the emperor felt at home, prayed, received, rested and changed, and from which he 'left' to take communion or to meet the patriarch on his own territory.[25] The *Story of the Construction of Hagia Sophia*, a largely legendary work probably composed in the ninth century, was not mistaken when it recorded that Justinian constructed the *diabatika*, when he was building St Sophia, so that he could visit the site more conveniently while remaining incognito and 'called *metatorion* the beautiful

---

[24] E. Antoniades, *Ekphrasis tes Hagias Sophias* (Athens, 1907), I, pp. 46, 50–1, and in particular Mango, *Brazen House* (n. 11), pp. 73–92.

[25] Ibid., pp. 60–70. Mango has made a detailed study, on the basis of the *De cerimoniis*, of the various communications between the side aisle *metatorion*, the Holy Well, the sanctuary and the gallery *metatorion*. Certain old doors are still visible in the masonry of the east wall of the aisle and gallery. Mango is surely right in thinking that the various rooms of the *metatorion* must have occupied the whole of the easternmost compartment of the south aisle (and corresponding portion of the south gallery), from the pillar south east of the cupola; see also R. J. Mainstone, *Haghia Sophia: Architecture, Structure and Liturgy of Justinian's Great Church* (London, 1988), pp. 225–6. The 'walls', which seem to have left no trace on the pavement, may have consisted of curtains and light screens. The attempt by T. F. Mathews to place the *metatorion* and 'the emperor's box' in the middle of the south side aisle, between the great south-east and south-west pillars, on the basis of marks on the ground, is not, in my view, wholly convincing: *The Early Churches of Constantinople: Architecture and Liturgy* (University Park/London, 1971), p. 96, figure 50 and plates 87–8.

gilded chamber he had constructed there for relaxation when he came to the church'.[26]

In both cases, therefore, the impression given is one of difficult communications with the public: long and careful at St Sophia, almost always indirect at the Hippodrome, unless the emperor risked descending to the level of the terraces and the *stama*, where he was separated from the people only by a symbolic line in the form of a pi, the *phina*, which could be crossed only on his orders,[27] and which has echoes of the last green marble line isolating the ambo and the *solea* outside the sanctuary of St Sophia.[28] Why were there so many precautions and so many real or symbolic barriers? Out of caution, no doubt, but also to signify that the movements of the emperor brought into contact worlds which were, and which should remain, foreign to each other.

But let us return to the starting point for the religious ceremonial which is our main concern here. The emperor prepared at length, communed with himself in the rooms of his palace that were most redolent of history, reviewed his men and armed himself. He was about to leave a place where Christ guaranteed his power, where the images and the Christian symbols were at his service, where the chapels were for his use, served by a special body of clergy known as the 'palace clergy', where the principal relics were Old Testament in origin, where the cross was that of the victory of Constantine and where, lastly, the imperial throne occupied in the apse of the Chrysotriklinos (whose plan and orientation were those of a church) the position of an altar or of the *synthronos* of a bishop, under the image of God made man. It was there that he prayed before proceedings began and there that he prayed on his return when everything was over. In fact, he was leaving a place where the emperor was both soldier and high priest, directly delegated by Christ to the government of men, for a place where all power belonged to Christ through the intermediary of the clergy and where the cross was not that of imperial victory (the *stauros nikopoios*) but a replica of that of Jerusalem.

It is as if the ceremonial was designed to accentuate the differences between two conceptions of Christianity before developing the strategy of an

---

[26] *Diegesis*, 6, ed. T. Preger, *Scriptores originum Constantinopolitanarum* (Leipzig, 1901–7), I, pp. 81–2; Dagron, *Constantinople imaginaire* (see ch. 1, n. 59), pp. 199, note 57, 207; for the position of the *diabatika*, see Mango, *Brazen House* (n. 11), pp. 87–91.

[27] From the Latin *finis*; see *De cerimoniis*, II, 20, p. 614, line 13 (where it is identified with the pi in front of the box of the Hippodrome).

[28] Majeska, 'St Sophia at Constantinople' (n. 19), pp. 299–308; see also Mathews, *Early Churches of Constantinople* (n. 25), p. 120; Dagron, *Constantinople imaginaire* (see ch. 1, n. 59), pp. 207, 254. The three most westerly *phinai* were rectilinear, but the most easterly was in the form of a U, so as to include the sanctuary, the *solea* and the ambo. For the unique *potamion* of St Sophia of Thessalonike, see J. Darrouzès, 'Sainte-Sophie de Thessalonique d'après un rituel', *REB*, 34 (1976), pp. 45–78.

encounter between them. In its palace chapels, its insignia and its talismans, the religion of the emperor was both very Constantinian and haunted by Old Testament images. There is no contradiction here. The chambers through which he proceeded almost all preserved the memory of the first Christian emperor, who was himself, according to more or less legendary traditions, the builder of many of the rooms and sanctuaries. Some of the objects exposed for devotion were believed to come from him or to preserve the form that he had originally given to his Christian 'vision'. But the emperor 'New Constantine' was also 'New Moses' and 'New David'. His palace shared with St Sophia, or disputed with it, some of the most significant of the Old Testament relics: perhaps the trumpets of Jericho, with which the angels would sound the Day of Judgement and of Resurrection;[29] in any case the celebrated rod, which the ceremonial associated with the cross of Constantine.[30] Not without reason, since the Christianisation of Roman power had been achieved in the fourth century largely through the deployment of biblical images. At the battle of the Milvian Bridge, Constantine had been Moses leading a new chosen people across the Red Sea;[31] victorious or enthroned, he was David. According to the *Patria* of Constantinople, when the holy rod of Moses was brought to his new capital, Constantine went out on foot to receive it at the Aimilianos Gate and placed it in an oratory, which he later made into a church, before transferring it to his palace.[32]

The first crossing, that of the gate of the Chalke, was made in a series of distinct stages which began in the quarter of the *scholae* and progressively involved various typically urban social categories – foreigners, the guilds, the medical corps, the gymnasts and, of course, the symbolic representatives of the townspeople, in the form of the Greens and the Blues, with their doubles, the Reds and the Whites. Without going into the details of the factional mechanisms, we should note the military setting of the 'peratic' factions (in principle recruited 'from the other side' of the Bosphorus, 'outside the city'), who played their part in the military quarter of the palace, and the civil setting of the 'politic' colours (recruited 'in the city'), who were involved in the section of the route corresponding to the Augustaion, a square supposedly 'public' but more or less annexed to the palace. The 'crossing of the city' was thus wholly symbolic. We may also note the slightly more prominent role of the 'Blues', colour of the

---

[29] *Diegesis*, 22, ed. Preger (n. 26), pp. 98–9; Dagron, *Constantinople imaginaire* (see ch. 1, n. 59), pp. 206, 248, note 162.

[30] See above, p. 84, and below, p. 216.

[31] Eusebios, *Hist. eccl.*, IX, 9, PG 20, col. 821. Other comparisons of Constantine with Moses or David in Eusebios, *Vita Constantini*, I, 1–4; 6–9; 12; 38; IV, 73–5 (*Life of Constantine*, trans. and comm. by Averil Cameron and S. G. Hall (Oxford, 1999), pp. 67–71, 73, 84–5, 182); *Hist. eccl.*, X, 1; 4; 9.

[32] *Patria*, III, 88, ed. Preger (see ch. 2, n. 52), p. 247.

imperial 'preference', whose receptions straddled those of the reputedly more turbulent 'Greens'. The schema suggests a rite of crossing triply interlocking:

1. Tribunal – democrat of the Blues – peratic Blues;
2. Triklinos of the *scholae* – democrat of the Greens – peratic Greens;
3. inside the gate – democrat of the Blues – peratic Blues passing through the Chalke;
4. outside the gate – demarch of the Blues – politic Blues (= Whites);
5. Augustaion – demarch of the Greens – politic Greens (= Reds);
6. Horologion – demarch of the Blues – politic Blues (= Whites).

These stages, distinct and punctuated by halts, comprised the longest and most restrictive itinerary, that taking the imperial procession from the Bronze Gate of the palace to the vestibule of the narthex of St Sophia. On its return, there were only five 'receptions' by the colours, which the emperor passed without stopping.

The entry to St Sophia and the progress to the altar also comprised three distinct stages, passing through three doors, the Beautiful Door of the vestibule, the Imperial Doors of the narthex (see plate 1) and the Holy Doors of the chancel barrier, whose name was enough in itself to indicate an approach to the sacred. In this rite of passage, the 'propylaea of the narthex' served as a sort of halfway house, where the ceremonial imposed a first transformation. Coming from the town, the emperor entered wearing his crown, but he removed it on the threshold of the palace of Christ the King, to receive it back again on leaving the church, in the halfway house constituted by the Holy Well. It was thus made plain to the Constantinian and Old Testament emperor that the *basileia* belonged to God incarnate alone, who delegated it provisionally to a person of his choice. The mosaic placed above the door opening on to the vestibule of the narthex was probably slightly later than the *Book of Ceremonies*, but was an illustration of it; it showed Constantine and Justinian crowned, the one offering his city and the other his church,[33] not directly to Christ, lord of St Sophia, but to the Virgin, the supreme intercessor, often described in Christian rhetoric as a 'door' (see plate 2).[34]

In crossing the threshold of the narthex, the emperor took note that he was not even the steward of this territory where he did not reign. The patriarch was there with his clergy, master of the house; he waited, welcomed and escorted his guest in a short *propompe* as far as the monumental triple door giving on to the central nave. Everything then demonstrated this duality: the court ceremonial combined with the liturgy, prayer of welcome and 'entry'; the representatives of

---

[33] Dagron, *Constantinople imaginaire* (see ch. 1, n. 59), p. 273 and plate 8; G. Prinzing, 'Das Bild Justinians I. in der Überlieferung der Byzantiner vom 7. bis 15. Jahrhundert', in *Fontes minores*, 7 (Frankfurt-am-Main, 1986), pp. 6–26.

[34] For example, *Greek Anthology*, I, 106 v. 8.

Plate 1. The Imperial Doors, St Sophia

Plate 2. Southwest vestibule mosaic, above the 'Beautiful Door', St Sophia: Constantine I conse-crates his city and Justinian I his church to the Virgin, late tenth century. Byzantine Visual Resources © 1995, Dumbarton Oaks, Washington DC

the 'two powers' performed in perfect synchrony the acts of devotion addressed to their unique sovereign, and in particular the *proskynesis* (a deep bow more than a true prostration) on the threshold of the central nave, under the mosaic of the lunette (to which we will return) which reproduced in image, almost redundantly, the gesture of greeting and of submission actually made by the emperor *servus dei* before the Christ *rex regnantium* (see plate 3).

This parity was still demonstrated when the emperor and the patriarch walked side by side the length of the church. It ceased as they approached the sanctu-ary. When the sovereigns came close to the Holy Doors, on a circular plaque of marble of porphyry (*omphalion*), the patriarch 'went inside the railings' alone. Now in control of the ritual, it was he who then introduced the emperor, ac-companied him to the altar, saw him presented with the liturgical vessels and relics, gave him the cloth to kiss, led him to the back of the apse before the cross and handed him the censer. The roles were clearly defined and hierarchical, but the emperor, too, entered the sanctuary. After crossing over the line of green marble which demarcated a first zone reserved for worship, after skirting the

Plate 3. Narthex mosaic, above the Imperial Doors, St Sophia: an emperor (probably Leo VI) kneels before Christ enthroned, with the Virgin and the archangel Michael in medallions, ?920. Byzantine Visual Resources © 1995, Dumbarton Oaks, Washington DC

ambo and proceeding along the *solea*, after repeating on the *omphalion* the triple *proskynesis* of the Imperial Doors, he passed through the chancel barrier and entered a space normally reserved for priests.[35] The problem this posed was not that of the rights of the emperor in the Church, nor that of his relations with the patriarch, but that of the sacerdotal nature of his office. The canonists of the twelfth century, as we will see, realised this, whether they tried to explain the 'privilege' by the fact that the emperor needed to approach the altar to be able to place his gifts on it, or whether they saw it as one argument among others to the effect that the emperor was not wholly a layman.

He was certainly a quasi-priest or quasi-bishop when, at the end of the liturgy of the 'entry' and at a pause in the ceremonial, he rejoined the patriarch behind the chancel; but it was no longer the case from the moment when, having taken his leave of the patriarch, he left the sanctuary for the last time and entered the rooms reserved for him at the extreme east end of the south aisle, which the text calls *metatorion* and which I have described as his apartments in St Sophia. When he left them for the offertory, the kiss of peace and communion, it was

[35] The *thysiasterion* is sometimes called *hierateion* in the *Typikon of the Great Church*, ed. Mateos (n. 17); see Index II, p. 298.

by the right-hand side of the church, and the ceremonial was careful to specify the respective positions of the patriarch and the emperor, now separated by the chancel barrier.[36] The former was the first of the clergy, the latter the first of the laity, as Symeon of Thessalonike was to say.[37] Retrospectively, the liturgy of the 'entry' took on the meaning of a transgression, an error quickly rectified, or, as had already been suggested by the bishops of the council in Trullo in 691–2, of a concession to autocracy.[38]

For the exit by the Holy Well, where the patriarch returned his crown to the emperor, for the journey back, again punctuated by the acclamations of the demes, and for the re-entry to the palace, where the sovereign resumed his throne beneath the image of Christ, the ceremonial repeated, in reverse order and speeded up, the scenario of preparation, procession and arrival in the vestibule. Normality was restored and everyone was back in their place.

SITES OF MEMORY

The true nature of a ceremonial of this type has long been misunderstood. Those who have studied it have been looking for the description of an 'imperial liturgy', the elements of a coherent ideology or the glorification of an emperor chosen by God, celebrated by his people and submissive, as a good Christian, to the Church. This is not so much wrong as of only minor interest. Such a reading is suggested, it is true, by the compilers of protocol collections, by Philotheos and Constantine Porphyrogenitus himself, who were seeking to restore the splendour of the *basileia* by re-establishing the immutable order of its ceremonies. But such an approach can only reveal for Byzantium, in the style specific to its civilisation, the theatricality with which kings everywhere and always have liked to surround themselves, a flawless display and a proliferation of symbols. The meticulously organised procession from the palace to St Sophia comes to resemble the impeccably stage-managed ceremonies of Versailles or Buckingham Palace. We need to dig a little deeper and uncover, beneath the peaceful and rather static surface of the ceremonial, a more dramatic ritual which was designed not only to glorify the person of the sovereign but to test the nature, limits and contradictions of his power, and to confirm his suitability to receive or to preserve it. This second reading makes it possible to see what was at stake, to count transitions and metamorphoses, to distinguish two spaces *a priori* impermeable one to the other, to perceive that an imperial Christianity that was Old Testament in tone was confronted by the

[36] *De cerimoniis* I, 32 [23], pp. 132–4, is even clearer on this subject than the chapter analysed here (I, 1).
[37] See below, p. 280.
[38] Canon 69, Rhalles–Potles, *Syntagma*, II, p. 466, analysed below with the commentaries of the twelfth-century canonists, pp. 260–1.

more New Testament-oriented Christianity of the clergy, and to realise that the central problem, clearly posed but never truly resolved, was that of the sacerdotal nature of kingship. But we need to go further still and introduce into the schema not only the tensions of the ritual but the turbulence of real life. In this chapter as elsewhere, Constantine Porphyrogenitus presents a tightly controlled scenario without one false note, where everyone has his place and his part already written; but it was accepted that the actors would sometimes improvise and step out of their conventional roles, that the people at the Hippodrome might boo the emperor instead of acclaiming him, that the patriarch might refuse to introduce the emperor into the church, and that the ceremony might go tragically wrong. One need only glance briefly at the chronicles and accounts, truthful or invented, to see that memories, *exempla*, fables or images were attached to every one of the key points in the processional itinerary, and emphasised their significance. The underlying ritual breathed life into the ceremonial; a few examples will show how this accumulation of memories gave it depth.

When, behind the portière in the vestibule, the emperor laid down his crown so as not to usurp a kingship which, within the church, was no longer his, his act prefigured that of the last emperor of Byzantium, who, the apocalypses said, would depart for Jerusalem to lay his crown on the reconstituted cross of Golgotha and return his power to Christ with the Second Coming in mind.[39] It also revived or affected some memories: the sin committed in 780 by Leo IV, who entered St Sophia wearing his crown and who was soon punished by fatal facial carbuncles;[40] or the surprise of the assembled faithful when, at Pentecost 866, they saw Michael III pass through the doors of the narthex wearing his crown, before they realised that he was going to use it for the coronation of Basil I.[41] The Great Church was an altar of repose for votive or disused crowns, for those which pious emperors expressly consecrated to Christ,[42] and for those, above all, with an eventful or scandalous history, such as the crown which Maurice, at Easter 601, suspended by a chain of gold above the altar to the dismay of his wife and mother-in-law who had procured it for him at great cost;[43] or that of Herakleios, which could have been the subject of a novel. In defiance of convention, Herakleios had chosen to wear it when he was buried on 11 February 641; Herakleios-Constantine had retrieved it from his father's tomb because it

[39] Dagron, *Constantinople imaginaire* (see ch. 1, n. 59), pp. 329–30.

[40] Theophanes, *Chronographia*, ed. de Boor (see ch. 1, n. 4), pp. 453–4 (p. 625 of Mango and Scott translation); a slightly different version in Constantine Porphyrogenitus, see n. 46 below.

[41] Leo the Grammarian, *Chronographia*, ed. Bekker (see ch. 2, n. 12), pp. 245–6; George the Monk Continued, ed. Bekker (see ch. 1, n. 101), pp. 831–2; see above, p. 57.

[42] *Diegesis*, 23, ed. Preger (n. 26), p. 100; Dagron. *Constantinople imaginaire* (see ch. 1, n. 59), pp. 206, 249–50; see also Khitrowo, *Itinéraires russes* (n. 20), p. 92.

[43] Theophanes, *Chronographia*, ed. de Boor (see ch. 1, n. 4), p. 281 (pp. 406–7 of Mango and Scott translation).

was worth seventy pounds of gold; a few months later, Martina, Herakleios' widow, dedicated it to God; but it was used again, when a popular uprising forced Heraklonas to crown Constans II.[44] It was almost certainly this same crown that aroused the greed of Leo IV and which, taken back from God and wrongfully worn, had seemed to cause its wearer's death, after which, Irene, Leo's widow, offered it solemnly to St Sophia in expiation on Christmas Day.[45] Constantine Porphyrogenitus claims, with some exaggeration, that the church dictated the choice of crown to be used in the ceremonial, that the patriarch sent to the palace the crown which was appropriate for each festival and that the emperor was obliged later to return it.[46] It remains the case that in the act of removing and resuming the crown, many sins or involuntary offences could be committed; this is what the ceremonial made clear, by its stirring evocation of memories, when the sovereign entered the church.

Next, when the patriarch went to meet the emperor in the narthex and passed, by his side, through the Imperial Doors (see plate 3), the ceremonial marked the exceptional importance of both this encounter and this crossing, without, of course, evoking any problems or blunders. But historical accounts, accumulating over time, quickly becoming *exempla* and emphasised by legends and images, remind us that the patriarch, at this precise moment, might refuse entry to the sovereign and that the latter had to submit to the power of the clergy 'to bind and to loose'. The earliest episode, which then served as a model in the version given by Theodoret of Cyrrhus, dates back to 390 and the scene was not the Great Church of Constantinople but the episcopal church of Milan, where the very orthodox Theodosius I presented himself after ordering the massacre of the rebellious population of Thessalonike in a fit of rage:[47]

> Having learned of this lamentable calamity, this Ambrose whose name I have often mentioned, when the emperor had arrived in Milan and was preparing, as was his custom, to enter the holy church, went to meet him outside the vestibule and prevented him from passing into the holy propylaea, addressing him as follows: 'You do not realise, it would appear, the gravity of the massacre which has been perpetrated, and you have not appreciated, once your anger has subsided, what you have dared to do. No doubt it is imperial

---

[44] Nikephoros, *Breviarium* (see ch. 1, n. 66), 30, 31, ed. and trans. Mango, pp. 80, 82; Theophanes, *Chronographia*, ed. de Boor (see ch. 1, n. 4), p. 299.

[45] *Ibid.*, pp. 453–4 (p. 627 of Mango and Scott translation).

[46] *De administrando imperio*, 13 ll. 24–72, ed. and trans. Moravcsik and Jenkins (see ch. 1, n. 117), pp. 66–9. For discussion of this passage, see below, pp. 214–15.

[47] Theodoret, *Hist. eccl.*, V, 18, 1–19, ed. L. Parmentier (Leipzig, 1954), pp. 307–12. This passage is repeated in full in the anonymous Greek *Life of St Ambrose* at §20–5, PG 116, cols. 872–7 (and see below, n. 69); for the episode itself see J.-R. Palanque, *Saint Ambroise et l'empire romain. Contribution à l'histoire des rapports entre l'Eglise et l'Etat à la fin du IVᵉ siècle* (Paris, 1933), pp. 227–50; C. Morino, *Chiesa e stato nella dottrina di S. Ambrogio* (Rome, 1963), especially ch. 6. Same story in Sozomen, *Hist. eccl.*, VII, 25, PG 67, col. 1496, and in all later Byzantine historiography.

might which prevents you from being aware of your sin and power which blinds your reason. You must learn, however, to know nature, your ancestor the dust from which we are all made and to which we will return; you must not be so dazzled by the purple that you remain ignorant of the frailty of the body which it conceals. You rule people of the same nature and subject to the same slavery as you. The sole master and emperor of all things is the universal creator. With what eyes, then, will you see the temple of our common master? With what feet will you walk on this holy pavement? What hands will you extend [towards God], still dripping with the blood of those criminal murders? How could you receive with these hands the holy body of Christ? How could you approach with your mouth his holy blood, you who have shed so much blood criminally in anger? Leave; do not try to aggravate your first crime by a second [entering the church by force] and receive the bond [of excommunication] which, from on high, God the master of all things decides jointly [with me] to inflict on you. It is a healing bond which will bring you health.' Yielding to these words, the emperor – who, raised in the Holy Scriptures, knew very well what was the province of the priests and what of the emperors – returned to the palace moaning and weeping.

Eight months later in the narrative, at most two in reality, it was Christmas, and the master of the offices Rufinus, who represents brute force, suggested to the afflicted emperor that he, Rufinus, should go to Ambrose and make him reverse his decision. Theodosius acquiesced, though not believing that the bishop would agree to break divine law out of respect for imperial power; and, in fact, Ambrose reproached Rufinus for having 'the impudence of a dog' and declared that he would prevent the emperor from passing through the doors of the narthex and that he would be content to die if the sovereign 'transformed [by forcing his way in] his *basileia* into a *tyrannis*'. It was a repentant emperor, accordingly, who appeared at the doors of the church, asked to be 'loosed' and signed a decree, prepared by Ambrose, which stipulated a delay of thirty days, the time anger took to subside before the execution of death sentences:

> After this, the divine Ambrose loosed the bond. And the most faithful emperor, daring to penetrate the interior of the holy temple, did not pray to the Lord standing, or even on his knees, but stretched out on the ground, repeating the words of David: 'My soul cleaveth unto the dust: quicken thou me according to thy word' (Psalm CXIX [CXVIII]: 25); holding back his hair with his hand, striking his forehead and flooding the ground with his tears, he asked to be pardoned.

Theodosius was history, but an almost contemporary event directly affecting Constantinople had revived memories of the fourth-century emperor and recalled the risk that the Byzantine sovereign ran of being refused 'entry'. Contravening the canons so that his son, the future Constantine VII Porphyrogenitus, could succeed him, Leo VI had taken his mistress as his fourth wife and,

having legitimised his child, refused to separate from her. The patriarch Nicholas
Mystikos, prompted by the metropolitans, then twice forbade him entry to the
Great Church, for the celebration of Christmas 906 and for the Festival of Lights
(Epiphany), on 6 January 907.[48] The *Life of the Patriarch Euthymios* reveals
both the theatricality with which the conflict was conducted and the speed with
which people began to treat it as exemplary. Borrowings from Theodoret made
explicit the parallels between Leo VI and Theodosius, across five centuries;
and the mosaic still in place above the door to the narthex, if it really does
represent the emperor Leo VI asking God's pardon for the crime of his fourth
marriage, lent significance to the event by drawing from it a sort of institutional
image:

> The day of the birth of our Saviour and Lord Jesus Christ came, and everyone
> went to the church at the same time as the holy senate and the reigning
> sovereign himself, believing that the latter was going to enter the nave. But
> the patriarch, going to meet him at the Imperial Doors, said: 'For the moment,
> may your majesty, without taking offence, enter by the right hand side aisle.[49]
> At the Festival of Lights, there will be a procession and reception and we will
> raise no objections. But if you advance, acting like a tyrant,[50] all of us [the
> clergy] are prepared to leave the church.' The emperor dissolved into tears
> and, having drenched the ground with his weeping, without saying a word,
> retraced his steps and reached the *metatorion* by the right hand aisle. He then
> summoned certain of the metropolitans and learned from them everything
> that had been said and the commitments entered into.[51] Heaving a heartfelt
> sigh, he said for their benefit: 'I place my hope in Christ, Son of God, who
> left the paternal bosom to come and save us, who are sinners. May he take
> pity on me, who am the most sinful of all. May he open his arms to me as to
> the prodigal son and may he count me as a member of his holy catholic and
> apostolic church thanks to the prayers of our common father the patriarch
> and of all your holy assembly [of the metropolitans].' And after the reading
> from the Holy Gospels, the emperor, groaning and shedding tears, urged
> those who were listening to weep and beat their breasts with him, not only
> the senators but the metropolitans too; then he returned to the palace without
> having uttered the slightest reproach, waiting for the patriarch to deliver his
> decision.

[48] Earlier, on 1 May 906, Leo had of his own accord prudently refrained from 'requesting entry'
for the festival of the 'dedication' of the *Nea*, main centre of the devotions of the Macedonian
dynasty: *Vita Euthymii Patriarchae*, 11, 12, 13, ed. and trans. P. Karlin-Hayter, *Life of Euthymios
the Patriarch* (Brussels, 1970), pp. 70–1, 78–9, 84–5.

[49] That is, by the side doors which made it possible to pass from the narthex into the south aisle of
the church, and so reach the great *metatorion* directly.

[50] The same expression as in Theodoret and the *Life of St Ambrose* with regard to Theodosius.

[51] This was in the *triklinos* of the *metatorion*, where the emperor received people and, as we have
said, felt at home.

The Festival of Lights arrived. The patriarch Nicholas Mystikos had not gone to the palace the previous evening, as was customary, for the blessing of the water, on the pretext that he was ill:

> Next day, the emperor was there, with the holy senate, at the church, requesting the entry which the hierarch had often promised him. But the patriarch justified [his new refusal] by saying: 'If the metropolitans are not in agreement, and principally the *protothronos* Arethas,[52] I can do nothing; and if you decide arbitrarily to enter, I will at once withdraw with all of my entourage who are here.' The emperor replied: 'It seems to me, my lord patriarch, that your words and your deeds are making mock of my kingship. Is it that you are awaiting the rebel Doukas of Syria?[53] Are you counting on him to the point of scorning me?' At these words, the patriarch stood his ground, saying nothing, in the middle of the Imperial Doors, neither allowing the entry nor withdrawing. Then the emperor Leo imperially acted in a truly imperial manner: he threw himself on the ground and, having wept at length, stood up and said to the patriarch: 'Enter [alone], master, I will thwart you in nothing. What I suffer is the just and worthy price of my innumerable sins.' After uttering these words, he made straight for the side door which led to the *metatorion*.[54]

The senators nevertheless proposed to the emperor that he enter the church behind the patriarch by mingling with them, but the emperor did not deign to reply and went, as on Christmas day, into the *metatorion* before returning to the palace. From beginning to end, the account conforms to the topographical directions for the ceremonial; unable to enter the central nave, the emperor reached his 'apartment' in the *metatorion* by the south aisle, then, unable to take communion, returned to the palace by the direct gallery of the *diabatika*. We will return to Leo VI's 'sin', but the institutional lesson is clear; this precise issue was a test of the sovereign's legitimacy and of the nature of his power in relation to spiritual power. An assault, always a possibility, would cause him to fall into 'arbitrariness', 'tyranny' and sacrilege, whereas his repentance, whatever the nature of his sin, paradoxically preserved him from humiliation and confirmed his legitimacy. In the case of Leo VI, the narrator even added

---

[52] Arethas of Patras, metropolitan of Caesarea, who was then the fiercest opponent of the 'fourth marriage'.

[53] The general Andronikos Doukas, slandered and compromised by a crony of the emperor, Samonas, had rebelled in 905, with his family, a few supporters and perhaps in collusion with Nicholas Mystikos, in the region of Iconium; then, strengthened by the Arab alliance, he had returned to Baghdad in 907: M. Canard, 'Deux épisodes des relations diplomatiques arabo-byzantines au Xᵉ siècle', *Bulletin d'études orientales de l'Institut français de Damas*, 13 (1949–50), pp. 55–62, repr. in M. Canard, *Byzance et les musulmans du Proche-Orient*, Variorum Reprints (London, 1973); R. J. H. Jenkins, 'Leo Choerosphactes and the Saracen Vizier', *Zbornik Radova*, 8 (1963), pp. 167–75.

[54] *Life of Euthymios the Patriarch*, 12, ed. and trans. Karlin-Hayter (n. 48), pp. 74–9.

further spice to the story by hinting at a counter-charge which Theodoret had carefully avoided and which suggested the interdependence of the two powers; while the repentant emperor became a model, the patriarch who 'bound' him was discredited by the suspicion of political treason.

And when an 'economy' on the problem of fourth marriages was accepted by Nicholas Mystikos' successor, Euthymios, in 907, Leo VI adopted until his death in 912 the posture of a penitent. On the customary feast days, he was present in the church, but 'on this side of the holy railings' of the chancel (that is, not entering the sanctuary), standing and weeping.[55] Arethas, in 907, stipulated a more humiliating treatment: the emperor must kneel throughout the service at the church door (in the narthex), imploring the pity of the faithful.[56]

Later still, we find analogies of form and meaning in the account of another episode occurring in 969. The patriarch Polyeuktos refused entry to St Sophia to John Tzimiskes, who had just murdered his predecessor and relative, Nikephoros Phokas, in collusion with the latter's wife. 'That same night', wrote John Skylitzes,

> the emperor went with a small company to the Great Church, wishing to receive the diadem from the hands of the patriarch; but when he arrived, Polyeuktos would not allow him to enter, saying that a person whose hands were still wet from the freshly spilled and still warm blood of a relative was unworthy to set foot in the divine temple, but that he must show his repentance without delay and that only then would he have the right to tread the ground of the church of the Lord. John humbly accepted the punishment and promised that he would comply with all these directions in an obedient spirit.[57]

He assured the patriarch, what is more, that he had not killed Nikephoros with his own hands and that everything had been arranged by the empress, speedily sent into exile, and redeemed his own sin by distributing his personal fortune to the poor; Polyeuktos then allowed him into the church, on Christmas Day.

It was well known, therefore, from these illustrious examples and these memories of several dramas, that entry might be refused; but people also liked to imagine that it might happen in circumstances that were unusual and of dubious propriety in religious terms. A well-known passage in the *Story of the Construction of Hagia Sophia* (?ninth century) gleefully describes Justinian's 'entry' for the inauguration of 'his' Great Church: having arrived with the patriarch Eutychios, he passed with him through the Imperial Doors, but then gave him the slip to rush forward alone and shout, under the dome: 'I have beaten

---

[55] Ibid., p. 109.
[56] Arethas, *Scripta minora*, ed. L. C. Westerink, I (Leipzig, 1968), p. 317; he was clearly remembering the attitude adopted by Theodosius I in Milan according to Theodoret.
[57] Skylitzes, *Synopsis*, ed. Thurn (see ch. 1, n. 39), pp. 285–6; see also Leo the Deacon, *Historia*, ed. C. B. Hase (Bonn, 1828), pp. 98–9.

you, Solomon!'[58] The author maliciously records that the cupola collapsed soon after, as if to punish the emperor for an offence that we can recognise by reference to the 'normal' ceremonial. The sin was pride, obviously: the builder was too proud of mere architectural success. It was also an error of timing: by competing with Solomon Justinian was defining himself as an Old Testament king, forgetting Christ and comparing his church to the forever-destroyed temple of Yahweh. Lastly, this was an abuse of power: once over the threshold of the church, the emperor should allow himself to be led by the priests; he could no longer invoke his Old Testament models and the privilege of priesthood he took from them. Through this incongruous 'entry', the popular imagination took its revenge on the presumptuous emperor portrayed by the mosaic in the vestibule as offering St Sophia to the Virgin, and it recalled that the man who had massacred the rebels of Nika had blood on his hands,[59] and that he, like the others, should have asked to be cleansed of it.

The final crossing, which took the emperor through the Holy Doors into a priestly space and acknowledged, for a brief moment, his quasi-priestly character, was also associated with a number of texts. The first, obviously, is the passage in Leviticus, 9: 23: 'And Moses and Aaron went into the tabernacle of the congregation, and came out, and blessed the people: and the glory of the Lord appeared unto all the people.' In the rhetorical eulogies of patriarchs, the comparison between the two pairs, emperor and patriarch, Moses and his brother Aaron, was the norm.[60] It was probably the key moment in the ceremonial, at least in its interpretation in an Old Testament context through the intermediary of Philo of Alexandria.[61] Moses, whom Philo calls prophet, king and priest, delegated his sacerdotal functions to his brother Aaron and introduced him into the tabernacle. The roles, of course, are reversed; Aaron and his sons were initiated by Moses into the service of the Lord, whereas the emperor was received into the holy of holies by the patriarch and his clergy. But it was as leader of the people and God's elect that the sovereign, like Moses, had the right to enter the sanctuary and act as a priest or even, as Constantine Porphyrogenitus several times put it in a revealing slip of the pen, 'to celebrate the liturgy' (*ten theian leitourgian telein/ektelein*).[62] It was not, at all events, as a simple spectator, and if certain canonists played down the importance of the crossing of the chancel barrier and access to the altar, the emperors saw it as recognition of their

[58] *Diegesis*, 27–8, ed. Preger (n. 26), pp. 104–5; Dagron, *Constantinople imaginaire* (see ch. 1, n. 59), pp. 207–8, 303–13.
[59] The suppression of the 'Nika' revolt in 532 involved, it was said, 30,000 deaths in the Hippodrome of Constantinople.
[60] See, for example, M. Loukaki, 'Première didascalie de Serge le Diacre. Eloge du patriarche Michel Autoreianos', *REB*, 52 (1994), pp. 164–9.
[61] *Life of Moses*, II, 153, ed. R. Arnaldez, C. Mondésert, J. Pouilloux and P. Savinel, *De vita Mosis* (Paris, 1967), p. 258.
[62] I, 34, 37, 39 [25, 28, 30], pp. 141 ll. 2–3, 159 l. 1, 169 ll. 24–170, 1 and *passim*.

legitimacy and confirmation of their title. The sources are not mistaken in this. At Edessa in 737, a would-be imperial heir could see no better way of asserting his rights than to 'enter the sanctuary and take communion with his own hands on the table of life, according to the custom of the Roman emperors'.[63] In the fictionalised history of the Himyarites of 'happy Arabia' (?seventh century), when the recently converted king, Abraha, is crowned by the very Christian king of the Ethiopians, Elesboam, they proceed together to the 'holy entry into the holy sanctuary' of the church of the Trinity.[64] This moment was awaited and closely observed; at Christmas 814 and at Epiphany 815, people watched to see if Leo V would kiss the effigy of Christ on the altar cloth, so dispelling the suspicion of iconoclasm.[65] In the highly authentic *Life of St Theophano*, Leo VI, having emerged from the prison in which he had been confined by his father, was not truly restored to his imperial dignity until the emperor had taken him by the hand to enter with him the 'holy of holies' of the church of the Asomatoi, end point of the imperial procession for the feast of that day.[66] And here, too, the patriarch might refuse entry; in 963, Polyeuktos prevented Nikephoros Phokas from crossing the chancel barrier to celebrate his marriage to Theophano in the Nea.[67]

The clergy were not slow to react. Constantine Porphyrogenitus himself points us towards the *exemplum* used to circumscribe the privilege and make it seem simply an indulgence: 'It should be known', he wrote,

> that in ancient times, after placing his gifts on the holy table, the emperor remained inside the holy sanctuary until the communion of the holy mysteries. Under the orthodox emperor Theodosius [I], this custom ceased by reason of the deed that is reported in the *Life* of the saintly and most glorious Ambrose, bishop of Milan.[68]

This Greek *Life*, that known to the Byzantines, was simply a selection of episodes concerning the saint taken from Theodoret's *Ecclesiastical History*, in particular those concerning his confrontation with Theodosius,[69] which ran as follows, after the passage quoted above:

---

[63] Michael the Syrian, *Chronicle*, trans. Chabot (see ch. 1, n. 6), II, pp. 503–4; *Chronicon ad annum 1234 pertinens*, 165, CSCO, Scriptores Syri 56, pp. 242–3.

[64] *Leges homeritarum*, PG 86, col. 569.

[65] *Scriptor incertus de Leone Armenio*, ed. Bekker (see ch. 1, n. 43), pp. 356–7.

[66] *Life of St Theophano*, 19, ed. Kurtz (see ch. 1, n. 81), p. 13.

[67] Skylitzes, *Synopsis*, ed. Thurn (see ch. 1, n. 39), pp. 260–1; see also Zonaras, *Annales*, ed. Pinder (see ch. 1, n. 29), III, p. 499.

[68] *De cerimoniis*, II, 27, p. 627.

[69] Not the Latin *Life* written by Paulinus and translated into Greek (*BHG* 67, ed. A. Papadopoulos-Kerameus, *Analekta hierosolymitikes stachyologias*, I (St. Petersburg, 1891), pp. 27–88), where the episodes of imperial repentance occupy relatively little space, but an anonymous Greek *Life* (*BHG* 68 and 68b, PG 116, cols. 861–81), which passed into the menologies at the date of 7 December; see A. Ehrhard, *Überlieferung und Bestand der hagiographischen und homiletischen Literatur der griechischen Kirche*, I (Leipzig, 1937), pp. 395, 517, 522.

And when the time came to place the gifts on the holy table, [Theodosius] rose to his feet, still in tears, and entered the sanctuary. And after laying down his gifts, he remained, as was his custom, inside the chancel. But once again the great Ambrose did not remain silent. He gave him a lesson by teaching him to distinguish places [those appropriate for the laity and those reserved to the clergy]. He began by asking him if he needed something, and when the emperor replied that he was waiting to participate in the holy mysteries [to communicate], he said to him through the intermediary of the head deacon: 'The interior [of the sanctuary], O emperor, can be trodden only by priests. No one else can have access to it or touch it. Leave, then, and join the others: the purple makes emperors and not priests.' The most faithful emperor accepted the explanation in a good spirit and made it known in return that it was not from arrogance that he had remained within the chancel, but that in Constantinople it was the custom he had been taught. 'I must thank you', he said, 'for this healing.' And he observed, on his return to Constantinople, the rules of piety that he had learned from the great hierarch. So when a holy festival had once again taken him to the divine temple, after laying his gifts on the altar, he withdrew. And when the leader of the Church – it was then [the patriarch] Nektarios – asked him: 'Why do you not remain inside? Is there something wrong?', he replied: 'It was hard for me to learn the difference between an emperor and a priest, it was hard for me to find a teacher of truth! Ambrose is the only one I know who deserves to be called bishop.'[70]

This error corrected was meant to illustrate a rule: the emperor was not a priest, so his place was not inside the sanctuary. But it emphasised most of all an ambiguity in the ceremonial, discreetly evoked by canon 69 of the council in Trullo at the end of the seventh century and made explicit by the canonist Balsamon in the twelfth,[71] which concerned the very definition of power. The lesson given by the bishop of Milan to a pious emperor only just readmitted to

---

[70] Theodoret, *Hist. eccl.*, V, 18, 20–25, ed. Parmentier (n. 47), pp. 312–13, repeated word for word in the anonymous Greek *Life* at §§26–7 (PG 116, col. 877). In Theodoret's story, and consequently in the Byzantine tradition, this episode occurred soon after the penance of 390. Sozomen (*Hist. eccl.*, VII, 25, PG 67, col. 1496) does not make the chronological link and refers only to the problem of the emperor's place during the office as another lesson given by Ambrose to the emperor. In fact, it seems that this episode should be dated to October 388, immediately on Theodosius' arrival in Milan, and not 390: F. J. Dölger, 'Kaiser Theodosius der Grosse und Bischof Ambrosius von Mailand in einer Auseinandersetzung zwischen Predigt und Messliturgie', *Antike und Christentum*, 1 (1929), pp. 61–3; A. Lippold, 'Theodosius I', *RE*, Suppl. XIII (1973), cols. 879–80; F. Kolb, 'Das Bussakt von Mailand: zum Verhältnis von Staat und Kirche in der Spätantike', in *Geschichte und Gegenwart. Festschrift K. D. Erdmann* (Neumünster, 1980), pp. 41–74.

[71] Rhalles–Potles, *Syntagma*, II, pp. 466–7 and see below, pp. 260–1. For the change in the liturgy attributed to the influence of Ambrose, see Treitinger, *Kaiser- und Reichsidee* (see ch. 2, n. 35), p. 136 and n. 4.

the church and too readily consenting may have revealed a divergence between West and East with regard to protocol and liturgy, but it principally revealed the need of the East in the tenth century, as in the fifth, to have recourse to western mediation to formulate the clerical thesis of the 'two powers' and deny the sovereign any sacerdotal privilege. True or false, the exemplary story told by Theodoret and readily adopted by the Greek tradition denounced Constantinople as a city of confusion and the patriarch Nektarios as a priest lacking in respect for his proper place; it was the emperor himself, bullied by the bishop of Milan, who was being asked to impose on the eastern church the reform which would laicise him. The aim was clear, since the Greek *Life* of Ambrose was fabricated with the express purpose of extirpating the notion of a priestly kingship; it was remarkably effective, since Constantine Porphyrogenitus, distant successor of Theodosius I, referred to the *exemplum* and revived it as grounds for a prohibition.

One understands, therefore, why the ceremonial which conducted the emperor from the palace to St Sophia on every major festival is worthy of even more attention than the exceptional ceremonial of the coronation, of which it was only a particular case. It was a reminder of the nature of imperial power, without offering the clear, balanced and accepted definition that one might find in a chapter of constitutional law or that would result from an ideological consensus; rather, it expressed in movements and gestures the tensions provoked by its absolute character. An emperor was nothing if he was not everything, and in particular if he was not the providential mediator between his people and God. But on this point, and this point alone, an effective resistance might be organised, and the ceremonial was obliged to compromise with the liturgy. To each step in the direction of imperial apotheosis corresponded a question or a refusal. You are emperor and priest, but only in appearance and for a while. You are David *redivivus*, but according to the Old Law which is dead. You enter the church, but without your crown. You pass through the Imperial Doors which lead you to God, but only after asking pardon for your sins from the priests, who alone have the power to bind and to loose. You enter the sanctuary, but only to present your gifts, because you do not really belong, or only a little, to the priestly order.

But what was the alternative to the absolute power of the emperor? Neither a law nor ideas, only an accumulation of memories, true or false, and images. The rituals studied by ethnologists are content for the most part to describe and to test the powers they challenge. But in Byzantium, a civilisation of remembering and commemoration,[72] ceremonial was also a powerful mechanism for evoking the past and for fixing the present, for selecting places charged with memories,

---

[72] For these two aspects of memory in the Christian middle ages, see the fine article by O. G. Oexle, 'Memoria und Memorialüberlieferung', *Frühmittelalterliche Studien*, 10 (1976), pp. 70–95.

which in their turn produced other memories. On this very spot, Justinian had compared himself to Solomon and the dome of the church had collapsed; over there, Leo VI could have forced the entry which was refused him, but preferred to prostrate himself and weep; and there, too, John Tzimiskes had been turned away because he had blood on his hands. These splendid stories or beautiful legends were more valuable than a constitution; they analysed in depth the phenomenon of power and curtailed it by the workings of memory. The ceremonial provided the canvas, but it was history that embroidered it. History created case law; it always had the last word.

THE REPENTANT EMPEROR

Let us return to the mosaic in the narthex which shows an emperor bowing low before Christ enthroned and, in two parallel medallions, a Virgin imploring and an archangel in the dress of a commander (see plates 1 and 3). Its style dates it to the late ninth or early tenth century; its position, in the lunette above the Imperial Door, where it probably replaced a simple cross in the almost aniconic decoration of Justinian, associates it with an important stage in the ceremonial and gives it a special significance. The Fossati brothers noticed and drew it during their restoration of the building in 1847–9;[73] Thomas Whittemore rediscovered it under the whitewash applied by the Turks in 1932 and published it[74]; it was re-examined in 1968 by E. J. W. Hawkins.[75] The conclusions of the archaeologists are not in doubt, but the iconographical interpretations and attempted identifications remained tentative until a recent article by Nicholas Oikonomides.[76]

[73] C. Mango, *Materials for the Study of the Mosaics of St Sophia at Istanbul* (Washington, 1962), especially pp. 24–5 and figs. 8–10.
[74] T. Whittemore, *The Mosaics of St Sophia at Istanbul. Preliminary Report on the First Year's Work, 1931–1932: The Mosaics of the Narthex* (Oxford, 1933).
[75] E. J. W. Hawkins, 'Further observations on the narthex mosaic in St Sophia at Istanbul' *DOP*, 22 (1968), pp. 151–66.
[76] N. Oikonomides, 'Leo VI and the narthex mosaic of St Sophia', *DOP*, 30 (1976), pp. 151–72. Of the earlier bibliography, note in particular A. Grabar, *L'Empereur dans l'art byzantin* (Paris, 1936), pp. 100–6 and *L'Iconoclasme byzantin. Dossier archéologique* (Paris, 1957), pp. 239–41, who relates the mosaic to the Annunciation on the basis of the fourth homily of Leo VI. In response to Oikonomides, see Z. A. Gavrilović, 'The humiliation of Leo VI the Wise (the mosaic of the narthex at Saint Sophia, Istanbul)', *Cahiers archéologiques*, 28 (1979), pp. 87–94, who tries to show that the scene represents the 'gift of the Spirit' and of 'Wisdom' to the emperor; see also R. Cormack, 'Interpreting the mosaics of St Sophia at Istanbul', *Art History*, 4 (1981), pp. 131–49, especially pp. 138–41, who accepts the iconographical interpretation, but leaves open the problem of the identification of the emperor, seeming to favour Basil I more than Leo VI. See also A. Schminck, '*Rota tu volubilis*. Kaisermacht und Patriarchenmacht in Mosaiken', in *Cupido legum*, ed. L. Burgmann, M. T. Fögen and A. Schminck (Frankfurt-am-Main, 1985), pp. 211–34, who assumes that the emperor is Basil I and that he was paired with an image of the patriarch Photios, effaced after a *damnatio memoriae*.

The work is unusual in its subject, an imperial *proskynesis*, which is rare;[77] it is also unusual in its clumsy but necessary dissymmetry, which leaves a blank space to the right of the divine throne that cannot be attributed to some reworking;[78] it is unusual, lastly, in the absence of any inscription identifying the emperor, which means it cannot be a dedicatory image or commemorate a specific event. In this position, evoking so many memories, the picture serves as a reminder. The message it delivers is addressed to the emperors present and future who are about to cross the threshold. Its significance is general, but it has nevertheless been achieved by an accretion of historical allusions, models and meanings. Christ, seated on a throne with a traditional lyre-back, blesses with his right hand and holds in his left an open book in which can be read: 'Peace be unto you. I am the light of the world', a juxtaposition of two sentences from St John's Gospel. 'Peace be unto you' is the greeting used on three occasions by Jesus when he appeared among his disciples, 'when the doors were shut', to pass on to them the Holy Ghost, to give them the power to 'remit' or 'retain' the sins of men and to make Thomas touch the wound in his side (John, 20: 19, 21, 26). 'I am the light of the world: he that followeth me shall not walk in darkness, but shall have the light of life' are words spoken by Christ to the Pharisees (John, 8: 12). Peace and light: two key words that express the 'wisdom of God' – that is, of Christ – to whom the Great Church was dedicated. The anonymous emperor bows very low, kneeling, his body bent as if he had just touched the ground with his forehead and was rising to address his prayer to God in a gesture of supplication. This goes further than was required by the ceremonial,[79] not only a humble submission of the earthly emperor before the celestial emperor, the *rex regnantium* whose slave he acknowledged himself to be, but probably also a request for pardon. This would explain the images of the Virgin and the archangel in two symmetrical medallions: not as has been suggested, an Annunciation, but a *deesis*, the Theotokos intervening with her Son on behalf of the supplicant, so that the archangel judge, probably St Michael, would suspend punishment. A comparable image of repentance and intercession, but with St John Baptist in the place of the archangel, according

---

[77] For the meaning of the *proskynesis* and its relatively rare iconographical transcriptions, see R. Guilland, 'La cérémonie de la *proskynèsis*', *REG*, 59–60 (1946–7), pp. 251–9, repr. in R. Guilland, *Recherches sur les institutions byzantines* (Berlin/Amsterdam, 1967), I, pp. 144–50; Treitinger, *Kaiser- und Reichsidee* (see ch. 2, n. 35), pp. 84–94. For the iconography, see Grabar, *L'Empereur dans l'art byzantin* (n. 76), p. 101 and n. 3, who gives only five examples of imperial *proskynesis*; C. Bertelli, *La Madonna di Santa Maria in Trastevere* (Rome, 1961), pp. 60–2, who cites fifteen examples before the eleventh century; and above all A. Cutler, *Transfigurations: Studies in the Dynamics of Byzantine Iconography* (University Park / London, 1975), pp. 53–65.
[78] According to the archaeological studies cited above, which invalidate the interpretation proposed by Schminck, '*Rota tu volubilis*' (n. 76).
[79] It is unlikely that the emperor prostrated himself at this point, but rather bowed very low.

to a more usual formula, was the subject of a verse dialogue composed by John Mauropous, in the eleventh century, in which the emperor addresses Christ in these words:

It is you who have made me master of your creatures
and ruler of my companions in servitude.
And I, who prove to be a slave to sin,
I fear, master and judge, the lashing of your whip.[80]

All these observations led Nicholas Oikonomides, in 1976, to establish that the emperor portrayed was, like the David of the Byzantine Psalters, in the posture of a penitent, to assert with confidence that he was Leo VI rather than Basil I, and to propose the date of 920. This was the year when the Tome of Union, issued by the synod and signed by the emperor,[81] sanctioned new legislation on remarriage, the victory of Nicholas Mystikos, restored to the patriarchate by Leo VI himself in 912,[82] and the necessity of the penance imposed on the dead emperor and of the divine pardon, which was assumed to have assured the salvation of a sovereign who had submitted to the orders of the Church. Rather than recapitulate here a solidly based argument, let us continue, from our own standpoint, our examination of an imperial power which we find easy to understand when it is acknowledging its inferiority to the divine majesty, but which we are surprised to find so ostentatiously proclaiming its guilt.

Veneration and simple humility can easily be understood as Christian virtues; the repentance of an anonymous emperor, that is, of any emperor, should not, however, come as a surprise. This was the 'truly imperial' act which the emperor could make 'imperially', as the author of the *Life of Euthymios* said of Leo VI,[83] and which could invoke so many illustrious precedents. Let us take first a model, that of David accursed, repentant and pardoned. It was for sending his general, Uriah, to a certain death, so that he could marry his wife, the beautiful

---

[80] John Mauropous, *Epigram* 75, ed. P. de Lagarde and J. Bollig, *Johannis Euchaitarum metropolitae ... quae supersunt* (Göttingen, 1882), p. 38, quoted by Oikonomides, 'The narthex mosaic of St Sophia' (n. 76), p. 158, note 24.

[81] Grumel-Darrouzès, *Regestes*, no. 669; Zepos, *Jus*, I, pp. 192–6; see now the ed. by L. G. Westerink, *Nicholas I Patriarch of Constantinople, Miscellaneous Writings* (Washington, 1981), pp. 56–85. Oikonomides ('The narthex mosaic of St Sophia' (n. 76)) notes that the word *eirene* and the verb *eireneuein* are found no fewer than fourteen times in the preamble of the Tome of Union, which should be related to the legend of the mosaic: 'Peace be unto you'. For the commemoration of this 'Union of the Church', the *De cerimoniis* stipulated a procession between St Sophia, church of the Wisdom of Christ, and St Irene, church of the Peace of Christ (I, 45 [36], pp. 186–7).

[82] N. Oikonomides, 'La dernière volonté de Léon VI au sujet de la tétragamie (mai 912)' and 'La "préhistoire" de la dernière volonté de Léon VI au sujet de la tétragamie', *BZ*, 56 (1963), pp. 46–52, 265–70; B. Flusin, 'Un fragment inédit de la Vie d'Euthyme le patriarche?', *TM*, 9 (1985), pp. 119–31 (text and translation) and 10 (1987), pp. 233–60 (discussion).

[83] See above, pp. 108–9.

Bathsheba, that the king had seen the first child of this union die 'on the seventh day'; but the second, Solomon, had been saved after the intervention of the prophet Nathan, thanks to David's repentance, which Psalm LI [L], the famous *miserere* of David, so magnificently expresses:[84]

Have mercy upon me, O God, according to thy lovingkindness: according unto the multitude of thy tender mercies blot out my transgressions. Wash me thoroughly from mine iniquity, and cleanse me from my sin. For I acknowledge my transgressions: and my sin is ever before me.

. . .

Behold, I was shapen in iniquity; and in sin did my mother conceive me.

. . .

Deliver me from bloodguiltiness, O God, thou God of my salvation...

For thou desirest not sacrifice; else would I give it...

Illustrations of this text in Byzantine Psalters offer the only convincing parallel to the image in the narthex; they show David in the same posture, saved from an angel of justice who threatens him by the intercession of the prophet Nathan and by awareness of his crime, the *metanoia* (repentance) personified in the form of a woman.[85] An inscription says only: 'I have sinned against the Lord' (see plates 4a and 4b). Text and image present us, therefore, with the guilty king and his earthly intercessor, the celestial agent of justice and the feeling of contrition which stays his arm, without anything being said or suggested as to the origin of the sin. Neither the death of Uriah nor David's amorous passion for Bathsheba are referred to; nor, later, would there be any reference to the decision to take a census which rekindled the divine wrath, allowed the exterminating angel to strike the people of Israel and prevented David from building an altar.[86] The biblical logic is not that of responsibility. It is God who forces into error in order to punish or pardon; the sin is only a pretext for repentance – it is in a sense the original sin of kingship, just as repentance is constitutive of royal legitimacy. The Old Testament says this of the founder of the dynasty, but Jewish legends extend the theme to Solomon, who was supposed to have wandered the world with a stick as his only possession as a result of his sins or of the loss of a magic ring, and who recovers his throne, occupied in his absence

---

[84] The episode is described in II Samuel [II Kings] XI–XII. David also expresses his repentance in Psalm XLI [XL]: 'Lord, be merciful unto me: heal my soul; for I have sinned against thee.' The theme of David's repentance for his double crime is used in the *Palaea historica*, in A. A. Vasiliev, *Anecdota graeco-byzantina*, I (Moscow, 1893), pp. 282–3.

[85] See the mss. *Parisinus gr.* 510 (880/883), fol. 143v; *Parisinus gr.* 139 (second half of tenth century), fol. 136v; *Marcianus gr.* 17 (from the reign of Basil II, 976–1025), fol. IVv.

[86] II Samuel [II King] XXIV; 1 Chronicles, 21–2; the biblical schema was applied to Justinian, builder of St Sophia, in an anonymous story, probably ninth century: Dagron, *Constantinople imaginaire* (see ch. 1, n. 59), pp. 293ff.

Plate 4. The repentance of David
(a) Paris psalter, Cod. gr. 139, fo. 136v, second half of the tenth century, © Bibliothèque Nationale, Paris
(b) *Homilies* of Gregory of Nazianzus, Cod. gr. 510, fo. 143v, 879–83, © Bibliothèque Nationale, Paris

by a demon or double, only after he has repented.[87] A verse in the Koran, in evoking the 'caliphate' of David on earth, picks up and transmits the message in all its simplicity:

To David we gave Solomon.

How excellent a servant!

He was filled with repentance.[88]

David suggested the pose and supplied the meaning, and when looking at the mosaic at that period, it must have been impossible not to think of him.[89] But it is certainly not David who is prostrating himself before Christ. It is one of the Christian emperors for whom he was the model, both as the Lord's anointed and as repentant sinner, a David *redivivus*, anonymous because exemplary, placed in this position on the occasion of some event. It is less important to be able to name the emperor represented, an 'identification' that has long divided the experts, than to be clear about when and why the decision was taken to create this image. It had, as we have said, a general significance and its potency was only increased by the existence of so many possible repentant sovereigns, even if one of them historically ranked higher than the others.

After David the model, comes the 'prototype', Constantine, subject of diverging traditions, but always found in a posture of repentance. According to the pagan Zosimus, he killed his own son and became a Christian only in the hope of obtaining a pardon from the priests.[90] Christian historiography and hagiography clear Constantine of this crime, but acknowledge one sin, that of a persecuting emperor struck down by God with leprosy and learning from Pope Sylvester that repentance and baptism alone could assure him a cure and legitimacy.[91] The Constantinopolitan folklore of the *Patria*, in the mid-tenth

---

[87] See the references and discussion in L. Ginsberg, *The Legends of the Jews*, IV (Philadelphia, 1913), pp. 123–76, especially pp. 165–72; firmly established on his throne and sure of his legitimacy, Solomon forgot the precepts of Deuteronomy, and God decided to punish him for his sins. In order to complete the Temple, Solomon captured Asmodeus, prince of the demons, but let himself be seduced by him and lost his ring, on which was written the name of God. Banished from his kingdom, he went begging from town to town, experienced humiliation, understood that God punished those he loved for their sins, repented, was pardoned and expelled Asmodeus, who was reigning in his place, passing himself off as Solomon.

[88] Koran, ch. 38: 30.

[89] To quote only one example of the Byzantines' familiarity with the Psalter: according to the author of her *Life*, St Theophano, first wife of Leo VI, learned the Psalms by heart at the age of six and, once empress, 'sang David' seven times a day (5 and 22, ed. Kurtz (see ch. 1, n. 81), pp. 3, 15).

[90] Zosimus, *Hist.*, II, 29, ed. and trans. F. Paschoud, *Zosime. Histoire nouvelle* (Paris, 1971), I, pp. 101–2.

[91] This is the version given by the *Actus Silvestri* and the sources which depend on it; see the Greek *Life* of St Silvester, ed. F. Combefis, *Sancti Silvestri Romani antistitis acta antiqua probatoria* (Paris, 1659), p. 279: Silvester asked Constantine, before the baptism, to fast for a week, remove his robes of purple, shut himself up in his room and prostrate himself on the floor, weeping and moaning, and admit before God that he had killed by blinding his holy servants, martyrs of his persecutions.

century, shows a founder bloody in victory, basing his 'monarchy' on murders, erecting statues of his victims in a dark cellar to implore their forgiveness and begging his children to do the same, repenting the assassination of his son, weeping over him for forty days without washing and 'begging God to pardon his sin'.[92]

After the founder of the Christian empire comes the very legitimate Theodosius I, the soldier emperor who definitively suppressed paganism and brought the orthodoxy of the *pars orientalis* into line with Rome, but also the autocrat too favourable towards the Jews, who wanted the synagogue of Kallinikon to be rebuilt by the Christians who had destroyed it,[93] the irascible despot who was excommunicated for massacring the inhabitants of Thessalonike,[94] and lastly, in at least part of the tradition, the emperor deranged by love of the beautiful Galla, his second wife.[95] *Rex judaicus, rex furiosus, rex lubricus*: it was more than enough to make him ask God's pardon. In the *exemplum* drawn from his reign, David is clearly the model. The *Life of Ambrose* by Paulinus, integrated into the Byzantine menology for December, makes the emperor say: 'Like David, I have committed a murder and an adultery', to which the holy bishop replies: 'If you have followed David in his errors, follow him also in putting things right.'[96] The version of the *Life* read by Constantine VII, which is closer to the mirrors of princes than to hagiography,[97] is organised round a single theme: the repentance of the emperor and his necessary humility, the price paid for his *dynasteia*.

Only a few years before Leo VI, his father Basil I (867–86) had made his own act of repentance. In rhetoric first, when he sent to the bishops assembled for the sixth session of the council of 869 a message in which he proposed to humble himself in order to avert a crisis within the Church, and so perfectly adopted the pose of the sovereign in the mosaic that he has been seen as its inspiration or its model. 'There is nothing shameful', he wrote,

in showing one's wounds and in seeking a place of repentance and healing. There is no shame, brothers, in prostrating oneself before God. They who prostrate themselves before him are they who submit to the Church and the spiritual Fathers. If you feel ashamed at this, let me be for you a model of such humiliation, I who have neither learning nor wisdom, for you who are the wise and the illustrious doctors. I who am steeped in sin, before you,

---

[92] Dagron, *Constantinople imaginaire* (see ch. 1, n. 59), p. 93.

[93] Kedrenos, *Historiarum Compendium*, ed. Bekker (see ch. 1, n. 5), I, pp. 571–2; Zonaras, *Annales*, ed. Pinder (see ch. 1, n. 29), III, pp. 87–9.

[94] See above, pp. 105–6.

[95] Zosimos, *Hist.*, IV, 44, ed. and trans. F. Paschoud, *Zosime. Histoire nouvelle*, II, 2 (Paris, 1979) pp. 312–13.

[96] *Life of St Ambrose* by Paulinus (*BHG* 67), 24, ed. Papadopoulos-Kerameus, *Analekta hierosolymitikes stachyologias*, I (n. 69), p. 55. It deals with the repression of Thessalonike; there is nothing to justify the accusation of 'adultery', except the comparison of Theodosius to David.

[97] See above, pp. 111–12 and n. 69.

the pure, who make a profession of virtue, I am first to throw myself on the ground. Walk on my face, pass over my eyes; do not hesitate to trample the back of an emperor. There is nothing I am not ready to endure if only I may see you united.[98]

Basil was accusing himself, with forced humility, only of faults common to all men, but the historians, polemicists and hagiographers of the tenth century assert that, at the end of his life, he was prey to a more personal terror and remorse. His reign and the dynasty he had wished to found had been besmirched from the beginning by the murder, on 23 September 867, of his predecessor Michael III, who had singled him out and shared his empire with him. The death of his elder son, Constantine, had reminded him of this crime and driven him to distraction;[99] as with David, it seemed that the loss of his first-born son could only be the consequence of the wrath of God and left him with no option but public repentance. The author of the *Life of St Basil the Younger* and Liutprand of Cremona record what was then being said in Constantinople. Basil had tried to expiate his crime by dedicating a church to the archangel Michael, celestial judge, patron saint of his victim and protector of the dynasty; on his deathbed, Michael III had appeared to him to ask: 'What had I done to you? Of what crime was I guilty that made you attack me and murder me without pity?'[100] Other sources say that what Basil regretted most was having followed the sorcerer Santabarenos down the path of magic and incantations, but his last words were also words of repentance: to avoid eternal damnation, he could count only on the pity of God.[101]

It is difficult to imagine that Basil I conceived the idea of expressing through an image the public avowal of his sin and repentance, or that he left his son Leo VI the task of representing him in the posture of a supplicant; nor is it likely that the ecclesiastical authorities took such an initiative after his death and against his memory. But it is clear that, at a time when the Macedonian dynasty was establishing itself, when its legitimacy was assured, and when the empire, the capital and even the Church bore its imprint, the reign of the founder assumed,

---

[98] Mansi, XVI, cols. 94 and 356.
[99] Niketas Paphlagon, *Life of the Patriarch Ignatius*, PG 105, col. 549. Basil made the bishops of the 879–80 council wait for many months before presiding over the session at which the acts were signed and promulgated. For Constantine's appearances to his father and the attempts at canonisation, see below, p. 202.
[100] *Life of St Basil the Younger*, ed. S. G. Vilinskij, *Žitie sv. Vasilija Novago, Zapiski imp. Novorossijskago Universiteta*, 7 (Odessa, 1911), pp. 284–5, 307; Liutprand, *Antapodosis*, I, 10; III, 33–4, ed. P. Chiesa, *Liudprandi Cremonensis Opera Omnia*, Corpus Christianorum, Continuatio Mediaevalis 156 (Turnhout, 1998), pp. 9–10, 83–4, where the apparition more logically precedes the construction of the church dedicated to St Michael. Whatever the sources say, the devotion of the Macedonians to St Michael was more than simply expiatory: see below, pp. 198–9.
[101] *Life of Euthymios the Patriarch*, 1, ed. Karlin-Hayter (n. 48), pp. 4–5; the Pseudo-Symeon (*Annales*, ed. Bekker (see ch. 1, n. 95), pp. 699–700) adds the name of Photios to that of Santabarenos.

in its turn, the form of an *exemplum*. It provoked 'eulogies', such as the *Life* written by Constantine VII, and epic narratives,[102] but also the more nuanced, though not necessarily hostile, portrait of a sovereign who, like so many others, reigned thanks to a crime of blood and died repentant. The image was based on accepted facts and was not inaccurate, but its value was primarily symbolic, and it was inspired less by historical reality than by the various myths and legends that subordinated the conquest of power to the elimination of a fellow emperor or rival, and consequently its legitimate exercise to a perpetual and impossible expiation – Romulus killing Remus or Constantine the Great eliminating the tetrarchs in order to reign alone.[103]

It was because Basil was in his way a founder that the shadow of Constantine loomed over him; and it was because Leo VI incarnated dynastic and religious legitimacy that his sin and his repentance were immediately and explicitly related to the *exemplum* of Theodosius.[104] Whatever the rumours regarding his birth,[105] and however reluctant his father had been to designate him as his successor after imprisoning him,[106] Leo was, almost to excess, an autocrat of perfect Christian legitimacy. He declared the law so that law and order would be restored, expounded tactical constitutions so that his armies would be again victorious, and wrote and delivered from the ambo of the churches of Constantinople homilies for the great festivals. He was convinced that, on any subject, the imperial word operated *per se*. He also believed that his power was sacred and that, as he wrote in the funeral oration for his father Basil, and as Justinian in his day had professed to believe, 'the *charismata* of kingship are not very far from those of priesthood', and that he was himself 'engaged to the Church', almost as strongly as his brother Stephen, appointed patriarch of Constantinople.[107] With him, there reappeared the notion of sacerdotal kingship, but in a context of orthodoxy and no longer in the wake of iconoclasm. The tonsure he received soon after his baptism conferred no sacred order;[108] but this could be misunderstood, and an Egyptian tradition made him a lector or

---

[102] G. Moravcsik, 'Sagen und Legenden über Kaiser Basileios I', *DOP*, 15 (1961), pp. 59–126; A. Markopoulos, 'An anonymous laudatory poem in honour of Basil I', *DOP*, 46 (1992), pp. 225–32.

[103] Dagron, *Naissance d'une capitale* (see ch. 2, n. 36), pp. 341–4; Dagron, *Constantinople imaginaire* (see ch. 1, n. 59), pp. 78–97.

[104] See, for example, Arethas, *Scripta minora*, ed. Westerink (n. 56), I, p. 17, l. 27, p. 138, ll. 1–4.

[105] Mango, 'Eudocia Ingerina, the Normans, and the Macedonian dynasty', *Zbornik Radova*, 14–15 (1973), pp. 17–27, for whom the doubts are well founded; a different interpretation in P. Karlin-Hayter, 'L'enjeu d'une rumeur. Opinion et imaginaire à Byzance au XIᵉ siècle', *JÖB*, 41 (1991), pp. 85–111.

[106] Flusin. 'Un fragment inédit?' (n. 82), pp. 128–9.

[107] *Funeral Oration of Basil I*, ed. and trans. Vogt and Hausherr (see ch. 1, n. 4), pp. 74–5. Justinian, *Novellae*, VII: 2, 1.

[108] *De cerimoniis*, II, 23, p. 622; see Dagron, 'Nés dans la pourpre' (see ch. 1, n. 56), pp. 121–2, 127–8.

deacon.[109] His Davidic priesthood gave him some right to regulate the Church, but it was known that he would always yield to the advice of the monks or the threats of the clergy. And it was this hieratic and inflexible sovereign, uncomfortable perhaps but recognised as more pious and 'wiser' than any other, who was to be a subject of scandal; he was accused of having abandoned himself to the lusts of the flesh and fallen into the most bestial debauchery, as a result of a fourth marriage that enabled him at last to legitimate a male heir,[110] The canonical problem of remarriage was not trivial, but it could be, and in this case, was, got round by an 'economy'. The problem did not justify the passions it aroused. For Leo VI, all the *topoi* of militant rhetoric and hagiography were unleashed; for him, the old dialectic of the legislator who should submit to the law was revived; a polemicist who got his dates wrong represents him slapping the face of the pious Niketas the Paphlagonian and 'lauding the beauty of women' in the hope of luring him away from monasticism.[111] The disproportion is obvious between the 'sin' and an 'affair' which looks like a formidable campaign designed to denounce the risks of sliding from legality into anomie, from the *basileia* into tyranny and from orthodoxy into heresy, and above all to establish a close link between sexuality and dynastic legitimacy.

This exaggeration was only possible because the sins were venial, because the target was less the emperor, who fell in with the process, than the imperial office, and because the 'Leo affair' was added to the 'Theodosius *exemplum*' with the same paradoxical result: a legitimacy contested when asserted by an act of sovereignty, but incontestable when it denied itself by an act of repentance. The repentance of Leo VI was sincere, certainly, but theatrical, and the penitence turned to apotheosis. The emperor used the same language as those who condemned him: 'Given that I committed the sin of tetragamy...', he wrote at the beginning of his last wishes, which restored Nicholas Mystikos to the patriarchate and accepted the condemnation of unions 'foreign to human nature'.[112] Poems were written soon after his death. One has Leo say: 'The tomb receives me, emperor without flesh. Put there this epitaph: Here lies Leo, who provoked more than any other man the wrath of God.' Another drew from the 'scandal' a sort of moral lesson:

Nature deferred the birth of a male child of a lawful union and a legal marriage. How profound are the judgements of God! Strange though it may seem, this was the will of providence on high. And it was in transgression of the law

[109] Eutychios of Alexandria (Sa'id ibn Batriq), trans. M. Canard, in A. A. Vasiliev, *Byzance et les Arabes*, II, 2 (Brussels, 1950), pp. 25–6; Al-Makin (Elmacinus), *Historia Saracenica*, Latin trans. by Thomas van Erpe, alias Erpenius (Lyon, 1625), p. 180.
[110] See, in particular, the letter from Nicholas Mystikos to Pope Anastasius III, Ep. 32, ed. and trans. R. J. H. Jenkins and K. G. Westerink, *Nicholas I, Patriarch of Constantinople, Letters* (Washington, 1973), pp. 228–33.
[111] Flusin, 'Un fragment inédit?' (n. 82).
[112] Oikonomides, 'La dernière volonté de Léon VI' (n. 82), pp. 48–9.

that the child was born. But the law, briefly suspended, has been enacted anew, and the decision has returned to the holy canon. The emperor washes himself clean of the stain in a flood of tears, and he attaches himself anew to his mother the Church.[113]

In sum, what Facundus of Hermiane said of Theodosius I could equally be said of Leo VI, 'the great emperor of happy memory, whose image lives indelibly in the memory of the Church', less as a result of his mighty deeds than of 'the humble and public penance he undertook for his errors, with courage and humility, having put aside all royal ostentation'.[114]

The mosaic in the narthex of St Sophia may well represent Leo VI, but it is the image of every Davidic emperor who wept for his lost legitimacy and recovered it only by renouncing the priesthood of Melchizedek, that of kings, and acknowledging to the priesthood of Aaron, that of the clergy, the privilege of binding and loosing. The fault of kings, which made them depend on the clergy, was not the ordinary sin of men; it was inherent in their power. A sexual offence for Leo VI, a crime of blood for Constantine, Theodosius I and Basil I, both for that perfect model which was David. This sin was judged exemplary only because it was recognised to be an inherent defect of the royal office, and all the more obvious when the guilty sovereign was just and pious. The empire was conquered and preserved by violence; it could be transmitted hereditarily only by a fleshly commerce which desacralised it. Power was absolute, did not allow itself to be confined within legal limits and was deemed sacred; but he who exercised it, whoever he might be, was never considered wholly innocent and might at any moment be convicted of illegitimacy. The Church was there to make him kneel, to bind him and to loose him. This is what the ceremonial of the 'festivals of the Lord' and the *exempla* associated with it recalled.

---

[113] I. Ševčenko, 'Poems on the deaths of Leo VI and Constantine VII in the Madrid manuscript of Scylitzes', *DOP*, 23–4 (1969–70), pp. 185–228 (the poems are pp. 197 and 202).

[114] Facundus Hermianensis, *Pro defensione Trium Capitulorum*, XII, 4–5, PL 67, cols. 849–50.

Part 2

The Emperors

4. *Constantine the Great: imperial sainthood*

The story of Constantine's baptism at Nicomedia [by a heretical bishop, and not at Rome by the pope] implies a quantity of slanders against a signal benefactor of the Church, a great age in Christian history, the Churches of Rome and of Constantinople and innumerable Catholic scholars and saints. It was probably concocted during an orgy of Valens's courtiers, more than forty years after Constantine's death. It had been forgotten by the dawn of the Middle Ages, but it was revived during the Protestant Reformation, from hatred of the miracle, of the divine supernatural and, above all, of Rome. It was then adopted by Jansenism and sceptical, materialistic and atheistic self-styled philosophy.

P. Philpin de Rivière,
Constantine the Great, his baptism and his Christian life[1]

CONSTANTINE, QUASI-BISHOP

When they approach the reign of Constantine, contemporary historians seem unable to avoid taking on the problematic of the first rhetoricians and historians of the Church. They differ from them only in tone and in a scepticism that sees itself as objectivity. The Christian emperor, they say, perhaps remained slightly pagan; if he refused to climb to the Capitol, he did, on the other hand, accept the title of *pontifex maximus* and have two temples built in his *Constantinopolis Christiana*; he believed as fervently in the *Sol invictus* (invincible Sun) as in the resurrected Christ. This watering down may go as far as outright attack, but it has to be shown by one means or another that the reign was a turning point and not just a link in a chain, that the empire became suddenly Christian, and that everything changed or began to change around 312 or 330. Constantine

---

[1] Paris, 1906; quoted by F. J. Dölger, 'Die Taufe Konstantins und ihre probleme', in *Konstantin der Grosse und seine Zeit, Gesammelte Studien. Festgabe zum Konstantins-Jubiläum 1913* ed. F. J. Dölger, Römische Quartalschrift, Supplement XIX (Freiburg im Breisgau, 1913), pp. 377–81; see p. 380, where Philipin should read Philpin.

has to be made an icon, even if the truth suffers in the attempt. To break out of this mind set, we have to stop scrutinising the conscience of the first Christian emperor and speculating about the sincerity or the depth of his faith; instead, we should turn our attention to such issues as the place he carved out for the new religion within the empire, the role he himself intended to play in it, the ways in which the history of his turbulent reign was gradually made exemplary, the ultimate assimilation of the Constantine 'phenomenon' into sainthood and the legitimacy which this sainthood of the founder guaranteed his successors, the 'new Constantines'.

Johannes Straub has said that the Church was not ready for an emperor like Constantine, that is, not ready to play an official role in a Christian empire; and he contrasted the state Christianity of Constantine with the more personal Christianity attributed by Eusebios and Orosius to the emperor Philip the Arab, supposed to have adhered to the Christian faith by a secret penance, who quietly avoided sacrificing to the gods of the Capitol for Rome's millennium but continued to perform the same imperial duties as before.[2] Constantine's desire to integrate Christianity into the empire caught the faithful unawares, accustomed as they were to their clandestine existence, and anxious, as the Gospel advised, to keep God and Caesar separate, even if Caesar supported their cause.

This opposition is seductive, if hardly convincing. It assumes from the outset the concept of a distinction between spiritual and temporal power which actually only later emerged as a way of limiting the influence of the emperor in doctrinal matters. Nor did it find a theoretician until a politically almost independent Roman papacy was made a centre of resistance to the empire of Constantinople. The legend of the secretly converted emperor, which persists in the historiography, was designed, on the contrary, to show that imperial Rome had been virtually Christian from the start and that the conversion of Constantine was not an absolute beginning but the moment when the schema of a temporal order planned from time immemorial and under way since Augustus emerged into the light of day. The legend of Philip the Arab, which is very old, derives from this desire to make the Christian age coincide with the beginning of the empire, and not with its Christianisation. There are many other legends, probably more recent, which tended in the same direction: that of Augustus, to whom

---

[2] J. A. Straub, 'Constantine as *koinos episkopos*. Tradition and innovation in the representation of the first Christian emperor's majesty', *DOP*, 21 (1967), pp. 37–55, especially p. 46. The legend of Philippus (Philip the Arab), successor of Gordian and predecessor of Decius, describes a Christian emperor very different from Constantine: Eusebios, *Hist. eccl.*, VI, 34: 'It is said that the emperor Philippus was a Christian and that on the day of the last Easter vigil, he wanted to take part with the crowd in the prayers said at the church'; as he was not baptised, the leader of the church imposed confession and penance, which Philip accepted, so demonstrating 'the sincerity and piety of his dispositions in what concerned the fear of God'; Orosius, *Histories against the Pagans*, VII, 20, 1–2, ed. and trans. M. P. Arnaud-Lindet (Paris, 1991), III, p. 55.

Pythia revealed that she had lost her prophetic power since the birth of a Hebrew child, and who then made haste to erect an altar to the *deus primogenitus*; that of Nero, admiring witness of St Peter's exploits before Simon the Magician, who had Pilate executed for having surrendered Jesus to the Jews; that of Vespasian and Titus, who fulfilled the prophesies of the Old Testament by destroying the Temple of Jerusalem; or that of Domitian, an admirer of St John, who had arrived in Rome from Patmos. In the sixth century, the chronicler Malalas brought together this body of pre-existing stories, inventing nothing.[3]

For the Church did not see itself as independent, but as victorious. From the moment when the conversion of Constantine made it official, it had a grand vision of the Christian empire and of a Christianity in the image of the empire, which Gregory of Nazianzus would later call 'royal priesthood' (*basileion hierateuma*), taking an expression from the First Epistle of Peter in order to reproach Julian the Apostate for having betrayed both the Christian faith and Rome itself.[4] But it remained to establish what precise position the Church was to occupy in the pre-existing structures of the empire and, even trickier, to define that of the emperor in the new ecclesiology. This was not done at one go, but gradually, by successive adjustments as problems emerged, in what was often a contradictory manner. To summarise in a few phrases dense volumes of debate, let us say simply that Constantine was expecting from the new religion what his predecessors had expected from the old (and what the Byzantine emperors continued to expect from the monks they supported): an advantage to himself and a contribution to the 'public good', the effective support of what the pious Leo VI was still calling, around 900, the *hieratike techne*, the liturgical 'technique' that was the business of the clergy, in effect assistance in war or peace on a par with that provided by the technical skills of engineers.[5] In 311, Galerius, Maximinus Daia and Constantine declared that the Christians

> by reason of the indulgence which [the emperors] show them, ought to pray to their God for our salvation, for that of the empire and for their own, in order that the integrity of the state should be restored everywhere and that they might live peacefully in their homes.[6]

A little later Constantine claimed to believe that if those whose 'function' was worship, and who were customarily called clergy, remained exempt from all public office so as not to be distracted from their service, 'a very great benefit for

---

[3] *Chronographia*, ed. Dindorf (see ch. 2, n. 107), pp. 231–2, 250–57, 260, 262.

[4] *Disc.* IV (*Against Julian I*), 35 and *Disc.* V (*Against Julian II*), 26, ed. and trans. J. Bernardi, SC 309 (Paris 1983), pp. 134–5, 344–5. The expression is taken from I Peter, 2: 9, where it is used for the Christians as a body; for the different exegeses, see below, pp. 239–40.

[5] *Tactica, epilogus*, 53 and 62, PG 107, cols. 1088, 1089.

[6] Lactantius, *De mortibus persecutorum*, XXXIV, 5, ed. and trans. J. Moreau, SC 39 (Paris, 1954), p. 118.

public affairs will ensue'.[7] This was the beginning of the special personal and fiscal status of the clergy,[8] and it explains why it was the duty of the emperor to intervene in a Church whose unity and stability mattered to the empire. Worship and the faith being an affair of state, the Donatist crisis and its consequences were sorted out 'in the Roman manner', by bishops to whom the emperor delegated the powers of *iudices*,[9] or by councils which the emperor summoned and which he might attend, but at which he did not vote, just as he summoned the senate and might attend its meetings without taking part in the voting.[10] This was the logic of Constantine; it was also that of the Church, as long as 'orthodoxy' and the emperor were on the same side.

It is much more difficult to discern how the Church itself defined the religious role of a sovereign who was for centuries described as 'divine', who was recognised as divine by the ceremonial of prostration and adoration, and who was, according to the Hellenistic ideology adapted by Rome, God's representative on earth, deriving his legitimacy directly from Him.[11] Until the time of Gratian he continued to bear the pagan title of *pontifex maximus*, inseparable from the Roman *basileia*, said Zosimus, since Numa Pompilius.[12] The Christianisation of the formulary and laudatory themes posed no insuperable problems. Such recycling was possible, at the cost of some fairly crude patching, even if the joins sometimes showed. As, for example, in the soldiers' oath reported by Vegetius (late fourth century):

> They swore by God, by Christ, by the Holy Spirit and by the majesty of the emperor who, immediately after God, ought to be venerated and adored by the human race. Because once he has received the name of augustus,

---

[7] Eusebios, *Hist. eccl.* X, 7 (letter from Constantine ordering that the clergy should be exempt from all public office); see also Eusebios, *Vita Constantini*, III, 21, 4; IV, 14, 2 ed. F. Winkelmann, pp. 94, 125 (*Life of Constantine*, Cameron and Hall (see ch. 3, n. 31), pp. 131, 158).

[8] See C. Dupont, 'Les privilèges des clercs sous Constantin', *Revue d'histoire ecclésiastique*, 62 (1967), pp. 729–52; F. Vittinghoff, 'Staat, Kirche und Dynastie beim Tode Konstantins', in *L'Eglise et l'empire au IV* siècle*, Fondation Hardt, Entretiens 34 (Geneva, 1989), pp. 1–34, especially pp. 14–15. For the forms of choice and ordination of bishops, see J. Straub, 'Zur Ordination von Bischöfen und Beamten in der christlichen Spätantike', in *Mullus, Festschrift Theodor Klauser*, *JAC*, Ergänzungsband 1 (Münster, 1964), pp. 336–45.

[9] See, for example, the letter addressed by Constantine to the vicar of Africa Aelafius in 313/14, published in the works of Optatus, ed. C. Ziwsa, *S. Optati Milevitani Libri VII*, CSEL 26 (Vienna, 1893), appendix 3, pp. 204ff.

[10] See F. Dvornik, 'Emperors, popes and general councils', *DOP*, 6 (1951), pp. 1–23; K. M. Girardet, 'Kaiser Konstantin der Grosse als Vorsitzender von Konzilien', in *Costantino il Grande dall'antichità all'umanesimo*, ed. G. Bonamente and F. Fusco, I (Macerata, 1992), pp. 445–9.

[11] See F. Dvornik, *Early Christian and Byzantine Political Philosophy: Origins and Background*, I–II (Washington, 1966).

[12] *Hist.*, IV, 36, ed. and trans. Paschoud (see ch. 3, n. 95) for Gratian's renunciation of the title. For the date, see below, p. 183 and n. 76; for the title, see G. Rösch, *Onoma basileias. Studien zum offiziellen Gebrauch der Kaisertitel in spätantiker und frühbyzantinischer Zeit* (Vienna, 1978), pp. 30–1, 85–8.

loyal devotion and unwavering submission are owed to the emperor, as to a physically present god (*tanquam praesenti et corporali deo*). In fact, it is God whom a civilian or a soldier serves when he faithfully cherishes he who reigns at God's instigation.[13]

It was usually necessary to resort to a subtler rhetoric to define the emperor's role in the Church, a rhetoric of 'as if' which does not always make it clear whether the Christian writers of the fourth century were producing an original ideology or revising the imperial ideology when they so clearly went beyond what was acceptable to Christianity in lauding the emperor.

This is the case with Eusebios. Difficult though it may be, we need to distinguish in his case between the thinker and the rhetorician, between the author of a 'political theology' which would give birth to 'caesaropapism' and the counsellor to the prince who offered advice when appropriate and criticism in the form of eulogy, at a period when nothing – neither New Rome, nor the Christianisation of the empire, nor Christian orthodoxy – was definitively settled.

As a theoretician, Eusebios had to respond to the massive problem of a Roman *universalitas* which had previously been political and was now religious. He devised a theological structure in which the supreme God was creator of the world, and where the Logos, His son, necessary mediator between divine unity and the multiplicity of creation, introduced into the world the principles of reason and order which saved it from anarchy. In exact parallel, the emperor who had been converted to Christ's doctrine was also an intermediary. Inspired by the true philosophy and *mimesis*, he modelled himself in the image of celestial kingship and was delegated by the Logos to govern humans, with a duty to save them from the proliferating cults by the eradication of paganism and from the discord of ethnic groups by uniting all the peoples of the world.[14] In this, Eusebios was not wholly original. He found the slogan he Christianised – one sole God, one sole emperor – in Hellenistic treatises on kingship and in ideas

[13] Flavius Vegetius Renatus, *Epitoma rei militaris*, II, 5, ed. A. Önnerfors (Stuttgart/Leipzig, 1995), p. 61.
[14] Of the many works on Eusebios and Constantine, I will quote only N. H. Baynes, *Constantine the Great and the Christian Church* (Oxford, 1929, repr. 1972); E. Peterson, *Der Monotheismus als politisches Problem* (Leipzig, 1935); R. Farina, *L'Impero e l'imperatore cristiano in Eusebio di Cesarea. La prima teologia politica del cristianesimo* (Zurich, 1966); Straub, 'Constantine as *koinos episkopos*'(n. 2); S. Calderone, 'Teologia politica, successione dinastica e consecratio in età costantiniana', in *Le Culte des souverains dans l'Empire romain*, Fondation Hardt, Entretiens 19 (Geneva, 1972), pp. 213–69; S. Calderone, 'Il pensiero politico di Eusebio di Cesarea,' in *I cristiani e l'impero nel IV secolo*, ed. G. Bonamente and A. Nestori (Macerata, 1988) pp. 45–61; J.-M. Sansterre, 'Eusèbe de Césarée et la naissance de la théorie "césaropapiste"', *Byz.*, 42 (1972), pp. 131–95, 532–94. For relations between Constantine and Eusebios: T. D. Barnes, *Constantine and Eusebius* (Cambridge, Mass., 1981), which accepts the argument that caesaropapism was linked to the Arian heresy; see also F. Heim, *La Théologie de la victoire de Constantin à Théodose* (Paris, 1992), especially pp. 57–92.

then in the air. But he was one of the first to have made the Logos of God
in his organising role central to his speculations, and to have constructed a
veritable 'political theology' not only on the correspondence between a unique
divine royalty and a unique human kingship, extended to the furthest limits of
earth, but also on a synchronism between the appearance of the Logos and the
establishment of the monarchy of Augustus. Admittedly, Eusebios presented
Constantine as the emperor chosen by God to reveal to the world the power
of the cross, but within a 'divine economy' in which the empire was already
the providential instrument of salvation. At one stroke, this political theology
imposed an unrivalled new coherence on all the various ideas which together
composed the oecumenicity of imperial power; but it gave Christian *Romanitas*,
at the cost of some obvious distortion, the same degree of political and religious
integration as Judaism and, more generally, as the civilisations in which religious
revelation and state organisation were merged. While we must recognise that
this fundamentalism represented a temptation for Byzantium, it is only fair
to note that it was resisted. Byzantium never adopted this ideology, however
simple and effective, in which the Logos remained an abstract notion, and was
not in any case quite Christ incarnate, in which only minimal space was left for
the Church between God and the emperor, and in which the rupture between
the time of Law and the time of Grace was insufficiently clear. This model of
Christian fundamentalism was no sooner sketched out than it was recognised
as impossible to follow through.

But the panegyrics in which Eusebios articulated these ideas can also be
read as exercises in rhetoric, intended to flatter the sovereign and make him
more susceptible to influence. In the discourse of the *Tricennalia* and *Life of
Constantine*, as in any set language, the nuances of the formulation may have
been more important than the overt themes, especially when it moved from
accepted truths, such as that of the sovereign 'imitator of Christ', to more
controversial issues, such as the imperial priesthood. This was a subject that
had to be tackled with great caution. Like Christ, wrote Eusebios, the emperor
is the priest of a pure and spotless sacrifice; he has learned to offer a sacrifice
without either fire or blood and no longer to sacrifice according to the ancient
rites, so God is delighted with the victim and admires the 'hierophant'.[15] The
comparison and the choice of words make it clear that the sacrifice of the
emperor-priest was only metaphorical, that the emperor 'sacrificed himself'
for the good of humanity, and that his priesthood, in any case, like that of

---

[15] *Tricennalia*, 2–3, ed. Heikel, p. 200. The *Triakontaeterikos logos* was probably spoken in Constantinople on 25 July 336, during the deferred festival for the *Tricennalia* of Constantine; to this
panegyric was added at an early date another *Basilikos logos*, spoken by Eusebios at Jerusalem
in 335/6. See T. D. Barnes, 'Two speeches by Eusebius', *GRBS*, 18 (1977), pp. 341–5; P. Maraval, *Eusèbe de Césarée. La théologie politique de L'Empire chrétien. Louanges de Constantin*
(Paris, 2001).

Christ, was not institutional.[16] Similarly, Constantine built his palace *as if* it was to be a church;[17] he withdrew every day to pray *as if* he was 'participating in sacred mysteries',[18] which implied only Constantine's presence at the mass, real or desired by Eusebios. This hierophant emperor had all sorts of revelations: 'You could, if you wished, mention hundreds of occasions when your Saviour appeared to you, hundreds of occasions when he was present in your dreams';[19] he had also received a 'science of God' which qualified him to be 'a sort of interpreter of the divine Logos' or of 'God the universal King',[20] at all events an expert in piety for the 'soldiers' and pagans. This was a way of confirming the miraculous nature of the imperial conversion and of the emperor's magisterium, while restricting the latter to government servants and pagans, who might be brought to the threshold of the Church by his decrees or his wars.

This is the context in which appear the expressions 'universal bishop' and 'bishop over those outside', found in passages in the *Life of Constantine* so famous that they must be quoted. Constantine 'was all things to all people (*koinos pros hapantas en*)', it says,

> But to the Church of God he paid particular personal attention. When some were at variance with each other in various places, like a universal bishop (*hoia tis koinos episkopos*) appointed by God he convoked councils of the ministers of God. He did not disdain to be present and attend during their proceedings, and he participated in the subjects reviewed (*koinonos ton episkopoumenon egineto*), by arbitration promoting the peace of God among all; and he took his seat among them as if he were one voice among many, dismissing his praetorians and soldiers and bodyguards of every kind, clad only in the fear of God and surrounded by the most loyal of his faithful companions. Then such as he saw able to be prevailed upon by argument and adopting a calm and conciliatory attitude, he commended most warmly, showing how he favoured general unanimity (*he koine panton homonoia*), but the obstinate he rejected.[21]

The expression 'universal bishop' was not only signalled as metaphorical by a *like*, but emptied of its institutional sense by a rhetorical play on the words *koinos*, *koinonos*, *koine homonoia*, and above all *episkopos*, *episkopein*, which devalued its meaning. For an emperor who believed himself *pontifex maximus* of Christianity it could hardly be stated more clearly that he was not really a

---

[16] See K. M. Girardet, 'Das christliche Priestertum Konstantins d. Gr.', *Chiron*, 10 (1980), pp. 569–92.

[17] *Vita Constantini*, IV, 17, ed. Winkelmann, p. 126 (*Life of Constantine*, Cameron and Hall (see ch. 3, n. 31), p. 159).

[18] Ibid., IV, 22, 1, ed. Winkelmann, p. 128 (*Life of Constantine*, Cameron and Hall (see ch. 3, n. 31), p. 160).

[19] *Tricennalia*, 18, ed. Heikel, p. 259.   [20] Ibid., 2 and 10, pp. 199, 222.

[21] *Vita Constantini*, I, 44, ed. Winkelmann, pp. 38–9 (*Life of Constantine*, Cameron and Hall (see ch. 3, n. 31), pp. 85–6).

bishop, and that, if he 'participated in the subjects reviewed' by the authentic bishops, it had to be by renouncing the military aspect of his power and by supporting the majority opinion. In a Christianity that had become the religion of the empire, this was to define a minimal role for the emperor. Later in the same *Life* we find the emperor receiving the bishops and telling them that he, too, was a bishop: 'You are bishops of those within the Church (*ton eiso tes ekklesias*), but I am perhaps a bishop appointed by God over those outside (*ton ektos*).' This was a neat formula, which Eusebios proceeded to interpret by adding that, in effect, 'he exercised a bishop's supervision (*epeskopei*) over all his subjects and pressed them all, as far as lay in his power, to lead the godly life'.[22] Once again, after the watering down of a conditional, the use of the verb *episkopein* (supervise, watch over) after *episkopos* (bishop) had the effect of making the words commonplace and defusing their charge; Constantine was using a significant and pleasing comparison to explain that it was the emperor's duty to watch over the citizens of the empire and, more particularly perhaps, to lead non-Christians to Christianity. The Byzantine emperors never ceased to pride themselves on this missionary duty within the empire and outside it, extending it sometimes as far as a form of *didaskalia*.[23]

It is by no means easy to tell from these panegyrics what Eusebios himself believed, even less to see how his beliefs fitted in with those of Constantine himself. Was the emperor being defined as the bishop of those who would, thanks to him, become Christians? Or as the bishop of the laity as opposed to the clergy? Or as he to whom the bishops gave responsibility for enforcing their decisions throughout the empire?[24] The very idea of a Christian empire was of necessity accompanied by a political theology and so led to an acceptance that the emperor had a divine mission and a sort of priesthood. But the connection between this royal priesthood and the institutional Church was and must always remain problematic. This fault line was quick to emerge and could only be concealed by the 'as if' of rhetoric or, as we will see, by the exegesis of a few scriptural models (Melchizedek, Moses and David). The phenomenon was not confined to the East. Almost contemporary with Eusebios, the western author of the *Quaestiones Veteris et Novi Testamenti* declared that the Christian emperor carried within him *Dei imaginem, sicut et episcopus Christi*;[25] and in the twelfth century Theodore Balsamon defended very similar formulae in the light

---

[22] Ibid., IV, 24, ed., Winkelmann, p. 128 (*Life of Constantine*, Cameron and Hall (see ch. 3, n. 31), p. 161).

[23] See below, pp. 265–6.

[24] R. Farina (*L'Impero e l'imperatore* (n. 14), pp. 312–19) is right to argue that *hoi ektos* cannot here mean 'the non-Christians' and to prefer *ta ektos* in the sense of 'matters external to the Church'; J. Straub and S. Calderone think rather in terms of a Church/state or clergy/non-clergy opposition.

[25] Pseudo-Augustin, *Quaestiones Veteris et Novi Testamenti CXXVII*, 35 and 91, 8, ed. A. Souter, CSEL (Vienna, 1908), pp. 63, 157.

of canon law.[26] The problem was central and probably insoluble. But one thing is clear: in opening the door to a conception of the emperor as *quasi-bishop*, Eusebios was closing it to a more radical conception which contemporaries attributed to Constantius II, son and successor of Constantine, that of the emperor *bishop of the bishops* (*episcopus episcoporum*).[27] It was Constantius who was on the throne when the *Life of Constantine* was written, soon after May 337, and we may suspect that the rhetoric of Eusebios was specifically intended to detach the new sovereign from 'caesaropapism' by systematically locating imperial priesthood within the Christian empire, certainly, but outside the Church, and by treating it as a metaphor.

CONSTANTINE 'EQUAL OF THE APOSTLES'

Our best hope of understanding the Christianity of Constantine and the way it was corrected in the writings of Eusebios is to study the texts describing the death of the first Christian emperor and his burial in the mausoleum of the Holy Apostles, which he himself had built. Coming to the end of his hero's life, Eusebios, aware of how much was at stake, knew that his account of Constantine's last days must assure the emperor of a reputation for sanctity and that his account of the funeral – the first of a Christian emperor – must establish the idea of a new ceremonial and of new relations between emperors and death and, more generally, between the imperial power and Christianity. He devoted a long and careful passage to this delicate subject, giving, in a sense, the official church version.[28]

The emperor felt the first onset of illness after passing the Easter of 337 in asceticism and fervour. From Constantinople, he went to bathe in the Hot Springs, then to Helenopolis, where he prayed in the sanctuary of the martyrs, before, sensing that death was near, being carried to a suburb of Nicomedia. There, he summoned the bishops and explained to them that it was time for him to receive baptism; he would have liked to be baptised in the waters of the Jordan, like Christ, but God – 'who knows what is good for us' – had decided otherwise. When he had been 'filled with divine light' and had received 'the seal that brings immortality', he retained his white garments and rejected the

[26] See below, pp. 259–67.
[27] Lucifer of Cagliari, *Moriendum esse pro Dei Filio*, 13, ed. G. Diercks, Corpus Christianorum, Series Latina 8 (1978), p. 293; F. Winkelmann, 'Die Beurteilung des Eusebius von Caesarea und seiner *Vita Constantini* im grieschichen Ost', in *Byzantinische Beiträge*, ed. J. Irmscher (Berlin, 1964); K. M. Girardet, 'Kaiser Konstantius II. als "episcopus episcoporum" und das Herrscherbild des kirchlichen Widerstandes', *Historia*, 26 (1977), pp. 95–128; G. Bonamente, 'La "svolta constantiniana"', in *Cristianesimo e istituzioni politiche di Augusto a Costantino*, ed. E. Dal Covolo and R. Uglione (Rome, 1995), pp. 91–116.
[28] *Vita Constantini*, IV, 61–75, ed. Winkelmann, pp. 145–51 (*Life of Constantine*, Cameron and Hall (see ch. 3, n. 31), pp. 177–82).

purple robe, in order to preserve until his death the purity and the cleansing of sins symbolised by the baptismal robe. That baptism should here take the form of a pre-funerary ritual, like later the assumption of a monastic habit, which had the same effect, was not unusual at this period. On the day of Pentecost, around noon, Constantine died, and Eusebios is careful to say, as if to cut short any speculation, that he bequeathed his body to mortals and united his soul to God.[29] The ceremonial then began; there were scenes of lamentation, the mortal remains were carried in convoy to Constantinople, the body, crowned and in imperial robes, was displayed on a high catafalque in the most splendid room in the palace – in fact with all the normal honours due to an emperor. But there was a political element, too – the fear or the reality of a conspiracy among the collateral branches of the family (Philostorgios goes as far as to say that Constantine had been poisoned by 'his brothers')[30] and the desire of the army not to be too hasty in declaring the empire vacant, so as to avert an attack and to await the arrival of the emperor's sons, all absent from Constantinople (in particular of Constantius II, who was warned that he should return with all speed from the east).[31] The funeral ritual reflected these preoccupations, but the practices adopted present some analogies with the funerals of Augustus,[32] Pertinax[33] and Severus[34] as they are described by ancient historians. A wax effigy was laid on top of or substituted for the body of the deceased, treated for a while as the living emperor, then burned at the time of the *consecratio*, that is, of the ascension of the *divus imperator* in the form of an eagle opportunely released.[35]

Over and above the political calculation, there was perhaps also, in the case of the first Christian emperor, an understandable uncertainty about how to adapt the traditional rituals to the requirements of the new faith. The *Life of Constantine* says that all the army commanders, the *comites* and the officers, who had previously prostrated themselves before the emperor, behaved as before. They were present round the coffin at set times, knelt and kissed the emperor after his death, 'as when he was alive', followed by the senators, dignitaries and representatives of the people. These scenes continued 'for a long time', perhaps for the three months intervening between the death of the emperor, on 22 May,

---

[29] Ibid., IV, 64, 2 (*Life of Constantine*, Cameron and Hall (see ch. 3, n. 31), pp. 178–9).

[30] *Church History*, II, 16–17, ed. J. Bidez (Berlin, 1981), pp. 26–8.

[31] See R. Klein, 'Die Kämpfe um die Nachfolge nach dem Tode Constantins des Grossen'. *ByzForsch.*, 6 (1979), pp. 101–50.

[32] Cassius Dio, *Roman History*, LVI, 31–42, ed. H. B. Foster, trans. E. Cary, Loeb Classical Library (London/Cambridge, 1924), VII, pp. 68–99.

[33] Ibid., LXXIV, 13; ibid., IX, pp. 146–7.

[34] Herodian, *History of the Roman Emperors*, IV, 2, ed. K. Stavenhagen (Leipzig/Berlin, 1922), pp. 109–10.

[35] For pagan imperial funerals, see, in particular, J. M. C. Toynbee, *Death and Burial in the Roman World* (London, 1971), pp. 56–61; J.-C. Richard, 'Recherches sur certains aspects du culte impérial: les funérailles des empereurs romains aux deux premiers siècles de notre ère', *Aufstieg und Niedergang der römischen Welt*, II, 16, 2 (1978), pp. 1121–34; J. Arce, *Funus imperatorum. Los funerales de los imperadores romanos* (Madrid, 1988).

and the official recognition by the Roman senate, on 9 September, of Constantine's three sons as augusti.[36] There were, as we have said, political reasons, but probably also religious implications. We sense this from the clumsy emphasis in Eusebios:

Alone of mortals, the Blessed One reigned even after death, and the customs were maintained just as if he were alive, God having granted this to him and no other since time began. Alone therefore among Emperors and unlike any other he had honoured by acts of every kind the all-sovereign God and his Christ, and it is right that he alone enjoyed these things, as the God over all allowed his mortal remains to reign among mankind, thus demonstrating the ageless and deathless reign of his soul to those with minds not stony-hard.[37]

The pagan imperial funerals had been preparing a subdued or ritualised 'deification' of the emperor by engaging in this sort of *pompa triumphalis*, and it is indeed the traditional iconography of the apotheosis that Eusebios evokes when he tells us that the people and senate of Rome dedicated to Constantine an image which portrayed him seated above the heavenly vault, a theme known in the third century as that of the *Aeternitas Augusti* and of the emperor *cosmocrator*;[38] similarly, he describes a coin type chosen by Constantius II – of which many examples survive – which bore on the obverse the veiled effigy of the dead emperor and on the reverse the image of the same emperor driving a quadriga up to heaven, from which the hand of God emerges to receive him.[39] Eusebios was careful not to dwell on the pagan origins of these representations, but one senses that Christianisation, making the notion of immortality respectable again, allowed the classical image of the imperial *consecratio*, although it had been abandoned for some eighty years, to be re-employed with a different meaning.[40] Images are slower to be invented than ideas.

[36] Klein, 'Die Kämpfe um die Nachfolge' (n. 31), pp. 104–5; on 2 August 337, the empire was still being administered in the name of the dead emperor: *CTh.*, XIII, 4, 2.
[37] *Vita Constantini*, IV, 67, ed. Winkelmann, p. 148 (*Life of Constantine*, Cameron and Hall (see ch. 3, n. 31), p. 180).
[38] Ibid., 69, 2, ed. Winkelmann, p. 149 (*Life of Constantine*, Cameron and Hall (see ch. 3, n. 31), pp. 180–1).
[39] Ibid., 73, ed. Winkelmann, p. 150, (*Life of Constantine*, Cameron and Hall (see ch. 3, n. 31), p. 182). For this coinage, see J. P. C. Kent, *The Roman Imperial Coinage*, VIII: *The Family of Constantine I, AD 337–364* (London, 1981), pp. 446–7, 449, and plates 1 (no. 44) and 21 (1P); C. Foss, *Roman Historical Coins* (London, 1990), p. 293 (no. 33 (a) and (b)). P. Bruun has suggested that the Christianisation of the theme of the *consecratio* was achieved via the ascension of Elijah ('The consecration coins of Constantine the Great', *Arctos*, NS 1 (1954), but, in Christian iconography, Elijah rising to heaven on his solar chariot always lets his cloak fall to earth for Elisha. In the case of Constantine's *consecratio*, there are no grounds for assuming this intermediary.
[40] For the imagery of the *consecratio*, see MacCormack, *Art and Ceremony* (see ch. 2, n. 31), pp. 93–158, who shows why the iconography of the *consecratio* lost its appeal in the third century and above all under the tetrarchy, once the emperors regarded themselves as directly chosen by God and 'divine' from their accession, and once the notion of capital, and hence of senatorial representation, disappeared. E. Bickerman has shown that the 'imperial cult' was

What the rhetoric of Eusebios is endeavouring to gloss over is probably less a conflict or a contamination between paganism and Christianity than the tentative preparation of what it is tempting to call an imperial Christian apotheosis. The burial of a *basileus* was unlike any other and did not fit easily into the ordinary Christian rules, because it called into question the *basileia* itself. When, between 1422 and 1610, the kings of France reverted to the funerary practices which substituted an effigy of the dead king and so prolonged his reign, it was for the same reason: to assure the transmission, without interruption or overlap, of a unique dignity which itself 'never died'.[41] That the theoreticians of French kingship invoked the ancient precedent and the example of Constantine,[42] and that they assumed, wrongly, a direct link, shows only that in a ceremonial of this type religion counts for less than politics.

A similar hesitation can be detected in Constantine's project for the Holy Apostles as it is described by Eusebios, once again an invaluable witness since he knew nothing of the rebuilding that completely transformed the initial programme between 356 and 370 (he died in 339).[43]

never institutionalised or extended to the whole of the empire. By the *consecratio*, a particular emperor was considered *divus* and included among the divinities of Rome, but the *declaratio* of the senate was not essential: '*Consecratio*' in *Le Culte des souverains* (n. 14), pp. 1–37.

[41] R. Giesy, *The Royal Funeral Ceremony in Renaissance France* (Geneva, 1960). For the funeral rituals of the Byzantine emperors, see P. Karlin-Hayter, 'L'adieu à l'empereur', *Byz.*, 61 (1991) (Mélanges Maurice Leroy), pp. 112–55.

[42] See the description of the funeral of Francis I by Jean du Tillet, clerk to Parlement (1547): Giesy, *Funeral Ceremony* (n. 41), pp. 224–5.

[43] Of an abundant bibliography, note in particular A. Heisenberg, *Grabeskirche und Apostelkirche*, 2 (Leipzig, 1908), which develops the idea of an architectural parallel between the Holy Sepulchre in Jerusalem (basilica and rotunda of the Anastasis) and the Holy Apostles of Constantinople (circular church and mausoleum); A. Baumstark, 'Konstantiniana aus syrischer Kunst und Liturgie', in *Konstantin der Grosse* (n. 1), pp. 248–54, who was the first to ask whether the theme of Constantine 'thirteenth apostle' might conceal a comparison with St Paul; O. Weinreich, *Triskaidekadische Studien. Beiträge zur Geschichte der Zahlen*, Religionsgeschichtliche Versuche und Vorarbeiten 16, 1 (Giessen, 1916), pp. 3ff, who develops the theme of Constantine 'thirteenth god'; A. Kaniuth, *Die Beisetzung Konstantins des Grossen. Untersuchungen zur religiösen Haltung des Kaisers* (Breslau, 1941); A. Grabar, *Martyrium. Recherches sur le culte des reliques et l'art chrétien antique*, I (Paris, 1946), especially pp. 227–44, who relates Constantine's foundation to the tradition of imperial mausoleums founded in the 'heart' of the city; G. Downey, 'The builder of the original Church of the Apostles at Constantinople: a contribution to the criticism of the *Vita Constantini* attributed to Eusebius', *DOP*, 6 (1951), pp. 51–80, who rightly defends the thesis that the basilica of the Holy Apostles was constructed by Constantius II and not by Constantine himself, but unjustifiably criticises the authenticity of the *Vita Constantini*; R. Krautheimer, 'Zu Konstantins Apostelkirche in Konstantinopel', in *Mullus, Festschrift Theodor Klauser* (n. 8), pp. 224–9, who sees Constantine as the founder of the church of the Holy Apostles and Constantius II as responsible for a rebuilding following the construction of the mausoleum; Dagron, *Naissance d'une capitale* (see ch. 2, n. 36), pp. 401–9, where some aspects of the architectural interpretation need correction in the light of the work of Cyril Mango; P. Stockmeier, 'Herrscherfrömmigkeit und Totenkult. Konstantins Apostelkirche und Antiochos' Hierothesion', in *Pietas. Festschrift B. Kötting*, ed. E. Dassmann and K. Suso Frank, *JAC*, Ergänzungsband 8 (Münster, 1980), pp. 105–13, who examines Constantine's religious

The emperor, wrote the panegyrist,[44] had set out to build in memory of Christ's apostles a church of 'unimaginable height', adorned internally with a facing of polychrome marble extending right up to a gilded coffered ceiling, and with a roof not of tiles but of bronze plaques. The roof was surrounded by a circular balustrade, also of bronze, with every sort of gleaming gilding. This rotunda was situated in the middle of a vast rectangular square, bordered by four porticoes, along which were rooms reserved for the emperors,[45] baths, other rooms for various purposes and houses for the custodians. The 'church' so described bears a strong resemblance, as Cyril Mango has observed,[46] to an imperial mausoleum of the age of the Tetrarchy, such as those of Diocletian at Split, of Galerius at Thessalonike and of Maxentius on the Via Appia. But Eusebios feigns surprise.[47] Constantine, he goes on, had consecrated the whole of this building to the Saviour's apostles, but he had had something else in mind, a scheme which at first remained hidden and emerged only as the building progressed. He intended to be buried in this building, to place his tomb in the central niche, in the middle of the *thekai* of the twelve apostles (burial sites, 'cenotaphs' or simply commemorative plaques?), hoping, in his exceptional zeal for the faith, that his mortal remains would in this way 'partake in the invocation of the Apostles' and that his soul would benefit from the prayers that would be addressed to them and from the liturgical services that would be celebrated on the altar placed in the centre of the church.

Constantine's Holy Apostles was, therefore, an attempt to reconcile an imperial cult and a Christian cult, at the price of a double anomaly that all the skill of Eusebios cannot quite conceal. An imperial mausoleum was not a church, and the burial of an emperor in the middle of the apostles, precisely where one would expect Christ, was incongruous. If Christian opinion, that of the clergy in particular, was not up in arms, it is difficult to understand why Constantius II, not long after, proceeded to redevelop the site by building a true church, with

intentions; C. Mango, 'Constantine's mausoleum and the translation of relics', *BZ*, 83 (1990), pp. 51–61, who establishes by a new analysis of the sources that the circular mausoleum really is the work of Constantine, whereas the cruciform church of the Holy Apostles is part of the rebuilding ordered by Constantius II with a store for relics; R. Leeb, *Konstantin und Christus. Die Verchristlichung der imperialen Repräsentation unter Konstantin dem Grossen als Spiegel seiner Kirchenpolitik und seines Selbstverständnisses als christlicher Kaiser* (Berlin, 1992), especially pp. 93–120, who reverts to the conclusions of R. Krautheimer, wrongly rejecting Mango's interpretation.
[44] Eusebios, *Vita Constantini*, IV, 58–60; 71 (*Life of Constantine*, Cameron and Hall (see ch. 3, n. 31), pp. 176–7, 181).
[45] This is the interpretation of Grabar (*Martyrium* (n. 43), p. 229) and Mango ('Constantine's mausoleum' (n. 43)). Krautheimer ('Zu Konstantins Apostelkirche' (n. 43), p. 225 and n. 6) believes it implies 'basilicas', that is, the four naves of a cruciform church.
[46] 'Constantine's mausoleum' (n. 43).
[47] *Vita Constantini*, IV, 60, 2; 71, 2 (*Life of Constantine*, Cameron and Hall (see ch. 3, n. 31), pp. 176, 181).

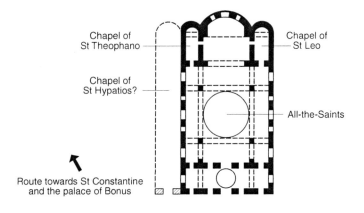

Chapel of St Theophano

Chapel of St Leo

Chapel of St Hypatios?

All-the-Saints

Route towards St Constantine and the palace of Bonus

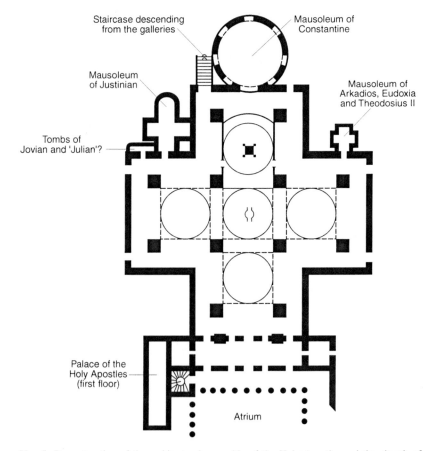

Staircase descending from the galleries

Mausoleum of Constantine

Mausoleum of Justinian

Mausoleum of Arkadios, Eudoxia and Theodosius II

Tombs of Jovian and 'Julian'?

Palace of the Holy Apostles (first floor)

Atrium

Plan 5. Reconstruction of the architectural ensemble of the Holy Apostles and the church of All-the-Saints at the time of Constantine Porphyrogenitus a cruciform plan, consecrated to the cult of the apostles alone, and with a reliquary, the original mausoleum becoming simply a funerary annex (see plan 5).[48] Had Constantine wanted to become a 'thirteenth god' on the Hellenistic or Roman model?[49] This supposes that the first Christian emperor had revived the pagan *consecratio* and apotheosis by giving them greater significance than they had ever possessed in pagan times. Is it all to be explained by *mimesis*,[50] by an 'imitation' of Christ, the model to whom the emperor looked for survival and resurrection, going so far as to envisage baptism in the Jordan and perhaps conceiving his Constantinople mausoleum on the pattern of the *Anastasis* in Jerusalem? If he was not aiming at deification or equivalence with Christ by *mimesis*, Constantine was at least seeking immortality, the immortality of an emperor, that which was assured by liturgical commemoration, the *mneme* which Eusebios emphasised in order to justify the apostolic connection. He was proposing a commemorative ritual associating the dead emperor with the constantly renewed memory of the apostles,[51] which explains his desire to have mass said on the very spot of his burial. It was usual for a hippodrome to be constructed close to the imperial mausoleums of pagan Rome, as if the ritual of the races, reproducing the natural and cosmic cycle of death and rebirth, could assure the dead sovereign perpetual survival. By attributing the same virtue to the Christian liturgy, Constantine showed that he had understood its meaning and that he intended, in the words of the *Life of Constantine*, 'to benefit from it'. He revealed, in short, that he had become a Christian, but that he intended to remain an emperor and that he still took his inspiration from the old models predating Christianity.

Whatever his true intentions, Constantine seems to have blundered. Eusebios is clearly aware of this, but just as he disguises as Christian novelties the fiction of a dead emperor honoured 'as if he was still alive' and the issue of the consecration coinage, he chooses to interpret as a sign of deep faith and an identification with the apostles what others denounced as an offence or a scandal.[52] So, in an attempt at mitigation, the theme of the emperor 'equal of the apostles', which developed in the fifth century and belongs to what I have called the rhetoric of 'as if', was launched.

This theme was felt to be dubious and was revived only with the utmost caution. The word *isapostolos* quite naturally described St Paul, converted and

---

[48] This is the most convincing hypothesis, put forward by Cyril Mango. The other fourth- and fifth-century sources, if they do not always corroborate this interpretation, never actually contradict it, contrary to the claims of R. Leeb (*Konstantin und Christus* (n. 43)).

[49] Weinreich, *Triskaidekadische Studien* and Kaniuth, *Die Beisetzung Konstantins des Grossen* (n. 43).

[50] As argued, in particular, by R. Leeb (*Konstantin und Christus* (n. 43)).

[51] Stockmeier, 'Herrscherfrömmigkeit und Totenkult' (n. 43).

[52] The strongest denunciations came from Philostorgios: *Church History*, II, 7, ed. Bidez (n. 30), p. 28.

summoned by God himself to preach the gospels, and for this reason the 'thir-teenth apostle'. The apostles of the second generation who set out to evangelise various countries were generally regarded as 'equals' of the twelve first disciples of Christ. So, by a rhetorical extension, were a handful of great figures whose more or less legendary image was linked to the life of Jesus (Mary Magdalen), or that of Paul (Thecla in the apocryphal *Paul and Thecla*), or the preaching of the earliest times (*Abercius*). One can understand that a sovereign who had Christianised his kingdom – even more so the universal Roman empire, cra-dle of Christ under Augustus and centre from which Christianity had spread throughout the whole world – had been able to lay claim to the title or receive it from the mouth of a panegyrist. It was, after all, quite possible to paint a portrait of Constantine that went some way to meet the required definition; after the many revelations and apparitions which Eusebios had already emphasised, he had been entrusted by God Himself with an apostolic function, that is, with responsibility for a *didaskalia* extending to all pagans and all Jews.

The word was hardly, therefore, surprising, but its implications were seen as dangerous, because unclear. Was this quasi-apostolate attached to the very function of the Christian emperor? Was it accompanied by a special priesthood? It was not at all clear how to reply. It might be possible in rhetoric, at the cost of some glossing over, to grant the emperor a sort of apostolic pre-eminence in the Church, but only in its own language, by making the emperor an almost-priest, granting him and denying him in the same phrase a sacerdotal character without which he could not be recognised as God's elect, but which must not give him the authority of a *pontifex maximus* or of a hierarch in the Christian Church. Certain historians, Socrates Scholastikos in the fifth century, Alexander the Monk in the sixth, and later the authors of some *Lives* of Constantine, may have imprudently gone down this path when they explained the project of the Holy Apostles by Constantine's desire not to deprive the 'emperors and priests' of the proximity of the apostolic relics.[53] Were these the beginnings of a recognition of sacerdotal kingship? They were very tentative, at all events, and provoked vehement reactions. Sozomen, with regard to the burial in the Holy Apostles of the emperors 'and the bishops' added: 'Because priesthood has the same rank, I believe, as kingship, or rather holds first rank in sacred places.'[54] John Chrysostomos, referring to the rebuilding which made the family mausoleum where the emperors were buried into an annex of the church which housed the relics of the apostles, pretended to see this as proof of the humility of the

[53] Socrates, *Historia ecclesiastica*, I, 40, PG 67, col. 180: 'hopos an hoi basileis te kai hiereis ton apostolikon leipsanon me apolimpanointo'; Alexander the Monk, *De inventione sanctae crucis*, PG 87, col. 4068: 'eis to thaptesthai ekeise tous basileis kai hiereis, hopos me osi makran ton apostolikon leipsanon'; Downey, 'The builder of the Church of the Apostles' (n. 43), pp. 57, 60. The *Life of Constantine* ed. H. G. Opitz, *Byz.*, 9 (1934), p. 590 (§72), repeats the text of Socrates. One may nevertheless ponder the accidental loss of an article which, if restored, would make the meaning 'the emperors and the priests'.
[54] *Hist. eccles.*, II, 34, 6, ed. Hansen (see ch. 1, n. 107), p. 100.

sovereigns, who 'considered that they should be content to be buried not next to the apostles [that is, inside the church] but in their "external antechamber", so becoming "their doorkeepers".'[55] A theme in direct contradiction to the theme of equality with the apostles was thus aired by the beginning of the fifth century. Symeon of Thessalonike echoed it six centuries later when he saw in the opposition between the tombs of the patriarchs, placed in the sanctuary of the Holy Apostles, and those of the emperors, relegated to the margins of the church, a sign of the true hierarchy between the leaders of the Church, true successors of the apostles, and the sovereigns, whom he considered to be 'laity'.[56]

It becomes all too clear that Constantine's initiative did not so much inaugurate a tradition as reveal the scale of the problem.

ST CONSTANTINE

What was at stake may have been appreciated in the fourth century; but an open debate was avoided by conferring on Constantine *personally* a sainthood that could justify the titles he had himself claimed or been given in Christian rhetoric, and by persuading his *successors* to interpret their role as Christian emperors in a more appropriate fashion.

Constantine was made a saint so as to avoid making him a model of kingship. The office of St Constantine, on 21 May, repeated more or less all the themes in Eusebios, but normalised and stripped of their rhetorical straitjacket by the 'canonisation' of the first Christian emperor. It contained the same mixture of Old and New Testament references: '[God] friend of men, you have given to your pious servant the wisdom of Solomon, the sweetness of David and the orthodoxy of the apostles.' Constantine was 'the equal of the apostles, the basis and pride of all the sovereigns [who had succeeded him], because, illuminated by the rays of the Spirit', he had united Christians, silenced the heretics at Nicaea and made the Church splendid. It was because he had 'emulated Paul' that he had the right to the 'same honours as an apostle'. The parallel with the thirteenth apostle Paul, which recurs on every page, was based on a specific event, the vision of the cross in the sky. 'It is not from men, Constantine equal of the apostles, that you received the call, but, like the divine Paul, from on high, from Christ God.'[57] Illumination of the Spirit, direct revelation, comparison

---

[55] *Contra Judaeos et gentiles*, 9, PG 48, col. 825; *In epist. II ad Corinth. homil*, XXVI, 10, PG 61, col. 582.

[56] *De ordine sepulturae*, PG 155, col. 677.

[57] Troparion of the feast of St Constantine (*Typikon of the Great Church*, ed. Mateos (see ch. 3, n. 17), I, pp. 296–7), which may be compared to the mosaic of the propylaia of the narthex of St Sophia showing Constantine offering 'his city' and Justinian 'his church' to the Virgin. On the liturgical poetry of 21 May: A. Luzzi, 'Il *dies festus* de Costantino il Grande e di sua madre Elena nei libri liturgici della chiesa greca', in *Costantino il Grande dall' antichità all' umanesimo*, ed. G. Bonamente and F. Fusco, II (Macerata, 1993), pp. 585–643; U. Zanetti, 'Costantino nei calendari e nei sinassari orientali', in ibid., pp. 893–914.

with Paul and title of 'apostle among the emperors' all led to the notion of imperial priesthood:

So, having received knowledge from the Spirit, anointed with oil both priest and emperor, you have fortified the Church of God, you the father of the orthodox emperors, you whose coffin produces cures. Constantine equal of the apostles, intercede for our souls!

Suspicions were dispelled in the language of the liturgy and of the hymns, with the sanction of supposed miracles, however vaguely defined.[58] The scandal of a cult or an imperial priesthood grafting itself on to the Christian religion was defused once the emperor had been made a saint. This way of eliminating 'from the top' the 'Constantine phenomenon' made it possible to place the line of succeeding emperors under a commendable patronage. This posthumous sanctification was probably conferred very early, by the fifth century, since some of the principal themes made commonplace in the saint's office, those of Constantine New Moses and New Paul, and of the 'non-human call', are found almost word for word in a hymn of the heretic Severos of Antioch (512–38), suggesting an earlier model incorporated into and transmitted by the orthodox tradition.[59]

With a similar rapidity and freedom, chroniclers and hagiographers rewrote the life of Constantine in such a way as to eliminate the awkward episodes and render it exemplary. The first notes, a sort of short *Life* known in many versions, seem to have appeared by the early sixth or even late fifth century,[60] at the same time as edifying accounts of the *Invention of the Holy Cross* or other episodes in which Constantine featured (for example, *Lives* of Metrophanes and Alexander, texts on the Fathers of Nicaea). The rewriting of the story had long been completed and the legend of Constantine solidly anchored to the *Acts* of Pope Sylvester, who served as his tutor, when the Macedonian dynasty encouraged a revival and exploited it to its own advantage.[61] The works of this period simply put into literary form popular versions already widely known, included in the *Synaxarion* and reflected in the ceremonial of the tenth century. All the contentious issues had already been ironed out, and an analysis of these 'corrections' helps to bring out not only what was lacking in Constantine's personal 'sanctity', but what was problematic in the general definition of a Christian 'saint emperor'.

---

[58] *Vie de saint Constantin*, ed. M. Guidi, *Rendiconti della R. Accademia dei Lincei*, Ser. V, 16 (Rome, 1907), pp. 654–5.

[59] See Baumstark, 'Konstantiniana aus syrischer Kunst und Liturgie' (n. 43); the text is in PO, VII, 5, *James of Edessa. The Hymns of Severus of Antioch and others*, II, pp. 663–5 (no. 200).

[60] F. Winkelmann, 'Ein Ordnungsversuch der griechischen hagiographischen Konstantinviten und ihrer Überlieferung', in *Studia Byzantina II* (Berlin, 1973), pp. 267–84; F. Winkelmann, 'Das hagiographische Bild Konstantins I. in mittelbyzantinischer Zeit', in *Beiträge zur byzantinischen Geschichte im 9.-11. Jh.*, ed. V. Vavrinek (Prague, 1978), pp. 179–203; and especially F. Winkelmann, 'Die älteste erhaltene griechische hagiographische Vita Konstantins und Helenas (BHG Nr. 365z, 366, 366a)', in *Texte und Textkritik*, ed. J. Dummer, Texte und Untersuchungen 133 (Berlin, 1987), pp. 623–38.

[61] See below, pp. 240–1.

One of the revisions which allowed the icon to emerge also clarified the problem of the succession by ascribing to Constantine the intention – which he may not have had, or not so clearly – of a patrimonial partition of the empire between his three surviving sons, 'heirs to his kingship'.[62] Helena, Constantine's mother, was introduced here; it was she, curiously, according to Eusebios, who had the idea of the partition,[63] and her body, it was claimed, against all likelihood, was buried in Constantinople or transferred from Rome to the Holy Apostles and placed by her son himself in the mausoleum, which made it a burial place like any other.[64] To emphasise in this way the immediate family and the patrimonial transmission made it possible both to play down certain aspects of the imperial cult and to signal more clearly a rupture between the 'monarchy' of Constantine and the Tetrarchy from which it had emerged.[65]

But it was with regard to the baptism that tradition effected the most complete transformation. Constantine was baptised at the time of his death, in accord with contemporary custom,[66] in a suburb of Nicomedia, probably by an Arian bishop, that is, a heretic.[67] But a consensus, immediate in the hagiography and

---

[62] The idea is already emphasised in Eusebios, *Vita Constantini*, I, 9, 1–2; IV, 51, 1–3 and 63, 3, ed. Winkelmann, pp. 19, 141, 146 (*Life of Constantine*, Cameron and Hall (see ch. 3, n. 31), pp. 71, 172–3, 178); see also Socrates, *Historia ecclesiastica*, I, 39, PG 67, col. 180. For the hagiography: Winkelmann, 'Vita Konstantins und Helenas', (n. 60) p. 636; *Vie de saint Constantin*, ed. Guidi (n. 58), pp. 653–4; *Life*, ed. Opitz (n. 53), p. 585 (§64). According to Calderone ('Teologia politica' (n. 14)), Constantine had intended to retain for himself, even after his death, the title of augustus, and allow his children only that of caesar. For patrimonial succession, see above, pp. 24–5.

[63] *Vita Constantini*, III, 46 (*Life of Constantine*, Cameron and Hall (see ch. 3, n. 31), p. 139): Helena died in Constantine's presence, leaving the empire to her son and dividing the world between her grandsons, the caesars, in her will.

[64] Helena died at the age of eighty, probably at Nicomedia in 330, on her return from Palestine: Socrates, *Historia ecclesiastica*, I, 17, PG 67; Theophanes, *Chronographia*, ed. de Boor (see ch. 1, n. 4), p. 27 (pp. 42–3 of Mango and Scot translation); Alexander the Monk, *De inventione sanctae crucis*, PG 87, cols. 4064, 4068. According to the unimpeachable testimony of Eusebios, her body was immediately escorted to Rome, where it was laid to rest in an imperial mausoleum, probably that of the Via Labicana: *Vita Constantini*, III, 46 (*Life of Constantine*, Cameron and Hall (see ch. 3, n. 31), p. 139). Socrates (*Hist. eccl.*, I, 17, PG 67) copies Eusebios while simplifying his style and understanding, or pretending to understand, that the 'imperial city' was Constantinople. Unwitting error or deliberate reinterpretation? It is hard to tell, but one sees how the burial of Helena in the Holy Apostles, preceding that of her son, had the effect of dispelling doubts as to Constantine's religious intentions and making the mausoleum a family burial place from the outset. A different eastern tradition accepts Helena's burial in Rome, but adds that Constantine himself had the body and the sarcophagus brought to his new capital two years later: *Life*, ed. Guidi (n. 62), pp. 652–3; Nikephoros Kallistos, *Hist. eccl.*, VIII, 31, PG 146, cols. 117–20. This return to the East before 337, about which Eusebios says nothing in his *Life of Constantine*, is unlikely. Either it never happened, or it happened when Constantius II deliberately transformed Constantine's rotunda into a family mausoleum.

[65] See above, p. 25.

[66] As baptism erased sins, it was customary to leave it as late as possible.

[67] See Eusebios, *Vita Constantini*, IV, 61–3 (*Life of Constantine*, Cameron and Hall (see ch. 3, n. 31), pp. 177–8), ed. Winkelmann, pp. 145–6; for this problem, see Dölger, 'Die Taufe Konstantins' (n. 1).

soon accepted by the chroniclers,[68] shifted the scene to Rome, a little before the foundation of Constantinople, and attributed the conversion and the administration of the sacrament to Pope Sylvester. Everybody gained by these changes, even the pagan tradition, probably transmitted by Eunapios and repeated by Zosimos, which established a direct link between the baptism of Constantine, the over-hasty pardon (by Bishop Ossius of Cordova or Sylvester) for the murder of his son, Crispus, and the emperor's break with eternal Rome, which gave rise to an illegitimate 'New Rome'.[69] In the Christian tradition, elaborated at greater length and more successfully on the basis of the *Life of St Sylvester*, the miraculous logic combined with exaltation of the Roman see. Thanks to the teaching of Sylvester, Constantine was brought to repentance; thanks to the baptism administered by Sylvester, he was miraculously cured of the leprosy from which he suffered; thanks to the collaboration between the bishop and the emperor, a Christian legislation was developed which recognised the privileges of the Roman Church and established that, throughout the empire, priests would have the pope as their leader, just as government officials had the emperor as theirs.[70] We see here in embryonic form the 'Donation of Constantine' (*Constitutum Constantini*), later grafted on to the Sylvester legend, which shows Constantine leaving the West for the East in order to leave to the pope his full imperial rights over Rome and Italy.[71]

One might have expected the eastern tradition to show some reluctance to accept a story so obviously fabricated, which made the Christian empire originate in Rome and stripped Constantinople of its aura; but it assimilated it very easily, just as it later assimilated the Donation of Constantine. The *Life of St Sylvester* was disseminated in Greek by the late fifth or early sixth century and almost a hundred manuscripts attest to the continued success of its various

[68] Socrates (*Historia ecclesiastica*, I, 39, PG. 67), Sozomen (*Historia ecclesiastica*, II, 34, PG 67), Theodoret (*Hist. eccl.*, I, 30 (see ch. 3, n. 47)), Evagrios (*Hist. eccl.*, III, 41, ed. J. Bidez and L. Parmentier (London, 1898, repr. Amsterdam, 1964), p. 141) and the *Chronicon Paschale* in the seventh century (ed. Niebuhr (see ch. 1, n. 58), p. 532) keep to Eusebios's version; but Malalas (see ch. 1, n. 107), pp. 316–17, by the sixth century, was spreading the version in the *Actus Silvestri*; Theophanes, believing that the eastern tradition had been corrupted by the Arians, opted for the western tradition: *Chronographia*, ed. de Boor (see ch. 1, n. 4), pp. 17–18; later, George the Monk raged against the 'Arian slanders': ed. de Boor (see ch. 1, n. 75), p. 525. The texts are discussed in Dölger, 'Die Taufe Konstantins' (n. 1).

[69] Zosimos, *Hist.*, II, 29 (see ch. 3, n. 90); see F. Paschoud, 'Zosime 2, 29 et la version païenne de la conversion de Constantin', in *Cinq études sur Zosime* (Paris, 1975), pp. 24–62. For the possible relations between the *Actus Silvestri* and the pagan tradition hostile to Constantine, see V. Aiello, 'Costantino, la lebbra e il battesimo di Silvestro', in *Costantino il Grande* (n. 10), I, pp. 17–58.

[70] 'Privilegium ecclesiae Romanae pontificique contulit [Constantinus] ut in toto orbe Romano sacerdotes ita hunc caput habeant sicut judices regem', *Actus Silvestri*, ed. Boninus Mombritius in *Sanctuarium seu Vitae Sanctorum* (Milan, in about 1480, repr. by the monks of Solesmes in 1910, and in New York, 1978), pp. 513, ll. 17–18.

[71] See below, pp. 241–3.

versions.[72] Malalas summarised it in his *Chronicle*; the continuator of Zacharias the Rhetor gave an abbreviated version of it in Syriac. The Christian East had no wish to miss out on the first act of that great spectacle which showed it the 'two powers' confronted, providentially but ambiguously reconciled, and rapidly placed at a safe geographical distance one from the other.

Nor did it wish to miss out on the second act which, in the same *Life of St Sylvester*, involved a problem of equal importance for the definition of a Christian kingship. Helena had supposedly written to her son, from Palestine or Bithynia, to congratulate him on having renounced idols, but also to ask him not to believe in the divinity of Jesus of Nazareth; rather, his new faith should lead the emperor to 'enter into possession of the *basileia* of David and the infinitely wise Solomon', and to take his place with them among the mouthpieces of God.[73] This blunder (another one, but this time invented to give greater emphasis to its correction) was rectified by a great debate between representatives of Judaism and Christianity, organised in Rome and presided over by the emperor. The theological controversy, Bible in hand, was quickly transformed into a battle between Zambi armed with magic and Sylvester armed with miracle. The latter resuscitated a bull which the former had caused to die; Sylvester triumphed, therefore, just as the apostle Peter had triumphed over Simon the Magician in the apocryphal Acts, and everyone rushed to be baptised. The real importance of this *disputatio*, however, which George the Monk included in his *Chronicle* and which remained a model of the genre,[74] lay in the ambiguous role it assigned to the first Christian emperor. Admittedly, he was wrong to believe himself the direct heir of Old Testament kingship, as if the age of Law had not succeeded to the age of Grace; but it was because he was a New David that the conversion of the Jews was his proper sphere. His main business was not, as might have been expected in Rome at this period, the conversion of the pagans to Christianity, which would happen naturally, but that fusion of the two chosen peoples which would be a sign of fulfilment. This was his eschatological and priestly mission. This is how it would be understood by the emperors who, in spite of the reservations or the hostility of the church, embarked on the forced baptism of Jews so as to hasten the realisation of the economy of salvation; by Herakleios, about 630, who wanted to preserve reconquered Jerusalem,

---

[72] W. Levison, 'Konstantinische Schenkung und Silvesterlegende', in *Miscellanea F. Ehrle*, Studi e Testi 38 (Rome, 1924), pp. 159–247; see also, on the *Actus Silvestri* in general, R. J. Loenertz, 'Actus Silvestri. Genèse d'une légende', *Revue d'histoire ecclésiastique*, 70 (1975), pp. 426–39; W. Pohlkamp, 'Textfassungen, literarische Formen und geschichtliche Funktionen der römischen Silvester-Akten', *Francia, Forschungen zur westeuropäischen Geschichte, Mittelalter*, 19, 1 (1992), pp. 115–96. The Greek *Life* is still accessible only in the edition of Combefis of 1659–60.

[73] *Vita Silvestri*, ed. Combefis, *Illustrium Christi martyrum lecti triumphi* (Paris, 1660), p. 290.

[74] George the Monk, ed. de Boor (see ch. 1, n. 75), pp. 491–9.

Leo III, a century later, who wanted to unify the empire of which he was 'emperor and priest', and Basil I, in 873/4, who defied the distinction between clergy and laity by himself engaging in debates, catechising and perhaps even baptising.[75]

The Constantine legend was not intended only to rewrite history and to make the first Christian emperor a paragon of virtue; it identified problems and explored possible routes forward, most of which were judged dangerous by the institutional Church. It also allowed into the Christian literature of the fifth century a strain of ferocious polemic which has continued to our day. This is first visible in the West, where the involvement of Constantine and above all of his son Constantius II on the side of the Arians was used to launch an all-out attack on what modern historians would call 'caesaropapism', to denounce the conception which made the emperor an *episcopus episcoporum* and to invoke for the first time in the debate the formula of Matthew, 22: 21: 'Render therefore unto Caesar the things which are Caesar's; and unto God the things that are God's.'[76] In the works of Ossius of Cordova, Lucifer of Cagliari and Hilary of Poitiers, all the Constantinian–Eusebian themes were turned on their heads. It was not for the emperor to act as a *didaskalos*; he was neither prophet nor apostle; he might be the 'false apostle' against whom Paul had warned, or the precursor of Antichrist.[77] In the work of Ambrose of Milan, these ideas acquired doctrinal form; the emperor is a son of the Church, in the Church and not above it, subject to the judgement of the bishops (*filius ecclesiae, intra ecclesiam non supra ecclesiam, ab episcopis judicatus*).[78] But as we will see, the East, though more aware of what the Christian empire actually was, did not remain deaf to these reproaches, which were revived and intensified every time that the emperor and the Church came into conflict over the faith.[79]

The first Christian emperor was made not only a saint, but an experimental model of imperial sainthood; a model for all purposes, which has served as icon or target up to our day.[80]

---

[75] G. Dagron, 'Introduction historique: entre histoire et apocalypse', in G. Dagron and V. Déroche, 'Juifs et chrétiens dans l'Orient du VIIe siècle', *TM*, 11 (1991), pp. 17–46; G. Dagron 'Le traité de Grégoire de Nicée sur le baptême des Juifs', ibid., pp. 314–57.

[76] Letter of Ossius of Cordova, in Athanasios of Alexandria, *Historia arianorum ad monachos*, 44, PG 25, cols. 744–8, 4, ed. Opitz, II, 1, pp. 207–8.

[77] Lucifer of Cagliari, *Moriendum est pro Dei Filio*, 13, ed. W. von Hartel, CSEL 14 (Vienna, 1884), p. 311; Hilary of Poitiers, *Contra Constantinum*, 1 and 5, PL 10, cols. 577, 581; Ossius of Cordova, fragment of letter in Athanasius of Alexandria, *Historia arianorum* (n. 76); see Girardet, 'Kaiser Konstantius II.' (n. 27).

[78] See in particular, Ep. 20, 8 and 19; 21, 4; *Contra Auxentium*, 36, PL 16, cols. 996–7, 999–1000, 1003–4, 1018, ed. M. Zelzer, *Sancti Ambrosii Opera*, CSEL LXXXII, Pars X, 3: *Epistularum Liber decimus* (Vienna, 1982), *Ep.* 75a, 75, 76, pp. 75–6, 106, 112, 118–19; see J. R. Palanque, *Saint Ambroise et l'Empire romain* (Paris, 1933), pp. 355–86.

[79] See below, pp. 299–300.   [80] See below, pp. 285–8.

HOLY EMPERORS

Constantine ranks high, obviously, in the category of holy kings who steered their people to Christianity and so deserved to be the equal of the apostles – a category which, after him, was accessible mainly to non-Byzantine sovereigns.[81] He is unquestionably their leader and their reference point, since it was the whole world and not just a kingdom or a people that his personal conversion brought into the economy of salvation. He played in Byzantium the role of *rex perpetuus* later allotted to St Edward in England, St Wenceslas in Bohemia, St Olaf in Norway, St Eric in Sweden and St Louis in France. He, on his own, sanctified all his successors, hailed as 'New Constantines';[82] his cross accompanied the reigning sovereign in the principal ceremonies; the emperors who founded or consolidated a dynasty gave their eldest sons his name, which conveyed legitimacy (Herakleios, Leo III, Leo V, Theophilos, Basil I). Nevertheless, the sanctity of the founder, loudly proclaimed though problematic, set no trend in Byzantium itself. Few saints were recognised among the *basileis* of Constantinople until the age of the Palaiologoi. If we exclude women, there were none, and this lack was an embarrassment.

In the West, until Pope Gregory VII tried to impose a degree of order on the process, sainthood was freely granted to kings, princes and their families – sufficiently freely, in fact, for historians to have suggested a typology.[83] Apart from the kings who converted peoples, there were 'martyr kings' who were unjustly killed, victims of treachery who faced death without resisting, such as Sigismund, king of the Burgundians, in 523, and, in medieval Russia, the *strastoterpci* (holy sufferers), Boris and Gleb; there were 'thaumaturgic' kings, who performed miracles before or after death; and lastly, there is the long list of kings who were recognised as saints for their piety, their irreproachable life, their charity or their generosity towards the Church, who were sometimes said to have acted *acsi boni sacerdotes*. But no Byzantine emperor fitted any of these definitions; none, notably, was renowned as a miracle-worker or a martyr. There were attempts to promote the cult of several sovereigns, but it is significant that they were few, that they were resisted by the Church or public opinion, and that they quickly fizzled out.[84]

---

[81] We should note, however, that Vladimir of Kiev, who converted his people, was not declared a saint, because he enjoyed banquets too much and because his tomb had not produced any miracles: V. Vodoff, 'Pourquoi le prince Volodimer Svjatoslavič n'a-t-il pas été canonisé?' *Harvard Ukrainian Studies*, 12–13 (Proceedings of the International Congress commemorating the Millennium of Christianity in Rus'-Ukraine) (1988–9), pp. 446–66.

[82] A symposium was devoted to this subject: *New Constantines: The Rhythm of Imperial Renewal in Byzantium, 4th–13th centuries*, ed. P. Magdalino (Aldershot, 1994).

[83] R. Folz, *Les Saints Rois du Moyen Age en Occident (VIe–XIIIe siècle)* (Brussels, 1984); see also A. Vauchez, *La Sainteté en Occident aux derniers siècles du Moyen Age* (Rome, 1981), (trans. J. Birrell, *Sainthood in the Later Middle Ages* (Cambridge, 1997), pp. 187–96).

[84] E. Patlagean, in a highly stimulating article ('Le basileus assassiné et la sainteté impériale', in *Media in Francia. Recueil de mélanges offert à Karl Ferdinand Werner* (Paris, 1988),

Justinian I might have joined Constantine as a saint. Towards the end of the tenth century, the mosaic of the propylaea of the narthex of St Sophia associated the two emperors and shows Constantine offering his city and Justinian his church to the Virgin.[85] The historian Prokopios tells us that certain toadies, including the jurist Tribonian, told Justinian they were afraid that they might see him fly up to heaven, so angelic had his piety made him.[86] The church historian Nikephoros Kallistos, in the fifteenth century, evoking the death of the builder of St Sophia and engaging in a sort of canonisation process, reached a negative conclusion. He noted first that the council in Trullo gave Justinian 'the condition of the blessed' (by naming him *ho tes makarias / theias lexeos*) and ranked him 'among the saints' (*ho en hagiois*), a vague formula that stops short of proper sainthood; he then added that, in the time of Alexios Komnenos and the patriarch John of Chalcedon, the annual commemoration at St Sophia, and incidentally at Ephesos, in two of the principal churches built by Justinian, had acquired or preserved the solemnity of a religious festival which attracted large crowds, but without it amounting to a cult.[87]

Maurice had the makings of a martyr; murdered by Phokas in 602, his executioner had first forced him to watch as his sons were killed before his eyes; yet he faced death courageously, saying only: 'Righteous art thou, O Lord, and upright are thy judgements' (Psalm CXIX [CXVIII]: 137). The account of his reign written by Theophylaktos Simokattes only a few years after the event reveals deep emotion and already records some legendary developments which were elaborated throughout the seventh and eighth centuries.[88] Maurice, it was said, had committed the grave sin of not redeeming 'Roman' prisoners; the Christ of the Chalke had appeared to him to ask him whether he wanted to pay in this life (by his own death and that of his family) or the other (by

---

pp. 345–61), has usefully posed the question of royal sainthood in Byzantium and assembled for the first time a large part of the documentation; in my view, however, she puts too much emphasis on similarities with the West. See also P. Schreiner, 'Aspekte der politischen Heiligenverehrung in Byzanz', in *Politik und Heiligenverehrung im Hochmittelalter*, ed. J. Petersohn (Sigmaringen, 1994), pp. 365–83.

[85] For the image of Justinian, see Prinzing, 'Das Bild Justinians I' (see ch. 3, n. 33).

[86] *Historia arcana*, XIII, 12, ed. J. Haury, *Procopii Caesariensis opera omnia*, III (Leipzig, 1963), p. 86.

[87] Nikephoros Kallistos, *Hist. eccl.*, XVII, 31, PG 147, cols. 300–1; he quotes the acts of the council in Trullo and a scholium of the time of John of Chalcedon, but reproaches Justinian for not combating the aphthartodocetist heresy and for persecuting the patriarch Eutychios, as Constantine had persecuted Athanasius of Alexandria. It is only recently, as Prinzing has observed ('Das Bild Justinians' (see ch. 3, n. 33)), that a surprising book has been devoted to *Justinian the Great, the Emperor and Saint* by a Greek historian, A. Gerostergios (Belmont, Mass., 1982).

[88] Theophylaktos Simokattes. *Hist.*, VIII, 11, ed. de Boor and Wirth (see ch. 1, n. 1), p. 305; for Maurice, see J. Wortley, 'The legend of the emperor Maurice', in *Actes du XVe Congrès international d'Etudes byzantines, Athènes, septembre 1976*, IV, *Histoire, communications* (Athens, 1980), pp. 382–91, whose conclusions I repeat here.

eternal damnation); the tragedy of 602 was thus the consequence of his free choice, courageously faced.[89] This development could easily have turned into hagiography, but did not; the official *Synaxarion of Constantinople* provides only for a commemoration of Maurice (called in error Markianos) and his children.[90] A Palestinian–Georgian calendar goes slightly further by awarding the emperor 'the condition of the saints'[91] and a Syriac document suggests a marginal cult,[92] which in any case never took root in the empire. Constantinopolitan orthodoxy took care to see that the life of this glorious soldier who piously accepted the cruellest of deaths gave rise only to a 'story of value to the soul', the *exemplum* of his vision of Christ, which presented him not as a martyr, but as a repentant sinner.[93]

The Macedonians tried hard to achieve success in this sphere, as we will see.[94] But Basil I failed to win official recognition for the cult of his eldest son, Constantine, who died prematurely, and contemporary writers record this attempt only because it seemed to them incongruous and discreditable to the patriarch (Photios) who had given it his support. They had to fall back on a daughter-in-law, 'St Theophano', a limited concession which even then had been difficult to obtain.

In the case of Nikephoros Phokas (963–9), matters went further. An Athos manuscript preserves an office in his honour (for 11 December, the date of his death),[95] and the *Life of St Athanasios the Athonite* devotes a chapter to a monk-cook from Lavra who had secretly asked for and received the posthumous assistance of the emperor, described by him as a martyr.[96] The office presents Nikephoros as an accepted saint, because the *myron* emanating from his tomb cured the sick (a necessary but minimal miracle); further, he was a great defender of the faith, since he had been the first to make the ancestral battle against the Arabs a sort of holy war, going so far as to propose that the soldiers killed in battle should be accorded the same honours as the martyrs.[97] He was a monk and an ascetic, since he had 'kept away from the stains of the flesh from birth' and because, before his marriage to the empress Theophano, widow of Romanos

---

[89] Theophanes, *Chronographia*, ed. Boor (see ch. 1, n. 4), pp. 284–5 (pp. 410–11 of Mango and Scott translation) gives the most developed version of the legend.

[90] *Synaxarion* for 28 November: V. Grumel, 'La mémoire de Tibère II et de Maurice dans le *Synaxaire de Constantinople*', *Anal. Boll.*, 84 (1966), pp. 249–53.

[91] G. Garitte, *Le Calendrier palestino-géorgien du Sinaiticus 34 (Xe siècle)* (Brussels, 1958), pp. 87, 315 (for 28 August).

[92] 'Légendes d'Abraham, martyr de Barsoma, et de Maurice, empereur des Romains', ed. F. Nau, PO V, pp. 773–8.

[93] *De Mauricio imperatore visio*, BHG 1322yb.   [94] See below, pp. 202–4.

[95] L. Petit, 'Office inédit en l'honneur de Nicéphore Phocas', *BZ*, 13 (1904), pp. 398–420.

[96] *Vita B*, 44, ed. J. Noret, *Vitae duae antiquae Sancti Athanasii Athonitae*, Corpus Christianorum, Series graeca 9 (Turnhout, 1982), pp. 178–9.

[97] Skylitzes, *Synopsis*, ed. Thurn (see ch. 1, n. 39), pp. 274–5; Zonaras, *Annales*, ed. Pinder (see ch. 1, n. 29), III, p. 506.

II, he had intended to leave the army to join St Athanasios and found with him the monastery of Lavra, of which he became, as emperor instead of monk, a generous benefactor. He was a martyr, lastly, because he was slain when defenceless. These were surely enough and sufficiently weighty justifications! The circumstances of his murder provoked deep emotion and pity. 'Placed at the head of your people as a priest and not as an emperor', wrote the author of the office, avoiding by a negative the dangerous theme of the emperor-priest, 'a horde of disreputable men, O emperor and ascetic, criminally and treacherously cut your throat.' Nevertheless, the cult of Nikephoros Phokas, which might have enthused hearts and minds, remained marginal and soon died out.[98] It was never approved, but on the contrary discouraged by an ecclesiastical hierarchy which had reproached the dead emperor for his laws on the finances of bishoprics and the foundation of monasteries, which it persuaded his successor to abolish immediately. The initiative had certainly came from Lavra, which had thereby demonstrated its gratitude and contrived another argument in support of its claim to supremacy on Athos; but it is unlikely that St Athanasios himself, who described his stormy relations with Nikephoros in a very different tone, was behind it. Nor does the cook in the *Life of St Athanasios the Athonite* conceal that there had been disagreement among the monks on the subject of the emperor's spontaneous 'canonisation'.

The reference to John Tzimiskes in a Georgian calendar from Iviron is evidence only of that monastery's gratitude to an emperor who had encouraged its establishment on Athos and generously endowed it.[99] It had purely local resonance. It was not until the age of the Palaiologoi that an emperor, John III Vatatzes, son-in-law of Theodore Laskaris, came close to official recognition as a saint by reason of his virtues and, above all, his charity. It has to be said, however, that his eulogy resembles an imperial panegyric, that his *Life* was written in the eighteenth century, that his office, composed by Nicodemos the Hagiorite, is more recent still, and that he was emperor of Nicaea, not of Constantinople.[100]

---

[98] There survives, in Slav popular and epic literature, a *slovo* which may date back to the fourteenth century: E. Turdeanu, *Le Dit de l'empereur Nicéphore II Phocas et de son épouse Théophanô* (Thessalonike, 1976); E. L. Vranoussi, 'Un "discours" byzantin en l'honneur du saint empereur Nicéphore Phocas transmis par la littérature slave', *Revue des études du sud-est européen*, 16 (1978), pp. 729–44. The piece is moving but in no way hagiographical.

[99] M. Van Esbroek, 'L'empereur Jean Tzimisces dans le calendrier de Georges l'Athonite', *Bedi Kartlisa*, 41 (1983), pp. 67–72: mention of Tzimiskes on 11 January; it is more of a commemoration. In contrast, in the *Apocalypsis Anastasiae*, 6, ed. R. Homburg (Leipzig, 1903), pp. 27–8, John Tzimiskes is, after his death, among the damned, as a result of his murder of Nikephoros Phokas.

[100] The text of George of Pelagonia, ed. A. Heisenberg, *BZ*, 14 (1905), pp. 193–233, is really a eulogy. See D. I. Polemis, 'Remains of an acolouthia for the Emperor John Ducas Batatzes', *Harvard Ukrainian Studies*, 7 (*Okeanos. Essays presented to Ihor Ševčenko*) (1983), pp. 542–7; R. Macrides, 'Saints and sainthood in the early Palaiologan period', in *The Byzantine Saint*, ed. Hackel (see ch. 1, n. 99), pp. 69–71.

The various surviving versions of the *Synaxarion of Constantinople* make it possible to take stock of the situation between the end of the ninth and the second half of the twelfth centuries.[101] They include, for dates which are usually, but not always, those of their death or their burial, commemorations of a number of emperors or empresses. Father Delehaye has asked whether these were liturgical, funerary or a mixture,[102] that is, whether they were intended for emperors recognised as saints, or for whom the Church wished to demonstrate particular esteem, or for whom the service provided an embryonic liturgy (a troparion) before the office of the dead, as was the custom in certain monasteries for the celebration of a founder. For Constantine (associated with Helena) and for Theophano, first wife of Leo VI, the adjective *hagios/hagia* leaves no doubt;[103] for the others, there are slight differences between formulae evoking simple 'piety' and those granting the deceased the 'condition of the saints', which, as we have seen, was not enough to signify sainthood. Nor is it easy to establish the criteria for the choice of the emperors and empresses mentioned. It can only be remarked that all the sovereigns who convened an ecumenical council are commemorated: Constantine the Great (Nicaea I, 325), Theodosius I (Constantinople I, 381), Theodosius II (Ephesos, 431), Marcian (Chalcedon, 451), Justinian (Constantinople II, 553), Constantine IV (Constantinople III, 680–1), the sinister Justinian II (Quini-Sext or in Trullo, 691–2, regarded as ecumenical in the East) and Irene (Nicaea II, 787).[104] It was not until the twelfth century, and then only tentatively, that the *Synaxarion* provided for the commemoration of Theodora, widow of Theophilos, regarded as a saint for having restored images, in 843, in agreement with the patriarch Methodios, but without convening an ecumenical council.[105] To this list should be added a few augustas, alone or associated with their husband, known for their many pious foundations or for having played a notable role (Flacilla, Eudokia, Pulcheria, Ariadne wife of Zeno then Anastasios, Theodora wife of Justinian),[106] and a

[101] A. Luzzi, 'Note sulla recensione del Sinassario di Costantinopoli patrocinata da Costantino VII Porfirogenito', *Rivista di Studi bizantini e neoellenici*, NS 26 (1989), pp. 139–86; A. Luzzi, 'Gli imperatori bizantini commemorati nel Sinassario di Costantinopoli', *XVIIIe Congrès international des études byzantines, Résumés des communications*, II (Moscow, 1991), pp. 684–5.
[102] *Synaxarium Ecclesiae Constantinopolitanae*, ed. H. Delehaye, *AASS, Propylaeum Novembris* (Brussels, 1902), p. LXXV.
[103] Ibid., cols. 697ff. (21 May), 314 (16 December). Every emperor and empress mentioned in the *Synaxarion of Constantinople* also appears in the *Typikon* of the Great Church.
[104] Ibid., cols. 205, 856, 472, 224, 12, 822, 872. The Empress Irene merits only a commemoration in the *Synaxarion*, but she had her hagiographer: W. T. Treadgold, 'The unpublished saint's life of the empress Irene (*BHG* 2205)', *ByzForsch.*, 8 (1982), pp. 237–51.
[105] *Synaxarium* (n. 102), col. 458 (only in manuscripts S and M, of the twelfth century). But there exists a *Life of St Theodora*, ed. A. Markopoulos, *Symmeikta*, 5 (1983), pp. 249–85.
[106] *Synaxarium* (n. 102), cols. 46, 890, 472 and 871ff, 912, 224.

few emperors of the fifth and sixth centuries, surprising (Leo I),[107] predictable (Maurice and his wife and children)[108] or thanks to their family ties (Justin I as uncle of Justinian).[109]

There was perhaps a shift in the sixth century towards a muted form of sainthood for orthodox emperors and empresses or at any rate an opening up the *Synaxarion* to the commemoration of sovereigns and their families. But a halt was called by the Church at the time of the Monothelete crisis and in particular of iconoclasm. After Herakleios, only Constantine IV and Justinian II, who had repudiated the religious policies of their predecessors, were commemorated, and two wives, Theodora, wife of Theophilos, and Theophano, wife of Leo VI. It had been possible to declare the latter saints on the grounds of a personal sanctity which did not risk reflecting glory on the imperial office itself. They had been very different from their husbands, whose sins they had redeemed – heresy and persecution in the case of Theophilos, sexuality and tetragamy in the case of Leo VI. The Church openly mistrusted the imperial power, accused of sullying the purity of the faith. This accusation, long implicit, was openly expressed at the time of the Monothelete crisis, in the mid-seventh century, and engraved on the memory at the time of iconoclasm, described as the 'imperial heresy'. The result in Byzantium was that clericalisation of sainthood and that demystification of lay power which was emphasised by Gregory VII, in the eleventh-century West, when he had compared the tiny number of kings who deserved their reputation as saints with the masses of prelates, clerics and monks who were worshipped with good reason.[110] The emperor 'saints' were above all those who had assembled the bishops in a council and bowed to their opinions. They were not, Constantine apart, true saints.

But the reluctance of the Church is not the whole explanation. If the emperors scarcely needed the individual sanctity that the *Synaxarion* found only in the first of them, it was because they all, whatever their merits, shared in another sanctity attached to their office.

The historian Pachymeres tells how, in 1281, sensing that death was near, the old patriarch Joseph made his will. As custom dictated, he mentioned the name of the emperor, Michael VIII Palaiologos, and prayed to God on his behalf; but he failed to add to his title of *basileus* the adjective 'holy' (*hagios*), 'which is traditionally borne by the emperors after they had been anointed with the *myron*'. This caused a scandal. Receiving his copy of the will, the emperor

---

[107] Ibid. It only appears in the *Synaxarion of Constantinople* in the twelfth century, but it is mentioned much earlier in the *Typikon* of the Great Church, ed. Mateos (see ch. 3, n. 17), I, pp. 199, 203.

[108] *Synaxarium* (n. 102), col. 264 (correcting 'Constantine, Marcian and their children' to 'Constantina, Maurice and their children').

[109] Ibid., col. 866 (correcting 'Justinian' to 'Justin').

[110] Letter to Bishop Hermann of Metz (15 March 1081), ed. E. Caspar, *MGH, Ep. select. ad usum scholar.*, II, p. 558; see Vauchez, *Sainthood* (n. 83), pp. 165–6.

expressed his indignation and instructed the city prefect and the new patriarch, John Bekkos, to investigate. Joseph, when questioned, extricated himself by the cowardly device of blaming the offence on the monks who had surrounded him, who were extremely hostile to the emperor because of his policy of union with the Latin Church, and produced – not very convincingly – a 'first draft' of the will in which appeared the phrase 'to my most powerful and holy emperor autokrator' (*to kratisto kai hagio mou autokratori*).[111] This anecdote confirms a rule. The adjective *hagios* was in general use and obligatory. To refuse it to the emperor was to consider him illegitimate, or at least as abandoned by God. If the emperors themselves did not speak of their sainthood, their correspondents and the official documents referring to them habitually used expressions such as 'holy masters' or 'holy emperors crowned by God'.[112] At most, it may be noted that the protocols of acclamations and of ceremonies preferred to associate the adjective 'holy' with 'kingship' itself; Emperor Leo I referred to himself by saying 'my holy and happy kingship',[113] and the demes wished that God might grant the sovereigns many years of 'holy kingship';[114] but this retreat into the abstract did not remove from the person what it seemed to attribute to the office.

To appreciate this sanctity, it may be useful to recall that the Roman emperor, his constitutions, his *nutus* and his gestures,[115] and the parts of his body, notably his feet which were kissed,[116] were considered 'divine'. But this Roman reference explains the adjective *divus/theios* and not the qualifier *sanctus/hagios*, which can only be understood in an Old Testament context. At the time of the 1281 episode summarised above, Michael VIII justified the title of 'holy' by the divine unction received directly from God at the moment of coronation, which conferred on the emperor quasi-sacerdotal as well as political powers. The same explanation is given in the fifteenth century by Symeon of Thessalonike, but with a restrictive gloss; emperors and bishops were called 'holy masters' because they were both anointed, but sainthood and unction were only 'symbolic' for the emperors, whereas they were accompanied by the grant of true *charismata* in the case of the bishops.[117] In order to glorify or simply to justify imperial 'sanctity', reference is made to a ceremonial already attested in the

---

[111] Pachymeres, *Hist.*, VI, 31, ed. and trans. Failler and Laurent (see ch. 1, n. 8), II, pp. 638–9. See also V. Laurent and J. Darrouzès, *Dossier grec de l'Union de Lyon (1273–1277)* (Paris, 1976), pp. 88–90, 508–17. And see below, pp. 254–5.

[112] See, for example, J. Darrouzès, *Epistoliers byzantins du Xe siècle* (Paris, 1960), pp. 144 (II, 79, l. 9), 167 (III, 11, ll. 11, 14), 213 (IV, 3, l. 9); Rhalles–Potles, *Syntagma*, V, p. 307 (*semeioma* of deposition of the patriarch Kosmas); Laurent and Darrouzès, *Dossier grec* (n. 111), pp. 135, 137, 377, 387.

[113] *De cerimoniis*, I, 100 [91], p. 412 ll. 12ff.: protocol of the fifth century.

[114] Ibid., I, 2 (pp. 36 l. 11, 37 l. 6, 38 l. 22); I, 3 (p. 43 l. 18); I, 9 (p. 61 l. 2); I, 92 [83] (p. 384 ll. 9ff.); II, 19 (p. 612 l. 13); II, 43 (pp. 650 l. 13, 651 l. 11).

[115] Ibid., I, 96 [87], p. 396 l. 3.   [116] Ibid., II, 52, p. 706 l. 16.

[117] Symeon of Thessalonike, *De sacris ordinationibus*, 207 and 218, PG 155, cols. 417, 432. See below, pp. 278–9.

tenth century, which arranged for the people, to shout 'Holy, Holy, Holy!' three
times after the coronation of the emperor by the patriarch.[118] What exactly was
the meaning of this triple invocation, derived from the song of the seraphim of
Isaiah (6: 2–3), repeated in the most classical Chrysostomian liturgy and heavy
with Trinitarian or Christological implications in the Byzantine formula of the
Trisagion?[119] I am not convinced that in the tenth century it was understood as
addressing the emperor himself; it seems to me rather to celebrate God, who
had just manifested himself by designating his 'anointed'. However that may
be, this generic sainthood linked to unction was deeply rooted in the Old Testament and barred the emperors from access to the sainthood of the Gospels,
which was not their sphere.

We see here one of the chief differences between East and West. A Byzantine
emperor, once invested with absolute power, had nothing more to prove or
disprove in relation to his worthiness for office; he took his place in a vast
divine plan and played the role which had been laid down for him from time
immemorial. The Roman empire, of which he was the temporary guardian, was
part of an eschatological schema which gave it a meaning and an end; it was
the last of the great universal monarchies predicted by the prophet Daniel (2
and 7) and St John, the last day of the worldly week of 7,000 years, a day
which would never end and would lead to the establishment on earth of the
kingdom of God, after the fleeting victory and then defeat of the Antichrist.[120]
The history of Rome was understood by the authors of Chronicles seeking for
a universal 'computation' as the progressive apocalypse of this Last Day. Some
historians and theologians made this final stage begin with the Christianisation
of the empire by Constantine; most of them went back to Augustus, who had
pacified the world, conducted the first census and so prepared the empire to be a
cradle where, under his rule, Christ would be born.[121] For them, the conversion

---

[118] *De cerimoniis*, I, 47 [38], p. 193 l. 4. The patriarch here only crowned and did not anoint the
emperor; the people shouted three times: 'Holy, Holy, Holy! Glory to God in the highest and
peace on earth.' Later, the patriarch performed the anointing by tracing a cross with the *myron*
on the emperor's head and saying in a loud voice 'Holy!', an invocation repeated three times
by the congregation: Pseudo-Kodinos, *De officiis*, ed. and trans. Verpeaux (see ch. 2, n. 16),
p. 258; and see below, pp. 279ff.

[119] The liturgical acclamation of the *trisagion* (*Hagios ho Theos, hagios ischyros, hagios athanatos,
eleeson hemas*) is obviously addressed to God; it had been made famous in the fifth century by
a Monophysite addition denounced at the council of Chalcedon (451).

[120] G. Podskalsky, *Byzantinische Reichseschatologie* (Munich, 1972); G. Podskalsky, 'Représenta-
tion du temps dans l'eschatologie impériale byzantine', in *Le Temps chrétien de la fin de
l'Antiquité au Moyen Age, IIIe–XIIIe siècles*, Colloques internationaux du CNRS, no. 604
(Paris, 1984), pp. 439–50.

[121] See, for example, Eusebios of Caesarea, *Hist. eccl.*, I, 5, 2 (birth of Christ in the forty-second
year of the reign of Augustus); IV, 26, 7 (where Eusebios states that Melito of Sardis was the
first to have noted the synchronism between the reign of Augustus and the birth of Christianity);
Eusebios, *Tricennalia*, 16, ed. Heikel, p. 249; Gregory of Nazianzus, *Disc.* IV (*Contra Julianum*

of Constantine was not an absolute beginning. Imperial Rome had already been virtually Christian; its principal dates were already part of the same timescale as Christian history. This overlap of timescales gave rise, as we have seen, to all sorts of legends indulgently repeated by Malalas, which aimed to transform the pagan emperors into crypto-Christians.[122]

What changed with New Rome and the Christian empire was that the count-down had officially begun, that people speculated that only a few years re-mained, that they scrutinised the face of every emperor or empress in an attempt to recognise the characteristic features of Antichrist or of the sovereigns, good or bad, who would precede his coming, and that every phase of contemporary history was studied to see if it had a place in the scenario of a pre-ordained end. Just as historical legends went back to the origins of the empire, so apocalyptic stories, constantly rewritten, looked forward to its spectacular end. Everyone looked for signs, and none were more obvious than the events of a reign or the face or words, even unconscious, of an emperor. At times of great tension, the language of politics became spontaneously apocalyptic; this was the case with those who experienced the restoration of paganism under Julian and the difficult successions of the fifth century, for those contemporaries of Anastasios, 'with his eyes of different colours', for those who suffered the plague and earthquakes and lived through the sinister end of the reign of Justinian, for those who wit-nessed the capture of Jerusalem by the Persians, the return of Herakleios with the wood of the Cross and the forced conversion of the Jews, followed by the Arab invasion, for the defenders of images under the first iconoclasts, Leo III and Constantine V, and for those who later fought against Michael VIII and the Union of the Churches.

The Byzantine emperors were not, therefore, 'saints', or even Christians, like others. They were seen, for better or worse, as players in a sacred history which went back to the Davidic alliance and not – or not only – as men whose conduct might be judged in terms of morality or piety. This is why the 'Christian' sainthood of Constantine, so problematic and ambiguous, had to remain an exception.

I), 37, ed. and trans. Bernardi, pp. 136–7: '[Constantius II] was well aware ... that the devel-opment of Rome coincided with that of Christianity and that the empire began with the coming of Christ, because never before had power been concentrated in the hands of one single man.' The idea goes back to Hippolytus, Melito and Origen. See J. Sirinelli, *Les Vues historiques d'Eusèbe de Césarée durant la période prénicéenne* (Dakar, 1961), especially pp. 239–45, 388–411; Dvornik, *Christian and Byzantine Political Philosophy* (n. 11), II, pp. 725ff.
[122] See above, pp. 128–9.

5. Leo III and the iconoclast emperors: Melchizedek or Antichrist?

A LITTLE PHRASE

'I am emperor and priest.' Authentic or invented, this little phrase caused a major stir and has ever since been debated by historians. It was a trap, and we need to see how it operated and why it was so effective. First, however, let us establish how it fitted into the long history of Byzantium. Between 726 and 730, when he declared the cult of images idolatrous, initiating the crisis which, a 120 years later,[1] would leave Byzantium frozen in its Orthodoxy and political legitimacy, Leo III, the 'heresiarch' emperor, is supposed to have issued this challenge to the Roman pontiff, first of all the hierarchs. More, perhaps, than any of his predecessors, Leo owed his position to his sword, but the power seized in the turmoil of battles and sieges invested him with a mission and endowed him with sacerdotal *charismata*. He was not bishop 'of those outside', like Constantine the Great, but of those inside; he was not the secular arm of the Church, but high priest as David's heir. The phrase was so successful because, by its shocking association of the two words, it stripped away the veil of rhetoric beneath which the Constantinian project and the ambiguity inherent in the Christian empire itself had been concealed. Its impact was so great because it was not uttered during one of the many conflicts internal to Constantinople between emperor and patriarch, but during a confrontation at a distance between a pope who prided himself on the independence of the

---

[1] For the beginnings and the development of iconoclasm, see, in particular, *Histoire du christianisme*, IV: 'L'iconoclasme et l'établissement de l'Orthodoxie', pp. 93–165; S. Gero, *Byzantine Iconoclasm during the Reign of Leo III with Particular Attention to the Oriental Sources* (Louvain, 1973); S. Gero, *Byzantine Iconoclasm during the Reign of Constantine V with Particular Attention to the Oriental Sources* (Louvain, 1977); *Iconoclasm, Papers given at the Ninth Spring Symposium of Byzantine Studies (Birmingham, March 1975)*, ed. A. A. M. Bryer and J. Herrin (Birmingham, 1977); H. G. Thümmel, *Die Frühgeschichte der ostkirchlichen Bilderlehre, Texte und Untersuchungen zur Zeit von dem Bilderstreit* (Berlin, 1992); L. Brubaker and J. Haldon, *Byzantium in the Iconoclast Era (ca. 680–850): The Sources, an Annotated Survey* (Aldershot, 2001), with useful bibliography.

Christian West and an emperor sure of his rights, whose reforms risked shattering the unity of the eastern Church. The time was ripe for the abscess to be lanced: on one side, a priest without an emperor, on the other, an emperor without priests.

The contentious expression appears in two letters from Pope Gregory II to Leo III which, despite their oddities, we should first read without subjecting them to critical scrutiny.[2] In the first,[3] the pope says that he has received annual professions of faith from Leo since his accession, ten in all, perfectly orthodox, which he has carefully stored in the Confession of St Peter.[4] But in this, the eleventh year (726), the lay sovereign has broken his promise to respect the definitions of the Fathers and scandalised Christians all over the world by attacking images and by issuing orders that they should everywhere be destroyed. The Old Testament prohibition on the adoration of any man-made object, on which Leo III based himself, and which he had probably cited in his letter, had been aimed at Jews who were suspected of idolatry, and God himself had frequently ordered it to be ignored, for example for the adornment of the Ark of the Covenant or the Temple.[5] The other arguments, theological or legendary, that Gregory II employed against Leo III are equally commonplace: Christ had offered himself to the sight of men with recognisable features, which might therefore be represented; his coming had ended idolatry, which need no longer, therefore, be feared; both in his lifetime and in apostolic times, images had been painted and disseminated, that of Edessa among others; these representations edified the faithful, helped instruct the young and the illiterate and led people to shed tears of contrition.[6] There was a continuous and ancient tradition of eight centuries (an approximation or a false date?), which only Leo's whim was interrupting. The pope accordingly requested the emperor to put aside his arrogance, to renounce heresy and to fear its inevitable consequences of excommunication and anathema. He told him of the astonishment of the western princes when they had learned of the destruction of the image of Christ on the church of the Chalkoprateia (in fact, the Christ ikon on the Chalke, the 'Bronze Gate' of the

---

[2] These letters have been edited, translated and discussed by J. Gouillard, 'Aux origines de l'iconoclasme: le témoignage de Grégoire II', *TM*, 3 (1968), pp. 243–307.

[3] Ibid., pp. 276–97. The letter appears to have been written between 726 and 730, after the Chalke affair.

[4] The presence of documents in this illustrious locale is known, but it was not a true archive; in any case, it is absurd to imagine that the emperor had sent the pope every year a declaration of orthodoxy which he in fact made only once, in Constantinople, at the time of his proclamation: Gouillard, 'Aux origines' (n. 2), p. 265.

[5] A commonplace of the iconophile literature, based in particular on Exodus, 31: 1–6 ('See, I have called by name Bezaleel the son of Uri ... of the tribe of Judah: And I have filled him with the spirit of God ... to devise cunning works, to work in gold, and in silver, and in brass') and on the description of the temple of Solomon: see, for example, George the Monk, ed. de Boor (see ch. 1, n. 75), p. 784.

[6] This was the traditional argument.

palace).[7] He twice made the ludicrous suggestion that, in order to save face, Leo should blame the error on the pope himself or on the patriarch Germanos. As regards the latter, now a wise old man of ninety-five, still in office though already in disgrace (he was removed in 730), Leo would have done better to have asked his advice. Above all, he should have followed the example of his predecessor, Constantine IV, who had not hesitated to disown his own father in order to bring to a close, by the sixth ecumenical council (680–1), the long and unhappy episode of the Monothelete heresy and to try to atone for the martyrdoms of Pope Martin and the monk Maximos (655, 662). This time, the council that Leo was asking for would be superfluous;[8] let the emperor say no more and everything would return to normal. The letter ended with an appeal for peace, but preceded by a strange piece of bravado. So Leo was threatening to come to Rome, smash the image of St Peter and arrest Gregory! Let him try! The pope only needed to retreat three miles into the interior of Campania and 'best of luck, chase after the wind!' The West, now Christianised and prosperous, would not take things lying down; it had its eyes on the successor of the apostle Peter whom it 'regarded as a god on earth'.[9]

The references to the Monothelete crisis and the sixth ecumenical council had earlier made it possible to raise the issue of the independence of the bishops in matters of faith:

> you know, Basileus, that the dogmas of the holy Church do not fall within the province of emperors, but of bishops, and require to be dealt with very prudently. It is for this that bishops have been established for the Churches, keeping apart from public affairs, and emperors similarly in order to keep apart from ecclesiastical affairs and apply themselves to those which have been entrusted to them. The harmony between emperors dear to Christ and pious bishops forms one single power when affairs are dealt with in peace and in charity.[10]

[7] The letter is almost the only document which speaks of the Chalkoprateia rather than the Chalke. The other sources relate how Leo III sent soldiers, under the command of a 'spatharocandidatus', to take down the famous image of Christ placed above this Bronze Gate of the palace. A crowd gathered and pious women, scandalised, toppled the ladder and killed the officer. *Life of St Stephen the Younger* by Stephen the Deacon, 10, ed. and trans. M. F. Auzépy, *La Vie d'Etienne le Jeune par Etienne le Diacre*, Birmingham Byzantine and Ottoman Monographs 3 (Birmingham, 1997), pp. 100–101; Theophanes, *Chronographia*, ed. de Boor (see ch. 1, n. 4), p. 405 (p. 559 of Mango and Scott translation); George the Monk, ed. de Boor (see ch. 1, n. 75), p. 743.

[8] Gouillard, 'Aux origines' (n. 2), pp. 292–3. This detail, like many others, suggests the second, rather than the first, iconoclasm: it was Leo V who, in 815, proposed an ecumenical council, which the supporters of images judged pointless and refused.

[9] Ibid., pp. 297. The formulation is strange, to say the least. 'The West had its eyes on...' is an expression that occurs in the *Acta Maximi* II, *Disputatio cum Theodosio*, PG 90, col. 161; ed. P. Allen and B. Neil, *Scripta saeculi VII vitam Maximi Confessoris illustrantia*, Corpus Christianorum, Series graeca 39 (Turnhout/Leuven, 1999) pp. 130–1.

[10] Gouillard, 'Aux origines' (n. 2), pp. 290–3.

Gregory had slipped from the veneration of images to the status of the emperor within the Church; and it was to this very point that Leo III was supposed to have returned in order firmly to assert the sacerdotal nature of his office. 'But you have persisted in your stubbornness and your natural passions. You have written: *I am emperor and priest* [*basileus kai hiereus eimi*].' This lapidary phrase was both repeated and refuted by the pope in a new reply, briefer and more caustic, wholly devoted to the issue.[11] One expects a traditional tirade on the difference between the priesthood and the empire, in the tone and style of the letter from Pope Gelasius to the emperor Anastasios,[12] and, to a degree, and with much repetition, this is what we find:

Take note of our humility, O emperor, cease, and preserve the holy churches as you found and received them. Dogmas are not a matter for emperors, but for bishops, because we have the mind of Christ (1 Corinthians, 2: 16). Instruction in the dogmas of the Church is one thing and the secular mind for secular administration another. The warlike spirit, unsophisticated and rough, which is yours, cannot be applied to the spiritual administration of dogma. I will describe to you the differences between palace and churches, emperors and bishops; understand, be saved and dispute no longer. If you were to be stripped of the imperial robes, the marble of porphyry, the diadem on your head, the purple and all the trappings of the court, you would assuredly appear to men without beauty or grace, insignificant, as you have done for the churches [by stripping them of their images]. What you yourself do not have [natural presence], you have taken away from the holy churches, which you have deprived of their beauty. Just as bishops do not have the power to interfere in the palace or appoint to imperial dignities, so the emperor does not have that to interfere in the churches and conduct elections among the clergy, or to consecrate or to touch the holy mysteries, or even to take communion without the assistance of a priest. 'Let every man abide in the same calling wherein he was called' (1 Corinthians, 7: 20). You see, emperor, the differences between bishops and emperors? If someone commits a crime against you, O emperor, you confiscate his house and strip him of his belongings, leaving him only his life, and then you hang him, behead him or exile him. Bishops do not do this, but when someone has sinned and confessed, instead of the gallows and beheading, they burden him with the gospel and the cross, they imprison him in the sacristies, they exile him in the *diakonika* and the *cathechoumena:* fasting for the belly, vigil for the eyes, doxology for the lips. When they have properly corrected him and subjected him to this diet, they give him the precious blood of the Lord and wash him in his holy blood and, having made

---

[11] Ibid., pp. 298–305. The letter is thought to have been written just before the deposition of Germanos.
[12] See below, pp. 182, 300–1.   [13] Gouillard, 'Aux origines' (n. 2), pp. 300–3.

him a new *chosen vessel* without sin, they lead him, pure and unsullied, to the Lord. You see, O emperor, the differences between churches [that is, the clergy] and emperors?[13]

But these familiar arguments are accompanied by others which express very different ideas. It was permitted for orthodox sovereigns to declare themselves 'emperors and priests', those, that is, who had demonstrated their orthodoxy in words and deeds, who had taken care of the churches 'in agreement with the bishops, seeking truth with the zeal and the love of orthodoxy: the great Constantine, the great Theodosius [I], the great Valentinian [III], the great Justinian [I] and Constantine [IV] father of Justinian [II]'. This is a familiar tirade, in which one recognises those sovereigns who had convened and presided over the ecumenical councils of Nicaea I (325), Constantinople I (381), Chalcedon (451, for which Marcian is more often credited than Valentinian) and Constantinople II (553) and III (680–1).[14] And the same idea, repeated in conclusion, this time jars as a massive logical flaw: 'We beg you, become bishop and emperor as you have written!'[15] One's first instinct is to allow for rhetoric or clumsiness and understand that Leo III was being invited to follow the example of several good emperors who had respected the clergy, and who might have called themselves priests because their reign had been so beneficial to the Church. But this is impossible; the contradiction is clear. The exposition of all that sharply differentiated the imperial office from the priestly office (the most important difference clearly being the power to bind and to loose) is followed by the model of a sovereign in whom the two are combined: pious, orthodox, legitimate, priest or even 'arch priest', that is, bishop. Gregory II, or whoever was hiding behind his name, was himself apparently so unconvinced of the possibility of separating *imperium* and *sacerdotium* that, while reproaching the emperor for having interfered in matters of faith, he suggests that he switch roles again and, to preserve his dignity, himself restore the worship of images by falsely imputing to the pope and the patriarch the initiative for the iconoclast heresy.[16] The first lesson to be drawn from these documents is not, therefore, that the assertion of the priestly character of kingship offended the political sensibilities of the Byzantines as the breaking of a political taboo, but rather that it was impossible, in Byzantium, for the distinction between the sacerdotal function and the imperial function to be fully thought through.

---

[14] Similarly, the synodal letter of the council of Rome, conveyed to Constantine IV and his brothers and signed by Pope Agatho and 125 bishops, asks the emperors to receive the delegation sympathetically, which would earn them a renown comparable to that enjoyed by Constantine, Theodosius, Marcian and Justinian: ed. R. Reidinger, *ACO*, Ser. II, vol. II, 1, pp. 134–7.

[15] Gouillard, 'Aux origines' (n. 2), pp. 304–5.

[16] This bizarre suggestion, made in both letters (ibid., pp. 292–3, 304–5), can only have come from an easterner who remembered that Herakleios 'had shifted onto his patriarch, Sergios, authorship of the *Ekthesis* and that Maximos the Confessor would have liked Constans II, in the case of the *Typos*, to do the same with Pyrrhos': ibid., p. 264; see also Maximos Confessor, *Relatio motionis*, PG 90, col. 125; ed. Allen and Neil (n. 9), pp. 40–1.

It is almost certain that the letters originated in Byzantium, not Rome. All the skill of those who have studied them has failed satisfactorily to explain letters which are full of anomalies, asperities, contradictory chronological allusions, erroneous scriptural quotations and borrowings from the whole 'iconodule' literature; but of some things we can be sure.[17] We know, from reliable western sources, that Leo III had informed Gregory II of his intentions, and that the pope had attempted to dissuade him and then reacted to the deposition of the patriarch Germanos.[18] But there is no trace of these authentic documents in the pontifical chancery; nor were they mentioned at the council of Nicaea in 787, even though every available argument was deployed there.[19] Theophanes, writing a little before 814, is the first to refer to them; he says that in a first letter, written in 726, the pope had advised his correspondent that it was not for an emperor to interfere in the faith or to overthrow the tradition of the Fathers; in the second, 'widely known' at the time of writing, he had condemned the ungodliness of the Byzantine emperor, who had recently sent Germanos into exile.[20] This passage may allow us to date to the first years of the ninth century the diffusion of documents which were certainly forged – but perhaps round a few authentic nuggets – and which were added, soon after iconoclasm, to the repertoire of edifying readings proposed for the Sunday of Orthodoxy, a feast instituted in 843 to celebrate the definitive victory of images. The faithful at the office and the monks at their meals heard what the *typikon* of the monastery of the Evergetis, in the middle of the eleventh century, called 'the letter of Gregory Dialogus [confusion with Gregory I] to Leo the Heretic'.[21] It becomes clear that the two texts had been devised or at least rewritten without historical scruple but, like so many other documents of the period, with considerable skill. The roles are deliberately reworked in order to make the first iconoclast emperor the archetypal autocrat, in whom the oriental despot is suddenly revealed, 'arrogant and stubborn', indulging his 'natural passions' and disqualified by his crudeness as a warmonger and scandalmonger, to show that he was guilty not only of an error of faith, but of political heresy, and to suggest that the one explained the other. He had a mistaken and exaggerated idea of his office and had violated a

---

[17] While Jean Gouillard, following L. Duchesne (*Liber pontificalis*, I (Paris, 1955), p. 413, note 45) and L. Guérard ('Les lettres de Grégoire II à Léon l'Isaurien', *Mélanges d'Archéologie et d'Histoire*, 10 (1890), pp. 59–60), is right to conclude they are not authentic, some of his predecessors (L. M. Hartmann, G. Ostrogorsky, E. Caspar) believed it to be an authentic document with many interpolations or a second authentic letter, on the basis of which a forger reconstituted the first; for these interpretations; see Gouillard, 'Aux origines' (n. 2), pp. 259–60, 306.

[18] Jean Gouillard (ibid., p. 260) quotes in particular the letter of Hadrian I to Constantine and Irene (Mansi, XII, col. 1061), the refutation by the same pope of the *Libri carolini* (ibid., col. 802) and the *Liber pontificalis* (ed. Duchesne, I (n. 17), pp. 404, 409).

[19] In particular, another forged letter of Gregory II addressed to the patriarch Germanos was invoked: Mansi, XIII, cols. 92–100.

[20] Theophanes, *Chronographia*, ed. de Boor (see ch. 1, n. 4), pp. 404, 408–9 (pp. 558, 565 of Mango and Scott translation).

[21] See the references to lectionaries on images in Gouillard: 'Aux origines' (n. 2), pp. 253–4.

taboo, committed what the ancient Greeks called an act of hubris, by questioning a fundamental distinction between two sorts of power; he had rendered himself illegitimate twice over. And it was for the pope of Rome, the successor of St Peter, to tell him that the development of the West now protected it from the violent assaults of the past, and it was the pope who therefore represented, in an apparent equilibrium and an independence based primarily on distance, the power of the clergy as opposed to that of the laity, and who was the high priest speaking 'of thy testimonies also before kings',[22] in the words of the psalm often quoted in Byzantium in such circumstances.

The fact that the roles have been rewritten and dramatised does not mean they are false. The historical Leo III fits reasonably well into the role assigned to him, and it is quite possible that, at the presumed date of the letters, the polemic on the sacerdotal or non-sacerdotal character of imperial power was expressed through a confrontation of Old Testament models on the great biblical stage, where everything to do with kingship was decoded. In the first letter of the Pseudo-Gregory, the most obviously forged passage is perhaps that which suggests the most skilful use by the forger of authentic documents. The pope is supposed to have replied to Leo:

> You have written: 'Uzziah, king of the Jews, after eight hundred years, re-moved the serpent of brass from the Temple, and I, after eight hundred years, have removed the idols from churches.' In truth, Uzziah was also your brother, and he was as stubborn; and he tyrannised the priests of his time as you do today, because it was the blessed David who had introduced this serpent into the Temple with the holy Ark.[23]

The references are incoherent. David never introduced the serpent of brass into the Temple, built after his reign; it was Hezekiah who melted it down because its cult was becoming idolatrous, and was praised for this as an act of piety; Uzziah, on the other hand, criticised for having usurped sacred functions, had nothing to do with the serpent. But the very absurdity suggests a hasty reading and invites us to correct the text as it has come down to us in such a way as to obtain a highly probable dialogue between a sovereign deciding to prohibit the worship of images and a clergy denying him this right. The emperor was saying, or being made to say 'Just as Hezekiah smashed into pieces the serpent of brass which Moses had made on Jahweh's orders (Numbers, 21: 8–9), because the sons of Israel had started burning incense to it and giving it a name, Nehushtan, as if it were an idol (II Kings [IV Kings], XVIII: 4), so I have excluded from Christian churches the images which, over time, have become the object of an idolatrous cult.' To which his opponents replied, 'By removing the images from the churches, you are comparable not to the pious

----

[22] Psalm CXIX [CXVIII]: 46; see below, p. 232.
[23] Gouillard, 'Aux origines' (n. 2), pp. 286–7.

Hezekiah intervening as pontiff in the organisation of the sanctuary, but to the sacrilegious Uzziah, portrayed in 2 Chronicles, 26: 16–20 as an immoderate sovereign usurping the privileges of the priests, sons of Aaron':

> But when he was strong, his heart was lifted up to his destruction; for he transgressed against the Lord his God, and went into the temple of the Lord to burn incense upon the altar of incense. And Azariah the priest went in after him, and with him were fourscore priests of the Lord, that were valiant men. And they withstood Uzziah the king, and said unto him, It appertaineth not unto thee, Uzziah, to burn incense unto the Lord, but to the priests the sons of Aaron, that are consecrated to burn incense: go out of the sanctuary; for thou hast trespassed; neither shall it be for thine honour from the Lord God. Then Uzziah was wrath, and had a censer in his hand to burn incense: and while he was wrath with the priests, the leprosy even rose up in his forehead before the priests in the house of the Lord, from beside the incense altar.[24] And Azariah the chief priest, and all the priests, looked upon him, and, behold, he was leprous in his forehead, and they thrust him out from thence; yea, himself hasted also to go out, because the Lord had smitten him.

The argument drawn from Hezekiah had become standard among the opponents of images; it is found in the *Libri carolini*[25] and it is refuted by Hadrian I,[26] and also by Theodore of Stoudios.[27] That derived from Uzziah seems to have been less common. As for the figure of 800 years, frequent in the sources which refer to the return to iconoclasm in 815, it is a further argument for dating the letters, in their present form, to the late eighth or very early ninth centuries.[28] But we should note, above all, that in this debate, and at the most authentic level, the ideas mattered less than the biblical models. Neither the liturgical arguments nor the political theories were enough to confer or deny legitimacy to the sovereign, unless they were combined with an identification with a particular just or unjust Old Testament king. With the aid of exegesis, the Old Testament text was no longer understood as a history of the Jewish people, but rather, as noted above,[29] as a repertoire of roles and situations, and

---

[24] A Byzantine reader would think of Constantine the Great attacked by and then cured of leprosy, and of the ceremonial which provided for the Byzantine emperor to cense the altar (see below, pp. 264–5).

[25] *Caroli Magni Capitulare de imaginibus*, I, 18, ed. H. Bastgen (Hanover/Leipzig, 1924), *MGH, Legum Sectio* II, *Concilia* II, *Supplementum*, pp. 42–4.

[26] *MGH, Ep.* V, *Epistolae Karolini aevi* III, pp. 27–8 (ch. 26), where the pope prefers to hark back to the reference to the serpent of Moses (Numbers, 21: 8–9) and hardly mentions Hezekiah.

[27] *Antirrheticus*, II, 39, PG 99, col. 380.

[28] Gouillard, 'Aux origines' (n. 2), pp. 286–9. The way the chroniclers calculated is pretty consistent: they count, on the basis of the Incarnation and the *didaskalia* of the Apostles, 736 years for the first iconoclasm under Leo III (George the Monk Continued, ed. Bekker (see ch. 1, n. 101), p. 739), 'almost 800 years' for the council of Nicaea II in 787 (Mansi, XIII, col. 228A), and more than 800 years for the renewed war against images under Leo V: George the Monk Continued, p. 767; *Life of St Nicetas of Medikion* by Theosteriktos, 35, *AASS*, April I, p. XXIX.

[29] See above, p. 50.

as the only typology which made it possible to judge the present and the future. Comparison weakened a link that was actually very strong; at the moment of his death at the hands of the Bulgarians, Nikephoros I was not led astray *like* Ahab, he saw himself *in the role* of Ahab.[30] Similarly, it was important to know which was the true face of Leo III – that of Hezekiah or that of Uzziah? The first letter suggests this dilemma; the second offers a different identification, this time veiled. To be able to say 'I am emperor and priest', you had to believe yourself Melchizedek.

But before we examine this great biblical model of sacerdotal kingship, we need to be clear as to its centrality to the debate. The sources from which the forger or his model drew their inspiration will, I hope prove the case.

MAXIMOS THE CONFESSOR AND THE MONOTHELETE SOURCES

Jean Gouillard has justly observed that the chief value of the letters of the Pseudo-Gregory is to shed light on a particular milieu, that of the defenders of images in Constantinople in the first decades of the ninth century.[31] It was a milieu with an active memory extending back to about 650. The historical allusions that stud the two texts are rare and cursory for earlier periods, but numerous and significant when they relate to the arrest and deportation of Pope Martin, the martyrdom of Maximos the Confessor,[32] the providential murder of Constans II at Syracuse in 668,[33] and the wisdom of his successor, Constantine IV, who left it to the bishops of the sixth ecumenical council, in 680–1, to define the Orthodox creed.[34] There are errors of detail, but one can detect the use, at

---

[30] Theophanes, *Chronographia*, ed. de Boor (see ch. 1, n. 4), p. 490 (pp. 672–3 of Mango and Scott translation). In the same author, the emperors Valens and Constantine V are also compared to Ahab (ibid., pp. 65, 439, pp. 100, 607 of Mango and Scott translation); George the Monk compares Leo V to Saul, who reigned two years 'according to the laws', then, deprived of the grace of God and seized by an evil spirit, took up arms against his benefactor David and massacred the priests (ed. de Boor (see ch. 1, n. 75), p. 777, in line with I Samuel [I Kings], 18–19 and 22: 17–19); he says the same 'of the race of Senacherim' (pp. 780–1); George the Monk Continued calls the same emperor 'New Caiaphas' (ed. Bekker (see ch. 1, n. 101), p. 783) and the *Scriptor incertus de Leone Armenio* (ed. Bekker, see ch. 1, n. 43) compares him to Pharaoh, p. 357.

[31] Gouillard, 'Aux origines' (n. 2), pp. 306–7.   [32] Ibid., pp. 294–5.

[33] Ibid. The author of the letter errs only in asserting that the emperor was murdered in a sanctuary (instead of a bath) by a certain Mezenxios (instead of Mezezios): Theophanes, *Chronographia*, ed. de Boor (see ch. 1, n. 4), p. 351 (p. 490 of Mango and Scott translation).

[34] Gouillard, 'Aux origines' (n. 2), pp. 290–2, 294–5, 298–9. Constantine IV never envisaged anathematising his father, as claimed in the letter, which very freely adapts the *sacra* in which Constantine simply gave assurances that the papal envoys would be well received and at liberty in their search for truth, that he himself would remain impartial and force no one, that he would accept the general opinion or, in case of disagreement, ask the pope to rule, and that he was responsible for the purity of the faith, and would, for this reason, preach union, but compel no one. See the *sacrae* of the emperor, in the Acts ed. R. Riedinger, *ACO*, II, 2, 1, pp. 2–13.

least indirectly, of a number of documents referring to Monotheletism, the presence of several borrowed formulae, and a deliberate intention to establish a link between two crises separated by half a century.

Let us briefly recall the facts.[35] Soon after his victory over the Persians, the emperor Herakleios (610–41), wishing to restore the unity of the empire which had been undermined by the religious opposition between 'Chalcedonians' and 'non-Chalcedonians', proclaimed a compromise statement of faith, which recognised in the single person of Christ two separate natures moved by one 'energy' (Monoenergism) or 'will' (Monotheletism). As its theological implications gradually emerged, they provoked rejection or resistance wherever the political influence of Constantinople was most contested, particularly in Palestine, Africa and Italy. In drawing back, the authorities only made matters worse, and the dictatorial measures taken by the patriarchs and even the emperors alone (*Psephos* of 633, *Ekthesis* of 638, *Typos* of 648) turned Monotheletism into a typical imperial heresy, against a backdrop of military defeat and religious discord. The victorious Arabs were advancing, Africa was liberating itself before succumbing in its turn, and Rome, now the focus of eastern resistance, adopted a provocative stance at the Lateran Council of 649. Constans II decided to use force, the last occasion on which – as the Pseudo-Gregory recalled – an eastern sovereign was in a position to take effective action against the Holy See, and also the most brutal. Pope Martin was arrested on 17 June 653, tried for high treason in Constantinople and exiled almost immediately to Cherson, where he died in 655. Maximos the Confessor was also seized, taken to Constantinople in May 655, exiled at Bizye in Thrace, then brought back to Constantinople in the spring of 662, by which time he was eighty-two years old. The synod anathematised him; his tongue was torn out and his right hand cut off. Deported to Lazike at the same time as his disciples Anastasios the Monk and Anastasios the papal legate *apokrisiarios*, but separated from them, he died soon after, in the fortress of Schemaris, on 13 August 662.

The author of Gregory II's letters shows considerable familiarity with the documents emanating from this long affair; they consisted of authentic letters and accounts written in the heat of the moment and intended to spread the news and foster, rather than direct opposition to the emperor, a far more effective surge of fervour surrounding the victims and soon-to-be martyrs – Martin, Maximos, a handful of clerics and laymen.[36] Rome was involved, of course, and

---

[35] *Histoire du christianisme*, IV, pp. 40–9, with bibliography. See also *Martino I Papa (649–653) e il suo tempo. Atti del XXVIII Convegno storico internazionale, Todi, 13–16 ottobre 1991* (Spoleto, 1992).

[36] See, in particular, R. Devreesse, 'Le texte grec de l'*Hypomnesticum* de Théodore Spoudée. Le supplice, l'exil et la mort des victimes illustres du monothélisme'. *Anal. Boll.*, 53 (1935), pp. 49–80.

Anastasius Bibliothecarius translated all the texts into Latin;[37] but only the East, including the easterners in the West, really mobilised to bring events to their dramatic climax and then to keep their memory alive. At the end of the seventh century, Anastasios Sinaites saw the defeat of the Christians by Islam as divine punishment for the sins of Constans II.[38] Pope Martin merited two notices in the *Synaxarion of Constantinople*[39] and his Greek *Life,* probably written under iconoclasm, knew nothing about him before his Lateran defiance and arrest.[40] In the same collection of documents, his later defenders found a marginal text which enabled them to travesty Maximos, by anticipation, as an iconodule;[41] but above all he became an exemplary figure through whom Rome helped the eastern opposition to stiffen its resistance and even win a double victory, that of the martyrdom which discredited the adversary and that of the ecumenical council which condemned him. The allegiance of a Byzantine to the papacy never went much further than this, even in Theodore of Stoudios, presented by Catholic historiography – with much exaggeration – as a convinced papist.[42] It was less a matter of ecclesiology than of strategy: when there was conflict in the East between the emperor and a section of the Church, Roman polarisation offered a model of independent ecclesiastical power and an ideal base from which to tell the sovereign that he was only a layman and that only bishops were qualified to define dogma and rule the Church. It is hardly surprising, therefore, that an eastern forger should glorify the memory of Pope Martin and make Gregory II his hero.

One of the documents in this Monotheletist collection can be recognised as the source of the principal themes and certain expressions in the second letter to Leo III. This was the account by a disciple, Anastasios Apokrisiarios, of the interrogation endured by Maximos immediately after his arrival in

---

[37] J. Sirmond, *Anastasii Bibliothecarii Sedis Apostolicae Collectanea* (Paris, 1620), also the new edition of Allen and Neil (n. 9).

[38] Anastasios Sinaites, *Sermo* III, PG 89, cols. 1156–7; see also ed. K.-H. Uthemann, *Anastasii Sinaitae sermones duo in constitutionem hominis secundum imaginem dei, necnon opuscula adversus monothelitas,* Corpus Christianorum, Series graeca 12 (Turnhout, 1985), II, 1, pp. 58–61.

[39] Ed. Delehaye (see ch. 4, n. 102), cols. 49–50 (16 September) and 599–602 (13 April).

[40] *BHG* 2259; ed. P. Peeters, 'Une Vie grecque du pape S. Martin I', *Anal. Boll.,* 51 (1933), pp. 225–62.

[41] In the *Disputatio cum Theodosio* (= *Acta Maximi* II), Maximos kisses images (18, PG 90, col. 156; ed. Allen and Neil (n. 9), p. 117) and invokes the judgement of God in the presence of the Gospels and images of Christ and the Virgin (ibid., 26, PG 90, col. 164; ed. Allen and Neil (n. 9), p. 133). These texts were invoked by the defenders of images. John of Damascus cites the first (*Contra calumniatores imaginum,* II, 65 and III, 131, ed. B. Kotter, *Die Schriften des Johannes von Damaskos,* III (Berlin, 1975), pp. 164, 196), both were read at the council of Nicaea II (Mansi, XIII, cols. 37–40) and Theodore the Stoudite invokes the first (*Antirrheticus,* II, 39, PG 99, col. 38) just after the refutation of the argument taken from Hezekiah (see above, pp. 164–5).

[42] See, for example, S. Salaville, 'La primauté de Saint Pierre et du pape d'après Saint Théodore Studite', *Echos d'Orient,* 17 (1914–15), pp. 23–42.

Constantinople, in May 655, which is clearly biased but written on the spot.[43]
In a hall in the palace, in the presence of the senate, the official conducting
the investigation avoided all theological debate and asked the prisoner how he
could be a Christian and hate the emperor. The formulation is surprising, but
the indignation is sincere; Maximos had defied and scorned he whom Christ
had placed at the head of the Christians. The reproaches piled up, exaggerated
or ill founded: Maximos had stirred up Africa, the Pentapolis and Egypt, so
facilitating the arrival of the Arabs; by recounting a dream, he had encouraged
the usurpation of the exarch Gregory in Africa; a witness told how, in Rome, he
had heard Maximos make insulting remarks about the person of the emperor.
The fourth grievance is of direct relevance to us:

> After him, they produced a fourth accuser, Gregory son of Photeinos, who
> declared: 'I had gone to the cell of the abbot Maximos, in Rome, and when I
> told him that the emperor was also a priest, the abbot Anastasios, his disci-
> ple, replied: "You must not accord him the dignity of priest!"' At once, the
> servant of God [Maximos] said to Gregory: 'Fear God, Lord Gregory! My
> companion said absolutely nothing during the conversation which bore on
> that.' And he threw himself to the ground, saying to the senate: 'Be gracious
> enough to listen to your servant and I will repeat to you what was actually
> said, and let him [Gregory] confound me if I lie. The lord Gregory, on ar-
> riving in Rome, was kind enough to come to your servant's cell. On seeing
> him, as was my custom, I threw myself to the ground and prostrated my-
> self before him, embraced him and asked him, after we were seated: "What
> is the reason for my lord's dear presence?" He replied: "Our good master
> who is upheld by God [the emperor], wishing to procure peace for the holy
> Churches of God, sent an order to the pope honoured by God, accompanied
> by an offering to St Peter, urging him to unite with the leader of the Church of
> Constantinople; and his pious Power was kind enough to send it through the
> intermediary of my mediocrity." I said to him: "Glory to God, who has made
> you worthy of such a mission. But in what way has His Serenity crowned by
> God ordered that union should be achieved? Tell me, if you know." And you
> said to me: "On the basis of the *Typos*." I replied: "This is, in my opinion,
> an impossible project, because the Romans do not accept that the words of
> the holy Fathers should disappear at the same time as those of the impure
> heretics, or that the truth should be extinguished at the same time as lies or
> that light should disappear at the same time as shadows[44] ... If, on the pretext
> of 'economy',[45] the saving faith is abolished at the same time as the evil
> faith, this sort of fake economy is a separation from God and not a union

---

[43] *Relatio motionis*, PG 90, cols. 109–29; ed. Allen and Neil (n. 9), pp. 1–51.
[44] The *Typos* prohibited all discussion of the two or the single wills.
[45] That is, a compromise; see glossary.

desired by God. And in effect, tomorrow the Jews of ill fame have only to say: Let us make the economy of peace between us; we, for our part, will do away with circumcision, and you, for your part, baptism, and we will cease to fight each other. It is this that in the past the Arians proposed in writing under Constantine the Great, saying: Let us suppress Consubstantiality and Heterogeneity, and let the Churches unite! But our God-loving Fathers did not accept this; they would rather be persecuted and die than keep silent about the word which defined the unique divinity, superior to substance, of the Father, the Son and the Holy Spirit. And this, when Constantine the Great had come to an agreement with those who had made such propositions, as is related by many authors who carefully recorded what happened. And no emperor has been able, by compromise formulas, to persuade the Fathers inspired by God to reach an agreement with the heretics of their day; they used clear and decisive expressions, corresponding to the dogma under discussion, and openly proclaimed that the study and definition of the salutary dogmas of the catholic Church were the province of priests alone."

You then said: "So what? Is not every Christian emperor also a priest?" To which I replied: "No, because he does not have access to the altar; and after the sanctification of the bread, he does not raise it, saying: *the holy things to the holy*; he does not baptise, nor does he perform initiation with the *myron*; he does not ordain, nor does he make bishops, priests and deacons; he does not consecrate churches by unction; he does not bear the symbols of priesthood, the *omophorion* and the Gospel, as he bears those of kingship, the crown and the purple." You objected: "And why does the Gospel say that Melchizedek is *king and priest* (Genesis, 14: 18; Hebrews, 7: 1)?" To which I replied: "It is of the unique king by nature, God of the Universe, become for our salvation hierarch by nature that Melchizedek is the unique prefiguration (*typos*). If you assert that another is king and priest of the order of Melchizedek, dare then to say what follows: *without father, without mother, without descent, having neither beginning of days, nor end of life* (Hebrews, 7: 3), and consider the disastrous consequences that might follow: such and such a person will be another God made man, bringing about our salvation as priest not of the order of Aaron, but of the order of Melchizedek. But what purpose is served by continuing? During the holy anaphora at the holy table, it is after the hierarchs and the deacons and the whole order of clergy that one remembers the emperors at the same time as the laity, the deacon saying: *and of the laymen who have died in the faith, Constantine, Constans etc.* He also mentions living emperors after all the clergy.' "

At these words, Menas cried: 'In saying that, you have started a schism in the Church.'[46]

---

[46] *Relatio motionis*, 4–5, PG 90, cols. 113–17; ed. Allen and Neil (n. 9), pp. 21–9.

There can be little doubt that the author of Gregory II's letters knew of this passage and exploited it with consummate skill. At the date of 729/730, we find the scenario of 655, but schematised, hardened and hieratic. The geographical polarisation has become a rupture between East and West, and the pope can now flout the emperor with impunity. The two protagonists no longer confront each other through officials and monks, but directly. The sovereign, by speaking in the first person ('I am emperor and priest'), transforms a not particularly remarkable formula into a provocative assertion, especially when addressed to the successor of St Peter. It was also incorrect, because there was a fundamental difference between the rhetorical glorification of sacerdotal kingship in ceremonial or a chancery formulary celebrating an orthodox sovereign and the claim of an exorbitant privilege by an emperor whose heresy had deprived him of legitimacy. Last but not least, the text of 655 suggested the ending: 'I am emperor and priest *like Melchizedek*', creating the impression of Leo III not only as an autocrat too sure of his own rights and disrespectful of those of the Church, but as a sort of sulphurous rival to Christ, because, for Maximos, the Antichrist and the general apostasy that would mark the end of the world were never far away. His letters foretell them with regard to the Persian conquest, the Arab invasion and the forced baptism of the Jews in 630;[47] his replies to the dignitaries who interrogated him brandish this threat;[48] he confronted martyrdom as one entering an apocalypse.

The account of Maximos' interrogation is by no means the first text to defend the idea that dogmas are the province of priests, that it was not for emperors to interfere or to use 'economy' in this sphere, and that those who had done so had fallen into heresy or would have led the Church astray but for the courage and sacrifice of the bishops. Maximos spiced up this traditional thesis with a dash of anti-Judaism, a virulent attack on Constantine the Great – essentially justified, but highly unusual in its form – and a roll call of all the heretical councils which had met on the initiative of emperors; but he was, above all, probably the first explicitly to oppose this distinction between the 'two powers' to the notion of sacerdotal kingship. The astonishment of his visitor, for whom an emperor was self-evidently a priest, like the reaction of the government, which saw in the refutation by Maximos an attack on imperial majesty, betrayed a real embarrassment. And this embarrassment was felt sufficiently keenly, even by the author of the *Life of Maximos*, now dated to the tenth century,[49] for him

[47] Ep. 8 and 14, PG 91, cols. 445, 537–41; with regard to the former, see R. Devreesse, 'La fin inédite d'une lettre de saint Maxime. Un baptême forcé de juifs et samaritains à Carthage en 632', *Recherches de sciences religieuses*, 17 (1937), pp. 25–35.

[48] *Disputatio cum Theodosio*, PG 90, col. 145; ed. Allen and Neil (n. 9), p. 93.

[49] *BHG* 1234; R. Devreesse, 'La Vie de S. Maxime le Confesseur et ses recensions', *Anal. Boll.*, 46 (1928), pp. 5–49; and above all, W. Lackner, 'Zu Quellen und Datierung der Maximosvita *BHG*³ 1234', *Anal. Boll.*, 85 (1967), pp. 285–316.

to modify the text of the account, which he otherwise servilely recopied or summarised:

> Next, they brought a third accusation against him, when they saw that the second had been refuted, an accusation that I did not feel I ought to include in my work, so much would it seem not only barely credible, but puerile and ridiculous. And as these good judges did not even refrain from a fourth intervention and fraud, they introduced a certain Gregory, who said that, in Rome, the saint's disciple had said to him that it was neither holy nor appropriate to call the emperor a priest, given what he had been taught by his master [Maximos]. But the holy man did not lack arguments to defend himself also of this, addressing this same Gregory face to face and proving that what had been said then did not correspond to what was being alleged against him today: 'With this man, when he went to Rome, it was a matter of union and of our [possible] acceptance of the *Typos* which decreed and promulgated the famous dogma. It was round this matter that our conversation and our meeting revolved, I expounding my views and what seemed to me useful. In any case, I know that what is being complained of against me did not come from me or from my disciple, who is accused and to whom I never – God be my witness – made such statements. I accept only that I said, not to my disciple but to Gregory himself, which he cannot absolutely deny without denying himself, that the defining of dogmas and the study of that subject was more the province of priests than of emperors, because it is to them that had been granted the privilege of unction [of baptism], of consecration [to ecclesiastical orders], of the offering of the bread, of presence at the altar and of all those acts with a sacred and secret character. That, I said then and I repeat today. It is on this point that whoever wishes it ought to absolve or condemn me.[50]

In this strange censorship, the hagiographer tried to reconcile the saint and an imperial power that was again orthodox. Maximos had not only never uttered words injurious to the emperor (the third complaint is not even spelled out), but he had never denied that the emperor was a priest, because the question had never been put to him. The witness who said so had lied; the conversation in Rome had dealt only with the definition of dogmas and the holy monk had done no more than defend the customary view of the Church, accepted by the emperors themselves. At the beginning of the tenth century a hagiographer lauding the martyrs of Monotheletism dared not raise openly the question of the priestly nature of kingship and preferred to avoid mentioning the name of Melchizedek. He smoothed over and corrected and, in so doing, helps us to understand certain oddities in the second letter from the Pseudo-Gregory to Leo III, drafted a century earlier. Its eastern author, too, was uneasy about bluntly asserting that the emperor was not a priest, which is why he maladroitly

---

[50] PG 90, col. 92.

suggested that he might become one if he was truly orthodox and consulted the bishops, which was virtually meaningless. He, too, made no reference to Melchizedek and bequeathed the explosive formula without the name of the model which had served him, Maximos is our witness, as catalyst.

MELCHIZEDEK, PRIEST AND KING

This silence was transparent. No one, either in the seventh century or the tenth, could fail to understand. For a Christian of the East, priestly kingship was neither an idea, nor a theory, but a person, that of the enigmatic Melchizedek, whose two brief appearances in the Old Testament were enough to provoke volumes of exegesis and a host of images.[51]

When Abraham returned victorious from what was called the massacre of the kings:

Melchizedek king of Salem brought forth bread and wine. He was priest of the most high God. And he blessed Abraham and said: 'Abraham is blessed by the most high God, who has created the heaven and the earth, and he is worthy of being blessed, the most high God who has delivered your enemies into your hands!' Abraham gave him the tenth part of all. (Genesis, 14: 18–20)[52]

This passage was probably inserted into the Pentateuch at a later date to mark a rupture or a link between an ancient local dynasty and the new Hebraic dynasty. It presented the exegetists with a paradox, very quickly perceived: a sovereign whose name meant 'my king is justice' and who reigned in Salem ('peace'), usually identified with Jerusalem, is called priest of the true God, that of Israel, without himself belonging to the chosen race. Long before the Levitical priesthood existed, this stranger, probably a Canaanite, served as intermediary

---

[51] See, in particular, G. Wuttke, *Melchisedech der Priesterkönig von Salem. Eine Studie zur Geschichte der Exegese*, Zeitschr. für die neutestament. Wiss., Beiheft 5 (Giessen, 1927); M. Simon, 'Melchisédech dans la polémique entre juifs et chrétiens et dans la légende', *Revue d'histoire et de philosophie religieuses*, 17 (1937), pp. 58–70, repr. in M. Simon, *Recherches d'histoire judéo-chrétienne* (Paris/The Hague, 1962), pp. 101–26; F. L. Horton Jr, *The Melchizedek Tradition: A Critical Examination of the Sources to the Fifth Century AD and in the Epistle to the Hebrews* (Cambridge, 1976). See also G. Bardy, 'Melchisédech dans la tradition patristique', *Revue biblique*, 35 (1926), pp. 496–509, and 36 (1927), pp. 25–45; J. Sirinelli, 'Quelques allusions à Melchisédech dans l'oeuvre d'Eusèbe de Césarée', in *Scripta Patristica*, VI, *Texte und Untersuchungen*, 81 (Berlin, 1962), pp. 233–47; J.-L. Ska, 'Melchisédech' in *DS* 10 (1977), cols. 967–72; J.-P. Mahé, 'La fête de Melkisédeq le huit août en Palestine d'après les *tropologia* et les ménées géorgiens', *Revue des études géorgiennes et caucasiennes*, 3 (*Hommage à Georges Dumézil*) (1987), pp. 83–125. See also the *Actes* of a conference held at Chartres, where the cathedral has several representations of Melchizedek: *Autour de Melchisédech, Mythes, réalités, symboles*, Association des amis du Centre médiéval européen de Chartres (Chartres, 2000).

[52] This is the translation of the text of the Septuagint according to *La Bible d'Alexandrie, LXX*, 1, *La Genèse*, by M. Harl (Paris, 1986), pp. 160–1; the title of 'priest', like the Hebrew term, is here more evocative of a pagan priesthood.

between God and the Jews; by paying him tithe, Abraham – the Christians would say – recognised himself his inferior.[53] The name of Melchizedek appears a second time in Psalm CX [CIX], which seems to have been written for the enthronement of a Davidic king or for the investiture of a charismatic leader, which reports this oracle of God:

> Sit thou at my right hand, until I make thine enemies thy footstool. The Lord shall send the rod of thy strength out of Zion: rule thou in the midst of thine enemies. Thy people shall be willing in the day of thy power, in the beauties of holiness from the womb of the morning: thou hast the dew of thy youth. The Lord hath sworn, and will not repent, Thou art a priest for ever after the order of Melchizedek.[54]

The image of the king-priest, already associated, in the Judaic context, with the idea of the king being adopted by God, had thus made its way to the day of his accession: 'I will declare the decree: the Lord hath said unto me, Thou art my Son; this day have I begotten thee. Ask of me, and I shall give thee the heathen for thine inheritance, and the uttermost parts of the earth for thy possession' (Psalm II, 7–8).[55]

Speculation was rife when St Paul tried to cut it short by suggesting a Christian interpretation in his Epistle to the Hebrews (7: 1–17). He based his argument on the unusual silence of the Scriptures regarding the filiation and descent and the birth and death of the king of Salem, to recognise in him Christ, of whom alone it could be said that he was 'without father, without mother, without descent, having neither beginning of days, nor end of life', and that he 'abideth a priest continually'. This was the origin of the distinction between being a 'priest after the order of Aaron', by belonging to a priestly caste, that of the tribe of Levi, and being a 'priest after the order of Melchizedek', 'not after the law of a carnal commandment, but after the power of an endless life'. Christ, who 'sprang out of Juda; of which tribe Moses spoke nothing concerning priesthood', prefigured by Melchizedek, had thus come to abolish the Levitical priesthood.[56] This anti-Hebraic interpretation was then repeated and refined. Justin had already recognised in Melchizedek a person uncircumcised announcing the triumph

---

[53] See, in particular, Simon, 'Melchisédech' (n. 51).

[54] Psalm 110 [109], 1–4. Some commentators think of the age of the Maccabees and draw a parallel with I Maccabees, 14: 41, which gives Simon the title of 'leader and high priest in perpetuity', but F. L. Horton has dismissed this hypothesis, pointing out that there was no longer prophecy at that period, and that it must therefore go back to the age of the Davidic dynasty.

[55] Horton (*The Melchizedek Tradition* (n. 51)) cites other passages illustrating the notion that the king becomes son of God and that he is invested with a sacerdotal *character* (in particular II Samuel [II Kings], 6: 14 and 17; Jeremiah, 30: 21), but he emphasises that the term used for the priesthood of Melchizedek is unique and that it indicates a *function* and not only a sacerdotal *character*.

[56] Horton (*The Melchizedek Tradition* (n. 51), pp. 152–72) shows how the ideas of St Paul, not properly understood, gave rise in their turn to a number of legends and heresies. See also the epilogue, below.

of Christianity over the descendants of Abraham and the law;[57] Augustine observed:

> The reason is, Aaron's priesthood and sacrifice are abolished; and now in all the world under Christ the Priest we offer that which Melchizedek brought forth when he blessed Abraham [the bread and the wine symbolising the Eucharist]. Who doubts now of whom this is spoken?[58]

In this way, a secondary and highly obscure person in the Old Testament became one of the key figures in Christian thought. But before and after the peremptory assertion of St Paul, this figure was enriched by very diverse interpretations, made possible by that very obscurity, which coexisted at very different levels: those of history, allegory and myth as well as of exegesis. No one doubted that Melchizedek, even 'prefiguration' of Christ, had also been a very real king of Jerusalem or of the place called Salem, near Sichem, where, in Jerome's day the ruins of his palace could still be seen.[59] This did not prevent him being made into an allegory. For Philo of Alexandria he was an allegory of the *basileus dikaios* (just king), led by the *orthos logos* (right word) whose perpetual priesthood was not a function but a quality inherent in his justice.[60] The same idea, but historicised, is found in Flavius Josephus, whose influence on Byzantium was huge; because he was just to the highest degree, King Melchizedek was the first to receive the priesthood.[61]

The drift into eschatology began very early. Manuscripts from Qumran present Melchizedek in the form of a celestial being engaged in the fight against Belial, a sort of archangel or *elohim* comparable to St Michael, avenger, liberator or judge, expected on earth on the Day of Atonement.[62] The 'Melchizedekians' were partly inspired by this. They claimed that Christ was never more than Melchizedek's delegate on earth, or that Melchizedek represented the true Word

---

[57] *Sancti Iustini Dialogus cum Tryphone*, 19 (Abraham the circumcised paid tithe to Melchizedek the uncircumcised), 33 (it is Christ priest and king, and not Hezekiah as claimed by the Jews, who fulfils the prefiguration of Melchizedek by becoming high priest of the uncircumcised and the circumcised): PG 6, cols. 516–17, 545. Against the Christian anti-Judaic exegesis, rabbinical exegesis tends generally to minimise the person of Melchizedek, attach him to the lineage of Abraham, identify him with Shem, or make him a prefiguration of the Messiah to come or of Elijah: Simon, 'Melchisédech' (n. 51), pp. 102–9.

[58] Augustine, *City of God*, XVII, 17.

[59] *Epist. ad Evangelum presbyterum de Melchisedech*, LXXIII, 1, 7–8, ed. and trans. J. Labourt, *Saint Jérôme, Lettres*, IV (Paris, 1954), pp. 19–26.

[60] *Legum allegoriae*, III, 25–6, 79–82, ed. and trans. C. Mondésert, *Œuvres de Philon d'Alexandrie*, 2 (Paris, 1962), pp. 182–5, 214–17. Philo repeats this idea of a sacerdotal kingship crowning the king's 'justice' with regard to Moses, prophet and leader of people, whom he also declares, contrary to the Old Testament, king and high priest, of a priesthood linked to his justice as opposed to that with which he invested his brother Aaron: *Life of Moses*, II, 66–69, 116, 187, ed. R. Arnaldez, C. Montdésert, J. Pouilloux and P. Savinel, *Œuvres de Philon d'Alexandrie*, 22 (Paris, 1967), pp. 222–4, 264, 274.

[61] *Jewish War*, VI, 438 (pp. 500–1 of Loeb ed.); *Jewish Antiquities*, I, 178–81 (p. 89 of Loeb ed.).

[62] See E. Puech, 'Notes sur le manuscrit de XI Q Melkîsédeq', *Revue de Qumran*, XII, 4 (no. 45) (1987), pp. 483–513.

and the Son of God before he entered Mary's womb, or that he merged with the Holy Spirit.[63] This heresy, regarded as 'Judaising', became fossilised in the treatises, but was still dangerous in the fourth century and lingered in the imagination subsequently. At the time of Cyril of Alexandria, we learn from the *Apophthegmata*, a pious monk could still wonder if Melchizedek was the Son of God and, to convince him that he was a human and historical person, God had to make appear to him in a dream, one after the other, 'all the patriarchs from Adam to Melchizedek'.[64] Melchizedek escaped from heresy only to enter legend, in the Syriac story of *The Cave of Treasures*, whose most ancient elements date back to the third century,[65] or in the Greek versions of the Pseudo-Athanasius and the *Palaia*.[66] Son of a pagan king and a queen of Salem, Melchizedek refused to provide the beasts required for an animal sacrifice, then prevented a massive human sacrifice by praying to God to swallow up the town and its inhabitants. The prince became a monk on Mount Tabor, and it was this Christian hermit, naked as the day he emerged from his mother's womb, his finger nails uncut and his hair hanging down to his waist, whom God, who loved him 'like a son', ordered to clothe himself more decently and go out and meet Abraham with the horn of oil of unction, the bread and the wine.

The Byzantine Melchizedek was a composite of all these ideas. The person had been contained by Orthodoxy, but not completely subdued. He remained evocative, sensed as vaguely dangerous. In the Pauline tradition as it was enriched by the Fathers, he was recognised as a 'prefiguration' of Christ; his act was that of the sacrifice without blood and he prefigured the Eucharist (see plates 5a and 5b).[67] In Christianity's stubborn determination to deny its Judaic descent while still claiming the Old Testament heritage, Melchizedek was a powerful argument. As Marcel Simon has shown, this uncircumcised person who gave his blessing to Abraham and obliged him to pay a tithe made it possible to assert the temporal anteriority (at least theoretical) of Christianity over Judaism, or at least the superiority of the Christian ritual over Jewish institutions. This staging post between Adam and Christ made it possible to reduce the history of the Jews to a simple digression, but at the same time to give solid anchorage in Jewish territory to Christian kingship. And this exegetic model

[63] Epiphanius, *Panarion*, LV, 1–5, ed. K. Holl, II, Griechische christliche Schriftsteller, 31 (Leipzig, 1922), pp. 324–31 ; Pseudo-Chrysostomos, PG 56, cols. 260–3; 61, cols. 740–2; Mark the Hermit (disciple of John Chrysostomos), PG 65, cols. 117–40; Horton, *The Melchizedek Tradition* (n. 51), pp. 90–101.
[64] *Apophthegmata Patrum*, PG 65, col. 160.
[65] *The Book of the Cave of Treasures*, trans. E. A. Wallis Budge (London, 1927).
[66] Pseudo-Athanasius (*BHG* 2268), PG 28, cols. 525–30; story of the Palaea (*BHG* 2269): A. Vassiliev, *Anecdota Graeco-byzantina*, I (Moscow, 1893), pp. 206–14.
[67] Clement of Alexandria is the first to have recognised the sacrifice without blood of the eucharist in the bread and wine of Genesis, 14: 18: *Stromateis*, IV, 161, 3, ed. A. van den Hoeck and C. Montdésert, *Les Stromates*, IV, SC 463 (Paris, 2001), pp. 324–5.

Plate 5. Christ giving communion to the apostles between David, who announced his coming, and Melchizedek, to whom Abraham offered the bread and wine in a prefiguring of the eucharist
(a) Chludov Psalter, Cod. Gre. 129, fo. 115r, ninth century. State History Museum, Moscow
(b) Theodore Psalter, BL. Add. MS. 19.352, fo. 152r, copied 1066. British Library, London

found a place and a date in the chronicles; in the seventh century, the *Paschal Chronicle* made him a man of the tribe of Shem, transplanted into the land of Canaan and leaving on God's orders to meet Abraham, a king so just that, although a pagan, he pleased God and became 'priest of the Most High'.[68]

From this mixture of history and exegesis there emerged an illustrated note, perhaps already present in the *Alexandrine Chronicle*,[69] which appears with its original iconography and a commentary in the *Christian Topography* of Cosmas Indicopleustes.[70] The *Paschal Chronicle* reproduces part of the same text; the *Chronicle* of George the Monk gives a different text, but with this appeal to the reader: 'Look at this person to whom Abraham gave the tithe', which marks the place of an illustration or a borrowing from another illustrated work.[71] Cosmas is therefore wholly representative of a tradition and may serve as our guide:

> Here is Melchizedek, sublime priest of the Most High, who levied the tithe on the priests of the law of Moses. Here is the king of peace and of justice, at the same time as priest of the Most High, made similar to the Son of God: he did not receive his priesthood by succeeding to other priests, nor transmit it to other priests. Here is he who celebrated the cult without following the law of Moses, exercising his priesthood by right of other and better alliances. Here is he who blessed the patriarch Abraham, he who had neither father, nor mother, nor genealogy going back to the Abrahamites, the only one to be king and priest, made similar to the Son of God and judged worthy, he too, of initiating into such good things.
>
> *Digression* – After the flood, when men had multiplied, Melchizedek was the only one among them to be proclaimed, by a special dispensation, priest of the Most High God and king of Jerusalem, in likeness to the Son of God, and he offered in sacrifice, following Scripture, the best of all things created which fortified and delighted the human race [the bread and the wine]. As king, he exhorted by every means the people governed by him to engage in these practices, while he continued to exercise his priesthood according to this dispensation and to pray to God for his people. A Canaanite by origin and king of the Canaanites, not descending from the race of the ancestors

---

[68] Ed. Niebuhr (see ch. 1, n. 58), pp. 90–2.

[69] See. A. Bauer and J. Strzygowski, *Eine alexandrinische Weltchronik. Text und Miniaturen eines griechischen Papyrus der Sammlung W. Goleniščev*, Denkschriften der k. Akad. der Wissensch. in Wien, Philos.-hist. Kl., 51 (Vienna, 1905). The notes of this chronicle, which seem to have been used by the *Paschal Chronicle* and George the Synkellos, do not go beyond 392, and there is reason to think that the author was writing soon after 412; among the miniatures (discussed pp. 119ff), there are representations of prophets praying, ancient kings and near contemporary personages. Obvious parallels with the old illustration of Cosmas Indicopleustes and the *Barbarus* of Scaliger (ms. *Parisinus lat.* 4884).

[70] *Christian Topography*, V, 95–8, ed. and trans. W. Wolska-Conus, II, *Cosmas Indicopleustès, Topographie chrétienne*, SC 159 (Paris, 1970), pp. 142–7.

[71] George the Monk, ed. de Boor (see ch. 1, n. 75), pp. 100–3; see also George the Synkellos, *Chronographia*, ed. W. Dindorf (Bonn, 1829), pp. 184–5.

of Abraham, but known to the lineage of the Abrahamites, such a man was celebrated among men as just, as king and as priest...

Scripture says that Melchizedek was without father, without mother, without genealogy, having neither beginning of days nor end of life, because he was not descended from the Abrahamites counted according to the genealogies; in this also he resembled the Lord Christ, because the latter was without father according to the flesh, without mother according to divinity, and similarly without genealogy; he had neither beginning of days, because he was without beginning according to divinity, nor end of life according to this same divinity, and also according to his humanity, because he became immortal and immutable...

In this unoriginal source, as in the others, Melchizedek is certainly a unique 'prefiguration' of Christ, but also a real king, hence a model of priestly kingship. To appreciate this, one need only look at the drawing that originally accompanied the text and which is probably faithfully reproduced in the three ancient manuscripts (the *Vaticanus gr.* 699 of the ninth century, the *Laurentianus Plut.* IX 28 and the *Sinaiticus gr.* 1186 of the eleventh century) (see plate 6). Melchizedek is here given all the attributes characteristic of the Byzantine emperor: crown (*stemma*) with pendants (*prependoulia*), *loros*, *tablion* and boots which were surely purple in colour. His pose in prayer attaches him to the lineage of the patriarchs or the saints, a few images of whom are preserved in the *Alexandrine Chronicle*, but the illustrator, required to choose between king and priest, opted for the king. It would not always be so. This iconography, the closest to Genesis, would be eclipsed by another, which kept closer to the Pauline exegesis of Psalm CX [CIX] and where one sees, on either side of Christ, David (presumed author of the Psalm) as king and Melchizedek as Old Testament priest (see plate 5).[72] The message is clear and also restrictive;

---

[72] For the Psalters, see, in particular Chludov Psalter (ninth century), fol. 115r: M. V. Ščepkina, *Miniatjury Hludovskoj Psaltyri, Grečeskij illjustrirovannyj kodeks IXogo veka* (Moscow, 1977); ms. *Parisinus gr.* 20 (?ninth century), fol. 25: S. Dufrenne, *L'Illustration des psautiers grecs du Moyen Age*, I (Paris, 1966), p. 46 and plate 45; ms. *Leningrad 265* (ninth century), fol. 4v (folios of the ms. *Pantocrator 61*, which were detached and taken to Russia by Porphyros Uspenskij): Dufrenne, *L'Illustration des psautiers grecs*, p. 34 and plate 25; ms. *London add.* 19. 352, fol. 152r: S. Der Nersessian, *L'Illustration des psautiers grecs du Moyen Age*, II (Paris, 1970), p. 52 and plate 89 (fig. 244); Genesis of Vienna: W. von Hartel and F. Wickhoff, *Die Wiener Genesis* (Vienna, 1895), plate 14; O. Mazal, *Kommentar zur Wiener Genesis: Faksimile-Ausgabe des Codex theol. gr. 31 der Österreichischen Nationalbibliothek in Wien* (Frankfurt-am-Main, 1980). For the mosaics, the representation of the meeting of Abraham and Melchizedek in the 'dome of Abraham' in St Mark's Basilica in Venice: O. Demus, *The Mosaics of San Marco in Venice*, II, 2 (Chicago/London, 1984), plates 48, 212. In decorative painting: P. A. Underwood, *The Kariye Djami*, II (New York, 1966), p. 84b; G. Millet, *Monuments de l'Athos*, I, *Les peintures* (Paris, 1927), p. 8 (Protaton); V. Lazarev, *Storia della pittura byzantina* (Turin, 1967), pp. 153, 199, 399 and n. 215 (St Sophia of Kiev, Cefalù in Sicily, St Theodore-the-Stratelates in Novgorod). When Melchizedek is represented alone, he is shown sometimes as king, sometimes as priest; another iconographical theme, especially in Russia, is Melchizedek and Aaron as the contrasting image of the two priesthoods.

Plate 6. Melchizedek, 'king and priest', represented as a Byzantine emperor in the *Christian Topography* of Cosmas Indicopleustes. Vatican. Cod. gr. 699, fo. 58r, ninth century. Biblioteca Apostolica Vaticana

kingship and priesthood were combined only in Christ; but the dominant image is that of a Christian Melchizedek emperor.

The illustration in Cosmas, the surprise of Maximos' interrogators, the embarrassed silence of his hagiographer and the little phrase attributed to Leo III all show how the images went naturally together. This historical Melchizedek who had abolished the Law and inaugurated by anticipation the time of Grace, this uncircumcised person whose right to make the Jews pay tithe had been recognised, this king come directly, like Constantine the Great, from paganism to the religion of Christ – who else could he be than a sovereign of the Christianised Roman empire? He was said to be without genealogy or descendants, and imperial legitimacy was not transmitted hereditarily; even when the crown fell to the son, it was by association and not by filiation, by virtue of a choice supposedly made by God. Priesthood of the order of Melchizedek was not, like priesthood of the order of Aaron, a function, bound up with membership of the tribe of Levi in Judaism or with clerical status in Christianity, but an indelible character, conferred directly by God on the 'just king' for a great historical mission. The emperor was not a specialist in sacred things, or of the clergy, but he was invested with a superior priesthood.

There was nothing here that was totally unacceptable. Exegesis and images, 'prefiguration' and 'model' might fail to coincide, but only as long as either a certain vagueness was maintained and rhetoric was employed or else levels of interpretation were carefully distinguished and no immediate short-circuit was provoked by asking with feigned ingenuousness or arrogance, was Melchizedek the model of the emperor or the figure of Christ? Am I not emperor and priest? For as soon as the exegetists were given free rein, the question was made into a trap. It ensnared the accuser of Maximos and then the emperor Leo III. And it was, it must be said, cleverly done. The Monothelete official and the iconoclast emperor said only what everybody thought, but they said it at the wrong moment, at a time of violence, injustice and heresy which immediately invalidated the parallel, explicit or implicit, with 'My king is justice'. This is the meaning of the reply of the Pseudo-Gregory, which did not argue from the orthodox exegesis of the person of Melchizedek, but told Leo III that he was no longer a just king.

PRECURSORS OF THE ANTICHRIST

The account of the 655 interrogation is not the first text to have tried to establish the nature of imperial power on the basis of the figure of Melchizedek. A treatise of Pope Gelasius (492–6) had already tackled the problem of the 'two powers' from this perspective, though without really opening up a debate, as it had little impact in the East and probably no direct influence on Maximos or the Pseudo-Gregory. The fifth-century pope was critical of emperors who 'accepted that their power was limited to human matters and not to divine matters', but 'ventured to judge those by whom divine matters are administered', that is, the bishops and the sovereign pontiff. He went on:

It is certainly the case that, before Christ's coming, certain men, symbolic figures but nevertheless engaged in earthly activities [by which we may understand 'historical persons'], were both king and priest; such was the holy Melchizedek, as sacred History tells. The devil followed this example in his own domain, he who always claims in a tyrannical spirit what is proper to divine worship, so that the pagan emperors were also called pontiffs. But when there came the only one who can truly call himself king and priest, the emperor ceased from then on to assume the name of pontiff and the pontiff to claim royal pomp. For, although it is said that the members of Christ true king and true pontiff [= the Christians], by reason of their participation in the glorious nature, have received each dignity thanks to the sacred generosity [of Christ], so that they are both a 'royal and priestly race',[73] nevertheless Christ, remembering human weakness and adjusting by a magnificent plan what pertains to the salvation of his own, separated the offices of the two powers and established for each proper activities and distinct dignities, wishing that his own should be saved by the remedy of humility and should not again be victims of human pride. So that the Christian emperors have need of the pontiffs for eternal life and the pontiffs abide by imperial measures for the conduct of earthly things. In this way, spiritual activities have been separated from earthly affairs ... and conversely, he who has responsibility for the affairs of the world should not appear to preside over divine things, so that the *modestia* of the two orders is respected, so that no one is so proud as to take on both at the same time and so that a particular competence is attached to the quality of the activities.[74]

The perspective here is clearly western; the *de facto* separation between pontifical Rome (subject in future to a Gothic king) and imperial Constantinople becomes a division by right. In the background, one senses the *City of God*, where, in his exegesis on Melchizedek, Augustine asserts that Christ is now the only mediator between God and men, the only one to have assumed eternal priesthood. In the days of Israel, the earthly kingdom 'represented' the spiritual kingdom, but, since the incarnation, the city of God has found its perpetual king.[75] The cut-off point is clear: before the coming of Christ, a priestly kingship was possible either by divine 'economy' (Melchizedek) or

[73] *Plebs sancta, regale sacerdotium*, I Peter, 2: 9, taken up notably by St Augustine in *City of God*, XX, 10. See below, pp. 239–40.
[74] *Tractatus IV (Tomus de anathematis vinculo)*, ed. A. Thiel, *Epistolae romanorum pontificum genuinae* (Brunsberg, 1868), I, pp. 567–8.
[75] See in particular *City of God*, X, 20; XVII, 17 and 20; XX, 10.

by diabolical counterfeiting (the Roman emperor *pontifex maximus*). After the coming of Christ, this same notion had lost its legitimacy; the *regale sacerdotium* was devolved to the Son of God and by extension to Christians as a body. The pope was taking some liberties with history by omitting to mention that the Roman emperors, pagans then Christians, continued to bear the title of *pontifex* until about 376 or 383,[76] but he did this to emphasise the idea of a radical separation between two ages. This had the major consequence that a true Christian emperor was not a Roman emperor converted or faithful to Christianity, or an emperor who would derive a new legitimacy from Old Testament models, but an emperor whose power had in part been confiscated by Christ. His sphere of competence had been modified by the establishment of Christianity; he had to adopt a pose of humility before those who now held spiritual power, and he would be constantly suspected of belonging to the 'earthly City', of having remained pagan, or of identifying, out of pride, with the Antichrist.

This analysis, as I have said, was western. But the East, from the seventh to the ninth centuries, also called in question imperial power as it had been conceived from Constantine to Herakleios. The Monothelete crisis and iconoclasm were the occasion for redefinitions, for theories which invoked tradition but in reality innovated, and for *exempla*, fictional stories or dialogues which, like the little phrase 'I am emperor and priest', established roles and painted portraits of devilish emperors. The dogma of the 'single will in Christ' was a minor deviation from orthodoxy; Pope Honorius saw nothing to object to in it and the conflict, lacking a serious patristic basis, would never have achieved such intensity if imperial power had not been in the line of fire, embarrassed under Herakleios, persecuting and stubborn under Constans II and contradicting itself under Constantine IV, as the Pseudo-Gregory recalled, exaggerating the contrasts to the point of caricature. By about 730, the cult of images shocked many Christians, especially the bishops of Asia Minor (Thomas of Klaudioupolis and Constantine of Nakoleia, at first regarded as having initiated the heresy), and provoked a sort of 'reform', in which the emperor took the lead; but the iconodule tradition gradually attributed the heresy to Leo III alone. He was not a heresiarch, but an Antichrist or the precursor of the Antichrist. This accusation was necessary to explain and avert a crisis which was not fundamentally a heresy, but a sort of schism internal to the Christian culture of the East, a crucial moment, a century in the preparing, when Christianity was still hesitant about relinquishing the 'God without a face' and cutting all links with Judaism.[77] It

---

[76] The date is debatable: F. Paschoud, *Cinq études sur Zosime* (Paris, 1975), pp. 63–99, argues for 376; Alan Cameron, 'Gratian's repudiation of the pontifical robe', *JRS*, 58 (1968), pp. 96–102, opts for 383.

[77] Dagron, 'Judaïser' (see ch. 1, n. 148), pp. 359–80.

was therefore decided at an early stage to make iconoclasm a 'scandal' and
an abuse of power, and to conceal real divisions by a direct confrontation between a Church claiming to be united and a sulphurous autocrat under Jewish
influence. This was the high point of 'imperial heresy', denounced for almost a
century and to be denounced for more than a century to come in various forms.
In reality, it was a trial of imperial power, to which heresy contributed only an
additional proof of illegitimacy.

Let us return to Leo III, whose stature, style and constant references to the
Old Testament made him an ideal victim. Like all his predecessors, he probably
believed he was 'emperor and priest', and there would be no reason to doubt the
authenticity of the phrase if the pope's letter had not been an obvious forgery or
if some echo of so striking a declaration had been found in an authentic work.
Among possible texts is the juridical collection of the *Ecloga*, in particular its
preface, which was probably written by the emperor. It is studded with biblical
references and reveals a sovereign convinced that he held from God alone the
right to proclaim the law and reform men. 'Since God', he wrote, 'in entrusting
to us imperial power, wished to provide proof of the love, full of fear, we bear
him, and ordered us, in the words of St Peter, the coryphaeus of the Apostles,
to feed his flock...' (I Peter, 5: 2).[78] The emperor was defining himself here
as a sort of bishop chosen directly by God in order to govern Christianity;[79]
elsewhere, as we have seen, he defined himself as a new Hezekiah melting down
the serpent made an idol. Melchizedek was never far away, and also dominated
the polemic, more so than a theology of the image which remained insubstantial
before the ninth century.

John of Damascus does little more than repeat, equally vehemently, the com-
plaints formulated by Maximos the Confessor. In his *Against the Calumniators
of the Holy Icons*, he suggested to the emperor that he write a Gospel according
to Leo, just as the Manicheans had written a Gospel according to Thomas, then
declared:

> We do not accept an emperor who tyrannically appropriates priesthood.
> Emperors do not have the power to bind and to loose. I remember Valens,
> who called himself a Christian emperor, but who persecuted the ortho-
> dox faith; I remember Zeno, Anastasios, Herakleios, Constantine of Sicily
> and Bardaniskes-Philippikos. I do not trust imperial canons to regulate
> the Church, but the written and unwritten precepts transmitted by the
> Fathers.[80]

[78] *Ecloga*, prooimion, ed. L. Burgmann, Forschungen zur byzantinischen Rechtsgeschichte 10
(Frankfurt-am-Main, 1983), p. 160, ll. 21–4.
[79] S. Gero usefully emphasises the Old Testament references in the *Ecloga* and the impression
they create that Leo III saw himself as a new David or a new Solomon: *Byzantine Iconoclasm*
(n. 1), p. 63; 'Notes on Byzantine iconoclasm in the eighth century', *Byz.*, 44 (1974), pp. 40–2.
[80] *Contra imaginum calumniatores*, II, 16, ed. Kotter (n. 41), pp. 113–14.

And again:

> We will not accept that a new faith should be taught…we will not accept
> that the custom which comes from the Fathers should yield to an imperial
> order which tries to overturn it. Because it is not the act of pious emperors
> to overturn ecclesiastical decisions…that is the province of synods, not of
> emperors, as our Lord said: 'Where two or three are gathered together in my
> name, there am I in the midst of them' (Matthew, 18: 20). It is not to emperors
> that Christ gave the power to bind and to loose, but to the apostles, to their
> successors, to the pastors and *didaskaloi*. 'Though an angel from heaven –
> says the Apostle Paul – preach any other gospel unto you than that which we
> have preached unto you…' (Galatians, 1: 8) We remain silent about what
> follows,[81] out of modesty, awaiting repentance.[82]

But most other sources do not use this line of argument, as one might have
expected, and instead attack the person of the emperor.

The oldest polemical work to have survived, the *Advice of the Old Man*,
written before 754, sets the tone. In its first part, the holy monk George announces that the time predicted by Daniel has arrived (8: 23–5), when a king of
fierce countenance and arrogant heart will destroy the holy people by force and
deception. It was necessary to 'choose between Christ and him', because this
Antichrist and Christ-Hater was rebelling against the Son of God and scattering
like a lion those whom Christ had brought together.[83] This apocalyptic portrait
was clear. And the discussion that followed between the bishop delegated by
the palace and the charismatic monk, though it makes it plain that there was
disagreement within the Church, constantly contrasts the orders of the emperor
(this time, Constantine V) and the teaching of Christ. 'Little phrases' which
emphasise the arrogance of the *basileus autokrator* are deliberately attributed
to Bishop Cosmas: he 'wished to keep the commandments of Moses' (in other
words, he was a Judaiser); he 'knew God's designs'; guided by God, 'his pure
thought sought the orthodox faith'; he behaved like an 'imitator of Christ' and
'whoever opposed him opposed God's orders'; the monk George 'had raised
his horn against him'. To the accusation of 'blaspheming against the emperor'
responded that of 'blaspheming against Christ'.[84] In the closing address, the
monk George evokes the Enemy who had pushed the Jews into the abyss by
telling them: 'He is not the Son of God but a deceiver, and he destroys the
customs of Moses'; and he added that it was this same Enemy, that is, the devil,
who was saying today: 'It is not the image of Christ, but an idol.'[85]

---

[81] The rest ('let him be accursed') would have condemned an emperor who John hoped would
reverse his decision. The quotation from St Paul was repeated by Theodore of Stoudios in the
dialogue in which he opposed Leo V: see below, p. 189.

[82] I, 66; II, 69, ed. Kotter (n. 41), pp. 166–7.

[83] *Nouthesia gerontos*, ed. B. M. Melioranskij, *Zapiski istoriko-filologičeskago Fakulteta Impera-
torskago S. -Peterburgskago Universiteta* 59 (St Petersburg, 1901), pp. V–VIII.

[84] Ibid., pp. VIII–XXVIII.   [85] Ibid., pp. XXX–XXXI.

Equally violent, but in a different tone, the invectives *Against Constantine Kaballinos* also impute the heresy to the emperors alone, even if they implicate the bishops collectively, turned wolves rather than shepherds, who had unanimously supported heresy at the council of Hiereia.[86] Here again the portrait takes precedence over theory. Leo III and his son Constantine V are not so much accused of unwarranted interference in matters of dogma as of a sort of original illegitimacy, revealed by several indisputable signs. The former had been deceived by a Jew and concluded through his intermediary a diabolical pact in return for the promise of a long reign; the latter had soiled the font on the day of his baptism.[87] Leo III had broken with the tradition of the good emperors not by examining the profundities of the faith but by an excess of pride, by claiming to do it better than them and by becoming the prey of that same Satan who had said to Adam: 'If you eat the fruit of this tree, you will be as God.'[88]

Leo III was assigned the role of sovereign brought down by pride, who believed he was living in the time of the Old Testament and whom the Jews made an Antichrist, a false Melchizedek; Constantine V was assigned the role of pagan tyrant and persecutor. An extraordinary scene in the *Life of St Stephen the Younger*, written in 807, brought a sovereign who loved banquets, women, the music of the zither[89] and the sound and fury of the Hippodrome, who readily roared with laughter, celebrated the pagan feast of the *Brumalia* and hissed like a dragon when anyone infringed his 'imperial majesty',[90] face to face with a monk who lived in silence, prayer and contrition; paganism was face to face with Christianity. Constantine V, who by his writings had inspired the iconoclast theology, was condemned less as a heretic than as a tyrant, who wielded an arbitrary and brutal power but who could do nothing against a monk prepared for martyrdom. And just as Corneille's Polyeucte overthrew altars, Stephen trampled underfoot the imperial effigy on a *nomisma* which he had produced from his cowl, 'as Jesus had done in the synagogue of the Jews', says his biographer,[91] forgetting that Jesus had actually sidestepped the provocation of the Pharisees by 'rendering unto Caesar the things which are Caesar's and unto God the things that are God's'.

There was violence and persecution, and the defenders of the 'two wills' or those of 'images' sincerely believed that the age of the martyrs whose Acts they had read had returned. But it was above all a time for rediscovering, and for rewriting almost unchanged, the roles in the *Passions* of the reigns

---

[86] *Adversus Constantinum Caballinum*, 14–15, PG 95, cols. 329–32.

[87] Ibid., 19–20, cols. 336–7.   [88] Ibid., 23, col. 341.

[89] The zither also appears in Gregory's letters to Leo.

[90] See M.-F. Rouan (Auzépy), 'Une lecture "iconoclaste" de la Vie d'Etienne le Jeune', *TM*, 8 (Mélanges P. Lemerle) (1981), pp. 425, 431.

[91] PG 100, cols. 1157–60. Stephen was attacked; the emperor intervened to ensure that he was not immediately killed but legally tried for the crime of lese-majesty.

of Decius, Diocletian or Maximian, still read at liturgical commemorations, where Christians defied the emperor here below, who ruled only over bodies, in the name of the emperor on high, who assured the salvation of souls.[92] The hagiographical texts of iconoclasm, which evoked or invented the new martyrs, put them in the same places (hippodrome or amphitheatre, tribunal or throne room), attributed to them the same formulae on the duty of disobeying a tyrannical sovereign to remain faithful to God, made them accuse the emperors of the same outrages and drove their persecutors to the same impotent rage. Reality submitted to the model. A *Life* like that of St Andrew *en Krisei*, very probably legendary, in which the martyr comes voluntarily to Constantinople for an encounter with the 'servant of Satan' and where Constantine V 'roars like a lion' and rolls 'the eyes of a dragon', clearly belongs to the genre of 'epic passions' whose influence soon spilled over into the Chronicles.[93] The psychological portrait of Leo III in the letters of the Pseudo-Gregory is of the same school. The emperor is a barbarian, a rustic and a man of violence untouched by Christian sweetness and humility; his 'warlike spirit' made him incapable of understanding the dogmas; all he knew was how to 'follow his obstinacy and his natural passions' by proclaiming himself 'emperor and priest'.

This literature was a formidable test bed for trying out formulae, devising antitheses, establishing roles and dramatising ideas which could not be artic-ulated in a theoretical form. Under cover of heresy, it was the imperial power itself that was being challenged. This was very clear in the years that followed the council of Nicaea II (787), when a large body of public opinion explicitly associated the hard-won but insolent triumph of images with a decline in im-perial dignity, and so relaunched iconoclasm. The final pages of Theophanes

---

[92] For example, the *Passio sanctorum Scilitanorum*, in which St Speratus, who was asked by the proconsul Saturninus, at Carthage, to swear in the name of 'the emperor our master', replied: 'I do not recognise kingship in this world, but I praise and worship my God, whom no man has seen ... for it is not possible to see him with eyes of flesh ... and if I do something, I am answerable to him': O. von Gebhardt, *Ausgewählte Martyrerakten* (Berlin, 1902), pp. 23–4. This commonplace of exclusive obedience to Christ the sole true king is found in almost all the Passions: martyrdoms of Justin and Chariton, of Polycarp and of Apollonius: ibid., pp. 4–5, 13–15, 18–21, 45–7; *Passio antiquior SS. Sergii et Bacchi, Anal. Boll.*, 14 (1895), pp. 375–95, where the Syrian martyrs, who were soldiers, declared that they had enrolled in the army of the sole true king, Christ, and were as a result accused of 'scorning the imperial dignity'. See also the *Passio* of St Athenogenus of Pedachthoe in Cappadocia, where insulting words are directed at the emperor, but with a corrective by Athenogenus himself: ed. and trans. P. Maraval, *Le Passion inédite de S. Athénogène de Pédachthoé en Cappadoce* (Brussels, 1990), pp. 50–1, 72–3.

[93] *AASS*, Oct. VIII, pp. 135–42. The Emperor Constantine V 'roared like a ferocious lion' and, in his fury, had 'dragon eyes' (5 and 7, pp. 137, 138); Andrew thirsted for martyrdom and came to Constantinople to provoke the tyrant, when he heard that the orthodox were persecuted (6, p. 137), in the palace of St Mamas where the verbal exchange took place; Constantine V reproached Andrew for opposing the 'masters of the universe' and treating them like atheists (8, p. 138). More historical, the *Lives* of Stephen the Younger (first iconoclasm) and Euthymios of Sardis (second iconoclasm) kept to the rules of the genre.

describe this decay of an empire, which might or might not find its saviour.[94] Constantine VI plotted against his mother, Irene blinded her son, Nikephoros I 'left his bones' in Bulgaria, Michael Rangabe was too weak and too pious and was booed in public, and the fires lighted in Thrace by the Bulgar Krum were visible from the ramparts of Constantinople. The shadow of the great emperor Constantine V loomed large, and demonstrations were organised around his tomb. The *strategos* of the Anatolikon, who became Leo V, seemed a providential figure; and since the idea of a strong imperial power, exercised over many years and transmitted to descendants, was now associated with iconoclasm, it was this course that the emperor prudently chose by proposing a new debate on images.[95] He invoked his function as mediator, arbiter and king-priest, which was again denied him.

The texts of this second iconoclasm, among which we should probably include the 'letters of Gregory II', reveal more clearly the real issues of the first. The *Life of St Niketas of Medikion*, compiled by a certain Theosteriktos before 840 and widely quoted in the Chronicles, meditates on the true nature of the iconoclast heresy. It observes:

> Some regard it as inferior and of little importance, which means they are easily taken in and carried away by it; some do not even think that it is a heresy, but a protest. I myself – in the same way, I imagine, as all men of good sense – regard it as particularly pernicious because it undermines the 'economy' of Christ. It may also be observed that the other heresies came from the bishops or lesser priests, whereas this one comes from those in power. *Know the difference between emperors and priests.* The old heresies started from a disagreement about dogma and gradually developed, whereas this one comes from the imperial office itself.[96]

This is emperor against Church, or a conception of the *basilike dynasteia* – presented as a recent perversion, but in reality that of the Christian empire since Constantine – against a supposed 'apostolic tradition'. Later in the same work,[97] for the historical date of 24 December 814, when Leo V summoned the patriarch Nikephoros and a few bishops and monks to urge them to consult with those who were 'scandalised' by images and come to an 'economy', the confrontation gave rise to a series of trenchant and widely disseminated 'little phrases', which outlined a new theory of imperial power. With this emperor of perfect legitimacy, who had as yet taken no action against images and wanted

---

[94] Ed. de Boor (see ch. 1, n. 4), pp. 464ff.

[95] *Scriptor incertus de Leone Armenio*, ed. Bekker (see ch. 1, n. 43), p. 349; George the Monk Continued, ed. Bekker (see ch. 1, n. 101), p. 771.

[96] *Life of Nicetas of Medikion*, 27, *AASS*, April I, p. XXVIII; the theme of 'imperial heresy' against the 'unity of the Church' is also found in the *Life of Nikephoros the Patriarch*, ed. C. de Boor *Nicephori Archiepiscopi Constantinopolitani opuscula historica* (Leipzig, 1880), pp. 166–7.

[97] *Life of Nicetas of Medikion* (n. 96), 34–6, pp. XXIX–XXX.

a council of bishops to address the problem, the clergy refused all debate. Aimilianos of Kyzikos told him: 'If there is an ecclesiastical problem, as you say, O emperor, let it be settled within the Church, as is the custom . . . and not in the palace', to which Leo replied that he, too, was a child of the Church and that he might serve as arbiter between the two camps. Michael of Synada then told him that 'his arbitration' was in effect 'tyranny'; yet others reproached him for his bias. Euthymios of Sardis invoked without batting an eyelid eight centuries of Christian images and enraged the emperor by repeating the quotation from St Paul already used by John of Damascus: 'But though . . . an angel from heaven preach any other gospel unto you than that which we have preached unto you, let him be accursed' (Galatians, 1: 8). The 'fiery teacher of the Church and abbot of Stoudios', Theodore, was the last to speak:

> Emperor, do not destroy the stability of the Church. The apostle has spoken of those whom God has established in the Church as 'first apostles, secondarily prophets, thirdly pastors and teachers . . .' (1 Corinthians, 12: 28), but he has not spoken of emperors. To you, O emperor, have been entrusted political stability and the army. Attend to them and leave the Church, as the apostle said, to pastors and teachers. Were you not to accept this and diverge from our faith . . . if an angel came from heaven to preach to us [another] Gospel, we would not hear him; even more so, you!

Leo V was furious and broke off the dialogue to embark on persecution. George the Monk, resuming this epic dialogue, paints a picture of the emperor not unlike that of Leo III in the letters of the Pseudo-Gregory; a semi-barbarian of unstable mind, a slave to his baser instincts, 'a monkey roaring like a lion'. George then launches into a violent diatribe against Constantinople, imperial city and town of iniquity, which had used the pretext of idols to rise up against the rest of the Christian world.[98]

The schema outlined by Theodore of Stoudios seems very similar to the western theory of the 'two powers', but it is only a caricature of it, deliberately offensive to an emperor obliged to emphasise that he, too, was part of the Church, and it was untenable. Elsewhere, this same Theodore insisted on the necessity of consultation between the emperor and the patriarch chosen by him, and reproached Michael II, Leo V's successor, for refusing to intervene in the debate about images.[99] In fact, the 'anti-establishment' Church was engaged in an all-out assault on an imperial authority which Constantine had not truly Christianised; it took advantage of the heretical context to try to ridicule the Constantinian rhetoric of the emperor who was 'quasi-bishop', 'imitator of Christ' and 'equal of the apostles'; it vigorously contested the Constantinian ideology

---

[98] George the Monk, ed. de Boor (see ch. 1, n. 75), pp. 778–80; George the Monk Continued, ed. Bekker (see ch. 1, n. 101), pp. 766–8.
[99] See below, p. 298.

which Herakleios and his successors, and even more the iconoclast emperors, had derived from this ambiguous rhetoric. The first Christian emperor had already been criticised by Maximos, who had emphasised his complicity with the Arian heresy;[100] he was attacked by George the Monk and several others through the medium of the capital which bore his name and was a hotbed of heresies.[101] The *Life of St Stephen the Younger* mocks the title of 'thirteenth apostle' adopted by Constantine V,[102] and the Continuator of Theophanes claims that an iconoclast monk who dabbled in magic had prophesied to Leo V that, if he followed the example of Leo III, he too would obtain this title, enjoy a long reign and found a dynasty, in other words, be a New Constantine.[103] At the iconoclast council of Hiereia (754), the emperors were called 'emulators of the apostles, because God appointed them and the Holy Spirit granted them wisdom', and an audacious similarity was established between the apostles whom Christ had sent out to combat idolatry and the pious emperors, 'emulators of the apostles', to whom he today deputed the suppression of the cult of images.[104] In direct opposition to this official phraseology, the council of Nicaea II (787) expressed its surprise that the iconoclasts could attribute to the assembly of clergy and the 'force of emperors' a liberation from the idolatry for which men were indebted only to Christ, and went on to denounce the extravagance of the flattery lavished on the emperors. They were credited with what came from Christ, when they should have been praised only for their concern for their subjects, their internal and external government, their victories or the rebuilding of cities.[105]

It was very obviously the Constantinian project that was under attack. And since history offered little prospect of a return to paganism, it was to the apocalypses, constantly being rewritten on the basis of the texts of the Pseudo-Methodios and the Pseudo-Daniel, that people turned to describe the coming of the impious emperor who would restore idols, have himself adored in place of Christ, empty the earthly Jerusalem, fill that in heaven with martyrs, and pave the way for the Antichrist, or himself assume that role, after a truly pious emperor had abandoned Constantinople to return his crown to the Christ of the Parousia.[106] Prokopios had already discerned in Justinian I the 'prince of the demons'.[107] Suspicion subsequently grew and fell in particular on the iconoclast

---

[100] See above, pp. 170–1.   [101] See above.
[102] Chapter 29, PG 100, col. 1121.   [103] *Chronographia*, ed. Bekker (see ch. 1, n. 4), p. 28.
[104] Mansi, XIII, col. 225; P. Chrestou, 'Ho basileus kai hiereus eis to Byzantio', *Kleronomia*, 3 (1971), p. 13.
[105] Mansi, XIII, cols. 353–6.
[106] See above, p. 104; the scenario is repeated in the later apocalypses, such as that of Leo of Constantinople, the earliest version of which dates back to the early ninth century: R. Maisano, *L'Apocalisse apocrifa di Leone di Costantinopoli* (Naples, 1975).
[107] *Historia arcana*, XXX, 27–34, ed. Haury (see ch. 5, n. 86), pp. 185–6.

emperors.[108] But even with regard to an orthodox emperor like Constantine VI and an unexceptional remarriage which he called adulterous, Theodore of Stoudios laid it down as a rule that an emperor whose wishes deviated from the Gospel paved the way for Antichrist, and came up with a phrase which hit home and would be repeated: 'The Antichrist too will be an emperor.'[109]

Whatever they did, the emperors were permanently suspect, caught in the mesh of a rhetoric of the 'almost-priest' and of a Melchizedekian model associated with the beginnings and with the historical development of their power since Constantine the Great, but which backfired on them at the slightest moral or religious 'sin'. The tradition which had attempted to Christianise the pagan emperors since Augustus by linking the birth of the empire to the coming of Christ,[110] was opposed by another which tended to paganise the Christian emperors and suspect them either of having remained *pontifices* in the Roman manner or of announcing the coming of the Antichrist by comparing themselves to Melchizedek. This explains the extreme caution of the ceremonial 'entry' to St Sophia; it had to concede to the emperor a quasi-sacerdotal character, without ever putting him in the position of uttering Leo III's 'little phrase' – 'I am emperor and priest' – which would immediately have disqualified him.[111]

---

[108] Germanos warned Leo III that he who suppressed images would be, as negator of the Incarnation, 'the precursor of the Antichrist': George the Monk, ed. de Boor (see ch. 1, n. 75), p. 741; Constantine V was 'the Antichrist born of Dan': ibid., p. 750; Leo V 'had become another Antichrist': *Scriptor incertus de Leone Armenio*, Bonn, p. 362.

[109] Theodore of Stoudios, *Ep.* 36 (to Euprepianos, of 809), ed. G. Fatouros, *Theodori Studitae epistolae* (Berlin, 1992), I, pp. 102–3; the *Panoplia* directed against Michael VIII, in the thirteenth century, changed the letter, but not the sense, of the formula, *kai ho antichristos basileusei*: A. Michel, *Humbert und Kerullarios. Quellen und Studien zum Schisma des XI. Jahrhunderts*, II (Paderborn, 1930), p. 248 (the editor wrongly believes that the *Panoplia* was written by Michael Keroularios, in the eleventh century).

[110] See above, pp. 128–9, 156–7.

[111] It should be remembered that access to the sanctuary was long forbidden to the emperors for the celebration of the feast of Orthodoxy, which closed the second iconoclasm: see above, p. 95.

6. *Basil the Macedonian, Leo VI and Constantine VII: ceremonial and religion*

SUPERNATURAL PROTECTORS, MODELS OF KINGSHIP AND DYNASTIC SAINTS

A story and an image, both composed for the purpose, will show us the usurper Basil legitimised even before he had won power, then, as reigning monarch (867–86), assisted by his supernatural protectors.

The story is found in the *Life* in the form of a classical eulogy which Basil's grandson, Constantine VII Porphyrogenitus, later composed on the subject of the founder of the dynasty; it constitutes a chapter in the Continuation of Theophanes. In distant Macedonia, the mother of the future emperor saw in a dream an old man with fiery breath, who told her that God would put her son in possession of the sceptre of the Romans and that she should encourage him to go to Constantinople.[1] Coming after several prophetic prodigies, this prophecy seems conventional enough; what followed was less so. Basil, having embarked on his journey, arrived one night at the Golden Gate, through which the emperors passed for their triumph or their coronation. Waiting for dawn, when he would be able to enter the city, he fell asleep at the door of the monastery of St Diomedes, situated just outside the walls. Three times, St Diomedes himself warned the *hegoumenos* that he should open the monastery door to the vagabond, 'because he had been anointed by Christ to become emperor'.[2]

Constantine Porphyrogenitus may have invented the marvellous signs and apparitions, which he based on Hermogenian models, but not the role of Elijah, which Basil himself took as accepted fact. He may have embellished the episode of St Diomedes with the aid of hagiographical *topoi*, but he had received it as established tradition, and this tradition marked with a legend a significant moment in the career of a future emperor. A note in the *Patria* of Constantinople,

---

[1] *Vita Basilii*, 8, in Theophanes Continuatus, ed. Bekker (see ch. 1, n. 4), Bonn, p. 222.

[2] Ibid., 9, pp. 223–4; in Glykas, it is an angel who appears to the monk: *Annales*, ed. I. Bekker (Bonn, 1836), pp. 546–7. For the variants of the St Diomedes episode, see Moravcsik, 'Sagen und Legenden', *DOP*, 15 (1961), pp. 59–126, especially pp. 90–3.

almost contemporary with the *Life of Basil*, helps make this clear: 'St Diomedes', we read, 'was founded by Constantine the Great. The emperor Basil rebuilt and enlarged it, adorned it, and endowed it with many properties, because it was there that he had received the oracle on the subject of kingship [*ton peri tes basileias chresmon*].'[3] For Basil at St Diomedes, as for Justinian at SS Sergios and Bakchos, and for other emperors, the 'oracle' was this first step of an ambitious man towards his future as an emperor – this sudden conviction, like a clarion call, that God had chosen, adopted and 'anointed' him, and that an irreversible mechanism had been set in motion, justifying, if need be, treachery and murder. At the first stage, that of the prediction made to Basil's mother, Elijah had revealed himself like a Christianised version of the 'Genius of the empire', now associated with an imperial destiny; the second stage was even more decisive. It made God's choice known to an unimpeachable witness. It fixed the historic spot, which would become a place of commemoration, where unction occurred (there was no second unction during coronation), where the man from nowhere became a Davidic king, founder rather than heir of a dynasty,[4] where the vagabond – later said to be descended from the Arsacids and Constantine the Great[5] – conquered the town, without anyone yet realising it. This was legend, certainly, but a legend that combined individual psychology, the paradox of the legitimacy of a usurpation and a very concrete understanding of the phenomenon of power. We may assume that Basil himself believed the story to be true.

The pictorial image is later. Probably between 879 and 883, an illuminated manuscript of the *Homilies* of Gregory of Nazianzus, the first imperial manuscript to have survived, was offered to or commissioned by Basil I.[6] On the verso of the first folio (Av) is painted Christ Pantocrator, second person of the Trinity, God with a human face, whose representation sealed the recent victory over iconoclasm. On the recto of the next folio (Cr, as a result of an accidental inversion of the second and third folios),[7] appears a foliate cross bearing the very Constantinian inscription 'Jesus Christ is victorious', and on

[3] *Patria*, III, 86, ed. Preger (see ch. 3, n. 32), pp. 246–7: the words in square brackets are a later addition to clarify the meaning: Dagron, *Constantinople imaginaire* (see ch. 1, n. 59), pp. 319–22.
[4] See above, pp. 36–7.
[5] It was Photios, we are told, who invented the genealogy that made Basil descend from Tiridates, king of Armenia: Niketas Paphlagon, *Life of the Patriarch Ignatios*, PG 105, cols. 565–8; Pseudo-Symeon, *Annales*, ed. Bekker (see ch. 1, n. 95), pp. 689–90; the legend was repeated with a degree of reserve in the funeral oration that Leo VI wrote for his father: see above, p. 37.
[6] Of the abundant literature concerning the ms. *Parisinus gr.* 510, see, recently: S. Der Nersessian, 'The Illustrations of the Homilies of Gregory of Nazianzus Paris gr. 510', *DOP*, 16 (1962), pp. 195–228; I. Spatharakis, 'The portraits and the date of the Codex Par. gr. 510', *Cahiers archéologiques*, 23 (1974), pp. 97–105; I. Spatharakis, 'A note on the imperial portraits and the date of Par. gr. 510', *JÖB*, 39 (1989), pp. 89–93; I. Kalavrezou-Maxeiner, 'The portraits of Basil I in Paris gr. 510', *JÖB*, 27 (1978), pp. 19–24.
[7] During rebinding in the seventeenth century, according to Sirarpie Der Nersessian.

the verso (Cv) a portrait of the emperor in *skaramangion*, *loros* and purple slippers, receiving the Constantinian standard (the *labarum*) from the hands of the prophet Elijah, on his right (our left), and the crown from those of the archangel (*archistrategos*) Gabriel, on his left (our right) (see plate 7). The metrical inscription which accompanies the image emphasises its significance; it makes Elijah the sure guarantor of a victory against the enemy and it makes Gabriel, crowning Basil master of the world, the harbinger of universal joy. The recto of the following page (now Br) shows the empress Eudokia with the two porphyrogeniti, Leo and Alexander, already promoted to the *basileia* and both called *despotai* (see plate 8). On the verso (Bv), the painter had executed another coronation scene, of a bearded emperor, Basil himself or his eldest son Constantine, flanked by two symmetrical figures, but then covered it over with a cross of victory similar to the first; it may be that he had wanted to represent the coronation of Constantine and the latter's death had necessitated a change of iconographical programme, or simply that the design had been botched and started again.[8]

The Macedonian family prided itself on its triumphant orthodoxy, but it had its official protectors in the divine world, saints – the prophet Elijah and the archangels – who had accompanied and protected Basil during his conquest of power, who continued to intervene in the principal episodes of imperial politics, and whose cults were gradually organised into a system of commemorations and processions. For three generations at least, the piety of the Macedonians was deliberately dynastic; it annexed or attempted to annex, with partial success, a few saints from within the family, and it created, if not a new religious architecture, at least a new architectural programme and a new organisation of worship, whose finest expression was the New Church (*Nea ekklesia*).

The illustrations in the *Homilies* were more than simply evocative. They authenticated a whole corpus of later texts, which made Elijah, Gabriel or Michael intervene at every key moment in the Macedonian saga. We have already seen how, in the *Life* of Basil, the prophet Elijah foretold his destiny to the mother of the future emperor; he may also have intervened in the St Diomedes episode.[9] Later, it was through the intermediary of the prophet Elijah and the archangel Michael that Basil asked God not to let him die before he had witnessed the death of Chrysocheir, leader of the Paulician heretics of Asia Minor.[10] In the

---

[8] The first explanation is that of Spatharakis ('Codex Par. gr. 510' (n. 6)), who accordingly dates the manuscript to 879; the second is that of Kalavrezou-Maxeiner ('Portraits of Basil I' (n. 6)).

[9] Some sources, in specifying that the convent had previously borne the name of Elijah (Genesios, ed. Lesmüller-Werner and Thurn, p. 108; Pseudo-Symeon, *Annales*, ed. Bekker (see ch. 1, n. 95), p. 656), are probably reflecting a tradition that Elijah had intervened.

[10] Constantine VII, *Vita Basilii*, 41, in Theophanes Continuatus, ed. Bekker (see ch. 1, n. 4), p. 271.

Plate 7. The emperor Basil I receiving the imperial standard from the prophet Elijah and crowned by the archangel Gabriel. *Homilies* of Gregory of Nazianzus, Cod. gr. 510, fo. Cv, 879–83, © Bibliothèque Nationale, Paris

Plate 8.   The empress Eudokia, wife of Basil I, between their two crowned sons Leo and Alexander. *Homilies* of Gregory of Nazianzus, Cod. gr. 510, fo. Br, 879–83, © Bibliothèque Nationale, Paris

Homilies of Gregory of Nazianzus, Elijah offers Basil not the crown but the guarantee of victory constituted by the Constantinian standard, and the promise of a place in the lineage of the successors of the first Christian emperor. The sources do not lie when they tell of Basil's extraordinary devotion to his guardian angel,[11] and of the many churches and oratories he consecrated to him in the palace (near Our Lady of the Pharos[12] and in the *Nea*),[13] in Constantinople (in the Petrion district)[14] and in the vicinity (in the monumental ensemble of the Pege, the Macedonians' retreat on the north shore of the Golden Horn,[15] and in the ancient palace of Hiereia in the Chalcedon region).[16] The protection of Elijah extended from the founder to his family: it was in the church of St Elijah that, on 20 July, Basil ended a conflict which marked the end of his reign and freed his son, Leo, whom he had unjustly imprisoned, and solemnly restored him to his rank of *basileus* and to his rights as successor, during a procession which went from a church of the 'Asomatoi', that is, of the archangels (in the palace?), to a church of St Elijah (of the Petrion?);[17] and it was in St Elijah that the sainthood of Theophano, wife of Leo VI, was revealed by a first posthumous miracle.[18] The festival instituted by Basil I in honour of his prophet,[19] charged with the memory of so many family events, was enriched by Leo VI; he commemorated his rehabilitation on that same date, wrote and proclaimed a homily in honour of Elijah in which he referred to his release,[20] and composed *troparia* which were preserved in the ceremonial until the next generation.[21] Why, of all the prophets, Elijah? According to Zonaras, Basil nurtured the hope that Elijah 'would take him with him one day and raise him in his chariot of

---

[11] Ibid., 83, in Theophanes Continuatus, ed. Bekker (see ch. 1 n. 4), p. 325; Ephraim (verse chronicler of the early fourteenth century), ed. I. Bekker, *Ephraemii monachi imperatorum et patriarcharum recensus* (Bonn, 1840), p. 113, verses 2581–3.

[12] *Vita Basilii*, 87, in Theophanes Continuatus, ed. Bekker (see ch. 1, n. 4), pp. 329–30; Janin, *Eglises et monastères*, pp. 136–7.

[13] *Vita Basilii*, 76 (as n. 12), p. 319; Janin, *Eglises et monastères*, p. 137.

[14] *Vita Basilii*, 82 (as n. 12), p. 325; Janin, *Eglises et monastères*, pp. 137–8.

[15] *Vita Basilii*, 91 (as n. 12), p. 337; Janin, *Eglises et monastères*, p. 138; Janin, *Constantinople byzantine*, p. 142.

[16] *Vita Basilii*, 91 (as n. 12), p. 337; Janin, *Eglises et monastères*, p. 36.

[17] *Life of St Theophano*, 19, ed. Kurtz (see ch. 1, n. 81), p. 13; Leo the Grammarian, *Chronographia*, ed. Bekker (see ch. 2, n. 12), p. 260; Pseudo-Symeon, *Annales*, ed. Bekker (see ch. 1, n. 95), p. 698; George the Monk Continued, ed. Bekker (see ch. 1, n. 101), Bonn, p. 847.

[18] *Life of St Theophano*, 25, ed. Kurtz (see ch. 1, n. 81), p. 17.

[19] *De cerimoniis*, I, 28 [19], pp. 114–18; and see below.

[20] And also to Elijah's action in transforming paternal hostility into affection: 'Discours d'action de grâces au prophète Elie à l'occasion de la libération de Léon VI emprisonné par son père', ed. Akakios Hieromonachos, *Panegyrikoi logoi* (Athens, 1868), *Hom.* 31, pp. 259–62; reed. T. Moschonas, *Deltion tes patriarchikes bibliothekes (Alexandrias)*, 3, no. 1 (1950), pp. 2–5; see also J. Grosdidier de Matons, 'Trois études sur Léon VI', *TM*, 5 (1973), pp. 190, 192, 198; T. Antonopoulou, *The Homilies of the Emperor Leo VI* (Leiden/New York/Cologne, 1997), pp. 25 (no. 34), 234–6.

[21] See below.

fire'.[22] This was no doubt a witticism on the part of the historian of the twelfth century at the expense of the emperor of the ninth, whom he criticised for having been more concerned with building churches than with equipping a fleet which might have saved Syracuse from the Arabs; but it remains the case that, in Christian belief, Elijah, like Enoch, did not die but ascended alive to Heaven at the end of his days, which had already given him a special role in apparitions in the Judaic literature. This great Old Testament figure was therefore a fit prophet of accession and perhaps a sure guarantor of imperial apotheosis.

Nor was Basil I crowned by an ordinary saint, but by the general of the celestial armies, sometimes Gabriel, more often Michael, which should probably be seen less as a significant indecision than as a commonplace duplication, as with Elijah and Elisha. When he was made co-emperor on 26 May 866, Basil, in accord with tradition, received the crown from the hands of Michael III; but, having murdered Michael on 23 September 867, he had himself crowned again, this time in the church of the Asomatoi (the 'bodiless' Michael and Gabriel), which he himself had restored, to make it absolutely clear that it was to God alone that he owed the empire, through the intermediary of his *archistrategoi*/archangels.[23] This interpretation is confirmed by the illustration in the Paris manuscript and by Basil's eagerness to revive the cult of St Michael in Constantinople; he rebuilt, inside the city, the church of the archangel in the Ta Steirou/Tzerou quarter, near the Arkadianai,[24] and outside it the famous but ruined sanctuary of the Sosthenion,[25] and he consecrated an oratory in the *Nea ekklesia* to the archangel, as also to the prophet Elijah.[26] There were many *michaelia* in Constantinople, often with a funerary associations, but it seems

---

[22] Zonaras, *Annales*, ed. Pinder (see ch. 1, n. 29), p. 42; see also II Kings [IV Kings], II: 1–14: Elijah is raised on a chariot of fire and lets fall his cloak, which is taken up by his son Elisha. The scene is portrayed in the ms. *Parisinus gr.* 510, the homily collection made for Basil I, at fol. 264v; see L. Brubaker, 'Politics, patronage and art in ninth-century Byzantium: the *Homilies* of Gregory of Nazianzus in Paris (BN Gr. 510)', *DOP*, 39 (1985), pp. 1–13, illustr. 5. It also appears in the ms. *Vaticanus gr.* 333 (eleventh-century), fol. 109v; see J. Lassus, *L'Illustration byzantine du Livre des Rois, Vaticanus graecus 333*, Bibliothèque des Cahiers archéologiques (Paris, 1973), pp. 83–4 and plate. In both cases, it is possible that the iconography is taken from the apse of the church of St Elijah.

[23] Genesios, *History*, ed. Lesmüller-Werner and Thurn (see ch. 1, n. 95), pp. 80, 92–3. There is some doubt about the second coronation: see Christophilopoulou, 'Ekloge' (see ch. 1, n. 73), p. 92. McCormick thinks the second coronation may have occurred on the occasion of one of Basil's triumphs: *Eternal Victory* (see ch. 2, n. 35), pp. 156–7; see above pp. 74, 80.

[24] *Life of St Basil the Younger*, ed. Vilinskij (see ch. 3, n. 100), pp. 164, 307; *Vita Basilii*, 93, in Theophanes Continuatus, ed. Bekker (see ch. 1, n. 4), p. 339; Genesios, *History*, ed. Lesmüller-Werner and Thurn (see ch. 1, n. 95), p. 80; *Patria*, ed. Preger (see ch. 3, n. 32), p. 225; Janin, *Eglises et monastères*, pp. 340, 345–6.

[25] *Vita Basilii*, 94 (as n. 24), pp. 340–1; Skylitzes, *Synopsis*, ed. Thurn (see ch. 1, n. 39), p. 165; Janin, *Eglises et monastères*, p. 347.

[26] *Vita Basilii*, 76 (as n. 24), p. 319; Skylitzes, *Synopsis*, ed. Thurn (see ch. 1, n. 39), p. 164; *Anonymou Synopsis Chronike*, ed. K. N. Sathas, *Mesaionike Bibliotheke*, VII (see ch. 1, n. 115), p. 145; Janin, *Eglises et monastères*, p. 343.

likely that the cult of the archangel to which Basil gave his dynastic stamp was intended, as Genesios suggested, to substitute for the patronage of Michael III that of his patron saint, and perhaps also to redeem the murder which had marked his accession and avert the celestial vengeance which the archangel customarily administered.[27] Leo VI continued the tradition by dedicating a chapel to St Michael in the church of the monastery he founded for the future patriarch Euthymios.[28]

Alongside these special devotions, there were models of kingship. That of David, first, since everything goes back to him and to the unction of which he was, if not the first, at least the most illustrious beneficiary, the only one under whose patronage a kingship both sacerdotal and hereditary could be conceived. It was in Old Testament terms that Basil I saw his imperial mission, as many sources attest. About 873, through the intermediary of the deacon and protonotary Theophanes, Basil questioned Photios, who had been removed from the patriarchate more than five years before but was beginning his return to favour, on the subject of certain exegetical difficulties concerning those whom Solomon 'surpassed in wisdom', and also about unction, the popular acclamations of the coronation of David and the leg of lamb which Samuel gave Saul to eat.[29] In three poems addressed to Basil, which are attributed to Photios and which date from the same period, there are frequent allusions to 'Wisdom', to David and to the Psalms.[30] A long panegyric in the *Laurentianus Plut.* IX 23, which may well be by the same author, who was restored to the patriarchate in 877, also emphasises the themes of unction and of David.[31]

Athanasios Markopoulos has noted how the Davidic model led on to a near identification with David.[32] Like David, Basil was of humble origins. This similarity appears even in the eulogies, enhancing the personal prestige of the

---

[27] This is the explanation given by the *Life of St Basil the Younger* (ed. S. G. Veselovskij, *Žitie svjatago Vasilija* (Odessa, 1911–13), p. 85; ed. S. G. Vilinskij (see ch. 3, n. 100), pp. 164, 307) and suggested by Liutprand (*Antapodosis*, I, 10; III, 33–4, ed. Chiesa, *Liudprandi Cremonensis opera omnia* (see ch. 1, n. 111), pp. 9–10, 83–4); see also Moravcsik, 'Sagen und Legenden' (n. 2), pp. 105–6. P. Magdalino puts forward the rather risky hypothesis that the archangel to whom Basil devoted a cult was Gabriel, and that Leo VI, at the same time as rehabilitating his true father, Michael III, diverted the cult to the other archangel, Michael: 'Observations on the Nea Ekklesia of Basil I', *JÖB*, 37 (1987), p. 60 and note 26.

[28] *Life of Euthymios the Patriarch*, 5, ed. Karlin-Hayter (see ch. 3, n. 48), pp. 28–9; the church itself is dedicated to the 'doctors who do not charge' (*anargyroi*), Cosmas and Damian: Janin, *Eglises et monastères*, p. 341 (no. 7).

[29] Photios, *Ep.* 241, ed. B. Laourdas and L. G. Westerink, *Epistulae et Amphilochia* (Leipzig, 1984), II, pp. 163–7.

[30] PG 102, cols. 577–84; they were probably written on the occasion of a birthday celebration or the accession of the emperor.

[31] A. Markopoulos, 'An anonymous laudatory poem in honor of Basil I', *DOP*, 46 (1992), pp. 225–32.

[32] A. Markopoulos, 'Constantine the Great in Macedonian historiography', in *New Constantines: The Rhythm of Imperial Renewal in Byzantium, 4th–13th centuries*, ed. P. Magdalino (London, 1994), pp. 159–70.

'private person' (*idiotes*) who owed his succession to the throne solely to his own merits but rather detracting from the success of the fabricated genealogy which attached the parvenu to the Arsacids.[33] On one of the mosaics decorating the Kainourgion, the 'New Chamber' of the palace, Basil's children thank God for having raised their father from his 'Davidic poverty' in order to 'anoint him with his spirit'.[34] Just as David succeeded to an unpopular king, Saul, so Basil replaced a discredited emperor, Michael III; just as David lost, in expiation of a crime of blood, the first son given him by Bathsheba and had as his successor the second, the 'Wise' Solomon, so Basil attributed to divine vengeance the loss in 879 of his eldest son, Constantine, and designated his second son, for whom he felt little affection, Leo 'the Wise'.[35] The 'metaphor' of a Davidic kingship developed and, in a sense, came true over at least three generations of the Macedonian 'divine dynasty'.

The Constantinian model, too, was important. Constantine is present in the iconography of *Parisinus gr.* 510 not only in the insignia of the *labarum*, but in the choice of certain images: the dream which made him see for the first time the cross, and the victory of the Milvian Bridge (fol. 440). At the council of 869–70, Basil was hailed as New Constantine and his wife Eudokia as New Helena.[36] David and Constantine come together in the background of the anti-Judaic policy, when Basil, about 873–4, following Herakleios in 630 and Leo III 722, launched a massive campaign for the baptism of the Jews and formally required them, as Constantine had done in legend, publicly to demonstrate the truth of their faith, or convert. The intention was perhaps to win over to the empire communities whose importance was increasing with the revival of the urban economy; but the emperor was also rediscovering the apocalyptic vision of his role which had been that of his predecessors and which continued to nourish the Constantinian myth: to assist the realisation of the divine plan by a reconciliation, predicted for the last days, between the old and the new chosen people, and to achieve a reunification which could only successfully be brought about by a successor of David and an emperor-priest. That this was a sensitive issue was made plain by the reaction of the church. On this occasion the traditional reservations of the clergy on the subject became a violent and provocative opposition to the conversion of the Jews and a denunciation of the abuse of power perpetrated by a 'lay' emperor who was meddling in religious debate, converting, teaching and perhaps even personally practising catechesis and baptism. Basil's initiative provoked a pamphlet by the finest theologian and canonist of the age, Gregory Asbestas, who was not content to defend the dogmas and canons but preached rebellion and threatened the emperor with

---

[33] See verses 82–8 of the poem cited in n. 30 above.

[34] *Vita Basilii*, 89, in Theophanes Continuatus, ed. Bekker (see ch. 1, n. 4), pp. 334–5.

[35] See some examples of comparisons with Solomon collected by S. F. Tougher, 'The wisdom of Leo VI', in *New Constantines* (n. 32), pp. 171–9.

[36] Mansi, XVI, col. 185; see also Markopoulos, 'An anonymous poem' (n. 31).

anathema.[37] It was not only two religious policies that clashed in this episode, but a religion of the Church and a religion of the emperor.

While Basil restored or constructed in Constantinople numerous churches dedicated to the founder, his grandson went further by orchestrating a revival of the Constantinian ideology, appropriating it to the benefit of the dynasty.[38] It was probably he who added to the genealogy that made Basil descend from the Arsacids through his father the 'firm rumour' which attached him to Constantine through his mother.[39] Poverty and obscurity on the Davidic model were forgotten; it was now the illustriousness of the ancestors and 'birth in the purple' that were emphasised. Liutprand of Cremona faithfully recorded in his *Antapodosis* what he had been told about Constantine VII Porphyrogenitus at the time of his first embassy to Constantinople in 949–50:

> Porphyrogenitus does not mean born in the purple, but born in a building that is called Porphyra. It was Constantine the Great who ordered this building to be constructed; he had wanted his descendants to see the light of day there and to be called *porphyrogenetes* for this reason. And some people say that this Constantine, son of Leo, is a blood descendant of Constantine I.[40]

One sees how the 'model' became an 'ancestor'. This biological relationship, in which no one could truly believe, was an amalgam of different elements: a homonymy of name which neither rhetoric nor Constantine VII could resist exploiting, the notion of a Constantinian legitimacy extending to the whole lineage of orthodox sovereigns, and the notion that Constantine himself, by ending the Tetrarchy, had based this new legitimacy on a dynastic principle which had failed to win acceptance in his own day but which had found success with Basil and his descendants.

Other cults bore the mark of the Macedonians: that of St Euphemia, dedicatee of the convent which Basil I founded for the burial of members of his family and where his daughters became nuns;[41] and that of St Demetrios, who had appeared to Leo VI in prison to announce his imminent rehabilitation.[42] Leo showed his

---

[37] Dagron, 'Le traité de Grégoire de Nicée', *TM*, 11 (1991), pp. 316–17, 347–57.

[38] A. Luzzi, 'Nota sulla recensione del Sinassario di Costantinopoli patrocinata da Costantino VII Porfirogenito', *Rivista di Studi Bizantini e Neoellenici*, 26 (1989), especially pp. 179–80.

[39] *Vita Basilii*, 3, in Theophanes Continuatus, ed. Bekker (see ch. 1, n. 4), pp. 215–16. For Constantine VII and the Constantinian ideology, see H. Ahrweiler, *L'Idéologie politique de l'Empire byzantin* (Paris, 1975), pp. 46–52; H. Ahrweiler, 'Ho Konstantinos Z' Porphyrogennetos kai he Konstantineia ideologia', in *Konstantinos Z' ho Porphyrogennetos kai he epoche tou, B'*, Diethnes Byzantinologike Synantese (Athens, 1989), pp. 1–14; Markopoulos, 'Constantine the Great' (n. 32), pp. 162–5.

[40] *Antapodosis*, I, 6–7; III, 30–1, ed. Chiesa, *Liudprandi Cremonensis opera* (see ch. 1, n. 111), pp. 8, 82. Liutprand wrote his account at a later date, between 958 and 962; the etymology he gives is probably incorrect.

[41] Theophanes Continuatus, ed. Bekker (see ch. 1, n. 4), pp. 264–5; *De cerimoniis*, II, 42, pp. 648–9; Janin, *Eglises et monastères*, p. 127.

[42] *Life of St Theophano*, 15, ed. Kurtz (see ch. 1, n. 81), pp. 10–11.

gratitude to St Demetrios in a variety of ways, composing three homilies in his honour,[43] dedicating a sanctuary to him in the palace, with a procession on 26 October,[44] and probably endowing his great church in Thessalonike with rich revenues from Bulgarian trade.[45] Above all, however, the Macedonian dynasty wanted to acquire for some of its own members a more human and more ordinary sainthood than that of celestial beings like the archangels, or that of the Old Testament prophets like Elijah, or that of the great models of kingship like David and Constantine.

In his *Life of the Patriarch Ignatios*, Niketas Paphlagon tells of the shameless-ness of Photios, who carried subservience to such lengths that he proclaimed the emperor's much-loved son a saint, on his own authority, after he had died prematurely about September 879, and who 'did not scruple to honour him with monasteries and sanctuaries'.[46] There are echoes of this in a chronicler who tells how the patriarch exploited his hold on the emperor in order to deceive him by simulating an apparition of the dead boy on a horse, in a wooded place to which his father was led; Basil believed he recognised the apparition as his son, and later dedicated a convent to him there.[47] The episode is perfectly possible and it was long thought, wrongly, that this St Constantine was commemorated in the *Synaxarion*.[48] In fact, the anomaly seems to have been quickly resolved; few sources refer to him and Constantine was quietly buried in a sarcophagus in the Holy Apostles.[49] But it seems that the abortive cult may have taken refuge be-hind the official cult of the first Christian emperor, then being revived; perhaps the church of St Constantine founded by Theophano, much-loved daughter-in-law of Basil, near the cistern of Bonus in Constantinople, exploited homonymy; perhaps the monastery of the apparition of Basil's son in the suburbs of the cap-ital should be identified with the church of St Constantine the Great built by Basil himself in the Pege palace and quietly rechristened.

The cult of Basil's son, Constantine, was short lived, but that of Theophano eventually succeeded. Sainthood came to the Macedonians, less directly and more discreetly, through the daughter-in-law of the founder and the 'female dy-nasty' of the Martinakioi – a further example of the role of marriage alliances.

[43] Grosdidier de Matons, 'Trois études' (n. 20), pp. 190, 192; Antonopoulou, *Homilies* (n. 20), pp. 25 (numbers 17–19), 132–6.
[44] Janin, *Eglises et monastères*, p. 91; *De cerimoniis*, I, 30 [21], pp. 121–4.
[45] P. Magdalino, 'Saint Demetrios and Leo VI', *ByzSlav.*, 51 (1990), pp. 198–201.
[46] PG 105, col. 573.
[47] Pseudo-Symeon, *Annales*, ed. Bekker (see ch. 1, n. 95), pp. 692–3.
[48] P. Halkin, 'Trois dates historiques précisées grâce au Synaxaire', *Byz.*, 24 (1954), pp. 14–17; contradicted by V. Grumel, 'Quel est l'empereur Constantin le Nouveau commémoré dans le Synaxaire au 3 septembre?', *Anal. Boll.*, 84 (1966), pp. 254–60. Halkin's interpretation still has its defenders: P. Karlin-Hayter, *Byz.*, 36 (1966), pp. 624–6; K. Mentzou-Meimare, 'Ho autokrator Basileios A' kai he Nea ekklesia. Autokratorike ideologia kai eikonographia', *Byzantiaka*, 13 (1993), pp. 85–7.
[49] *De cerimoniis*, II, 42, p. 643.

Theophano, 'beauty queen' of 882, had been chosen to become the wife of Leo VI more on account of her 'royal blood' and connection with the empress Eudokia than her personal charms, to which her young husband Leo was immune.[50] She was devout and had ceased all conjugal relations after the death of her only son; she was hardly distinguished, therefore, as a source of heirs, but might make a tolerably good saint when she died, probably on 10 November 895 or 896.[51] It needed all the powerful support of her family and of Leo VI himself, however, to achieve this; indeed, Leo put as much effort into getting her sanctified as he put into searching for substitutes for her, in her lifetime and after her death, in the form of more attractive women who might also prove more fruitful. The task was far from easy, as is emphasised by the anonymous author of her *Life*, probably a cleric who was related to or a client of the Martinakioi. He was reluctant to take on the task and to add to his work two laudatory canons, normally read during the office in honour of a saint. After all, he wrote before making up his mind, Theophano lacked the virginity of a true nun, the bloody end of a martyr and the miracles of a saint. Nevertheless, he collected together a few meagre incidents occurring from the fortieth day after her death, the time when sanctity began to reveal itself on earth after the soul's journey into the beyond and its appearance before God, which he claimed he had himself witnessed – the relief of minor ills and strokes of luck that Theophano's family or he himself or his family had experienced.[52] The bishops resisted, deeming this hasty sanctification more a consequence of 'family love' than of true 'divine zeal', but eventually capitulated.[53]

The battle for the 'canonisation' was won, that for the relics was only just beginning, with numerous transfers and compromises between the imperial family and the episcopal hierarchy.[54] Theophano was first provisionally laid in the mausoleum of Constantine at the Holy Apostles, while efforts were made to demonstrate that her body was performing miracles. Meanwhile, Leo VI, in accord with his original plans, had constructed nearby, in great haste and with

---

[50] *Life of Euthymios the Patriarch*, 7, ed. Karlin-Hayter (see ch 3, n. 48), pp. 39–41: Leo told Euthymios all he had suffered on account of Theophano, how she had accused him of deceiving her with Zoe Zaoutzaina and how his father, Basil, in a fit of rage, had struck his son so hard that he had drawn blood and thrown him to the ground. Leo added: 'The whole senate knows that it was against my will and in great sorrow that I married her.'

[51] V. Grumel ('Chronologie des événements du règne de Léon VI (886–912)', *Echos d'Orient*, 35 (1936), pp. 22–32), opted for 897; P. Karlin-Hayter argues that the only possible years were 895 and 896: 'La mort de Théophano (10.11.896 ou 895)', *BZ*, 62 (1969), pp. 13–19.

[52] *Life of St Theophano*, 24–31, ed. Kurtz (see ch. 1, n. 81), pp. 16–23.

[53] *Life of St Theophano* by Nikephoros Gregoras (fourteenth century), 24, ed. Kurtz (see ch. 1, n. 81), p. 43.

[54] See the excellent article by G. P. Majeska, 'The body of St Theophano the Empress and the convent of St Constantine', *ByzSlav.*, 38 (1977), pp. 14–21; G. Dagron, 'Théophanô, les Saints-Apôtres et l'église de Tous-les-Saints', *Symmeikta*, 9 (*Mélanges à la mémoire de D. A. Zakythènos*) (1994), pp. 201–18.

salvaged materials, a church dedicated to her to which he wanted her remains to be transferred.[55] But the opposition of the clergy obliged the emperor to abandon his scheme and the promotion of the cult of Theophano in the splendid church he had built for her, except under the camouflage of a general dedication to 'All-the-Saints'.[56] Until the next generation, that of Constantine VII, Theophano continued to lie in the mausoleum of the Holy Apostles, where her official feast was celebrated on 16 December,[57] while a side chapel in the church of All-the-Saints was dedicated to her, without her relic. Much later, her body was transferred to the church of the monastery she had founded, St Constantine of the Cistern of Bonus,[58] proof both that her cult had rapidly developed and that it remained closely linked to the memory of the dynasty.

It was the first time that an imperial family had attempted to achieve for its scions this personal sanctity, which was usually denied them, as we have seen. Overall, it had been a very partial success, but developments in ceremonial soon made up for this.

CEREMONIAL AND DYNASTIC RECOVERY

The various centres of 'Macedonian' devotion and sanctity, only a few among the many cults in the capital, were given coherence and dynastic meaning by the processional routes of the ninth and tenth centuries. These are described in two groups of chapters in the *Book of Ceremonies* and constitute an easily identifiable strategy, corresponding to innovations of Basil I or his successor Leo VI and to protocols assembled or instituted by the latter or by his son, Constantine VII. The first group concern the celebrations of St Elijah, the anniversary of the dedication of the New Church (*Nea*), Basil I's great foundation, of St Michael and of St Demetrios; the second group is presented as the 'new ceremonial' for the commemoration of St Constantine and the procession for the feast of 'All-the-Saints'; on one hand the patron saints of the dynasty, on the other the models and saints of the imperial 'family'.

Let us begin with the latter. The title of the ceremonial of 21 May emphasises a recent change in the ceremonial, which it was hoped would be perpetuated by being committed to writing: 'How there should be preserved, in its present form, the annual commemoration of St Constantine the Great and the dedication of the holy crosses placed in the new palace of Bonus.' A few days beforehand, there

---

[55] *Patria*, III, 209, ed. Preger (see ch. 3, n. 32), pp. 280–1; Pseudo-Symeon, *Annales*, ed. Bekker (see ch. 1, n. 95), pp. 702–3; Zonaras, *Annales*, ed. Pinder (see ch. 1, n. 29), III, p. 446.

[56] *Life of St Theophano* by Nikephoros Gregoras, 24, ed. Kurtz (see ch. 1, n. 81), pp. 42–3.

[57] *Synaxarium* of Constantinople, ed. Delehaye (see ch. 4, n. 102), col. 313; *Typikon* of the Great Church, ed. Mateos (see ch. 3, n. 17), I, p. 132; *De cerimoniis*, II, 6 and 42, pp. 533, 643.

[58] Probably after the pillage of the Holy Apostles in 1204: Majeska, 'The body of St Theophano' (n. 54), who notes that the name of Theophano eventually eclipsed that of Constantine.

was a procession to the palace of Bonus. The evening before, in the church of St
Constantine in this same palace, situated in the northern part of Constantinople,
there was a 'private' vigil beside the precious and holy crosses. On the day itself,
the emperors went from the nearby palace to the Holy Apostles, entered the
narthex, then, after changing their robes, proceeded as far as the holy doors of the
sanctuary, where they gave thanks to God by a triple bow, but did not enter. They
went straight to the mausoleum of Constantine, in the extension of the east end of
the church. The patriarch, who was waiting for them at the communicating door,
advanced with them and gave the censor to the senior emperor for him to cense
the sanctuary of the mausoleum, the tombs of 'Leo the orthodox sovereign',
of the holy empress Theophano, of Basil, 'orthodox and good emperor' and,
lastly, of 'Constantine I the Great, holy and glorious emperor'. After a prayer
from the patriarch and the singing of a *troparion*, the sovereigns crossed the
court connecting the mausoleum and the church of All-the-Saints and returned
by a direct route to the palace of Bonus. This time it was the emperor who
waited for and welcomed the patriarch and went with him to venerate the cross
in the double sanctuary dedicated to Constantine and his mother, Helena. The
sovereigns then 'mounted' to the palace of Bonus where, the service over,
they dined with the patriarch and a selection of senators and metropolitans.[59]

For the feast of 'All-the-Saints' (first Sunday after Pentecost),[60] the sovereigns started from the Great Palace, proceeded on horseback to the Holy Apostles
and, after the usual preparations, met the patriarch at the chancel barrier of the
Holy Apostles, entered with him into the sanctuary, then followed him to reach,
a few dozen metres to the east, the church of All-the-Saints, where the liturgy
of the 'dedication' was celebrated. The sovereigns and the patriarch entered the
central *bema*, passed to the right into the chapel of a mysterious martyr Leo,
then crossed by the round end of the principal apse into the symmetrical chapel
dedicated to St Theophano, where they changed their robes. After listening
to the Gospel in the central part of the church dedicated to 'All-the-Saints',
they returned to the side chapel of St Theophano, where the guest list for
the subsequent banquet was displayed and which served as a sort of chamber
and cloakroom, a *metatorion*, like the extreme east end of the south aisle in
St Sophia. They then went out into the east court of the Holy Apostles, crossing
the atrium of a chapel of St Nicholas which must have been contiguous with
the church of All-the-Saints, and climbed an external wooden staircase which
enabled them, by the galleries, to reach directly the few state rooms which
were called the 'palace of the Holy Apostles', where the inevitable banquet
followed.[61]

---

[59] *De cerimoniis*, II, 6, pp. 532–5.
[60] This is, to the best of my knowledge, the only church in Constantinople with this dedication,
which would seem to confirm that it served as an alibi for the cult of Theophano.
[61] *De cerimoniis*, II, 7, pp. 535–8.

All this detail is necessary if we are to understand how the first emperors of the dynasty exploited the sanctity of Constantine to their own advantage while at the same time restoring their reputation, which had been tarnished by iconoclasm. It began with the reopening of the circular mausoleum of Constantine, which, after the burial of Anastasios in 518, had been regarded as full; it had been replaced by the cruciform mausoleum which Justinian had built for himself and his successors to the east of the north crossing, when he had rebuilt the Holy Apostles without touching Constantine's rotunda.[62] This second mausoleum was probably also overcrowded with sarcophagi; further, the presence of sovereigns from the iconoclast dynasties may have earned it the ambivalent reputation of a cemetery of 'orthodox and heretical' emperors. But if the iconoclasts lay in the mausoleum of Justinian, with the exception of Constantine V who had been removed from it long after his death, there were many Arian emperors in that of Constantine, beginning with his son, Constantius II. It was not on account of their sanctity or their orthodoxy but their office that they lay, in the words of John Chrysostomos, 'in the antechamber of the apostles'.[63] When Constantine's rotunda was reopened on the death of Basil in 886, or perhaps of his son Constantine in 879,[64] having been closed for more than three centuries, this was in an attempt to graft the new dynasty onto the old imperial stock.

But there was more. The two chapters of the *Book of Ceremonies* which have just been discussed show that the place of burial became more or less a place of worship, and in this way it rediscovered the vocation assigned to it by the founder in an initial schema which the church had succeeded in modifying. Constantine Porphyrogenitus twice calls it St Constantine, as if it was a church; he tells us that it had a *bema* and a central altar for a funerary or Eucharistic liturgy, as its founder had wished; and he shows, lastly, how the ceremonial allowed for the sovereigns to cense – the act of a priest – the tombs of Leo, Theophano, Basil and Constantine the Great going backwards in time, as if they were all of the same family, rendered illustrious by two official saints.

The dynastic rehabilitation was accompanied by a fraudulent attempt at sanctification, in which Theophano played a decisive role. In the revised ceremonial, she was everywhere present; she was the founder of the church of St Constantine of the palace of Bonus, from which the procession of 21 May departed and to which it returned; her body lay in the mausoleum of Constantine, where her hagiographer tells us it performed miracles; she was honoured in the church built for her under the front of All-the-Saints, where a side chapel bore her name and where a symmetrical chapel, dedicated to a notably obscure martyr

[62] See *De cerimoniis*, II, 42, pp. 642–5; P. Grierson, 'The tombs and obits of the Byzantine emperors', *DOP*, 16 (1962), pp. 1–60, especially pp. 21–3. For the construction of the Holy Apostles, see above, pp. 138–41.

[63] See above, pp. 142–3.

[64] Constantine, dead before his father, had a special sarcophagus, but was probably transferred there after 886.

Leo,[65] seemed to recreate the imperial couple Leo VI–Theophano. Having failed to promote a St Constantine of their own blood, the descendants of Basil gave this relative by marriage the task of retransmitting the sanctity of the founding emperor.

In fact, the Macedonians took over the whole remodelled site of the Holy Apostles. The mausoleum of Constantine, which they reactivated and which received their tombs with few exceptions until the extinction of the dynasty, became the centre of an architectural ensemble comprising, to the west, the church dedicated to the apostles and the adjacent palace, to the east, the church of All-the-Saints, whose ample proportions have been revealed by the recently exposed foundations, and towards the north-east, not far away, the monastery of Theophano and her church of St Constantine, integrated by Romanos Lekapenos into the architectural ensemble of the 'palace of Bonus'[66] (see plan 5).

The processions in honour of the patron saints reveal another aspect of the piety of the first Macedonians: the organisation of cults in churches with multiple dedications integrated into their palace ensembles.

For the feast of St Elijah, which a scholium notes was introduced into the ceremonial by Basil I, but which was redefined and orchestrated by Leo VI, the senators assembled at the Hippodrome the previous evening, entered the palace, reached the church of the Theotokos of the Pharos built on one of its terraces, followed the office of vespers, heard as the final prayer a *troparion* composed by Leo VI, which was sung by alternate choirs composed of the personnel of the Chamber and the imperial clergy, and each received a silver cross. On the day itself, while the official procession went to wait for the sovereigns in the narthex of the 'New Great Church', the *Nea*, the emperor welcomed the patriarch in his apartments. Together, they descended to the church of the Theotokos of the Pharos, then passed into that of St Elijah, where the same *troparion* was sung; they then passed through the Theotokos of the Pharos once more to join the senators and dignitaries who were waiting for them in the narthex of the *Nea*, via the terrace of the Heliakon and the staircase of the Boukoleon. It was here that the liturgy proper began. First the sovereigns went with the patriarch into the oratory of this church dedicated to St Elijah, entered the sanctuary, and kissed the holy doors, the altar cloth and the principal relic, the prophet's sheepskin cloak; they laid their offering on his altar, then performed the same acts of devotion at the other altars, working their way round the church; they eventually passed by the north aisle in order to light candles before an 'image

---

[65] Unless it was Leontius, one of the brothers of the 'healing saints', Cosmas and Damien, and martyred at the same time?

[66] W. Müller-Wiener, 'Zur Lage der Allerheiligenkirche in Konstantinopel', in *Lebendige Altertumswissenschaft, Festgabe zur Vollendung des 70. Lebensjahres von Hermann Vetters dargebracht von Freunden, Schülern und Kollegen* (Vienna, 1985), pp. 333–5 and plate XLI; Dagron, 'Théophanô' (n. 54).

of Basil, the sovereign friend of Christ'.[67] They then took their leave of the
patriarch, entered an 'oratory', heard the Gospels in the narthex facing the sea,
which seems to have served as their apartment, and dined there with a few
guests before regaining the centre of the palace by the same route.[68]

For the commemoration of the consecration of the *Nea*, on 1 May – also
instituted, says the same scholiast, by Basil I, builder of the church – the preparations were very similar and the ceremonial also required the procession of
dignitaries and senators to wait in the narthex of the *Nea*, while the sovereigns,
the patriarch and the personnel of the Chamber began with a private visit to the
Theotokos of the Pharos, which they reached directly from their apartments.
From it they proceeded to the *Nea* without, in this case, deviating by the church
of St Elijah. The entry and presentation of the offering took place at the principal
altar of the New Great Church, after which the sovereigns visited the secondary
altars, including that of St Elijah, then lit candles before the image of Basil
and reached the narthex facing the sea for the Gospels and the banquet. The
protocol goes on:

> Let it be known that the feast of the *archistrategos*, on 8 November, is
> celebrated according to the order and the ceremonial of this feast [of the
> consecration]. Let it also be known that on this feast of the *archistrategos*,
> the celebration takes place in the oratory of the church, that is, in the oratory
> of the *archistrategos*.

This oratory must be one of the secondary altars, dedicated to St Michael
Archangel.[69]

It is clear that it was Leo VI who officially integrated the feast of St Demetrios
(26 October) into the imperial calendar and who determined its form, in order
to thank the saint who had announced his release and rehabilitation in 886. The
ceremonial is appreciably different from the others, but has a similar structure.
The sovereigns began their devotions in the palace sanctuary of St Peter; as
they left, the cantors intoned a troparion composed 'by the most wise and good
emperor Leo' in honour of St Demetrios; the procession then moved to the
martyr's church, built by Leo VI immediately next to the Theotokos of the
Pharos.[70] There followed 'the usual office, that is, that of the dedication'.[71]

The processions organised round the mausoleum of Constantine took the
emperors into the heart of the city, quite a distance from their palace, and

---

[67] It is difficult to tell from the text whether this image was located in the north aisle, as argued by
R. J. H. Jenkins and C. A. Mango ('The date and significance of the tenth homily of Photius',
DOP, 10 (1956), p. 134) or in the narthex at the level of the north aisle, which the emperor was
obliged to cross.

[68] *De cerimoniis*, I, 28 [19], pp. 114–18.   [69] Ibid., I, 29 [20], pp. 118–21.

[70] See J. Ebersolt, *Le Grand Palais de Constantinople et le Livre des cérémonies* (Paris, 1910),
pp. 143–6: the church of St Demetrios communicated with that of the Theotokos. Like it, it was
preceded by a vestibule giving directly onto the terrace of the Pharos. Its dome was supported
by four columns with gilded capitals; its plan was that of the period, an inscribed cross.

[71] *De cerimoniis*, I, 30 [21], pp. 121–4.

made a bridge between dynastic sanctity and official religion. Those discussed immediately above took place within the narrow confines of the very short route leading from the throne room to the places of worship built on the south terraces of the palace ensemble; they assigned an important role to the palatine clergy on the fringes of the patriarchal hierarchy and established a distinction between an official procession and an imperial retinue, so strengthening the impression of a family devotion and a privatisation of the cults.

Everything was organised round two poles, the church of the Theotokos of the Pharos, restored by Michael III and inaugurated by the patriarch Photios in 864,[72] and the New Church, built by his successor and murderer, Basil I, and consecrated by the same patriarch on 1 May 880.[73] This at first suggests an opposition between one building which bore the mark of the last of the 'Amorians' and another which the first of the 'Macedonians' had wanted to make the monument of his new legitimacy. But this approach leads nowhere. Basil added a chapel dedicated to his protector Elijah to the Theotokos of the Pharos and Leo VI added a sanctuary alongside dedicated to St Demetrios. It was not a matter of dynastic rivalry but of a complementarity of cults taking many forms. First, topographical: the two churches were within the palace perimeter, but on either side of a boundary which defined an interior and an exterior part of the palace. The Theotokos of the Pharos was directly linked to the apartments and the throne room by a gallery; it was 'right in the middle of the palace', wrote Photios,[74] and western pilgrims were not wholly mistaken in calling it the chapel of the emperor (*capella imperatoris*)[75] as it was where the 'private' phase of the ceremonial took place and was used by Leo VI for the celebration of imperial marriages, previously held in the palace chapel of St Stephen. As for the *Nea*, it was both inside and outside; at about this period, Constantine Porphyrogenitus placed it 'in the palace'[76] and Liutprand 'next to the palace' (*iuxta palatium*);[77] it had its own status, economy and revenues; it was served by an autonomous clergy, separate from the palace clergy.[78]

Superposed on this topographical and functional separation was another, noted by Paul Magdalino:[79] one of the two churches was 'New Testament', the other 'Old Testament'. According to pilgrims who visited it before the great pillage of 1204 and to Nicholas Mesarites, the Theotokos of the Pharos

[72] Photios, *Homily* 10 (delivered for the inauguration of the church), ed. B. Laourdas, *Photiou Homiliai* (Thessalonike, 1959), pp. 99–104; trans. and discussed by C. Mango, *The Homilies of Photius Patriarch of Constantinople* (Cambridge, Mass., 1958), pp. 177–90. See also Janin, *Eglises et monastères*, pp. 232–6.
[73] Ibid., pp. 361–4; Mentzou-Meïmare, 'Ho autokrator Basileios' (n. 48); C. Mango, *Byzantine Architecture* (London, 1986) (pp. 196–7 of French trans. of 1981).
[74] *Homily* 10, ed. Laourdas (n. 72), p. 100, line 24; Jenkins and Mango, 'Tenth Homily of Photius' (n. 67).
[75] Comte Riant, *Exuviae sacrae Constantinopolitanae*, II (Geneva, 1878), pp. 211–17.
[76] *Vita Basilii*, 83, in Theophanes Continuatus, ed. Bekker (see ch. 1, n. 4), p. 325.
[77] Liutprand, *Antapodosis*, I, 10, ed. Chiesa (see ch. 1, n. 111), pp. 9–10.
[78] Magdalino, 'Nea Ekklesia' (n. 27), pp. 61–3.   [79] Ibid., pp. 57–60.

possessed all sorts of relics of the Passion: crown of thorns, whip used in the flagellation, scrap of purple, reed, tunic, nail from the cross, bandages from the sepulchre, footprints of Christ on this earth; it also owned the 'Holy Tile' and the sandals of Christ; in 944, the Holy Face of Edessa was placed there with much ceremony. In contrast, the *Nea* specialised in Old Testament relics, some of which had been taken from St Sophia: at least one of the trumpets of Jericho and the horn of Abraham's ram (two instruments which would serve to sound the hour of the Resurrection), the horn with which Samuel anointed David, the rod of Moses (perhaps at a later date, as the ceremonial of the tenth century says that it, like the cross of Constantine, was kept in the palace chapel dedicated to St Stephen), the table of the *philoxenia* or hospitality of Abraham, a cross carved in the vine planted by Noah after the Flood and the olive branch brought him by the dove, not to speak of the sheepskin cloak which the prophet Elijah let fall to Elisha as he ascended in his chariot of fire.[80] The church of the Virgin was more intimate and more personal; it was more like a stage of personal prayer and intercession, a *deesis*, before the return to the sources of Judaic kingship symbolised by the *Nea*, where a few souvenirs of Constantine (his cross and his shield, according to pilgrims) recalled that the Christian *basileus* succeeded to David and Solomon *by* unction and *for* the eschatological conclusion of the Second Parousia, that is, the return of Christ on the Last Day.

These contrasts made the processional route which led from the throne room (the Chrysotriklinos, which had the architecture of a church) to the *Nea* by way of the Virgin of the Pharos, an institutional journey comparable to that which took the emperor to St Sophia,[81] and a sort of active meditation on sacred history and its emperor-priests. But, at each halt, the piety itself was ordered according to surprisingly similar forms, in which we see all the Macedonian obsessions. The New Church, like St Sophia, was dedicated principally to Christ, but its cross-in-square plan, with five domes and many annexes, favoured a more complex liturgical use and an ambulatory devotion. Christ was central, certainly, but in order to serve as a prop for the cults of St Elijah, probably in the south apse, and of the archangels Michael and/or Gabriel, perhaps in the north apse; it is significant, also, that both the western ambassador Liutprand of Cremona and later the Russian pilgrim Antony of Novgorod described the *Nea* as a church of St Michael.[82] The sources also refer to an oratory dedicated to the Virgin and

[80] A. Heisenberg, *Nikolaos Mesarites. Die Palastrevolution des Iohannes Komnenos* (Wurtzburg, 1907), pp. 29–31; Antony of Novgorod (1200), Khitrowo, *Itinéraires russes* (see ch. 3, n. 20), pp. 97–9; 'Anonymous of Mercati' (English pilgrim of the late eleventh century), ed. K. N. Ciggaar, *REB*, 34 (1976), pp. 245–6; Leo the Deacon, *Historia*, ed. Hase (see ch. 3, n. 57) pp. 71, 166; E. von Dobschütz, *Christusbilder. Untersuchungen zur christlichen Legende* (Leipzig, 1899), p. 85**. See also Janin, *Eglises et monastères*, pp. 235, 362–3.

[81] See above, pp. 84–95.

[82] *Antapodosis*, I, 10, ed. Chiesa (see ch. 1, n. 111), pp. 9–10; Antony of Novgorod, trans. Khitrowo, *Itinéraires russes* (see ch. 3, n. 20), pp. 98–9.

another dedicated to St Nicholas, both located in the central body of the church, but present them as secondary.[83] Whatever the details of its arrangement, the architectural ensemble should be read like the coronation image in *Parisinus* 510: Christ, 'on high', is flanked by the two patrons of the dynasty, and he whom he has crowned, the emperor Basil, is represented 'below', at the level of the narthex, by a mosaic or painted portrait which, like a holy icon, received the prayers of the imperial procession and the honour of lighted candles. As for the Theotokos of the Pharos, after the additions of Basil I and Leo VI it too served as a prop for dynastic cults, that of Elijah and that of Demetrios, which later gave its name to the whole group of cults on the site, just as, in the end, St Michael indicated the *Nea* as a whole.

It is difficult to define the role of each emperor in this surprisingly coherent political programme, which altered the balance of cults and reorganised the ceremonial to dynastic ends. Basil was probably its initiator and it was codified by Constantine Porphyrogenitus. But Leo VI, between the two, was its organiser. It was to him that the treatise composed in 899 by Philotheos on the order of banquets, before the *Book of Ceremonies*, attributed the orchestration and the development of the feasts of 1 May (dedication of the *Nea*) and 20–23 July (St Elijah), and of other dynastic anniversaries.[84] It was he who had the task of managing a power that had long become patrimonial and of transforming into a network of alliances, and into a religion, the occasional assistance of the patron saints of his father Basil. He was their cantor; he wrote *troparia* about them and pronounced homilies from the ambo of their churches.

ST SOPHIA AND THE *NEA*

The church founded by Basil I was not called *Nea* only because it was recent and because its architecture was up to the minute, but because it 'renewed' the

---

[83] Constantine Porphyrogenitus, *Vita Basilii*, 83, in Theophanes Continuatus, ed. Bekker (see ch. 1, n. 4), p. 319: Christ, Michael and Elijah; p. 325: Christ, Gabriel and Elijah 'and in addition' the Virgin and Nicholas; Skylitzes, *Synopsis*, ed. Thurn (see ch. 1, n. 39), p. 158, mentions only Christ, the archistrategos and Elijah the Thesbite. The homage to the Theotokos is easily understood; that to Nicholas might evoke the accession of Basil I, foretold by Elijah and sanctioned by the archangels, if it is true that the monk who opened the door of the convent of St Diomedes to Basil and received from him all sorts of honours was called Nicholas: Pseudo-Symeon, *Annales*, ed. Bekker (see ch. 1, n. 95), p. 691; Leo the Grammarian, *Chronographia*, ed. Bekker (see ch. 2, n. 12), p. 256; George the Monk Continued, ed. Bekker (see ch. 1, n. 101), p. 256.

[84] Oikonomides, *Listes*, pp. 214–15 (dedication of the *Nea*), 216–19 (St Elijah), 220–3 (procession to St Diomedes, memory of Basil, *autokratoreia* of Leo and Alexander); see also pp. 212–13 ('anniversary feast of the coronation of the emperor'). Leo VI may have been responsible for changes which were further integrated into the palace processions which, in the time of Basil I, seemed still to have gone out into the town and, to celebrate St Elijah, went as far as the remote district of the Petrion, on the Golden Horn: see P. Magdalino, 'Basil I, Leo VI, and the Feast of the Prophet Elijah', *JÖB*, 38 (1988), pp. 193–6; and see the feast described in the *Life of St Theophano*, 19, ed. Kurtz (see ch. 1, n. 81), p. 13.

pact concluded since the time of David between God and the imperial power. It was part of the *renovatio imperii*, a cyclical renewal which had long been purely Roman in inspiration,[85] but which, accompanying the appearance of a new dynasty, took on a different meaning and resounded with biblical echoes. Constantine Porphyrogenitus usually used the full title, 'New Great Church', and says it had been chosen by Basil himself.[86] The *Nea* was defined, therefore, in relation to St Sophia, the old Great Church of Christ, which continued in use and remained a fixed point in ceremonial.

There were similarities between the two churches at a number of levels. Just as the 'opening' (*ta anoixia*) and 'second dedication' (*ta egkainia*) of St Sophia had their own feast days in the *Synaxarion* and the *Typika*, on 22 and 23 December,[87] so the dedication of the *Nea* was commemorated, with the same liturgy, at a date (1 May) that was not associated with any other liturgical feast.[88] Like St Sophia, the *Nea* was not an isolated church. As Paul Magdalino has shown, it was the principal element, in a sense the mainspring, of an architectural complex which also included a race course and playing field, the Tzikanisterion, where, according to Constantine VII, the emperors and their 'happy children' had acquired the habit of 'push ball on horseback' (polo), and probably also baths, the whole adorned with statues taken from various public places; similarly, the baths of Zeuxippos and the Great Hippodrome formed part of the same urban complex as the Great Church.[89]

But the similarities emerge even more clearly if we consider the legendary texts which associate Basil and Justinian, or the pamphlets which criticise the latter in order to attack the former. This is probably the case with a story which seems to date from the second half of the ninth century and which presents the builder of St Sophia deciding to erect the new Temple of Christianity in Constantinople and identifying with Solomon, who had built that of Jerusalem. While not quite a *roman à clef*, this highly amusing little story may well have been aimed at the founder of the *Nea*. It shows Justinian supervising the building works in person and lending a hand, as Basil had done, according to contemporary sources.[90] The Justinian of the story appropriates

[85] P. Alexander, 'The strength of empire and capital as seen through Byzantine eyes', *Speculum*, 37 (1962), pp. 339–57, repr. in P. Alexander, *Religious and Political History and Thought in the Byzantine empire* (London, 1978); Magdalino, 'Nea Ekklesia' (n. 27).

[86] George the Monk Continued, ed. Bekker (see ch. 1, n. 101), p. 845; Leo the Grammarian, *Chronographia*, ed. Bekker (see ch. 2, n. 12), p. 258.

[87] *Synaxarion of Constantinople*, ed. Delehaye (see ch. 4, n. 102), cols. 338 (commemoration of the opening of St Sophia, 22 December 537) and 340 (commemoration of the second dedication, 23 December 562).

[88] Ibid., col. 648; Magdalino, 'Nea Ekklesia' (n. 27), pp. 55–6.

[89] *Vita Basilii*, 86, in Theophanes Continuatus, ed. Bekker (see ch. 1, n. 4), p. 328; *Patria*, II, 85, ed. Preger (see ch. 3, n. 32), pp. 194–5; Magdalino, 'Nea Ekklesia' (n. 27), pp. 62–3; P. Magdalino, 'The Bath of Leo the Wise and the "Macedonian Renaissance" revisited: topography, iconography, ceremonial, ideology', *DOP*, 42 (1988), pp. 97–118.

[90] Especially *Vita Basilii*, 83, in Theophanes Continuatus, ed. Bekker (see ch. 1, n. 4), p. 325.

for the benefit of *his* church all the resources of the empire and all the materials he can lay his hands on; Basil, we are told, mobilised for his purposes
a fleet which would have been more useful to a besieged Syracuse. Just as
all private contributions, except that of the widow Anna, were refused by Justinian, who had no wish to share the plaudits for his achievement, so the *Nea*
was exclusively imperial, apart from the gift of a few carpets from the rich
widow Danelis.[91] Justinian inaugurating his master-work with the patriarch
(Menas), on 27 December 537, with much pomp and lavish distributions of
silver, bears a strong resemblance to Basil proceeding to the dedication with
the patriarch Photios, on 1 May 880.[92] Last but not least, when Justinian gave
Menas the slip and got to the dome first to shout, 'I have beaten you, Solomon!',
we are reminded of something the chroniclers tell us about the reign of Basil.
The emperor had his name put on a statue of Solomon which had previously
stood in the basilica and had it buried in the foundations of the *Nea* in a simulated act of self-sacrifice assuring the solidity of the building, but also to
make even more marked the similarities between his foundation and that of the
Temple of Jerusalem, and between his *basileia* and the kingship of David.[93]

This Old Testament tone suggests a humorous but also clear-sighted critic
of the religion of the emperors. In a different style but in the same legendary
context, the Chronicle of Ahima'atz (eleventh century) tells of a discussion that
took place in Constantinople between Basil and the representative of the Jews
of the Italian town of Oria, Rabbi Shefatiya, comparing the costs of the Temple
of Solomon and of St Sophia.[94] This text reminds us that the great imperial
dream of equalling David and Solomon had as its corollary a very real project
for the authoritarian conversion of the Jews, which the Church did not want
at any price. (Not only did it violate consciences and lead to a profanation of
the sacraments, but it eliminated a rupture and a division felt to be necessary,
relocated Jews and Christians in the same history and made the emperor something quite other than a 'lay' sovereign.) This was why the representative of
the clergy, Gregory Asbestas, rose up in order to 'speak of [God's] testimonies
also before kings, and . . . not be ashamed' (Psalm CXIX [CXVIII]: 46).[95]

Iconoclasm had proved revealing; its 'orthodox' conclusion had not eliminated
an imperial ideology which went back to Constantine, but it had prevented
it from being expressed too openly and made compromises necessary. The
foundation of the *Nea* was one of these. Directly attached to the imperial power,
it was clear that the New Great Church expressed a new religious policy; but it

---

[91] Ibid., 76, p. 319.   [92] *Diegesis*, 26–7, ed. Preger (see ch. 3, n. 26), pp. 102–5.
[93] Leo the Grammarian, *Chronographia*, ed. Bekker (see ch. 2, n. 12), p. 257–8; Pseudo-Symeon,
    Annales, ed. Bekker (see ch. 1, n. 95), p. 692.
[94] M. Salzman, *The Chronicle of Ahimaaz* (New York, 1924), pp. 70–4; J. Starr, *The Jews in the
    Byzantine Empire, 641–1204* (New York, 1939), pp. 127–31.
[95] Dagron, 'Le traité de Grégoire de Nicée' (see ch. 4, n. 75), pp. 316–17, 334–9, 357.

did not encroach upon St Sophia, now identified with the patriarchate, which had emerged victorious from the crisis. Constantine Porphyrogenitus gives an example of this prudent duplication, which verges on duplicity, in a passage in his treatise on the administration of the empire.

If, he wrote,[96] the Khazars, Turks, Rus' or other Nordic and Scythian peoples asked, as often happened, that they be sent one of the vestments, one of the emperors' crowns or robes, they should be refused with the following explanation. These robes and crowns had not been commissioned by men and were not the product of artisans. According to ancient and secret histories, they had been brought by an angel to Constantine, when God made him the first Christian emperor, to be kept in St Sophia and not used every day but only on the occasion of the great religious feasts. So it was by divine decree that the crowns were held in St Sophia, suspended above the holy altar table in the holy sanctuary, serving to adorn the church. As for the items of clothing, they were laid out on the altar. When one of the Lord's feasts arrived, the patriarch chose from among these robes and crowns those which were appropriate for the feast in question and had them taken to the emperor, who put them on 'as servant and deacon of God' for the duration of the ceremony only, and who then returned them to the church, where they were once more stored. A curse of Constantine the Great was written on the altar table, recording the divine prescripts transmitted by the angel, against any emperor who took one of these ornaments, for whatever reason, in inappropriate circumstances, whether for his personal use or to serve as a gift to a foreigner. If an emperor wanted to have other similar items made, it was the Church which should receive them, too, in the presence of the bishops and the senate. Neither the emperor nor the patriarch had the right to remove these robes and crowns from the church of God. The emperors felt a very real fear at the idea of contravening these divine orders. In fact, an emperor by the name of Leo, who had taken a Khazar wife (Leo IV), in an act of extraordinary folly, had taken one of these crowns on an occasion other than a feast of our Lord and without the patriarch's consent; he had immediately afterwards been afflicted with carbuncles on his face and died before his time in terrible agonies. Since this act of divine vengeance, the following rule had been established: the emperor, just before being crowned, ought to swear that he would neither conceive of nor do anything contrary to the precepts preserved by hallowed tradition, and it was after this oath that the patriarch crowned him and proceeded to the ceremonial of the feast in question.[97]

[96] *De administrando imperio*, XIII, ed. and trans. Moravcsik and Jenkins, *Text*, pp. 66–9, ll. 24–72, *Commentary*, pp. 64–6 (see ch. 1, n. 117); see A. Christophilopoulou, 'Hai eis tous naous tes Konstantinoupoleos autokratorika stemmata', *Hellenika*, 15 (1957), pp. 279–85.

[97] The text makes it clear that this was not the oath and profession of faith which preceded the enthronement and coronation of an emperor; it was rather an oath sworn each time that the patriarch crowned the emperor for a feast of the Lord.

Constantine Porphyrogenitus himself was not deceived by this story, which he presented as a diplomatic untruth for the benefit of non-Christian foreigners, who were particularly dangerous, insistent and obsessed, like many 'barbarians', with the insignia of the 'Roman' *basileia*. There was of course, no curse carved by Constantine on the altar table of St Sophia – which had, in any case, been rebuilt by Justinian – concerning the robes and the crowns, any more than there was a prohibition on communicating the formula for Greek fire, as Constantine Porphyrogenitus claimed a little further on. The oath sworn by the emperors to the church was sworn once and for all at the time of their investiture and was not renewed at every feast of the Christian calendar. The imperial robes were not used as altar cloths. The emperors had no need of the patriarch's permission before having crowns, robes or mantles made or reproduced in their workshops, or before using them as gifts for the sovereigns of friendly peoples who put themselves within the Byzantine sphere of influence by asking for and accepting them.[98]

We are in the land of make believe, but not one lacking all credibility. One does not invent at random to justify a refusal, and it is interesting that Constantine Porphyrogenitus could imagine, even in such a distorted a form, an imperial institution so wedded to its Constantinian origins – which is not too surprising – but above all, so hamstrung by the Church. Everything was decided in St Sophia. The emperor was held in suspicion by the clergy. He could take no initiative; the insignia of his power were at the discretion of the patriarch, who had them in his care, who alone had the right to choose them and who surrendered them only for the duration of a ceremony and in return for a repeated oath, not only of orthodoxy, but of submission to ecclesiastical tradition. This was, of course, a gross exaggeration, but the ceremonial of the 'feasts of the Lord' which took the emperor from his palace to the Great Church seems to point in the same direction.[99]

What exactly was the position with regard to the imperial insignia, and in particular the crowns? As we have seen, the emperor never entered St Sophia wearing his crown, except in the exceptional circumstance of being about to perform the coronation of a co-emperor; he removed it before entering the narthex and the patriarch returned it to him at the end of the ceremony – all signs of sovereignty were abandoned in the house of the King of kings. But there is nothing in the ceremonial to suggest that the crown that was removed and resumed was kept in St Sophia and provided by the patriarch; his representative, the *referendarios*, went to the palace before every major festival to inform the emperor of the ecclesiastical *ordo* of the ceremony, but did not take with him

[98] In the sixth century, the emperors of Constantinople sent the king of the Laz, who had become a Christian, a crown and a white *chlamys*: Agathias, *Historiarum libri quinque*, III, 15, 2, ed. R. Keydell (Berlin, 1967), p. 103; *Chronicon Paschale*, ed. Niebuhr (see ch. 1, n. 58), pp. 613–14.
[99] See above, pp. 84–95.

any insignia. There was, however, a legend, very close in date and in inspiration, which may be compared with the passage in Constantine Porphyrogenitus, to the effect that Justinian had consecrated a hundred crowns to St Sophia, so that the emperor could change his crown for every festival.[100] In fact, the Great Church, like the capital's other sanctuaries, held only votive crowns specially made or crowns offered by the emperors in their lifetime or by their family after their death, like those of Maurice and Herakleios,[101] or trophies seized from enemy kings, like the Bulgarian crowns brought home by John Tzimiskes in 972.[102] The prohibition which Constantine Porphyrogenitus generalised to support his own thesis applied only to the return into profane hands of these objects consecrated to God: this was the offence of Leo VI, who, overcome by a passion for the precious stones, according to Theophanes, seized a crown from St Sophia, probably that of Herakleios, and was miraculously punished.[103]

It was the palace which had charge of its insignia; and it was in its sanctuaries that these 'pledges of empire' (*pignora imperii*), whose sacredness must be preserved and maintained, were kept. The *Book of Ceremonies* lists them. In the chapel of St Theodore, adjoining the Chrysotriklinos, were the rod of Moses which the emperor carried when proceeding to St Sophia, and also the rods, chains, swords and lances of the officials and dignitaries. The cross of Constantine the Great, imperial insignia par excellence, was kept in St Stephen in the Daphne Palace and the new cross made by Constantine VII, probably on the same model, was kept in the Theotokos of the Pharos. The church of Our Lord, near the quarter of the Excubitors, housed the 'sceptres', banners and standards;[104] it was usually there that the *praepositus* placed the crown on the emperor's head when he went in procession to a church outside the palace, and where it was removed on his return.[105] In these palatine church repositaries not only were the imperial insignia sacralised, but they merged with the relics regarded as authentic whose form they reproduced, rod of Moses or cross of

---

[100] *Diegesis*, 23, ed. Preger (see ch. 3, n. 26), p. 100; Dagron, *Constantinople imaginaire* (see ch. 1, n. 59), pp. 206, 249–50; we should remember that in this account the St Sophia of Justinian bears a strong resemblance to the *Nea* of Basil I. In 1200, the Russian pilgrim, Antony of Novgorod, saw under the ciborium of St Sophia the 'crown of Constantine', and with it some thirty others that were smaller, but these must have been other small crowns: Khitrowo, *Itineraires russes* (see ch. 3, n. 20), p. 92.

[101] Theophanes, *Chronographia*, ed. de Boor (see ch. 1, n. 4), p. 281 (pp. 406–7 of Mango and Scott translation); Nikephoros the Patriarch, *Breviarium* (see ch. 1, n. 66), 30, 31, ed. and trans. Mango, pp. 80, 82; and see above, pp. 104–5.

[102] Leo the Deacon, *Historia*, ed. Hase (see ch. 3, n. 57), pp. 158–9; Skylitzes, *Synopsis*, ed. Thurn (see ch. 1, n. 39), pp. 410–11.

[103] Theophanes, *Chronographia*, ed. de Boor (see ch. 1, n. 4), pp. 453–4 (p. 625 of Mango and Scott translation).

[104] *De cerimoniis*, II, 40, pp. 640–1. The word 'sceptre' probably means here, as elsewhere in the collection, a standard, a sort of *vexillum*.

[105] Ibid., I, 19 [10], 26 [17], 39 [30], 46 [37], pp. 84, 99, 107, 168–9, 188.

Constantine. The vestimentary symbolism made the ceremonial not only a ritual but a representation, a sort of medieval 'mystery play'. The inventory of the palace insignia was preceded by a short text explaining the double meaning of the robes and insignia which the emperor wore or distributed to be worn by a dozen *magistroi* or patricians chosen by him, on Easter Day. Historically, they came from the Roman consuls and victors; symbolically, they indicated Christ resurrected (the role taken by the emperor) and his disciples ('played' by the twelve high dignitaries). With the *loros* which encircled his body like funerary wrappings, and which was gilded like the sun, the 'emperor was comparable, making due allowances, to God', wrote Constantine VII without batting an eyelid in a passage which is almost certainly his.[106] This was not pretentious; ceremonial, like liturgy, was a simulation.

In a chapter devoted to the sovereigns' dress for the great religious festivals to which they went in procession, but also for a few civil feasts, the same Constantine Porphyrogenitus does not bother to refer to the patriarch when deciding which crown or robes should be worn by the emperor. He distinguishes, according to the silk lining, the cap, or more likely the stone inserted in the middle, a 'white', a 'blue', a 'green' and a 'red' crown, and specifies when each one should be used, setting out and returning, depending on the nature of the festival or the sanctuary in Constantinople to be visited. The symbolism and the criteria for choice are not clear.[107] But the same crowns recur in another chapter which describes the reception of Arab ambassadors:[108] the white crown, which went back at least to Leo VI, was on the head of the emperor seated on the 'throne of Solomon' in the reception room of the Magnaura; the others, which are explicitly said to have been made by Constantine Porphyrogenitus, were displayed in the Chrysotriklinos. These are, we are told, the crowns of the 'Theotokos of the Pharos and the other palace churches', in particular of St Demetrios[109] and the Holy Apostles (not the city Holy Apostles, but that 'of the palace', in the quarter of the *scholae*).[110]

The grandson of Basil I has no difficulty, therefore, in visualising a hamstrung Christian empire in which everything depended on the goodwill of the patriarch and the power of the clergy to bind and to loose; but he codified a different solution and a different partition, previously introduced, which abolished all incompatibility between the religious and the political, between ecclesial structures and palace structures and between crowns consecrated to God and

[106] Ibid., II, 40, p. 637–9.
[107] It may be noted that the four colours are those of the demes of the Hippodrome, which also had their own symbolism.
[108] *De cerimoniis*, II, 15, pp. 580–1, 586–7.
[109] Janin, *Eglises et monastères*, pp. 91–2 (no. 7): this was the church built by Leo VI immediately adjacent to the Theotokos of the Pharos.
[110] Ibid., p. 50 (no. 4): it may be noted that this church was a meeting place of the deme of the Greens, and that the crown kept in this church was 'green'.

those worn freely by the emperor. The *Nea* had a role here. It was not, strictly speaking, a palace church, but the emperor controlled it and took from it the essential pieces from among the chains, chandeliers and works of art when he received foreign ambassadors in the Magnaura or the Chrysotriklinos;[111] it was not annexed, but sufficiently privatised for the emperor to be able to enter it without the many transitions which made the distance between the palace and St Sophia almost infinite. It was not the seat of the patriarchate but the last refuge of the emperor-priest, even though the patriarch went to it in procession with the emperor and officiated there.

Emperor-priest? The phrase was no longer tenable and the first 'Macedonian' emperors avoided using it. Their policy was remarkably consistent. They annexed a large number of cults, relics and religious ceremonials to the dynasty and palace, but assumed the posture of repentant sinner, submissive to the clergy. Constantine VII followed closely in his father's footsteps. He was, ex officio, preacher, hagiographer, initiator of the *Synaxarion of Constantinople*, a great organiser of celebrations and author of a complete restructuring of places of worship and an unprecedented transfer of relics, but he was careful not to 'use his imperial power arrogantly' or trespass on the domain of the clergy. The return to Constantinople of the body of Gregory of Nazianzus is a case in point. The emperor appropriated the saint and his relics. He attributed the recovery of his imperial rights in 944–5 to a miraculous intervention by Gregory, like Leo VI with a similar intervention by St Demetrios. He had Gregory write a fictitious letter humbly beseeching him to allow his remains to be returned to the capital; he personally carried the silver reliquary and deposed it in the sanctuary of the church of the Holy Apostles; and he pronounced a panegyric in which he again 'promoted' the old fourth-century bishop to the patriarchal see. He turned the saint into a new protector of the dynasty and his cult into a personal matter; but he was careful to specify that he was acting with the humility of a slave and that he was not unaware of 'what separates kingship from the priesthood'.[112]

Iconoclasm left its mark, but the two problems it had helped to expose, that of the image and that of the Christian legitimacy of the emperor, were obscured or received only symbolic responses. Just as the theological debate on the figurative representation of Christ was regarded as definitively closed after 842,

---

[111] *De cerimoniis*, II, 15, pp. 566–98.

[112] Our knowledge of these matters has been transformed thanks to the work of B. Flusin, 'L'empereur et le théologien. A propos du retour des reliques de Grégoire de Nazianze (*BHG* 728)', in I. Ševčenko and I. Hutter, ed., *Studies in Honour of Cyril Mango, Presented to him on April 14 1998* (Stuttgart/Leipzig, 1998), pp. 137–53; B. Flusin, 'Le panégyrique de Constantin VII Porphyrogénète pour la translation des reliques de Grégoire le Théologien (*BHG* 728)', *REB*, 57 (1999), pp. 5–97; B. Flusin, 'L'empereur hagiographe. Remarques sur le rôle des premiers empereurs macédoniens dans le culte des saints', in *L'empereur hagiographe. Culte des saints et monarchie byzantine et post-byzantine*, ed. P. Guran (Colegiul Noua Europa, Rumania, 2001), pp. 29–54.

and Orthodoxy came to be defined by a religious practice, the veneration of the icon, so no one now reflected on the place of the *basileus* in the structure of Christianity except within a correct or corrected ceremonial. Constantine Porphyrogenitus managed to normalise a fairly chaotic situation, but he did not clarify it. A 'junior emperor' with little legitimacy who became, after 945, *autokrator* and theoretician of imperial grandeur, in the *Book of Ceremonies* he constantly returned to the distinction between clergy and laity, noting the error of past emperors who remained inside the sanctuary until communion, and emphasising the role and respective positions of the emperors and metropolitans during the promotion and consecration of the patriarch.[113] His sensitivity in such matters enabled him to define good practice and enunciate a 'flawless' ceremonial with all the pride of the good pupil, but not to achieve an overall conception. He ostentatiously respected a few Christian taboos, but pursued the great Davidic dream of his predecessors. What the imperial institution lost in abandoning the impossible model of Melchizedek, it gained by assuring its mastery of the less theoretical but more certain sphere of the management of the sacred.

[113] *De cerimoniis*, II, 14 and 38, pp. 564–6, 635–6; II, 26, p. 627. These and many other chapters reveal Constantine's personal interest in these problems, or at least the directions he gave to those responsible for compiling the supporting documentation.

Part 3

The Clergy

7. The kingship of the patriarchs (eighth to eleventh centuries)

FROM THEODORE OF STOUDIOS TO PHOTIOS: IN THE WAKE OF ICONOCLASM

Let us now consider what three churchmen have to say about the patriarchate and the influence that it exerted or aspired to exert over the emperors. The first is Theodore of Stoudios, not the great reformer of eastern monasticism but the man of the Church and man of influence who, at the end of the first iconoclast crisis and before the second, at the very beginning of the ninth century, took advantage of a political vacuum to propose new rules; the second Photios, the patriarch execrated by Rome, who provided the idea and perhaps outlined the programme, after his rehabilitation in 879–80, of what a sovereign pontiff of the Christian East might be; and the third the patriarch Michael Keroularios, who, in another context of schism, in the mid-eleventh century, tried – or so it was said – to usurp the purple. Three periods, three men as different as it is possible to be and three ways of opposing to the tenacious model of priestly kingship that of royal priesthood, by rousing the patriarchate from the somnolence to which it was usually condemned by its deep orthodoxy and relative powerlessness *vis-à-vis* the emperors.

Everything began to change in the period between the first and the second iconoclasm, between the sulphurous iconoclasm of the emperor-priest and the more adroit and solidly based iconoclasm of the emperor-arbiter surrounded by a clerical elite. The period between the two saw a series of public misfortunes, lost wars and invasions; emperors and empresses proved spineless or unpopular; a council to restore images, Nicaea II, in 787 – held away from Constantinople to avoid the general hostility – indulged in set language and self-criticism and revealed the theological poverty of the new hierarchy.[1] What was needed was a man of destiny who would save the empire; this was to be Leo V, a general

---

[1] For an overview of the period, see *Histoire du christianisme*, IV, pp. 135–9.

unanimously hailed as 'most legitimately'[2] sovereign until, in 815, he revived the war on images.

In this confusion, new voices made themselves heard; those of Theodore, his family and his monks, who had recently taken possession of the old convent of Stoudios in the middle of the capital. They were a clan, explained the chronicler Theophanes, who had seen them in action and had little liking for them. They were a clan whose aims were not quite clear, but who attacked the old hesychast tradition, were justifiably denounced for their ambition and made effective use of allegations of 'scandal' (a word which then entered the everyday vocabulary of politics) with regard to facts which the representatives of the older generation found it difficult to deny – the remarriage of the emperor Constantine VI to his mistress, a proposal for peace with the Bulgars, the death sentences imposed on unrepentant Paulician heretics, and the accession to the patriarchate of candidates chosen from the laity and hastily ordained (though this was quite normal in the East).[3]

For Theodore of Stoudios, obviously, these were problems of conscience; objectively, however, they were primarily 'affairs' which promoted 'schism', that is, where the disagreement went so deep that it led to a severing of communion between the supporters of 'acribie' and those of 'economy', that is, between those who demanded strict respect for the canonical prohibitions, precipitating a trial of strength, and those who would accept a compromise that made it possible to get round the obstacle. If we add to the debates in which Theodore engaged all those which led, after his death, to rifts of a similar type (the confrontation between the patriarchs Ignatios and Photios, the dispute about the fourth marriage of Leo VI), it becomes clear that the Church was for more than a century in a situation comparable to that experienced by the empire in the sixth and early seventh centuries. This was when the demes, in other words the Green and Blue factions, abandoned the role which had been assigned to them in the Hippodrome, and took turns at rebellion. Incongruous though it might seem, the analogy between these repeated 'schisms' and the violence of 'democracy', also denounced as a dangerous rupture of the consensus, is not arbitrary. In the sources, the two anomalies are called by the same word, *stasis*. It is noted that the adversaries sometimes changed sides, as if the ideas being upheld counted for less than the casual alliances, and these chronic but structurally unstable divisions are described as pure mechanism, a phenomenon with neither cause nor meaning. Prokopios, writing in the sixth century about the 'colours', compared it to a 'sickness of the soul', and the bishops in their

---

[2] Theophanes, *Chronographia*, ed. de Boor (see ch. 1, n. 4), p. 502 (p. 685 of Mango and Scott translation).

[3] Ibid., pp. 481, 484, 495, 498; *Life of St Ioannikios* by Sabas, *AASS*, November II, 1, pp. 371–2, by Peter, ibid., pp. 404–5, 422, 431.

turn, when they were seeking to restore peace within the Church in 920 by a 'Tome of Union', described it as an invention of the devil.[4]

However violent at the personal level, these conflicts were 'political' and did not really split the Church in two, any more than the battles of the Greens and the Blues had split the *populus constantinopolitanus* into two. On the contrary, they helped it to move on from the centuries-old rift between the monks and the episcopal hierarchy, which the reforms of Theodore of Stoudios deliberately ignored; they reinforced the solidarity of the clergy in the face of the lay world – another of Theodore's great themes – and divided the clergy among themselves only on issues of strategy. These crises should be seen not as real conflicts of ideas or between parties, but as battles for power in which the Church, like the imperial institution, was either paralysed or shocked into action.

For the Church, by the end of the first iconoclasm, had indeed become a power, and patriarchs of Constantinople who ruled it alongside weak emperors were expected to have authority and the means to exercise it. For the first time, selection procedures were an issue. They were the subject of a letter which Theodore, implicitly a candidate, addressed to the emperor Nikephoros in 806, discussing a replacement for the deceased patriarch Tarasios.[5] God, he wrote, has made your piety reign over Christianity not only so that the secular power should be renewed, but also so that ecclesiastical affairs might benefit, if necessary, from a similar renewal and that there should come about, between the two, a new 'mixture'. It was therefore essential that the future hierarch was invested only after an indisputable and 'legitimate' selection. The emperor had asked for his advice, so he replied by observing, first, that the Church was not short of intelligent and worthy men, but that what was needed for such a position was someone also able to interpret with a perfect heart the decrees of God, who had passed through all the ecclesiastical grades from the lowest to the highest (which had not been the case with Tarasios, nor would be the case with the future patriarch Nikephoros, or, later still, with Photios, all three being products of the imperial beaurocracy), and who could give others the benefit of the widest possible experience; someone who would stand out from the others like a sun from the stars. Theodore (himself, we should remember, in the running) knew of no such person and so did not venture to state a preference, but he suggested a procedure. The emperor should assemble bishops, abbots, 'stylite' and 'immured' ascetics – for, he added, in a dig at solitary asceticism,

---

[4] Prokopios, *De bello persico*, ed. J. Haury, *Bella*, I (Leipzig, 1963), pp. 123–4, I, 24. Tome of Union of 9 July 920: Grumel-Darrouzès, *Regestes*, no. 715; Zepos, *Jus*, I, pp. 192–3; ed. and trans. L. G. Westerink, *Nicholas I Patriarch of Constantinople: Miscellaneous Writings* (Washington, 1981), 200, pp. 56–85. The text of 920 is followed by an appendix dating from the reigns of Basil II and Constantine VIII, which shows that the schism within the clergy was only really ended at the very end of the century.

[5] *Ep.* 16, ed. Fatouros (see ch. 5, n. 109), I, pp. 46–8 (between February and April 806).

the stylites would have to descend from their columns and the immured emerge from their sequestration for the common good – and selected clergy, from whom only those outstanding for their intelligence, their wisdom and their morality should be retained. It was they who should chose the most worthy candidate. Were they to act in this way, the sovereigns, 'imitators of Christ', would be triply blessed; their *basileia* would be strengthened and their name exalted from generation to generation. God had given Christians the priesthood and kingship, and they fashioned the earthly world in the image of the heavenly world; if either one of them declined, both would suffer. Nikephoros could earn no higher praise than by giving to the Church a *proedros* with, if such a thing was possible, as much merit as he.

This text implicitly contains or explicitly formulates some new ideas, in particular that of a single government of the Church, which should operate at the same level as that of the empire, that is, it should be ecumenical. It painted an ideal picture, a sort of 'mirror of patriarchs', probably the first of its kind, which shows the extent to which hopes were pinned on the creation of a strong patriarchate to end the crisis. It outlined a procedure which did not challenge the right of the emperor to appoint, but which made the choice itself a matter involving all the clergy, apparently chosen in two stages, and only the clergy. The pairing of priesthood and kingship was a commonplace already employed by Justinian;[6] we should note only that here it did not lead to postulating a distinction, but to advocating an ill-defined 'mixture', which would reproduce on earth the heavenly harmony.

This, then, was what Theodore, and no doubt many others, were hoping for in 806. From the perspective of a happy coming together of the two ecumenical powers, no reference was made either to Rome or to the pentarchy, which may seem surprising. The division of the Church into five patriarchates of equal status, effectively ended by the Arab conquests, which had left in Christian territory only Rome and Constantinople, was now little more than a tactical argument in time of need. As for the papacy, Theodore turned to it when he was at odds with the emperor or the patriarch, but for him it was primarily an ecclesiastical court of appeal, forgotten as soon as there was the prospect of the two powers marching in step where they naturally coexisted, in Constantinople.

Photios represents the complete antithesis of the model outlined by Theodore the Stoudite half a century earlier, in the lull in the iconoclast crisis. He came from the imperial bureaucracy which he had directed as *protasekretis*; after his appointment as patriarch by the emperor Michael III, this lay civil servant rose in five days through all the ranks of ordination (on the first day he became a monk, on the second a lector, on the third a subdeacon, on the fourth a deacon and on the fifth a priest) so that, on the sixth, he could be ordained and give

---

[6] Justinian, *Novels* 6, pr.; 7, chapter 2, 1.

his blessing to the faithful in St Sophia. Let us note only the three principal phases of his turbulent patriarchate. In 858, he took over from a predecessor Ignatios, who refused to resign, and was condemned by Pope Nicholas I, whom he excommunicated in his turn; in 867, he was deposed by the new emperor, Basil I, then treated as a criminal by a first council (869–70); but he returned to favour, was restored to his position in 877 and lauded as 'supreme pastor' by a council of rehabilitation (879–80).[7] At least in the West, these ups and downs and the polemic have for centuries created an enduring impression of an unscrupulous intriguer, devoted to secular power and ferociously hostile to Rome. It is by no means clear what to put in place of this caricature, so much does the man seem to have played all roles at the same time and so much have his ideas been distorted by extravagant rhetoric and unreliable reminiscences. But we can at least be sure that he was more authentically a man of the Church than his enemies and Catholic historiography would have us believe. Further, brought up during the second iconoclasm in a family which had played an active part in the conflict and included a patriarch, Tarasios, his uncle, he was keenly aware of the role that had devolved to the patriarchal office. It is this aspect alone which is our concern.

The notes in his *Bibliotheca*, which reveal his choice of reading, and also, sometimes, aspects of his character,[8] suggest a particular interest in Jewish history and, within Jewish history, in everything to do with high priests. Reading Diodoros of Sicily, Photios first dealt with 'the man and the work' in a single note,[9] but later returned at length to a selection of texts concerning events in the second century before Christ (the discoveries of Antiochos IV Epiphanes when he entered the Temple, the capture of Jerusalem by Antiochos VII Evergetes) and the laws and customs of the Jews.[10] He was particularly interested in Moses, guide and law-maker, interpreter of the God without a face. Citing or paraphrasing now lost passages in Diodoros – whom he described, in the end, as a liar – he noted:

> Among the citizens, [Moses] chose the most refined and those who would be most capable of ruling all the people, and he appointed them priests... he made them guardians of the laws and customs; that is why the Jews never have a king and why the government of the people is still entrusted

---

[7] For the two patriarchates of Photios, see *Histoire du christianisme*, IV, pp. 169–86.

[8] The *Bibliotheca* is a collection of 279 reading notes which Photios agreed to compile at the request of his brother Tarasios on the eve of his departure on an embassy. P. Lemerle dates this embassy to 838: *Byzantine Humanism, the First phase: Notes and Remarks on Education and Culture in Byzantium from its Origins to the 10th Century*, trans. A. Moffatt (Sydney, 1986), pp. 35–41, 186–90; W. T. Treadgold suggests the date of 845: *The Nature of the Bibliotheca of Photius* (Washington, 1980), pp. 35–6. It is likely that the embassy was only a starting point and that Photios continued to work on the *Bibliotheca*, which reveals the preoccupations of a man of the church, until his second patriarchate: C. Mango, 'The availability of books in the Byzantine empire, AD 750–850', in *Byzantine Books and Bookmen* (Washington, 1975), pp. 40–3.

[9] *Bibliotheca, Cod.* 70, ed. R. Henry (Paris, 1959–77), I, pp. 102–4.

[10] *Bibliotheca, Cod.* 244, ed. Henry, VI, pp. 126–74, especially pp. 132–7.

to whomsoever among the priests is regarded as the most intelligent and the most virtuous. It is he whom they call the High Priest, and they believe that he is for them the messenger of the divine commandments.[11]

Photios clearly had more confidence in Flavius Josephus, to whom he devoted four notes. The *Jewish War* interested him in particular for the omens that preceded the capture of Jerusalem and for the dissension between zealots and sicarians which accompanied it;[12] these were familiar Byzantine themes. He showed his greatest interest in *Jewish Antiquities*, a book so assiduously read, pondered and sometimes rewritten by Christians that Hardouin called it the 'fifth gospel'. Photios based on Book XX a first, fairly brief note, which primarily emphasised the powers of the high priests,[13] although other passages in the same book might have attracted his interest as exegete, such as those describing the machinations of the high priest Ananias against James, 'brother of our lord'. In a much longer note, he returned to the same passages, which he had reread in another manuscript or in an interpolated version.[14] This fascination with Jewish history is not in itself surprising, but it was focused on specific subjects, touching on the definition and the heredity of the high priesthood. We may suspect that Photios was searching among the chosen people for Old Testament models of priesthood just as the emperors were searching for models of kingship. This was when the patriarchate was in the middle of the disturbances we have already described, when it was sometimes subject to imperial arbitrary power, sometimes stood up to the emperor as counter-power, and when the patriarchs, in imitation of the emperors, required the bishops and the clergy to sign oaths of allegiance[15] and involved their families in their own success or failure. With the fall of Photios, his nephew, the future patriarch Nicholas Mystikos, chose to go into exile, just as he would have been obliged to do had he been the scion of a fallen dynasty.

---

[11] Ibid., p. 136.   [12] *Bibliotheca, Cod.* 47, ed. Henry, I, p. 333.

[13] *Bibliotheca, Cod.* 76, ed. Henry, I, pp. 155–8, corresponding to *Jewish Antiquities*, XX, 224–51 (pp. 507–23 of Loeb ed.).

[14] *Bibliotheca, Cod.* 238, ed. Henry, V, pp. 152–5; see also J. Schamp, 'Flavius Josèphe et Photios. A propos d'une singulière lecture des *Antiquités judaïques', JÖB*, 32/3, pp. 185–96. For the use by Photios of Jewish and Roman history, see A.-J. Bousquet, 'The references to Josephus in the Bibliotheca of Photius', *Journal of Theological Studies*, 36 (1935), pp. 289–93; J. Bompaire, 'Réflexions d'un humaniste sur la politique: le patriarche Photius', in *La Notion d'autorité au Moyen Age, Islam, Byzance, Occident. Colloque international de la Napoule* (Paris, 1982), pp. 44–55; D. Mendels, 'Greek and Roman history in the *Bibliotheca* of Photius: a note', *Byz.*, 56 (1986), pp. 196–206; D. Mendels, 'Hecataeus of Abdera and a Jewish *patrios politeia* of the Persian period (Diodorus Siculus XL, 3)', *Zeitschrift für die alttestamentliche Wissenschaft*, 95 (1983), pp. 96–110; M. Maas, 'Photius' treatment of Josephus and the High Priesthood', *Byz.*, 60 (1990), pp. 183–94.

[15] See, for example, the references to the oaths sworn to Ignatios or Photios in the *Life of the Patriarch Ignatios* by Niketas Paphlagon, PG 105, cols. 505, 540, 572; reacting against this custom, canon 8 of the anti-Photian council of 869–70 prohibited the patriarch of Constantinople from making the clergy sign oaths of allegiance.

The Old Testament might suggest examples of priest-kings to oppose to those of king-priests, but Rome offered a much more obvious example, which many ambitious patriarchs hoped to imitate. Photios seems to have been the first. Whatever his disagreements with Rome, it was on the Roman model that he proposed to reform the see of Constantinople during his second patriarchate, which coincided with a period when imperial power, still in the hands of Basil I, had become very vulnerable. He noted that Christendom was now split in two, and that the pentarchic ideal, still invoked at the 'anti-Photian' council of 869–70,[16] might be relegated to the repertoire of memories or devious arguments. The first canon promulgated by the council of 879–80 stipulated that if the clergy who were responsible to the pope were excommunicated or condemned, they would be treated as such by the patriarch of Constantinople and vice versa.[17] It thus explicitly denied to the pope the right of appeal that he claimed and which he had misused, it must be admitted, during the crisis that was drawing to a close. This was a big step towards the recognition of two Christian spheres of influence, each with its sovereign pontiff.

A TWO-HEADED POWER?

The new stature of the patriarchate of Constantinople in relation to Rome, other patriarchates and the emperor is described in greater detail in the preamble and first three 'titles' of a legal manual, the *Eisagoge*,[18] compiled between 879 and 886 to accompany a first version of the great codification undertaken by the Macedonians, and later given the name of *Basilika*. Photios has quite plausibly been suggested as the author of these introductory pages, which discuss the organisation of the two powers before the strictly legal chapters, and which date, at all events, from a period when the patriarch was in a position to make his ideas prevail.[19] He had just been rehabilitated by a council which had hailed him with the title 'supreme pastor' and recognised his sphere of responsibility to extend to the 'whole world', and the papal representatives had joined, willynilly, in this chorus of flattery, as had the patriarchates in Islamic territory. In addition, the depression which afflicted Basil I and the intrigues which had led

[16] Mansi, XVI, cols. 140–1; and see F. Dvornik, *Byzantium and the Roman Primacy* trans. E. A. Quin (New York, 1966), p. 102.

[17] Rhalles–Potles, *Syntagma*, II, p. 705.

[18] The correct name of the collection usually known as the *Epanagoge;* the title indicates as emperors Basil, Leo and Alexander, so we must assume that Constantine was already dead, which puts its date between September 879 and 29 August 886: see A. Schminck, *Studien zu mittelbyzantinischen Rechtsbücher* (Frankfurt-am-Main, 1986), pp. 1–15, who narrows down the possibilities to 885/6.

[19] This attribution, already suggested by Zacharias von Lingenthal, is based on a marginal note in the ms. *Bodleianus gr.* 173 and an argument on philological grounds by J. Scharf: 'Photios und die Epanagoge' and 'Quellenstudien zum Prooimion der Epanagoge', *BZ*, 49 (1956), pp. 385–400; 52 (1959), pp. 68–81; see also Schminck, *Studien* (n. 18), pp. 14, 70ff.

or would lead, in 883, to the imprisonment for a full three years of the heir to the throne, Leo VI, can give the impression that the patriarchate, in spite of the secession of several clergy, had succeeded in elevating itself, as Theodore of Stoudios had wished, to the same level as the imperial power and that it would be called on to compensate for its deficiencies.

The preamble presents man as both a spiritual and a corporeal being, composed of conflicting elements whose mixture is willed by God and guaranteed by his law.[20] It is the Law which ensures the unity of the whole and governs, like a monarch, the duality. This comes from God, is proclaimed by God and is written with His finger, not on tablets of stone as in the time of Moses, but in our souls in letters of fire; thus, one should acknowledge its 'autocracy'. In this flamboyant introduction, we may observe borrowings from various authors of Ancient and Christian Hellenism, perhaps Isidore of Pelusium in particular. It is hardly surprising that Title I should then be devoted 'to the law and justice',[21] but it turns out to consist of little more than articles extracted from the *Digest*, cited in a Greek paraphrase from the time of the *antecessores* and strung together in a notably careless fashion.[22] We have to ask, therefore, whether this mishmash of quotations expresses an idea or simply repeats a well-worn *topos*; whether we should recall that Photios had in the past made notes of an anonymous dialogue advocating under the name of *dikaiarcheia* a sort of 'state of law', a constitution combining monarchy, aristocracy and democracy under the rule of law,[23] or whether it is simply a case of unsystematic rhetoric.

The answer probably lies somewhere in between. In this trompe-l'oeil structure, primacy was conceded to the law only for it to be more surely removed from the emperor; the law occupied the apex of the pediment in order to leave space at either side of its base, at the same level and in exact parallel, for imperial power and for patriarchal power, the subjects of Titles II and III.[24]

The first surprise is that the emperor is defined as a 'legitimate authority' (*ennomos epistasia*),[25] contrary to the Hellenistic and Roman tradition which declared him 'above the laws' and himself 'living law', submitting to the law only by conscious choice.[26] The compiler of Title II retains only one term of this customary dialectic of absolute power and restrictive virtue, of the emperor

---

[20] To be read in the edition of Schminck (ibid.).   [21] Zepos, *Jus*, II, p. 240 (Epanagoge).

[22] D. Simon, 'Princeps legibus solutus. Die Stellung des byzantinischen Kaisers zum Gesetz', in *Gedächtnisschrift für Wolfgang Kunkel*, ed. D. Nörr and D. Simon (Frankfurt-am-Main, 1984), p. 471; S. Troianos, 'Ho megas Photios kai hai diataxeis tes Eisagoges', in *Ekklesia kai Theologia*, 1 (1989–91), p. 495.

[23] *Bibliotheca, Cod.* 37 ed. Henry (n. 13); see above pp. 15–16 and n. 11. H.-G. Beck, in *Res Publica Romana. Vom Staatsdenken der Byzantiner*, Sitzungsberichte der Bayerische Akademie der Wissenschaften, Philosophisch-historische Klasse, 2 (Munich, 1970), pp. 28–30, is perhaps too impressed by the 'democratic' emphasis of this passage.

[24] Zepos, *Jus*, II, pp. 240–3.

[25] The expression seems to have been borrowed from *Ep.* 143 of Isidore of Pelusium, PG 78, cols. 1224–5.

[26] See above, p. 19.

nomos empsychos and the *basileia ennomos*, and so contradicts a rhetoric established by centuries of usage, whose juridical expression was repeated in the Macedonian codification.[27] His bias emerges even more clearly a little further on in an article where the emperor is subject not only to the gospel precepts and the canons of the ecumenical councils, which was usual, but to the 'Romaic' laws, that is, to the legislative tradition and the law in the process of codification, which was a surprising and essentially absurd novelty. The ulterior motive concealed behind Title II emerges as we read Title III, in whose first article the patriarch is defined as an 'incarnate and living image of Christ, who, by his words and his deeds, expresses the truth [*eikon zosa Christou kai empsychos, di'ergon kai logon charakterizousa ten aletheian*]'. The formulation is original,[28] but all the words are coded; the verb *charakterizein* comes from the iconoclast dispute where it emphasised the very strong relationship existing between the image and its model; *empsychos* belongs, as we have seen, to imperial rhetoric and ideology. Everything the patriarch gained was stolen from the emperor. The emperor traditionally called – as in Theodore the Stoudite's letter – 'imitator of Christ' is replaced by a patriarch in the image of Christ, the emperor traditionally 'living law' by a patriarch 'living truth'.

If we pursue this further, we note that this first article of Title III seems to be inspired by Maximos the Confessor, who wrote in the *Ambigua*:

The great Melchizedek, by reason of the divine virtue placed in him, was chosen to be the image of Christ our God and of his ineffable mysteries [the Eucharist], image of Christ towards whom all the saints converge as to the cause of all the good which each has in him, and above all the one [Melchizedek], who bore in him more than any other the features of Christ.[29]

It is quite possible, therefore, that the author was not only making the patriarch a sort of saint, image of Christ, but that he was giving him Melchizedek as a model. The idea of an emperor-priest, condemned in the person of Leo III, was replaced by a cautious but clear evocation of a patriarch-emperor, or at least of a high priest to whom all the attributes of sovereignty would fall. If he was the living image of Christ, the patriarch shared like him in the two powers.[30] He was a New Moses and a New Melchizedek.

Other articles outline an insubstantial and unoriginal philosophy of the relations between the emperor and the patriarch, giving the former responsibility for bodies and the latter for souls, along familiar lines; it is primarily intended to concentrate all spiritual power in the hands of the patriarch and avoid mentioning any of the better-established rights of the emperor to intervene in the church:

[27] *Basilica* II, 6, 1 repeats, in effect, *Dig.* I, 3, 31: 'Princeps legibus solutus est'; and *Basilica* II, 6, 2 repeats *Dig.* I, 4, 1: 'Quod principi placuit, legis habet vigorem'.
[28] Schminck, '*Rota tu volubilis*' (see ch. 3, n. 76), p. 213, rightly emphasises that this is an original fragment which is the key to the whole.
[29] PG 91, col. 1141; the phrase is followed by an exegesis of the person of Melchizedek. The connection was made by Scharf: 'Quellenstudien zum Prooimion' (n. 19), p. 80.
[30] See below, pp. 313–18.

The *politeia* being constituted, like men, of members and parts, the most important and the most necessary are the emperor and the patriarch; that is why the peace and happiness of subjects, according to the soul and according to the body, reside in friendly relations and harmony on all points between the emperor and the patriarch.[31]

A pious wish was left to resolve all the conflicts which would inevitably result from this dangerous two-headedness and which are predicted in another article, where we read that the patriarch will speak out before the emperor 'and will not be ashamed', so as to defend the truth or the dogmas against him. The expression is taken from the Psalm 119, but Gregory Asbestas had used it in 878/9, a few months or a few years before the author of the *Eisagoge*, to denounce the very 'Constantinian' policy of converting the Jews pursued by Basil I.[32]

It was the duty of the emperor to safeguard and preserve 'present things', to 'recover lost things' and to acquire by 'just victories' the 'missing things' – in other words, to mount an effective defence of the territories under his control, to win back from the Slavs and the Arabs the 'Roman' countries they had conquered in Europe and Asia, and even, by future conquests, to draw closer to an ideal universality. This article had an exact counterpart in the one describing the duties of the patriarch;[33] to preserve orthodoxy by eliminating from the empire all traces of deviation, to cause the heretics who had left it to return to the Church, and to summon unbelievers to the true faith. There are three levels here, too: the elimination of Judaising or dualist sects within the empire, reconciliation with the Armenians and the Jacobite Syrians formerly within the empire or within its orbit, and missionary activity among the Slavs. This programme tallies very closely with the preoccupations of Photios. A homily of his of 867 quoted the reintroduction into the church of a small community of 'quartodeciman' Judaisers, probably in Asia Minor,[34] he composed a whole anti-Paulician and anti-Manichean corpus,[35] he wrote to the *catholicos* of Armenia in the hope of winning his support,[36] and he sponsored the Byzantine missions in Great Moravia, Bulgaria and among the Varangians.[37] In this, the

---

[31] *Eisagoge*, III, 8; Zepos, *Jus* II, p. 242.

[32] Psalm CXIX [CXVIII]:46; Dagron, 'Le traité de Grégoire de Nicée' (see ch. 4, n. 75), p. 317 (§1). See above, pp. 147–8, 200–1.

[33] II, 2; III, 2.

[34] *Hom.* 17, of 876, ed. Laourdas (see ch. 6, n. 72), pp. 165–6, trans. and comm. See Mango, *Homilies of Photius* (see ch. 6, n. 72), pp. 279–82, 288–9; J. Gouillard, 'L'hérésie dans l'empire Byzantin des origines au XIIe siècle', *TM*, 1 (1965), pp. 307–12.

[35] PG 102, cols. 16–264. See C. Astruc et al., 'Les sources grecques pour l'histoire des Pauliciens d'Asie Mineure', *TM*, 4 (1970), pp. 1–227; P. Lemerle, 'L'histoire des Pauliciens d'Asie Mineure d'après les sources grecques', *TM*, 5 (1973), pp. 1–144.

[36] J. Darrouzès, 'Deux lettres inédites de Photius aux Arméniens', *REB*, 29 (1971), pp. 137–81; J.-P. Mahé, in *Histoire du christianisme*, IV, pp. 492–5, which casts serious doubt on the authenticity of the document.

[37] Photios, *Ep.* 2, ed. Laourdas and Westerink (see ch. 6, n. 29), I, pp. 41, 50.

patriarch was only doing his job; but it was a job that was eminently political since, over and above the conversion of pagans and the return of dissidents, it involved the extension of Constantinople's sphere of influence in competition with Rome on the one hand and Baghdad on the other. About 880, it was very clear that the frontiers of the patriarchate might not coincide with those of an empire barely emerged from recession, and that the spiritual arm was more effective than the 'temporal' arm for redefining an eastern Christianity.

In fact, the notion of *christianon ethnos* now assumed a concrete meaning, but it was limited to an eastern Christianity with New Rome as its centre and the patriarch as its sole head. In the *Eisagoge*, the power of the latter, like imperial power itself, is not institutional in nature. The articles on the bishops, the clergy and ecclesiastical property, that is, on the Church as an institution, are relegated to Titles VIII–X; Title III accepts no division of authority between the patriarch and the metropolitans, who nevertheless constituted, on their own ground, a relatively autonomous rank and, in synod or assembly, a structure with which the patriarch increasingly had to reckon.[38] The rights of the metropolitans, which were already and would continue to be the subject of fierce debate, are here passed over in silence, because patriarchal authority was exercised at a different level, ecumenical in a way that was in theory unlimited and extending in practice to all the territories of the old empire of the East.

In support of its arguments, the *Eisagoge* relies on canons 3 of the council of Constantinople (381), 28 of the council of Chalcedon (451) and 36 of the council in Trullo (691–2). These had gradually brought Constantinople recognition as second among the patriarchates, after Rome but before Alexandria, Antioch and Jerusalem, because New Rome was 'honoured by the presence of the emperor and the senate, and enjoyed privileges equal to those of Rome'.[39] It was the principle of making ecclesiastical geography conform to imperial geography which had suggested elevating Constantinople to this position in the hierarchy of the five patriarchates. But it was a quite other principle that caused the author of the *Eisagoge*, at the end of the ninth century, to distort these canonical texts and offer this strange resumé:

> The see of Constantinople being distinguished by the emperor, it has been declared first by decision of the holy councils. In accord with this, the sacred laws decree that contentious cases arising in the other [patriarchal] sees should be brought to its knowledge and submitted to its judgement.[40]

The fact that Rome was ignored signifies not that it had lost its supremacy and should be subject to Constantinople, but that the compiler was deliberately adopting a logic of separation between a Christian East and a Christian West, and that he was granting the two Christian capitals equal rights over whichever

---

[38] See below, pp. 250–1, 309–11.   [39] Rhalles–Potles, *Syntagma*, II, pp. 280–1, 387.
[40] *Eisagoge*, III, 9; Zepos, *Jus*, II, pp. 242–3.

part of Christendom they governed. This ecclesiastical Yalta put Antioch, Alexandria and Jerusalem within Constantinople's sphere of influence and awarded it not only the right of appeal for all ecclesiastical cases in the East, but the right to summon and hear any case and to intervene in any matter it chose, which was exactly the right the pope had been claiming at the time of the quarrel between Ignatios and Photios.[41] In 879–80, the council for the rehabilitation of Photios had taken the first step in the direction of this equalisation of Rome and Constantinople and this downgrading of the eastern patriarchates, by abolishing the appeal to Rome for condemned easterners. At the same time or a few years later, the *Eisagoge* showed where this first measure had led: to the definitive abandonment of the old pentarchic ideal, to recognition of a solidarity among Christians of the East and to a partition of Christendom.

What exactly is the significance of the *Eisagoge*, this 'introductory' treatise to an ongoing legal reform, which was probably officially promulgated but soon set aside, and which it would be mistaken to see as the keystone of a political ideology or as an original conception of the balance of the 'two powers'? It – or rather the first three titles, the only ones in which the direct influence of Photios can be detected, what follows being no more than a rehash of the juridical tradition – is a text produced for the occasion, which fossilised a transitory situation. It deprived the imperial office, suspect since iconoclasm, of some of its sacred nature. It indicated that the emperor might well be put under the tutelage of a self-confident patriarch. The only 'ideological' originality of this hastily drafted theory lay in what it had borrowed from the Roman pontifical model; and this was also its weakness. Theodore of Stoudios, for whom Rome had been a recourse in his perpetual *stasis* against the authorities, was the first to imagine a patriarch who, without substituting himself for the pope, would have a legitimacy almost equal to that of the emperor and so constitute himself a power. Photios went further down the same path, perhaps dreaming of a sacerdotal kingship on the Judaic model, at any rate drawing on the Roman example to define a sort of eastern ecumenicism. The *Eisagoge* simply expressed the same idea by giving the patriarch pontifical stature. But it did not succeed in establishing a bicephalous power, being content to juxtapose a 'temporal' power arbitrarily laicised and a 'spiritual' power endowed with all sorts of regalian attributes, as if an emperor and a pope could cohabit in the same capital.

The epilogue reveals the fragility of this conception. A few months after the 'publication' of the *Eisagoge*, the emperor Basil died; his son Leo VI wasted no time in forcing Photios to resign, on 29 September 886, and replacing him with his own brother, Stephen, whom he enthroned on 18 December of the same year, himself delivering the homily for the occasion from the ambo of

[41] Letter from Pope Nicholas I to Michael III, dated 28 September 865: see Dvornik, *Byzantium*, (n. 16), p. 109.

St Sophia.[42] In his funerary eulogy for his father, Leo explained that Basil had found no other way of restoring peace to the Church and ending the rivalry between competing patriarchs than to 'sacrifice' one of his children to God, as Abraham had done.[43] The problem of a power with two heads was solved by the tie of blood; and Leo VI was certainly closer than the author of the *Eisagoge* to Byzantine conceptions when he mounted the pulpit, ruled on problems of canon law and declared, in Novels which erased the last juridical vestiges of Roman 'republicanism', that in future imperial 'providence', with God's help, would 'control and govern everything'.[44]

MICHAEL KEROULARIOS AND THE PURPLE SANDALS

Men come and go, ideas have long lives; and that of a near parity between the patriarchate and the papacy had no need of an ambitious hierarch to take root. It corresponded to a reality. The see of Constantinople was well suited, as we have said, to become a sort of eastern papacy in the context of a religious partition dating back to the seventh century, just as Constantine's capital was well suited to become New Rome in 330 as a result of a political partition, less to emphasise a rupture than to mitigate its effects by giving a duality the form of a duplication.

Nothing divided the two capitals when there occurred a minor but significant incident, which can serve as a staging post between the posturings of Photios and of Michael Keroularios. The Burgundian monk, Raoul Glaber,[45] later repeated by Hugh of Flavigny,[46] tells of an eastern embassy which caused something of a stir in about 1024. It came to present Pope John XIX with a joint request from the patriarch Eustathios and the emperor Basil II, asking that 'with the approval of the Roman pontiff, the Church of Constantinople should be called and recognised as universal in its world (*in orbe suo*) as Rome had been in the whole world'. The gifts borne by the 'Greeks' soon dissipated the unease of the pope and his advisers, and after discreet discussions consent was on the point of being given, when there was an outcry (*tumultus, commotio*) in Italy which reverberated through more vigilant Christian circles. William of Volpiano, from St Benignus of Dijon, dispatched a letter to the pope, the text of which is given and which reads very much like a demand. The political power of the Roman empire may have been fragmented into many sovereignties, but that to 'bind

[42] Grosdidier de Matons, 'Trois études', pp. 198–207; Antonopoulou, *Homilies* (see ch. 6, n. 20), pp. 25 (no. 22), 245–7. In his homily, Leo exalted brotherhood and reminded hesitant bishops of his right to elect the patriarch.

[43] *Funeral Oration of Basil I*, ed. and trans. Vogt-Hausherr (see ch. 1, n. 4), p. 65.

[44] Novel 47; see also 46, 78, 94.

[45] *Hist.*, IV, 1–4, PL 142, cols. 670–1, ed. and trans. N. Bulst, J. France and P. Reynolds *Radulfi Glabri Historiarum libri quinque* (Oxford, 1989), pp. 172–6. See Grumel-Darrouzès, *Regestes*, no. 828.

[46] *Chron.*, II, 17, PL 154, cols. 240–1.

and to loose on earth as in heaven' was an inviolable gift made to the sole magisterium of Peter; their vanity and their foolish presumption had caused the Greeks to forget this. John XIX had to retract and eventually found himself in the role of principal culprit.

It is a little surprising that the eastern sources preserve no trace of this request, which had certainly not been the main purpose of the embassy and was hardly revolutionary. It had perhaps been an incidental plea, yet again, for the title of 'ecumenical' patriarch, disputed by Rome since the time of John the Faster at the end of the sixth century, or for confirmation of the principle of a jurisdiction of appeal of the type envisaged in the canon of 879–80 and the *Eisagoge*, which would have given Constantinople supremacy over the other eastern patriarchates. If the embassy had really been charged by an emperor at the peak of his power and a rather undistinguished patriarch to champion a religious policy, it could only have been a renewal of that championed in the past by Photios for a restructuring of the patriarchate of Constantinople, but in a low-key, pragmatic manner, without the customary sabre-rattling. This is shown by the imbalance which left Rome with an undisputed primacy and a superior right of appeal and gave Constantinople, in a derivative but contradictory formula, an ecumenical role limited to its own sphere of influence, primacy after Rome within an eastern subdivision.

The novelty was not a sudden surge of Byzantine 'caesaropapism', but a wind of reform which had begun to blow in western Christendom and was, as we have seen, quick to catch out an 'unworthy' pope in dealings with caricatured 'Greeks'. On the Byzantine side, these were still the days of a low-key patriarchate which derived most of its importance from the presence of the emperor in Constantinople. But it was precisely this that made the East the ideal target for western reformers; it represented in their eyes the model of an imperial Church, whose privileges were based only on an alignment of the spiritual with the temporal. In fact, what they knew of Byzantium, which barely extended beyond Italy, predisposed them neither to indulgence nor understanding: a cunning diplomacy, a pretentious and ineffectual authority, religious particularisms given the name of Orthodoxy. The new ideas also made some aspects appear as serious anomalies – the prohibition of the Latin rite in the dioceses of Apulia and Calabria, the direct attachment to Constantinople of an ecclesiastical province of southern Italy with Otranto as metropolis, and the direct appointment by the Byzantine emperor of the archbishop of Bulgaria.[47]

But everything changed when, a few decades later, with the slow extinction of the Macedonian dynasty, relations were reversed between an imperial power

[47] In the ancient empire of Tsar Samuel of Bulgaria (died 1014), gradually pacified and annexed (1020), the patriarchate had been abolished and replaced by an autocephalous archbishopric whose occupant was directly appointed by the emperor.

which had become unstable and a patriarchate which now had the advantage of longevity (between 1025 and 1075, there were a dozen emperors and only four patriarchs), which often posed as arbiter in political conflicts, and which could once again dream of a quasi-imperial power. The exceptional personality of Michael Keroularios was a factor here and acted as catalyst.[48] In 1043, the new patriarch still bore the stigma of a failed usurpation attempt which had driven his brother to suicide. His ecclesiastical career and sudden promotion seemed almost a compensation for this thwarted ambition. He was certainly ambitious, as determined to extend his authority as to find positions for the nephews who followed in his footsteps. After the 'schism' of 1054, to which we will return and which established his power vis-à-vis the emperor Constantine IX Monomachos, he was the *éminence grise* of the coup d'état which, in 1057, drove Michael VI into a monastery and placed on the throne the rebel general, Isaac Komnenos; he proceeded to treat the new emperor with contempt, reminding him at every turn that, having made him, he could unmake him. So much so that Isaac 'went on the attack rather than submit', had the patriarch and his nephews arrested, with great caution and in secret, in their suburban monastery and sent them into exile; he then prepared a trial which was averted only by the sudden death of the accused and which might well have triggered a popular uprising in Constantinople.[49] Keroularios troubled and disturbed his contemporaries; his initiatives gave the impression summed up in Ancient Greece by the word hubris, one of psychological excess and religious transgression. To convey this muffled disapproval, the sources make frequent allusions to his past as a conspirator and hint that he aspired to become emperor himself.[50] In reality, like Photios before him, his aim was to make the high priest the supreme power in the empire, also taking his inspiration, like Photios, from the Roman pontifical model.

The Continuator of Skylitzes says that the patriarch

went as far as to wear sandals dyed purple, claiming that this was a custom of the *ancient* priesthood and that the hierarch ought to preserve the usage in the *new*, too, because between the priesthood and the empire there was no difference or only a negligible difference, which gave the former more honour and certainly prestige.[51]

[48] The most recent studies are F. Tinnefeld, 'Michael I. Kerullarios, Patriarch von Konstantinopel (1043–1058). Kritische Überlegungen zu einer Biographie', *JÖB*, 39 (1989), pp. 95–127; J.-C. Cheynet, 'Le patriarche *tyrannos*: le cas Cérulaire', in *Ordnung und Aufruhr im Mittelalter. Historische und juridische Studien zur Rebellion*, ed. M. T. Fögen (Frankfurt-am-Main, 1995), pp. 1–16.
[49] Psellos, *Chronographia*, ed. Renauld (see ch. 1, n. 47), II, pp. 106–7; Attaliates, *Historia*, ed. Bekker (see ch. 1, n. 29), pp. 56–9; Skylitzes, *Synopsis*, ed. Thurn (see ch. 1, n. 39), pp. 496–500; Skylitzes Continued, ed. Tsolakes (see ch. 1, n. 39), pp. 103–6; Zonaras, *Annales*, ed. Pinder (see ch. 1, n. 29), III, p. 660–70.
[50] See, for example, the *Accusation against Michael Kerularios*, Psellos, *Scripta minora*, ed. Kurtz and Drexl (see ch. 1, n. 132), pp. 284–5, 287–9, 312–14.
[51] Skylitzes Continued, ed. Tsolakes (see ch. 1, n. 39), p. 105.

'Ancient' and 'new' can hardly oppose here, as so often, Jewish high priests and Christian hierarchs, but rather – as Balsamon also understood, as we shall see – the pope of old Rome, who wore regalian insignia, and the patriarch of New Rome, who ought to enjoy the same privileges. Justinian had already asserted, while formally distinguishing the priesthood and the *basileia*, that they were very close to each other;[52] Keroularios may have remembered this, but tipped the balance in favour of the Church and away from the empire. To justify the wearing by the patriarch of purple, that is imperial, sandals, which so offended Byzantine sensibilities, the Roman example was the obvious one. Keroularios was not thinking, therefore, of usurping the empire, but of recovering for the patriarch the imperial prerogatives of which the papacy boasted as if they were a Constantinian heritage. It was the wind of Roman reform which had, rather tardily, reached Constantinople, a reform whose consequence in the East was to liberate the patriarchate from political subjection and so make it the pope's rival as well as imitator.

There is every reason to think that the ambitious Keroularios, in 1057–8, took his arguments from the dispute between Constantinople and Rome that had erupted a few years earlier, in 1053–4; this conflict has been called a 'schism' because it seemed violently to oppose the two Churches, but the real issue had been, in the East itself, a new distribution of power between the patriarch and the emperor, between a patriarch as he was described in the *Eisagoge* and an emperor who, once again, exploited the Roman alliance. When the new pope, Leo IX (1049–54), surrounded himself with reformers and took as his principal adviser in eastern affairs a Hellenist monk from the diocese of Toul, Humbert de Silva Candida, raised to the dignity of cardinal, provocations suddenly multiplied on both sides.[53] When informed by Peter, newly appointed patriarch of Antioch, of his election in 1052,[54] the pope immediately offered his assistance in defending his authority and rank against Constantinople.[55] When, at the end of 1052 or early in 1053, a letter was sent by Leo of Ohrid to the Greek bishop, John of Trani, which urged the Latins to abandon practices described as 'Judaic', such as using unleavened bread in communion and fasting on Saturdays,[56] it sparked off the train of events that would lead to rupture, that

---

[52] *Novels* 7, chapter 2, 1.

[53] The new Roman policy and its repercussions for relations between Rome and the East are analysed by E. Petrucci, 'Rapporti di Leone IX con Constantinopoli. Parte I: per la storia dello scisma del 1054', *Studi medievali*, 3rd ser., 14 (1973), pp. 733–831; E. Petrucci, *Ecclesiologia e politica di Leone IX* (Rome, 1977). For Cardinal Humbert, see U.-R. Blumenthal, 'Humbert von Silva Candida', in *Theologische Realenzyklopädie*, XV (1986), pp. 682–5.

[54] C. Will, *Acta et scripta quae de controversiis ecclesiae graecae et latinae seculo undecimo composita extant* (Leipzig / Marburg, 1861, repr. Frankfurt-am-Main, 1963), pp. 227–8.

[55] Jaffé, *Regesta*, no. 4297.

[56] Ed. Will (n. 54), pp. 56–60 = PG 120, cols. 835–44; Grumel-Darrouzès, *Regestes*, no. 862. Not by accident, the Latin translation imputes this letter to both Michael Keroularios and Leo of Ohrid.

is, to the double and highly theatrical excommunication, in Constantinople on Saturday 16 July 1054, of Michael Keroularios and of the papal legates.

It has become a commonplace that this fierce quarrel erupted in a welter of hotheadedness and improvisation, without any real understanding of the theological issues or any coherent ecclesiological conception. Insults flew thick and fast and the debate got bogged down in controversial matters involving rites and the hierarchy. The 'Judaising' Latins were like the leopard, 'whose coat is neither wholly black nor wholly white'; the unruly East was responsible for 'more than ninety heresies' and had appointed eunuchs and even, it was said, a woman, to the patriarchate; Niketas Stethatos, who had come to the aid of Keroularios, was 'more stupid than a donkey' and ought to 'live in a brothel'. Neither Leo IX nor Cardinal Humbert had an eastern policy; they had a vision of Rome in the Christian world which undermined the legitimacy of an eastern Church by recognising no foundation other than Peter for the universal Church and by relegating Constantinople to below the level of Alexandria, Antioch and Jerusalem.

Among all this jumble of words, however, a few phrases and ideas stood out. Leo IX's long reply to Michael Keroularios and John of Trani, composed in September 1053 with the assistance of Cardinal Humbert,[57] attempted to impose obedience by a plethora of the usual scriptural quotations, such as Matthew, 16: 18–19: 'Thou art Peter, and upon this rock I will build my church... and I will give unto thee the keys of the kingdom of heaven', or Romans, 13: 1–5: 'For there is no power but of God... wherefore ye must needs be subject.' He added that the eastern rebels ought to be content with these testimonies 'to the power both earthly and heavenly, or better, to the royal priesthood, of the Roman and apostolic see (*de terreno et coelesti imperio, imo de regali sacerdotio romanae et apostolicae sedis*)'.[58] The expression *regale sacerdotium* (royal priesthood) merits particular attention. It is taken from the First Epistle of Peter, who had himself taken it from Exodus, 19: 6. In the Old Testament, priesthood (*hierateuma*) meant only that the chosen people of Israel had been separated from the rest of humanity as priests were from other people, and it was called royal, or kingly (*basileion*), simply by reference to divine kingship; the Epistle applies the same idea to the baptised as a whole, 'scattered throughout Pontus, Galatia, Cappadocia, Asia, and Bithynia', 'strangers', but whose 'sanctification of the spirit' had made them 'a chosen generation, a royal priesthood, an holy nation... the people of God' (I Peter 1: 1–2, 2: 9–10).[59] This often repeated and often glossed formula had a different significance, clearly, when it was applied

---

[57] Ed. Will (n. 54), pp. 65–85; Jaffé, *Regesta*, no. 4302.
[58] Ibid., 12, p. 72; the expression *regale sacerdotium* occurs earlier (11, p. 71) but not explicitly applied to the Roman see.
[59] See J. Blinzler, '*Hierateuma*. Zur Exegese von 1 Petr. 2, 5 u. 9', in *Episcopus. Studien über das Bischofsamt. Festschrift M. Kardinal von Faulhaber* (Regensburg, 1949), pp. 49–65.

not to the tiny minority of the baptised of apostolic times, but to triumphant Christianity and the universal Church;[60] nevertheless, its meaning had never been stretched to the point of applying to the Roman see, of serving as standard for the reformed papacy and justification for the combination of temporal and spiritual power.

A formula alone would not have been convincing nor, perhaps, attracted sustained attention. But a document was introduced into the scripture-based argument which was designed to justify the new interpretation of the *regale sacerdotium*. This was a constitution signed by Constantine's own hand and sealed with a golden bull; in it the Christian emperor, a few days after his baptism, left to Pope Sylvester his crown and some lands and imperial rights and announced his departure for another capital, declaring that 'it was not right for the earthly emperor to exercise power there where the heavenly emperor had established the reign of the priests and the head of the Christian religion'.[61] This ancient forgery, the *Constitutum Constantini*, or Donation of Constantine, was for the first time quoted almost in full. It was certainly a powerful argument. It appeared that Constantine had not left Rome a spiritual power distinct from the temporal power which had emigrated, out of modesty, to another capital, but a *regale sacerdotium* with a *terrena potestas* which, as a result, was not subject to the *judicium* of the other Churches or of the emperor himself. In a letter of January 1054, the emperor Constantine IX Monomachos was invited to follow the example of his predecessor and namesake and ensure respect for the regalian privileges of the sovereign pontiff.[62]

It is hardly surprising that Keroularios was able to turn this assertion of the dual power of the hierarchs to his own advantage. The *regale sacerdotium* of the pope corresponded in the East to an idea which had passed in and out of favour but which was old, and for which the *Constitutum Constantini* provided a justification. It explains, some years later, the patriarch's 'purple sandals'.

THE USE IN THE EAST OF THE DONATION OF CONSTANTINE

Was the *libellus* signed by Leo IX, a prisoner of the Normans in Benevento when it was drawn up by the pope and Cardinal Humbert, ever sent, or was it taken to Constantinople some months later by the legates? It has recently been

---

[60] See, for example, the text of Gregory of Nazianzus, quoted above, p. 129, n. 4; Michael of Alexandria's letter read at the council of 879–880: Mansi, XVIIA, col. 429.

[61] 'Unde congruum prospeximus nostrum imperium et regni potestatem orientalibus transferri ac transmutari regionibus . . . quoniam ubi principatus sacerdotum et christianae religionis caput ab imperatore coelesti constitutum est, justum non est ut illic terrenus imperator habeat potestatem': ed. Will (n. 54), p. 74.

[62] Ibid., pp. 85–9; Jaffé, *Regesta*, no. 4333.

claimed that it never reached its destination, that the text of the *Constitutum Constantini* remained unknown to the emperor and the patriarch, and that the conclusions based on it by Rome were, in 1054, neither registered nor refuted.[63] But none of the arguments for this thesis is wholly convincing. That this crucial document failed to enter the polemic, except allusively in a letter addressed by the pope to the emperor,[64] shows only that it was not open to debate. Accepted as a historical document – perhaps with a scintilla of doubt – it was not in any case seen as an anti-Byzantine weapon, but rather as an argument against the protectionist ambitions of the western empire. It formed the final layer of that solidly based construction which was the Constantinian legend, built, certainly, in the Latin West, but with the immediate and active assistance of the Greek East. In 1053–4, the emperor of Constantinople could only be flattered by the role devolved to his illustrious predecessor and by the Christian humility which had led him to grant independence and power to the pontiff of Rome. As for the patriarch of New Rome, he hoped to benefit from at least some of the privileges granted to the Church by the first Christian emperor, and there are indications that the person of Sylvester was sometimes used, in the middle of the eleventh century, to exalt the superiority of the spiritual over the temporal and to humble the pride of kings.[65] There was nothing in it, therefore, to contest.

The legend developed of its own accord. As we have seen, at an early stage in its life, Constantine was no longer baptised on his deathbed at Nikomedia by a heretical bishop, but soon after his vision of the 'sign of victory' and conversion, in Rome, and by the hand of the pope who had instructed him.[66] This was a crucial modification, because it gave the founding emperor a political as well as a religious orthodoxy. The *Actus Silvestri*, composed in Rome in the second half of the fifth century and soon known and disseminated in Greek, had given this episode a historical base and had already touched on the problem of the relations between the imperial power and the Church by briefly noting that

---

[63] H.-G. Krause, 'Das Constitutum Constantini im Schisma von 1054', in *Aus Kirche und Reich. Studien zu Theologie, Politik und Recht im Mittelalter. Festschrift für Friedrich Kempf*, ed. H. Mordek (Sigmaringen, 1983), pp. 131–58. A full discussion would be inappropriate here.

[64] Ed. Will (n. 54), p. 88, lines 6–25.

[65] An illuminated psalter dated to 1059, *Vaticanus gr.* 752, puts unusual emphasis on the adultery and repentance of David, shows David judged by Christ and has many anachronistic images of St Silvester intervening in the great Old Testament king's 'penitence': I. Kalavrezou-Maxeiner, 'Silvester and Kerularios', *JÖB*, 32/5 (1982), pp. 453–8, a preliminary study expanded in I. Kalavrezou-Maxeiner, N. Trahoulia and S. Sabar, 'Critique of the emperor in the Vatican Psalter gr. 752', *DOP*, 47 (1993), pp. 195–219. A similar argument can no longer be based on the 'cross of Michael Keroularios', which shows St Silvester and St Michael, but whose dating to the eleventh century is extremely dubious: R. J. H. Jenkins, 'A cross of the Patriarch Michael Cerularius', followed by E. Kitzinger, 'An art-historical comment', *DOP*, 21 (1967), pp. 233–49; and the critique of the dating by C. Mango, 'La Croix dite de Michel le Cérulaire et la croix de Saint-Michel de Sykéôn', *Cahiers archéologiques*, 36 (1988), pp. 41–9.

[66] See above, pp. 145–6.

on the fourth day [after his baptism], [the emperor] had granted a privilege to the Church of Rome and to its pontiff, stipulating that throughout the Roman world, the priests would have as their leader the pope, just as the judges had a king,[67]

that is, just as the representatives of the civil authority recognised the sole authority of an emperor. It was this phrase that was picked up by the *Constitutum Constantini* and one understands why, of the eight measures which the *Acts* present as the very first legislation of the Christianised empire, the reference to this privilege in particular attracted the attention of a forger who was probably a clerk in the Roman chancery in the second half of the eighth century and keen to strengthen the political and territorial foundations of the Roman Church against threats which came, not from an increasingly remote East, but from a turbulent West.[68] So he fabricated an imperial constitution along the lines indicated, summarising in an initial *confessio* the material in the hagiography, justifying the Donation by the healing of the emperor's body and the salvation of his soul thanks to the preaching of St Sylvester, and enunciating the principle that the successors of St Peter should have a superior *potestas* to that of the emperor. In the text, this historical summary is followed by concrete measures. The papacy received not only primacy but *judicium* over the patriarchates of Antioch, Alexandria, Jerusalem and Constantinople; Constantine gave it the palace of the Lateran and the right to wear the imperial vestments and insignia (the crown or diadem, the *phrygium* = tiara, the *superhumerale* or *loros* = pallium,[69] the purple *chlamys*, the sceptres and standards); the pope's escort would be that of an emperor; the Roman clergy, like the imperial senate, would have their

---

[67] *Actus Silvestri*, repr. of ed. Mombritius (see ch. 4, n. 70), p. 513, lines 17–18: 'Quarta die privilegium ecclesiae romanae pontificique contulit, in toto orbe romano sacerdotes ita hunc caput habeant sicut omnes judices regem.' On the *Acts* of Silvester strictly speaking, see, among others, R.-J. Loenertz, 'Actus Sylvestri. Genèse d'une légende', *Revue d'Histoire ecclésiastique*, 70 (1975), pp. 426–39; W. Pohlkamp, 'Textfassungen, literarische Formen und Geschichtliche Funktionen der römischen Silvester-Akten', *Francia, Forschungen zur westeuropäischen Geschichte, Mittelalter*, 19/1 (1992), pp. 115–96.

[68] The *Constitutum Constantini* has been edited by H. Fuhrmann (Hanover, 1968), who is also the author of fundamental works: 'Das frühmittelalterliche Papsttum und die konstantinische Schenkung', *Settimane di studio del centro italiano di studi sull'alto medioevo XX, 1972, Problemi dell'Occidente nel secolo VIII* (Spoleto, 1973), I, pp. 257–92; *Einfluss und Verbreitung der pseudo-isidorischen Fälschungen*, Schriften der *MGH* 24, I–III (Stuttgart, 1972–4), especially II, pp. 354–407. See also W. Levison, 'Konstantinische Schenkung und Silvester-Legende', in *Miscellanea F. Ehrle*, II, Studi e testi 38 (Rome, 1924), pp. 159–247; R.-J. Loenertz, 'Constitutum Constantini. Destination, destinataire, auteur, date', *Aevum*, 45 (1974), pp. 199–245.

[69] The *loros* was a long embroidered scarf, based on the consular *trabea* and triumphal clothing, which the emperors and certain high dignitaries wore over the *divitesion*, hence the comparison with the *superhumorale* and the pallium. At the time of Constantine Porphyrogenitus, it was believed that the *loros*, worn especially at Easter, identified the emperor with Christ himself, whose death and resurrection it symbolically represented: *De cerimoniis*, II, 40, pp. 637–9. In part of the tradition, the term was no longer understood and the *loros* was identified with a hat: Loenertz, 'Constitutum Constantini' (n. 68), pp. 202–3.

dignities and offices; in ceremonial, the *ordo romanus* and senators would ride horses with white caparison, and would wear the sandals with white stockings of senators (*campagi* with *udones*). As Sylvester had refused the crown of gold which Constantine had removed from his own head to do him homage, it was the tiara that the emperor used for a sort of coronation prefiguring the protocol of the processions of the future – *ad imitationem imperii nostri*, specified the emperor – who retained in Rome only the humble office of 'squire of St Peter' (*beati Petri stratoris officium*), responsible for holding the reins of the pope's horse. Further to strengthen the power of the papacy, Constantine gave it by this same constitution, along with the city of Rome and the western provinces, many unspecified lands and cities, and he announced his intention of transferring his capital to the East, regarding it as improper that the 'earthly emperor should exercise his power there where the heavenly emperor had established *principatus sacerdotum et Christianae religionis caput*'. By a confusion of names in a consular date, the act is associated both with the year 315 and the year 330, just after the legendary Roman baptism and just before the foundation of Constantinople, at a date that was fictitious, but strategic, when a redefinition of powers was of particular significance.

In September 1053, Leo IX was the first to extract this document from the archives or from the pseudo-Isidorian *Decretals* in which it had been included about 850, and to quote from it at length and expound its meaning. We know neither when nor how the 'Greeks', well prepared to receive it, effectively became aware of it. References to the Donation have been detected in the discussions in 968 between the ambassador Liutprand of Cremona and his Constantinople hosts, in particular when the western bishop praises his master Otto for having restored to the Roman see the western territories which he had been given by Constantine, and when his eastern interlocutor admits that the emperor of Constantinople would have performed this role, had Rome and the papacy not rebelled.[70] One detects in this passage a strand in the Sylvestrine and Constantinian legend, but perhaps predating the *Constitutum*. Paul Alexander finds the first certain allusion to the Donation of Constantine in a rather confused passage in Kinnamos, written in the 1160s, where it is utilised against the idea of a division of the empire and the pope's claim to create a western emperor.[71] But it is difficult to believe, as we have said, that the Donation was not known in Constantinople, either directly through the *libellus* of 1053, to whose argument it is crucial, or indirectly during the various forays of Cardinal Humbert to the

---

[70] *Legatio*, 51, ed. Chiesa, *Liudprandi Cremonensis opera* (see ch. 1, n. 111), pp. 209–10; see P. Alexander, 'The Donation of Constantine at Byzantium and its earliest use against the Western Empire', *Zbornik Radova*, 8 (1963) (Mélanges G. Ostrogorsky), pp. 11–26.

[71] Kinnamos, *Epitome* V, 7, ed. Meineke (see ch. 1, n. 125), pp. 219–20. The passage concerns the years 1162–4; the *Constitutum Constantini* is used against the pope and against the ideology of the Hohenstaufen.

eastern capital. Even if the Greek translations known to us are all much later and seem not to derive directly from the Latin text quoted by Leo IX,[72] it is almost certain that the document was known at least in outline in 1054.

Balsamon, the great canonist of the end of the twelfth century, whom I will discuss more fully in the next chapter, never doubts for a moment that the document had long been known in Constantinople. Head of the patriarchal chancery (*chartophylax*), he was the first to unearth a Greek text that corresponded exactly to the extract quoted by Leo IX, which he did not see as a chance discovery, and to give an authorised interpretation. In his commentary on *Nomokanon*, VIII, 1, he muses on the privileges of Ancient Rome granted to Constantinople by the council of Chalcedon and on the official name of 'Rome' which was recognised by imperial legislation. He adds, in the form of an additional scholium:[73] 'We learn what were the privileges of the Holy Church of Ancient Rome from the written ordinance addressed by St Constantine the Great, equal of the apostles, to St Sylvester who was then pope of Rome, thus...' There follows the text of the Donation proper. 'Note', he continues:

> that since the present imperial edict or order (*prostagma*) of St Constantine the Great, the pope of Rome has the right to avail himself of all the imperial prerogatives with the sole exception of the crown. That is why in all the processions organised for him and in the exercise of his sacred liturgical duties, he has his head covered by the *loros*,[74] wears shoes of true purple,[75] rides with a harness of true purple, like the emperors, and honours those who serve him with imperial dignities. As the second council [that of Constantinople I, 381] gave the archbishop of Constantinople all the privileges of the pope of Rome, certain patriarchs, the lord Michael Keroularios and others, have tried to avail themselves of the same privileges; but the attempt turned out badly. There is nothing to prevent the clergy of Constantinople from being honoured with dignities, but with lesser dignities. Since the present edict [still the *Constitutum*], the *chartophylax* has the right to ride, for the feast of the Notary saints, on the patriarch's horse with a white caparison. He ought, as cardinal of the patriarchate,[76] to cover his head with the gold

---

[72] The two Greek versions of the *Constitutum* are known to us later from Demetrios Kydones in the fourteenth century, and Maximos and Andrew Chrysoberges in the fifteenth century; they emanate, therefore, from 'Latinophrones' who, at the time of the Latin empire or of the council of Ferrara-Florence, were in league with the Dominicans of Pera and anxious to orient the Greek Church towards union and submission to Rome.

[73] Rhalles–Potles, *Syntagma*, I, pp. 144–9.

[74] Balsamon seems here to have fallen victim to the confusion which made the *loros* a sort of hat: see n. 69 above.

[75] 'True' purple was a violet purple, in principle extracted from the *murex*, as opposed to a deep red purple. The *Constitutum Constantini* does not refer to the purple shoes, but adds more generally to the list of specific insignia *et diversa ornamenta imperialia*.

[76] The comparison of the *chartophylax* of Constantinople (the office held by Balsamon) to a cardinal of the patriarchate is amusing.

tiara which is kept in the *chartophylakion*. But the successive patriarchs of
Alexandria also have acquired the right, after the present edict, to officiate
with the *loros*. St Cyril of Alexandria received this permission from the pope
of Rome Celestine, when he went to Ephesos to combat Nestorios [at the
council of 431]. In fact, as Celestine was unable to be present at Ephesos to
judge Nestorios, it was agreed to allow St Cyril to preside over the council
in his stead. To make it plain that he held the right from the pope of Rome
Celestine, he sat with the *loros* and condemned Nestorios. Since then, the
patriarchs of Alexandria officiate and process with the same *loros* without
suspecting the reason. Read the letter of St Celestine on this subject, which
is found in the Acts of the third council.

We are better able to understand the position of Keroularios, who based the
claim of a *regale sacerdotium* not only on the text of the Donation, which
concerned Rome alone, but on the extension to Constantinople, in 381 and
451, of all the privileges of the Roman Church; and we learn incidentally that
other patriarchs thought like him, even if he was alone in pushing this logic
to its conclusion. Balsamon did not approve of such an extreme claim, but
seems hardly to have doubted the authenticity of the *Constitutum*, any more
than the right of the Roman see to take advantage of it. If he saw limits to its
brutal application to the patriarchate of New Rome, he noted several imperial
privileges which the eastern clergy already possessed or might claim and which
related directly or indirectly to the 'edict' of Constantine. The document meant
different things in different circumstances: Keroularios thought primarily of the
advantage the patriarch might derive from the *Constitutum* in its confrontation
with the emperor; a century and a half later, Balsamon based on it an argument
in favour of the 'ecclesiastical archontes', their emancipation and their status
as high dignitaries.[77]

He returned to the subject in his commentary on canon 28 of the council of
Chalcedon. 'The present canon', he then[78] wrote,

> specifies that the archbishop of Constantinople should enjoy the privileges
> of the pope of Rome and should be honoured like him in all ecclesiastical
> matters, in accord with the third canon of the second council [Constantinople
> I, 381]. Some, aware that he receives none of the marks of consideration which
> are the privilege of the pope – because he does not cover his head with the
> imperial *loros*, does not process with a sceptre, banners and standards, does

---

[77] V. Tiftixoglu, 'Gruppenbildungen innerhalb des konstantinopolitanischen Klerus während der
Komnenenzeit', *BZ*, 62 (1969), pp. 60–72.

[78] Rhalles–Potles, *Syntagma*, II, pp. 285–6; see also III, pp. 149–50, Balsamon's commentary
on canon 12 of Antioch on the right of appeal, where we find the following argument: the
Donation of Constantine gave imperial rights to the pope, and the councils of Constantinople I
and Chalcedon gave Constantinople the same privileges as Rome, hence the patriarch, like the
emperor, should not have his decisions questioned.

not confer imperial dignities, does not wear authentically imperial garments and does not process on horseback, as laid down in the ancient imperial decretal addressed by St Constantine the Great to St Sylvester, pope of Rome, and to his successors – say that the canons are now obsolete, basing their argument on the fact that one does not find in the *Basilika*, compiled after a rewriting and a purging [of the juridical texts], the laws specifying that the holder of the see of Constantinople has the privileges of the pope of Rome, as we ourselves have shown in Title VIII, chapter 1 of the present work. But I, who am a well-born citizen of Constantinople and who have been by the grace of God an important member of the most holy see of Constantinople [*nomophylax* and *chartophylax* before becoming patriarch of Antioch], I hope and desire that the patriarch of Constantinople will have without scandal all the privileges which have been granted to him by the sacred canons.

This is further proof that the *Constitutum Constantini* was discussed in relation to the canons that elevated Constantinople to the level of Rome. It had occurred to some people that Basil I and Leo VI, in their codification and purification of the old laws, might knowingly have rejected measures that risked giving the patriarchate of Constantinople the appearance of *regale sacerdotium*; one thinks here, obviously, of Photios. Balsamon criticised them only from an avowed patriotism, and his pious wish was accompanied by a clear disapproval of the man who had caused a scandal in an attempt to impose his rights: Michael Keroularios.

The *Reflections on the Privileges of the Patriarchs* perhaps reveals the essence of Balsamon's thinking; with regard to the adjective 'ecumenical', included exclusively in the titulatures of the pope and of the patriarch of Constantinople, he declared, not without humour, that the demon of arrogance had cut the pope of Rome off from all the other holy patriarchs and isolated him in the West:

As for [the patriarch] of Constantinople, I do not see him adorned with any of the privileges of the pope – he is not clothed in the *loros* of the emperor by virtue of the decree attributed to St Constantine,[79] he does not appear in purple boots as has been laid down [for the pope], and he uses none of the other privileges granted to old Rome – and for this reason *his foot standeth in an even place* (Psalm XXVI [XXV]: 12)...and the Father [the patriarch of Constantinople] does not add importance to his signature by proclaiming himself ecumenical, even though he is addressed and glorified by us with this title.[80]

[79] Perhaps the formulation reveals a very slight hesitation as to the authenticity of the *Constitutum Constantini*; but this is the only passage where this is the case and it is going too far to say that its authenticity is seriously questioned: Tiftixoglu, 'Gruppenbildungen' (n. 77), pp. 68–9, criticising F. Dölger, 'Rom in der Gedankenwelt der Byzantiner', repr. in F. Dölger, *Byzanz und die europäische Staatenwelt* (Ettal, 1953), p. 110, n. 65.
[80] Rhalles–Potles, *Syntagma*, IV, pp. 552–4.

Constantine's decree serves once again as reference point, with perhaps a slight hesitation as to its authenticity, but in order to establish a very clear difference between on the one hand a *regale sacerdotium* giving the pope imperial privileges and robes (including the famous red boots, implicitly or explicitly mentioned in the Greek version of the *Constitutum*), which affirmed his temporal power and flattered his typically western vanity, and on the other the spiritual power exercised by the patriarch of Constantinople, glorified and recognised by all on condition that he remained modest, did not exploit his regalian privileges and renounced the Roman model. It was not only the pope who was being condemned but Keroularios too.

8. *The canonists and liturgists (twelfth to fifteenth centuries)*

THE 'EPISTEMONARCHIC' EMPEROR

From the late eleventh to the early thirteenth centuries, or, to be more precise, from the pontificate of Gregory VII (1073–85) to that of Innocent III (1198–1216), it was in the West, in the entourages of popes and secular princes, that the question of whether the power of kings and the emperor was lesser or greater than that of bishops or the pontiff of Rome was posed and fiercely debated.[1] The Gregorian reform, the investitures struggle and the recurring problem of the Holy Empire gave rise to all sorts of *libelli*[2] which are full of formulae and definitions regarding old problems, which the East had long ago explored but rarely posed in theoretical terms. Was the king also in his way a priest or was he simply a layman? Was royal unction of the same nature as the unction given to bishops, and did it confer on whoever received it, symbolically or materially, some of the episcopal *charismata* or privileges? To fuel this impassioned debate, the parties invoked the enigmatic Melchizedek, priest and king of Genesis, exhumed the legend of pope Sylvester receiving the crown from the hands of Constantine the Great to whom he returned only a limited temporal power, and claimed that the Roman pontiffs could intervene in the appointment of emperors ever since. The story of St Ambrose preventing Theodosius I from entering the episcopal church of Milan and imposing a public penance on him was told yet again.[3]

None of these arguments, which appear, for example, in the treatise *Summa Gloria* written soon after 1123 by Honorius Augustodunensis,[4] seems to have

---

[1] For the significance of the Gregorian reform, see the useful historiographical analysis of P. Toubert, 'Eglise et état au XIe siècle: la signification du moment grégorien pour la genèse de l'état moderne', in *Etat et église dans la genèse de l'état moderne* (Madrid, 1986) (Casa de Velazquez), pp. 9–22.

[2] The *Libelli de lite imperatorum et pontificum sec. XI et XII*, published in three volumes in *MGH* between 1891 and 1897.

[3] See above, p. 105.

[4] Ed. I. Dieterich, *MGH, Libelli de lite*, III (Hanover, 1897), pp. 63–80.

248

come, at least directly, from Byzantium, even though they had often been employed there. The West drew on a heritage of texts that were ancient, and so to a large extent common to both East and West, but in order to account for a configuration of political and religious powers which was unique to it. Never had the fundamental question of the sacerdotal nature of kingship been so starkly posed; but the responses, at first clear cut, were soon qualified. It was realised that to answer yes or no was impossible without compromising either the legitimacy of power or the authority of the Church. As Marc Bloch,[5] Percy E. Schramm[6] and Ernst Kantorowicz[7] have shown, it was necessary to resort to compromises and to accept toned-down formulae. Kings were no longer treated as bishops, but nor were they relegated to the ranks of the laity; they were generally acknowledged to have the status of quasi-clergy by virtue of unction, and they were symbolically accepted into the ranks of ecclesiastical officials, but at the lowest possible level. The desire for a radical distinction between Church and political power led only to the tracing of a rather imprecise boundary. Kings were 'mitred' and pontiffs 'crowned'.[8] Paradoxically, the emergence of the modern state, in its conception and its imagery, owed far more to this interchange of symbols than to a separation, highly laudable but recognised as to a degree illusory, between the power of the clergy and that of the politicians.

It is doubtful whether this great debate in the West had any influence on the East, which was probably hardly aware of it. But in Byzantium, too, 'reform' was in the air, if we mean by this a revival of the Church as an institution and of religious culture and feeling, not only the assertion of the independence of the Church, which meant different things in different places. The origins of these changes lay in the eleventh century, not in the confrontation between the patriarch Michael Keroularios and the emperors of his day, a fleeting episode with no long-term consequences, but in a major renaissance of spirituality associated with the name of Symeon the New Theologian and viewed with some suspicion by the hierarchy, and in the appearance of an elite of learned

---

[5] M. Bloch, *Les Rois thaumaturges. Etude sur le caractère surnaturel attribué à la puissance royale, particulièrement en France et en Angleterre* (Strasbourg, 1924), trans. J. E. Anderson as *The Royal Touch: Sacred Monarchy and Scrofula in England and France* (London, 1973).

[6] P. E. Schramm, 'Sacerdotium und Regnum in Austausch ihrer Vorrechte: *imitatio imperii* und *imitatio sacerdotii*. Eine geschichtliche Beleuchtung des Dictatus papae Gregors VII', *Studi Gregoriani*, 1 (1947), pp. 403–57; P. E. Schramm, *Herrschaftszeichen und Staatssymbolik. Beiträge zu ihrer Geschichte vom dritten bis zum sechzehnten Jahrhundert*, Schriften der *MGH*, 13, I–III (Stuttgart, 1954–6); P. E. Schramm, 'Kaiser, Könige und Päpste', in his *Gesammelte Aufsätze zur Geschichte des Mittelalters*, IV, 1 (Stuttgart, 1970), pp. 57–140.

[7] E. Kantorowicz, *The King's Two Bodies. A Study in Mediaeval Political Theology* (Princeton, 1957); E. Kantorowicz, 'Mysteries of state: an absolutist concept and its late mediaeval origins', *Harvard Theological Review*, 48 (1955), pp. 65–91, repr. in his *Selected Studies* (New York, 1965), pp. 381–98.

[8] E. Kantorowicz, 'Mysteries of state' (n. 7), p. 381.

and able clergy. The latter took on the task of instruction for the first time, occupied key positions in the patriarchate (the four or five posts of ecclesiastical 'archontes'),[9] often kept the patriarchs, to whom they rather condescended, at a distance, and were themselves destined to fill the most prominent metropolitan sees.[10] The permanent synod of the capital, composed of the metropolitans and archbishops present in Constantinople, also played an important role; it no longer promulgated canons but synodal sentences making case law on the whole range of social problems. This intense reforming activity developed not in opposition to the emperor, who encouraged and soon led it,[11] but in opposition to the most conservative elements in the episcopal hierarchy, who clung to their privileges and feared a Constantinopolitan centralism that was encouraged by the loss of several bishoprics in Asia Minor which had fallen into Turkish hands.

As soon as government stabilised with the Komnenoi and until the great crises of the declining empire of the thirteenth century (seizure of Constantinople by the crusaders, Arsenite schism against Michael VIII, mobilisation against the Union of the Churches), reform was dependent on the emperor and the clergy of St Sophia. The edict of Alexios I on the reform of the clergy, addressed to the patriarch Nicholas Grammatikos and to the synod in June 1107, outlined behind the rhetoric a sort of programme. The emperor was alarmed by the condition of the Church, by the indolence and ignorance of the clergy and by the negligence of the provincial bishops, who regularly dispensed with the obligation of the annual synod; he proposed a revision and stricter application of the *Nomokanon* and laid down new rules for the selection and promotion of the *didaskaloi*.[12] There was much criticism, sometimes well founded, of the requisition of sacred vessels melted down to finance the war, the frequent grants of ecclesiastical property to laymen, for life or conditionally, and the transfers of bishops. But the organised opposition of what might be called, for simplicity, the 'metropolitan party' concealed behind the pretext of resistance to imperial encroachments hostility to all reform. The *Diatribes* of John the Oxite set the tone, blaming the military failures of the empire and all the ills of the day on the injustices of the reign, the violence of the seizure of power in 1082, taxation and the lifestyle of the imperial family. John called for penitence and recalled the time in 860, when the emperor Michael III and the patriarch Photios had brought about the destruction of the Russian fleet besieging Constantinople by

---

[9] These were the posts of *megas oikonomos, megas sakellarios, megas skeuophylax, praepositus* at the Sakelle and *chartophylax*, the first four of which directed financial matters and the last, the most important (see below, with regard to Balsamon), had charge of the archives and the Chancellery.

[10] See the study of V. Tiftixoglu, 'Gruppenbildungen' (see ch. 7, n. 77), pp. 25–72.

[11] Well brought out by E. Patlagean, in *Histoire du christianisme*, V, pp. 50–1.

[12] P. Gautier, 'L'édit d'Alexis Ier Comnène sur la réforme du clergé', *REB*, 31 (1973), pp. 165–201.

making a procession with the *maphorion* of the Virgin.[13] The enemy was more clearly identified in the invectives of Niketas of Ankyra against the clergy of the Great Church: 'Briareus, torrent that sweeps everything away, polyp that clings to the rocks, leech . . .'.[14] Traditional historiography concludes that Alexios took advantage of the conflict between the metropolitans and the clergy of St Sophia to strengthen his hold on the Church, but it can equally well be argued that the oligarchy of the metropolitans took advantage of the slightest weakness in the government to make vain claims of absolute autonomy and to try to relegate the emperor to the sidelines.

Manuel Komnenos, too, was a reformer. He founded the convent of Kataskepe, near the Black Sea, to set up a model community without lands in opposition to the traditional monasticism now immersed in the rural economy,[15] rather as Nikephoros Phokas had encouraged the rise of Athos. He wanted to die in the habit of a monk.[16] He was not content to surround himself with theologians, with teachers and clergy from St Sophia,[17] but himself preached, ventured into exegesis and theology,[18] and summoned and presided over synods which condemned alleged heretical deviations and defined Orthodoxy.[19] He was active in the Church in many different, often ill-timed, ways, which has to some extent sullied his image as a reformer; but he acted in accord with an ecclesiology that conformed to the twelfth-century conception of the Constantinian model.

The principle of 'economy' would have been enough to justify imperial interference. It authorised the emperor temporarily to lift the application of the laws and – some said – the canons for the 'common good', that is, to carry out his policies; it concealed arbitrary power, therefore, behind a discreet veil – at any rate it dispensed with the need for a theory to justify a long established practice. In fact, the word was brandished by certain obliging jurists or canonists to explain that, for example, the sovereign was free to entrust profane duties to the clergy in spite of the canons, or to authorise marriages between relatives contrary to the synodal prohibitions. But the notion of 'economy' had unhappy associations, reviving memories of recognised abuses and evoking great saints, Maximos the Confessor and, above all, Theodore of Stoudios, who had wanted to restrict its

---

[13] P. Gautier, 'Diatribes de Jean l'Oxite contre Alexis Ier Comnène', *REB*, 28 (1970), pp. 5–55.

[14] J. Darrouzès, *Documents inédits d'ecclésiologie byzantine* (Paris, 1966), pp. 44, 200.

[15] Niketas Choniates, *Historia*, ed. J. L. Van Dieten (Berlin, 1975), pp. 206–7.

[16] Ibid., pp. 221–2.

[17] Niketas Choniates gives the names of Soterichos Panteugenes, Michael of Thessalonike and Nikephoros Basilakes, all condemned by the synod in 1156–7.

[18] See the 'funeral oration' in which Eustathios of Thessalonike emphasises his *didaskalia* and theological competence, claims that he had succeeded in assuring the unity of the Church and compares him to St Paul: §35, 37–40, ed. G. L. E. Tafel, *Eustathii metropolitae Thessalonicensis opuscula* (Frankfurt-am-Main, 1832), pp. 204–5; see also below, pp. 265–6.

[19] J. Goulliard, 'Le Synodikon de l'Orthodoxie', *TM*, 2 (1967), pp. 210–26.

application and whose intransigence still had its admirers. The contemporaries of the Komnenoi and the generation following resorted to 'economy' relatively rarely and seized each favourable opportunity to debate the emperor's rights to intervene and to justify them by a title. It was Theodore Balsamon who travelled farthest down this path, but let us take here the example of Demetrios Chomatianos, who, at the beginning of the thirteenth century and thinking of Manuel I, compiled a list of these rights:[20] the emperor presided at synodal debates and gave them executive force, formulated the rules governing the ecclesiastical hierarchy, legislated regarding the 'life and status' of the clergy, including those of the *bema*, and regarding ecclesiastical jurisdiction, elections to vacant sees and the transfer of bishops,[21] and he could promote a bishop to the rank of metropolitan 'to honour a man or a town'. The list annexed on behalf of the emperor several disputed and disputable areas, but in the name of a right which gave the emperor his status and his title of 'common *epistemonarches* of the Churches'.

We need to look carefully at this term,[22] which Chomatianos did not invent. It had appeared in the official terminology since Manuel Komnenos and corresponded to an attempt at clarification comparable to that which had led in the time of Constantine the Great to the formulae 'universal bishop' and 'bishop over the outside', which it seemed to revive but in a muted way, with a rather lame substitute. In the monastic context, the word *epistemonarches* had, to begin with, a precise meaning. The *epistemonarches* was responsible for the external conduct of the monks, for their attendance and their punctuality at the offices; he applied the disciplinary rules without any involvement in formulating them and like the ecclesiarch, punished only formal derelictions of duty, without ever encroaching on the direction of the monastery. As it had appeared almost continuously from the sixth to the twelfth centuries in the *typika* of St Sabas,[23] of Stoudios as reformed by Theodore,[24] of the Athonite Great

---

[20] Ed. J. B. Pitra, *Analecta sacra et classica Spicilegio Solesmensi parata*, VI (Paris, 1891), col. 632 (no. 157, Reply 4 to Kabasilas); Rhalles–Potles, *Syntagma*, V, p. 429. For the rest of the text, copied from Balsamon, see below, p. 269.

[21] This was the issue raised by the letter from Constantine Kabasilas, bishop of Dyrrachion, to which Chomatianos replied. He quoted the case of Manuel Komnenos ordering the synod by a *prostagma* to accept the resignation of Eustathios from the see of Myra and his transfer to that of Thessalonike.

[22] See, in particular, B. K. Stephanides, 'Hoi horoi episteme kai epistemonarches para tois Byzantinois', *EEBS*, 7 (1930), pp. 153–8; R. Macrides, 'Nomos and Kanon on paper and in court', in *Church and people in Byzantium*, ed. R. Morris (Birmingham, 1990), pp. 61–85, especially pp. 63–4.

[23] Ed. A. Dmitrievskij, in the periodical of the Academy of Theology of Kiev (1890), pp. 170ff (ch. 5).

[24] *Hypotyposis*, PG 99, col. 1709; *Epigram*, 8, ed. and trans. P. Speck, *Theodoros Studites, Jamben auf Verschiedene Gegenstände* (Berlin, 1968), p. 129, where Theodore of Stoudios mentions several *epistemonarches*. See also J. Thomas and A. Constantinides Hero, *Byzantine Monastic Foundation Documents*, Dumbarton Oaks Collection XXXV (Washington, 2000), I, pp. 93, 107.

Lavra,[25] of the monastery of the Evergetis or that of the Virgin *Kecharitomene* in 1118,[26] the office was relatively minor. Revived metaphorically as a title justifying certain disciplinary interventions by the temporal power in the ecclesiastical sphere, the word might express the idea that the emperor was the secular arm of the Church and correspond to the oath later sworn by the sovereigns at the time of their coronation, according to the *Treatise on the Offices* of the Pseudo-Kodinos (fourteenth century), to be *defensores* of the Church. But the twelfth-century emperors clearly did not understand it in this way. In the synodal record of the deposition of the patriarch Kosmas, guilty of having received communion with the Bogomil Niphon (1147), it was specified that Manuel engaged in the interrogation of the accused 'by virtue of his competence and his wisdom as *epistemonarches*'.[27] In the *prostagma* of 1166 which ordered that marriages to the seventh degree should be prohibited and punished with the separation of the spouses, Manuel explained that the synod had put this proposal to him and wished to consult him out of respect for his 'right as *epistemonarches*';[28] and in the account of the reading of this *prostagma*, in the synod of 25 April of the same year, the *chartophylax* John Hagiophlorites repeated and amplified the expression in a rhetoric in which the emperor was compared implicitly to Moses and explicitly to Solomon, and in which God himself had entrusted him with an 'epistemonarchic power' over his Church, which went far beyond a simple matter of record-keeping.[29] Nor did Isaac Angelos see himself in the role of simple executant when, in a Novel of 1187 which laid down the conditions for valid synodal elections, he chose to specify that the metropolitan of Kyzikos had wanted his complaint to be examined jointly by him and the patriarch, given that 'he had received the "rank of *epistemonarches* of the Church from he who had anointed him and made him emperor", so granting him the right to correct whatever did not conform to the ecclesiastical canons'.[30]

In the literature of the period there are also several attempts to add greater lustre to a word to some degree devalued in everyday language, by etymological

[25] P. Meyer, *Die Haupturkunden für die Geschichte der Athosklöster* (Leipzig, 1894), p. 125. There should be one and if possible two *epistemonarches*. See Thomas and Constantinides Hero, *Foundation Documents* (n. 24), I, pp. 216, 224.

[26] Ed. and trans. P. Gautier, 'Le Typikon de la Théotokos Evergétis', *REB*, 40 (1982), pp. 21–3, 39, 71–3; 43 (1985), pp. 73–5. See Thomas and Constantinides Hero, *Foundation Documents* (n. 24), II, pp. 492, 655, 684.

[27] Rhalles–Potles, *Syntagma*, V, p. 309, lines 8–10.

[28] Zepos, *Jus*, I, p. 409, lines 6–7; Dölger, *Regesten*, no. 1468.

[29] D. Simon, 'Ein Synodalakt aus dem Jahre 1166', in *Fontes minores*, 1 (Frankfurt-am-Main, 1976), p. 125, ll. 11–12; Grumel-Darrouzès, *Regestes*, no. 1072; discussed in depth by H. Hunger, 'Kanonistenrhetorik im Bereich des patriarchats am Beispiel des Theodoros Balsamon', in *Byzantium in the 12th Century: Canon Law, State and Society*, ed. N. Oikonomides (Athens, 1991), pp. 37–59, especially pp. 55–9.

[30] Zepos, *Jus*, I, p. 430; Rhalles–Potles, *Syntagma*, V, p. 314; Dölger, *Regesten*, no. 1572 (which wrongly gives the date of 10 September 1186).

sleight of hand. Anna Komnene congratulated Alexios I on having invented new titles, in particular that of *sebastos*, and added:

> If one considers the art of government to be a body of knowledge [*episteme*] and a science of great importance ... one must admire my father as a scholar [*epistemon*] and an architect for having invented in the empire these functions and these titles. The only difference is that the masters of the sciences of discourse have invented the different names with a view to clarity, whereas Alexios, that *epistemonarches* of kingship [*tes basileias*], instituted all that in the interests of the empire.[31]

Since Anna was writing in the 1140s, we might conclude it was then, rather than in the reign of her father, that this formula was launched. But it is with the reign of Manuel Komnenos that the work of Eustathios of Thessalonike is linked, and he readily uses the rare word *epistemonarches* and its derivatives in connection with God himself or the patriarchs of the Old Testament; when he applies them to the emperor, he seems to link them to the 'sanctity' which derives from unction.[32]

That the word should be so elevated and explicitly associated with the political ideology of the Komnenoi probably explains why it was taken up by Michael VIII Palaiologos after the reconquest of Constantinople and used as an argument against the attacks of the Church. To the patriarch Arsenios, who objected in 1265 to a trial being held in the emperor's presence, his response was that 'ever since the emperor had the right, in his capacity as *epistemonarches*, to be present in ecclesiastical cases, it had been neither right nor reasonable to debate such questions, which were of the highest importance, without his intervention'.[33] In a *prostagma* of 1270, Michael VIII again invoked his title of *epistemonarches* of the Church to compel the patriarch Joseph I to give the deacon Theodore Skoutariotes, on whom the emperor had conferred the imperial title of *dikaiophylax*, a corresponding rank in the hierarchy of the archontes of the Church.[34] To settle this trivial affair, Michael, imbued with the spirit of the Komnenoi and the doctrines of Balsamon, did not hesitate to assert that the choices of the patriarch should fall into line with those of the emperor and that ecclesiastical offices were only carbon copies of imperial offices, as the Donation of Constantine showed. One sees the context in which the title of *epistemonarches* was used and what it implied. But the word had lost some of its magic. The Church was no longer tacitly consenting; it took advantage of the major crisis of the Union to restrict the title to its most modest temporal

---

[31] Anna Komnene, *Alexios*, III, 4, 2, ed. and trans. B. Leib (Paris, 1967), I, p. 114.

[32] Ed. Tafel, *Eustathii metropolitae Thessalonicensis opuscula* (n. 18), pp. 21, ll. 8, 50, ll. 20–1, 66, ll. 77–8, 87, ll. 13–14, 145, ll. 55–6, 230, ll. 80–1, 257, ll. 87–8.

[33] Pachymeres, *Hist.*, IV, 4, ed. and trans. Failler and Laurent (see ch. 1, n. 8), II, pp. 340–1.

[34] See the two *prostagmata* ed. in Zepos, *Jus*, I, pp. 502–4 (p. 503, l. 15 for the title of *epistemonarches*); Dölger, *Regesten*, nos. 1972–3; for the affair itself, see J. Darrouzès, *Recherches sur les Offikia de l'Eglise byzantine* (Paris, 1970), pp. 109–10.

dimensions. Job Iasites, in the name of the patriarch Joseph, soon after 1273, offered this definition:

> It is true that he who wears the diadem has personally received the responsibilities and the title of *epistemonarches* of the holy Churches; it does not consist, however, of electing, deposing, imposing excommunication or performing any other action or attribution of the bishop, but, according to the meaning of the word *epistemonarches*, it consists [for the emperor] of wisely maintaining in order and in rank the leaders of the Churches,[35] and of conferring the force of law, by his confirmation of the canonical decrees they issue. If these decrees are truly canonical, it is not in his power, as *epistemonarches*, to oppose or frustrate them by virtue of the superiority of his position, because nor would it be in accord with his learning to set aside canons. This role of *epistemonarches* is given to him because he is recognised as pious and most Christian: it is his duty, therefore, to repay to his mother the Church the cost of his education, to protect her and support her with great gratitude in exchange not only for the milk she gave him, the basic initiation in piety, but for the bread he has eaten, that of piety, in full initiation into the dogmas, the manly nourishment.[36]

And it was not by chance that, venturing one step further and provoking a scandal, the same patriarch Joseph omitted in his statement the adjective 'holy' which was traditionally applied to the emperor and which was justified by the unction directly received from God.[37]

In this way we return to the classical schema of the two powers, but the independence of the Church sounded the death knell of the reforming spirit.

BALSAMON AND THE IMPERIAL *CHARISMATA*

The title of *epistemonarches* was, in short, no more than a convenient but ambiguous label, a screen which avoided the necessity of justifying more or less recognised rights. Happily, one of those cultivated clergy whose importance in the twelfth century we have emphasised, the great canonist Theodore Balsamon, offered a rather more penetrating analysis. Balsamon's personal contribution to the debate on the sacerdotal nature of the emperor was of such importance that it may be helpful first to consider his character.[38]

---

[35] That is, assure respect for the ecclesiastical hierarchy as it has been established.

[36] 'Réponse du patriarche Joseph sur les propositions faites en faveur des Latins', in V. Laurent and J. Darrouzès, *Dossier grec de l'Union de Lyon 1273–1277* (Paris, 1976), pp. 236–9. The *Response* was written by Job Iasites soon after the *Tomos* containing the emperor's proposals in 1273.

[37] Pachymeres, *Hist.*, VI, 31, ed. and trans. Failler and Laurent (see ch. 1, n. 8), II, pp. 638–9. For the connection between the title of 'holy' and unction, see above, pp. 154–5 and below, pp. 267–76.

[38] Apart from articles in encyclopedias, all out of date, and a rather mediocre monograph (G. P. Stevens, *De Theodoro Balsamone. Analysis operum ac mentis iuridicae* (Rome, 1969)) there are

His biography remains vague until the time when, in the 1170s, he emerged as 'perfect deacon', *nomophylax* and *chartophylax* of the patriarchate of Constantinople; since the reforms of Alexios Komnenos, the holder of this office had become a sort of vicar general of the patriarch, his authorised representative and official intermediary in all relations with the clergy, not only responsible for the archives but head of the chancery, drawing up, authenticating and dispatching letters and acts, exercising administrative control over ordinations and – burning issue of the day – the regularity of marriages, exercising the rights that belonged to the patriarch in his capacity as bishop.[39] Balsamon was proud of and knew how to exploit a power that was all the greater in that patriarchal decisions and imperial legislation often dealt with the same subjects; the *chartophylax* operated at the strategic point where the problems arising from this overlap were resolved. Balsamon was ambitious; he was very particular, at any rate, with regard to questions of etiquette. Appointed patriarch of Antioch soon after 1180, an essentially honorific title since he was unable (and had no wish) to take up his position in Islamic territory, he spares us no detail of the prerogatives attached to his new position and holds forth at length in order to establish his right to move formally to Constantinople with the double-branched candlestick of the *didaskalos*. His opportunism sometimes made his contemporaries smile. Niketas Choniates tells how the emperor Isaac II Angelos consulted him to find out if he could appoint one of the patriarchs in exile to the vacant see of Constantinople, in spite of the canons. Assuming he was the patriarch in question, Balsamon hastened to justify such a transfer and to influence the synod's decision to this effect; he was then extremely chagrined to see the appointment go to Dositheos of Jerusalem (February 1189).[40]

Balsamon was born in Constantinople (about 1130/40?). He claimed to be 'of the city' (*polites*) and he wrote at length on the question of the supremacy of the New Rome, its law, traditions and liturgy in an East that was politically divided, and where most Christians lived under Arab or Turkish rule. This situation posed some problems of pure ecclesiastical administration to which the canonist frequently returned: that, for example, of sees left vacant and of the status in exile and the transfer of bishops appointed *in partibus infidelium*, who were unable to go to their sees. It also posed fundamental problems that had emerged in the second half of the eleventh century and lost none of their urgency. What sort of links should be established between these different parts

on Balsamon and the genesis of his work as a canonist a number of articles published in *Byzantium in the 12th Century* (n. 29), in particular, C. Gallagher, 'Gratian and Theodore Balsamon: two twelfth-century canonistic methods compared', pp. 61–89; K. Pitsakes, 'He ektase tes exousias henos hyperoriou patriarche. Ho patriarches Antiocheias sten Konstantinoupole ton 120 aiona', pp. 91–139; V. Tiftixoglu, 'Zur Genese der Kommentare des Theodoros Balsamon. Mit einem Exkurs über die unbekannten Kommentare des Sinaiticus gr. 1117', pp. 483–532.

[39] Darrouzès, *Les Offikia* (n. 34), especially pp. 336–49.

[40] Niketas Choniates. *Hist.*, ed. Van Dieten (n. 15), pp. 407–8.

of the Christian and Orthodox world, which were no longer subject to the same political rule? What degree of harmonisation was desirable? Where should the frontier lie between regional particularisms that were tolerable because purely cultural, canonically dubious practices and deviations from the faith? What, in the last analysis, actually was Christian 'Romanitas'? These issues exercised all Christians. The patriarch of Constantinople and the synod had to respond to a series of *Questions posed, at the request of the Christians who live in the lands and the possessions of the Saracens, by the most humble patriarch of Alexandria, Mark*, almost all of which suggested harmonisation with Constantinople:

> Are the liturgies which are read within the competences of Alexandria and Jerusalem, and which are said to have been written by the holy apostles James, brother of Our Lord, and Mark, accepted by the holy and universal Church, or not?[41].... The sixty books of the laws which are called *Basilika* are not widely known in our lands. For this reason, there is uncertainty in their regard and we wish to know if this is reprehensible.[42].... Is it safe for the orthodox Syrians and Armenians, but also the faithful of other countries, to say the office in their own language, or are they obliged to officiate with books written in Greek?[43]

A first draft of a reply, drawn up by John of Chalcedon, seemed to the synod too slipshod in form and fundamentally lax, and Balsamon performed the task with a firmer hand, in February 1194. He dismissed the liturgies of James and Mark, allowed the use of vernacular languages in the liturgy only where they translated authorised Greek models and recalled, lastly, that the ultimate definition of the *Romaioi* who had become politically dependent was to live according to 'Roman' law. Balsamon was not a centraliser from narrow authoritarianism; he saw reference to Constantinople, to its Church, its emperor and its tradition as the only way to preserve a semblance of unity in a Christendom that was falling apart. It was a little like the western reform but in reverse; here the unity of Christianity was assured by the recognition of imperial power, there by the supremacy of pontifical power.

As we have seen, Balsamon had little sympathy for the pope, whose pride had isolated him from the other patriarchs, but he projected the Roman model on to Constantinople by a simple line of argument. The Donation of Constantine had granted imperial rights to the pope of Rome; the second and fourth ecumenical councils had conceded the same prerogatives to the see of Constantinople as to the see of Rome; so, whenever the texts spoke of Rome, Constantinople should be understood, and the patriarch of Constantinople, too, might claim

---

[41] Question 1, Rhalles–Potles, *Syntagma*, IV, p. 451, where Balsamon's answer should be read together with his commentary on canon 32 of the council in Trullo: ibid., II, pp. 377–8.
[42] Question 4, ibid., IV, p. 451.   [43] Question 6, ibid., pp. 452–3.

quasi-imperial privileges. If he wisely refrained, it was because the Roman emperor, having left Rome, exercised power in New Rome and retained quasi-episcopal rights. The chief problem, therefore, was to define and reconcile these two powers, either by radically differentiating between them or by bringing out their close kinship.

This was the starting point for Balsamon's great work, his *Commentaries* on the *Nomokanon*, that is, on a compilation conceived towards the end of the sixth century and revised in 883, which, even in its form, juxtaposed a pre-existing canonical collection[44] and an imperial legislation which freely addressed the same subjects and postulated *a priori* harmony and compromises. Without going into detail, let us say simply that Byzantine law had two forms and two sources, but that there was no true duality in that the emperor promulgated the canons with the bishops and recognised in principle their superiority over the civil laws. The aim, therefore, was to eliminate potential contradictions, and care was taken to avoid defining distinct spheres. In fact it was to a joint request from the emperor Manuel and the patriarch Michael of Anchialos that Balsamon was responding, between 1170 and 1178, as a result of a divergence of interpretation. He was asked not to revise the *Nomokanon*, but to explain, in a free commentary, the obscurities and possible contradictions, and to indicate the ancient laws (those of the codification and the Novels of Justinian) which, not having been included in the last codification of the *Basilika* (a revision carried out by Basil I and Leo VI at the end of the ninth century), had lost validity by virtue of the principle of according preference to the most recent law: *lex posterior derogat legi priori.*

The canonist was confronted, therefore, with a global juridical tradition which he did not have to constitute, like Gratian in the West, but to consolidate and show to be coherent, and which was the ultimate reference point of eastern 'Romanitas' and provided a model of unity/duality of powers that could easily be generalised. We should not therefore be surprised if the role of the emperor within the Church was one of the subjects to which Balsamon constantly returned, nor attribute only to flattery or opportunism a theory of the emperor quasi-bishop which has been seen as the official expression of eastern caesaropapism.[45] It was a matter of circumstances as much as of temperament, but also of intelligence; Balsamon's great merit was to have moved beyond the false problem of a distinction between Church and state and to have broken out of the narrow view of the 'traditional' prerogatives of the emperor,

---

[44] Formally constituted in canon 2 of the council in Trullo.

[45] See the opinion of S. Troïtzky, reported by C. Gallagher ('Gratian and Theodore Balsamon' (n. 38), p. 79) and discussed below, p. 294 and n. 43: it was Balsamon who was responsible for the deepening of the schism between the East and the West, even more than Photios or Keroularios; his argument based on the unction of kingship was an innovation of the twelfth century.

which had been that of his predecessor Zonaras, in order to outline a sort of theory of eastern practice. If the emperor acted in many situations like a bishop, it was because his power was twofold. His double competence, spiritual and temporal, could only be understood by the quasi-sacerdotal nature of kingship, based on unction. Eight centuries after Constantine, the rhetoric of 'as if' had become a theoretical approach based on a threatened tradition. Balsamon remained cautious in his conclusions; his thinking was refined over the years and expressed in a complex process of writing and revising, which has now been carefully analysed. He was aware that he was not expressing a consensus on these burning issues. He was challenged very close to home, as the manuscript tradition shows; *Sinaiticus gr.* 1117 reproduces his work with a commentary written before 1195, whose anonymous author distances himself on a number of key points.[46]

By taking phrases out of context and by oversimplifying a fluid and sometimes contradictory line of thought, Balsamon's arguments may be summarised as follows. The Church is subject to the authority of the emperor and to that of the patriarch or patriarchs. That is a given. But on what is the authority of the emperor based? On his role as *epistemonarches*, was the usual reply, that is, on his acknowledged disciplinary function. Balsamon did not reject this explanation; in fact he sometimes used it, for example with regard to the right of appeal to the emperor in ecclesiastical matters, to show that the decisions of the patriarchal court were without appeal by reason of the elevation of the see, but that it was for the emperor, as *epistemonarches* of the Church, to judge the patriarch if he was personally accused of sacrilege (*hierosylia*) or heterodoxy.[47] There was nothing here that was particularly new. More provocative was the opinion attributed by Balsamon to others, but which he seems to have approved,[48] to the effect that the emperor was subject neither to the laws nor the canons. This extended to the sphere reserved to the Church the old dialectic of the emperor 'living law',[49] and postulated in principle that the 'norms of power' – as Demetrios Chomatianos would later call them – were superior to the 'norms of law'.[50] Looked at more closely, however, all Balsamon was doing was justifying a certain number of acknowledged imperial rights (that, in particular, to remodel the ecclesiastical geography and hierarchy)[51] and generalising the liberty the emperor had always possessed to proceed to an 'economy', that is, to excuse himself from canonical rules by virtue of a higher interest (for example,

---

[46] Tiftixoglu, 'Kommentare des Theodoros Balsamon' (n. 38).

[47] Commentary on canon 12 of Antioch: Rhalles–Potles, *Syntagma*, III, pp. 146–50, especially p. 149, where Balsamon expresses his personal opinion.

[48] Commentary on canon 16 of Carthage: Rhalles–Potles, *Syntagma*, III, pp. 342–51, especially pp. 349–50.

[49] See above, p. 19 and n. 30–1.   [50] See above, p. 20 and n. 33.

[51] See below, pp. 307–8.

he wrote, to entrust to the clergy or monks administrative or political offices or responsibilities in principle incompatible with their status). But Balsamon's originality only really appeared when he added to these justifications, which he felt to be insufficient, the idea that the emperor had 'episcopal rights',[52] that his authority within the Church was exercised over souls as well as over bodies and that it was, in a sense, superior to that of the patriarchs with whom he shared the honour of blessing with the double candle the *dibamboulon* still used in the orthodox liturgy.[53]

Balsamon returned, therefore, to the problem which had seemed to be definitively obscured, that of sacerdotal kingship, and ordered his arguments around two points which were, in effect, strategic: access to the sanctuary and unction.

With regard to the former, we have already seen how the ceremonial of the tenth century, which continued unchanged in the twelfth, registered a sort of hesitation, allowing the emperor to enter the sanctuary at the time of the 'entry', then firmly keeping him at a distance for the rest of the liturgy. This intermediate solution had already been supported by the bishops of the council in Trullo (691–2). Wishing to restore order to devotional practices and to distinguish more clearly between the sacred and the profane, and between clergy and laity, they had formally pronounced in canon 69: 'Let it be permitted to no one from the laity to penetrate the interior of the holy sanctuary (*thysiasterion*).' But they had made an exception for the *basileus* by adding, without transition: 'The power and the sovereignty of the emperors are in no way subject to this rule each time that the emperor wishes to offer gifts to the creator, according to a very ancient tradition.'[54] So entering the sanctuary was a privilege, and by virtue of a tradition, not a right, and in specific circumstances – for the laying of gifts on the altar on the occasion of the 'entry'.[55] The canonists of the twelfth century realised that this exception posed the problem of the religious status of the emperor and reacted according to temperament. The commentary of John Zonaras, historian, canonist and polymath of the generation preceding Balsamon,[56] was fairly terse:

---

[52] The expression, which we will encounter again, had already appeared in the commentary on canon 16 of Carthage: Rhalles–Potles, *Syntagma*, III, p. 350.

[53] See the treatise of Balsamon 'On the prerogatives of the patriarchs': Rhalles–Potles, *Syntagma*, IV, pp. 544–5. In the Orthodox Church, the bishop still, on the most official occasions, carries in his left hand a small candelabrum with three branches (*trikerion*) symbolising the Trinity, and in his right a small candelabrum with two branches (*dikerion*) symbolising the union of the two natures in Christ, with which he blesses. This *dikerotrikerion* should not be confused with the *dibamboulon*, a large candelabrum with two branches carried before the patriarch when he officiates.

[54] Rhalles–Potles, *Syntagma*, II, p. 466, with the commentaries of Zonaras and Balsamon, pp. 466–7.

[55] Not at the time of the offertory, but at the conclusion of the 'entry', as is shown by the *De cerimoniis*, I, 1, I, pp. 15–16; ed. Vogt (see ch. 2, n. 1), I, pp. 11–12; and see above, pp. 92–3.

[56] He died about 1159.

Those who accord this privilege to the emperor invoke, by way of an excuse, his power and his sovereignty, saying more or less that the emperor, as a layman, ought not to have the right to enter the sanctuary, but that by reason of his power and his sovereignty, this privilege has been conceded to him from the beginning by a tradition going back to the ancient Fathers.

Theodore Balsamon's summary was along the same lines, clear and concise:

> The present canon prohibits the laity from entering the holy sanctuary, which is reserved to the consecrated clergy alone.[57] But to the emperor, even though he is a layman, this concession is made – says the canon – when he is intending to bring his gifts to God, according to an ancient tradition.

The canonist then gives his thoughts free rein. He marvels at some dispensations or lapses which amaze him. Absolutely anyone, he writes, can get into the sanctuary of the Church of Christ of the Chalke; he has no idea (like us) why. He knows – or thinks he knows – that the Latins, both men and women, enter the sanctuary and sit down there, even when the officiants are standing; this was a point of contention which had appeared some years earlier in a letter from Niketas Stethatos to Gregory the Sophist,[58] and which became a habitual complaint in the anti-Latin polemic, for example in the pamphlet of Constantine Stilbes,[59] soon after 1204. A little later, rereading his text, Balsamon drew on his experience as patriarch of Antioch established in Constantinople:

> Take careful note of this canon, and use it not to allow the laity to go into the holy sanctuary in any circumstances. But for my part, despite my best efforts to prevent the laity from entering the holy sanctuary of my most holy mistress the Virgin Hodegetria, I failed, the laity claiming that it was an old custom and that they ought not to be prevented.[60]

---

[57] That is, the clergy in major orders (above sub-deacon), otherwise known as 'clergy of the *bema*'.

[58] Niketas Stethatos, *Ep.* VIII, 3, ed. J. Darrouzès, *Opuscules et lettres* (Paris, 1961), p. 282: 'If, in fact, the divine Fathers forbade entry to the altar to all lay people – because only the emperors bearing gifts have received their permission to enter – how can it be so freely permitted to the laity to approach the altar?'

[59] J. Darrouzès, 'Le mémoire de Constantin Stilbès contre les Latins', *REB*, 21 (1963), pp. 75–6 (grievances 55 and 56), commentary, pp. 96–7: among the Latins, 'the altar is accessible to all comers, whatever their age, sex and rank, even during the mass ... sometimes also women sit down in the congregation, so well do the most pious men among them know how to distinguish the sacred from the profane! ... among them, even when the holy gifts advance, those who chose remained seated'. The importance of this last remark on sitting and standing emerges very clearly in a Novel of Constantine Doukas (dated 1065) forbidding the emperors to change the hierarchy of the ecclesiastical sees, where this curious argument is found: 'While [in the church] the emperor is standing and the priest seated, how can he who is standing make a gift of a higher see to he who is seated?' (Zepos, *Jus*, I, pp. 276–8 = Rhalles–Potles, *Syntagma*, V, pp. 274–6).

[60] This last addition, put into square brackets by Rhalles–Potles, may very well be by Balsamon himself and correspond to a version of the text 'later than 1180'. The monastery of the Virgin Hodegetria was the residence and property of the patriarch of Antioch in Constantinople, and so where Balsamon lived: Janin, *Eglises et monastères*, p. 202; above all, Pitsakes, 'He ektase tes exousias henos hyperoriou patriarche' (n. 38), pp. 117–33.

The tone changes when Balsamon expresses his personal opinion on the question of whether the emperors were truly equivalent to the laity:

As regards the emperors, some [commentators] have claimed, by taking the canon literally, that they are permitted to enter the sanctuary only when they go to offer a gift to God, and not when they wish to enter to perform simple devotions. That is not my opinion. For the orthodox emperors, due to the fact that they promote the patriarchs by invoking the Holy Trinity,[61] and that they are the Lord's anointed, may enter the holy sanctuary when they wish without being prevented.[62]

Returning later to his text,[63] he added new arguments which had since occurred to him and which enabled him to turn his opinion into a thesis:

And they [the emperors] cense and bless with the triple candle, just like the bishops; they even engage in instruction of a catechetical type,[64] which is permitted only to the local bishop.[65] And one also finds in the nineteenth

---

[61] For the implications of the term *probole/problesis*, see *De cerimoniis*, II, 14, pp. 564–6; Darrouzès, *Documents inédits* (n. 14), pp. 142–3 and note 1. At a first reading of the text edited by Rhalles and Potles, it seems that the words *di'epikleseos tes Hagias Triados* refer to the appointment of the patriarch. But the ceremonial laid down for this occasion (*De cerimoniis*, II, 14, pp. 564–6) attributes to the emperor only a banal and scarcely sacramental formula: 'The grace of God and the kingship which I have received from it appoint such a patriarch', whereas the invocation of the Holy Spirit is habitual, in Balsamon and elsewhere, with regard to unction.

[62] It seems that, in a first version of his commentary, Balsamon stopped at this point and returned, by a simple remark, to the particular case of the church of the Chalke. This first version, dated 'about 1179' by V. Tiftixoglu, ends with the following phrase: 'And to the very holy patriarch Theodosios, who prevented the entry of the laity into the holy sanctuary of the holy church of Our Lord and Saviour Christ at the Chalke, there were some who said that, from the time when the canon did not lay down any penalty against those who transgressed its dispositions, the laity were then authorised to enter freely into the sacred sanctuary. But they could not convince the aforesaid holy man, who declared that all those who, in one way or another, transgressed the canons are punishable by canonical *epitimiai*, left to be decided by the local bishop.' I thank my colleague Dieter Simon for communicating to me the conclusions of his research at Frankfurt on the manuscripts of Balsamon, which I am happy to reproduce here.

[63] This second version, which dates from about 1180, adds to the first the passage corresponding to ed. Rhalles–Potles, *Syntagma*, II, p. 467, lines 2–12.

[64] It was probably by virtue of this catechetical role that Basil I chose, about 879, to engage personally in the instruction of the Jews he wished to baptise (Dagron, 'Le traité de Grégoire de Nicée' (see ch. 4, n. 75), pp. 336–7, 356), that Leo VI pronounced homilies from the ambo of some of the principal churches in Constantinople (Grosdidier de Matons, 'Trois études' (see ch. 6, n. 20), especially pp. 189–201) and that the emperor addressed 'the people', in the hall of the Magnaura, on the first Monday in Lent, to urge them to pass Lent in purity and fear of God (*De cerimoniis*, I, 36 [27] and II, 10, pp. 155, 545–8; see also Treitinger, *Kaiser – und Reichsidee* (see ch. 2, n. 35), pp. 141–3). Some emperors seem to have used this privilege more than others: Leo VI, who, in 912, already sick, could hardly speak (Theophanes Continuatus, ed. Bekker (see ch. 1, n. 4), p. 377; Leo the Grammarian, *Chronographia*, ed. Bekker (see ch. 2, n. 12), p. 285) and Manuel Komnenos, in Balsamon's time, who liked to make 'catechetical addresses' in public, and even to organise debates on matters of exegesis and dogma (Niketas Choniates, ed. Van Dieten (n. 15), p. 210).

[65] Canon 20 of the council in Trullo prohibited, on pain of deposition, a bishop from preaching publicly in a town for which he was not responsible: Rhalles–Potles, *Syntagma*, II, p. 349.

Book of the *Jewish Antiquities* of Flavius Josephus an imperial titulature composed as follows:[66] *Tiberius Claudius, Caesar Augustus, Germanicus, pontifex maximus (archiereus megistos), tribunicia potestate, cos. II.* Since the successive emperors are declared the Lord's anointed by the unction of kingship and since Christ [= the Anointed], our God, received among other titles that of bishop, it is only right that episcopal *charismata* should be ascribed to the emperor.[67]

Beneath its complicated expression, the argument is simple: the Anointed par excellence, Christ, is called by us bishop,[68] hence the emperors, who also receive unction, should equally be regarded as bishops.

This constant revision reveals how the theoretical problem of sacerdotal kingship was posed and developed. It clearly preoccupied Balsamon, who began by putting the promotion of the patriarchs and unction, a privilege and a *charisma*, at the same level, but changed his mind and listed a certain number of properly priestly acts which the emperor, because he was 'the Lord's anointed', was qualified to perform. His thinking is more precise and his arguments better organised in a passage in his *Response on the rights of patriarchs,* where he unequivocally states that it was by reason of the power [of the Spirit] conferred by unction, that 'our faithful sovereigns and *autokrators* address catechetical homilies to the people who bear the name of Christ, cense like the priests and bless with the double candle', which was, for them as for the patriarchs and the bishops, the symbol of the 'dignity of *didaskalos*' *(didaskalikon axioma).*[69] There was probably some interaction between this text written in one go and the various versions of the commentary on canon 69 of the council in Trullo. One senses Balsamon's ideas gradually deepening and clarifying.

Imperceptibly, we have passed from one logic to another. The rights of intervention that the Church acknowledged to the emperor were no longer seen as exceptional privileges, but as a manifestation of the quasi-episcopal nature of imperial power. Taken together, they gave the temporal power a special status and led inexorably to the conclusion that, if the emperor was not strictly speaking a priest 'in the order of Aaron', nor was he simply a layman. As against a purely juridical conception, Balsamon proposed, not without caution, a charismatic conception of imperial power. To 'promote' the patriarch, he suggested, was not simply to choose him from a list of, in principle, three names submitted by the assembly of metropolitans, or to impose him on this same assembly in case of disagreement, as envisaged by a chapter in the *Book of Ceremonies;*[70]

---

[66] *Jewish Antiquities*, XIX, 287 (p. 351 of Loeb ed.). It prefaces an imperial edict of Claudius dealing with the Jews of Alexandria (the second quoted by Josephus).
[67] Balsamon, *Syntagma*, II, p. 467. This is symbolism run riot, as Christ was only metaphorically a bishop.
[68] For the priesthood of Christ, see below (epilogue). [69] Rhalles-Potles, *Syntagma*, IV, p. 544.
[70] II, 14, pp. 564–6.

it was, above all, to 'create' him – before the religious consecration performed by the metropolitans the following Sunday in St Sophia – either by invoking the Holy Spirit, as Balsamon said, or by using the rather more neutral formula preserved in the ceremonial of the tenth century: 'Divine Grace and the Kingship which we have received from it promotes the most pious person before us patriarch of Constantinople.' The 'appointment' of the patriarch was a political prerogative, like the reorganisation of dioceses and the promotion of episcopal sees, which the emperor had the right to perform without appeal in the interests of a closer harmony between the spiritual and the temporal powers; but his 'promotion by invocation of the Spirit' was a religious, if not a liturgical, act, which only *charismata* could justify. It would be interesting to carry the enquiry further by analysing the religious vocabulary used in the ceremonial for the promotions to dignities regarded as 'lay', in particular the term 'consecration' (*cheirotonia*), which equated the promotion by the emperor of a caesar or a *nobelissimos* to a sort of ordination,[71] and the formula used for the appointment of the caesar or of certain high dignitaries: 'In the name of the Father, the Son and the Holy Spirit, my kingship given by God promotes you [to such and such a dignity].'[72]

The *Book of Ceremonies* sheds further light on Balsamon's thinking by revealing the specific circumstances in which the emperor blessed by making the sign of the cross and censed. At the Hippodrome he three times blessed, with the fold of his *chlamys*, the demes and the assembled people, who shouted 'Holy' three times,[73] that is, recognised him as 'the Lord's anointed'; he blessed the person he was promoting to the rank of caesar by making the sign of the cross with the crown of a caesar which he was about to place on his head;[74] he three times blessed the assembled dignitaries when he went to preach at the beginning of Lent in the Magnaura;[75] and he blessed the town and then said a prayer over it when he departed on campaign.[76] In the ceremonial of the principal feasts, he censed, with a censor handed to him by the patriarch or by a deacon, the sanctuary, the altar table, the cross at the back of the apse and the liturgical vessels of the *skeuophylakion* of St Sophia,[77] and also the sanctuary and altar of the Blachernai,[78] the altar of the Holy Apostles and the tombs of

---

[71] *De cerimoniis*, I, 52–3 [43–4], pp. 217–29.

[72] Ibid., I, 52 [43], I, pp. 220, 225 (for the caesar, whom the emperor blessed as he pronounced the invocation of the Trinity); II, 3–5, for promotions to the offices of *domestikos* of the *scholae*, *strategos*, *droungarios* of the fleet, rector and *synkellos*.

[73] I, 52 [43], 72 [63], 73 [64], 75 [66], 77 [68], 78 [69], 79 [70], 81 [72], 82 [73]; II, 21, pp. 222–3, 280, 291, 299, 307, 316–17, 325, 344, 347, 365, 614.

[74] I, 52 [43], pp. 220, 225.   [75] II, 10, p. 545.

[76] Haldon, *Constantine Porphyrogenitus* (see ch. 2, n. 41), pp. 88 (Text B, line 91) and 114 (Text C, line 324).

[77] I, 1; I, 44 [35]; II, 10; II, 19, pp. 16, 28, 34, 182, 609.   [78] I, 43 [34]; II, 12, pp. 179, 552.

Leo VI, Theophano, Basil I and Constantine the Great.[79] His blessing then had a more particular meaning, since he used the triple candle that symbolised the illumination of the Holy Spirit and the gift of *didaskalia*, that is, the right to teach the faith by reason of divine *charismata*.

This, as Balsamon was well aware, was an important and a controversial point. We have noted the vehemence with which Gregory Asbestas reproached Basil I for having meddled in the conversion of the Jews by himself acting as a *didaskalos*, which was the province of the bishops. Balsamon must have known this late ninth-century text, which was reproduced in many of the heresiological collections; but he put himself in the place of the emperors and turned the traditional argument on its head. Since they shared so many privileges with the clergy, including that of *didaskalia*, why should the emperors be regarded as laymen? How were they not superior to the bishops themselves, since they could be universal *didaskaloi*, unlike the bishops, who were restricted to their own diocese?

It is clear that the sovereigns valued this function of teaching and preaching very highly. Leo VI, son of Basil I, mounted the ambo of the churches of Constantinople on the principal religious feasts and ceremonies to deliver the homilies which he had written for the occasion and which have survived, only allowing them to be read by someone else when it was absolutely unavoidable.[80] The *Book of Ceremonies* describes in two places the way in which the emperor, on the first Monday in Lent, held a public assembly (*silentium*) in the Magnaura, climbed the steps of the hall as one climbed those of the ambo or of the *synthronon*, and addressed the congregation, whom he blessed, on the necessity of passing Lent in purity and fear of God, before going in procession to St Sophia.[81] It is likely that the ceremonial employed the term *demegoria* on this occasion, which equated the sermon to a rhetorical exercise and was unambiguous; but certain chroniclers preferred to speak of the 'catechetical addresses' which the emperors who were lovers of rhetoric and, above all, keen to fulfil their religious function liked to compose. Leo VI, we are told, in the year of his death, 912, 'could only with great difficulty deliver in public the usual Lenten address;[82] or Manuel Komnenos, who, according to Niketas Choniates, loved to write and deliver this sort of catechesis, and whose penchant led him to go well beyond rhetoric and 'discuss divine dogmas, discourse upon God' and raise

---

[79] II, 6; II, 13, pp. 533, 558–9, 563.
[80] One finds, in the title of some of his homilies, statements such as: 'spoken before the people by a secretary . . . because the presence of the emperor was prevented by decisions which occupied him without allowing him any free time': Grosdidier de Matons, 'Trois études' (see ch. 6, n. 20), p. 191.
[81] I, 36 [27], p. 155; II, 10, I, pp. 545–8.
[82] Leo the Grammarian, *Chronographia*, ed. Bekker (see ch. 2, n. 12), p. 285; Theophanes Continuatus, ed. Bekker (see ch. 1, n. 4), Bonn, p. 377.

thorny exegetical and theological problems.[83] With Manuel Komnenos we are
in the very period when Balsamon was not only recognising that the emperor
had 'episcopal *charismata*', but making him a model and reference point for
the patriarchs themselves: 'Like the emperors', he wrote, 'the patriarchs are
honoured with *didaskalikon axioma* by the power of sacred unction.'[84]

Such a turnabout of opinion makes the argument based on the title of *pontifex
maximus* which had been born by the emperors until about 380 slightly less
surprising.[85] It is true that Balsamon was not the first Christian author to gloss
this word. Isidore of Seville wrote in the seventh century:

> The pontiff is the first of the priests, as it were the way for those who follow. He
> is the supreme priest and he is called *pontifex maximus*. It is he, indeed, who
> makes the priests and the Levites; it is he who disposes of all the ecclesiastical
> orders; it is he who shows what each one should do. Previously, one was
> both pontiff and king. In fact, it was the custom of the ancients that the
> king was also priest or pontiff. That is why the Roman emperors were called
> pontiffs.[86]

But this philological commentary hardly suggested transferring the religious
functions of the pagan emperors to the Christian emperor. Nor did Gratian, when
he copied the passage into his *Decretum*,[87] encourage such a confusion, and
when it reappears, in the thirteenth century, in a summary of liturgical knowledge, Guillaume Durand's *Rationale divinorum officiorum*,[88] it is no more than
a memory of little consequence. If the expression *imperator pontifex maximus
dictus est*, taken out of context, succeeded in the West, and if it was not until
Guillaume Budé that it was exorcised, as we are reminded by Ernst
Kantorowicz,[89] it is because it was inoffensive and not exploited. In the East, on
the contrary, it carried an explosive charge. In order to bolster the notion that the
accumulation of the 'two powers' was diabolical before the coming of Christ
and sacrilege after the Incarnation, Pope Gelasius (492–6) had already invoked
the Christian exegesis of Melchizedek in a letter to the emperor Anastasios; and
he added that the pagan emperors had assumed the title of *pontifex maximus* at
the instigation of the devil, but that, 'since the coming of the true king and pontiff

[83] *Hist.*, ed. Van Dieten (n. 15), p. 210.   [84] See above, p. 263 and note 69.
[85] See above, p. 183, n. 76.
[86] 'Pontifex princeps sacerdotum est, quasi via sequentium. Ipse et summus sacerdos, ipse et
pontifex maximus nuncupatur. Ipse enim efficit sacerdotes et Levitas, ipse omnes ordines ec-
clesiasticos disponit, ipse quid unusquisque facere debeat ostendit. Antea autem pontifices et
reges erant. Nam majorum haec erat consuetudo ut rex esset etiam sacerdos vel pontifex. Unde
et Romani imperatores pontifices dicebantur': *Etymologiarum sive originum libri XX*, VII, 12,
13–14. ed. W. M. Lindsay (Oxford, 1989–91).
[87] *Decretum magistri Gratiani, Distinctiones*, XXI, 1 §8 ed. E. Friedberg, *Corpus iuris canonici*,
I (1879), col. 68: the whole passage is copied without comment or reservation. In this new
context, the expression became ambiguous.
[88] II, 11, with the final phrase 'Unde et Romani imperatores pontifices dicebantur'.
[89] Kantorowicz, 'Mysteries of state' (n. 7), p. 387, n. 29.

[Christ], no other emperor had awarded himself the title of pontiff [sic] and no other pontiff had claimed the royal dignity'.[90]

There is nothing to suggest that Balsamon knew this text, but his remark about the imperial title of *pontifex*, if it was not intended to provoke the Roman pontiff, was at all events evidence of a profound difference between West and East. The Constantinople canonist knew that there had been no religious continuity from paganism to Christianity, and he would never have equated a pagan priest with a bishop simply on the basis of an identity of name. But the emperor-*archiereus* was not only a Christian emperor; he was part of that chain of kings who, from Melchizedek to David, from David to Augustus and from Augustus to Constantine, had consciously or unconsciously played a role in the economy of salvation. For this Old Testament priesthood, as we have already said, Christianisation was not truly a rupture, since it was only the revelation of a hidden purpose; consequently it was not absurd to base an argument on the titulature of Claudius, especially if it appeared in a passage in the *Jewish Antiquities* of Flavius Josephus, book of truth, and in the context of Roman policy towards the Jews.

THE UNCTION OF KINGSHIP

Balsamon's commentary on canon 12 of the council of Ankyra confirms that he was maintaining a thesis, that of the sacerdotal or quasi-sacerdotal nature of the imperial office, and that this thesis was based, in the last analysis, on the notion that the emperor, by the sole fact of being emperor, had received unction from God. Tradition was sufficient to justify recognition that the *basileus* possessed a number of 'episcopal rights' (*archieratika dikaia*), just as it was enough to justify recognition that the pope – and by extension, as we have seen, the patriarch of Constantinople – possessed 'imperial rights' (*basilika dikaia*);[91] but this was to go no further than that formal exchange of symbols and prerogatives between the two powers which, by other routes, closed the debate in the West. With royal unction, Balsamon was aiming to give this fragile edifice its keystone, to demonstrate that the episcopal rights of the emperor were well founded and to establish that they truly were *archieratika charismata*.[92]

Responding to a preoccupation of the fourth century, canon 12 of Ankyra had declared that Christians not yet baptised who had sacrificed to false gods might, after receiving baptism, be promoted to the priesthood, because baptism erased the previous sins. After a literal explanation, Balsamon gave this 'other interpretation', in fact, an additional comment:

[90] *Tractatus IV (Tomus de anathematis vinculo)*, ed. Thiel, *Epistolae Romanorum pontificum genuinae* (see ch. 5, n. 74), I, pp. 567–8; and see above, p. 182.
[91] Rhalles–Potles, *Syntagma*, I, pp. 143–9; II, pp. 285–6; IV, p. 553.   [92] Ibid., II, p. 467.

It was on the basis of this canon that the patriarch Polyeuktos, having excluded the emperor John Tzimiskes from the very holy Great Church of God
because he had murdered the emperor Nikephoros Phokas, later received
him.[93] He said, in fact, with the holy synod, in the synodal act which was
then passed and which is preserved in the archives, that, since the unction of
holy baptism had erased the sins previously committed whatever their nature
or their number, so the unction of kingship had wholly erased the murder
committed by Tzimiskes before becoming emperor.[94]

Balsamon was not debating the decision, but the claim of some other canonists,
who wanted to make bishops, too, enjoy remission of their sins by reason of
episcopal unction, and who asserted: 'Just as emperors are called and are really
the Lord's anointed, so bishops are too, and receive the same name.' These
people, Balsamon continued, base their argument on the fact that the prayers
said for the imperial coronation and for the consecration of bishops both invoke
the power of the Holy Spirit:

> In the place of the oil of unction with which the kings and the hierarchs were
> anointed according to Ancient Law, they say that the yoke of the Gospels
> placed on the nape of the neck and the blessing of the officiant by the invo-
> cation of the Holy Spirit is sufficient today for bishops.[95]

Balsamon accepts this and cites a passage in Gregory of Nazianzus developing
the idea that the virtue of unction operated as well on an unworthy bishop – if he
led a life of purity after his consecration – as on a worthy bishop.[96] With regard
to the other clergy, Balsamon cites various conciliar canons and concludes
that the consecration of bishops, as much as the anointing of emperors, erased
previous sins, but that for the priests and the clergy of lower rank, consecration
erased only venial sins. He added that consecration and unction gave not only
the 'apostolic', but the 'prophetic' *charisma*: 'That is why Saul counts among
the prophets and Caiaphas prophesied despite himself.'[97] Balsamon took this
remark from the same passage in Gregory of Nazianzus; it allowed him to

[93] See above, p. 109.
[94] Grumel-Darrouzès, *Regestes*, no. 794; the act is of December 969 or early 970; it is known only
from Balsamon, but the evidence of a *chartophylax* of the patriarchate is unimpeachable. On
the refusal of the patriarch to allow 'entry' to Tzimiskes, see above, p. 109.
[95] In the East, bishops were consecrated, not by a material unction, but by the placing of the hands
of the celebrant and of the Gospels on the nape of the neck: see below, p. 272.
[96] *Orationes* IX, PG 35, cols. 820–5.
[97] Rhalles–Potles, *Syntagma*, III, pp. 43–6. The Old Testament reference occurs in the passage
quoted from Gregory of Nazianzus. Balsamon's text is discussed in Tiftixoglu, 'Zur Genese
der Kommentare des Theodoros Balsamon' (n. 38), especially pp. 506–12, 530–1. Tiftixoglu is
puzzled by the reference to the act of Polyeuktos ending in absolution for Tzimiskes by reason
of unction, when the historical sources enumerate the penances imposed by the same patriarch
on the future emperor before his coronation (especially Skylitzes, *Synopsis*, ed. Thurn (see ch. 1,
n. 39), p. 285). But the contradiction is only apparent, because the penance and the repentance
might be devised after the erasing of the sins, and divine unction was granted to the emperor
from the moment of his accession to power and not at his coronation.

conclude on an Old Testament note which fitted perfectly with his theory of royal unction as a model for all others.[98]

Balsamon was not the only one at this period in the East to defend this extreme position. A few years later, Demetrios Chomatianos repeated the same arguments almost verbatim when responding to different 'Questions' from Constantine Kabasilas, bishop of Dyrrhachion, concerning transfers of bishops by the emperor, which he did not judge to be irregular since the emperor was the 'common *epistemonarches* of the Churches'.[99] Chomatianos then moved from the rights of the emperor in the Church to the priestly nature of his office, in a conclusion which might come straight from Balsamon: 'With the exception of the liturgy, the emperor reproduces the other episcopal privileges, insofar as he acts in accord with the laws and the canons.' The 'episcopal *charismata*' of Balsamon have become 'privileges' which the emperors possessed only metaphorically. The proof was accordingly less strong, but it was no less close in inspiration and concludes – if the text is not interpolated – with a word for word reproduction of the quotation from Flavius Josephus and Balsamon's daring conclusion on the anointed emperor and Christ.[100] This elicited from the modern editor, Monseigneur Pitra, already troubled by the 'priestly *charismata*' but revolted by the comparison with Christ, this outraged exclamation: *Heu! piget pro decore Graecorum non plura variari, sed de sequentibus magis pudendum.* In another reply to Constantine Kabasilas, Demetrios Chomatianos paraphrased Balsamon's argument on unction, but without adding anything new.[101]

Chomatianos followed Balsamon's lead, but others jibbed. The anonymous commentator of *Sinaiticus* 1117, a near contemporary, was surprised by the 'novelty' of Balsamon's thesis on the unction that erases sins. He noted:

---

[98] This reference to Saul and Caiaphas is repeated in the treatise 'On the prerogatives of the patriarchs' (Rhalles–Potles, *Syntagma*, IV, p. 547) to illustrate the same theory of unction.

[99] Pitra, *Analecta sacra et classica* (n. 20), VI, col. 632 (no. 157, Reply 4 to Kabasilas); Rhalles–Potles, *Syntagma*, V, p. 429. For the rights of the emperor as *epistemonarches*, see above, pp. 252–3.

[100] This textual similarity clearly poses a problem: are we to believe that a glossator has introduced a passage from Chomatianos into Balsamon's commentary or, more simply, that Chomatianos had directly appropriated an argument and expressions of Balsamon that pleased him without quoting his source, which often happened: D. Simon, 'Balsamon zum Gewohnheitsrecht', in *Scholia. Studia ad criticam interpretationemque textuum Graecorum et ad historiam iuris graeco-romani pertinentia, viro doctissimo D. Holwerda oblata* (Groningen, 1985), especially p. 130 and note 60.

[101] Pitra, *Analecta sacra et classica* (n. 20), VI, cols. 645–6 (no. 168, Reply 14 to Kabasilas). Kabasilas wanted to know if, when one changed confessor, it was necessary to ask for absolution for sins already remitted. Chomatianos said not; he then passed to the case of priests and bishops. For the latter, he argued that unction erased earlier sins, cited Gregory of Nazianzus, summarised the case of John Tzimiskes and emphasised 'the relationship and equality of strength of the two unctions', royal and episcopal.

What you have written seems to me rather audacious, at odds with and contradicting the canons, not to say the whole Christian tradition. An emperor will get no assistance from his coronation to erase his sins, any more than the bishop from his consecration, if it is not followed by repentance and everything that God has decreed. And for this reason, he must be accountable...[102]

To find in the West a formal criticism of the decision of the patriarch Polyeuktos, tacitly approved by Balsamon, we must move forward more than four centuries to the *De idolatria politica et legitimo principis cultu commentarius* of Jean Filesac,[103] a theologian at the Sorbonne, who wrote in 1615:

What Balsamon wrote with regard to Canon 12 of the council of Ankyra is surprising: that royal unction in consecration is no less effective [than baptismal unction] in erasing previous sins. He bases himself on the example of the emperor of Constantinople, John Tzimiskes, who, because he had murdered the emperor Phokas, had not been allowed into the church by the patriarch before his coronation, but had been once he had been crowned, as if he had been absolved of the parricide he had committed. Our theologians cannot accept this. Mortal sins can be erased only by the power and the virtue of the sacraments, and royal unction should be regarded only as a sacramental.[104]

How could royal unction cleanse of a mortal sin, when it was not a sacrament, but at most a sacramental? It is this question that we must now answer in order to appreciate both the gulf between East and West and that between the twelfth century and the end of the middle ages.

Filesac was not entirely mistaken. Unction, as it was described in the Old Testament, was not a sacrament but a rite marking the presence of God, signalling that in a particular place, on a particular object or a particular person, God had intervened on man's behalf. When Jacob woke after a divine apparition, he said: 'Surely the Lord is in this place; and I knew it not'. Frightened, he went on: 'How dreadful is this place! this is none other but the house of God, and this is the gate of heaven.' Then he set up as a pillar the stone from his bedhead and 'poured oil upon the top of it'.[105] This is the first anointing

---

[102] Fol. 209v, text ed. in Tiftixoglu, 'Zur Genese der Kommentare des Theodoros Balsamon' (n. 38), pp. 509–10.

[103] *De idolatria politica et legitimo principis cultu commentarius Ioannis Filesaci Theologi Parisiensis* (Paris, 1615), p. 73. For Jean Filesac, whose fluctuating opinions earned him the nickname 'Monsieur Le voici, Le voilà', see *DTC* V, 2, cols. 2303–8, under Filesac.

[104] 'Mirum vero quod scripsit Balsamon in canonem 12 Concilii Ancyrani, regiam unctionem in consecratione non minoris esse efficaciae ad delenda peccata prius admissa, probatque exemplo Ioannis Zimiscae imperatoris Constantinopolitani, qui propter a se interfectum Phocam imperatorem a Patriarcha non fuerit admissus in ecclesiam ante coronationem, qua peracta postmodum admissus est, veluti accepta venia parricidii ab eo patrati. Haec nostri Theologi probare non possunt; nec enim lethalia peccata nisi sacramentorum vi et energia purgari queunt, ipsa vero unctio regia sacramentale quiddam tantummodo censeri debet.'

[105] Genesis, 28:16–18.

described in the sacred text: the oil, symbol of strength, of life, of light and of spiritual purity, did not create sacredness, but only recognised it or preserved its memory. When Moses received the order to make a special oil and pour it on the head of his brother Aaron, it was to seal an eternal pact concluded with the latter's descendants and to symbolise, once again, the presence of the Spirit of God in those who were to become his priests.[106] Lastly, when God revealed to Samuel that he had chosen Saul 'that he may save my people out of the hand of the Philistines' and would send him to Samuel so that he could 'anoint him to be captain over my people Israel', the prophet poured the oil from his vial over the head of the new king, saying, was it not 'the Lord [who] anointed thee king over Israel?'[107] For Saul as for David, the first unction was secret, preceding recognition by the people; and for David it was followed by two public anointings, one carried out by the men of Judah so that he might reign over them,[108] the other at Hebron for the kingship over Israel.[109] This repeated anointing was clearly not, to begin with or in essence, a sacrament conferred by the priests, but the external manifestation, by a prophet or the community, that men had perceived the divine message. Royal unction, as it was later administered to Solomon on David's orders by Zadok the priest and Nathan the prophet, with the horn of holy oil stored in the Tabernacle,[110] perhaps more closely resembled a royal consecration; but the word 'unction' served primarily to indicate a choice by God that had no need of holy oil to be operative. The 'Lord's anointed', 'messiah' (*mashiah*) or 'christ' (*christos*), could be recognised as such without material unction. This was, as we shall see, the case with the Byzantine emperors and with the 'Anointed' *par excellence*, Christ, whose purely spiritual unction signified that he had received the Spirit and the Power directly from God.[111]

The Old Testament texts were fairly clear about the consequences of unction. With the gift of the Spirit, so emphasised by Isaiah, 11, came a profound change and a divine adoption. God says through Nathan of Solomon: 'I will be his father, and he shall be my son.'[112] Psalm II, on the 'anointed' king, expresses the same idea: 'I will declare the decree: the Lord hath said unto me, Thou art my Son; this day have I begotten thee.' Unction made the recipient 'another man';[113] it broke the ties of natural kinship in favour of a much stronger and more restrictive spiritual filiation, whose importance for the Byzantine succession process we have already discussed.[114] It established he who had received it, with or without holy oil, in the lineage of the kings Saul, David and Solomon, creating a sort of ideal dynasty which weakened the role of hereditary ties or compensated for their absence.

---

[106] Exodus, 29: 7; 30: 25–32; Leviticus, 16: 32; Psalm CXXXIII [CXXXII]; Ecclesiastes, 45: 15.
[107] I Samuel [I Kings], IX: 16, X: 1; XV: 1, 17; Ecclesiastes, 46: 13.
[108] II Samuel [II Kings], II: 4, 7; III: 39.   [109] II Samuel [II Kings], V: 3, 17 etc.
[110] I Kings [III Kings], I: 34, 39, 45.   [111] Luke, IV: 18; Acts, IV: 27, X: 38.
[112] II Samuel [II Kings], VII: 14.   [113] I Samuel [I Kings], X: 6.   [114] See above, pp. 49–50.

The distinction between the anointing of kings, of priests and of prophets that commentators later attempted to establish is barely detectable in a reading of the Old Testament, where the direct link that was set up between God and his anointed appears, on the contrary, to sanction a whole range of monarchical, sacerdotal or prophetic themes.[115] The king 'begotten' by Yahweh had not only a sacred character, but also, by right, a sacerdotal function, that of intermediary between God and men. Saul built altars;[116] David 'danced before the Lord ... girded with a linen ephod', sacrificed and received the gift of prophecy;[117] his children were called 'priests'.[118] This priesthood was not the Levitical priesthood, but it conferred on the king, in the 'order of Melchizedek', as Christian exegesis would later say, some of the attributes devolved to the descendants of Aaron. A good example of this parallelism which justifies, if not claims of equivalence, recognition of similarities, is blessing. David, the anointed king, 'blessed the people in the name of the Lord',[119] just as the Levites were, by the anointing of Aaron, authorised by God to 'bless his people in his name'.[120] Balsamon remembered this.

Since the Byzantine emperors drew their legitimacy from the Davidic model, they could legitimately be regarded as quasi-bishops or quasi-patriarchs and, with the implicit sanction of the Old Testament, the priestly acts which unction authorised them to perform could be enumerated. Some unease was no doubt experienced when it became necessary to pass from Old Testament proof to Christian practice and explain how Davidic anointing could still act on the emperor after the coming of he whom David had announced, and how the Christian sovereign could invoke the example of Melchizedek without becoming – as we have seen – Antichrist. For it was true that the coming of the Son precluded from then on the tie of filiation which 'unction' had established between the king and God; in a sense, it dried up unction, transformed it into a sacrament of the Church and doomed all ideology of kingship to be no more than metaphorical, from the Christian perspective. But if one accepted the anachronism or the utopia of reference exclusively to the Old Testament, it was true, as Balsamon suggested, that unction provided the only coherent explanation of imperial power as it had been exercised in Constantinople, and that its value was all the greater in that it was conferred not by the Church with holy oil on this or that historical individual, but directly and once and for all by God on the imperial office itself, or rather, on that perpetual reincarnation of power that was – to translate as closely as possible the Greek expression *ho kata kairous basileus* – 'the successive emperor'.

---

[115] When a Byzantine reader found in Daniel, 9: 26 that unction will be destroyed, he did not know whether the prediction concerned a person 'anointed as priest or as king': *Les Trophées de Damas*, IX, 24, PO XV (Paris, 1920), p. 265.

[116] I Samuel [I Kings], XIV: 35.   [117] II Samuel [II Kings], VI: 13–20.

[118] II Samuel [II Kings], VIII: 18.   [119] II Samuel [II Kings], VI: 18.

[120] Ecclesiastes, 45: 15.

It can no longer be doubted that material unction came to Byzantium only at a fairly late stage.[121] When Theophanes, at the beginning of the ninth century, refers to the coronation of Charlemagne and says, wrongly, that the pope crowned the new western emperor 'after anointing him with oil from head to toe',[122] it was in order to emphasise and mock an oddity; and when Constantine Manasses, in the twelfth century, repeated this statement in his verse chronicle, he specified that unction was performed 'according to the custom of the Jews' and wondered why.[123] When Photios, about 864/6, told the porphyrogenitus Michael III that God 'had created him and anointed him in his cradle as emperor of His People', he was sticking very close to his biblical source and the accepted significance of 'birth in the purple';[124] and when, a few years later, the same patriarch more familiarly reminded the parvenu Basil I that he owed his unction and consecration to him, he was simply saying that it was he who had allowed his sudden elevation to the throne.[125] Material unction was confined to dreams. To show that his heroine was destined to become empress, the author of the ancient *Life* of St Theophano (first wife of Leo VI) made her, when still a child, enter a church where she fell asleep and dream that the Virgin, whose icon she had kissed, had anointed her 'all over her body' with the oil from the lamp; when she emerged, her servants saw that her white chiton had turned purple.[126] In the *Book of Ceremonies*, compiled in the tenth century, the unction discreetly evoked in the acclamations was that which God gave directly to the emperor 'New David', as he had given it to Christ at the time of his baptism in the Jordan, and the oil was only the symbol of power

---

[121] For the date at which unction began to be performed materially during coronation, see F. E. Brightman. 'Byzantine imperial coronations', *Journal of Theological Studies*, 2 (1900–1), pp. 359–92, especially pp. 383ff., where it is argued that unction was already material under Manuel Komnenos; M. Jugie (*Theologia dogmatica christianorum orientalium*, 3 (Paris, 1930), pp. 151–70) thinks that unction by the patriarch was introduced after 1204 (perhaps in 1208 for Theodore I Laskaris), in imitation of the West; G. Ostrogorsky ('Zur Kaisersalbung und Schilderhebung im spätbyzantinischen Krönungszeremoniell', *Historia*, 4 (1955), pp. 246–56) agrees; D. M. Nicol ('*Kaisersalbung*. The unction of emperors in late Byzantine coronation ritual', *Byzantine and Modern Greek Studies*, 2 (1976), pp. 37–52) distinguishes an unction with oil, perhaps western in origin, which may have appeared before 1204, and an unction with the *myron* which was later. See also L. Bréhier, *Les Institutions de l'empire byzantin* (Paris, 1949), pp. 13–15; A. Michel, *Die Kaisermacht in der Ostkirche (843–1204)* (Darmstadt, 1959), pp. 10–13; Bloch, *Les Rois thaumaturges* (n. 5), pp. 460–77; C. Walter, 'The significance of unction in Byzantine iconography', *Byzantine and Modern Greek Studies*, 2 (1976), pp. 53–73.
[122] Ed. de Boor (see ch. 1, n. 4), p. 473, ll. 1–3.
[123] *Breviarium historiae metricum*, ed. I. Bekker (Bonn, 1837), p. 193, verses 4517–19.
[124] *Homily X*, for the inauguration of the Virgin of the Pharos, ed. Laourdas, p. 104, trans. Mango, *Homilies of Photius* (see ch. 6, n. 72), pp. 179–81. For the concept of 'birth in the purple', see above, pp. 41ff.
[125] *Ep.* 98 (c. 868), ed. Laourdas and Westerink (see ch. 6, n. 29), I, pp. 133, 136.
[126] *Life of St Theophano*, 6, ed. Kurtz (see ch. 1, n. 81), p. 4. The incident occurs in Constantinople, in the church of the Theotokos in the quarter of Ta Bassou, where Theophano had taken shelter after a storm. It should be noted that the saints intervened through the intermediary of their images, not directly.

and prosperity.[127] Unction was believed to occur not during the course of a ceremony, but at the moment when God had chosen and revealed his choice. The martyr Diomedes, appearing in a dream, told the abbot of his convent to open the gate to Basil I, then still a vagabond, 'because he *had been anointed* by Christ to become emperor'.[128] There was later a tendency to make unction by God coincide with the ceremony of coronation by the patriarch, as if the 'consecration' happened simultaneously on earth and in heaven – what Psellos neatly called the fulfilment 'of the mystery of kingship'.[129] It is probably significant that at the end of the twelfth and beginning of the thirteenth centuries, while Niketas Choniates uses the expression *eis basilea chriesthai* in the sense of 'to be appointed emperor',[130] he employs the active form to say that the patriarch 'anointed' the emperor;[131] but for him it was probably still only a metaphor, as it was in the synodal ordinance of 24 March 1171 imposing an oath of loyalty on Manuel Komnenos and his descendants, which includes the usual play on words between the emperor who was 'the Lord's anointed' (*christos kyriou*) and Christ.[132] At the very end of the twelfth century, the imperial unction on which Balsamon based his theory in the passages discussed above was no more material than the episcopal unction which was its counterpart;[133] but nor was it 'symbolic', since it was the basis of the emperors' 'episcopal rights'. Through it, God himself renewed the Davidic alliance for each emperor, and above all for each dynasty which was attempting to establish itself.[134]

---

[127] *De cerimoniis*, I, 3, p. 43, line 4 (ed. Vogt (see ch. 2, n. 1), I, p. 36); I, 72 [63], p. 281; I, 82 [73], p. 368; I, 87 [78], p. 375.

[128] *Vita Basilii*, 9, in Theophanes Continuatus, ed. Bekker (see ch. 1, n. 4), pp. 223–4.

[129] *Chronographia*, ed. and trans. Renauld (see ch. 1, n. 47), I, p. 88 (of Michael V): 'Kai teleitai epi to Kaisari to tes basileias mysterion'.

[130] For example, of Alexis III Angelos in 1195 (ed. Van Dieten, p. 457), and of Nicholas Kannabos, 'anointed emperor' in spite of himself by the mob in 1204 (ibid., p. 562); see also the *Discourse* of Niketas Choniates, ed. K. N. Sathas, *Mesaionike Bibliotheke*, I (Athens/Paris/Venice, 1872), pp. 105ff, 113, where the emperor is Theodore Laskaris, but where Davidic unction remains a metaphorical notion. See Ostrogorsky, 'Zur Kaisersalbung und Schilderhebung' (n. 120), pp. 247–9; the contrary opinion is argued most notably by Christophilopoulou, 'Peri to problema' (see ch. 1, n. 76), pp. 382–5, who thinks that unction had become material by the twelfth century, possibly by the coronation of Manuel Komnenos.

[131] Michael II Kourkouas, promoted patriarch by the emperor Manuel Komnenos in 1143, 'anointed he who had anointed him': ed. Van Dieten, p. 52; the expression is doubly metaphorical.

[132] A. Papadopoulos-Kerameus, *Analekta hierosolymitikes stachyologias* (see ch. 3, n. 69), IV, p. 110; for this act, see Grumel-Darrouzès, *Regestes*, no. 1120.

[133] F. Brightman ('Byzantine imperial coronations' (n. 120)), Nicol, ('*Kaisersalbung*') and Marc Bloch (*Les Rois thaumaturges* (n. 120)) all believe, wrongly, that Balsamon refers to material unction as early as 1180/90. The contrary opinion was argued by Ostrogorsky ('Zur Kaisersalbung und Schilderhebung' (n. 38), p. 247, n. 1) and, more recently and at greater length, by V. Tiftixoglu ('Zur Genese der Kommentare des Theodoros Balsamon', p. 506, n. 103), who adds that the anonymous commentator of *Sinaiticus* understands imperial unction in the same way as Balsamon, and concludes that about 1195 unction was still not material.

[134] Walter, 'Significance of unction' (n. 120).

The Fourth Crusade probably marked a turning point. The coronation of Theodore Laskaris, on 6 April 1208, was perhaps the first which was accompanied by an unction performed by the patriarch with the holy chrism or *myron*, solemnly prepared on Maundy Thursday, three days before.[135] The western-style coronation of Baldwin I, in Constantinople on 23 May 1204, may have served as a model. Far from the historic capital, in the more modest context of Nicaea, it may have seemed necessary to give material form to the 'mystery of kingship'. The Church, now the only unitary power capable of holding secessionist tendencies in check, was able to use this occasion to put its mark more firmly on imperial coronation. Taking advantage of the request of the clergy of Constantinople who wanted a council to meet for the appointment of a patriarch, Theodore Laskaris, not yet officially emperor, chose a date that would allow the newly appointed patriarch to prepare the sacred chrism (*to theion tou myrou chrisma*) at the 'usual' time, that is, during Easter week.[136] For his part, Michael Autoreianos, almost immediately after his election on 20 March 1208, took a number of initiatives designed to strengthen imperial authority, exhorting the army in a circular which contains surprising echoes of holy war, remitting the sins of the soldiers and of the emperor, and requiring the bishops assembled in Nicaea to swear an oath of dynastic fealty.[137] The circumstances were favourable, therefore, for a modification of the ceremonial, but the first certain evidence is a little later. It comes in a letter from the patriarch Germanos II reproaching Demetrios Chomatianos, archbishop of Bulgaria, for having crowned Theodore Angelos Doukas at Thessalonike in 1225 or 1227, so creating a rival to the emperor of Nicaea, John III Vatatzes. Germanos asked the archbishop, with rather laboured irony, from which wild olive tree he had procured the oil of unction, from which perfumery he had purchased this precious but ineffective myrrh and what made him think he had the right to perform the 'consecration of the *myron*'. Imperial unction, he said, was a sacrament of the same order and the same efficacy as the others, it was comparable to baptism without being quite its equal, and in normal times one used not the *myron* but an oil specially sanctified by the patriarch.[138]

---

[135] For the consecration and composition of the *myron* or chrism using oil and some fifty-seven aromatic substances, see L. Petit, 'Du pouvoir de consacrer le Saint Chrême', and 'Composition et consécration du Saint Chrême', *Echos d'Orient*, 3 (1899–1900), pp. 1–7, 129–42. More recently, P. Menebisoglou, *Meletemata peri hagiou myrou* (Athens, 1999).

[136] A. Heisenberg, *Neue Quellen zur Geschichte des lateinischen Kaisertums und der Kirchenunion, II: Die Unionsverhandlungen vom 30. August 1206; Patriarchenwahl und Kaiserkrönung in Nikaia 1208*, Sitzungsb. Bayer. Akad. d. Wiss. Philos.-philol. und hist. Kl. 1923, 2 (Munich, 1923), pp. 35–46.

[137] N. Oikonomides, 'Cinq actes inédits du patriarche Michel Autoreianos', *REB*, 25 (1967), pp. 17–24; Laurent, *Regestes*, nos. 1205–7.

[138] Pitra, *Analecta sacra et classica* (n. 20), VI, cols. 483–6 (no. 113), with Chomatianos' response, pp. 487–98 (no. 114); Laurent, *Regestes*, no. 1244; confirmation in Nikephoros Gregoras, who

Whatever its precise date, the change is noticed in the Chronicles, where we find the emperor 'anointed by the patriarch', and in the new ceremonial, which the fourteenth-century sources describe with very minor variations.[139] In the ambo where they are both standing, the emperor bares his head then bows it, and the patriarch pronounces in a low voice the following prayer:

> Emperor of reigning emperors and Lord of lords, you who have, by your prophet Samuel, anointed with your sacred oil your servant David king and captain of your people, send... your power by my sinful hands and anoint this person as our emperor, captain of your faithful people!

The patriarch then anoints the emperor by tracing a sign of the cross on his head with the divine chrism, and proclaims the word 'Holy' in a loud voice, repeated three times by those on the ambo, then by all present. Lastly, he crowns the sovereign. In the case of the son of a living emperor, his father crowns him, but it is always the patriarch who anoints. At the end of a long evolution, the Byzantine coronation had become a consecration and the leader of the Church was asked not only to provide the support of his prayers and the solemnity of his Church,[140] but to administer a sacrament.

FROM THE ROD OF MOSES TO THE ROD OF THE VERGER

Unction did not gain in importance by becoming a sacrament. On the contrary, it was, so to speak, taken over by the clergy. The role of the patriarch, alone qualified to prepare the sacred chrism, broke the direct link which unction had signalled between the emperor-priest and God. Rather than being the model for others, imperial unction was now seen as no more than a pale imitation of baptismal or episcopal unction. Paradoxically, while it had been possible to

---

wrote more than a century after the event: *Historia Romana*, ed. L. Schopen and I. Bekker, I (Bonn, 1829), p. 26. G. Prinzing, 'Die *Antigraphe* des Patriarchen Germanos II. an Erzbischof Demetrios Chomatenos von Ohrid und die Korrespondenz zum nikäisch-epirotischen Konflikt 1212–1233', *Rivista di Studi byzantini e slavi*, 3 (1983) (*Miscellanea A. Pertusi*), especially pp. 58–60; G. Prinzing, 'Das byzantinische Kaisertum im Umbruch. Zwischen regionaler Aufspaltung und erneuter Zentrierung in den Jahren 1204–1282', in *Legitimation und Funktion des Herrschers vom ägyptischen Pharao zum neuzeitlichen Diktator*, ed. R. Gundlach and H. Weber (Stuttgart, 1992), especially pp. 162–3.

[139] The late manuscripts of the Euchologion, noted by Goar in the commentary on his *Euchologion*, p. 729; the story of the coronation of Andronikos III Palaiologos in 1325, in Johannes Kantakouzenos, *Historiae*, I, 41, ed. L. Schopen, I (Bonn, 1828), pp. 196–204. (for unction, p. 198); the *Treatise on the offices* of Pseudo-Kodinos, written between 1347 and 1390, chapter 7, ed. Verpeaux, *Traité des offices* (see ch. 2, n. 16), p. 252ff. (for unction, p. 258); the protocol of Manuel II's coronation in 1391/2, published by Verpeaux after the *Treatise on the offices*, pp. 353–61. See also M. Arranz, 'L'Aspect rituel de l'onction des empereurs de Constantinople et de Moscou', in *Roma, Costantinopoli, Mosca. Da Roma alla Terza Roma, Studi I, Seminario 21 aprile 1981* (Naples, 1983), pp. 407–15.

[140] See above, pp. 80–3.

consider unction without oil as real unction, unction with oil was only symbolic. It soon ceased even to be a sacrament.

In the West, where trends were set, the change was marked and almost continuous from the end of the twelfth century. In a letter addressed in 1204 to the archbishop of Tirnovo, leader of the Bulgarian Church, Pope Innocent III explained that he had anointed an eastern bishop in Rome because the East, unlike the West, and wrongly, did not accompany episcopal consecration with material unction.[141] He went on to develop the idea that it was important to distinguish two aspects of episcopal unction: bodily unction, external and material, and spiritual unction, that of the heart. The latter was not only a sign but a sacrament, which had an efficacy of its own if it was worthily received; the former, both by the composition of the chrism and by the way it was administered to the head and hands of the bishop, symbolised the intervention of the Spirit and the powers it conferred. The unction of kings, similar in the Old Testament to that of priests and of prophets, was no longer, since Christ's coming, performed on the head, but on the arm or shoulder. It was to the pontiff, head of the Church, and to the Church itself, body of Christ and *regale sacerdotium*, that the kingship of the Son of God had passed. There was, accordingly, a big difference between the *auctoritas* of the pontiff and *potestas* of the prince.[142] This theory had its opponents – Robert Grossetête, in the second half of the thirteenth century, and above all Jean Golein, in the fourteenth century. In his *Traité du Sacre*, Jean invoked Samuel's words to Saul when he anointed him: 'Thou...shalt be turned into another man' (I Samuel [I Kings], X: 6), or clumsily tried to show that 'when the king divests himself, this signifies that he relinquishes the worldly state, in anticipation of taking that of the royal religion' and that 'he is as completely cleansed of his sins as he who first enters a tested religion' (that is, who becomes a monk).[143] But, this rearguard action notwithstanding, a new sacramental doctrine prevailed, which drew a fundamental distinction between the sacraments (*sacramenta*) by which God granted his sanctifying grace and the sacramentals (*sacramentalia*) instituted by the Church in imitation of the sacraments for the spiritual benefit of those who received them.[144] Royal unction was simply a 'sacramental', a symbolic ceremony conceived and orchestrated by the Church, which controlled it, in imitation of episcopal and baptismal unction. How, therefore, in the words of

---

[141] See above, p. 268.

[142] 'In capite vero pontificis sacramentalis est delibutio conservata, quia personam capitis in pontificali officio repraesentat. Refert autem inter pontificis et principis unctionem, quia caput pontificis chrismate consecratur, brachium vero principis oleo delinitur, ut ostendatur quanta sit differentia inter auctoritatem pontificis et principis potestatem': the letter is inserted into the *Decretales*, I, 15 (*De sacra unctione*), ed. E. Friedberg, *Decretalium collectiones*, Corpus juris canonici, II (Graz, 1959), cols. 131–4 (col. 133 for the passage quoted).

[143] Bloch, *Les Rois thaumaturges* (n. 5), p. 197.

[144] See 'Sacramentaux' in *DTC*, XIV, 1 (1939), cols. 465–82.

Filesac, in the seventeenth century, criticising Balsamon's commentary, could a murderer-emperor have his crime erased by an unction which was not even a sacrament?

In the West, the Roman reform established a more-or-less coherent and continuous tradition. It was different in the East, where the same questions (Should different types of unction be distinguished? Was imperial unction a sacrament?) received different answers. Nicholas Kabasilas, in the first half of the fourteenth century, drew on the sources of Byzantine spirituality when he defended the unity of the 'mystery of the most holy *myron*', which, like a sacrament and whatever its form, 'made active the spiritual activities'. He wrote:

> Whereas the Ancient Law anointed kings and priests in the same fashion, the rule of the Church consecrates the chief emperors by the *myron* whereas it lays hands on priests while invoking the grace of the Spirit; this is to show that both rites amount to the same thing and that both have the same efficacy. Further, the two rites share the same name, as the latter may also be called unction (*chrisma*) and the former communication of the spirit (*pneumatos koinonia*). In fact, the consecration [without material unction] of priests is called unction of priests by the most holy authors and, conversely, for those who are initiated by the mystery of the *myron* [the emperors, but also the baptised, who receive a material unction], one prays they will have and one believes they obtain communication of the Holy Spirit. And to show to the initiated what this initiation may be, it is called the seal of the gift of the Spirit: which is, in fact, the formula that is pronounced for those who are anointed.[145]

At the beginning of the fifteenth century, however, Symeon of Thessalonike developed a very different approach, that of a defender of ecclesiastical prerogatives. In the *De sacro templo*,[146] he asked: 'Why is the emperor anointed with the *myron* and consecrated with prayers?', a surprising question, which implicitly puts the imperial office at a distance from the *sacerdotium* and allows the Church sole control of anointment. His answer confirms this; it emphasised the role of the patriarch and resorted to an exclusively Christological symbolism. The hierarch, after obtaining from the future emperor a written and autograph commitment to follow Orthodoxy, hands him, in the ambo, the insignia of power and then anoints him in the form of the cross, in order to make it plain that it is Christ who confers the Spirit, makes him participate in his victory, bestows on him his power and, by describing him as 'Holy', recognises him as the leader of the 'sanctified' [= the baptised]. In the *De sacris ordinationibus*,[147] Symeon

---

[145] Goar, *Euchologion*, pp. 290–1 (prayer for baptism); Nicholas Kabasilas, *The Life in Christ*, III, 1–2, ed. and trans. M.-H. Congourdeau, *La vie en Christ*, SC 355 (Paris, 1989), I, pp. 236–8. Kabasilas seems to believe that imperial unction was still performed with the chrism, unlike the purely spiritual episcopal unction.

[146] 146, PG 155, col. 353.   [146] 207, PG 155, col. 417.

is more specific. He explains that the patriarch is called 'Holy master' and that
he is credited with an 'eminent sanctity' because he is consecrated in the Holy
Spirit; and he adds that the patriarch, when he anoints the emperor, also proclaims him 'Holy', but that this is simply a manner of speaking justified by the
circumstances and by the unction of the *myron*, that same unction which had
led St Paul to call all baptised Christians 'Holy brethren'. In reality,

> the emperor has none of the *charismata* of the priests, nor of the apostles,
> the prophets or the *didaskaloi*. He is called 'holy' only by the unction of the
> *myron*; whereas the patriarch receives, at the same time as the *charismata*,
> the fact of being 'holy' by the prayers of consecration.

This amounted to a clear and word for word refutation of the arguments of
Balsamon. The spiritual unction of the bishops (and in particular of the patriarch)
is a true sacrament which confers *charismata* on them; the material unction of
the emperor is much inferior and a primarily symbolic reiteration of that of
baptism, which does not allow him to claim any ecclesiastical privileges. A
little further on,[148] Symeon evokes the ancient custom, changed in his day,
which required a newly consecrated bishop or patriarch to go to the emperor,
read a prayer for his salvation, cense and bless him while he bowed his head,
and himself salute him with an inclination of the head 'because of temporal
power'. This was a good opportunity to compare 'the Lord's anointed by the
Spirit' and 'the Lord's anointed by the *myron*', but with nuances and examples
(*Life of Amphilochios, Life of Ambrose*, deferential attitude of Constantine the
Great to Pope Sylvester and the bishops of Nicaea I) which left no doubt as to
the relative importance of the two unctions.

With or without prejudice, the whole coronation ceremonial was downgraded
and accompanied by reductive commentaries. The *Treatise on the Offices* describes the new version with balletic precision.[149] The emperors and their wives
took up positions on a platform. Before the *trisagion*, the patriarch left the
bema and mounted the ambo by the east staircase, with the principal archontes
of the Church. The emperor who was to be crowned joined him by climbing
the west staircase, the one that 'faced the Beautiful Doors'[150] – a significant
difference, since, once anointed and crowned, the emperor descended by the
east staircase, 'facing the *solea* and the *bema*', where, according to Symeon of
Thessalonike,[151] the clergy in minor orders stood 'excluded from the *bema*'.
When the moment of the Great Entry arrived, the most important of the deacons
invited the emperor to accompany them as far as the *prothesis*:

---

[148] *De sacris ordinationibus*, 218, PG 155, cols. 429–32.
[149] Chapter VII, ed. and trans. Verpeaux (see ch. 2, n. 16), pp. 252–73.
[150] Verpeaux (p. 259, note 2) wrongly identifies these as the doors in the chancel barrier, whereas
it should be those between the narthex and the central nave.
[151] PG 155, 345.

> While he is still outside the *prothesis*, the sovereign puts a golden cope over his robe of silk (*sakkos*) and his belt (*diadema*). In the right hand, he holds the cross which he customarily carries when he is wearing the crown [*stemma*], in the left, he holds a rod (*narthex*). He then occupies the ecclesiastical rank which is called that of the *depotatos*. Holding both the cross and the rod, the emperor precedes all [the procession of] the 'entry'...After making, according to custom, a tour of the nave, [the procession] goes as far as the *solea*. All the others remain standing outside, while the emperor, crossing the *solea*, goes as far as the patriarch, standing before the Holy Doors. They both remain standing, the patriarch on the inside [of the *bema*], the emperor on the outside.

The emperor only went through the chancel barrier to enter the sanctuary when he received communion.[152] There followed some of the liturgical acts emphasised in the old ceremonial and seized on by Balsamon; the sovereign censes the altar and the patriarch, he removes the *stemma* from his head and communicates in both kinds, himself lifting the chalice to his mouth, 'in the manner of the priests (*hosper kai hoi hiereis*)'.

To this significant but fairly neutral description we may add the commentaries of Symeon of Thessalonike, much more 'committed' and again illuminating.[153] More than two centuries later, they reply, in effect, to those of Balsamon by emphasising the emperor's place in the Church, after the clergy and in the first rank of the laity. The emperor communicates before the unordained monks 'because of the second unction' (that is, the unction with the *myron* which repeated, at the coronation, baptismal unction). Except during his coronation, when tradition authorised him to enter the sanctuary, the emperor normally received communion on a portable altar (*antiminsion*) without passing through the chancel barrier; he received the bread from the hand of the patriarch, like the deacons, and drank from the patriarch's chalice, again like the deacons. This relative privilege derived from unction, which gave the emperor an ecclesiastical rank equivalent to that of *depotatos*[154] and the title of defender of the Church. In the palace of Christ, sole eternal king, the emperor was answerable to the patriarch, who alone was qualified to confer the insignia of power and to sanctify kingship, because he possessed on earth the power of the Holy Spirit. Anointing by the patriarch signified that the emperor was recognised as Christ's representative and promised to act in conformity with this divine model, as *christomimetes* (imitator of Christ). He was clothed in a liturgical garment, that of *depotatos*, which symbolically signified that he would ensure that order prevailed in the

---

[152] Verpeaux (p. 267) translates 'the emperor goes towards the sanctuary' instead of 'enters the sanctuary'.

[153] *De sacro templo*, 142–50, PG 155, cols. 352–6.

[154] In the faulty edition of the PG, *despotatos* clearly should be corrected, here and elsewhere, to *depotatos = deputatus*.

Church, and he held in his hand a flexible, light rod (*rabdos*), which signified that he would punish with sweetness and indulgence, and not with anger and harshness.

Let us linger for a moment on this significant detail or rather this loss of significance of a reductive ceremonial. It was a breathtaking fall, in which the emperor was reduced from the rank of quasi-bishop, or, at an already lower level, of quasi-*epistemonarches*, to the status of quasi-laity, so breaking the direct link which had made him answerable to God alone. A somewhat similar downgrading has been noted in the West, when the pope ceased to confer clerical status on the emperor he had consecrated, so as to equate him with a 'canon of St Peter' or sub-deacon.[155] But in that part of Christendom, the debate about the emperor-priest involved different issues, was dissipated in the multiplicity of kingdoms and scarcely went beyond the level of symbolism. It was not the same in the East, where the sole emperor, anointed and recognised as sacred by the grace of unction, believed himself and called himself not only chosen, but invested by God alone. His Christian legitimacy was dependent on this, that is, it made sense only in the context of a continuity between the Old and the New Testament or a projection of one onto the other. That is why theoreticians of imperial power, from Eusebios to Balsamon, were doomed to use the word 'quasi' (quasi-priest, quasi-episcopal *charismata*), probably less in order to water down the assertion of the sacerdotal nature of the imperial function than to intimate that it was wholly true only in the Old Testament register. The 'priesthood' of the emperor was in no way symbolic, but it was 'metaphorical' in the sense that it had to be 'transposed' from one register to another.

All it needed, consequently, to downgrade the emperor, was to break the chain that linked him to David, to cause the grace of unction to be conveyed by the hands and the oil of the patriarch, and to drag the emperor from the Judaic past into Christian times. Later commentators set out to do this by systematically eliminating from the revised ceremonial all the Old Testament references of the old ceremonial and by now offering only Christological interpretations. The unction was no longer that of Saul but that of Christ in baptism; the emperor was no longer a New David but an imitator of Christ subject to the Church; and in spite of the word *rabdos* which was no longer able to deceive, the miraculous rod of Moses was now seen as no more than the beadle's staff or a policeman's truncheon. Deprived of all *charisma*, the emperor still retained an ecclesiastical function, at the very lowest level, without which he would no longer even be a Christian monarch; but, once 'priest and king' in the order of Melchizedek, he was now simply a verger in the Church of Christ.

[155] Bloch, *Les Rois thaumaturges* (n. 5), pp. 201–3.

9. 'Caesaropapism' and the theory of the 'two powers'

'EASTERN CAESAROPAPISM'

Where should we situate Byzantium in the spectrum of political systems that are largely identified with a religion, where the separation between the spiritual sphere and the temporal system is not wholly effective and where the sovereign claims to be chosen by God? Our examination of its history and texts has revealed a number of shifting and contrasting answers, often non-answers, which we must now relate to a summary classification in which an eastern model of theocracy and caesaropapism is opposed to a western model based on the autonomy of the 'two powers': non-separation on the one hand, separation on the other.

To understand what 'caesaropapism' means, we need to start from the precise notion to which this more fluid notion has both been added and opposed – that of theocracy.[1] A society that is directed by God, over which He 'reigns' (I Samuel [I Kings] VIII: 7) and where He decides everything by making His will known directly or indirectly may be described as theocratic. The word was coined by Flavius Josephus in connection with the Jewish people,[2] who provide the best reference point for all forms of theocracy – original theocracy of the Covenant, dominated by the great figure of Moses, theocracy of the anointed kings, theocracy of the high priests. The rigidity of the system was only slightly relaxed by the creation of the Levitical priesthood and the emergence of a political power; it was still God who decreed and the prophet who spoke in His name, or interpreted the Law that was His expression. Thomas Hobbes,

---

[1] See the valuable collective work *Religionstheorie und politische Theologie*, ed. J. Taubes, I–III (Munich/Paderborn/Vienna/Zurich, 1987), especially B. Lang, 'Theokratie: Geschichte und Bedeutung eines Begriffs in Soziologie und Ethnologie', III, pp. 11–28.

[2] *Against Apion*, II, 165: p. 804 of *The Works of Josephus*, trans. William Whiston (London, 1860, revised ed. Peabody, 1987): 'our legislator [Moses] had no regard to any of these forms [monarchy, oligarchy, democracy] but he ordained our government to be what, by a strained expression, may be termed a Theocracy, by ascribing the authority and the power to God' (p. 359 of Loeb ed.).

and later Spinoza, admirably described this model and the contract with God it supposes and transfer of Law it imposes. But whereas Spinoza declared that the time of the prophets was over and warned against any interference in the state by ministers of religion,[3] Hobbes derived from the Jewish example a 'Christian Common-Wealth' in which the sovereign would occupy 'the same place... that Abraham had in his own family', would alone know 'what is, or what is not the Word of God', and would be by divine right the 'supreme pastor', with responsibility for his flock and governing the Church in his kingdom.[4] Such speculations and analyses have led sociologists, going beyond Jewish history, to distinguish between political organisations based on a revelation and closely bound up with a religion; those where the priests are content to legitimate temporal power (hierocracies); those where the chief priest or leader of the community of believers holds ex officio supreme power (theocracies properly speaking); and those where the temporal sovereignty more or less annexes the religious sphere (forms of caesaropapism).[5] Thus, theocracy is opposed to caesaropapism, and a priest-king model to a king-priest model.

The word 'caesaropapism' was intended, therefore, to condemn any 'lay' sovereign who saw himself as a pope. It had a sociological content, but an obviously polemical aim. When Iustus Henning Böhmer (1674–1749), professor at the University of Halle, devoted a passage in his manual of Protestant ecclesiastical law to the two principal abuses of power in religious matters, 'Papo-Caesaria' and 'Caesaro-Papia', it was in order to denounce and dismiss, in the name of the reformed Church, both the pope who arrogated to himself political power and the lay sovereigns who assumed responsibility for religious problems, as Justinian had done long ago.[6] Of these two expressions, only the second caught on; it was increasingly used in the second half of the nineteenth century, less as a theoretical notion than as a well-aimed insult targeting Byzantium and its Orthodox heirs, identifying 'Constantinian' or 'Justinian' interventionism as the principal cause of the 'schism' between Christian East and Christian West, and pushing to the point of incompatibility the distinction between the spiritual and the temporal 'power'. This imprecise concept was above all a killer word, and it should not be toned down by being given too conciliatory a definition; nor can its significance be appreciated without reference

[3] Spinoza, *Theological-Political Treatise*, especially ch. 17 and 18; see E. Balibar, *Spinoza et la politique* (Paris, 1985), pp. 55–62.

[4] Thomas Hobbes (1588–1679), *Leviathan*, part 3: 'Of a Christian Commonwealth'; see, in particular, ch. 40 ('Of the rights of the Kingdom of God, in Abraham, Moses, the High Priests and the Kings of Judah') and 42 ('Of power ecclesiastical'), pp. 312–21, 329–90 in Worlds Classic Paperback (Oxford, 1996).

[5] Distinctions made by Max Weber in *Wirtschaft und Gesellschaft*, 5th ed. (Tübingen, 1976), p. 689, and discussed by Lang, 'Theokratie' (n. 1), pp. 21–2.

[6] I. H. Boehmer, *Ius ecclesiasticum protestantium*, 5th ed., 1 (Halle, 1756), pp. 10–11: 'Iustinianus, a clero deceptus, sub praetextu salutis ecclesiasticae mirum in modum Caesaro-Papiam exercuit'. I am grateful to my colleague Bernhard Lang for this reference.

to the various strands of thought that led to its stark formulation and explain its survival. A rapid historiographical survey is thus a precondition for an in-depth analysis.

Neither the issues nor the connections can be understood without reference to the double divide of the Reformation and Counter-Reformation, that is, a confrontation which gave birth to Christian historiography in response to a critical reflection on the 'truth' of Christianity before it got embroiled in history. The Protestants were instinctively mistrustful of all historical legitimacy, of an evolution that had distinguished the clergy from Christians as a whole, and of a tradition that had made the Church into a power. In his tracts *Of the Liberty of a Christian Man* (1520)[7] and *Of Temporal Authority* (1523),[8] Luther pushed to the point of paradox the distinction between the spiritual and the temporal, grafted on to that between the 'two kingdoms' of St Augustine; the Christian who belonged to both the spiritual and the temporal kingdoms is both absolutely free and absolutely enslaved. If God had instituted two rules, it was because only a tiny elite of true Christians belonged to his kingdom; the vast majority had need of the 'temporal sword' and should submit to it according to the teaching of Paul (Romans, 13: 1: 'For there is no power but of God') and Peter (I Peter, 2: 13: 'Submit yourselves to every ordinance of man'). But, though temporal princes derive their power from God and though they are often Christian, they cannot aspire 'to govern in a Christian way' and in accord with the Gospels. 'It is impossible for a Christian reign to extend to the whole world, or even to a whole country.' It was impossible to reconcile a religion conceived as primarily personal and a state defined as primarily repressive; and Luther mocked both the temporal sovereigns 'who arrogate to themselves the right to sit on the throne of God, regulate consciences and the faith and... bring the Holy Spirit into the classroom' and the popes and bishops 'become temporal princes' who claim to be invested with a 'power' and not simply a 'function'. This radical distinction between the temporal and the spiritual did not lead, consequently, to the recognition of two powers, 'because all Christians belong truly to the ecclesiastical estate' and there was no reason to refuse Christian princes the 'titles of priest and bishop'.[9] Such principles proved difficult to handle, and disturbances of the peace sometimes caused Lutheranism to evolve in the direction of caesaropapism (and Calvinism in the direction of theocracy); but this new approach to 'religion' indubitably stimulated debate and made

---

[7] *Von der Freiheit eines Christenmenschen*; see the bilingual edition of M. Gravier, *Luther. Les grand écrits réformateurs* (Paris, 1955), pp. 252–301.

[8] *Von weltlicher Obrigkeit. Wie weit man ihr gehorsam schuldig sei*. See the bilingual edition of Luther's works on this subject: *Luther et l'autorité temporelle, 1521–1525, Textes allemands originaux, traduction, introduction et notes* by J. Lefebre (Paris, 1973).

[9] *To the Christian nobility of the German nation (An den christlichen Adel deutscher Nation)* (1520), ed. M. Gravier (n. 7), pp. 82–3. The passage concludes that the separation of the two powers has no basis.

possible in the nineteenth century the radical reappraisal of the origins of the Christian empire.

The Council of Trent (1545–63) proposed no doctrine directly on this issue, but by inserting the church as intermediary between Christians and God, and by giving as much weight to tradition as to the scriptures, it bound together what Luther had set out to separate. During the course of the council and after, more effort was put into uniting the two powers than into differentiating them; a conciliatory policy attempted to achieve a difficult balance between religious universalism and the national churches, with the Jesuits upholding the thesis of the 'indirect power' of the popes in political matters. Above all, history was summoned in support. The thirteen volumes of the Lutheran Croat Matthias Vlačič/Flacius Illyricus and the 'centuriaters of Magdeburg' (1559–75), which had raised high the flag of rebellion by calling Gregory VII a 'monster' and spread consternation in Roman circles, were eventually countered by the dozen tomes of Caesar Baronius's *Annales Ecclesiastici* (1588–1607).[10] In this history of Christianity, Constantine the Great became a key figure. Baronius saw him through the eyes of Eusebios of Caesarea, his apologist, but accepted the orthodox and clerical amendments to the legend according to which the first Christian emperor had been baptised in Rome by Sylvester and the temporal power of the popes and their regalian privileges were based on an imperial donation.[11] It is hardly surprising that the successive volumes of the *Annales*, all dedicated to lay princes or Roman pontiffs, were warmly welcomed in the Orthodox world, at the cost of some revisions instituted by the Russian hierarchy.[12] The union of the temporal and the spiritual was no more disputed in Catholic Europe than in eastern Christendom, and Constantine was its symbol. When, in 1630, Jean Morin, priest of the Oratory, dedicated a *History of the Deliverance of the Christian Church by the Emperor Constantine* to the king of France,[13] and, in opposition to Baronius, rejected the Roman baptism and the Donation,[14] it was

[10] For the production of the *Annales ecclesiastici* in response to the 'Centuriaters of Magdeburg', see, in particular, A. Walz, 'Baronio *Pater Annalium ecclesiasticorum*' in the collective work *A Cesare Baronio, Scritti varii* (Sora (= birthplace of Baronius), 1963), pp. 259–87; F. P. Sonntag, 'Matthias Flacius Illyricus und die Magdeburger Centurien', ibid., pp. 289–98. More generally, C. K. Pullapilly, *Caesar Baronius, Counter-Reformation Historian* (Notre Dame, Indiana/London, 1975).

[11] *Annales ecclesiastici*, annis 322–30; vol. IX of the original edition was devoted to Constantine and dedicated to the king of France, Henri IV, on whose behalf Baronius had intervened when he had been under excommunication.

[12] Pullapilly, *Caesar Baronius* (n. 10), pp. 62–3.

[13] The full title is even longer and more explicit: *Histoire de la délivrance de l'Eglise chrestienne par l'empereur Constantin, et de la grandeur et souveraineté temporelle donnée à l'Eglise romaine par les roys de France* (History of the deliverance of the Christian Church by the Emperor Constantine, and of the greatness and temporal sovereignty given to the Roman Church by the Kings of France) (Paris, 1630).

[14] He denounced the 'fraud' of the Donation, fabricated – he believed – to subject the spiritual and temporal authority of the popes to the Germans, and noted that Balsamon was the first Greek writer to refer to it: ibid., p. 449.

only to maintain that it had been in France that the emperor had been converted and seen the cross, that he had been catechised by French bishops and that the kings of France were 'the sole authors of the greatness and temporal power of the Holy See'. Ultramontanism and Gallicanism championed different interests, but were as one with regard to the beginnings of the Christian empire.[15]

It was many years before a Lutheran spirit seriously damaged the Constantinian myth by a fundamental critique of 'political Christianity', which was to lead to the condemnation of caesaropapism in Protestant countries. Santo Mazzarino,[16] that thorough researcher, noted that a certain Johann Christian Hesse, at Iena in 1713, had submitted a thesis with the revealing subtitle *De discrimine christianismi veri et politici*.[17] It was perhaps this that set the ball rolling. Constantine was now the villain of the piece; he had opted for Christianity for political reasons and had made religion serve what he perceived as his own interests. In 1853 a work by Jacob Burckhardt presented the case against this false Christianity in the service of power, hardened the psychological portrait of a deceitful and unscrupulous Constantine, and criticised Eusebios for having travestied the truth.[18] By choice a western humanist, by instinct typically Protestant, Burckhardt could imagine only a perpetual tension between religion and power; he rejected all forms of state Christianity and analysed with obvious antipathy the system he called 'Byzantinismus', which would soon be given the name 'caesaropapism'. He compared it to Islam, that is, rejected it as un-European.[19] The historical interpretation here played upon on all sorts of moral opposites: sincerity and opportunism, religion and politics, Church and state and already, in the background, West and East.

In much the same way, the moral critique of 'political Christianity' later gave way to a more fundamental critique of 'political theology'. Erik Peterson set out to define and eradicate this perversion in a brilliant essay on *Monotheism as a Political Problem*.[20] It was published in Leipzig in 1935, in the context of Nazi Germany, with immediately apparent allusions to the dangers of a monolithic

[15] M. Fumaroli, 'Cross, crown and tiara: the Constantinian myth between Paris and Rome (1590–1690)', in *Piero della Francesca and his legacy*, ed. M. A. Lavin (Hanover/London, 1995), pp. 89–102.

[16] 'Burckhardt politologo. L'età di Costantino e la moderna ideazione storiografica', in Santo Mazzarino, *Il basso impero: antico, tardoantico ed èra costantiniana*, 1 (Bari, 1974), pp. 32–50.

[17] J. C. Hesse, *Dissertatio historico-pragmatica, qua Constantinum Magnum ex rationibus politicis christianum . . .* (Iena, 1713). The president of the jury before whom the thesis was defended was Burkhard Gotthelf Struve.

[18] J. Burckhardt, *Die Zeit Constantin's des Grossen* (Basle, 1853, 2nd ed. Leipzig, 1880).

[19] A. von Martin, *Die Religion Jacob Burckhardt. Eine Studie zum Thema Humanismus und Christentum*, 2nd ed. (Munich, 1947), especially pp. 112–29; A. von Martin, *Nietzsche und Burckhardt, zwei geistige Welten im Dialog*, 4th ed. (Munich, 1947); W. E. Kaegi, *Jacob Burckhardt. Eine Biographie*, I–III (Basle, 1947–1982); J. Irmscher, 'Jacob Burckhardts Konstantinsbild', in *Jacob Burckhardt und die Antike*, ed. B. Betthausen and M. Kunze (Mainz, 1998), pp. 89–96.

[20] *Der Monotheismus als politisches Problem. Ein Beitrag zur Geschichte der politischen Theologie im Imperium Romanum* (Leipzig, 1935). E. Peterson is also the author of *Heis Theos.*

and charismatic power, and with aims that the author spelled out in 1947, once the storm had passed. The spotlight had shifted from Constantine, now relegated to the sidelines, to Eusebios of Caesarea. The theologian, historian and panegyrist was transformed for the purpose into a dangerous ideologue (and as such discredited), who wanted to situate Christianity in the continuation of the Hellenistic-Judaic philosophy of Alexandria and integrate it into Roman history. The notion of divine monarchy, which the Arians and Eusebios developed and which the Trinitarian dogma combated, should not be understood as a theological response to the problem of divinity, but as a political response to the risks of a break up of the Roman empire. This is why the case of Eusebios was exemplary, and why it was liberating to proclaim the one and threefold God; this straightaway located the religion of Christ beyond Judaism, making it impossible to project on to temporal government, in this world, models of Christian kingship and 'peace' which could only be fulfilled in God. To the erroneous eschatology of Eusebios, which exaggerated the importance of the empire in the history of salvation, Erik Peterson opposed the separation of the 'two cities' and made his choice even clearer by dedicating his book to St Augustine. He thus sketched out a confrontation, which others would pursue with less subtlety, between a secretly arianising and totalitarian East and a West which had been able to rid itself of the political theology consequent upon monotheism and so deny all justification to a contamination of religion by politics. Erik Peterson was neither the first nor the last to make a connection between Arian 'subordinationism'[21] and the ideal of a monarch who, like the Byzantine emperor, received his sacredness and his mission to lead men to salvation directly from God; but he was the only one who, starting from this historical perception of a caesaropapism dating back to the fourth century, proceeded to a general condemnation of all political speculation based on Christian theology. Carl Schmitt responded in 1969–70 in a text which was unconvincing when it dealt with history, but more interesting, if violent and confused, when it claimed for sociology the right to study the secularisation of Christian concepts and models.[22]

Whether they had read the 1935 essay or not, many historians opted for this approach, making Eusebios, whose Arianism was nevertheless condemned, the inspiration and spokesperson of 'Byzantinism', that is, of caesaropapism; they

---

Epigraphische, formgeschichtliche und religionsgeschichtliche Untersuchungen (Göttingen, 1926).

[21] That is, the tendency to subordinate the Son to the Father in the Trinity instead of accepting their equality and their 'consubstantiality'.

[22] C. Schmitt, *Politische Theologie II. Die Legende von der Erledigung jeder politischen Theologie* (Berlin, 1970, repr. 1984); reprinted in part with the title, 'Eusebius als Prototyp politischer Theologie', in *Die Kirche angesichts der konstantinianischen Wende*, ed. G. Ruhbach (Darmstadt, 1976), pp. 220–35. Carl Schmitt had already published *Politische Theologie, Vier Kapitel zur Lehre von der Souveränität* (1922, 2nd ed. 1934, repr. Berlin, 1985).

conformed to the inverted myth of a cynical Constantine the Great and opposed a western to an eastern 'mentality'.[23]

While one can quite reasonably trace a line of thought that leads from the Reformation to Burckhardt and Peterson,[24] and that developed the concept of caesaropapism on the basis of a critique of all religious power, a denunciation of 'political Christianity' and a rejection of all 'political theology', it remains difficult to see a more specifically French historiographical trend, sometimes slightly tinged with Catholic anti-clericalism, and which reached similar conclusions on the basis of an analysis of 'modernity', as anything other than academic in origin. The starting point was probably the last chapter of *The Ancient City* of Fustel de Coulanges (1864), where he set out to show how Christianity had 'altered the conditions of government' and 'marked the end of ancient society'.[25] He emphasised both the universality of a religious message which broke the ties linking cults to the family and the city, and the internalisation of faith and prayer, which enfranchised the individual and made him conscious of his liberty. What had been the privilege of a tiny elite of Stoic philosophers became the prerogative of humanity as a whole – a separation between 'private and public virtues':

> [Christianity] professed that the state and religion had nothing in common; it separated what the whole of Antiquity had combined. It may also be remarked that, for three centuries, the new religion existed wholly outside of the operation of the State, was able to manage without its protection and even to fight against it: these three centuries established a gulf between the sphere of government and that of religion. And as the memory of this glorious epoch has never faded, it has followed that this distinction has become a common and indisputable truth, which the best efforts of a sector among the clergy have been unable to eradicate.

Here, history is given a role in the separation of the temporal and spiritual powers, and a certain resistance is attributed to the ecclesiastical hierarchy; in the end, however, it is principles inherent to Christianity that led to the attribution of natural, rather than religious, foundations to the law, ownership and the family, and so to the tracing of a boundary 'that separates ancient politics from modern politics'. With an enthusiasm that earned him accusations of 'clericalism',[26]

---

[23] See, for example, H. Berkhof, *Kirche und Kaiser. Eine Untersuchung der Entstehung der byzantinischen und der theokratischen Staatsauffassung im vierten Jahrhundert* (Zurich, 1947) (= German translation of a book published in Dutch, Amsterdam, 1946). For a rather more moderate position, see J.-M. Sansterre, 'Eusèbe de Césarée et la naissance de la théorie "césaropapiste"', *Byz.*, 42 (1972), pp. 131–95, 532–94.

[24] Although Peterson apparently converted to Catholicism.

[25] *La Cité antique*, 5th ed. (Paris, 1974), pp. 472–81.

[26] F. Hartog, *Le XIXᵉ siècle et l'histoire. Le cas de Fustel de Coulanges* (Paris, 1988), pp. 35–8. Fustel defended himself rather ineptly by emphasising his lack of belief.

Fustel de Coulanges skipped lightly over the centuries, leaving to others the task of examining in greater detail the phenomenon of caesaropapism, sequel to ancient paganism in a Christian empire of the East, where change had been slower and remained incomplete.

These few pages in *The Ancient City* had almost as much influence in France as the work of Burckhardt in Germany. They were quoted in many articles and studies on the relations between Church and State.[27] In particular, the ideas of the master were repeated and developed by one of his disciples, Amédée Gasquet, in a doctoral thesis, *De l'Autorité impériale en matière religieuse à Byzance*, which he dedicated in 1879 to 'M. Fustel de Coulanges, membre de l'Institut'.[28] The scholarly apparatus may have been weak, but the expression was nuanced and academic in tone, carefully avoiding the term 'caesaropapism'. At all events, the argument was clear. The separation of political and religious power, explained Gasquet, with reference to *The Ancient City*, then in its fifth or sixth edition, was unknown to ancient societies. The Christian emperors of Byzantium, abdicating none of the rights of their pagan predecessors, aspired to rule both ecclesiastical and lay society. They assumed the title of priest-king, and claimed sanctity just as the pagan emperors had claimed apotheosis. Having accepted Christianity, they believed they could reform it at will and bend 'the immutable text laid down by the great councils' to their whim. But Rome effected against the caesars the major revolution of the separation of powers; 'the pope, vicar of Christ, stripped the imperial majesty of this borrowed title'. In this perpetual struggle, amid the revolutions unleashed by 'the caprice of the eastern sovereigns', 'the centre of Catholicism moved from Constantinople to Rome'. There was general alarm. 'By a bold usurpation', the pope resorted to distributing crowns in a West which was loyal to him; this was political schism, soon matched by religious schism. From it emerged the modern world, with a rift between those who remained faithful to the Byzantine tradition and those who accepted the separation of the two powers and the superiority of the spiritual over the

---

[27] See, for example, 'Caesaropapism' in the encyclopedia *Catholicisme. Hier, aujourd'hui, demain*, II, cols. 846–53 (Paris, 1949), ed. J. Lecler, author of a book entitled *L'Eglise et la souveraineté de l'Etat* (Paris, 1946); H.-X. Arquillière, *L'Augustinisme politique. Essai sur la formation des théories politiques du moyen age* (Paris, 1934), pp. 111–12.

[28] Amédée Gasquet, born in Clermont-Ferrand in 1852, received into the Ecole normale supérieure in 1870, was effectively the pupil of Fustel de Coulanges, who exercised a decisive influence on him. His first thesis (*De l'Autorité impériale en matière religieuse à Byzance*) appeared in Clermont-Ferrand in 1879, his second, *De translatione imperii ab imperatoribus byzantinis ad reges Francorum*, the same year. He held the chair of History and Geography in the University of Clermont, before becoming the town's mayor (in 1888), rector of the University of Nancy, then *directeur* at the Ministry of Education. He died in 1914. Of his very eclectic career as a historian, the most notable survivals are *L'Empire grec et les barbares* (1887) and *L'Empire byzantin et la monarchie française* (1888), books which are deservedly forgotten but assured him a certain notoriety.

temporal. This separation, audaciously carried to extremes, was the principle that had 'awakened the western nations sunk in barbarism'.[29]

A dedication does not necessarily signify blanket approval, and it is by no means certain that all of Gasquet's assertions would have won the wholehearted approval of Fustel de Coulanges. But it is easy to see how the essentially correct idea of a distinction between the spiritual and the temporal intrinsic to Christianity could give rise to the erroneous idea that this distinction was that of 'two powers', and how the vision of a modern world emerging from their separation could lead to 'caesaropapism' being seen as a pagan heritage preserved in a stagnant East, from which a liberated West had rapidly broken away. The presentation, conciliatory or provocative, matters little. The image of an emperor never wholly cleansed of his paganism and too accustomed to being *pontifex maximus* has permeated almost all historiography since.[30] For good measure and to revive the analyses of Peterson, it has also been argued that the ideology of the Hellenistic king, cleverly applied by the heretic Eusebios of Caesarea to the Christian monarch, served as intermediary and gave an appearance of new religious legitimacy to the successors of Augustus.[31] But the conclusion is always the same, open or implied: the conversion of Constantine did not fundamentally christianise the empire; where the imperial tradition survived, in the East, the government was crypto-pagan. This is exactly what the polemical literature had set out to imply when, at the time of iconoclasm or of the Union of the Churches, it had travestied any Byzantine emperor imbued with his religious role and anxious to extirpate the last vestiges of paganism from the Church, by calling him a persecuting tyrant or Antichrist.[32]

A more 'Roman' historiographical tradition has amended this model in a number of ways. In a highly influential book, the abbé Luigi Sturzo took as his starting point the 'novelty of Christianity as compared with other religions', which consisted of having 'broken all duty of relations between religion, on the one hand, and family, tribe, nation or empire on the other, and put these relations on a personal basis'.[33] He went on: 'Dualism was innate' for a Christian, between the spiritual life and the worldly life, between the religious and supernatural

---

[29] See in particular Gasquet's introduction; the book is worthy in some respects but based on unreliable quotations.

[30] See, for example, M. Meslin and J. Grosdidier de Matons. 'Caesaropapisme' in the *Encyclopedia Universalis*, IV (Paris, 1968), For the true significance of the title of *pontifex maximus* in the late Roman empire, see R. Schilling, 'A propos du Pontifex Maximus. Dans quelle mesure peut-on parler d'un remploi par les chrétiens d'un titre prestigieux de la Rome antique?', in *Diritto e religione da Roma a Costantinopoli e Mosca*, Da Roma alla Terza Roma, XI Seminario internazionale di studi storici, Rome, 21–22 avril 1991 (Rome, 1994), pp. 75–90.

[31] See in particular Dvornik, *Christian and Byzantine Political Philosophy* (see ch. 4, n. 11).

[32] See above, pp. 181–91.

[33] Trans. into French as *L'Eglise et l'Etat* (Paris, 1937), p. 25. This analysis is very close to that of Fustel de Coulanges, though the extent to which it was inspired by *La Cité antique* is unclear.

purposes of the Church and the earthly and natural purposes of the state; but if unification was always improper, diarchy, 'a fact of life', represented not so much a separation of powers as their mutual accommodation. 'From the Edict of Constantine to the creation of the Carolingian empire ... there developed two types of religious and political diarchy: the Byzantine caesaropapist type and the Latin organising type.' The former is the

> politico-religious system in which the authority of the State becomes, for the Church, an effective, normal and centralising authority, although external to it, and where the authority of the Church participates directly (although never autonomous) in the exercise of a certain temporal power.

This had been the situation of the eastern Church since Constantine, which had resulted in a loss of autonomy, subjection to the state and the preservation of the economic and political interests of a lay elite and a privileged caste of clergy. Conversely, in the 'Latin organising diarchy', the Church,

> while invoking the assistance of the civil government and while according sovereigns certain powers, rights and privileges within the ecclesiastical system, almost always reacts against any effective dependence and asserts, according to circumstances, its independence.[34]

Sturzo, who goes on to analyse in detail the Reformation, the Counter-Reformation, the development of national Christianities and the policy of 'concordats', clearly found unacceptable the crude opposition, over the centuries, of a non-separation of powers inherited from antiquity and a separation imposed by Christian modernity; but he maintained a distinction between an eastern model (more contemporary than medieval) and a western model, which his knowledge of the facts prevented him from oversimplifying.

Nuance gave way to polemic in a more openly confessional literature, one of whose last representatives was Father Martin Jugie, an expert on the East but a great scourge of schismatics: 'Caesaropapism', he wrote,

> as the word indicates, is Caesar, the State or the civil government in general replacing the pope in the supreme government of the Church; it is the totalitarian State assuming absolute power over the sacred as well as the profane, over the spiritual as well as the temporal, virtually ignoring the difference between civil power and spiritual power, or at least subordinating the latter to the former.

The roots of this evil went back deep into the pagan past:

> The pagan empire was caesaropapist in the full meaning of the word. The separation of the two powers was unknown to it. The pagan emperor, called *summus pontifex*, was both fully a priest and in full control of the clergy and sacred matters. This absolute caesaropapism was incompatible with the Christian religion, where we find a hierarchy invested with special liturgical

---

[34] *L'Eglise et l'Etat*, pp. 51–6.

powers, which cannot belong to a layman . . . a Christian leader of the State cannot be a sovereign pontiff, because he would always lack the power of order [given by ordination]. But he may usurp the role of the pope in the Catholic Church.

Such intrusions had happened everywhere:

> But it is primarily in the East that caesaropapism flourished, and since the fourth century, from the very day that Constantine declared himself protector of the Christian religion . . . the fateful example set by the first Christian emperor was followed by his successors, above all by those who governed the eastern part of the empire after it had been divided into two halves . . . it is true that imperial caesaropapism often served the interests of the Church . . . but, from the point of view of the unity of the Church, it had three disastrous consequences: the nationalisation of the Church, the enslavement of the clergy and a silent or open hostility to the popes . . . unlike the western Church, which, in spite of short-lived periods of weakness, found in the popes intrepid defenders of its independence, the Byzantine Church had too few fighters, although it was not entirely without. In general, the eastern episcopate proved extremely docile in the face of the dogmatic fancies or political heresies of its *basileis*.[35]

An ecumenical spirit and simple historical objectivity have made such prejudices less fashionable and they are no longer common in clerical circles.

The success of the word 'caesaropapism' was definitively assured by a strand within Roman Catholicism, but with the support of reformist Russian Orthodoxy. In the last decades of the nineteenth century, Vladimir Soloviev had already denounced tsarist absolutism and its claim that the eastern Church had 'renounced its own power' in order to return it to the state. In particular, he accused the Orthodox Church itself of having become a 'national Church', thereby forfeiting the right to represent Christ, to whom all power over earth and heaven had been entrusted. 'In all countries reduced to a national Church', he wrote, 'the secular government (whether it is autocratic or constitutional) exercises all power absolutely, and the church as an institution appears only as a special ministry dependent on the general administration of the State.' The finger was pointed at Byzantium once again for having, in the ninth century (in other words, in the time of Photios), claimed to be itself the centre of a universal Church and in practice set in motion a drift towards nationalisms.[36] Rather

---

[35] *Le Schisme byzantin* (Paris, 1941), pp. 3–7.
[36] V. Soloviev, *La Russie et l'Eglise universelle*, 2nd ed. (Paris, 1889), pp. 67–77. For the importance of Vladimir Soloviev (1853–1900) in the renaissance of Russian spiritualism and his influence before 1917, see for example, P. Pascal, 'Les grands courants de la pensée russe contemporaine', *Cahiers du monde russe et soviétique*, III/1 (January-February 1962), pp. 10–12; J. Scherrer, 'Les "sociétés philosophico-religieuses" et la quête idéologique de l'intelligentsia russe avant 1917', *Cahiers du monde russe et soviétique*, XV/3–4 (July-December 1974), pp. 297–314. The mystical philosophy of Soloviev lay beyond institutional churches.

more recently, Cyril Toumanoff argued along similar lines when he evoked a 'Byzantine sickness' which had developed on three fronts (absence of a clear boundary between the spiritual and the temporal, effective superiority over the former granted to the latter and 'the assumption by Caesar of the things which are God's'). In this connection he also described Russia as 'a provincialised and barbarised Byzantium', noting in passing what he regarded as a significant collusion between the Russian style of caesaropapism and Protestant ideology.[37] The problem this time had shifted, and if the idea of a lingering paganism in the Constantinian empire persisted, caesaropapism was now supposed to have emerged a little later, during the schism, in the explosion of a 'Greek' nationalism that conflicted with Christian universalism.

The 'Easterners', their feelings wounded and their convictions and concern for the truth impugned, attempted to counter these various attacks. It was not too difficult for them to qualify this crude picture of a retrograde 'Byzantinism' and to show that 'caesaropapism' was an offensive word, an anachronism which wrongly projected on to the East the western notion of papacy, and on to the middle ages a separation of powers unthinkable before the modern period.[38] Byzantium had never denied the distinction between the temporal and the spiritual,[39] nor ever officially accepted that an emperor might be a priest:[40] the autocrats who had ventured to suggest this had been treated as heretics, and those who had encroached on the rights of the Church – or worse, laid hands on its property – had been denounced as ungodly. So much for the refutation. Historians also made distinctions: the interventions of the empire in the Church had not all been of the same order; some were acceptable (convening and presiding over councils, promulgating laws and canons, maintaining or modifying the ecclesiastical hierarchy), others reprehensible (appointing bishops, defining the Creed). They then lapsed into casuistry: the Byzantine emperor was within his rights when he was content to enforce canons or synodal decisions; he was scarcely exceeding them when he took the initiative for legislation concerning the Church which corresponded to its express wishes (like Justinian and Leo VI in their Novels); he was committing a minor offence when he imposed his personal decisions on the consenting Church, but a flagrant abuse when he imposed

---

[37] C. Toumanoff, 'Caesaropapism in Byzantium and in Russia', *Theological Studies*, 7 (1946), pp. 213–43.
[38] F. Dölger, *BZ*, 31 (1931), pp. 449ff; 42 (1943–9), pp. 261ff, 283–7; F. Dölger, *Byzanz und die europäische Staatenwelt* (Ettal, 1953), pp. 9–33; G. Ostrogorsky, 'Otnošenie cerkvi i gosudarstva v Vizantii', *Seminarium Kondakovianum*, 4 (1931), pp. 121–32; A. W. Ziegler, 'Die byzantinische Religionspolitik und der sog. Cäsaropapismus', in *Münchener Beiträge zur Slavenkunde. Festgabe für Paul Diels* (Munich, 1953), pp. 81–97; A. Michel, *Die Kaisermacht in der Ostkirche (843–1204)* (Darmstadt, 1959), pp. 1–2, with bibliography; D. J. Geanakoplos, 'Church and state in the Byzantine empire: a reconsideration of the problem of caesaropapism', *Church History*, 34 (1965), pp. 381–403; H.-G. Beck, *Das byzantinische Jahrtausend* (Munich, 1978).
[39] H. Ahrweiler, *L'Idéologie politique de l'empire byzantin* (Paris, 1975), pp. 129–33.
[40] L. Bréhier, 'Hiereus kai basileus', in *Mémorial Louis Petit* (see introduction, n. 4), pp. 41–5.

them not only without consultation, but with the support of only a minority of the bishops, in particular in matters of faith. Only the two latter instances constituted an assault on the independence of the Church; the two former, though based on the same juridical principle, at least abided by the rules of the game.[41] Theologians and canonists are often less indulgent than historians; but they contrasted actual interference with a legal distinction, engraved in the canons and constantly referred to. So they looked for and identified those responsible for abuses – the authoritarianism of Constantius II rather than of the irreproachable Constantine, the compulsive law-making of Justinian, the 'imperial heresy' of the iconoclasts, or even more the *Commentaries* of Balsamon, which, as we have seen, toyed with the idea of an emperor quasi-bishop. The interpretation of the canonical heritage given at the end of the twelfth century and repeated by Matthew Blastares had concealed without really damaging a continuous tradition. If there was deviation, the eastern church was not – or not always – consenting; it had been obliged to battle with the 'paganism' which remained associated with the imperial ideology and of which the titles of *epistemonarches* or *defensor* still bore the mark.[42]

At all events, the word 'caesaropapism' was an irritant. It was like a slap in the face. It was imputed to the 'Latins' without any recognition of the fact that the evidence for the indictment had been fabricated throughout the Byzantine middle ages; and the response was to oppose western 'papo-caesarism' to eastern caesaropapism.[43]

All in all, it was a feeble riposte, which got sucked into the polemic instead of exposing its mechanisms, as our brief historiographical survey suggests should have been done. Byzantium was not entirely above suspicion in this matter, but clearly served as a foil. The most contradictory elements colluded in the artificially concocted notion of caesaropapism. At its birth, Roman fundamentalism entered into a strange alliance with the Reforming spirit; the radical distinction between the spiritual and the temporal, which was intended to separate religion from politics, had the unlikely consequence of ending in the recognition of a

---

[41] B. K. Stephanides, 'Hai en to byzantino kratei scheseis ekklesias kai politeias, kai he Neara tou autokratoros Konstantinou Douka (1065)', *BZ*, 30 (1930), pp. 420–4; J. Meyendorf, 'Justinian, the empire and the Church', *DOP*, 22 (1968), pp. 43–60, especially pp. 50–1, who also emphasises the juridical aspect and the fact that the Church and the empire formed a unified society, in which the former had *auctoritas* and the latter *potestas*.

[42] See, in particular, S. Troïtzky, 'Théocratie ou césaropapisme', *Messager de l'Exarchat du patriarche russe en Europe occidentale*, 19 (1954), pp. 165–77 (French trans. of Russian text published ibid., 16 (1953), and repr. in *Contacts*, new ser. 22 (July-August 1958), pp. 55–9); see also C. Gallagher, 'Gratian and Theodore Balsamon. Two twelfth-century canonistic methods compared', in *Byzantium in the 12th Century* (see ch. 8, n. 29), pp. 79–80. H. S. Alivisatos' communication 'Caesaropapismus in den byzantinischen Kirchengesetzen und den *Canones*', *Akten des XI. Internationalen Byzantinistenkongresses (München, 1958)* (Munich, 1960), pp. 15–20, is very superficial.

[43] See above, p. 283 and n. 6.

clerical 'power'; the founder of the Christian empire was reproached for having lacked an ideal of laicity. It is clear that its history, geography and culture now made it impossible for Europe to understand medieval Byzantium.

THE THEORY OF THE 'TWO POWERS'

It may be useful to recall a few obvious facts. The 'Church and state' pair can only oppose or cause to interact a temporal power that is more or less laicised and confined to one nation, and a Church that is identified with its clergy. It misrepresents what is original about a Christian empire: its universality, at least in theory, and its role – as political structure, as society and as history – in an economy of salvation. To encompass in these two words all the interrelations and problems of overlap which might bring the Byzantine emperor into dispute with the ecclesiastical hierarchy is an obvious methodological error. To show this, I will return to some of the problems already discussed in the previous chapters.

As a sinner (*ratione peccati*) – the popes and the ecclesiastical hierarchy never ceased to repeat – the emperor was a son of the Church, that is, subject to the power 'to bind and to loose' that was possessed by the bishops alone. This power was never contested by the emperors, who were exposed to it like everybody else and who were its most spectacular victims. They were frequently threatened; a few cases were made an example of in order to illustrate a notion that was constantly reiterated in the liturgy, the ceremonial and the 'mirrors of princes'. The emperors were sons of Adam, their omnipotence did not distinguish them from the rest of humanity and obliged them more particularly to repent for the 'crimes' they had committed or of which they were *a priori* suspected.[44] The excommunications of Theodosius I by Ambrose of Milan and of Leo VI by Nicholas Mystikos, and their repentance, reproduced the divine curse which had struck David and from which the anointed king had escaped by penitence. The support of this great Old Testament model was enough to transform the humiliation of the monarchs into the royal virtue of humility and to indicate the necessity of mediation, by the prophet in the past, by the pontiff in the present. There was nothing here to object to. The power to bind and to loose gave the priesthood a formidable weapon, but a power of limited punishment or release, derived from God but operating rather in the same way as the power of a saint when serving as intermediary to the miracle or of the magician when producing marvels. The liturgy abounded in special prayers to try to lift the punishment of those who had died in a state of excommunication when he who had 'bound' them had been unable or unwilling

<hr>

[44] See above, pp. 36, 123–4.

to 'loose' them – because it had to be the same person.[45] All sorts of *exempla* show them 'imprisoned' in the hereafter, no longer enjoying any bodily or spiritual faculty. Whatever the legitimacy of the sentence pronounced against them, their bodies could no longer dissolve but remained swollen, black and stinking. They suffered the special fate and treatment endured in antiquity by those struck by lightning.[46] To demonstrate the effects of the anathema, the example of the body of Michael VIII Palaiologos, who had the distinction of recovering Constantinople, but the misfortune of being excommunicated by the patriarch Arsenios, was invoked.[47] To force the prince of Smolensk to submit, in June 1370, the patriarch Philotheos reminded him that excommunication would prevent his corpse from dissolving.[48] This power, before which the emperors usually gave way, was terrifying, but it was hardly comparable, at least in the minds of contemporaries, with what is understood today by 'spiritual power'.

The problem of the emperor's involvement in the definition of the faith, in particular when the bishops were meeting in ecumenical or general councils, 'illuminated by the Spirit', had been acute since Constantine and Constantius II; one senses, through the rhetoric of Eusebios when he is lauding the impartiality of the former and through the invectives of the *homoousians* (defenders of the consubstantiality of the Father and the Son) against the pressures of the latter, that a division of responsibilities was soon worked out. This gave the emperor the role of arbitrating but not deciding, of implementing as the 'secular arm' decisions taken by the bishops but not enacting his own, and of guaranteeing the unity of Christianity and not encouraging its divisions. To illustrate what might have been a sound doctrine, it is usual to quote the letter sent to the Council of Ephesos in 431 by the absent rulers Theodosius II and Valentinian III. They explained to the bishops that they had instructed the *comes* Candidianus to

> join their very holy synod but take no part whatsoever in the enquiries and proposals which would be made there on the subject of the dogmas, as it would be contrary to religion for someone not belonging to the list of holy

[45] Goar, *Euchologion*, pp. 543–8; see also the act by which the patriarch Isidore, about 1350, lifted all the curses and excommunications pronounced by him on the occasion of internal disputes, for all those, living or dead, who had been struck: F. Miklosich and I. Müller, *Acta et diplomata*, I, no. 129, pp. 286–7; see also the *exempla* collected by Glykas, *Annales*, ed. Bekker (see ch. 6, n. 2), pp. 523–5.

[46] They too, it was said, did not become corrupted: see the references collected by F. Cumont, *Lux perpetua* (Paris, 1949), pp. 329–31. The *Life of St Andrew Salos* suggests that those struck by lightning were good Christians in whom a demon had tried to find shelter, but whom God had nevertheless chosen to strike with his lightning (ed. and trans. L. Rydén, *The Life of St Andrew the Fool* (Uppsala, 1995), II, pp. 218–20).

[47] Philotheos of Selymbria, *Oratio in sanctum Agathonicum*, PG 154, cols. 1237–9.

[48] Miklosich-Müller, *Acta et diplomata* (n. 45), I, no. 269, p. 525; see also Dositheos of Jerusalem, *Tomos agapes kata Latinon*, 1698, pp. 29–31 of the 'Prolegomena'.

bishops to meddle in the discussion of ecclesiastical matters, and to forbid all manner of access to the town to the laity and to the monks who had already gathered for the council or who were about to gather, because those who were not absolutely necessary to the analysis of dogma which was about to take place should not be allowed to obstruct the decisions that your holy assembly must take, and to see that nothing was allowed to aggravate a difference born of antipathy.[49]

Fine words, indeed, for a council which was hardly a model of calm. Another letter could also be cited, that sent by the emperor Constantine IV to the pope requesting the council to end the Monothelete crisis in 680–1, in which he declared that he had no wish to influence the decisions of the bishops; so could the attitude of neutrality adopted by Basil I during the 'Photian' and 'anti-Photian' councils of 869–70 and 879–80. Conversely, there are quoted as instances of authoritarianism or caesaropapist deviations the decisions taken in matters of faith by certain emperors on their own authority or under cover of the patriarch – the *Enkyklion* of Basiliskos in 476, the *Henotikon* of Zeno in 482, the decisions of Justinian against the theopaschites, the Origenists and the 'Three Chapters', the *Ekthesis* of Herakleios in 638 launching the formula of the 'single will'. Another example was the *Typos* that in 648 prohibited discussion of this theological problem, and which Constans II promulgated, as one who was 'accustomed to see to everything that was useful to the Christian *politeia* and especially everything to do with the immaculate faith'.[50] There was a wish for consensus within the Orthodox Church and an authoritarianism leading inevitably to heresy in certain sovereigns who, like Constantius II, believed or said that '[their] will had the weight of a canon'.[51]

On this point, historiography has ceased to be confessional without wholly ridding itself of clerical cant or of the providential conception of an Orthodoxy mapped out in advance and inevitably triumphant. Historians will add nuance. They can cite a few 'Orthodox' councils which, like Nicaea II, were imperial forced takeovers leading to Stalinist show trials. Above all, they can point to the violence which has always characterised confrontations within the Church, and to the splits which would inevitably have occurred if the Church had not been firmly linked to the empire, and which actually happened everywhere when this link was loosened or broken, obliging the emperor, who was officially responsible for summoning councils and for approving, signing and applying their decisions, to act as mediator between parties who would stop at nothing. The same Theodosius II who left the task of defining dogma at Ephesos to the bishops wrote to Cyril of Alexandria to ask him to cease his intrigues, and to assure him that 'the Churches and the *basileia* were one, and that, on his orders

---

[49] ACO, I, 1, 1, p. 120.   [50] Mansi, X, cols. 1029–32.
[51] Athanasios of Alexandria, *Historia arianorum ad monachos*, 33, PG 25, col. 732.

and with the providence of God the Saviour, would continue to be only one'.[52]
In the iconoclast period, which has been seen as the triumph of caesaropapism,
the opposition was not between orthodoxy and heresy, but between a reforming
movement which was 'scandalised' by the unchecked development of the cult of
images and a mass of Christians attached to practices of worship which legend
dated back to the age of the apostles. It was two Churches, or at least two interpretations of the ecclesiastical tradition, that confronted each other, and it is difficult to see how the emperors could have avoided being drawn into the conflict.
Leo III and Constantine V did so as autocrats, Leo V as a sovereign wishing
to impose an 'economy', that is, a compromise solution. Theodore of Stoudios
had fiercely defended the independence of the clergy against Leo V and asked
the pope to summon an ecumenical council, but he hastened with a delegation
of bishops and monks to his successor Michael II, who was thought to be better
disposed, to ask him to intervene and was bitterly disappointed when Michael
replied that the problem did not concern him and that he would leave each one
to act as he pleased.[53]

The emperor could not remain neutral. He was the guarantor and often the
principal architect of the unity of the Church. Thus, the councils, 'orthodox' or
'heretical', unanimously celebrated the sovereign who was 'watched over by
God' by freely bestowing on him the titles of '*didaskalos* of the faith', 'new
Paul' and 'equal of the apostles, illuminated like the bishops by the Holy Spirit'.
At the end of the fourth session of the council held in Constantinople in 536, the
bishops were expressing the general opinion when they declared that, 'under
an orthodox emperor', the empire had nothing and no one to fear. The patriarch
Menas concluded: 'It is right that nothing of what is discussed in the holy Church
should be decided against the opinion and the orders [of the emperor].'[54] The
iconoclasts were scarcely more emphatic when they acclaimed Constantine V
and his son Leo at the Council of Hiereia in 754:

> It is thanks to you that the universal Church has rediscovered peace. You
> are the lights of orthodoxy ... preserve, O Lord, he who is orthodox from
> birth ... It is you who have strengthened the dogmas decreed by the six holy
> ecumenical councils.[55]

Christian literature in the Greek language, like that in Latin, includes many
analyses and fine pieces of prose which set out a general distinction between
the affairs of the world, which were the province of the emperor, and those
of God, which were the exclusive province of the bishops. But all these many
texts do not have the same significance, and instead of lumping them together
we need to establish whether the author had wished to distinguish the temporal
from the spiritual according to a classical schema, the affairs of the Church

---

[52] Document produced at the council: ACO, I, 1, 1, p. 74, lines 3–5.
[53] *Life of St Theodore Stoudite* by Michael, 60, PG 99, col. 3167.
[54] Mansi, VIII, col. 970B.   [55] Mansi, XIII, cols. 352–3.

from those of the state as two functions, or the Church and the state as two powers. It is also necessary to take into account the geographical position of the author in relation to Constantinople and the nature of his contacts with the imperial power. An easterner who rehearsed the arguments for separation might be expressing a genuine conviction or simply making a strategic reply on the subject of Rome vis-à-vis the seat of the empire; he might be pondering the place of a Christian sovereign in the church or, in the heat of debate, see in the emperor no more than a 'pagan persecutor' and Antichrist. I will cite just a few examples.

Athanasios of Alexandria preserves and presents in evidence a letter in which Ossius of Cordova, in the thick of the Arian conflict, fiercely attacks Constantius II:

> Cease, I beg you, and remember that you are a mortal man. Fear the Day of Judgement. Keep yourself pure for that day. Do not meddle in ecclesiastical affairs and do not give us orders regarding them, but rather learn of them from us. God has given you the *basileia*, to us he has entrusted the affairs of the Church; and just as he who encroaches on your power contravenes the decrees of God, so fear lest in taking upon yourself the affairs of the Church you lay yourself open to a grave charge. It is written: Render therefore unto Caesar the things which are Caesar's; and unto God the things that are God's. We are not permitted, therefore, to govern on earth, but nor are you to cense. I write this with your salvation in mind.[56]

The threat, if not of excommunication by the church, is at least of condemnation by God; the distribution of roles already reveals a tendency peculiar to the West, but it neither extends the sphere proper to the church beyond faith and worship nor confers on it a 'power'.

Though both equally resistant to imperial power, a disparity is already visible by the late fourth and early fifth centuries between the formulations of the western Ambrose of Milan and the eastern John Chrysostomos. The former assumes a distinction between Church and state by declaring that 'the emperor is responsible for the affairs of the Palace and the clergy for the affairs of the Church';[57] the latter does not rule out state intervention in the 'temporal' affairs of the Church when he declares, with a rhetorical flourish, that 'to the king are entrusted bodies and to the priest souls'.[58]

A passage in the Epistle to the Romans recommending Christians to be obedient to an ungodly power inspired this commentary from Theodoret of Cyrrhus:

> Paul does not urge us to obey even if we are constrained into ungodliness; in fact, he clearly defined the function of power and the way in which God has ordered human things in such a way that the promulgation of laws contrary

---

[56] Quoted by Athanasios of Alexandria, *Historia arianorum ad monachos*, 44, PG 25, cols. 745–8.
[57] See above, p. 148 and n. 78.   [58] *In illud vidi Dominum*, Hom. IV, 4, PG 56, col. 126.

to piety is not a product of the function of power, but of the will of those who exercise power badly. For what concerns God is not for the judgement of those who exercise power; they were not established for that; they were established as intercessors and guarantors of justice in what concerns the affairs of men and their mutual rights.[59]

The claim that all authority comes from God and that one should submit to it (John, 19: 10–11; 1 Peter, 2: 13–16; Romans, 1: 1 and 13: 1–6; 1 Timothy, 2: 2) is tempered here by a restriction of the sphere of the temporal authority which excludes, even when the empire had become Christian, at least the faith, the sacraments and worship.

At the time of Monotheletism and iconoclasm, far more radical declarations appear, which we have already discussed; those of Maximos the Confessor, of the 'letters of Pope Gregory II' to Leo III, of John of Damascus and of the bishops and *hegoumenoi* confronting Leo V.[60] But it is difficult to interpret them as other than routine indictments of the imperial institution itself. This suspicion on principle left lasting traces, as we have seen, but it never led to a viable project.

The first rough outline of what is called the 'theory of the two powers' was not made spontaneously by a theologian or canonist, but at a time of schism between East and West and by a pope who would be judged 'arrogant' and whose rigidity would prevent the crisis from being ended. This was at the end of the fifth century; the distance between Rome and Constantinople had become an estrangement without yet amounting to a rupture. In 482, the patriarch Akakios had approved the decree of Zeno designed to win over the Monophysites (*Henotikon*) and had been excommunicated and anathematised by Felix II in 484. This incident provided Gelasius, head of the pontifical chancery and later pope (492–6), with the opportunity to develop Petrine claims, demanding for the papacy the right to have any case referred to it and decide it without discussion in council, downgrading the see of Constantinople in the hierarchy, and denying the emperor the right to intervene in ecclesiastical matters. Gelasius, who was still only a deacon, wrote to the eastern bishops in 488, during the reign of Zeno:[61]

> And if you say to me, 'But the emperor is universal', I might reply to the emperor, without wishing to offend him, that he is a son and not a hierarch of the Church: in religious matters, it becomes him to learn, and not to teach; he has the privileges of the power (*potestas*) that he has received from God to

---

[59] PG 66, col. 864, commenting on Romans, 13: 5–6: 'Wherefore ye must needs be subject, not only for wrath [that is, the wrath of the rulers], but also for conscience sake. For this cause pay ye tribute also.'

[60] See above, pp. 158ff., 169–70, 184–5, 188ff.

[61] *Ep.* 1, ed. Thiel, *Epistolae Romanorum pontificum genuinae* (see ch. 5, n. 74), I, pp. 292–3.

administer public affairs; but let him take care, not contenting himself with the privileges received, to usurp nothing that is contrary to the dispositions of the celestial order. For God wished the task of governing the Church to fall to the bishops and not to the earthly powers. If these powers are exercised by Christians, God wished them to be subject to his Church and to the priests. There is nothing particularly new in this assertion of the supremacy of the Church in religious matters and of the need for the laity to submit to priests. The general theory was formulated a little later, in 494, in a letter from Gelasius, now pope, to the emperor Anastasios:[62]

There are two things, august emperor, by which this world is principally ruled: the sacred authority of the pontiffs and royal power (*auctoritas sacrata pontificum et regalis potestas*). And of the two, the priests have a heavier burden in that they are accountable before God for the kings themselves. You know this, most merciful son, even though in dignity you are at the head of the human race, you nevertheless piously bend the neck before the hierarchs responsible for divine things, and it is from them that you seek the means of salvation. And so as to receive the celestial mysteries and administer them as is right, you recognise that you must submit to the rule of religion rather than command, and that consequently, for such matters, you depend on the judgement [of the bishops], and cannot claim to bend them to your will. If, in fact, in what concerns the sphere of public order, the religious leaders recognise that the empire has been given to you by a provision from on high and if they also obey your laws, not wishing, in the affairs of this world, to appear to go against your irrevocable decisions, how should you not, I ask, obey those who are responsible for administering the venerable mysteries?... Your Piety is obviously aware that no one can ever, by any human pretext, elevate himself above the privilege and the recognition of he whom the word of Christ has placed above the entire world, whom the venerable Church has always recognised and devoutly placed in the first rank.

And, as if to reply to a question of Anastasios which was almost the same as that later attributed to Leo III: 'But am I not emperor and priest?', Gelasius went on to evoke Melchizedek, Old Testament king and priest, the diabolic combination of the 'two powers' under the pagan empire, which had made the emperor a *pontifex maximus*, and their definitive separation with the coming of Christ:[63]

So that the Christian emperors have need of the pontiffs for eternal life and the pontiffs abide by imperial provisions for the conduct of temporal things. So, spiritual activities have been separated from worldly affairs... and, conversely, he who is responsible for worldly affairs does not appear to preside over divine things.

---

[62] *Ep.* 12, ibid., pp. 350–2.
[63] *Tractatus IV (Tomus de anathematis vinculo)*, ibid., pp. 567–8; and see above, p. 182.

With the exception of the assertion of Rome's exclusive rule over the 'pentarchic' Church, the principles enunciated here can hardly have surprised or shocked an emperor like Anastasios. The exegesis of Melchizedek as prefiguration of Christ and not model of human kingship was perhaps explicitly made for the first time, but it was already there in St Paul. One point alone might have caused surprise but not real unease: the distinction between the *auctoritas* of the pontiffs and the *potestas* of the emperors. The words were not chosen at random, certainly, but it was a matter of emphasis rather than a coherent distinction. Gelasius had recognised that the hierarchs also possessed the power (*potestas*) to bind and to loose, subject of the debate, and it is unlikely that he was meaning to challenge the *auctoritas* that justified the emperor's right to legislate, leaving him only the *potestas* of a magistrate or civil servant, that is, simply an executive role.[64] To have ascribed *auctoritas* to the clergy and *potestas* to the laity with deliberate intent would have been not only to distinguish two powers, but to situate them at two very different levels and postulate the basis of a theocracy. Later interpretations tended in this direction,[65] and western historiography has seen an ideological revolution where perhaps there had been no more than skilful rhetoric.[66]

The success of Gelasius' ideas in the West and their transformation into a system came about largely because they followed so naturally in the wake of St Augustine, that is, of his reflections, which retained their topicality, on an empire that had been Christianised but was disintegrating. The 'two powers' were more or less equated with the 'two cities', which opposed the spiritual and the temporal, certainly, but not the Church and the state. St Augustine found it good that there had been a Christian state, at least temporarily, because it had favoured the City of God during its peregrinations here below; he advised that it should be obeyed, approved its intervention against heretics and was content for it to legislate on ecclesiastical matters.[67] The opposition between the earthly city, naturally and fundamentally bad, and the heavenly city of the Christians, which Davidic kingship had 'prefigured', but which had been wholly spiritualised since the coming of Christ, was of another order. Between

---

[64] See, for example, A. Magdelain, *Auctoritas principis* (Paris, 1947), pp. 2–7, 18, 77–87, 98, where *auctoritas* is defined as a power of direction and initiative, which belonged in ancient Rome to the senate and passed to the *princeps*, and *potestas* as an executive power. The originality of the imperial system was to combine *auctoritas* and the *imperium/potestas* in the hands of the emperor.

[65] Like that of Jonas of Orleans the ninth century: J. Reviron, *Les Idées politiques d'un évêque du IXe siècle. Jonas d'Orléans et son 'De institutione regia'* (Paris, 1930).

[66] In particular E. Caspar, *Geschichte des Papsttums von den Anfängen bis zur Höhe der Weltherrschaft*, II (Tubingen, 1933), pp. 65ff, 753ff; for a more measured view, see Dvornik, *Christian and Byzantine Political Philosophy* (see ch. 4, n. 11), pp. 804–9; P. Toubert, 'La théorie gélasienne des deux pouvoirs. Propositions en vue d'une révision', in *Studi in onore di Giosuè Musca*, ed. C. Damiani Fonseca and V. Sivo (Bari, 2000), pp. 519–40.

[67] *Contra epistolam Parmeniani*, I, 8, 13; 9, 15, PL 43, cols. 43–4.

these two cities, there might be open warfare or intermittent skirmishing, but never alliance and even less complementarity.[68] It was only by simplifying and distorting his ideas according to a new situation in the West that it has been possible to derive political Augustinianism from St Augustine and tag onto it the 'Gelasian theory of the two powers'.[69]

In the East, the same subjects had neither the same meaning nor the same repercussions. They were part of a different historical and geographical reality. Justinian seemed to be following in Gelasius' footsteps[70] when he declared, in the preamble to his Novel 6 regulating the election of bishops and clergy: 'The greatest gifts of God, given to men by the philanthropy from above, are the priesthood (*hierosyne*) and the empire (*basileia*). The former is at the service of divine matters, it is for the latter to direct and take care of human affairs.' But he advocated the union and not the separation of these two distinct principles, which had the same divine origin and which both worked for the happiness of men:

> That is why nothing is more important to the emperors than that the priests command respect, inasmuch as the latter pray constantly to God on their behalf. In fact, if [the priesthood] is in all things without fault and enjoys the confidence of God, and if [the empire], for its part, with rectitude and propriety, makes the *politeia* which has been entrusted to it more beautiful, there will be an excellent harmony, which will secure for the human race everything that is necessary to it.

The distinction between the priesthood and the empire, which is here added to that between the spiritual and the temporal, was incorporated without difficulty into the imperial discourse. John Tzimiskes repeated it when, on 13 February 970, he chose as patriarch Basil Skamandrenos.[71] But it opposed neither two 'powers',[72] nor two independent entities, but at most two functions, that of

---

[68] See, in particular, book 19 of *The City of God* with a useful commentary in *Oeuvres de saint Augustin*, Bibliothèque augustinienne, vol. 37, 'note complémentaire 18', pp. 748–52. See also Dvornik, *Christian and Byzantine Political Philosophy* (see ch. 4, n. 11), pp. 840–50, who shows how the views of St Augustine were opposed to those expressed at the same period by Orosius: *Historiae adversum paganos*, especially VI, 20–22; VII, 2, ed. K. F. Zangemeister (Vienna, 1882), pp. 418–21, 426–30.

[69] Arquillière, *L'Augustinisme politique* (n. 27).

[70] Particularly, *Ep.* 12 of Pope Gelasius: 'Duo quippe sunt quibus principaliter mundus hic regitur: auctoritas sacrata pontificum et regalis potestas': ed. Thiel, *Epistolae romanorum pontificum genuinae* (see ch. 5, n. 74), I, pp. 350–1.

[71] Leo the Deacon, *Historia*, ed. Hase (see ch. 3, n. 57), VI, 6–7, Bonn, pp. 101–2: 'I know – the emperor is supposed to have said – only one principle, the highest and first power, which made emerge from nothing and brought into existence the whole of the visible and invisible world. But, in this life and in this earthly wandering, I distinguish two, the *hierosyne* and the *basileia*, to which the creator has entrusted, to the former the care of souls, to the latter the care of bodies, so that one of the parts does not drag compared with the other, but that they form together a complete and appropriate whole.'

[72] It should be remembered that the word *arche* could also mean 'principle' as well as 'power'.

the priest, who controlled the liturgy and was expected to provide effective intercession, and that of the emperor, who should rule the world justly and in orthodoxy. The emphasis was on unity, on the harmonisation of what had just been separated, and on a twofold integration of the Church into the state and of the state into the Church. To see what Justinian really believed, one need only, in any case, turn a few pages and read, in Novel 7 (2, 1), that the emperor might engage in transactions involving ecclesiastical property, in principle inalienable, 'because there is little difference between the priesthood (*hierosyne*) and the empire (*basileia*) and between sacred property and the property of the community or state'.

The distinction between *hierosyne* and *basileia* should be seen in a different context, and it derives from a different genre, that of the memorable moral maxims already discussed,[73] which went beyond mere rhetoric without aspiring to theoretical coherence, and which made sense only as part of the paradox or the dialectic of which they formed only one term. Thus it was said in the 'mirrors of princes' that the king, by the nature of his body, was the equal of any man, only to add that, by his power, he was the equal of God who ruled all things, and so he should not, as a mortal man, give way to vanity or, as a god, succumb to anger;[74] or that the emperor was above the laws, but that, if he was legitimate, hence just, he submitted to the law.[75] In the same collections, and in the same spirit, an idea already articulated in the *Testaments of the twelve patriarchs*,[76] the *Apostolic Constitutions*,[77] and the work of a few Fathers of the Church is ubiquitous,[78] namely that the priesthood is superior to kingship just as heaven is superior to earth and the soul or spirit to the body. But the second term inexorably follows: 'Every just king has the rank of a priest.' This aphorism, which had its roots in ancient Greece, passed by way of Irenaeus and John of Damascus to culminate, in the eleventh and twelfth centuries, in Antony 'Melissa', where it nicely complemented those celebrating the superiority of the priesthood over the empire.[79] Let us recall that Melchizedek meant 'my king is justice' and that, according to Philo of Alexandria, he was a priest because he was just.[80] All it needs is for 'just' to be replaced by 'orthodox' for what we saw as a logical flaw in the Pseudo-Gregory's letter to the emperor Leo III to reappear.

---

[73] See above, pp. 17–19.

[74] Antony Melissa (so called because he gathered nectar from the *sententiae* like a bee), *Loci communes*, II, 2 PG 136, col. 1012.

[75] See above, pp. 19–20.

[76] *Testament of Judah*, 21, ed. H. de Jonge, *The Testaments of the Twelve Patriarchs* (Leyden, 1978), pp. 73–4.

[77] II, 34, 4, ed. J. B. Pitra, *Iuris ecclesiastici Graecorum historia et monumenta* (Rome, 1884), I, pp. 178–9.

[78] John Chrysostomos, *In illud vidi Domini*, Hom. IV, 4, PG 56, col. 126; *In II Cor.*, Hom. XV, 5, PG 61, col. 507.

[79] *Loci communes*, II, 2 and 3, PG 136, cols. 1012, 1017.   [80] See above, pp. 173, 175.

It listed the differences between the imperial and the priestly functions only to conclude: you are not emperor and priest, but become so by defending the true faith.[81]

This was rather more than an illogicality. The distinction between the two powers was never so clearly formulated as when there was dissension between them. When there was agreement or hope of harmonisation, the celebration of, or nostalgia for, unity prevailed. No one objected when the synod which condemned the heretic Eutyches at Constantinople in 448 acclaimed Theodosius II by saying: 'Great is the faith of the emperors! Long live the guardians of the faith! Long live the pious emperor, long live the emperor-bishop (*to archierei basilei*).'[82] Nor did anyone object, a little later, at the council of Chalcedon, to acclaiming Marcian 'priest and emperor', as well as 'restorer of the Church, *didaskalos* of the faith, New Constantine, New Paul and New David'.[83] At the same period, Pope Leo the Great congratulated Theodosius II, then Marcian, for their *sacerdotalis industria*, their *sacerdotalis animus* and the *sacerdotalis palma* with which God had rewarded them,[84] and told Leo I that he was inspired by the Holy Spirit in matters of faith.[85] Except during periods of tension, the adjective *sacerdotalis* was part of the formulary of the pontifical chancery for letters addressed to the emperors of Constantinople. The eulogists were as busy in the West as in the East. Prokopios of Gaza emphasised that Anastasios had been chosen to be a bishop before being appointed emperor, and that he therefore combined in his person 'that which is most precious in men, the splendour of an emperor and the mind of a priest';[86] Ennodius of Pavia (472–521) proclaimed Theoderic 'prince and priest';[87] Venantius Fortunatus, in the second half of the sixth century, called Childebert I '*Melchizedek noster, merito rex atque sacerdos*';[88] an anonymous panegyric of about 645 described Clothair I as *quasi sacerdos*;[89] in 794, Paulinus, bishop of Aquileia, encouraged Charlemagne to be '*Dominus et pater, rex et sacerdos*'.[90] To justify the canonisation of a king, it

---

[81] See above, p. 162.   [82] ACO, II, 1, 1, p. 138.

[83] Ibid., II, 1, 2, pp. 155 [351], 157 [353].

[84] 24, 1 (to Theodosius); 111, 3 (to Marcian); 115, 1 (to Marcian); PL 54, cols. 735, 1023, 1031–3; *ACO*, II, 4, p. 88; see Caspar, *Geschichte des Papsttums* (see n. 66).

[85] *Ep.* 162 and 165, PL 54, cols. 1145, 1155. Vigilius writing to Justinian used almost the same formula to rejoice at finding in him 'a soul of priest and of prince': *Epistulae imperatorum pontificum aliorum inde ab a. CCCLXVII usque ad a. DLIII datae. Avellana quae dicitur collectio*, ed. O. Günther, CSEL 35/1 (Vienna, 1895), p. 348, ll. 18–20.

[86] *Panegyric of Anastasios*, 3–4, ed. and trans. A. Chauvot, *Procope de Gaza, Priscien de Césarée, Panégyriques de l'empereur Anastase Ier* (Bonn, 1986), I, pp. 6–8, 28–30.

[87] PL 63, col. 181. For the western examples, see F. Kampers, 'Rex et sacerdos'. *Historisches Jahrbuch*, 44 (1924), pp. 495–515.

[88] *MGH, Auct. ant.* IV, p. 40.

[89] *MGH, Ep.* III, p. 459; the anonymous bishop was addressing Clovis II or Sigebert III and praising their grandfather.

[90] PL 99, col. 166; *MGH, Concilia* II, p. 142.

was said that he had conducted himself during his reign *acsi bonus sacerdos*.[91] We are in the realm of rhetoric, but that does not mean that anything could be said or that taboos could be violated. Even if the words had a metaphorical and an incantatory meaning, and even if their association was not without an element of provocation, there was nothing abnormal in asserting that the *ideal* emperor was also a priest.

BYZANTINE ECCLESIOLOGY

It might be assumed that letters, acclamations, eulogies and collections of maxims had kept alive for a while old ideas that had been inadequately Christianised and now lacked justification. But even a rapid analysis of Byzantine ecclesiology makes clear that the notion of imperial priesthood found a basis in the very structures of the eastern Church. Balsamon was one of the very few canonists, perhaps the first and certainly the last, to have appreciated this. Beyond the pages of his *Commentary* and after him, the problem was not faced head on, and we find only a few lists and a few stormy but largely fruitless debates about the traditional rights of the emperor to intervene in the Church.[92] There is scarcely more than a handful of precedents giving rise to discussion and variations, which aimed only to codify customs and preserve a status quo without seeking an explanation except in metaphors or vague terms such as *epistemonarches*.

A thirteenth-century marginal note, for example, probably by John Chilas and in connection with the Arsenite schism, lists the privileges conceded to the emperors by the Church in addition to the free choice of their spiritual father.[93] They were acknowledged to have a sacred nature which equated them with the bishops: before being crowned, they signed, like the bishops, a profession of faith; they were anointed with the *myron*, which corresponded to the placing of the Gospel on the head of the hierarchs; they took communion inside the sanctuary, like the priests (at least on the day of their coronation), and they censed the altar table by making the sign of the cross with the censer. Also, they had judicial powers over the church – over the confirmation and signature of conciliar decisions and canons, the promotion or demotion in the hierarchy

[91] The formula was used for St Gontran, king of the Franks (Gregory of Tours, *Historia Francorum*, IX, 21) and for St Ethelbert, king of East Anglia (*Life of Ethelbert* (*BHL* 2627) 12); see also R. Folz, *Les saints Rois du Moyen Age en Occident (VIe–XIIIe siècle)* (Brussels, 1984), p. 58.

[92] Hence the contradictory viewpoints of Makarios of Ankyra (end fourteenth-early fifteenth century), who in a treatise against the Latins, put the emperor at the head of the Church and above the patriarchs, then, in his polemic against Matthew I, confined his role to secular affairs: V. Laurent, 'Le trisépiscopat du patriarche Matthieu I (1397–1410)', *REB*, 30 (1972), pp. 1–87, with bibliography. See also Allatius, *De Ecclesiae occidentalis et orientalis perpetua consensione* (Cologne, 1648), col. 219, citing Makarios of Ankyra, for whom 'the emperor is the Lord's anointed, is holy by the fact of this unction with the *myron*, is one of the clergy of the sanctuary, is bishop, priest and *didaskalos* of the faith'.

[93] Darrouzès, *Documents inédits* (see ch. 8, n. 14), pp. 411–12.

of episcopal sees and the right to authorise a bishop to perform liturgical acts outside his diocese in the presence of the local bishop. Last but not least, they appointed the patriarch, leader and father of the whole church.

Well on in the next century, in 1380, the emperor John V Palaiologos convened the permanent synod in the Constantinopolitan monastery of Stoudios and instructed the patriarch Neilos to set down in writing the number and nature of his prerogatives in the government of the Church. Coming from a sovereign whose empire had shrunk to the proportions of a petty Balkan state and whose prestige now rested only on a still powerful eastern Church, this was a strange request. The synod's reply consisted of nine articles:[94]

1. The emperor had the right to veto the election of a metropolitan who did not please him.
2. He could modify as he saw fit the hierarchy of episcopal sees, make transfers of bishops and, sign of the times, grant bishoprics as benefices.
3. He ratified appointments to the chief ecclesiastical offices, that is to the upper ranks of the patriarchal administration.
4. He ensured that the boundaries of the dioceses, as established by him, were respected.
5. He would be free from all patriarchal censure (excommunication, deposition), and if an archon and member of the senate infringed a canon, the patriarch would impose a punishment only through his intermediary, who would represent his role as defender of the Church and the canons.
6. He could retain in Constantinople or send back to their diocese bishops who had come or been summoned to Constantinople on important business without the patriarch having the right to object.
7. He might demand from every new bishop a promise of loyalty to his person and to the empire.
8. He could require all the bishops to approve and sign the synodal acts.
9. The bishops were obliged to take note of these articles and should not propose for election to an episcopal see anyone who was not a friend of the emperor.

This sinuous and awkwardly drawn frontier recognised strategic points won or lost by each side in the long war of position. They were not all, clearly, of equal importance. The role of the emperor in convening councils and promulgating canons had never been contested.[95] Originally in control of the *cursus publicus* and secular arm of the Church, the emperor was here exercising this latter function; the challenges, in particular during the 'Photian' and 'anti-Photian' councils of the ninth century, had concerned only pressures exerted by the sovereign and his continuous or occasional presence. The problem of deciding

[94] V. Laurent, 'Les droits de l'empereur en matière ecclésiastique', *REB*, 13 (1955), pp. 5–20.
[95] Dvornik, 'Emperors, popes and general councils' (see ch. 4, n. 10).

what constituted an ecumenical council, bone of contention at the time of iconoclasm and the restoration of images, had become a theoretical problem, since
only the patriarchal synod of Constantinople, the deliberative assembly of the
Church, now functioned. It no longer promulgated canons but decrees, some of
which, particularly in the eleventh century, were co-signed by the emperor and
those bishops present, or had the status both of synodal decision and imperial
law.[96] The remodelling of the ecclesiastical geography by the emperor was also
generally accepted. It was based on the principle of making the ecclesiastical
hierarchy conform to the administrative hierarchy that had been outlined by
canon 17 of the council of Chalcedon and repeated, in a context of territorial
retreat, by canon 38 of the council in Trullo; it was not seriously contested
when disagreements broke out in connection with vacant bishoprics, such as
the affair of the metropolitans of Basilaion and Madyta under Alexios I Komnenos. At most, it may be noted that on this occasion imperial 'law' became a
'privilege', that the emperor was urged not to base his decision on any partisan
or personal considerations, and that a canonist like Balsamon could turn the
argument on its head and refer to the 'episcopal rights' of a sovereign who
was not subject to the canons.[97] Lastly, the oath of loyalty by the clergy to the
emperor had become common during iconoclasm, at the same time as other personal commitments which were used and abused during the great crises of the
eighth and ninth centuries, and it became the norm under the Komnenoi,[98] but
with recognised limits which avoided embroiling the clergy in purely political
swings of fortune. When, in 803, Euthymios of Sardis was 'despite himself'
compromised in the usurpation of Bardanes Tourkos and the emperor wanted
to depose him, the patriarch successfully protested;[99] the synodal tome of 1026
(also considered an imperial Novel) which stipulated anathema against clergy
participating in a usurpation was fiercely criticised and quickly invalidated.[100]
Manuel Komnenos was equally unsuccessful when he took a similar initiative in
1171.[101] In 1295, the Church granted Andronikos II an oath of loyalty in favour
of his recently crowned son, but refused to accompany it with an anathema
against rebellious clergy.[102] Conversely, contemporaries were highly critical of
the patriarch Michael Keroularios when, in 1057, he gave official support to
the usurper Isaac Komnenos and authorised the clergy by a synodal decision to

---

[96] For example, an act of 1079 co-signed by the emperor, the patriarch and thirty-seven bishops:
J. Gouillard, 'Un chrysobulle de Nicéphore Botaneiatès à souscription synodale', *Byz.*, 29–30
(1959–60) (Mélanges C. Giannelli), pp. 29–41.
[97] Rhalles–Potles *Syntagma*, II, pp. 393–4; III, pp. 349–50.
[98] N. Svoronos, 'Le serment de fidélité à l'empereur byzantin et sa signification constitutionelle',
REB, 9 (1951), pp. 106–42.
[99] *Life of Euthymios of Sardis*, 5, ed. and trans. J. Gouillard, *TM*, 10 (1987), pp. 24–7.
[100] Rhalles–Potles, *Syntagma*, III, pp. 97, 103; Grumel-Darrouzès, *Regestes*, no. 830.
[101] Ed. Papadopoulos-Kerameus, *Analekta Hierosolymitikes stachyologias* (see ch. 3, n. 69), IV,
pp. 109–13; Grumel-Darrouzès, *Regestes*, no. 1120.
[102] Pachymeres, *Hist.*, IX, 3, ed. and trans. Failler and Laurent (see ch. 1, n. 8), III, pp. 222–3;
Svoronos, 'Le serment de fidélité' (n. 98), pp. 114–16.

take his side.[103] The difference between the institutional and the political was well understood.

All these points make it possible to see the extent to which emperor and Church were bound to one another. They gave little cause for dispute, but did not go to the heart of the problem, that is, the quasi-episcopal sacrality of a sovereign who was nevertheless deemed to be lay, as was noted, after Balsamon, by John Chilas.

To take the argument further and so as to appreciate more clearly the place of the emperor in ecclesiology, let us return to his right of intervention in ecclesiastical elections, subject of almost all the controversies from the tenth century on and of numerous contradictory treatises.[104]

The rules for promotion to the patriarchate of Constantinople are well known. They are sometimes invoked as the classic example of caesaropapism. The patriarch was not only chosen but 'promoted' by the emperor, in principle from among three candidates put forward by the synod, then consecrated the following Sunday in St Sophia by the metropolitans.[105] At least, this was the institutional schema which was gradually established, as practice varied. The choice might be preceded by open consultation among the bishops and abbots, as happened for the replacement of Tarasios in 806 and for the appointment of Methodios in 842; but the emperor was just as likely to appoint one of his own men without seeking the advice of the clergy – a close relative whose opposition he need not fear, like Stephen brother of Leo VI and Theophylaktos son of Romanos Lekapenos, or an administrator trained in his own government departments and hastily elevated through successive ecclesiastical orders, like Nikephoros, Tarasios and Photios, or an unknown and non-threatening anchorite, like Basil in the time of John Tzimiskes. This right of *problesis*, which was, astonishingly, ignored in the synodal document of the patriarch Neilos, was never seriously challenged, even if it was never clear whether it should be interpreted as a 'privilege' conceded by the Church to a secular sovereign or a consequence of his 'episcopal *charismata*'. The only contentious points, in times of crisis, were the 'scandal' of 'laymen' promoted to the patriarchate, which, in any case, shocked westerners far more than easterners, and the right of the emperor to depose the patriarch he had promoted, by the use of violence or by appeal to the principle of 'economy'.

The election of a metropolitan, conversely, was regarded as an exclusively ecclesiastical matter. The process was initiated by the patriarch; he arranged a synodal assembly of the metropolitans and archbishops present in the capital, and might express his own preference before the deliberations and the

---

[103] Attaliates, Bonn, pp. 57–8; Grumel-Darrouzès, *Regestes*, no. 874.

[104] Darrouzès, *Documents inédits* (see ch. 8, n. 14); also J. Darrouzès, *Recherches sur les Offikia dans l'Eglise byzantine* (Paris, 1970), pp. 469–72.

[105] See *De cerimoniis*, II, 14, 38, pp. 564–6, 635–6.

vote, in which he did not participate; he eventually chose one from among the three candidates nominated by the synod. There might be an impasse, if the metropolitans failed to include the name put forward earlier by the patriarch or if the latter, who controlled convocation and consecration, rejected the candidates proposed. The metropolitans then had to justify their opposition and, if the disagreement persisted, the synod was opened to the lay archontes and imperial arbitration was requested. But except in such extreme cases and except for a right of veto after the election, only slowly and reluctantly recognised, imperial interventions, though probably frequent, were regarded as an abuse. When Nikephoros Phokas, sick of votes based purely on favouritism and weary of the unending warfare between the patriarch Polyeuktos and the metropolitans, decided that no consecration should take place without his agreement, the Church reacted violently and put a stop to this abuse of power at the earliest opportunity.[106] What was really at issue here was the role of the patriarch, who was believed by some to have only an ill-defined power, half secular and half ecclesiastical, and no right to encroach on the autonomy of the metropolitans by his interventions;[107] but others said he had control over the election and the metropolitans who were regarded as his suffragans.[108]

These procedures, together with the disagreements about competences, show first and foremost the ambiguous position of the patriarch of Constantinople: sometimes simply a link between palace and Church, made and unmade by the emperor, a cleric for the occasion with only the primacy of an exarch, sometimes leader and father of the eastern Church, almost on a par with the pontiff of Rome. To the patriarchs dominated by the emperor we may contrast those who, like Nicholas Mystikos in the affair of the tetragamy of Leo VI, submitted to the assembly of metropolitans, or those who, like Michael Keroularios, set themselves up as rivals to the emperors. The whole history of the patriarchate reflects this ambiguity, which was a consequence not only of individual temperament, but of a structural duality. An understanding of Byzantine ecclesiology has to start from two fixed points: the existence of the metropolitans, masters of their provinces and united in synod where they formed a powerful oligarchy; and the power of the emperors, controlling the palace clergy and the appointment of the ecclesiastical archontes, usually relying on a very Constantinopolitan and socially coherent ecclesiastical elite. It was both the strength and the weakness of the patriarch to have had a foot in both camps; it was not the role of the emperor that was ill defined in Byzantine ecclesiology, it was that of the patriarch.

[106] Zonaras, *Annales*, ed. Pinder (see ch. 1, n. 29), p. 505; Skylitzes, ed. Thurn, p. 274; Darrouzès, *Documents inédits* (see ch. 8, n. 14), p. 17.
[107] See, in particular, the anonymous treatise of the second half of the tenth century which upholds an extreme point of view: Darrouzès, *Documents inédits* (see ch. 8, n. 14), pp. 21–9, 116–59; and, at the end of the eleventh century, the writings of Niketas of Ankyra, ibid., pp. 37ff, 176ff.
[108] This was the response of Niketas of Amaseia to the previously mentioned treatise: Darrouzès, *Documents inédits* (see ch. 8, n. 14), pp. 29–36, 160–75.

It is an error, therefore, to speak of caesaropapism with regard to election to the patriarchal throne and the relations between the emperor and the patriarch which were by their very nature equivocal. It was not here that the problem lay. The independence of the clergy should be judged at the well-organised and coherent level of the metropolitans, ever ready to contest authority. The unity of the Church can only be conceived at the level of the imperial institution itself, with its indelible sacrality and its unadmitted priestly character. In the structures specific to the East, the emperor of Constantinople occupied almost the same place as the pope of Rome. By projecting on to the middle ages the modern notion of the separation of Church and state, and on to the East a clericalisation of all ecclesial structure specific to the West, an imperial right can be too hastily labelled as encroachments. It was generally accepted and assumed, but rarely presented within an overall theory.

This theory can only be explained by seeing Christianity within history, or rather within the timescale which is specific to it, with its ruptures, its backward looks, its past and above all its culmination. The rupture was the Incarnation, which inaugurated the time of Grace, but within a political order willed by God, since the empire of Augustus was the cradle of the new religion. The backward looking was the astonishing projection of the Judaic past on to the Christian present, which made Byzantium and its emperors exist at two levels, that of Old Testament models which had no other reality in Jewish history than that of 'prefigurations' of a Christian future, and that of a Christian history which was simply their realisation. The culmination was the programmed end foretold by Daniel and all the apocalypses, which turned Christian time, from the reign of Constantine on, into a countdown, and in which the empire provided the setting and the emperor took the leading role. The notions of 'worldliness', 'state' and 'temporal power' could usefully delimit the sphere of the imperial institution in the face of the institutional Church which was in the care of the clergy. But they do not allow for that alchemy of time and that sacred history, of which the emperor was a sort of high priest, and which gave certain 'orthodox' or 'heretical' Byzantine emperors the status of religious reformers struggling against the conservatism of a hierarchy of bishops.

Until the very end, even when Byzantium had lost all its territorial basis and was reduced to a capital under siege, the feeling that the church and the empire were indissociable prevailed. In a justly famous letter written in 1393, the patriarch of Constantinople, Antonios IV, reproached the Grand Duke of Moscow, Vasilij, for treating him in cavalier fashion and for refusing allegiance to the emperor, while accepting the theoretical superiority of the patriarchate.[109] The position of Byzantium in the world, he wrote, did not justify this scorn or this revolt, because it challenged the very structures of the Church, and not the

---

[109] Miklosich-Müller, *Acta et diplomata*, II, pp. 188–92; Darrouzès, *Regestes*, no. 2931.

relative power of a state. To define his own dignity, Antonios used expressions which Photios would not have disowned: he sat 'on the very throne of the Lord'; he was owed the same respect as Christ, whose place he occupied. But the patriarch was primarily angry that the Christian prince had forbidden the metropolitan of Moscow to mention the Byzantine sovereign in the diptychs and had declared on this occasion: 'We have a Church [the one with the patriarchate of Constantinople as its centre], but we do not have and do not recognise an emperor.' 'The holy emperor,' the patriarch explained,

> occupies an important position in the Church and it is not possible to equate him with local rulers and sovereigns, because from the beginning the emperors have consolidated and strengthened piety throughout the whole world, convened ecumenical councils, given effect to the divine and sacred canons concerning the orthodox dogmas and the life of Christians by stipulating that they should be piously respected, and fought long and hard against heresies. They have established by their imperial decrees the hierarchy of episcopal sees, the spheres of responsibility of the provinces and the distribution into dioceses. It is for all these reasons that they are held in high regard and occupy a position within the Church. Even if God has permitted the Nations to encircle the seat of imperial authority, the emperor has nevertheless still received until now the same consecration on the part of the Church, the same rank and the same prayers; he is anointed with the prestigious *myron*, consecrated as *basileus* of the Romans, that is, of all Christians, and his name is commemorated everywhere by all the patriarchs, metropolitans and bishops, wherever people call themselves Christians, which is the privilege of no other local prince or sovereign.

The Latins themselves conformed to the rule, even though they were not in communion with the Easterners; all the more reason for the Orthodox to do the same. The evils of the day, that is, the decline of Byzantine power and the disintegration of a single power into a multitude of Christian kingdoms, changed nothing: 'It is not right, my son, to say, as you do, "We have a Church but not an emperor", because there is a profound unity and community between the *basileia* and the Church, and it is not possible to separate one from the other.' Quoting, in conclusion, from the First Epistle of St Peter (2: 17), 'Fear God. Honour the king', he argued from the apostle's use of the singular that he, not dwelling on the paganism of the rulers of his day, foreseeing the future and expressing an order from God, had clearly indicated that Christians ought to have only a single *basileus*, a *basileus* whose economy of salvation was a keystone of ecclesiology.

Epilogue *The house of Judah and the house of Levi*

Over the centuries, the debate about the single or dual power, and about the king-priest, the priest-king or the king and the priest has been enriched by history, rationalised and politicised. Let us return it to the pure, that is, the mythic form which it long retained and which 'modernity' has obscured: that of a messianic genealogy, or rather of a transgression by messianism of genealogical rules imposed by the official religion. The question posed had been more or less this. Would the Messiah come or had he come from the tribe of Judah as an heir to Davidic kingship, or from the tribe of Levi as a descendant of the priesthood of Aaron, or from a 'mixture' of the two tribes as a sovereign reunifying the power which Moses had divided after having exercised it in full and as one?

The answers were based first on the many Old Testament texts which, starting with II Samuel [II Kings], VII: 8–16, evoked God's promise to David that his house and his kingship would last for ever. Psalm CXXXII [CXXXI]: 11 echoes this: 'Of the fruit of thy body will I set upon thy throne.' A late passage in Genesis (XLIX: 8–10)[1] describing Jacob's farewells to his sons also predicted that kingship would remain in the tribe of Judah at least until the coming of the Messiah:

> Judah, thou art he whom thy brethren shall praise: thy hand shall be in the neck of thine enemies; thy father's children shall bow down before thee. Judah is a lion's whelp: from the prey, my son, thou art gone up: he stooped down, he couched as a lion, and as an old lion; who shall rouse him up? The sceptre shall not depart from Judah, nor a lawgiver from between his feet, until Shiloh come; and unto him shall the gathering of the people be.

After this coming, another division might prevail, or else a union between kingship and priesthood prefigured in the person of Melchizedek and to which the Jewish communities spontaneously gave a genealogical transcription. It is in the 'intertestamentary' writings, later than the Old Testament and already

---

[1] For a French translation of the Septuagint text and bibliography on its Christian interpretation, see M. Harl, *La Bible d'Alexandrie. La Genèse* (Paris, 1986), pp. 308–9.

heralding the New, that we find these at first rather hesitant speculations. The *Rule of the Community*, an Essene text from Qumran, announces two Messiahs, a Messiah-priest and a Messiah-king: '[The members of the community] will be ruled by the first ordinances... until the coming of the Prophet and of the Anointed of Aaron and of Israel'.[2] These two Messiahs, who would restore in their simple legitimacy the sacerdotal and regalian powers, were merged in a text with the same origin, the *Writing of Damascus*, which refers in the singular to 'the coming of the Anointed of Aaron and of Israel.'[3] The *Testaments of the Twelve Patriarchs*, which can be compared to the passage from Genesis quoted above, since it consists of the last recommendations and predictions of the twelve sons of Jacob to their respective children, is evidence of continuing uncertainties in the messianic tradition several decades before Christianity took over.[4]

In the *Testament of Simeon* we find:
And now, my children, be obedient to Levi and to Judah, and do not rise up against these two tribes, because it is from them that we will receive God's salvation. For the Lord will raise up someone from Levi, as high priest, and from Judah, as king, God and man. It is he who will save all the nations and the race of Israel.

Is this two Messiahs or one? The clumsy wording shows signs of a rewriting that was not necessarily Christian.[5]

The *Testament of Levi* foretells, through two visions described by the patriarch, the coming of a unique Saviour descended from a mixing of the two tribes: 'Through you [Levi] and Judah, the Lord will reveal himself to men, himself saving the whole human race'; but this mixture is strongly qualified by the celebration of a 'new' priesthood, subject of the second vision:
Levi, your descendants will be divided into three principles, to signal the glory of the Lord who is coming. The first portion will be great, and there will be no other above it. The second will be in the priesthood. The third will be called by a new name, for, as a king, he will rise up from Judah and will exercise a new priesthood for all the nations. His coming will be cherished

[2] IX, 10–11, trans. Dupont-Sommer in *La Bible. Ecrits intertestamentaires*, ed. A. Dupont-Sommer and M. Philonenko (Paris, 1987), p. 35. See also the 'General Introduction' by A. Caquot and M. Philonenko, ibid., pp. XLIV–XLVI.
[3] XII, 23-XIII, 1, ibid., p. 175.
[4] Each of the 'patriarchs', addressing his descendants, prophesies the faults that will be punished by the exile, return and, finally, emergence of the tribes of Levi and of Judah, from whom salvation will come. It was long thought that these *Testaments* were written, or at least interpolated, by Christians; but they are probably Essenian in origin, datable, in their actual state, to the second half of the first century before Christ, and if a few alterations by Christian copyists cannot be ruled out, the messianic inspiration does not come from them. See *Ecrits intertestamentaires*, 'General Introduction', pp. LXXV–LXXXI, and the commentaries of the last editor, De Jonge, *Testaments of* (see ch. 9, n. 76).
[5] VII, 1–2, ed. De Jonge (n. 4), p. 22; trans. Philonenko, *Ecrits intertestamentaires* (n. 2), p. 832.

like that of a prophet of the Most High, born of the descendants of Abraham, our father.[6]

In parallel and conversely, the *Testament of Judah* claims salvation only for the kingship of Judah revived by the Messiah:

Among strangers will my kingdom end, until the arrival of the salvation of Israel, until the coming of the God of Justice . . . it is he who will preserve the power of my kingdom for ever, for the Lord has sworn to me by oath never to remove the kingship from my descendants.[7]

The *Testament of Dan* soberly and abstractly foretells the mixed nature of one or more Saviours: 'The salvation of the Lord will rise up for you from the tribe of Judah and of Levi.'[8] The *Testament of Gad* does the same: 'You too, say this to your children, so that they will respect Judah and Levi, for it is from their tribes that the Lord will bring about the salvation of Israel.'[9]

The last recommendations of Joseph provide the conclusion: 'You, then, my children, observe the commandments of the Lord and honour Levi and Judah, because it is from their descendants that there will arise for you the lamb of God who, by grace, will save all the nations of Israel.'[10]

It was subsequently the Christians who pondered and constructed genealogies to show that Christ was indeed born of Judah and that He could therefore be seen as the beneficiary of the promise made to His ancestor David. They also tried to reply to the Jewish polemic, repeated by some pagans, portraying Mary as a woman of humble origins, a 'hairdresser', a seller of peas, a prostitute or, at any rate, as a debauched and adulterous person whom it was ridiculous to make the descendant of a royal race and whose son could hardly be the Messiah.[11] Contradictory lines of descents were devised, culminating in Joseph, the father 'according to the [Jewish] law', or in Mary, the mother 'according to the flesh'. The evangelist Matthew gives one (1: 15–16), Luke another, revealing a scintilla of doubt as to its accuracy (3: 23–4). John implies that Jesus himself believed he was descended from David: 'When Jesus therefore perceived that they would come and take him by force, to make him a king, he departed again into a mountain himself alone' (6: 15). And St Paul in his turn firmly asserted that Jesus was 'made of the seed of David' (Romans, 1: 1–4). Once Jewish

---

[6] II, 11 and VIII, 11–15, ed. De Jonge (n. 4), pp. 26, 34; trans. Philonenko (n. 2), pp. 837, 844.

[7] XXII, 2–3 and XXIV, 1–5, ed. De Jonge (n. 4), pp. 75, 76–7; trans. Philonenko (n. 2), pp. 871–4.

[8] V, 10, ed. De Jonge (n. 4), p. 108; trans. Philonenko (n. 2), p. 897.

[9] VIII, 1, ed. De Jonge (n. 4), p. 133; trans. Philonenko (n. 2), p. 913.

[10] *Testament of Joseph*, XIX, 6–7 (11–12), ed. De Jonge (n. 4), pp. 165–6; trans. Philonenko (n. 2), pp. 933–4.

[11] M. Lods, 'Etude sur les sources juives de la polémique de Celse contre les chrétiens', *Revue d'histoire et de philosophie religieuses*, 21 (1941), pp. 1–33, especially pp. 6–7. By the second century, the Davidic origin of Jesus was asserted in writings of anti-Jewish polemic, for example, in Justin, *Apologia pro Christianis*, I, 32; *Dialogus cum Triphone Iudaeo*, 43, 45, 100, 120, PG 6, cols. 377, 380, 568, 572, 739.

criticism, still fairly powerful and resurgent in the seventh century,[12] no longer risked undermining the credibility of the new religion, it was left to Christian exegesis to explain and interpret the divergences between Matthew and Luke. Genealogical schemas culminating in Mary circulated from this period till the end of the middle ages in Christian literature in the Greek, Georgian and Slav languages.[13] The oldest and most frequently repeated appeared in a letter from Sextus Julius Africanus, written about 240, which can be reconstituted on the basis of the lengthy extracts given by Eusebios,[14] with a few additions found in catenae.[15]

In fact, the problem for Julius Africanus – and for everyone after him – was twofold: to explain by a remarriage and a different culmination (Mary instead of Joseph) the contradictions between the genealogy of Matthew which went back to David via Solomon, and that of Luke which went back to David via Nathan; and to establish at the same time that these two genealogies, once harmonised, revealed not only a descent from David attaching the Virgin and Christ to the tribe of Judah, but a 'mixing of the races' (*mixis ton genon, epimixia*) which made the Messiah and his mother belong both to the tribe of Judah, repository of kingship, and to that of Levi, repository of the priesthood. Julius Africanus criticised those who, in his own day, from lack of faith, attempted to prove by physical descents a union of priesthood and kingship in the Messiah, which had been solemnly foretold by the patriarchs and the prophets; but his letter still attributed this fusion to a mixing of the tribes of Judah and Levi that had occurred very early, with the marriage of Aaron to Elisheba, daughter of Judah (Exodus, 6: 23), and more recently, with the marriage of Elizabeth, cousin of Mary and mother of St John Baptist, to the Levite Zacharias (Luke, 1: 36). This was the 'divine economy' which assured the Messiah, among Christians as well as among Jews, the double title of king and priest.

For some, the priesthood was no less important than kingship. St Augustine battled fiercely against the Manichean Faustus, who placed Mary and her father Joachim in the tribe of Levi.[16] Similar in aim was a tradition which, failing Jesus himself, made his 'brother' James, believed to be the son of Joseph's first marriage, a Jewish priest who later became a Christian bishop.[17] A legend

---

[12] As in the *Doctrina Jacobi*, I, 41–2, ed. and trans. V. Déroche, in G. Dagron and V. Déroche, 'Juifs et Chrétiens dans l'Orient du VIIe siècle', *TM*, 11 (1991), pp. 130–5, 251.

[13] M. Van Esbroeck, 'Généalogie de la Vierge en géorgien', *Anal. Boll.*, 91 (1973), pp. 347–56, where the problem is treated as a whole. For Byzantium, see in particular John of Damascus, *Expositio fidei*, 87 (IV, 14), ed. B. Kotter, *Die schriften des Johannes von Damaskos*, II (Berlin, 1973) pp. 198–200; Epiphanios the Monk, *De vita sanctissimae Deiparae*, PG 120, cols. 188–9.

[14] *Hist. eccl.*, I, 7, 1–17.

[15] W. Reichardt, *Die Briefe des Sextus Iulius Africanus an Aristides und Origenes*. Texte und Untersuchungen 34/4 (Leipzig, 1909), especially pp. 28–41 (introduction), and 53–62 (text of the *epistola ad Aristidem*).

[16] *Contra Faustum*, VI, 23, ed. J. Zycha, CSEL 25 (Prague/Vienna/Leipzig, 1892), pp. 707–17.

[17] *Panarion*, XXIX, ed. K. Holl, *Ancoratus and Panarion*, I (Leipzig, 1915), p. 324.

which emerged in the seventh century in the context of the anti-Jewish polemic, and which was enormously successful throughout the Christian East and in the West up to modern times, told how Jesus, by reason of the 'mixing of races' from which he came, had been elected to the college of Jewish priests and had for a time performed priestly duties in the Temple of Jerusalem.[18]

Jesus, king of the Jews, Jesus, Jewish priest. The legend, even if it lived on into modern times, is easily demolished at the level of scholarly exegesis, and the genealogies of Mary and Joseph were gradually marginalised in the Christian literature. But from all these texts and speculations, we may at least extract two lessons: with its mixture of the two tribes, Jewish messianism offered Christian history a model of mixed power; and a whole current in Christian thinking had been anxious to establish continuity between Judaism and Christianity instead of emphasising rupture, to attach value to the Jewish past instead of devaluing it, and to re-Judaise Christianity instead of de-Judaising it.

In the end, the most official exegesis opted for rupture. This is already visible in St Paul, who asserts that the previous order had been abolished, that Melchizedek had neither genealogy nor descendants, and that the priesthood of Christ, like his kingship, could not be transmitted.[19] In St Augustine, Christ is for ever king of the City of God, which will recognise no other; after His coming, priestly kingship loses all legitimacy. The Gelasian theory followed this well-marked path. It came to be accepted that the Incarnation marked a rupture, that it left the kings of this world only a much reduced power, shared with the Church and sacralised through the intermediary of the clergy, and that it broke the direct line, so strongly expressed in the Old Testament, between the ruler of the chosen people and God. Christ had reunited the two heritages in his own person only to separate them in the human world.

This negative interpretation was not peculiar to the West, but there it took the form of 'modernity', of a political revolution which accompanied the division and then disintegration of the empire in the fourth and fifth centuries, and their

---

[18] *BHG* 810–12: 'De sacerdotio Christi'; the text, in its 'middle' version, probably the most widespread in Byzantium, is found in the *Souda*, see under *Iesous*, ed. A. Adler *Suidae lexicon* (Stuttgart, 1967), II, pp. 620–5, and given in two different versions in A. Vassiliev, *Anecdota graeco-byzantina*, I (Moscow, 1893), pp. XXV–XXVII, 58–72. For the whole eastern and western manuscript tradition of this text and its 'long' version preserved in the Georgian homily collections and partly in Greek, see G. Ziffer (its future editor), 'Una versione greca inedita del *De sacerdotio Christi*', in *Studi per Riccardo Ribuoli* (Rome, 1986), pp. 141–73; G. Ziffer, 'Contributo allo studio della tradizione slava della *Confessione di Teodosio*', *Orientalia Christiana Periodica*, 54 (1988), pp. 331–51. In twelfth-century Byzantium, the legend was criticised at length by Michael Glykas, *Aporiai*, 54, ed. S. Eustratiades *Eis tas aporias tes theias graphes* (Alexandria, 1912), II, pp. 92–107. See also G. Dagron, 'Jésus prêtre du judaïsme. Le demi-succès d'une légende', in *LEIMON. Studies Presented to Lennart Rydén on his Sixty-fifth Birthday*, ed. J. O. Rosenqvist (Uppsala, 1996), pp. 11–24.

[19] Hebrews, 7: 18–24.

corollary: the constitution of the Church as a spiritual 'power'. In the East, the response was neither so rapid nor so simple, and the debate remained haunted by the survival of messianism, by the notion of eschatological fulfilment and by the memory of genealogical taboos and transgressions. For Epiphanios, great Old Testament scholar and perhaps product of a militant Judaism, Christ reunited the throne of David and the priesthood of Levi only to transmit both to the Church, that is, to the bishops;[20] a theocracy looms. During the shock of iconoclasm, the iconodule Church supported the separation of the two 'powers'. The emperors, if they only rarely dared loudly to proclaim their priesthood 'in the manner of Melchizedek', believed they were invested with a mission to administer this twofold heritage, Davidic and Levitic, which Christ had claimed when He came into the world made flesh, at the time of the first 'Parousia', but which he would take possession of only when he definitively established his kingdom, at the time of the imminent end of the world that was called the second 'Parousia'. Priestly kingship in Byzantium kept the messianic spirit alive in this intervening period, which was exactly that of the Christian empire.

On this subject as on all the others – it need hardly be said – history does not take sides. At most, it makes it possible to understand the justifications of the past and, in the present, to appreciate the various degrees of duplicity, the deviations, and then the 'lie' – to borrow the term in the *Brothers Karamazov* quoted at the beginning of this book – generated by all history that becomes tradition, then by all tradition that becomes ideology. The West, for which Judaism has rarely been a basic reference point and which profited from the ruin of the empire, made a virtue of necessity. It misunderstood or dismantled the great temporal structure produced by the encounter of the Roman and Jewish traditions; it separated the 'powers' in order to create, outside modern states, not so much a spiritual power as an impotent theocracy. The East, meanwhile, pursued a grandiose and arid dream, already illusory in the empire of the second Rome, which served as an alibi for a retrograde autocracy in the Russian empire of the third Rome, and which sometimes assumes the grimacing form of nationalism in the world of today, where Orthodoxy matters primarily as a national particularism or a form of religiosity. The political aporia 'priest and king', 'priest or king' is one of the fundamental problems of humanity, but its historical solutions are only ever the avatars of different acculturations.

---

[20] *Panarion*, XXIX, ed. Holl (n. 17), pp. 321–5, with regard to the heresies of the 'Nazoreans'; this particularly difficult chapter is excellently discussed in A. Pourkier, *L'Hérésiologie chez Epiphane de Salamine* (Paris, 1992), pp. 415–75, especially pp. 419–38.

Glossary

acheiropoietos: not made by the hand of man; said of images brought miraculously into existence and replicated according to a miraculous prototype

ambo: pulpit, usually situated towards the middle of the church, reached by a single or double staircase, used for the reading of the Gospels, for preaching and for certain ceremonies such as coronations

Antichrist: diabolic person who, in the scenario of the apocalypses, will impose his power for a time and will persecute the just, before Christ returns to judge men and make his kingdom triumph

apokombion: sum of money offered to the patriarch by the emperor when he made an official visit to St Sophia

Augustaion: semi-public open square situated at the end of the main street of Constantinople (Mese, qv), between the palace and St Sophia

Augusteus: state chamber of the old Constantinian palace (Daphne, qv)

autocephalous (Church): an ecclesiastical diocese granted complete autonomy, no longer dependent on a patriarchate and with the right to elect its own 'head' by its own suffragans

basileus: king, emperor

Basilika: new codification of Roman law translated into Greek; the *Basilika* were started under Basil I (867–86) and completed under Leo VI (886–912)

bema, sometimes translated as 'sanctuary': the part of a church containing the altar, which was reserved for the higher orders of clergy (the 'clergy of the *bema*'); it was raised a few steps up and closed off by the chancel barrier (qv)

Blues: supporters of one of the two principal factions or demes (qv) of the Constantinople Hippodrome (the other faction being the Greens)

catholicos: head of the Armenian Church

Chalcedonians: Christians faithful to the definition of faith of the council of Chalcedon (451), which recognised in Christ incarnate two *natures* (human and divine) united in one single *person* 'without confusion, change, division or separation'

Chalke: 'Bronze gate' of the Great Palace, the most solemn, through which the emperor passed to go to St Sophia. The portrait of Christ on the façade above it served as emblem and focus of hostilities in the iconoclast dispute

chancel barrier: openwork barrier pierced by doors which demarcated the *bema* (qv). The barrier was gradually made taller and closed in, developing into the *templon* (= screen), then the iconostasis (qv), completely separating the sanctuary from the nave, as in Orthodox churches today

chartophylax: head of the chancery (*chartophylakion*) of a church, especially the patriarchal church (St Sophia)

chlamys: outer garment fastened on the right shoulder by means of a fibula; the purple *chlamys* was, with the *stemma*, the principal symbol of imperial dignity

chrysobull: the most solemn document of the imperial chancery, bearing a complete date, autograph signature of the emperor in cinnabar (purple ink) and golden bulla attached by a silk cord

Chrysotriklinos: '*triklinos* of gold', large domed octagonal reception hall, built by Justin II (565–78); its mosaic decoration was restored immediately after the iconoclast crisis, under Michael III (842–67). It again became the centre of the palace under the Macedonian emperors; it had the shape and icono-graphical programme of a church, the imperial throne being situated in the eastern apse, under a representation of Christ

Consistorium: hall where the dignitaries of the empire met, adjacent to the Triklinos of the Nineteen Couches (qv)

Daphne: oldest part of the palace, dating back to Constantine the Great

deesis: intercession, epecially of the Virgin and/or a saint with Christ on behalf of a sinner

demarchs (*demarchoi*): leaders of the White and Red demes (qv) (politic Blues and politic Greens)

demes (*demoi*), also called 'colours' or 'factions': division at first exclusive to the Hippodrome, where the two principal colours, Blue and Green, associ-ated with the two secondary colours – White with Blue and Red with Green – served as badges for the four competing teams. This organisation, quadripar-tite but in reality dualist, soon broke out of the context of the Hippodrome and imposed its structures on the capital during the 'factional' disorders which marked the fifth to seventh centuries. In the tenth century, the demes, now pacified, had a role in the ceremonial, where the representatives of the principal colours, the Blues and the Greens, were regarded symbolically as 'peratics', that is, 'external' to the city, and the representatives of the sec-ondary colours, the Whites and the Reds, as 'politics', that is, constituents of the city. Hence the customary designation of the Whites as 'politic Blues' and the Reds as 'politic Greens'

diakonikon: sort of sanctuary flanking the central apse of the church to the south (the equivalent in the north being the *prothesis*, qv)

didaskalia: religious teaching, especially with a view to baptism, entrusted by the Church to *didaskaloi*

divetesion: tunic or robe of silk worn beneath the *chlamys* or the *sagion*

domestikos of the *scholae*: commander in chief of the army of the West and the East

droungarios: commander of the fleet

'economy' (*oikonomia*): a sort of management or compromise; 'to make an economy' was to relax the application of a rule in the light of circumstances and particular cases, or dispense with a rule for a greater good. From the theological point of view, the first of the 'economies' was the Incarnation of Christ, keystone of the divine plane of salvation. From the political point of view, the principle of 'economy' often allowed the monarch to impose his will or his interests against the laws and canons

epistemonarches: title given to a monk responsible for discipline within a monastery; by analogy, title given to the emperor to justify his intervention, at least disciplinary, in ecclesiastical affairs

euchologion: liturgical book containing the ordinary of the masses, the sacramental rites and the prayers of the different offices

Excubitors: palace guard

Great Church: St Sophia of Constantinople, the patriarchal church

Greens: supporters of one of the two principal factions or demes (qv) of the Constantinople Hippodrome; the other faction was the Blues

Hebdomon: place situated at the 'seventh' milestone from Constantinople, which was first, with its 'Campus Martius', a place of exercise, parade and assembly of the imperial troops, then, with this military connotation, the point of departure for a ceremonial (the *adventus*) taking the victorious general or emperor who was to be crowned from the outside to the inside of the city

hegoumenos: superior of a monastery (like an abbot)

Holy Well: construction in the chevet of St Sophia (south-east), where certain relics were preserved, including the rim of the well of Jacob (near which Christ had met the Samaritan), and which communicated between the 'passage' (*diabatika*) leading from the palace and the south aisle and gallery

iconoclast: one opposed to the veneration of images

iconodule or iconophile: defender of the veneration of images

iconostasis: wooden screen separating the sanctuary or *bema* from the central nave, on which icons were fixed

idiotes: as opposed to 'born in the purple', a 'private person' become emperor though neither the son of an emperor, nor born before his father became emperor

Jacobites: Syrian Monophysites, called after Jacob Baradaeus (sixth century); the term was sometimes applied to Monophysites in general

kampagia: shoes or sandals (Latin: *campagi*) attached by straps; when gilded, they were the privilege of victors and emperors

katechoumena: galleries of churches

kathisma: suite of rooms on three stories comprising the imperial box in the Hippodrome of Constantinople

kombina: programme of races in the Hippodrome which laid down the composition of teams and possible switching of horses

labarum: Roman standard which Constantine the Great Christianised by adding the 'chrismon', that is the letters Chi (X) and Rho (P) (the first two letters of Christ), to it in ligature

logothete: high functionary or minister at the head of a major public service, usually to do with state accounts

loros: ancient consular *toga picta* or *trabea*; this triumphal Roman garment was compared, in Christian symbolism, to the winding sheet of Christ dead and resurrected. It consisted of a long golden scarf studded with precious stones, which was draped several times round the shoulders and upper body. The emperor and also certain high dignitaries chosen by him wore the *loros* in specific circumstances, especially at Easter

magistros: holder of the old office of *magister officiorum*, become simply a dignity (fifth in hierarchic order)

Magnaura: ceremonial hall situated close to the Mese and the Augustaion, where the emperor gave audience to foreign ambassadors, held the most solemn assemblies (*silentia*, qv) and harangued the dignitaries by pronouncing a homily for the beginning of Lent

Menologion: collection bringing together the *Lives* of the saints commemorated during the same month in the liturgical calendar

Mese: 'central' avenue of Constantinople, along which were many monumental squares; it started from the Milion, or 'golden milestone', that is, the Augustaion and the Great Palace, and crossed the city as far as the Golden Gate, with a branch leading towards the church of the Holy Apostles

metatorion: room in - or curtain behind - which the emperor changed his robes during ceremonies

metropolitan: bishop of a provincial capital, or metropolis, depending directly on the patriarch and with authority over the suffragan bishops of the province

miliaresion: silver coin

Monophysitism: doctrine which, contrary to the definition of the faith of the council of Chalcedon (451), emphasised the unity of the *person* of the Incarnate Christ so strongly as no longer to distinguish his two *natures* (divine and human)

Monotheletism/Monoenergism: doctrine recognising in the Incarnate Christ the existence of one 'will' or 'energy' beyond the duality of the *natures*, according to a compromise formula put forward during the reign of Herakleios (610–41) and condemned by the council of Constantinople III (680–1)

myron: chrism, that is, a perfumed liquid (a mixture of oil, balsam and fragrant substances) made for certain festivals or miraculously emanating from the bodies of saints

mystikos: office created in the ninth century for a confidant or adviser of the emperor

Nestorianism: doctrine which, with the patriarch Nestorios (condemned in 431 by the council of Ephesos), so strongly emphasised the duality of the human and divine *natures* of the Incarnate Christ that it found it difficult to accept the unity of his *person*

nobelissimos: (Latin *nobelissimus*) dignity reserved for the descendants of the imperial family

nomisma: gold coin

Nomokanon: juridical collection putting imperial laws and ecclesiastical canons in parallel

nomophylax: 'guardian of the law', office created in the ninth century in connection with the reform of legal studies which soon became an office of the patriarchate reserved for canonists such as Theodore Balsamon

Novel: 'new' law issued by an emperor

omphalion: circular disk of marble or porphyry marking, in ceremonial, the place at which a particular dignitary or the emperor should stop

parakoimomenos: eunuch responsible for the imperial 'chamber'

Parousia: 'presence' of Christ in this world: the first Parousia corresponded to the Incarnation, the second to the return of Christ for the establishment of his kingdom at the end of time

Patria: collection of more or less legendary stories evoking the past of a city or town. The *Patria* of Constantinople are a model of urban folklore

patrician (*patrikios*): dignity (seventh in hierarchic order) often associated with an office such as that of *strategos*

pentarchy: ancient organisation of the Church into five patriarchates, those of Rome, Constantinople, Alexandria, Antioch and Jerusalem; the pentarchic idea and tradition are primarily invoked in the East in order to limit the domination of Rome and allow to the pope only an honorific primacy in a college of five patriarchs

peratics (*peratikoi*): see demes

phina: (Latin *finis*) demarkated area which it was forbidden to enter, or where entry was subject to rules

politics (*politikoi*): see demes

porphyrogenitus (*porphyrogennetos*): child of an emperor born 'in the purple' (or in the room in the palace called 'Porphyra'), that is, after the father had become emperor

praepositus: court official in charge of imperial ceremonial

prependoulia: pendants attached to the crown and falling to ear level

problesis: appointment, promotion, especially that of the patriarch by the emperor

proskynesis: gesture of respectful greeting or of reverence, which ranged from full prostration to genuflection or a simple bow

prostagma: imperial order

protasekretis: head of the imperial chancery

prothesis: sort of sanctuary flanking the central apse of the church to the north (the equivalent in the south being the *diakonikon*, qv)

protospatharios: holder of the dignity of 'first sword-bearer', eighth in the hierarchic order

reception: halt during an imperial procession, during which the emperor was 'received' by a constituted body (representing the demes, senate, etc.)

Romaioi: word used by the Byzantines for themselves

Romania: designation, by the seventh century, of the Christian empire of the East and of Byzantium

sagion: outer garment, shorter and less official than the *chlamys*

scholae: one of the palace guards and the quarter reserved to them near the 'Bronze Gate'; by extension, the military quarter of the palace

sekreton: administrative and financial office

senate, senators: no longer, after the seventh century, an institution and its members, but a class of dignitaries associated with different parts of the ceremonial

silentium: solemn assembly convoked by the emperor

skaramangion: tunic or robe of silk, less luxurious than the *divetesion*, sometimes worn with the belt and sword

skeuophylax: 'keeper of the treasure' (*skeuophylakion*) of a church, especially a high official of the patriarchate assigned to keep the sacred vessels, books and liturgical vestments

solea: pathway marked on the ground or, more often, raised by a step, linking the sanctuary (*bema*, qv) to the ambo (qv)

spatharios: holder of the dignity of sword-bearer, eleventh in the hierarchic order

stama: rectangular space situated in the arena of the Hippodrome just in front of the imperial box; where those who wished to address the emperor directly stood

stemma: imperial crown, usually surmounted by a cross and ornamented with pearls or enamels, originally without a cap. The form it assumed in the seventh century remained unchanged for hundreds of years, contrasting with the simple diadem of the Late Empire and the heavy crown in a half circle which appeared in the twelfth century

Stoudite: monk of the monastery of Stoudios in Constantinople

strategos: civil and military leader of a theme qv

Synaxarion: calendar of liturgical feasts, usually accompanied by brief hagio-graphical notes

synkellos: permanent assistant and adviser of the patriarch, usually appointed by the emperor; the office tended to develop into a simple dignity

synod, permanent (or 'endemic'): synod attended by all the metropolitans (qv) present in the capital and the patriarch of Constantinople; this assembly met occasionally to judge or record patriarchal decisions

tablion: rectangular fabric panel of a particular colour and embroidered; sewn onto the garment from the shoulder to the waist, front and back

tagmata: units of the central army employed for major military operations, offensive or defensive, and commanded by the *domestikos* of the *scholae*; the *tagmata* were opposed to the *themata* (qv); the palace guards were also called *tagmata*

templon: development of the chancel barrier (qv), originally surmounted by an entablature, then closed by a partition supporting icons

tetragamy: fourth marriage, forbidden by the canons

theandric: adjective used after iconoclasm to indicate Christ 'perfectly man and perfectly God', and pictorial representations in which his divinity cannot be dissociated from his humanity

themata: military units established in each theme (qv), in principle recruited locally and whose role was primarily defensive

theme: military circumscription become a territorial unit, replacing, after the invasions and conquests of the seventh century, the Roman division into provinces

Theotokos: the Virgin, 'Mother of God'

triklinos: hall for receptions, as opposed to the 'chamber' (*koiton*)

Triklinos of the Nineteen Couches: large reception hall which owed its name to the nineteen state beds on which the guests reclined

trisagion: hymn or liturgical formula declaring Christ thrice Holy

troparion: versified and sung hymn, gradually integrated into the liturgy

typikon: 1. act of monastic foundation usually including the operating rules and the calendar of the commemorations stipulated by the founder 2. group of liturgical rules and calendar governing a church

tzitzakion: outer garment, like the chlamys or the sagion, but less often worn, which appeared in the eighth century under Khazar influence

Index

Aaron, priesthood 'in the order of' 5, 110, 124, 165, 170, 181, 263, 271, 272, 313–14
Abbasids, dynasty of 52
Abd al-Malik, caliph (685–705) 52
Abraham, Old Testament patriarch 173–5, 176–9, 210, 235, 283, 315
Abu-Bakr, caliph (632–4) 52
acclamations 28, 45, 49, 55–7, 69, 73, 81, 91, 103, 104, 273
Ahab, 'New Ahab' 50, 166
acribie (exactitude in respect for the canons) 224
Adam 20, 51, 176–8, 295
Advice of the Old Man 185
adoption 38, 40, 42, 45–9
adoratio 130
adventus principis 61, 64–5, 67, 69, 73, 78
Africa, exarchate of 167–9
Agapetos, deacon 17–18
Agnellus 26
Aimilianos of Kyzicos 189
akakia 18, 36
Akakios, patriarch (472–89) 300
Alexander, Paul 243
Alexander, emperor (912–13) 33–4, 43, 80
Alexander the Monk 142
Alexandria, patriarchate of 233–4, 239, 242, 245, 257
Alexandrine Chronicle 178–9
Alexios I Komnenos, emperor (1081–1118) 150, 250–1, 254, 256, 308
al-Mamun, caliph (813–33) 52
altar cloths 77, 93, 95, 101, 111, 207
ambo 54–8, 72–3, 76–7, 82, 93, 97, 102, 122, 211, 234, 265, 276, 278–9
Ambrose of Milan 105–6, 148, 248, 295, 299
Life of 111–13, 120, 279
Amorion, dynasty of 14, 33, 41, 209

Anastasios I, emperor (491–518) 27, 40, 59, 65–8, 81–2, 157, 161, 184, 206, 266, 301–2, 305
Anastasios II-Artemios, emperor (713–15) 71
Anastasios Apokrisiarios 167–8
Anastasius Bibliothecarius 168
Anastasios the Monk 167
Anastasios Sinaites 168
anathema 78, 159, 167, 201, 296, 300, 308
Anatolios, patriarch (449–458) 60, 81
Andrew *en Krisei*, *Life* of St 187
Andronikos II, emperor (1282–1328) 42, 308
Andronikos, second son of Constantine X Doukas 44
Anna Komnene, daughter of Alexios I 254
Antichrist 6, 148, 156–7, 171, 183, 185–6, 190–1, 272, 290, 299
Antioch, patriarch of 233–4, 239, 242, 256, 261
antiquity 1, 3–4, 47, 288, 291
Antonios IV, patriarch (1389–90, 1391–7) 311–12
Antony of Novgorod, pilgrim 93, 210
Antony 'Melissa' 304
Aphrodisias 27
apocalypses 22, 104, 156–7, 171, 185, 190, 200, 311
apokombion 94
apostles, 'equal of the' 135–44, 149, 189, 244
apotheosis, imperial 137–8, 141, 198, 289
appeal, court or right of 226, 229, 234, 236, 259
Arabs, Arab conquest 167, 171, 226, 232, 256
Arcadius, emperor (395–408) 26
archangels, feasts and sanctuaries of 114, 115, 198
Michael 115, 121, 175, 194–9, 204, 210–11
Gabriel 194–8, 210

326

Past and Present Publications

General Editors: LYNDAL ROPER, *University of Oxford,* and
CHRIS WICKHAM, *University of Birmingham*

* Also published in paperback
† Co-published with the Maison des Sciences de l'Homme, Paris

Printed in the United States
119982LV00004B/103-105/A